**Sapling Plus**

Pre-class Tutorials

Introduce new topics in a more manageable, less intimidating way, to help students better retain what they've learned for class time.

Everything You Need in a Single Learning Path

SaplingPlus is the first system to support students and instructors at every step, from the first point of contact with new content to demonstrating mastery of concepts and skills. It is simply the best support for teaching economics.

Classroom Activities

Foster student curiosity and understanding through "clicker" questions (via iClicker Campus) and curated active learning activities.

Test Bank

Multiple-choice and short-answer questions to help instructors assess students' comprehension, interpretation, and ability to synthesize.

Developing Understanding

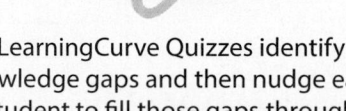

LearningCurve Quizzes identify knowledge gaps and then nudge each student to fill those gaps through an enhanced e-Book, videos, and interactives.

Assessment

Homework Assignments—with an intuitive approach to graphing—offer multi-part questions and targeted feedback.

For more information on SaplingPlus, visit www.macmillanlearning.com.

Dedication

To my favorite professors: Robert and Elizabeth Anderson

Survey of Economics

David A. Anderson

Centre College

worth publishers
Macmillan Learning

New York

Senior Vice President, Content Strategy: Charles Linsmeier
Program Director, Social Sciences: Shani Fisher
Executive Program Manager: Simon Glick
Development Editor: Amy Ray
Assistant Editor: Courtney Lindwall
Editorial Assistant: Amanda Gaglione
Marketing Manager: Andrew Zierman
Marketing Assistant: Chelsea Simens
Director of Media Editorial: Noel Hohnstine
Associate Media Editor: Stephany Harrington
Media Project Manager: Andrew Vaccaro
Assessment Manager: Kristyn Brown
Lead Content Developer: Joshua Hill
Director, Content Management Enhancement: Tracey Kuehn
Senior Managing Editor: Lisa Kinne
Senior Content Project Manager: Vivien Weiss
Senior Photo Editor: Cecilia Varas
Photo Research: Kerri Wilson, Lumina Datamatics, Inc.
Director of Design, Content Management: Diana Blume
Design Services Manager: Natasha A. S. Wolfe
Text Designer: Amanda Kavanaugh
Cover Designer: John Callahan
Senior Workflow Project Manager: Paul W. Rohloff
Production Supervisor: José Olivera
Composition: Lumina Datamatics, Inc.
Printing and Binding: LSC Communications
Cover Illustration: Evelyn Pence

Library of Congress Control Number: 2018942110

ISBN-13: 978-1-4292-5956-9
ISBN-10: 1-4292-5956-6

Printed in the United States of America

1 2 3 4 5 6   23 22 21 20 19 18
Worth Publishers
One New York Plaza
Suite 4500
New York, NY 10004-1562
www.macmillanlearning.com

Robert Boag/Centre College

David A. Anderson received his BA in economics from the University of Michigan and his PhD in economics from Duke University. His research focuses on economic education and the economics of law, crime, and public policy. Dr. Anderson has taught the Survey of Economics course, among others, since 1992 at Centre College and Davidson College, and he is currently the Paul G. Blazer Professor of Economics at Centre College. His 14 books include *Explorations in Economics, Economics by Example, Economics for AP, Favorite Ways to Explore Economics,* and *Environmental Economics and Natural Resource Management.*

A Message to Students from Dave Anderson

Every economics professor was once an economics student. As a college student choosing a major, I had several false starts: first in pre-law, then in English, and finally in business—for which economics was a required course. Perhaps like you, I sat in an Economics class expecting to major in something else. When I discovered how the tools of economics reveal specific answers to critical questions about scarcity, public policy, and the well-being of society, that was my aha moment—I knew I had found my path. With this book, I hope to make your experience learning those invaluable tools easier and more enjoyable.

Over my 27 years of teaching the Survey of Economics course, I have worked with wonderful students but mediocre textbooks. Many textbooks are too long, uninteresting, and unclear in their coverage of challenging topics. I wrote this book to address the needs of the type of student I see most often in my classroom—the student I was, and, perhaps, the student you are.

Three observations shape my approach to building a better textbook:

Dave Anderson

- **Most of us are visual learners.** *Survey of Economics* emphasizes visual stories with eye-catching photos, colorful diagrams, and clear graphs. Chapter narratives revolve around a particular industry or product that is easy to visualize, such as pizza, cotton clothing, or hairstyling.
- **Most of us have tight time constraints.** That makes it important for a textbook to be concise without skipping key content or rushing through difficult material. This book covers all the standard elements of a college survey course in brief, manageable chapters and in only about 300 pages. Relative to what you'll find in longer books, the streamlined chapters save you time by focusing on the truly important concepts.
- **Most of us find economics challenging.** This book weaves engaging explanations and real-world applications into the flow of the text to highlight the relevance of economics to our lives. Distracting application boxes and other superfluous elements are minimized.

My goal was to create an economics textbook that answers the question, "Why should I care?" I've written the book to be straightforward and fun to read, with design elements that make learning easier, and without unnecessary length or fluff. I hope this course sparks your interest in economics like it did mine, and that the tools of economics lead you to many important answers to life's pressing questions.

Yours,

Dave Anderson

Distinguishing Elements:
A Student-Centered Approach

This text was written specifically for the survey course, rather than being carved out of a principles of economics textbook. No other text provides the brevity, clarity, or visual emphasis of *Survey of Economics*, which offers fresh perspectives at a low switching cost. The coverage reflects the current state of this social science. For example, IS–LM and the kinked demand curve are out, game theory and behavioral economics are in, externalities matter, and discussions of macroeconomics emphasize AD–AS analysis. Explanations are delivered with real-life stories and specific examples that connect to students' lives.

Survey of Economics delivers on its promise to appeal to visual learners in a streamlined format, with an emphasis on student engagement. A story-based narrative surrounds simple explanations and memorable visual aids, all of which highlight the intersections of economics and daily life. The next few pages provide a sampling of what students will encounter.

Foundations of Economics

1

LEARNING OBJECTIVES
In this chapter, you will learn to:

1. Describe the problem of scarcity
2. Explain the purpose of specialization and exchange
3. Illustrate opportunity cost with a production possibilities frontier
4. Identify the three fundamental economic questions
5. Define several types of economics

Americans spend more than $38 billion each year on pizza. Every day, some 700,000 workers in U.S. pizza restaurants serve 100 acres of pizza spread with 1 million pounds of pepperoni. If you're like the average American, you will eat 6,000 slices of pizza in your lifetime. These uses of money, time, and resources result from the answers to three fundamental questions that must be addressed in every economy: What should be produced? How should it be produced? And for whom should it be produced? In this chapter, you will learn about these questions, and about how *economics* is at the heart of all such matters.

Early in each chapter, "Why Should I Care?" sections cultivate interest in the topics that students are asked to learn. What's in it for them? How does the content relate to their lives?

Why Should I Care?

Before you spend your valuable time studying economics, you deserve to know why it's worthwhile. The *Why Should I Care?* section in each chapter briefly explains how the economics you're about to dive into matters to you.

You've probably heard that economics is related to money, banks, and businesses. That's true! But economics also applies to issues involving poverty, crime, pollution, education, health care, the legal system, transportation systems, water shortages, wilderness areas, sustainable development, and energy, among many others. At an individual level, economics is about making decisions that give you as much satisfaction as possible. Every day you make decisions about how to use things that are in limited supply, such as time, clothing, closet space, and pepperonis. Whether or not they involve money, these are economic decisions. **In this book, you will learn how economic reasoning can help you make all sorts of wise decisions. You will also learn about money, economic policy, and strategies that help businesses and governments achieve their goals.**

▲ A Chicago-style pizza can cost $25 or more. Should these people be standing in line to buy one? The tools of economics help people decide how best to use scarce time, money, and resources.

The chapter openers engage students with true stories and relatable themes that run throughout each chapter. For example, demand is explained in the context of a real café, and elasticity is explained with stories about a small company that builds guitars. Clear learning objectives help students focus on what is important.

Abundant visuals cater to visual learners, conveying concepts in an intuitive way. Useful images and diagrams reinforce comprehension and retention while making the learning experience more enjoyable.

Price Controls

The market equilibrium determines the price for a good or service in the absence of intervention. Sometimes, however, governments control prices by putting upper or lower limits on them. These *price controls* have their benefits, but as you'll discover in this section, they also create problems of their own.

PRICE CEILINGS

A **price ceiling** is an artificial upper limit on the price of a good or service. The governments of Argentina, Russia, China, and France are among those that have capped prices on bread or rice in attempts to help the poor. In the United States, price ceilings aimed at curbing inflation have included caps on wages and food prices in the 1940s, and caps on oil prices in the 1970s. President Richard Nixon imposed a more general freeze on wages and prices in 1971. And millions of Americans live in apartments and mobile home parks whose rents are controlled by the government.

To have any effect on the price consumers pay, a price ceiling must be set below the equilibrium price in a market. A price ceiling set above the equilibrium price has no effect because firms don't want to charge more than the equilibrium price anyway! Recall that a price above the equilibrium price causes a surplus and leads firms to lower their price. For example, a price ceiling of $120 in the market for tires shown in Figure 5.5 would not affect tire sellers because they prefer the lower equilibrium price of $100.

We've seen that when the price set by firms is below the equilibrium price, a shortage results. A price ceiling set below the equilibrium price has the same effect: it drives the quantity demanded above the quantity supplied. But when a price ceiling is imposed, firms cannot raise their price to eliminate the shortage. Figure 5.5 shows that a price ceiling of $60 in the tire market would prevent firms from raising the price to the $100 equilibrium price.

Other than creating shortages, what's wrong with artificially low prices that result from price ceilings? Let's look into some of the problems they cause.

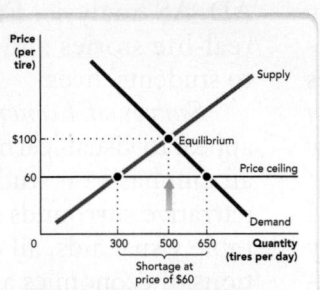

Visualize a house below the equilibrium point to remember where a price ceiling should be.

FIGURE 5.5 How a Price Ceiling Creates a Shortage
A price ceiling set below the equilibrium price causes the quantity demanded to exceed the quantity supplied, and firms cannot raise their price to eliminate the resulting shortage.

Black Markets. As Figure 5.5 shows, with a price ceiling of $60, firms are willing to supply only 300 tires. But consumers are willing to pay more than $60 for the first 649 tires. We know this because the demand curve lies above $60 for the first 649 tires. The willingness of customers to pay more than the going price can lead some sellers to charge prices above the price ceiling in an illegal market known as a **black market.** Black markets tend to emerge when there are price ceilings, and when the sale of particular goods or services is prohibited. For instance, black markets are common when sports teams cap their ticket prices below the equilibrium level so that students and others with limited incomes can attend games. At the Olympics, black-market scalpers sometimes sell tickets for 10 times their original price. To reduce this problem during the 2016 Olympics in Rio de Janeiro, the government of Brazil imposed scalping fines as high as 100 times the original ticket price.

price ceiling
An artificial upper limit on the price of a good or service.

black market
An illegal market.

When a price change causes a change in the quantity supplied, this is a *movement along the supply curve.*

fewer units will be supplied at each price. (A decrease in supply is sometimes described as an upward shift of the supply curve because when supply decreases, firms require a higher price for each unit.) Figure 4.5 illustrates an increase in supply and a decrease in supply.

Oversized pull quotes emphasize key points that deserve repeating, or highlight intriguing facts that will draw students into the broader text.

Q&A boxes address common questions that can trip students up. Carefully crafted explanations cut to the chase and clear up confusion that could otherwise prevent students from understanding important concepts.

Stores sometimes offer lower prices when consumers buy a larger quantity. Does that contradict the law of supply?

Volume discounts—that is, discounts for buying a larger quantity of a product—are common, but they do not contradict the law of supply. The supply schedule indicates the *most* a firm would be willing to supply at a given price. When a tire store offers to sell 1 tire for $150 or 4 tires for $125 each, it is not saying that it will sell *at most* 1 tire for $150 and *at most* 4 tires for $125 each. In fact,

the store would happily sell 4 tires for $150 each instead of $125 each. Beyond that, the store would probably be willing to sell even more tires for $150 each than it would for $125 each. Because this pricing policy does not indicate the largest quantity the firm would supply for either $125 or for $150, it does not reveal the shape of the supply curve. Rather, the volume discount shows that the firm recognizes that consumers' *demand* curves are downward sloping, and that buyers will purchase more tires at the lower price.

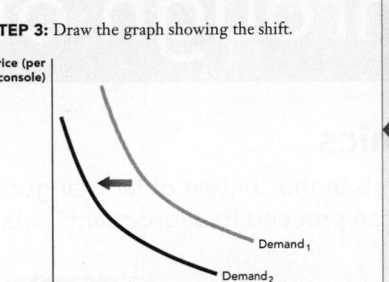

PROBLEM 3
The price of Xbox consoles, a competing product, decreases.

STEP 1: Does the change in the price of Xbox consoles shift the demand curve for PS4 consoles? Yes! Xbox consoles are a substitute in consumption for PS4 consoles. When the price of Xbox consoles decreases, some people who would have bought a PS4 console will buy an Xbox console instead.

STEP 2: In which direction does demand shift? The price decrease for Xbox consoles causes consumers to buy fewer PS4 consoles at any given price. So the demand for PS4 consoles decreases and the demand curve shifts to the left.

STEP 3: Draw the graph showing the shift.

Step-by-step problem-solving techniques give students a simple framework for tackling problems, which helps them avoid common pitfalls, such as confusing a change in demand with a movement along the demand curve.

---

36   Chapter 2

SUMMARY

The factors of production—land, labor, capital, and entrepreneurship—are the building blocks of goods and services. Households sell the factors of production to firms in exchange for income in the form of wages, rent payments, and profits. Households use their income to purchase goods and services from firms. The circular flow diagram illustrates the resulting payments as a flow of money from firms to households via the factor markets, and then back to firms via the product markets. The government also purchases goods and services in the product markets and inputs in the factor markets. These purchases, along with the transfer payments that are part of some government programs, are funded with tax collections from households and firms.

If you become an entrepreneur, you will have several options for the type of firm you operate. If you want tight control over decision making, you could create a sole proprietorship controlled by you alone, or a partnership owned and run by you and one or more partners. If you start a corporation, it will be a distinct legal entity, separate from you and the other owners for the purposes of taxes and legal liability. If your firm is a limited liability company (LLC), the owners will be shielded from legal liability and you

will have fewer paperwork requirements than corporations have. Unlike a corporation, however, you cannot sell stock to fund an LLC.

Economists generally approach decisions of what, how, and for whom to produce with the goal of efficiency in mind. An efficient combination of goods and services is produced if no alternative combination would make society better off. Production is efficient if no more of one good could be made without making less of another good. Goods are distributed efficiently if there is no way to make some people better off without making other people worse off.

The source of economic decisions depends on the type of economic system in place. In traditional economies, decisions are made as they were made in the past. In a market economy, or capitalist economy, incentives created within markets guide decision making. In the command economies of communism and socialism, governments or citizen groups decide what, how, and for whom to produce. Each of these systems has significant pros and cons. Today, most economies take a mixed approach that combines aspects of traditional, market, and command economies.

Chapter summaries reinforce learning with transparency about how economic concepts apply to the real world. Lists of key terms remind students of the vocabulary they need to know. Problems for review include prompts for critical thinking, which help students take the leap from simply memorizing models to actually applying the economic way of thinking to important questions.

KEY TERMS

factors of production, p. 26
land, p. 26
labor, p. 26
capital, p. 26
entrepreneurship, p. 26
household, p. 27
firm, p. 27
sole proprietorship, p. 27
partnership, p. 27

corporation, p. 28
stock, p. 28
shareholders, p. 28
dividends, p. 28
limited liability company (LLC), p. 28
government, p. 29
transfer payments, p. 29
circular-flow diagram, p. 29

factor markets, p. 29
product markets, p. 29
efficient, p. 30
traditional economy, p. 32
market (capitalist) economy, p. 32
command economy, p. 33
communism, p. 33
socialism, p. 35
mixed economy, p. 35

PROBLEMS FOR REVIEW

1. Printed versions of textbooks are manufactured using printing presses, workers, and paper. Identify the category of factors of production in which each of these inputs belongs.

2. Draw a simple circular flow diagram (without government) and use the relationships shown in the diagram to explain how producers' optimism about future sales can lead to an increase in future sales.

Understanding Graphs   17

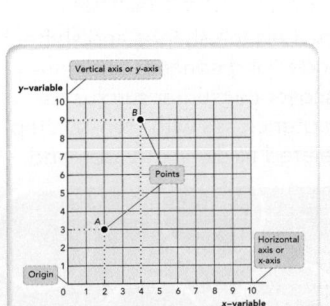

FIGURE 1A.1 Variables, Points, and Axes

Values of the x-variable are measured along the horizontal axis, or x-axis. Values of the y-variable are measured along the vertical axis, or y-axis. The two axes meet at the origin. Each point on the graph represents both a value of the x-variable and a value of the y-variable.

FIGURE 1A.2 A Demand Curve

Economists make frequent use of curves that show the relationship between two variables. For example, the demand curve shows the relationship between the price of a good and the quantity of that good demanded by consumers. Unlike this particular demand curve, some curves are actually straight lines.

An appendix on understanding graphs gives students a user-friendly reminder of (or introduction to) the workings of economists' favorite visual tools.

first is the value of the x-variable at that point, and the second is the value of the y-variable at that point. For example, point A can be identified by the coordinates (2, 3) and point B can be identified as (4, 9). The origin is found at (0, 0).

Graphs are commonly set up so that the x-variable is the independent variable and the y-variable is the dependent variable. When it comes to supply and demand graphs, however, economists follow a tradition begun by nineteenth-century economists Leon

A Walk-through of This Book

I. Introduction to Economics

These chapters explain basic economic tools in the context of familiar goods and everyday decisions. With this foundation, students can proceed to subsequent parts in any order.

1 FOUNDATIONS OF ECONOMICS

A case study of pizza showcases the scarce building blocks of all goods and services. Students discover how the production possibilities frontier illustrates opportunity costs and economic growth. The fundamental questions of what, how, and for whom to produce motivate further inquiry into optimal decision making.

Rawpixel.com/Shutterstock.com

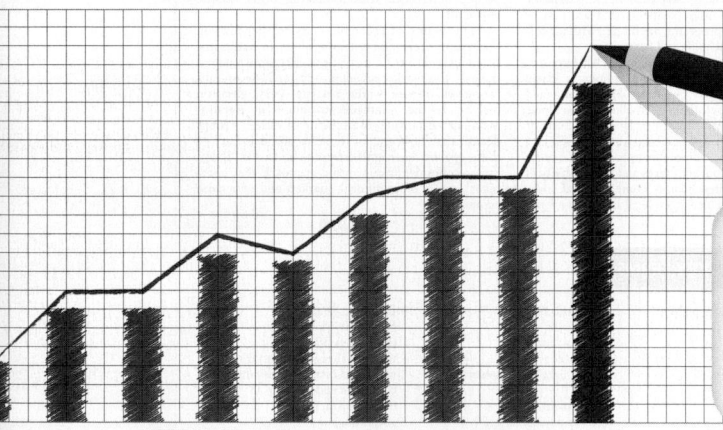

USBFCO/Shutterstock.com

1A UNDERSTANDING GRAPHS

This appendix explains economists' favorite visual tools. Students learn how curves on graphs convey relationships among variables. Coverage includes the interpretation of slopes and the calculation of simple areas. The appendix also explains the use of bar charts, pie charts, and scatter diagrams.

2 MARKETS AND ECONOMIES

Stories about chocolate and roller coasters tie efficiency goals to the fundamental questions of what, how, and for whom to produce. A circular flow diagram links the components of the economy together. Traditional, market, and command economies are compared with regard to decision making and efficiency.

3 DEMAND

A case study of the coffee market reveals the shapes and shifters of demand curves, as well as the underlying concept of diminishing marginal utility. Students discover consumer surplus as the true goal of purchases. The chapter closes with step-by-step instructions for solving problems related to consumer demand.

Susana Gonzalez/Bloomberg via Getty Images

Jason Salmon/Shutterstock.com

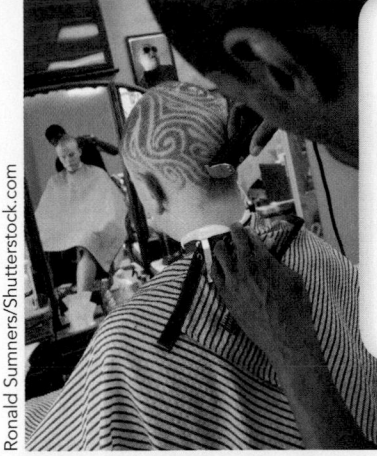

Ronald Sumners/Shutterstock.com

4 SUPPLY

Reality-based stories about hair-stylists introduce marginal cost and other underpinnings of the supply schedule. Intuitive explanations highlight the influences that cause movements along the supply curve or shifts in the curve. The last section provides a step-by-step approach to supply-related problem solving.

5 MARKET EQUILIBRIUM

Examples from the tire industry bring together the concepts of supply and demand to show how market equilibrium determines price and quantity. Students see the effects of price ceilings, price floors, and changes in supply or demand. Step-by-step guidance helps students solve problems involving market equilibrium.

C.O. Mercial/Alamy Stock Photo

II. Microeconomics

These chapters apply economics to many of the trade-offs students face daily, and shine light on everyday decisions made by individuals and firms. This part also explains the behavior of firms and the relevance of firm behavior to consumers, employees, and owners.

6 ELASTICITY

A case study of guitars demonstrates how responses to price and income changes are relevant to individuals, firms, and policy makers. Tables summarize useful interpretations of the price elasticity of demand, the price elasticity of supply, the cross-price elasticity of demand, and the income elasticity of demand.

Bruce yuanyue Bi/Alamy Stock Photo

Cafe Terrace, riace du Forum, Arles, 1888 (oil on canvas)/Gogh, Vincent van (1853–90)/BBC INFORMATION & ARCHIVES/Rijksmuseum Kroller-Muller, Otterlo, Netherlands/Bridgeman Images

7 CONSUMER BEHAVIOR

Fast food and posters frame discussions of the spending strategies that lead to the most happiness. Topics include budget constraints, income and substitution effects, and individual rationality. The included lessons on behavioral economics, which some textbooks omit, will make students better consumers.

Robert F. Leahy/Shutterstock.com

8 PRODUCTION COSTS

This chapter describes the cost of production in the context of a bakery intent on making some dough. Topics include diminishing marginal product, explicit and implicit costs, and economies of scale. Students also learn about the irrelevance of sunk costs and the cost-minimizing combination of inputs.

Chris Bennett, Farm Press

9 PERFECT COMPETITION

Cotton fields provide pathways for exploration into competitive markets. Students learn how firms in competitive markets make decisions to maximize profit. Considerations include the shutdown price, short-run and long-run behavior, and the efficiency of perfectly competitive markets.

10 MARKET POWER

We examine the forms, sources, and repercussions of market power with reference to the oil market. Students learn many ways that limited competition affects their lives. Visuals complement explanations of the differences between a monopoly and a perfectly competitive industry with regard to price, quantity, and efficiency.

Justin Sullivan/Getty Images News/Getty Images

11 FACTOR MARKETS

Stories about jeep tours introduce the workings of factor markets. Topics include derived demand, labor supply, and income distribution. The chapter explains why wages differ across individuals. Students also learn why minimum wage laws can, but don't necessarily, have a large effect on unemployment rates.

Terry Harris/Alamy Stock Photo

ArtFamily/Shutterstock.com

12 MARKET FAILURE AND GOVERNMENT FAILURE

Students learn about market failure through the lens of common experiences. Discussions cover both the role of governments in limiting market failure and the potential for governments themselves to fail. Examples include neglected costs or benefits of T-shirts, trees, immunizations, eBay, and college.

III. Macroeconomics

Using the book's highly visual approach, these chapters convey the macroeconomic concepts students see in the news, such as inflation, unemployment, interest rates, and macroeconomic policy. Coverage includes measures of economic progress, the Great Recession, and the relevance of economic ups and downs to students' lives.

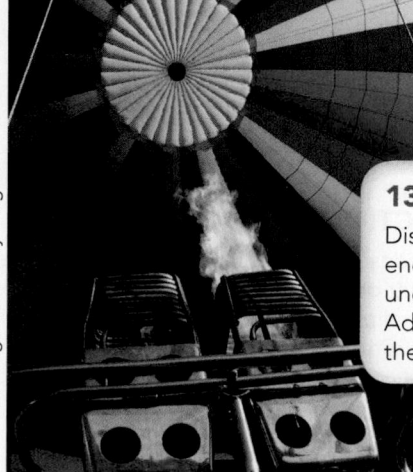
davelogan/E+/Getty Images

13 MEASURING AN ECONOMY'S PERFORMANCE

Discussions of balloon inflation and hamburger prices clarify the difference between real and nominal values. Students will develop a better understanding of gross domestic product, inflation, and unemployment. Additional topics include alternative measures of economic progress and the consumer price index.

14 AGGREGATE DEMAND AND AGGREGATE SUPPLY

We explore a workhorse of macroeconomic analysis: the aggregate demand and aggregate supply model. A narrative about familiar products from the American West—steaks, hats, and more—provides clear explanations of multiplier effects and self-corrections in the economy.

Franck Fotos/Alamy Stock Photo

Deposit Photos/glowimages.com

15 FISCAL POLICY

Students learn how a downturn in the economy affects them personally, and discover differing schools of thought on the appropriate fiscal policy response. Discussions cover past and present efforts to moderate the economy, pros and cons of fiscal policy, supply-side fiscal policy, and automatic stabilizers.

Michael Weber/imageBROKER/REX/Shutterstock.com

Illustration/Kristin Hambridge and Shutterstock.com

16 MONEY AND BANKING

This chapter links the roles of money and banks to students' lives. Discussions highlight local financial institutions as access points into the national banking system. Topics include the evolution of banking institutions in the digital age, the characteristics of money, interest rates, and the time value of money.

17 MONETARY POLICY

Students learn the story of the Federal Reserve, the reasons for its existence, and its behind-the-scenes role in students' own financial transactions. We explore the tools of monetary policy, challenges to Federal Reserve policy making, and new strategies adopted by the Federal Reserve during the Great Recession.

IV. Global Economic Issues

These chapters explain economic activity and growth from the perspective of the world economy. Students discover challenges facing developing countries and connections between economies large and small.

18 ECONOMIC GROWTH AND DEVELOPMENT

Perspectives on the United States and Jamaica illuminate the sources of economic growth, common barriers to productivity, and specific policies used to overcome economic stagnation. Discussions emphasize the importance of economic development as it relates to students' quality of life.

Layne Kennedy/Getty Images

John Moore/Getty Images

19 INTERNATIONAL TRADE AND FINANCE

A case study of bobblehead dolls clarifies the meaning of comparative advantage, absolute advantage, and mutually beneficial terms of trade. Balance of payments accounts are explained in simple terms. The determination of foreign exchange rates is likened to the determination of prices for the products students buy.

Engaging Students Beyond the Book

 **Sapling**Plus

SaplingPlus combines powerful multimedia resources with an integrated e-book and the robust problem library of Sapling Learning, creating an extraordinary new learning resource for students. Online homework helps students get better grades with its targeted instructional feedback tailored to the individual. Personalized support from a PhD or Master's level colleague trained in Sapling's system saves instructors the time spent preparing for and managing a course.

Pre-Lecture Tutorials give students a basic understanding of core economic concepts before they ever set foot in class. Developed by two pioneers in active-learning methods—Eric Chiang, Florida Atlantic University, and José Vazquez, University of Illinois at Urbana–Champaign—this resource is part of the SaplingPlus learning path. Students watch Pre-Lecture videos and complete Bridge Question assessments that prepare them to engage in class. Instructors then receive data about student comprehension that can inform their lecture preparation.

LearningCurve Adaptive Quizzing is embraced by students and instructors alike. This incredibly popular and effective adaptive quizzing engine offers individualized question sets and feedback tailored to each student based on correct and incorrect responses. Questions are hyperlinked to relevant e-book sections, which encourages students to read and use the resources at hand to enrich their understanding.

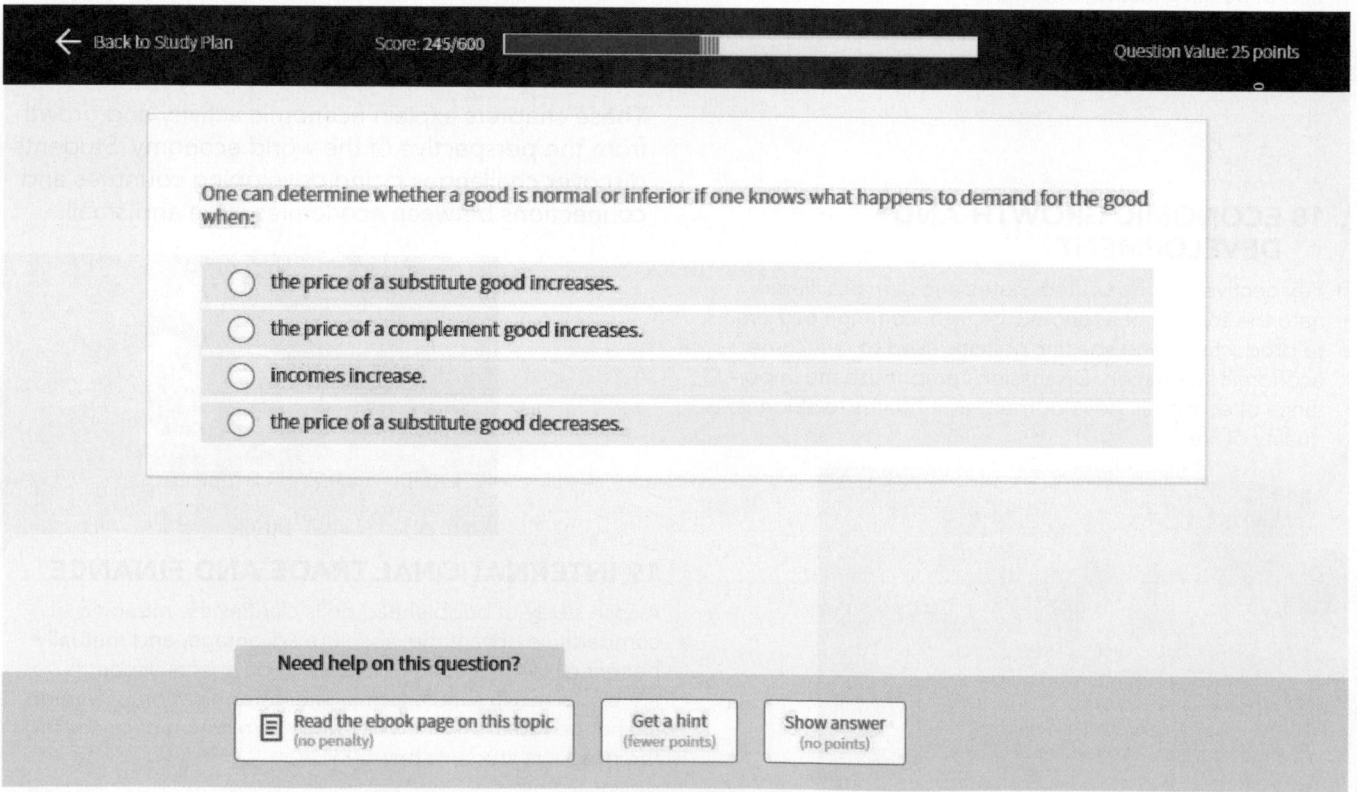

Graphing Questions are powerful multistep graphing exercises paired with helpful feedback to guide students through the process of problem solving. Students demonstrate their understanding by simply clicking, dragging, and dropping a line to a predetermined location. The graphs have been designed so that the students' entire focus is on moving the correct curve in the correct direction, virtually eliminating grading issues for instructors.

Supply and Demand End of Chapter Problem

16. Use the accompanying diagram to illustrate how the following event affects the equilibrium price and quantity of pizza.

a. The price of mozzarella cheese rises.

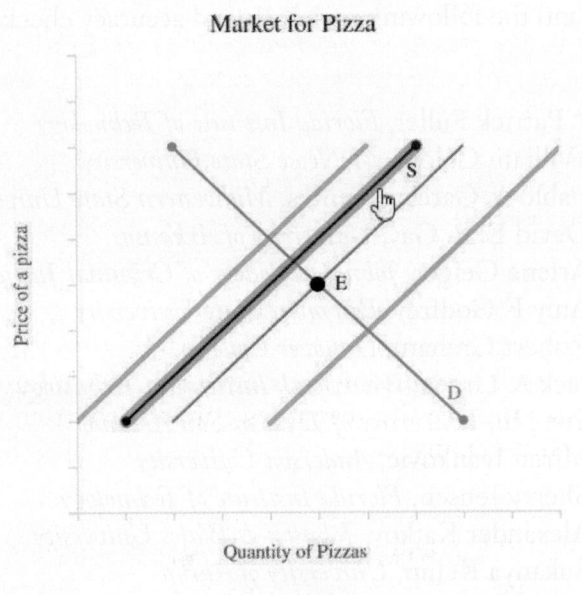

Market for Pizza

Instructor Resources

- An Instructor's Resource Manual is the perfect tool for busy instructors who want to make the survey of economics course more engaging for their students. The manual includes Tools and Tips for the Instructor, helpful web resources, and in-class activities. It also includes sample syllabi from the author and other educators who teach the survey course.
- A Solutions Manual includes suggested answers to the end-of-chapter questions for easy grading.

- Lecture slides for each chapter complement the readings and feature tables, graphs, figures, and notes on key concepts.
- A file of chapter photos, figures, and tables provides access to all the key materials from the text, giving instructors the option to create their own slides for class.
- A test bank contains multiple-choice and short-answer questions to help instructors assess students' comprehension, level of interpretation, and ability to synthesize concepts.

Acknowledgements

Textbook creation showcases the gains from specialization. Consider the graphs in this book, which began as glimmers on my computer monitor. Someone wiser than I improved on their colors; another expert redrew each graph; and then many reviewers checked every curve. Other specialists inserted the graphs into the text, made it all into a book, and got that book to you. It takes a dedicated team with wide-ranging insights to build a textbook worth switching to. My sincere thanks to everyone who lent their ideas, talents, creativity, and expertise to this project, including the Worth Economics Team and the following reviewers and accuracy checkers.

Carlos Aguilar, *El Paso Community College*
Olugbenga Ajilore, *University of Toledo*
Basil Al-Hashimi, *Mesa Community College*
Len Anyanwu, *Union County College*
Bettina Berch, *Borough of Manhattan Community College*
Anoop Bhargava, *Finger Lakes Community College*
Barbara Blake Gonzalez, *Tidewater Community College*
Jared Boyd, *Henry Ford Community College*
Elizabeth Breitbach, *University of South Carolina*
John Cadigan, *Gettysburg College*
Valbona Cela, *Tri-County Technical College*
John Clark, *Midlands Technical College*
Matthew T. Cole, *California Polytechnic State University*
Paula M. Cole, *University of Denver*
Dixie Dalton, *Southside Virginia Community College*
Dale DeBoer, *University of Colorado, Colorado Springs*
Eric Dodge, *Hanover College*
Leslie E. Doss, *University of Texas at San Antonio*
Justin M. Dubas, *Texas Lutheran University*
Archana Dube, *Indiana University–Purdue University Indianapolis*
Ron Dunbar, *Madison Area Technical College*
Mohammadmahdi Farsiabi, *Wayne State University*
Justin Fisher, *Jefferson State Community College*
Paul Fisher, *Henry Ford Community College*
Kaya Ford, *Northern Virginia Community College*
Cynthia Foreman, *University of Hawaii Maui College*
Melanie Fox, *Thomas More College*
Matthew Franchetti, *University of Toledo*

J. Patrick Fuller, *Florida Institute of Technology*
William Galose, *McNeese State University*
Pablo A. Garcia-Fuentes, *Midwestern State University*
David E. R. Gay, *University of Arkansas*
Arlene Geiger, *John Jay College of Criminal Justice*
Amy F. Godfrey, *Fairmont State University*
Robert Graham, *Hanover College*
Jack A. Green, *Wentworth Institute of Technology*
Yue Hu, *University of Texas at San Antonio*
Miren Ivankovic, *Anderson University*
Sherry Jensen, *Florida Institute of Technology*
Alexander Katkov, *Johnson & Wales University*
Sukanya Kemp, *University of Akron*
Roshan Khattry, *Spokane Falls Community College*
Teresa Laughlin, *Palomar College*
Jane Lopus, *California State University, East Bay*
Kimberly Mencken, *Baylor University*
Catherine P. Mulder, *John Jay College of Criminal Justice*
ABM Nasir, *North Carolina Central University*
Nasrin Nazemzadeh, *Rowan–Cabarrus Community College*
Ronald C. Necoechea, *Roberts Wesleyan College*
Greg Chidi Obi, *Purdue University Northwest–Calumet Campus*
Grace Onodipe, *Georgia Gwinnett College*
Tomi Ovaska, *Youngstown State University*
Lawrence Overlan, *Wentworth Institute of Technology*
Sezar Altin Pehlivan, *Irvine Valley College*
Kenneth Peterson, *Furman University*
Ravi Radhakrishnan, *Centre College*
Reza Ramazani, *Saint Michael's College*

Agne Reizgeviciute, *California State University, Chico*

Jean Rodgers, *Wenatchee Valley College*

Clark Ross, *Davidson College*

Rashida Rowther, *Northern Virginia Community College*

Prakarsh Singh, *Amherst College*

Stephen Slice, *University of South Carolina*

Richard Stahnke, *Moravian College*

Mark St. Clair, *Saginaw Valley State University*

Christopher Stevens, *Ohio University Eastern*

Taylor Stevenson, *East Tennessee State University*

James Stotter, *Ohio University*

Edward F. Stuart, *Northeastern Illinois University*

John D. Susenburger, *Mohawk Valley Community College*

Rick Szal, *Northern Arizona University*

Alexander Tanter, *Tarleton State University*

Eric Taylor, *Central Piedmont Community College*

Ross S. van Wassenhove, *University of Houston*

Rubina Vohra, *New Jersey City University*

Susan Washburn Taylor, *Millsaps College*

King Yik, *Idaho State University*

Kristen L. Zaborski, *State College of Florida, Venice Campus*

Contents

PART II   Microeconomics

PART III   Macroeconomics

Foundations of Economics

igordutina/Fotosearch LBRF/AGE Fotostock

LEARNING OBJECTIVES

In this chapter, you will learn to:

1. Describe the problem of scarcity

2. Explain the purpose of specialization and exchange

3. Illustrate opportunity cost with a production possibilities frontier

4. Identify the three fundamental economic questions

5. Define several types of economics

Americans spend more than $38 billion each year on pizza. Every day, some 700,000 workers in U.S. pizza restaurants serve 100 acres of pizza spread with 1 million pounds of pepperoni. If you're like the average American, you will eat 6,000 slices of pizza in your lifetime. These uses of money, time, and resources result from the answers to three fundamental questions that must be addressed in every economy: What should be produced? How should it be produced? And for whom should it be produced? In this chapter, you will learn about these questions, and about how *economics* is at the heart of all such matters.

Why Should I Care?

Before you spend your valuable time studying economics, you deserve to know why it's worthwhile. The *Why Should I Care?* section in each chapter briefly explains how the economics you're about to dive into matters to you.

You've probably heard that economics is related to money, banks, and businesses. That's true! But economics also applies to issues involving poverty, crime, pollution, education, health care, the legal system, transportation systems, water shortages, wilderness areas, sustainable development, and energy, among many others. At an individual level, economics is about making decisions that give you as much satisfaction as possible. Every day you make decisions about how to use things that are in limited supply, such as time, clothing, closet space, and pepperonis. Whether or not they involve money, these are economic decisions. **In this book, you will learn how economic reasoning can help you make all sorts of wise decisions. You will also learn about money, economic policy, and strategies that help businesses and governments achieve their goals.**

▲ A Chicago-style pizza can cost $25 or more. Should these people be standing in line to buy one? The tools of economics help people decide how best to use scarce time, money, and resources.

Deposit Photos/Glowimages

Scarcity: It's Why You Can't Always Get What You Want

scarcity
A condition that exists when the supply of something doesn't satisfy everyone's desires for it.

economics
The study of decision making under conditions of scarcity.

opportunity cost
The value of the next-best alternative you have foregone by making your choice.

If you can't have all of the pizza, shoes, or vacations you want, *scarcity* is the problem. **Scarcity** exists when the supply of something doesn't satisfy everyone's desires for it. The limited availability of workers, raw materials, and machinery results in scarcity. Even preparing a meal takes scarce time, money, and ingredients.

Scarcity forces you to make difficult decisions about how to use what you have. Should your Saturday evening be used to work, study, or hang out with friends? Should you save your money or buy a new car? Should you use your backyard as a vegetable garden or a soccer field? **Economics** is the study of decision making under conditions of scarcity. Given the many decisions you must make every day about time, money, and other scarce things, economics has direct relevance to your life.

Decisions are made difficult by what you must give up when you choose one thing over another. If you choose to read for the next hour, you can't spend that time hiking. When you choose to spend $1 to add pepperoni to your pizza, you give up the opportunity to use that $1 to buy a new smartphone app. And while you are attending class, you can't earn money working at a pizzeria. The foregone hiking, app, and earnings are examples of *opportunity costs*. In each case, the **opportunity cost** is the

▲ The selection of a college is complicated by the fear of missing out on the opportunities other colleges have to offer. Indeed, every decision involves opportunity costs.

value of the next-best alternative you have foregone by making your choice. As in the examples of vegetable gardens foregone for soccer fields and hikes foregone for reading time, opportunity costs do not always involve money. Part of the opportunity cost of attending your favorite college is that you cannot attend your second-favorite college, and part of the opportunity cost of spending an evening at a basketball game is that you cannot spend that time at the library.

Scarcity forces policymakers to deal with opportunity costs as well. For example, during a recent drought in California, government officials faced the opportunity cost of losing wild salmon if they allowed farmers to divert river water to their almond trees. And the money a government spends on education cannot be spent on national defense. Even so, the government of Finland spends enough money on education to allow students to attend college without paying tuition. Policy decisions such as this, as with so many of your personal decisions, are best made with careful attention to the associated benefits and opportunity costs. This chapter introduces the economic tools that help decision makers examine opportunity costs and achieve the greatest possible level of satisfaction, even if they can't always get what they want.

Specialization: It Brings You More of What You Want

Your instructor teaches economics and probably doesn't sell pizza. The founders of Blaze Pizza, Elise and Rick Wetzel, manage a restaurant chain and do not teach economics. That's a good thing, because if instructors and restaurateurs divided their time between classrooms and boardrooms, the quality and availability of both education and pizza would decrease. Consumers are best served when producers specialize in what they do relatively well and exchange their goods or services for those things that other producers can provide at a lower opportunity cost.

Markets allow people to sell the goods and services they specialize in producing and buy what

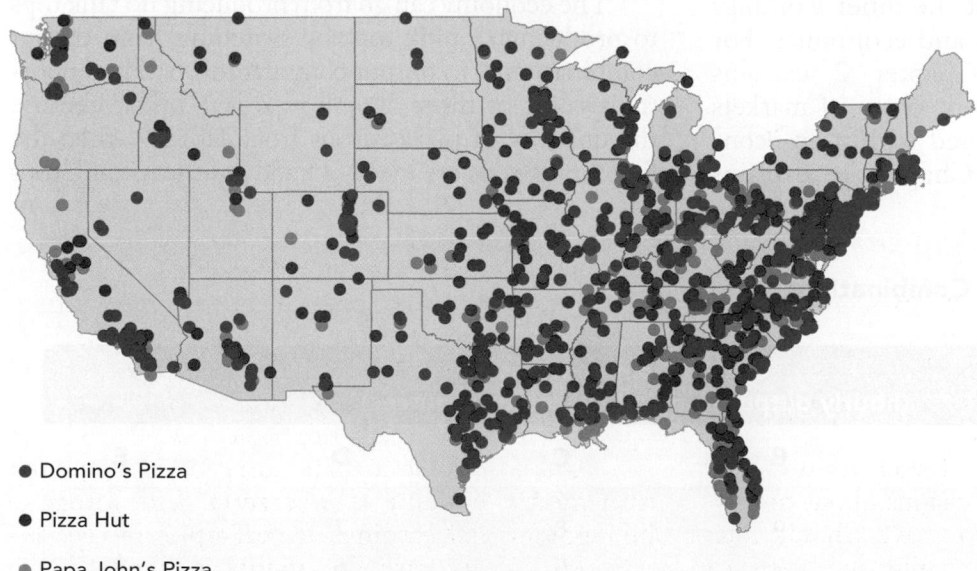

● Domino's Pizza

● Pizza Hut

● Papa John's Pizza

◀ A market is a collection of buyers and sellers of the same good or service. Few markets are found in just one place; you can typically buy the same goods and services in locations spread across the economy. Do you want a pizza? This map shows where the most popular pizzerias are located all over the country.

▲ If an economy uses all of its resources to make pizzas and tank tops, the opportunity cost of making more tank tops is the loss of some pizzas.

other people specialize in producing. A **market** is a collection of buyers and sellers of the same good or service. Few markets are found in just one place—buyers and sellers of cell phone service, for example, are spread across the country. The same is true for the markets for workers, education, Italian food, and other popular goods and services. Today many products, from Girl Scout cookies to illegal drugs, are bought and sold in neighborhoods far from "brick-and-mortar" stores. And the Internet brings the markets for most goods right into your home.

Markets are part of an **economy,** a system for coordinating the production and distribution of goods and services. In this book, you will learn about the inner workings of markets and economies. For example, Chapter 2 explains how different types of markets are connected within an economy. And Chapter 18 explains

market
A collection of buyers and sellers of the same good or service.

economy
A system for coordinating the production and distribution of goods and services.

how international markets facilitate specialization and exchange across economies.

Opportunity Costs and the Production Possibilities Frontier

Just as your leisure-time activities and purchases have opportunity costs, so does the production of goods and services. *Resources* such as land, workers, and equipment are needed to produce goods and services, which places resource scarcity at the heart of economic problems. Unless there are idle resources such as unemployed workers or unused equipment in the economy, increasing the production of one good draws resources away from the production of another good or service. Suppose an economy uses all its resources to produce pizzas and tank tops. An increase in tank top production necessitates a decrease in pizza production. Why? Because some of the workers, machines, and land currently used to produce pizza would have to be used to produce tank tops instead. In this case, the opportunity cost of having more tank tops is the loss of some pizzas.

Table 1.1 shows some possibilities for the quantities of tank tops and pizzas that a fictional economy could produce in an hour. If the economy doesn't produce any tank tops, it can produce 10 pizzas, as shown by output combination *A*. If no pizzas are produced, the economy can produce 8 tank tops, as shown by output combination *E*. Comparing the output combinations from left to right, we see that producing smaller quantities of pizza frees up resources to produce larger quantities of tank tops.

The economy can go from producing no tank tops to producing 3 tank tops by switching from output combination *A* to output combination *B*. The opportunity cost of those 3 tank tops is 1 pizza, because the quantity of pizzas drops from 10 to 9 when the first 3 tank tops are made. To add another 3 tank tops

Table 1.1 Possible Output Combinations

	Output Combinations (hourly output using all available resources)				
Product	A	B	C	D	E
Pizzas	10	9	8	7	0
Tank Tops	0	3	5	6	8

Hluboki Dzianis/Shutterstock

▲ A city map is one example of a model. By simplifying a real-life situation, a map helps people find their way around. Graphical models likewise simplify the analysis of economic relationships.

to its hourly output—for a total of 6 tank tops—the economy must switch to output combination *D*. The switch from combination *B* to combination *D* lowers the quantity of pizzas from 9 to 7. Notice that the opportunity cost increased from 1 pizza for the first 3 tank tops to 2 pizzas for the next 3 tank tops.

To better understand the concept of increasing opportunity cost, we can use a favorite tool of economists: a *model*. A **model** is a simplified representation of a real-life situation. Models are popular outside of economics as well. For example, a city map is a model in which lines are simplified representations of real roads that can take you from here to there.

Most maps don't show details such as trees, cars, or weather patterns, but when you're trying to find your way around, a map that keeps things simple can help you reach your destination. The models in this textbook are in the form of graphs. The lines on these graphs help us examine real-life situations while leaving out details that might get us lost before we reach a conclusion.

To help simplify our work with economic models, we will frequently make the assumption of *ceteris paribus,* Latin for "other things remaining unchanged." Suppose Tour de France winner Chris Froome is biking down a mountain at 40 miles per hour when he gets a flat tire. How will this affect his speed? Many factors might come into play. If the tire blew out as Chris flew over a guardrail and went into a free fall, his speed would increase. A collision or fatigue would reduce his speed and reinforce the influence of the

flat tire. So some people might just throw up their hands and say it's impossible to know how a flat tire would affect Chris's speed. An economist, on the other hand, is more likely to say, "*Ceteris paribus,* the bike will slow down." The economist is assuming that, except for the blowout, other factors—the biker's path, his energy level, and so on—will remain the same.

Likewise, when we use a model to examine the influence of a particular factor on the economy, we assume that other factors remain unchanged. For example, when we examine the effects of technological advances on production levels, we make the *ceteris paribus* assumption that no other determinant of production levels changes. Without that assumption, a change in technology could be accompanied by changes in management, worker training programs, and other factors that affect production. The *ceteris paribus* assumption allows us to address the issue in question without having to sort through a more complex set of changes.

A **production possibilities frontier (PPF)** is a model that shows all the alternative combinations of two goods that could be produced in an economy within a given time period using every available resource *efficiently*. If resources are used efficiently, the only way to make more of one good is to make less of another good, because every resource is already being used to its full potential.

> **model**
> A simplified representation of a real-life situation.
>
> *ceteris paribus*
> A Latin phrase that means "other things remaining unchanged."
>
> **production possibilities frontier (PPF)**
> A model that shows all the alternative combinations of two goods that could be produced in an economy within a given time period using every available resource efficiently.

Quantity of
Tank Tops
(per hour)

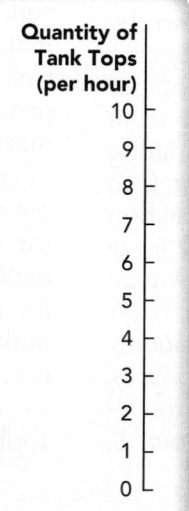

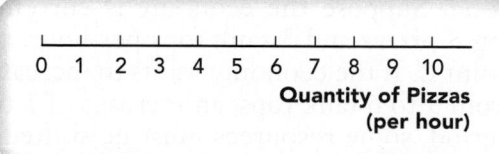

Figure 1.1 on the next page shows the PPF for an economy that uses all its resources to produce pizzas and tank tops. (If you haven't worked with graphs before, see the appendix to this chapter for a thorough introduction.) The horizontal axis (shown above) measures the quantity of pizzas produced per period, which in our example is an hour. The vertical axis (shown at left) measures the quantity of tank tops produced per

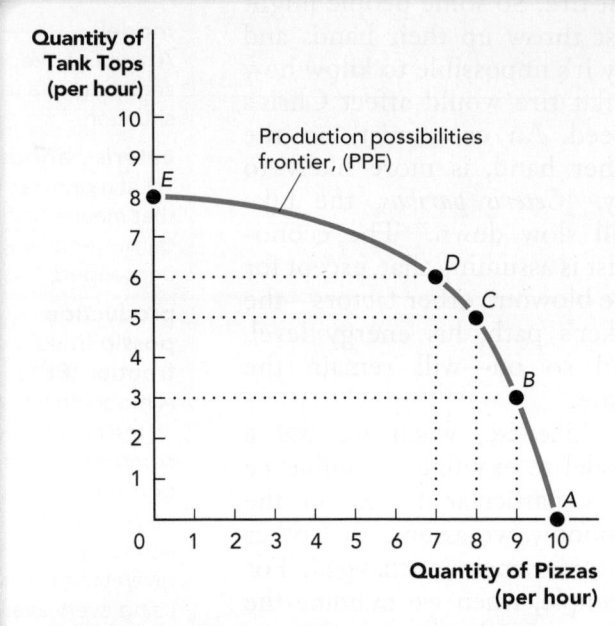

FIGURE 1.1 The Production Possibilities Frontier

This production possibilities frontier (PPF) shows all the combinations of tank tops and pizza the economy could produce in an hour using every available resource efficiently.

period. Point *A* in Figure 1.1 shows that if the economy devoted all its resources to making pizzas, it could produce 10 pizzas per period. Point *E* shows that if it produced no pizzas, the economy could produce 8 tank tops per period. Using all of its resources, the economy could also produce any other combination of pizzas and tank tops along the production possibilities frontier.

By looking at the PPF, we can identify the opportunity cost of producing each unit of each good. Suppose the economy is currently producing 8 pizzas and 5 tank tops per hour, as shown by point *C*. If the economy wants to increase its output from 5 to 6 tank tops, an increase of 1 tank top per period, some resources must be shifted away from pizza production. As the economy moves up along the PPF, from producing 5 tank tops at point *C* to producing 6 tank tops at point *D*, pizza production drops from 8 pizzas to 7 pizzas. This loss of 1 pizza is the opportunity cost of making the additional tank top.

Starting at point *C* again, suppose the economy wants to increase the quantity of pizzas it produces. As it moves to the right along the PPF, from producing 8 pizzas at point *C* to making 9 pizzas at point *B*,

production drops from 5 tank tops to 3 tank tops. This loss of 2 tank tops is the opportunity cost of producing an additional pizza.

THE SHAPE OF THE PRODUCTION POSSIBILITIES FRONTIER

Production possibilities frontiers are typically shaped like the one seen in Figure 1.1. This shape can be described as *bowed-out* or *concave to the origin*. The reason for that shape is the increasing opportunity cost of making more of either good. For example, notice that the opportunity cost of producing another pizza—the drop in the number of tank tops that can be produced when one more pizza is produced—increases as the quantity of pizzas increases. The opportunity cost of the first pizza is a small fraction of a tank top. By the time the 8th, 9th, and 10th pizzas are produced, the opportunity cost has grown to 1, 2, and 3 tank tops, respectively. This increasing opportunity cost causes the production possibilities frontier to fall by more and more as the quantity of pizzas increases, thus giving the PPF a concave shape.

The increasing opportunity cost of producing pizzas, tank tops, and most other goods and services results from the *specialization of resources*. Particular workers, land, equipment, and entrepreneurs are better suited for producing some things than they are for producing others. It takes different skills to produce pizzas and tank tops, and few workers are good at producing both. Loam soil in moderate climates is well suited for growing wheat for pizza dough, while sandy soil in warm climates is better for growing cotton for tank tops. And sewing machines are far more useful for making tank tops than for slicing pizza.

If the economy produces only tank tops, the resources specialized for making pizzas—like loam soil, pizza chefs, and pizza cutters—are used to make tank tops instead. The opportunity cost of the first few pizzas is small because the pizzas can be produced with resources that are better for making pizzas and don't contribute much to the production of tank tops. As more pizzas are made, resources better suited for tank top production must be adapted for use in making pizzas. The last few pizzas are made with the resources that are the least useful for making pizzas and the most useful for making tank tops, so the opportunity cost of the last pizzas is relatively large.

A similar story of increasing opportunity cost applies to increases in tank top production. As more tank tops are produced, resources increasingly ill-suited for tank top production and well suited for pizza production must be used. You can imagine what happens when the pizza chefs go to work sewing tank tops: a lot of pizzas are given up for each tank top, so the opportunity cost of making each tank top grows large.

It would be nice to have more pizzas and more tank tops by producing at a point beyond the PPF, such as point *F* in Figure 1.2. Unfortunately, that's not possible with the resources and production methods currently available. The points on the frontier can be achieved only if all resources are fully employed; points beyond the PPF are unattainable. Over time, more points become attainable if the PPF shifts outward, as we'll discuss shortly.

If some resources are idle, production occurs below the PPF at a point such as point *G* in Figure 1.2. Starting from points below the frontier, it is not necessary to produce fewer of one good to make more of another. Production at points below the PPF is inefficient because the idle resources

▲ Many resources are specialized for the production of particular goods. One example is a sewing machine, which is useful for making tank tops but not so useful for making pizzas.

rgbdigital/Getty Images

could be used to make more of one or both goods with no opportunity cost. For example, more pizza could be made without giving up any tank tops by moving from point *G* to point *B*. More tank tops could be made without giving up any pizza by moving from point *G* to point *D*. Or more of both goods could be made by moving from point *G* to anywhere on the PPF between points *B* and *D*, such as point *C*.

It is possible, but not common, for a production possibility frontier to be straight, as shown in Figure 1.3. Consider a PPF that indicates all the possible quantities of pizzas and calzones an economy can produce per hour. A calzone is basically a pizza folded in half, so the opportunity cost of each pizza is one calzone. Because there is no specialization of resources between calzones and pizzas, this one-to-one trade-off exists no matter how many units of each good are produced. The PPF for pizzas and calzones in Figure 1.3 is therefore a straight line. This PPF indicates that when resources are fully employed, the production of each additional pizza causes the loss of one calzone. Likewise, another calzone comes at the cost of a pizza.

ECONOMIC GROWTH

When you were 12 years old, you probably couldn't write as many good research papers in a school year as you can now. Over time, you developed knowledge that made you more productive. Also,

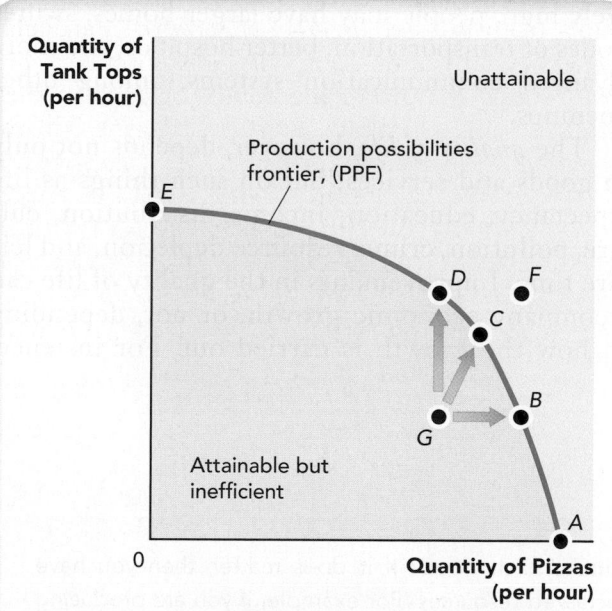

FIGURE 1.2 Inefficient and Unattainable Points

Production at a point below the PPF is inefficient because more of either or both goods could be made by using all of the economy's resources to their full potential. Points beyond the PPF are unattainable with the currently available resources and technology.

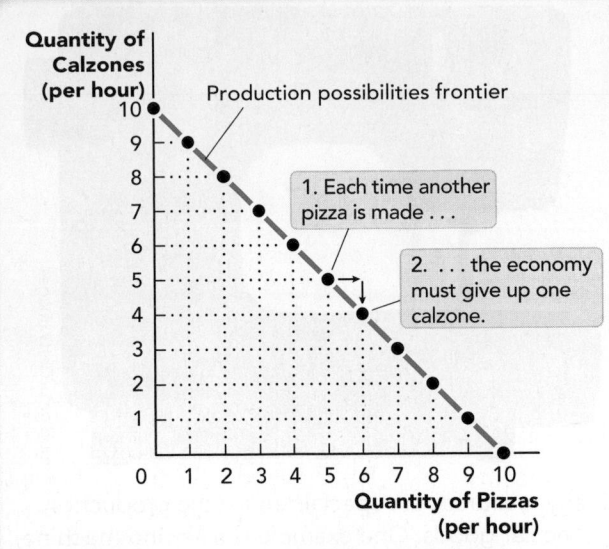

FIGURE 1.3 A Production Possibilities Frontier Without Specialized Resources
With no specialized resources, the opportunity cost remains the same at each level of production, and the production possibilities frontier is a straight line.

economic growth
An increase in the maximum amount of output an economy can produce over a period of time.

standard of living
A measure of the material wealth available to help people live comfortably.

that an economy can produce over a period of time. *Ceteris paribus*, economic growth comes from advances in knowledge or technology, or from increases in the availability of machinery, workers, or other resources that make higher output levels possible. However, an increase in output achieved by employing previously idle resources—such as unemployed workers—is not considered economic growth. Rather, the use of resources that were idle brings the economy a step closer to producing the maximum possible amount of output. If there has not been an increase in that maximum achievable output, there has not truly been economic growth.

Economic growth makes more goods and services available. This improves citizens' **standard of living,** a measure of the material wealth available to help people live comfortably. Chapter 13 explains that a country's standard of living is usually measured in terms of the amount of goods and services the average person produces. The standard of living can vary dramatically across countries. For example, the standard of living in the United States is 11 times higher than in Honduras and half as high as in Qatar. Where the standard of living is relatively high, people may have larger homes, swifter modes of transportation, better hospitals, and more advanced communication systems, among other amenities.

technological advances have resulted in better computers and websites, which enable people like you to write better research papers—and more of them. The productive capacity of an economy can increase in similar ways. **Economic growth** is an increase in the maximum amount of output

The *quality of life*, however, depends not only on goods and services, but on such things as life expectancy, education, income distribution, culture, pollution, crime, resource depletion, and leisure time. Improvements in the quality of life can accompany economic growth, or not, depending on how the growth is carried out. For instance,

How do I know whether to make the PPF curved or straight?

To determine whether a PPF is curved or straight, consider whether any of the resources used to make the goods are more useful for the production of one good rather than the other. The PPF is concave if some resources are specialized for making a particular good, whereas the PPF is straight if no resources are specialized. To determine whether any resources are specialized, imagine you are going to make some of both goods. Does it matter which workers, equipment, land, and other resources are used

to make each good? If it does matter, then you have specialized resources. For example, if you are producing bread and milk, and you have bakers and dairy farmers, it matters which workers produce each good: you want the bakers to make the bread and the dairy farmers to produce the milk. Because some resources are specialized, the PPF for bread and milk is concave. Now suppose you are producing ceramic mugs and ceramic bowls. The same workers—potters—can make either good with the same clay, glazes, and kilns. In this case, because there is no specialization of resources, the PPF is straight.

economic growth achieved by making everyone work in a factory for 16 hours a day would increase the standard of living, but *not* the quality of people's lives.

Economic growth shifts the production possibilities frontier outward. In Figure 1.4, the light green line recreates the PPF from Figure 1.1. The dark green PPF shows that as a result of economic growth, the economy can produce as many as 10 tank tops or as many as 11 pizzas per hour. Suppose the economy was originally at point C. After the economy has grown, it could produce the same quantity of pizzas as before, as well as more tank tops than before, moving to point H. Another option would be to keep the quantity of tank tops the same but produce more pizzas, moving to point I. Or the economy could produce more of both goods, moving to a point such as F.

The production possibilities frontier can also shift inward. In many countries, this has been the result of wars or natural disasters. Suppose an earthquake destroys many of the sewing machines and ovens used to make tank tops and pizzas. With fewer resources, there are fewer options for the production of goods. Figure 1.5 shows the resulting inward shift of the PPF. After the earthquake, the economy can produce at most 6 tank tops or 8 pizzas per hour. The question of how much of each

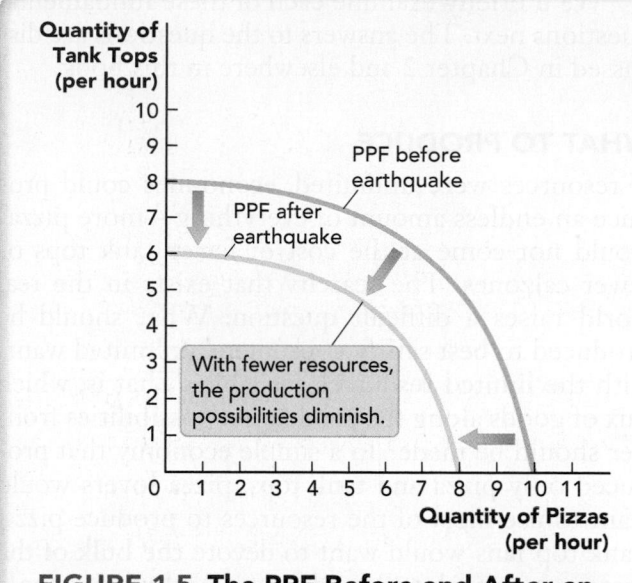

FIGURE 1.5 The PPF Before and After an Earthquake

The production possibilities frontier shifts inward when resources are destroyed by, for example, a natural disaster or a war. This shift indicates that the economy does not have the capacity to produce as much as it could before.

good to actually produce is one of the three fundamental questions that must be answered in every economy, as we'll discuss next.

The Three Fundamental Economic Questions

You and other members of society face questions every day about the use of time, money, and resources. Your decisions, and theirs, affect the answers to the following three broader questions that must be answered for economies as a whole:

1. What should be produced?
2. How should it be produced?
3. For whom should it be produced?

Answers to the fundamental questions of what, how, and for whom to produce determine the availability of the goods and services we need for our survival and comfort. The wrong answers can lead to shortages of goods and services and missed opportunities for a better life. For instance, economies that devote few resources to medicine, education, or food can end up with relatively large problems with illness, illiteracy, or starvation.

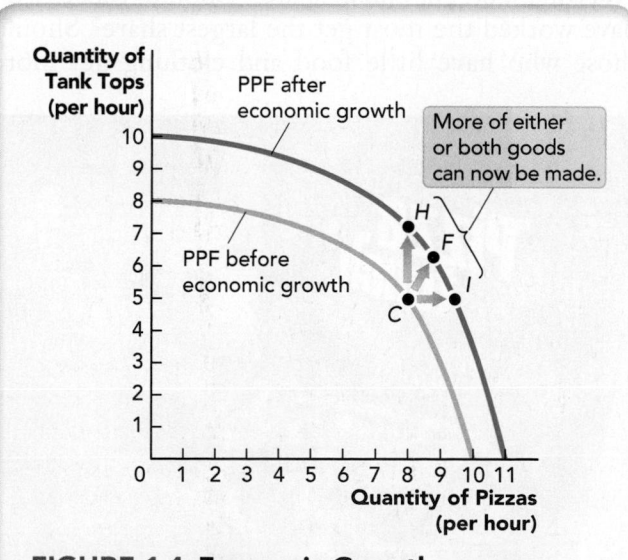

FIGURE 1.4 Economic Growth

Economic growth shifts the production possibilities frontier outward. This means that the economy has the capacity to produce more of either or both goods than before.

We'll briefly examine each of these fundamental questions next. The answers to the questions are discussed in Chapter 2 and elsewhere in this book.

WHAT TO PRODUCE

If resources were unlimited, economies could produce an endless amount of everything—more pizzas would not come at the cost of fewer tank tops or fewer calzones. The scarcity that exists in the real world raises a difficult question: What should be produced to best satisfy consumers' unlimited wants with the limited resources available? That is, which mix of goods along the production possibilities frontier should be made? In a simple economy that produced only pizza and tank tops, pizza lovers would want to use most of the resources to produce pizza. Tank top fans would want to devote the bulk of the resources to tank top production. And many people in between would push for still different combinations of the two goods.

In real-world economies, which produce hundreds of thousands of goods and services, the decisions are more complicated, but market forces can provide a helping hand in the form of *incentives*. An **incentive** is a reward or punishment that guides a decision. Incentives influence what people do with their time, money, and resources. Would you be studying right now if it weren't for the incentives of knowledge acquisition, good grades, and future career success? Would you drive faster if police didn't issue speeding tickets? Your favorite professional athlete might talk about giving "110 percent" to the team, but the truth is that athletes have many interests, including families, charities, and vacation homes. It would take a monumental incentive to get a mere 100 percent out of an athlete, so players are given all sorts of performance incentives. A professional football player might earn an extra $100,000 for rushing more than 1,000 yards in a season, $10,000 for catching six touchdown passes, or $300,000 for being on the roster for at least 15 games.

In 1776, Scottish economist Adam Smith pointed out that markets give consumers and producers incentives to make decisions that both benefit them personally and create benefits for society as a whole. These incentives, Smith said, guide people toward optimal decisions as if they were "led by an invisible hand." For example, when a product such as Chicago-style pizza is popular, the high demand drives up its price. High prices for the goods that many people desire provide incentives for producers to supply more of those goods. So the selfish pursuit of profit leads to consumers getting more of what they want. In this book, you will become familiar with the workings of supply and demand. You will also learn how incentives influence the answers to all three of the fundamental economic questions.

incentive
A reward or punishment that guides a decision.

HOW TO PRODUCE IT

Pizzas can be made mostly by hand, entirely by a pizza vending machine, or by various combinations of workers and equipment. Tank tops can be hand sewn or machine sewn. The cotton used to make clothing can be harvested either by hand, by a picking machine that pulls the cotton off the plant, or by a stripping machine that cuts the plant and then separates the cotton from the rest of the plant. Most other goods and services can be made in many different ways as well. Decisions about production methods help determine the cost and availability of your favorite goods and services. If the wrong production methods are used, the economy is operating at a point below its production possibilities frontier. In that case, it would be possible to make more output with the same resources by adopting improved production methods. Chapter 7 explains how the tools of economics help producers find production methods that make the most of the available resources.

FOR WHOM TO PRODUCE

Suppose we've produced the best possible mix of pizzas and tank tops. Who should get them? Should everyone get an equal share? Should those who have worked the most get the largest share? Should those who have little food and clothing get more

▲ Producers must make decisions about how to produce each good and service. This automatic pizza cooking and vending machine proves that there's more than one way to make a pizza.

Paul Hennessy/Newscom/Polaris Images/Lakeland/Florida/United States than those who have plenty? Chapter 2 explains that different types of economies have different mechanisms for deciding who gets what. Sometimes goods and services go to the people who are willing and able to pay the highest prices in the marketplace. Sometimes government leaders distribute goods and services. In most economies, a combination of these influences determines who gets what.

In some cases, tradition determines who gets what. Perhaps the distribution of goods at your home works similarly. Maybe it's a tradition for your family to have turkey on Thanksgiving and for you and your brother to get the turkey legs. The cook earns the privilege of tasting everything before the rest of the family even sits down at the dinner table. And your parents probably make sure that some of the turkey is shared with the youngest and oldest members of the family, who might have trouble fending for themselves.

Categories of Economics

Economics comes in many flavors. One kind of economics is strictly about facts; another is about suggestions that involve judgments. Economics can examine the big picture of what is going on in the nation's economy, or it can zoom in on the decisions that individuals like you are making. This section explains these four broad categories of economics.

POSITIVE AND NORMATIVE ECONOMICS

The cost of attending college in the United States has doubled over the past three decades, even after adjusting for inflation. This has led some policymakers to propose increased financial support for college students. Data on college cost increases and proposals for student aid are examples of two distinct ways that economics influences decisions. The first is that it establishes facts about *the way things are* in the economy. For instance, by tracking tuition costs economists provide a glimpse of important facts. This fact-based, descriptive side of economics is known as **positive economics.** Reports on the unemployment rate and the price of oil are considered positive economics, as are the findings that 69,386 pizzerias operate in the United States and that U.S. households consume about 45 million turkeys each Thanksgiving.

The second way that economics influences decisions is by addressing controversies about the way things *should be.* Should college students receive more financial support? What policies should be

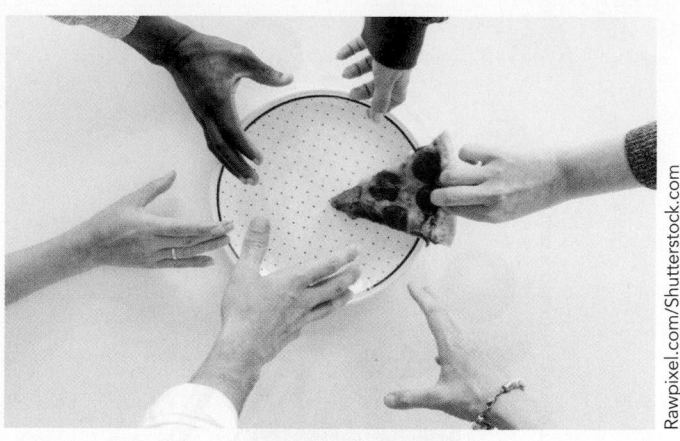

▲ When more people want something than can have it, economic systems determine who gets what.

adopted to promote job creation and decrease the unemployment rate? Should there be a tax on pizza? This type of economics, dealing with judgments about the way things should be, is known as **normative economics.**

Positive economics often influences normative economics. That's what happened when rising tuition costs led to calls for tuition assistance. Even more compelling is the example of heart disease, which takes the lives of about 610,000 Americans each year and imposes an annual financial burden in excess of $320 billion. Such facts have led to judgments that Americans should exercise more and eat healthier diets.

MICROECONOMICS AND MACROECONOMICS

Microeconomics is the study of scarcity and choice at the level of individual decision makers. What purchases will make you as happy as possible? How should the members of your household divide their time between work and leisure? What products, staffing levels, and prices will make a store as profitable as possible? And what output level should a factory select? The tools of microeconomics apply to these and many other decisions made by individuals, households, and businesses.

Whereas microeconomics focuses on small elements of the economy, *macroeconomics* steps

positive economics
The fact-based, descriptive side of economics.

normative economics
The type of economics that deals with judgments about the way things should be.

microeconomics
The study of scarcity and choice at the level of individual decision makers.

▲ Microeconomics examines the behavior of individual decision makers.

macroeconomics
The study of the economy as a whole.

back and looks at the big picture. **Macroeconomics** is the study of the economy as a whole. What you hear on the national news about consumer spending, inflation, unemployment, and

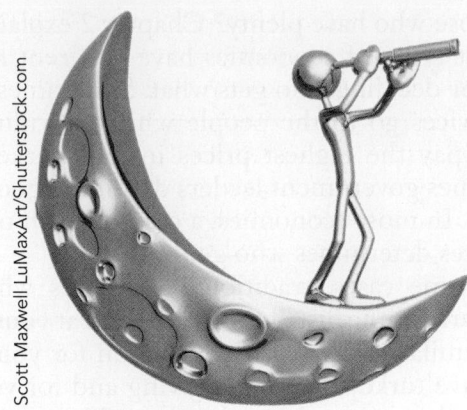

▲ Macroeconomics is the study of the entire economy.

interest rates is all about macroeconomics. Government policies designed to promote economic growth are macroeconomic policies because they affect the economy as a whole. Macroeconomic policy is in action when the nation's central bank, the Federal Reserve, increases the money supply in hopes of helping the economy out of an economic downturn. Later in this book, you will learn to make sense of macroeconomic information in the news and discover how macroeconomic policies work. But first we will explore the *trade-offs* people have to make between alternative choices at every level of the economy.

SUMMARY

The economic way of thinking provides insights into daily dilemmas. Economic literacy may contribute to your financial success by guiding relevant decisions. It is even more likely to help you appreciate the workings of the overall economy and the world around you. As you study economics, you will learn analytical tools that help policymakers, business leaders, and college students achieve their goals. Even if your own goals have little to do with money, they are likely to have much to do with economics.

Economics is about scarcity and choice. We all have needs and wants that are constrained by the scarcity of resources. Even those delightful things that require few if any resources, such as friendships, the arts, and hikes in the woods, take our scarce time. So we must make decisions about the use of time and resources made difficult by opportunity costs. If more time is spent on education, less time is available for recreation. If more resources are devoted to food production, fewer are available for clothing production. Given the scarcity that constrains our well-being, unwise decisions about resource allocation

limit the satisfaction of our needs and wants. Economic literacy can help you make wise decisions.

To deal with the problem of scarcity, producers specialize in what they do relatively well. Markets allow people to exchange what they've specialized in making for money they can use to buy what other people have specialized in making. International markets provide opportunities for specialization and exchange across countries.

Economists use models to simplify and better understand real-life situations. A production possibilities frontier (PPF) is a model of the alternative combinations of two goods that could be produced in an economy within a given period of time using all available resources. With this model you can determine the opportunity cost of producing more of either good. The opportunity cost typically rises as more of a good is produced, because increased production eventually draws on resources that are better suited for making something else.

Every economy must answer three fundamental questions: What should be produced? How should it be produced? And for whom should it be produced? In most modern economies, the answers to these big questions come from many smaller decisions you and other individuals make. In this book, you will learn how to make wise economic decisions and how to make sense of the bigger stories in the economy that result from decisions like yours.

Economics can be about the way things are or the way things ought to be. Positive economics involves descriptions of the way things are. If you say, "The average economics major earns more than the average math major," you have made a positive statement because it is factual and descriptive. Normative economics involves prescriptions for the way things

should be. If you tell someone, "You should major in economics," you've made a normative statement because it is based on your own judgment (and good judgment at that!).

Microeconomics focuses on individual decision makers. It is about how decisions are made to reach goals such as happiness for individuals and profit for businesses. Macroeconomics looks at an economy's big picture. The policy tools of macroeconomics influence interest rates, taxes, government purchases, and the money supply. The goal of macroeconomic policy is to make society better off by moderating inflation and unemployment and by encouraging economic growth.

KEY TERMS

scarcity, p. 2
economics, p. 2
opportunity cost, p. 2
market, p. 4
economy, p. 4
model, p. 5

ceteris paribus, p. 5
production possibilities frontier
   (PPF), p. 5
economic growth, p. 8
standard of living, p. 8
incentive, p. 10

positive economics, p. 11
normative economics, p. 11
microeconomics, p. 11
macroeconomics, p. 12

PROBLEMS FOR REVIEW

1. Consider the following statement: "Economics is all about money and banks." What part of the statement is true? What part is false? Provide a better explanation of what economics is about.

2. Which of the following items are typically scarce? Do particular people specialize in producing the scarce items? Explain how specialization helps reduce the problem of scarcity.
   a. paintings
   b. oranges
   c. hip hop concerts
   d. clean floors
   e. air

3. Assume that there is no difference in the resources used to make hats and belts, except that two belts can be made with the same amount of resources needed to make one hat. Fill in the accompanying table and then draw a graph showing the associated production possibilities frontier, with the quantity of hats on the horizontal axis and the quantity of belts on the vertical axis.

Output Combinations
(hourly output using all available resources)

Product	A	B	C	D	E
Hats	4	3	2	1	0
Belts	0				

   a. Would the production of 3 hats and 1 belt be inefficient, efficient, or unattainable?
   b. Would the production of 2 hats and 5 belts be inefficient, efficient, or unattainable?

4. Suppose an economy produces televisions and turkeys. The accompanying table shows several of the economy's efficient output combinations. Draw the production possibilities frontier for this economy on a graph with the quantity of televisions on the horizontal axis and the quantity of turkeys on the vertical axis. Label this curve PPF_1.

Output Combinations (hourly output using all available resources)					
Product	A	B	C	D	E
Televisions	4	3	2	1	0
Turkeys	0	4	7	9	10

Now suppose that economic growth allows the economy to produce the output combinations shown in the following table. Draw the new PPF on the graph you have already created for this economy and label it PPF_2. Identify one type of change that makes economic growth possible.

Output Combinations After Economic Growth (hourly output using all available resources)					
Product	F	G	H	I	J
Televisions	8	6	4	2	0
Turkeys	0	6	10	13	15

5. Suppose an economy in a cold climate makes sweatshirts and pizzas. The accompanying table shows several of the economy's efficient output combinations. Draw the production possibilities frontier for this economy on a graph with the quantity of pizzas on the horizontal axis and the quantity of sweatshirts on the vertical axis. Label this curve PPF_1.

Output Combinations (hourly output using all available resources)					
Product	A	B	C	D	E
Pizzas	16	12	8	4	0
Sweatshirts	0	8	14	18	20

Now suppose new oven technology increases pizza production by 50%. In other words, for each quantity of sweatshirts that can be made, the quantity of pizzas that can also be made is 1.5 times higher than before. Draw the new PPF and label the new points F, G, H, I, and J, from right to left. Label this curve PPF_2. Explain why one point on PPF_1 is also on PPF_2.

6. What is one thing that could cause the production possibilities frontier in your economy to shift inward?

7. Some people end their formal education with a high school degree, some finish with a college degree, and some go on to obtain a graduate degree. Beyond the ability to pay tuition, what are some reasons people stay in school for different lengths of time? How might the nonmonetary cost of college differ among individuals? How might the benefits differ?

8. What is the opportunity cost (not the dollar value, but the foregone activity) of you going to economics class?

9. Explain how incentives influenced something you did this week, how you did it, or for whom you did it.

10. How do incentives influence your study habits? Why do students often ask, "Is this going to be on the test?" Why would it be unwise for an education-maximizing instructor to answer, "No, it isn't"?

11. Can you tell when a salesclerk works on a commission basis (meaning that the clerk's earnings are based on the volume of sales)? Do people who work for tips behave differently from those who do not?

12. Suppose tickets to a basketball game with broad appeal are inexpensive, but you can only obtain them by standing in line for many hours. The tickets may not be transferred from one person to another. Who would be more likely to buy tickets to this game: college students or leaders of major corporations? Explain your answer.

13. Suppose the members of your family are fighting over a slice of pizza. Identify three ways to determine who gets the slice. Would any of these ways help assure that the person who most wants the slice of pizza gets it? Explain your answer.

14. Which of the following are positive economic statements?
    a. The unemployment rate is 5.4 percent.
    b. The price of bottled water is too high.
    c. The average college tuition last year was $35,000.
    d. The inflation rate is rising.
    e. It is improper to sell 64-ounce sodas to children.

15. Classify each of the following as a topic of either microeconomics or macroeconomics.
    a. Your family's decision to buy a house.
    b. The Kellogg company's hiring decisions.
    c. The economy's supply of money.
    d. Your large investment in stocks.
    e. The falling U.S. unemployment rate.

Understanding Graphs

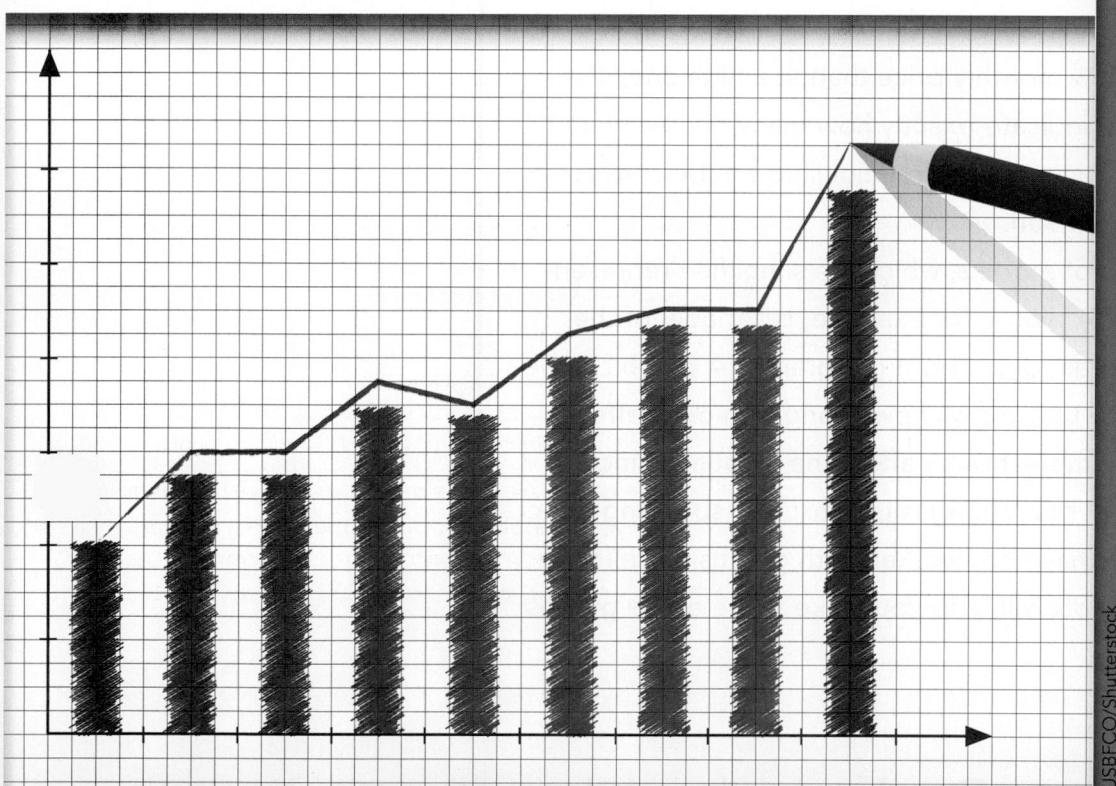

LEARNING OBJECTIVES

In this appendix, you will learn to:

1. Interpret the meanings of points and curves on graphs
2. Determine the slope of a line and understand its significance
3. Calculate the size of rectangular and triangular areas on graphs
4. Understand bar charts, pie charts, and scatter diagrams

When great ideas come up, it is wise to jot them down, even when a sheet of paper can't be found. For example, the success stories of Southwest Airlines, the song "Louie, Louie," and several popular mobile apps all began as scribbles on napkins, toilet paper, or envelopes. When economists feel compelled to write down a great idea, they often capture it in the form of a graph or equation. Why? Because these tools convey so much information in so little space. A classic example arose when economist Arthur Laffer and President Gerald Ford's Chief of Staff Donald Rumsfeld held a dinner meeting to discuss how changes in tax rates would affect tax revenues. Laffer wanted to illustrate his thoughts about rising and falling tax revenues with a graph, and being in a restaurant, Laffer drew the graph on a cocktail napkin. The controversial result, now known as the Laffer curve, became the basis for much of President Ronald Reagan's economic policy. In this chapter, an ample supply of paper is used to explain the essentials of graphs—the economist's favorite tool.

Why Should I Care?

When it comes to detailed information, a graph or equation makes a long story short. Consider the relationship between the monthly price of a Spotify Premium music-streaming subscription and the number of people who decide to subscribe. It's easy to explain that Spotify will have more subscribers at a low monthly price than at a high one; it's much harder to use words to indicate exactly how many people would subscribe at every possible price. Yet this relationship can be conveyed quickly with a graph or an equation.

Economists are also fond of *models*, which are simplified representations of real-life situations. A globe, for example, is a model of the world that can teach you a great deal about geography. A graph can be a model of the economy, one that shows how changes in price affect music sales, how changes in interest rates affect the amount of money people borrow for college, or how changes in consumer spending affect the inflation rate. Even if you have not worked with graphs much in the past, don't worry. This appendix will help you make sense of the graphs you will see in the book.

Coordinate Graphs

variables
Measures that can take on more than one value.

horizontal axis (x-axis)
The solid horizontal line along which the x-variable is measured in a coordinate graph.

vertical axis (y-axis)
The solid vertical line along which the y-variable is measured in a coordinate graph.

origin
The point at which the two axes in a coordinate graph meet and the value of each variable is zero.

You might be interested in the relationship between the number of miles you run and the weight you lose. Managers are interested in the relationship between the prices they charge and the quantities of their products that consumers want to buy. Measures that can take on more than one value—such as miles run, weight lost, prices, and quantities sold—are called **variables.** The graphs we will work with in this book involve two variables, identified in general terms as the *x-variable* and the *y-variable*. As Figure 1A.1 shows, the *x*-variable is measured along the solid horizontal line called the **horizontal axis,** or the **x-axis.** The *y*-variable is measured along the solid vertical line called the **vertical axis,** or **y-axis.** The two axes meet at the **origin,** the point at which the value of each variable is zero.

Each **point** on a graph represents a value for both the *x*-variable and the *y*-variable. Consider point *A* in Figure 1A.1. Because it lies above the value of 2 on the horizontal axis, the value of the *x*-variable at point *A* is 2. Because it has the height of 3 on the vertical axis, the value of the *y*-variable at point *A* is 3. Suppose the *x*-variable is the number of radio advertisements the Rough Smoothie Shop runs per week and the *y*-variable is the average number of customers that visit the shop per hour. Then point *A* tells us that if 2 ads are run per week, the shop will average 3 customers per hour. Likewise, point *B* indicates that if 4 ads are run, the shop will average 9 customers per hour.

Each point on a two-dimensional graph can be identified by a pair of numbers or *coordinates*: The

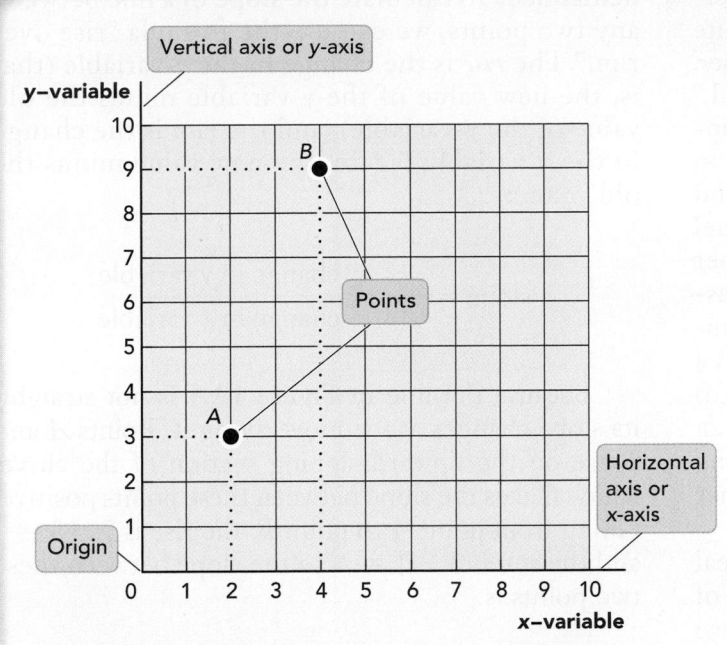

FIGURE 1A.1 Variables, Points, and Axes

Values of the *x*-variable are measured along the horizontal axis, or *x*-axis. Values of the *y*-variable are measured along the vertical axis, or *y*-axis. The two axes meet at the origin. Each point on the graph represents both a value of the *x*-variable and a value of the *y*-variable.

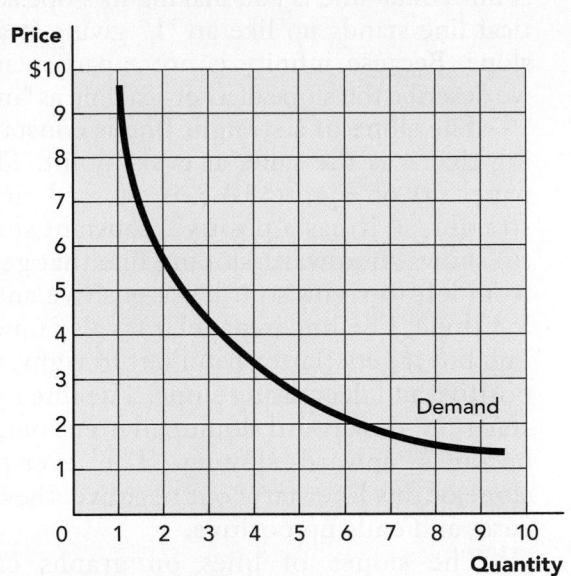

FIGURE 1A.2 A Demand Curve

Economists make frequent use of *curves* that show the relationship between two variables. For example, the demand curve shows the relationship between the price of a good and the quantity of that good demanded by consumers. Unlike this particular demand curve, some curves are actually straight lines.

first is the value of the *x*-variable at that point, and the second is the value of the *y*-variable at that point. For example, point *A* can be identified by the coordinates (2, 3) and point *B* can be identified as (4, 9). The origin is found at (0, 0).

Economists make frequent use of lines on graphs called *curves*. A curve represents the relationship between two variables. For example, Figure 1A.2 shows a *demand curve*, which illustrates the relationship between the price of a good and the quantity of that good demanded by consumers. In this book you will see many other useful relationships displayed as curves. Some curves really are curved; other curves are actually straight lines. Although curves pass through many points, depending upon what's being illustrated, sometimes the black dots that represent points don't appear at all on a graph. Or, they may only mark particular points that are the focus of discussion.

Most graphs show the relationship between an **independent variable**—one whose value is not influenced by the other variable—and a **dependent variable**—one whose value *is* influenced by the other variable. In our Rough Smoothie Shop advertising example, the number of advertisements is the independent variable and the number of customers per hour is the dependent variable.

Graphs are commonly set up so that the *x*-variable is the independent variable and the *y*-variable is the dependent variable. When it comes to supply and demand graphs, however, economists follow a tradition begun by nineteenth-century economists Leon Walras and Alfred Marshall of reversing that convention. As Figure 1A.2 shows, price is the *y*-variable on a demand graph, even though it influences the quantity demanded, which is the *x*-variable.

Slopes

You're reading this text from left to right. Descriptions of lines on graphs assume the same left-to-right viewing. The rate at which a line rises or falls from left to right is described by its **slope.** A downward-sloping line falls from left to right, so it has a negative slope. An upward-sloping line rises from left to right, so it has a positive slope.

point
A value for both the *x*-variable and the *y*-variable on a coordinate graph.

independent variable
A measure whose value is not influenced by another variable.

dependent variable
A measure whose value is influenced by another variable.

slope
The rate at which a line rises or falls from left to right.

A horizontal line is flat, making its slope zero. A vertical line stands up like an "l," giving it an infinite slope. Because infinity is not a particular number, we describe the slope of a vertical line as "undefined."

The slope of a straight line is constant, meaning that it is the same at every point. The line in panel (a) of Figure 1A.3 is upward sloping and straight, so it has a positive, constant slope. Panel (b) shows an upward-sloping line that gets steeper from left to right, so it has a positive and increasing slope. The line in panel (c) is also upward sloping, but it gets flatter from left to right, so it has a positive and decreasing slope. The line in panel (d) starts out downward sloping, flattens out, and then becomes upward sloping. The ever-increasing slope of this line starts out negative, then becomes zero, and ends up positive.

The slopes of lines on graphs can reveal important information, such as how much of one good an economy must give up to produce more of another good, or how a price change will affect the quantity of a good that is supplied and demanded. To calculate the slope of a line between any two points, we can use the formula "rise over run." The *rise* is the change in the y-variable (that is, the new value of the y-variable minus the old value of the y-variable), and the *run* is the change in the x-variable (again, the new value minus the old value):

$$\text{slope} = \frac{\text{rise}}{\text{run}} = \frac{\text{change in } y \text{ variable}}{\text{change in } x \text{ variable}}$$

Because the line in Figure 1A.4 is not straight, its slope changes as we move along it. Points A and B are on the upward-sloping section of the curve, which makes the slope between these points positive. Going from point A to point B, the rise is $7 - 3 = 4$ and the run is $3 - 1 = 2$, so the slope between these two points is

$$\text{slope} = \frac{4}{2} = 2$$

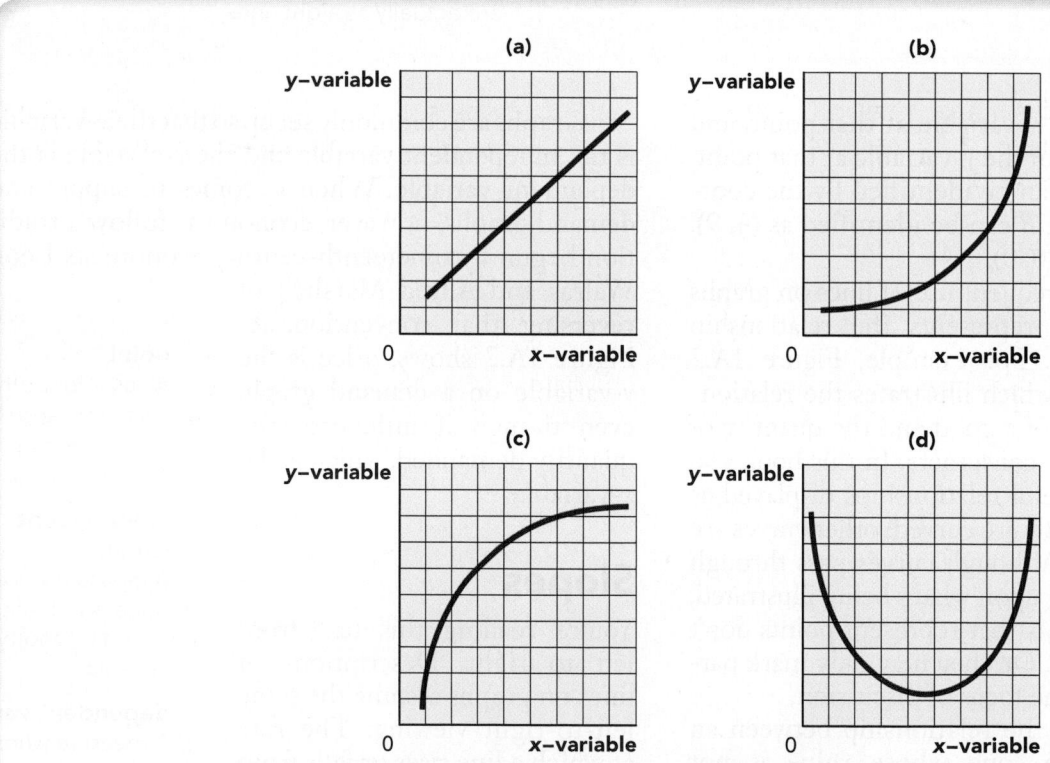

FIGURE 1A.3 Curves with Varying Slopes

An upward-sloping line can have a constant slope as in panel (a), an increasing slope as in panel (b), a decreasing slope as in panel (c), or a slope with some combination of these characteristics. Panel (d) shows a line that starts out downward sloping and ends upward sloping, but has an increasing slope from beginning to end.

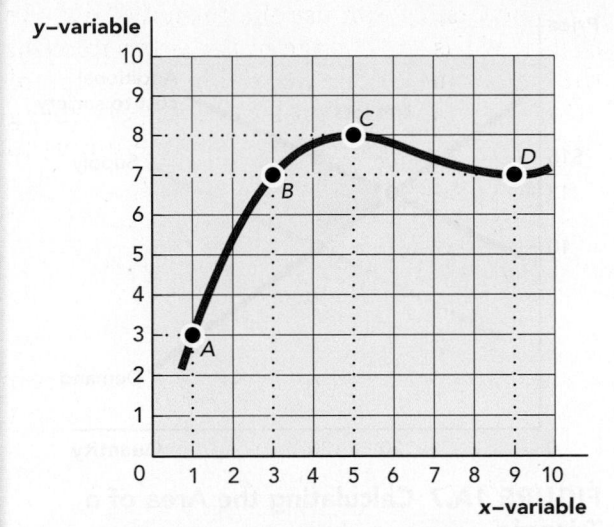

FIGURE 1A.4 Calculating a Slope

The slope of a line between two points is found by dividing the rise (the change in the y-variable) by the run (the change in the x-variable). Between points A and B, the rise is 4 and the run is 2, so the slope is $\frac{4}{2} = 2$. Between points C and D, the rise is −1, and the run is 4, so the slope is $\frac{-1}{4} = -0.25$.

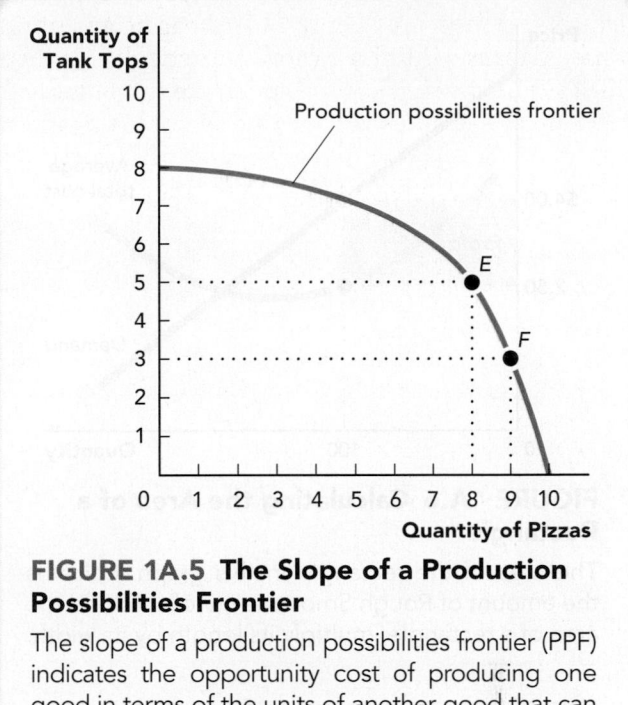

FIGURE 1A.5 The Slope of a Production Possibilities Frontier

The slope of a production possibilities frontier (PPF) indicates the opportunity cost of producing one good in terms of the units of another good that can no longer be produced.

The line is downward sloping between points C and D, so as the x-variable increases, the y-variable decreases. In our slope formula, we indicate the decrease in the y-variable by giving the rise a negative value. Going from point C to point D, the rise is $7 - 8 = -1$ and the run is $9 - 5 = 4$. Plugging these values into the slope formula gives us

$$\text{slope} = \frac{-1}{4} = -0.25$$

To see how slopes can be useful, consider the production possibilities frontier (PPF) explained in Chapter 1, a version of which appears in Figure 1A.5. The opportunity cost of the good measured on the horizontal axis—pizzas, in this case—is the absolute value (the value without the negative sign) of the PPF's slope. Going from point E to point F, for example, the "run" of 1 that has us making 1 more pizza is accompanied by a "rise" of −2, which represents the loss of 2 tank tops that can no longer be produced. The slope between points E and F is thus $\frac{-2}{1} = -2$. The negative value of the slope indicates a *negative* or *inverse relationship* between these two variables, meaning that as one of the variables increases, the

other decreases. The specific value of the slope, −2 in this case, tells us that the opportunity cost of the additional pizza is 2 tank tops.

Areas

In addition to the information conveyed by points and slopes, areas on graphs indicate important values such as the value of a firm's profit, a government's tax revenue, or a consumer's net gain from buying a good. When the areas of interest are rectangles or triangles, we can use simple formulas to determine their size. Figure 1A.6 shows a rectangle that represents profit for the Rough Smoothie Shop. A later chapter talks more about this graph, which appears here to show you how *areas* are relevant to the economic concepts you will be studying. To find the area of a rectangle, use the following formula:

$$\text{area of a rectangle} = \text{length} \times \text{width}$$

The length of the rectangle in Figure 1A.6 is 100 and the width is $4.00 − $2.50 = $1.50, so Rough Smoothie's profit is $100 \times \$1.50 = \$150$.

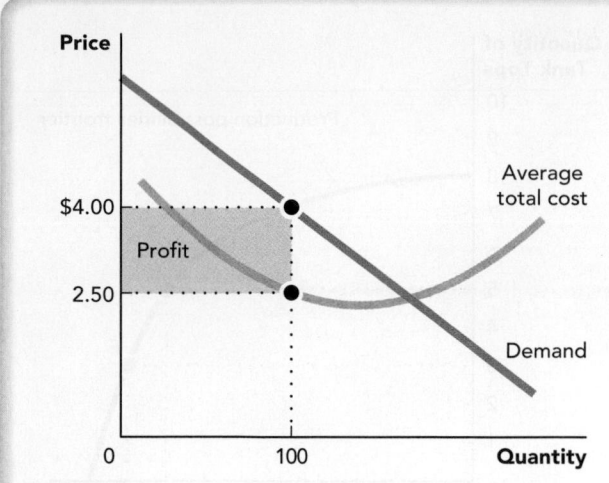

FIGURE 1A.6 Calculating the Area of a Rectangle

The area of the rectangle in this graph indicates the amount of Rough Smoothie's profit. To find the area of a rectangle, multiply its length by its width.

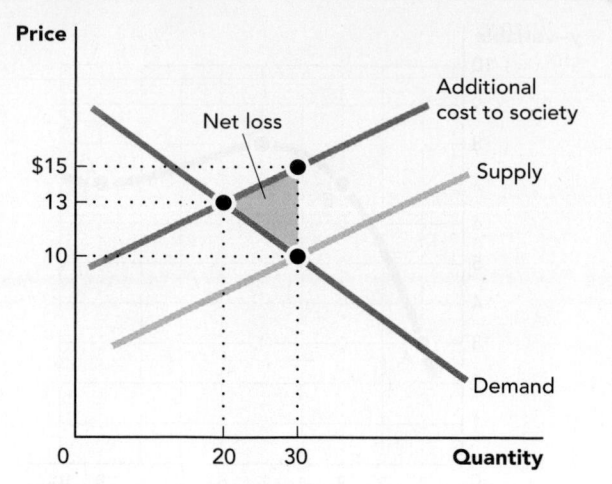

FIGURE 1A.7 Calculating the Area of a Triangle

Triangular areas on graphs indicate values such as the net gain to consumers from the purchase of a good or, as in this graph, the net loss to society from the overproduction of a good. The area of a triangle is found by multiplying one-half of its base times its height.

The areas of triangles on graphs can also represent important values and are not hard to calculate. To find the area, first pick one side of the triangle for which you can find the length, and call that side the *base*. Then determine what the height of the triangle would be if it were resting on that base. With that information you can find the area as:

$$\text{area of a triangle} = \frac{1}{2} \times \text{base} \times \text{height}$$

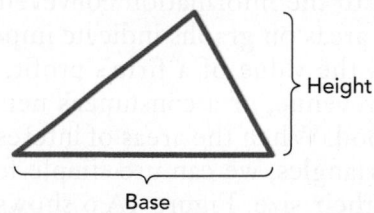

Now consider the triangle in Figure 1A.7, a graph you will see again in a later chapter. The yellow triangle represents a net loss to society due to the overproduction of a good. Let's call the right side of the triangle the base, because it is easy to determine its length from the information on the graph. The base starts at a price of $10 and ends at a price of $15, so the base is

bar chart (bar graph)
A chart in which rectangular bars indicate the value of a dependent variable for each value of an independent variable.

$15 − $10 = $5 long. The height of the triangle if it rested on its base would be 30 − 20 = 10, so the area of the triangle—the net loss to society from the overproduction—is $\frac{1}{2} \times \$5 \times 10 = \$25$.

Other Types of Graphs

Useful graphs come in many shapes and styles. In addition to graphs with curves, you will see bar charts, pie charts, and scatter diagrams in your economics-related readings. This section provides an overview of each of these types of graphs.

BAR CHARTS

In a **bar chart,** or **bar graph,** rectangular bars indicate the value of a dependent variable for each value of an independent variable. If you open a seller's account on eBay, you will receive sales reports in the form of bar charts. Major retailers use similar charts to track their sales over time. In those charts, the independent variable is a measure of time, such as months or years, and the dependent variable is a measure of sales during the designated time periods. In Figure 1A.8, each bar is situated over a particular year, and the height of the bar indicates how many dollars' worth of

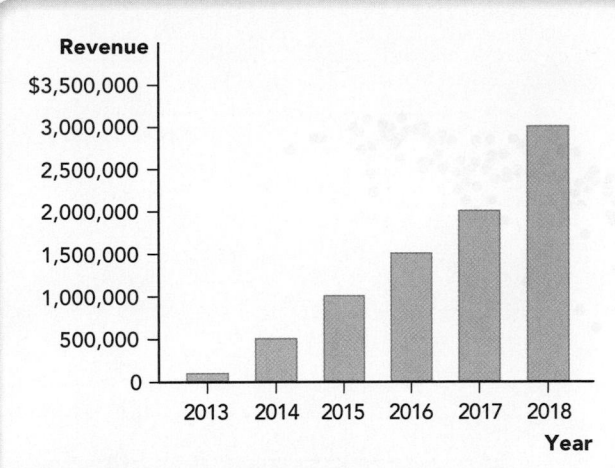

FIGURE 1A.8 A Bar Chart of Rough Smoothie's Annual Sales

A bar chart clearly indicates the value of a dependent variable for each value of an independent variable. In this chart, the dependent variable is sales by the Rough Smoothies Shop and the independent variable is the year.

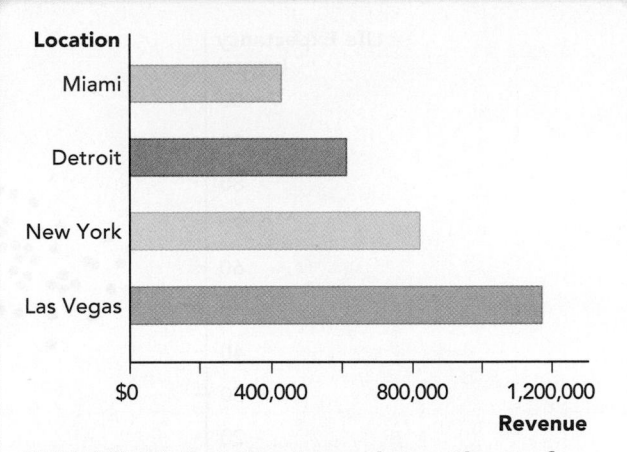

FIGURE 1A.9 A Horizontal Bar Chart of Rough Smoothie's 2018 Sales by Location

The bars in bar charts can be either horizontal or vertical. In this chart the length of the horizontal bars indicate Rough Smoothie's sales by location.

smoothies were sold in that year. For example, Rough Smoothie sold $2 million worth of smoothies in 2017, and $3 million worth in 2018.

Bar charts are useful for many types of comparisons. For example, the owners of Rough Smoothie could use a bar chart to compare the sales of peach, strawberry, and banana smoothies in the same year; the weekly sales made by each of the firm's employees; or the company's electricity usage for each month of a year. Some bar charts have horizontal bars and indicate the values of the dependent variable by the lengths of the bars instead of their heights. In Figure 1A.9, horizontal bars show the 2018 sales volume at each Rough Smoothie location.

PIE CHARTS

A **pie chart** is a circular chart made up of shapes that resemble slices of a pie. The slices show a larger value broken down into smaller pieces. Figure 1A.10 shows the breakdown of Rough Smoothie's expenses among the costs of advertising, equipment, ingredients, payroll and benefits, rent, and utilities. Although the same information could be presented in a table, the pie chart helps us visualize the relative size of each cost component. Pie charts are used to show everything from the percentage of energy that comes from different energy sources to the percentage of students who select each of the various majors in college.

SCATTER DIAGRAMS

A **scatter diagram** shows many points with no connecting lines. Sometimes the points form a pattern that can convey useful information about any relationship that may

> **pie chart**
> A circular chart made up of pie-shaped slices that show a larger value broken down into smaller pieces.

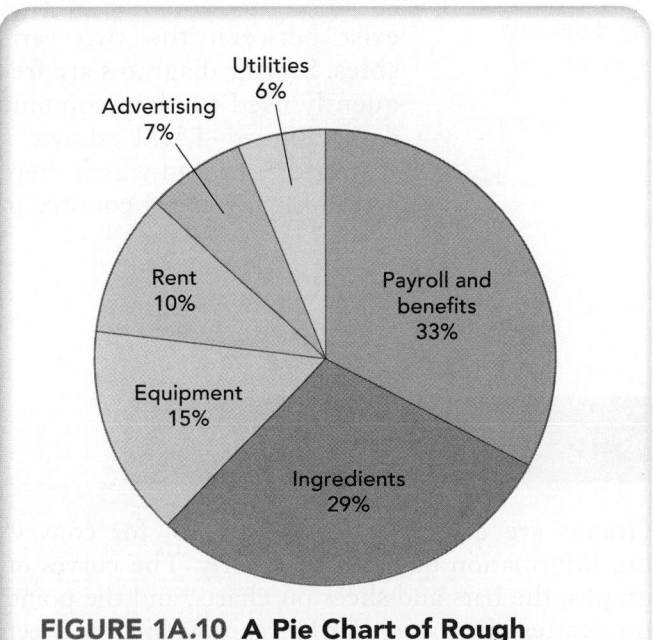

FIGURE 1A.10 A Pie Chart of Rough Smoothie's Expenses

The slices on a pie chart show how a larger value is broken down among many smaller parts.

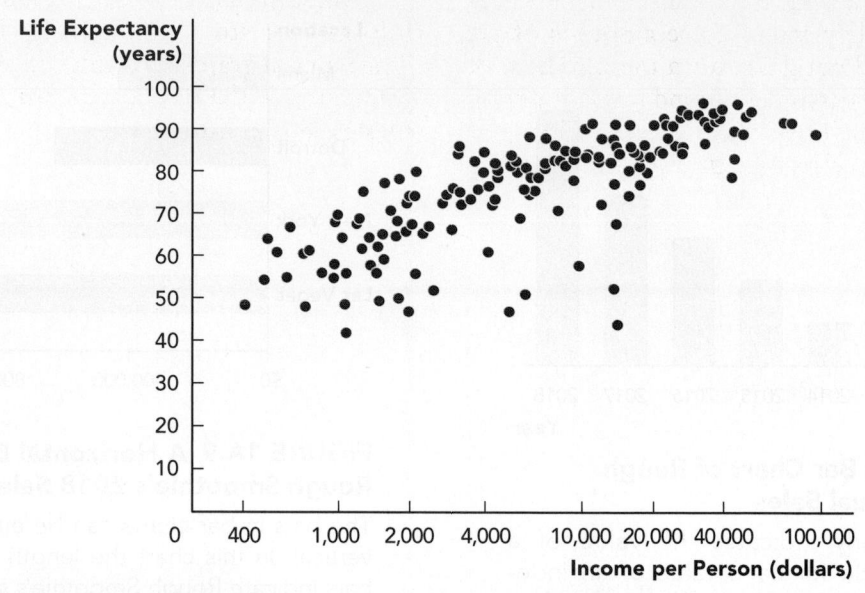

FIGURE 1A.11 A Scatter Diagram

The rising pattern of the points in this scatter diagram shows that there is generally a positive relationship between income per person and life expectancy in a country.

Note: Income per person is measured using a log scale, so that each increment along the *x*-axis represents the same percentage change in income per capita.

Source: World Bank.

scatter diagram
A chart containing many data points that may or may not show a pattern that indicates a relationship among them.

exist between the two variables. Scatter diagrams are frequently used to plot economic data. Figure 1A.11 shows a scatter diagram in which there is a point for every country in the world. The *x*-variable indicates the income per person and the *y*-variable indicates the life expectancy. The upward pattern of the points reveals that there is a *positive relationship* between the two variables—countries with more income per person generally have higher life expectancies.

SUMMARY

Graphs are economists' favorite tool for conveying information quickly and clearly. The curves on graphs, the bars and slices on charts, and the points on scatter diagrams clarify relationships between variables in ways that no small number of words could achieve.

Each point on a coordinate graph represents two values—one for the *x*-variable, which is measured along the horizontal axis, and one for the *y*-variable, which is measured along the vertical axis. The slope of a line shows the amount by which the *y*-variable changes when the *x*-variable increases by 1. By using the simple "rise over run" formula to calculate the slopes of certain lines, you can determine useful values, such as the opportunity cost of making another unit of a good, the price decrease needed to sell another unit of a good, and the additional output gained from hiring another worker.

Areas on graphs provide important information as well. For example, they indicate the amounts of tax revenues, profits, and net gains from the purchase of goods. The area of a rectangle is found by multiplying its length by its width. The area of a triangle is found by multiplying one-half its base times its height.

Your familiarity with the elements of graphs will inform your study of topics far beyond economics. The types of graphs explained in this appendix appear frequently in the news, on websites, in research summaries, and in business reports.

KEY TERMS

variables, p. 16
horizontal axis (*x*-axis), p. 16
vertical axis (*y*-axis), p. 16
origin, p. 16

point, p. 16
independent variable, p. 17
dependent variable, p. 17
slope, p. 17

bar chart (bar graph), p. 20
pie chart, p. 21
scatter diagram, p. 22

PROBLEMS FOR REVIEW

1. Draw the points (3, 6) and (2, 7) on a graph. Label the origin, the *x*-axis, and the *y*-axis.

2. Calculate the slope of a line going from (3, 6) to (2, 7).

3. On a new graph, draw a line that begins with a positive slope, ends with a negative slope, and always has a decreasing slope.

4. Identify the independent variable in each of the following pairs of variables.
   a. years of work experience *and* current income
   b. hours of lost sleep at night *and* coffee consumption the evening before
   c. heart rate of a public speaker *and* audience size

5. For each pair of variables in I, II, III, and IV, indicate the shape of the curve that correctly depicts the relationship between the two variables. Choose from the following shapes:
   a. upward-sloping
   b. downward-sloping
   c. horizontal
   d. vertical
   e. U-shaped

   Assume that the first variable is measured on the horizontal axis of a graph and the second variable is measured on the vertical axis.

   I. The temperature outside; the number of iced drinks you consume per day
   II. The temperature outside; the number of letters in the alphabet
   III. The number of times you brush your teeth per week; the number of cavities you'll have at your next dental checkup
   IV. Your age; the number of seconds it takes you to run 100 yards

6. The rectangle in the accompanying graph represents tax revenue. Calculate the area of the rectangle.

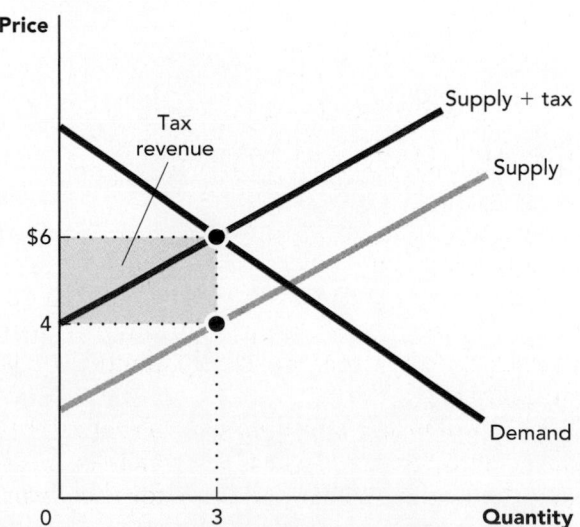

7. The triangle in the accompanying graph represents the net gain to consumers from purchasing a good. Calculate the area of the triangle.

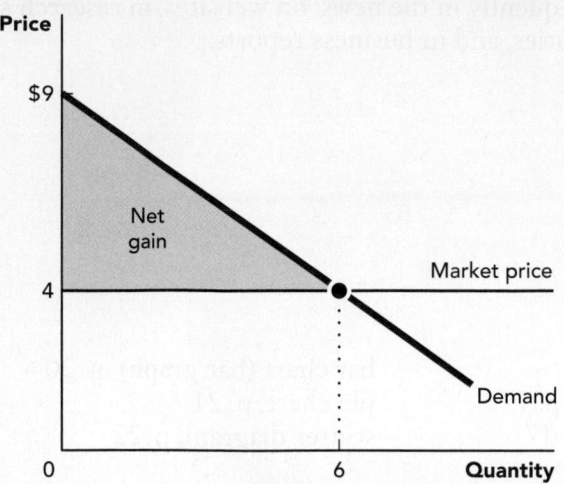

8. Draw a bar chart showing the number of hours you spent studying during each of the last seven days.

9. Choose one of the types of graphs described in this appendix to illustrate the most you would be willing to pay for your first, second, and third cup of coffee in one day.

10. The following table lists the percentage of the population between the ages of 15 and 24 and the annual population growth rate in four countries. Illustrate this information on a scatter diagram with population growth rate on the vertical axis.

Country	Population 15–24 Years Old	Population Growth Rate
Canada	12.7%	0.76%
Greece	9.8	0.01
Venezuela	18.8	1.42
Yemen	21.1	2.72

Source: CIA World Factbook

Markets and Economies

2

Cary Kalscheuer/Shutterstock

A few years ago the Rocky Mountain Construction Group provided 35 workers with truckloads of wood, steel, and equipment and had them build the world's fastest, steepest, and tallest wooden roller coaster at Six Flags Great America in Gurnee, Illinois. The same welders, carpenters, and engineers could have built a bridge, a ballpark, or a boardwalk. Why did they build a roller coaster instead? Because the entrepreneurs at Six Flags saw people pay $60 admission fees to stand in long lines to ride great roller coasters. When a good is in high demand relative to the available supply in a *market economy* such as our own, market forces stimulate an increase in the supply of that good. In this chapter, you will learn about the market participants and the resources they have to work with. You will also learn what mix of influences guides economic decisions in several types of economies.

Why Should I Care?

The U.S. economy produces about $20 trillion worth of goods and services each year. **The products available for you to purchase and the money at your disposal to spend result from a crucial flow of resources and money through the economy.** That flow is not planned by a central authority. Rather, it is orchestrated largely by market forces, with some government involvement. Fortunately, markets tend to offer consumers what they need and want. This chapter explains the ins and outs of markets that put money in your pocket, goods in your home, food on your table, and an occasional trip to the amusement park in your summer plans.

factors of production
The resources or inputs used to create goods and services.

land
The earth and everything drawn from it, including water, minerals, plants, and animals.

labor
The physical and mental contribution of people to the production process.

capital
The manufactured goods used to produce other goods or services.

entrepreneurship
The willingness and ability to take risks, initiate activities, innovate, and organize the other factors of production to provide goods and services.

Factors of Production

Factors of production, also known as *resources* or *inputs*, are the building blocks of goods and services. It may only take people to create a song, a physical therapy session, or the M&M'S® slogan: "Melts in your mouth, not in your hands." It takes many factors of production to provide the mountain bikes, blue jeans, Milky Way bars, and amusement park rides that we buy.

To keep things simple, economists group the factors of production into four general categories: land, labor, capital, and entrepreneurship.

- **Land** represents the earth and everything drawn from it, including water, minerals, plants, and animals. Because the wood used to make roller coasters comes from the land, it falls into the land category.

The cacao beans used to make chocolate also fall into the land category.

- **Labor** is the physical and mental contribution of people to the production process. Engineers, songwriters, physical therapists, and chocolatiers all contribute labor to the creation of goods and services.

- **Capital** refers to the manufactured goods used to produce other goods or services. Construction equipment, factories, delivery trucks, and chocolate molds are all examples of capital.

- **Entrepreneurship** is the willingness and ability to take risks, initiate productive activities, innovate, and organize the other factors of production in order to provide goods and services. There would be no Disney amusement parks and no Hershey's chocolate if it weren't for the entrepreneurship of Walt Disney and Milton Hershey.

The absence of one critical factor of production can block the availability of a good. For example, the land, labor, and capital needed for a fondue restaurant like The Melting Pot is probably available where you live. But if you lack an entrepreneur willing and able to open a fondue restaurant, there will be no Melting Pot fondue for you!

▲ It takes all four factors of production—land, labor, capital, and entrepreneurship—to bring a fondue restaurant to your town.

An Economy's Participants

The factors of production are the economy's building blocks, but who owns them and who transforms them into goods and services? These are among the roles of the economy's participants, which include households, firms, and the government.

HOUSEHOLDS

A person or group of people living together and sharing income constitute a **household.** Your family makes up a household; so do individuals living on their own. Members of the 126 million households in the United States own the factors of production that firms need to produce goods and services. Working household members provide labor and entrepreneurship to firms. Some land and capital is owned directly by households, and some is owned by firms that are owned by households. For example, the land used to grow cacao beans for the Original Hawaiian Chocolate Factory is owned by the household of Bob and Pam Cooper. The mixers used to make Hershey's chocolate are owned by the Hershey Company, which is owned by a large group of households. In exchange for the factors of production, households receive income in the form of wages for their labor, rent payments for their land and capital, and profits as a reward for their successful entrepreneurship.

FIRMS

A **firm** is any enterprise that employs factors of production and sells goods or services. The Rocky Mountain Construction Group, the Nestlé company, your doctor's office, and the college you attend are all examples of firms. Suppose you decide to open a chocolate shop. You could organize your firm in many different ways. For example, in 1765, James Baker and John Hannon formed a *partnership* to sell Baker's Chocolate. That firm was later acquired by a *corporation* called Kraft Foods. Your best choice among these and other types of firms would depend on how you feel about taking risks, sharing profit, and controlling decisions. In this section we explore the pros and cons of some of the most popular types of firms that entrepreneurs like Baker, Hannon, and you should consider when deciding which type of firm to form.

Sole Proprietorships and Partnerships. Kee's Chocolates is a **sole proprietorship,** which means it is owned and controlled by an individual—Kee Ling Tong. Although about 75 percent of all businesses are sole proprietorships, only 5 percent of the money spent at businesses is spent at sole proprietorships, so this type of firm is common and typically small. A **partnership** like the original Baker's Chocolate is similar to a sole proprietorship, except that two or more people own and control it. This means that the risks, obligations, and rewards of running the firm are shared.

The owners of these relatively simple types of firms can take action quickly. They can launch a business, troubleshoot, and change policies without the board meetings and paperwork hurdles associated with more complicated business types. The

household
A person or group of people living together and sharing income.

firm
Any enterprise that employs factors of production and sells goods or services.

sole proprietorship
A business owned and controlled by an individual.

partnership
A firm that is similar to a sole proprietorship, except that two or more people own and control it.

▲ Kee's Chocolates is a sole proprietorship. This type of firm is owned and controlled by one individual.

taxation of these firms is relatively simple, too. Sole proprietorships and partnerships are not taxed separately from their owners. Rather, the owners pay taxes on their business income as part of their personal income taxes.

On the downside of sole proprietorships and partnerships, their owners are personally liable for the debts, court judgments against the firms, and other legal obligations of their businesses. Also, the sources of funding for these firms are limited. The owners can apply for loans but cannot sell stocks or bonds to raise money for the operation and expansion of their businesses, as some corporations do.

Corporations. A **corporation**, such as Nestlé, is a type of firm that exists as a legal entity distinct from its owners. Corporations make up about 20 percent of all businesses in the United States and receive more than 85 percent of all spending at businesses. To create a corporation, business leaders file *articles of incorporation* with a state government that specify the firm's name, leadership, location, and purpose. Incorporation can bring a firm more prestige, more sources of funding, and less personal liability for its owners in the event of a lawsuit. Creditors and litigants with claims against a corporation must go after the assets of the firm; they usually cannot access the money, homes, and other assets of individuals within the firm.

To raise funds for business expenses, corporations can sell shares of ownership, or **stock,** to investors known

Susana Gonzalez/Bloomberg via Getty Images

▲ Corporations such as Nestlé are legal entities distinct from their owners, which helps to protect the owners from creditors and litigants.

as **shareholders.** For example, you could become a shareholder, and thus own part of the Hershey Company, by purchasing Hershey stock. The shareholders elect a board of directors to make key strategic decisions. The directors appoint a president, secretary, and treasurer, among other officers, to oversee the corporation's day-to-day operations. If the firm performs well, the shareholders generally benefit from an increase in their stock's value. Many corporations also distribute a portion of their profits to shareholders in payments called **dividends.**

Like a corporation, a **limited liability company (LLC)** is a distinct legal entity that shields its owners from creditors and litigants. The owners of LLCs are called *members* rather than shareholders. Although LLCs cannot sell stock to raise funds, they face fewer paperwork requirements than corporations and enjoy similar legal benefits.

corporation
A type of firm that exists as a legal entity distinct from its owners.

stock
A share of ownership in a corporation.

shareholders
Investors who buy a corporation's stock.

dividends
A portion of profits a firm distributes to its shareholders.

limited liability company (LLC)
A firm that does not sell stock, and is a distinct legal entity that shields its owners from creditors and litigants.

Q&A

What is a nonprofit organization?

Most firms seek profit, which they distribute to their owners or reinvest in the firm to improve its profitability. A *nonprofit organization* is any firm, association, or society that formally brings people together to accomplish a goal other than profit, such as to support the arts, the environment, education, research, health care, sports, peace, or religion. The government itself is a nonprofit organization. Most churches, hospitals, colleges, and charities are nonprofit organizations. Fair Trade USA is a nonprofit organization that certifies that certain chocolate makers and

other food producers pay farmers fair wages and don't employ children or slaves. Other nonprofit organizations include the U.S. Olympic Committee, Greenpeace, and the Corporation for National Research Initiatives.

Nonprofit organizations generate revenues through donations or the sale of goods and services. All receipts go toward operations, salaries, and other expenses rather than being disbursed as profits to owners. There are tax advantages to being a nonprofit organization. Most nonprofits are exempt from state and federal income taxes, property taxes, and sales taxes, and most donations to nonprofit organizations are tax-deductible.

GOVERNMENT

A **government** is an organization of individuals that has the authority to lead and govern. The government collects taxes from households and firms to support spending on its programs and operations. The U.S. government's purchases include everything from schools and aircraft carriers to the materials and labor needed to make license plates, mint currency, and conduct safety inspections in factories. The government also provides households and firms with **transfer payments,** payments that are not made in exchange for goods or services. Examples of transfer payments include grants for college students, social security payments to retired workers, unemployment insurance benefits, and subsidies for farmers.

The Circular Flow

If you have a job, you receive money in a paycheck and then spend money on goods and services. This flow of money through your hands is part of a larger cycle of receiving and spending by market participants. Figure 2.1 shows the **circular-flow diagram** that illustrates the give and take of goods and services, money, and factors of production in an economy. The lower half of Figure 2.1 shows that households provide the factors of production—land, labor, capital, and entrepreneurship—to firms in exchange for income. These transactions occur in the **factor markets,** which are made up of all of the buyers and sellers of factors of production in the economy. If you work at one of the Six Flags amusement parks next summer, you will be a seller in the factor market for labor and Six Flags will be a buyer in the same market.

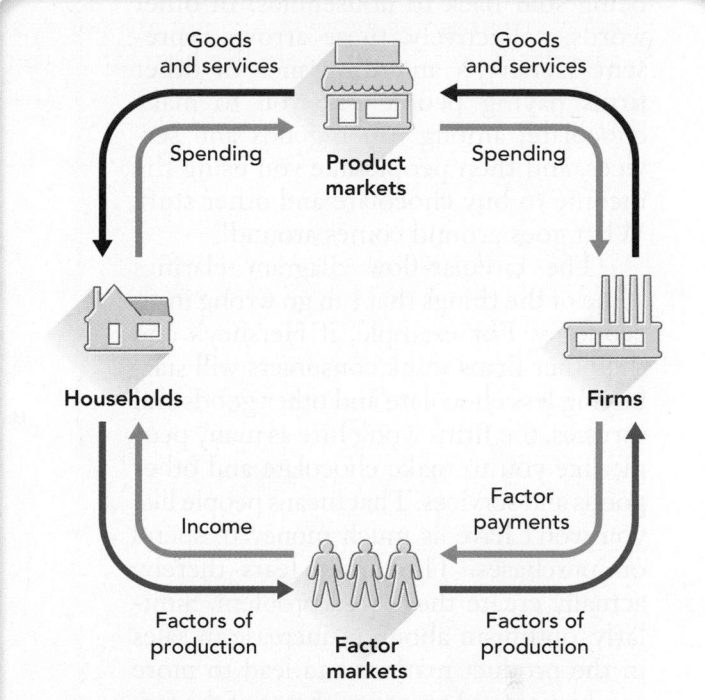

FIGURE 2.1 The Circular-Flow Diagram

The circular-flow diagram shows that when it comes to money in the economy, what goes around comes around. Households sell factors of production to firms in exchange for income, which households use to purchase goods and services from firms.

The upper half of Figure 2.1 shows that households purchase goods and services from firms. These transactions occur in the **product markets,** which are made up of all of the producers and consumers of goods and services in the economy. When you purchase a Hershey's chocolate bar, you are a buyer—and the Hershey Company is a seller—in the product market for chocolate.

The green arrows in Figure 2.1 illustrate how money flows from households to firms when consumers make purchases in the product markets, and then flows back to households as payments for factors of production in the factor markets. The blue arrows represent factors of production flowing from households to firms. The purple arrows show the goods and services that firms make out of the factors of production

▲ The government collects taxes from households and firms, makes purchases in the factor and product markets, and provides goods, services, and transfer payments to households and firms. For example, this photo shows license plates being made in a government-owned prison in California.

government
An organization of individuals with the authority to lead and govern.

transfer payments
Government payments that are not made in exchange for goods or services.

circular-flow diagram
A diagram that shows how goods, services, and money flow throughout an economy.

factor markets
All of the buyers and sellers of factors of production in the economy.

product markets
All of the producers and consumers of goods and services in the economy.

being sold back to households. In other words, collectively, these arrows represent Hershey's and thousands of other firms paying people like you to make chocolate, among other goods and services, and then people like you using the income to buy chocolate and other stuff. What goes around comes around!

The circular-flow diagram clarifies some of the things that can go wrong in an economy. For example, if Hershey's and the other firms think consumers will start buying less chocolate and other goods and services, the firms won't hire as many people like you to make chocolate and other goods and services. That means people like you won't have as much money to spend on purchases. The firms' fears thereby actually create the feared problem. Similarly, optimism about an increase in sales in the product markets can lead to more production and more purchases of the factors of production from households, and therefore more income that households can use to make purchases in the product markets. Again, the expectation creates the reality, which makes expectations an important driver of economic activity.

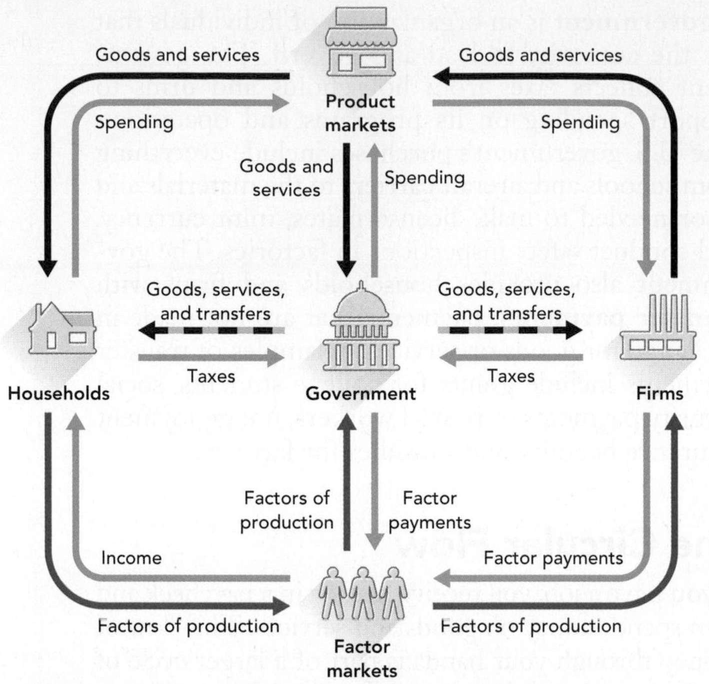

FIGURE 2.2 The Circular-Flow Diagram with Government

This expanded circular-flow diagram shows how households and firms interact with each other and with the government. The government collects taxes from households and firms and uses the money to pay for factors of production, goods, services, and transfers needed for government programs.

GOVERNMENT AND THE CIRCULAR FLOW

The circular flow diagram in Figure 2.2 includes the government's exchanges with households, firms, and each type of market. The blue arrow pointing from the factor markets to the government shows that some of the households' factors of production flow to the government via the factor markets. In exchange, the government makes payments to the factor markets, as shown by the green arrow pointing downward. These payments are returned to household members like you and your family as income in the form of wages, rent payments, and profits.

Figure 2.2 also shows that the government collects taxes from households and firms. In order to operate, the government uses some of the tax revenues to buy factors of production in the factor markets and goods and services in the product markets. In this simplified model of the economy, the government's budget is always balanced, so there is no debt for the government to repay. The remainder of the tax revenues can therefore be used to provide goods, services, and transfer payments to households and firms as part of government programs.

efficient
A condition that is satisfied when no alternative allocation of a resource can make some people better off without making other people worse off.

The Goal of Efficiency

Efficiency is a central objective when households, firms, or governments make economic decisions. Economists follow the efficiency guidelines of Italian economist Vilfredo Pareto (1843–1929), who deemed an allocation of resources to be **efficient** if no alternative allocation could make some people better off without making other people worse off. Suppose you like wooden roller coasters and your friend likes steel roller coasters. At the end of a dizzying day at the amusement park, you have two tickets to allocate between you and your friend—one for each type of coaster. If your friend gets the ticket for the Wooden Woosher roller coaster and you get the ticket to the Steel Looper, that allocation would be inefficient because it is possible to make some people (the two of you in this case) better off without making anyone worse off. You and your friend could achieve efficiency by switching tickets, so that you can each ride your favorite type of roller coaster.

Under the right conditions, markets create incentives for efficient answers to three fundamental economic questions:

1. What should be produced?
2. How should it be produced?
3. For whom should it be produced?

We will touch upon these critical questions next and revisit them later in the book.

WHAT SHOULD BE PRODUCED?

If an economy answers the *what* question by allocating resources to the production of an efficient mix of goods and services, no alternative mix of goods and services would make society better off. In the next few chapters you will learn more about how the market forces of supply and demand can lead to efficiency in resource allocation by guiding firms to produce more of the goods and services that consumers most need and want. You will also learn various circumstances under which market forces can lead to inefficient outcomes.

HOW SHOULD IT BE PRODUCED?

If the *how* question is addressed by developing efficient production methods, no more of any one good or service could be produced without making less of something else. Efficiency in production is achieved when firms employ the capital, labor, and other inputs that minimize the cost of producing

the desired quantity of output. For instance, when it comes to picking the cacao pods used to produce chocolate, machines aren't good at spotting a ripe pod and gently removing it from the tree; workers can harvest cacao pods at a lower cost per pod than machines can. But machines can mix together the ingredients in chocolate at a lower cost per pound than workers can. Many other stages of the production process, such as the transportation of ingredients, involve both workers and machines. Each firm minimizing its production costs leads to efficiency in production for the economy as a whole. Chapter 7 explains exactly how a firm chooses input and output levels to minimize its production costs.

FOR WHOM SHOULD IT BE PRODUCED?

Efficiency in distribution is achieved when the people who receive particular goods and services are the ones who place the highest value on them. Consider the lottery used to divvy up some of the entry slots for the New York City Marathon. Thousands of runners are picked at random from among those who apply. But the lottery does not distinguish between runners who *really really* want to run in the race and those who just kind of want to run in it. Because the winners of lotteries are determined by luck rather than by need or desire, lotteries do not distribute goods and services efficiently.

Other methods of distribution are better than lotteries at getting items to those who value them the most. For example, the First Universalist Society of Harland, Vermont, holds an annual chocolate auction. Auctions distribute goods to whoever is willing and able to pay the most for them. Other things being equal, the person who is willing and able to pay the most for an auctioned item is the one who places the highest value on it. In that case, the chocolate auction achieves efficiency in distribution by getting each chocolate Bundt

▲ To achieve efficiency in production, firms must choose the right combination of inputs to minimize the cost of producing each unit. For instance, workers can harvest cacao pods at a lower cost per pod than machines can, but machines can mix together the ingredients in chocolate at a lower cost than workers can.

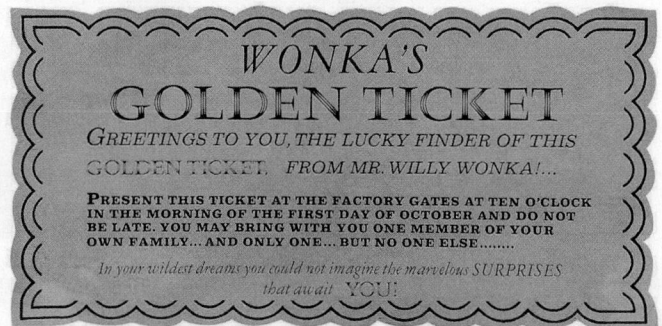

▲ In Roald Dahl's story of *Charlie and the Chocolate Factory*, five lucky people win a factory tour and a lifetime supply of chocolate by finding a golden ticket in their candy wrappers. The trouble with distribution on the basis of luck is that those who get the least value out of a good might be the ones who end up getting it.

cake and chocolate-dipped banana to the person who is willing and able to place the highest bid on it.

Efficient outcomes aren't necessarily fair or *equitable*, however. Chapter 12 explains how the goal of efficiency can conflict with the goals of helping people cope with unemployment, injury, and poverty. For example, consider a tax that would collect $1 from the richest person in the world and transfer it to the poorest person in the world. This transfer might be equitable, but it would not be efficient by Pareto's standard because, while making the poorest person better off, it would make the richest person worse off. The next section describes how goods are distributed under various economic systems.

Economic Systems

What goods and services are produced, *how* they are produced, and *for whom* depends on the economic system that is in place. The economic systems in most countries contain elements of traditional economies, market economies, and command economies.

> **traditional economy**
> An economy in which economic decisions are made on the basis of precedent.
>
> **market economy (capitalist economy)**
> An economy in which households own the factors of production.

TRADITIONAL ECONOMIES

In a **traditional economy,** economic decisions are made on the basis of precedent. For thousands of years, Native Americans followed the traditions of their ancestors. They cooked traditional foods, sewed traditional clothing, and built traditional housing. Their production methods were based on tradition, with men hunting and women crafting clothing out of animal hides. The distribution of goods and services to women, men, children, elders, and chiefs was based on tradition as well. There are still some traditional economies today. The Amish, for instance, still make many economic decisions on the basis of precedent, as do some Native Americans and some peoples living in rural areas of South America, Africa, and Asia. Traditional economies can serve the needs of small, simple societies. In recent centuries, most societies have grown larger and more complex, which has led to expanding roles for markets and governments in economic decision making.

MARKET ECONOMIES

In a **market economy,** or **capitalist economy,** households own the factors of production. Negotiations between employees and management determine wage rates. Firm owners make production decisions in the pursuit of profit, and buyers and sellers come together in markets to trade at prices determined on the basis of supply and demand.

Market economies distribute goods to the people who are willing to pay the going prices for them. The resulting distribution is efficient as long as the people who most value a good or service are willing to pay the most for it. The exception to this efficiency is when the people who most value a good or service cannot afford it. For example, some of the people who would get the most benefit out of a college education cannot afford the price of tuition.

The prices established in markets also promote efficiency in the allocation of resources. Producers

Brooks Kraft/Sygma/Getty Images

◀ In the traditional economy of an Amish community, economic decisions in the present are made in the same way they were made in the past.

▲ The high demand for U.S. amusement park tickets among Asian tourists was a signal to the Disney Company that it could earn more profit by building amusement parks in Japan and China.

and consumers respond to prices that reflect the relative scarcity and the benefits of inputs and products. When supply is low relative to demand, high prices motivate entrepreneurs to take risks, innovate, and organize businesses that help satisfy consumers' needs and desires. For instance, after the Disney Company noted that throngs of Asian tourists were among those willing to pay high prices to visit amusement parks in the United States, it built Disneyland resorts in Tokyo and Hong Kong.

Low prices also send important signals in market economies. New York City's Coney Island used to be the home of the Luna, Dreamland, and Steeplechase amusement parks. But as visits to these parks declined, so did the prices the parks' owners could charge for tickets. Entrepreneurs replaced the amusement parks with hotels and apartments that were in high demand relative to the supply, and that commanded correspondingly high prices.

Prices also lead consumers in market economies toward efficient decisions. When the production of a good requires large quantities of inputs, or particularly scarce inputs, the high cost of making the good will push its price upward and cause consumers to consider alternative goods that are less expensive. For example, it takes a lot of labor to harvest cacao (an ingredient in chocolate), which in turn makes chocolate with a high cacao content expensive. A chocolate bar that is 65 percent cacao costs about $5. Hershey's milk chocolate bars are about 11 percent cacao and cost about $1. The lower price of Hershey's bars steers many customers away from the higher-priced bars made with more cacao.

Market systems are not without challenges. Chapter 11 explains that market-based economies look to the government to fill gaps in the provision of goods and services whose benefits are shared by many consumers, including military and police protection, roads, schools, parks, and health-care systems. A pure market system also lacks safety nets. For instance, people disadvantaged by unemployment, poverty, disease, old or young age, bigotry, or disability can find themselves in desperate situations, with negative repercussions for all of society. Most market systems, however, operate under a government with the authority to protect people's rights, regulate trade, and provide tax-supported social programs such as unemployment insurance, workers' compensation, food assistance, and social security.

COMMAND ECONOMIES

In a **command economy,** decision making about what, how, and for whom to produce is centralized. The government or citizen groups, rather than market forces, guide the allocation of resources. The factors of production are collectively owned, and decisions are made in line with goals that include jobs for all workers and an equitable distribution of income. Command economies exist under *communism* and *socialism.*

Under **communism,** legislators from a single political party—the Communist party—determine production levels and wage rates. Factories, farms, and other productive enterprises are owned by the government, and goods and services are divided among citizens according to their needs. Because there are no private firms that compete for customers, fewer resources are expended on advertising. And because all firms have the same owner, the benefits of research and development can be shared by all producers. The ultimate goal is to allow everyone to share equally in the gains from productive activities and to eliminate the distinctions of social class.

A potential pitfall of communism is that this sharing gives people less of an incentive to

command economy
An economy in which economic decision making is centralized and decisions are made by the government or citizen groups rather than market forces.

communism
An economic system under which legislators from a single political party—the Communist party—determine production levels and wage rates.

◀ The communist country of North Korea has a command economy in which decisions about what, how, and for whom to produce are made by government leaders, such as Supreme Leader Kim Jong-un, pictured here.

STR/AFP/Getty Images

work hard, to take risks on behalf of their firms like entrepreneurs do, and to innovate to create new products and production methods. Consider what would happen to your study efforts if the exam scores for every student in your class were averaged and everyone received the average score. A series of long nights in the library might boost your own score by 10 points, but if there are 30 students in your class, your extra effort would raise the average score by only $10 \div 30 = 0.33$ points. You probably wouldn't spend as many long nights studying for a 0.33-point increase as you would for a 10-point increase. Likewise, when citizens in an economy receive roughly equal portions of the output, the rewards for extra effort are spread too thin to provide strong incentives.

Under capitalism, the possibility of becoming the next Milton Hershey, Henri Nestlé, or Walt Disney is more likely to motivate people to make risky investments in new businesses, work long hours, invent new products, and find better ways to make things. When the government owns the firms and divides the earnings, the incentives for groundbreaking work aren't as strong. Perhaps that's why the world's greatest inventions all came from predominantly market-based economies (see Table 2.1).

In the last century, communist economies existed throughout Eastern Europe, Africa, and Asia. A more recent shift toward market economies ended communism in many countries and accompanied the dissolution of former communist countries, including East Germany, which merged with West Germany in 1990, and the Soviet Union, which split into 15

Table 2.1 Origins of the World's Greatest Inventions

Invention	Year	Country
World Wide Web	1990	United States/ United Kingdom/ France
Computer	1936	Germany/United Kingdom
Penicillin	1928	United Kingdom
Radio	1895	Italy
Film	1890	United Kingdom/ United States
Automobile	1885	Germany
Television	1884	Germany/United States
Telephone	1875	Italy/Germany/ United States
Sewing machine	1830	France
Camera	1814	France
Light bulb	1809	United Kingdom/ Germany
Cotton gin	1794	United States
Steam engine	1698	United Kingdom
Printing press	1440	Germany

◀ Over the past 25 years, Russia has transitioned from a command economy with state-owned factories and farms to a mixed economy with strong elements of socialism and capitalism.

separate countries in 1991. Today, only China, Cuba, Laos, North Korea, and Vietnam retain strong elements of communism.

Socialism shares with communism the public ownership of capital, the interest in fair distribution, and the stumbling block of inadequate incentives. The questions of what, how, and for whom to produce are answered differently, however. Under the most basic socialist system, general assemblies and councils of workers and consumers make economic decisions, sometimes with oversight by a central government. Although some socialists advocate state ownership of key industries, under socialism, this is done within a free-market structure that includes profits for entrepreneurs and prices established by supply and demand.

The many countries with a substantial degree of socialism include Belgium, Finland, Iceland, the Netherlands, New Zealand, and Sweden. The tax rates in these countries are relatively high in order to pay for publicly funded health care, education, and other services. These countries also rank near the top among those whose citizens are the happiest, according to the World Happiness Report and similar studies of satisfaction.

MIXED ECONOMIES

Because each type of economic system has pros and cons, virtually no modern economy operates under a purely traditional, capitalist, or command system.

Most countries, including the United States, have a **mixed economy,** one made up of what they hope are the best characteristics of each type of economic system. The command economies of countries that include China, Cuba, Laos, Russia, and Vietnam have now evolved into mixed economies that allow private control of some businesses. The market-based economies of Canada and many European countries have significant socialist elements, as does the United States to a smaller degree. In these countries, governments provide at least some of the transportation systems, schools, police and fire protection, health care, national defense, and assistance for poor, disabled, and elderly residents.

Tradition still plays a role in some economic decisions in every country, including decisions made by the government, households, and firms in countries that lean toward capitalism. In Japan, for example, following a tradition of lifelong employment, some companies do not lay off workers, even after a dramatic drop in sales. And Taza Chocolate in Somerville, Massachusetts, embraces traditional chocolate production techniques even though modern methods would be cheaper.

socialism
An economic system under which general assemblies and councils of workers and consumers make economic decisions, sometimes with oversight by a central government.

mixed economy
An economic system that has characteristics of traditional, market, and command economies.

SUMMARY

The factors of production—land, labor, capital, and entrepreneurship—are the building blocks of goods and services. Households sell the factors of production to firms in exchange for income in the form of wages, rent payments, and profits. Households use their income to purchase goods and services from firms. The circular flow diagram illustrates the resulting payments as a flow of money from firms to households via the factor markets, and then back to firms via the product markets. The government also purchases goods and services in the product markets and inputs in the factor markets. These purchases, along with the transfer payments that are part of some government programs, are funded with tax collections from households and firms.

If you become an entrepreneur, you will have several options for the type of firm you operate. If you want tight control over decision making, you could create a sole proprietorship controlled by you alone, or a partnership owned and run by you and one or more partners. If you start a corporation, it will be a distinct legal entity, separate from you and the other owners for the purposes of taxes and legal liability. If your firm is a limited liability company (LLC), the owners will be shielded from legal liability and you will have fewer paperwork requirements than corporations have. Unlike a corporation, however, you cannot sell stock to fund an LLC.

Economists generally approach decisions of what, how, and for whom to produce with the goal of efficiency in mind. An efficient combination of goods and services is produced if no alternative combination would make society better off. Production is efficient if no more of one good could be made without making less of another good. Goods are distributed efficiently if there is no way to make some people better off without making other people worse off.

The source of economic decisions depends on the type of economic system in place. In traditional economies, decisions are made as they were made in the past. In a market economy, or capitalist economy, incentives created within markets guide decision making. In the command economies of communism and socialism, governments or citizen groups decide what, how, and for whom to produce. Each of these systems has significant pros and cons. Today, most economies take a mixed approach that combines aspects of traditional, market, and command economies.

KEY TERMS

factors of production, p. 26
land, p. 26
labor, p. 26
capital, p. 26
entrepreneurship, p. 26
household, p. 27
firm, p. 27
sole proprietorship, p. 27
partnership, p. 27

corporation, p. 28
stock, p. 28
shareholders, p. 28
dividends, p. 28
limited liability company (LLC), p. 28
government, p. 29
transfer payments, p. 29
circular-flow diagram, p. 29

factor markets, p. 29
product markets, p. 29
efficient, p. 30
traditional economy, p. 32
market (capitalist) economy, p. 32
command economy, p. 33
communism, p. 33
socialism, p. 35
mixed economy, p. 35

PROBLEMS FOR REVIEW

1. Printed versions of textbooks are manufactured using printing presses, workers, and paper. Identify the category of factors of production in which each of these inputs belongs.

2. Draw a simple circular flow diagram (without government) and use the relationships shown in the diagram to explain how producers' optimism about future sales can lead to an increase in future sales.

3. Explain two ways in which your own activities are part of the economy's circular flow. Which part of the circular-flow diagram in Figure 2.2 represents these activities?

4. Wonka chocolate bars are actually sold by the Nestlé corporation, but in the story of *Charlie and the Chocolate Factory*, Willy Wonka's company was a sole proprietorship. Discuss the advantages and disadvantages of these two types of firms, and indicate which type you would favor if Mr. Wonka handed you the keys to his factory.

5. Pair each type of firm on the left with one advantage on the right.

Nonprofit organization	Owners control decision making
Partnership	Owners protected from creditors
LLC	Is tax-exempt

6. Suggest an improvement in each of the following situations that could lead to efficiency.

   a. A college allocates its football tickets by lottery.

   b. A country with millions of unemployed workers invests heavily in expensive vending machines.

   c. A city whose buildings have been devastated by an earthquake uses the available cement to build a landing strip for the mayor's airplane.

7. Suppose all income in an economy with 100 workers is shared equally. Explain one advantage and one disadvantage of this system relative to a capitalist system.

8. If all income in an economy with 100 workers is shared equally, the rewards for extra effort are equivalent to the rewards for working under a tax on output of what percent? (*Hint:* When you produce $1 worth of output, what portion of the value of that output do you get to keep? The other portion is what you give up as if there were a tax.)

9. Explain how the decision of how much chocolate to produce is made in communist, socialist, and capitalist systems.

10. The chapter mentions that, "other things being equal," the person who places the highest value on a good will be the one willing and able to pay the most for it. What types of things might not be equal that could prevent the person who most values a good from being willing and able to pay the most for it?

Demand

Dave Anderson

3

LEARNING OBJECTIVES

In this chapter, you will learn to:

1. Interpret a demand schedule
2. Work with models of individual and market demand
3. Identify influences that shift the demand curve
4. Explain the importance of consumer surplus

Coffee fans flock to the Hub Coffee House at sunrise to grab a cup of hot java. Fifty-four percent of Americans drink coffee daily. Worldwide, coffee consumption exceeds 500 billion cups annually. The tremendous demand for coffee makes it the most traded commodity after oil, and the most popular beverage after water. In this chapter, you will learn how the value consumers place on coffee translates into the market demand for this cherished good. In later chapters, you'll see how demand and supply join forces to determine the market price and the quantity sold.

Why Should I Care?

Do you like lattes? Pizza? Liverwurst? Ice Cream? Trombone lessons? Wigs? Are these goods and services sold near where you live? It's more than luck if the things you like are available nearby and the things you don't like are not. **As products become popular, the growing demand creates opportunities for profit that motivate firms to action.** Indeed, growing demand for lattes spurred entrepreneur Jim Davis to open the Hub Coffee House in Danville, Kentucky, and sell lattes rather than wigs or liverwurst. Demand helps to determine the items on Davis's menu, the prices he charges, the quantities he supplies, the number of workers he hires, and the café's hours of operation. Demand's influence on these decisions helps you get what you want. In later chapters, you will learn more about demand's critical influence on the markets that serve you lattes and most everything else. But first, this chapter will get you well acquainted with the concept of demand.

The Demand Schedule

A jitterbug latte is a mixture of caramel, espresso, and steamed milk. As irresistible as that may sound, latte lovers are willing to pay only so much for coffee drinks. The quantity they buy depends on the price. We can summarize this relationship between the quantity and the price with a **demand schedule**, which is a table that indicates the quantity of a good or service that would be demanded in a given period at various prices. To keep things simple, suppose Aaron, Brian, and Cienna are the only customers in the local latte market and that all of the lattes are identical. Table 3.1 shows the *individual demand schedule* for each of the customers and the *market demand schedule* for all of them put together.

demand schedule
A table that indicates the quantity of a good or service that would be demanded in a given period at various prices.

On any given day, Aaron would be willing to pay up to $6 for his first latte. This does not mean he would *prefer* to pay $6 for a latte. His preferred price is $0, and the lower the price the better. But if he *had to*, Aaron would pay $6 for his first latte because he receives $6 worth of satisfaction out of it. So Aaron's demand schedule shows that he would buy zero lattes for $7 and 1 latte for $6. He would buy a second latte if the price fell to $4 and a third latte if the price fell to $2. Because additional lattes would not give him any satisfaction, he would buy no more than three lattes in a day, regardless of the price.

Brian would pay up to $5 for his first latte, so his demand schedule shows that he would buy zero lattes for $7 or $6, and 1 for $5. He would buy a second latte if the price fell to $1. After that, additional lattes would be of no interest to him at any price. Cienna would pay up to $7 for her first latte and buy a second if the price fell to $3, but she would not buy more than two lattes even if the price fell to $0.

Table 3.1 Individual Demand Schedules and the Market Demand Schedule for Lattes

Price per Latte	Quantity Demanded by Aaron	Quantity Demanded by Brian	Quantity Demanded by Cienna	Quantity Demanded in the Market
$7	0	0	1	1
6	1	0	1	2
5	1	1	1	3
4	2	1	1	4
3	2	1	2	5
2	3	1	2	6
1	3	2	2	7
0	3	2	2	7

The last column of Table 3.1 is the *market demand schedule*. It indicates the total quantity demanded in this market at each price. At a price of $7, only Cienna would buy a latte, so the quantity demanded in the market would be 1. For $6, Cienna would again demand only 1 latte, but Aaron would purchase 1 as well, making the market demand 2. Lower prices would lead to additional sales until the price fell to $1 or below, at which point 7 lattes would be sold in the market.

DIMINISHING MARGINAL UTILITY

Aaron, Brian, and Cienna are willing to pay more for a first latte than for a second or third. Is this true for you as well? Economists expect so because your first latte serves greater needs than any that follow. With no lattes, you may be particularly thirsty, cold, and in need of a caffeine boost. Such reasons make Cienna willing to pay $7 for her first latte. After she drinks a latte, she will be less thirsty, less cold, and less lethargic. She will value her second latte less than her first because the second latte satisfies less urgent needs. After drinking two lattes, Cienna will be full, warm, and perky. A third latte would serve no purpose for her, so she would not be willing to pay anything for it.

As with lattes, the value of having another unit of most goods and services falls as more units are

Dave Anderson

consumed within a given time period. Consider newspapers, bagels, and visits to the hairstylist. The most you would pay for your first one in a day is probably more than the most you would pay for your second, which is probably more than you would pay for your tenth. All-you-can-eat buffets provide another example. Despite being able to eat endlessly for one fixed price, people don't stay at all-you-can-eat buffets forever. Sooner or later, yet another chicken leg or slab of meatloaf provides no satisfaction.

Economists refer to the satisfaction or happiness that individuals feel as **utility**. It is difficult to measure utility directly, and to compare the utility of different people. Does drinking a latte make you happier than it makes your best friend? That may be hard to judge. But both of you make consumption decisions with utility in mind, and it is the value of the utility you each receive from each latte that determines your demand schedules for lattes. So, to gain an understanding of demand, we begin by examining what happens to utility as more of a good is consumed.

The utility received from consuming one more unit of a good is called **marginal utility**

utility
The satisfaction or happiness that individuals feel.

marginal utility
The utility received from consuming one more unit of a good.

because it is the utility gained *on the margin* between two quantities—the current quantity and that quantity plus one. Think about the additional satisfaction you would receive from one more cup of coffee today. In economic terms, you would describe that as your marginal utility from coffee.

Diminishing marginal utility refers to the decrease in the marginal utility a consumer receives from a good as more of it is consumed. If you enjoy your second cup of coffee less than your first, you are experiencing diminishing marginal utility. In rare cases, diminishing marginal utility does not set in immediately. You might enjoy reading a novel or watching a movie even more the second time than the first, due to your familiarity with the characters and your ability to anticipate exciting sections. And you might enjoy your second ride on a roller coaster more than your first because the second time you're less paralyzed by fear. However, it is even harder to find examples in which marginal utility does not *eventually* decrease. You probably wouldn't want to read any novel 100 times, and no one in the world has chosen to ride a roller coaster more times than Richard Rodriguez, who holds the world record of almost 8,000 rides in 401 hours.

Now we can make better sense of the numbers in the demand schedule. The value of marginal utility is the basis for consumers' willingness to pay for each unit. Due to diminishing marginal utility, consumers are willing to pay less and

> **diminishing marginal utility**
> The decrease in the marginal utility received from a good as more of it is consumed.
>
> **demand curve**
> A curve that illustrates the relationship between the price of a good and the quantity demanded.

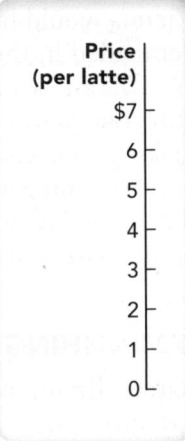

▲ As you consume more and more of a good within a fixed period of time, the appeal of consuming yet another unit of that good is likely to diminish.

less for each additional unit of a good. For example, Aaron receives $6 worth of marginal utility from his first latte, so the demand schedule indicates that he would pay at most $6 for one latte. As marginal utility diminishes for the second and third lattes, so does the highest price Aaron would pay for those lattes—down to $4 for the second latte and down to $2 for the third. Going forward, understanding the connection between marginal utility and demand will also help you identify changes that affect demand schedules and demand graphs.

The Demand Graph

We can make the information in a demand schedule more useful and easier to interpret visually by showing it in a graph. A **demand curve** illustrates the relationship between the price of a good and the quantity demanded. The first demand "curves" we will discuss aren't curves at all, but jagged lines. The pages that follow explain why some demand curves resemble staircases and others are smooth lines. We will also examine the characteristic downward slope of demand curves and the changes that shift demand curves around.

Figure 3.1 shows the *individual demand curves* for Aaron, Brian, and Cienna, and the *market demand curve* for all three of them combined. These curves are graphical representations of the demand schedules in Table 3.1. The vertical axes on the graphs (like the one shown at right) measure the price per latte. The horizontal axes (like the one shown below) measure the quantity of lattes per day. The $6 height of Aaron's demand curve above a quantity of 1 indicates Aaron is willing to pay at most $6 for his first latte. The $4 height of the curve above a quantity of 2 indicates that he would pay at most $4 for a second latte. Aaron's willingness to pay up to $2 for the third latte gives his demand curve a height of $2 at a quantity of 3.

By looking at the demand curves, you can determine the quantity of lattes demanded per day

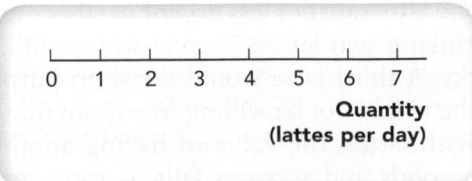

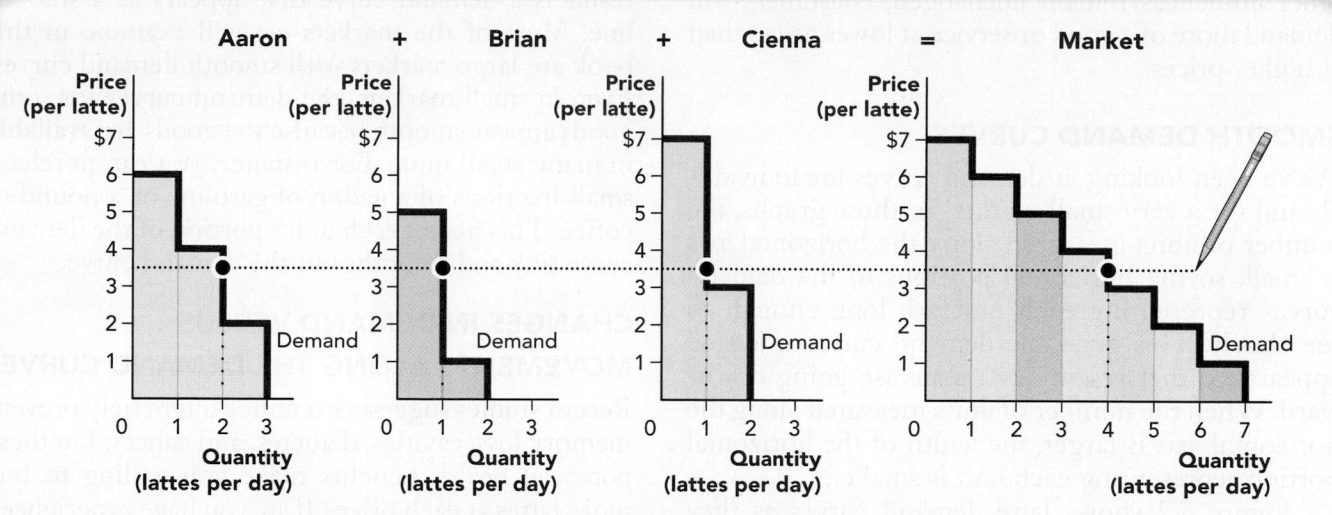

FIGURE 3.1 Individual Demand Curves and the Market Demand Curve

A demand curve indicates the relationship between the price of a good and the quantity demanded. To see the quantity demanded at a particular price, draw a horizontal line with a height of that price. Look directly below the intersection of the price line and the demand curve to find the quantity demanded.

at each price. To find the quantity demanded by each individual and the market at a price of, say, $3.50, draw a horizontal dotted line with a height of $3.50 across the graphs, as shown in Figure 3.1. The quantity demanded is found directly below the intersection of the dotted line and each demand curve. For instance, the dotted price line intersects Aaron's demand curve above the quantity of 2, so we know that Aaron would demand 2 lattes for $3.50. The quantity demanded in the market when lattes are $3.50 is the sum of the quantities demanded by each individual at that price. Aaron demands 2 for $3.50, Brian demands 1, and Cienna demands 1, so the market demand is 2 + 1 + 1 = 4. The same number can be found by looking below the intersection of the $3.50 price line and the market demand curve.

The downward slope of a typical demand curve results from diminishing marginal utility. You've seen that diminishing marginal utility makes each latte less satisfying to consume than the one before. As marginal utility diminishes, so does the amount consumers are willing to pay for another latte. With that in mind, it becomes clear why consumers demand a larger quantity at lower prices. As the price of a latte falls, it becomes lower than the value of more lattes, so more lattes are purchased.

This inverse relationship between the price and the quantity demanded gives the demand curve its downward slope. The **law of demand** summarizes this relationship: When

law of demand
States that when other influences remain unchanged, consumers will demand more of a good or service at lower prices than at higher prices.

Q&A

I buy more $60 Polo-brand polo shirts than $15 Walmart-brand polo shirts. Doesn't this violate the law of demand?

No, this does not violate the law of demand. The inverse relationship between the price and the quantity demanded is expected to hold for the *same* good, but not for two goods with real or perceived differences. Even

if Polo-brand shirts and Walmart-brand shirts were otherwise identical, consumers would not consider them to be the same shirts. The demand for Polo-brand shirts is relatively high due to consumers' perceptions of higher quality and prestige associated with the Polo brand. So it is not surprising that you would buy more Polo-brand shirts even though their price is higher.

other influences remain unchanged, consumers will demand more of a good or service at lower prices than at higher prices.

SMOOTH DEMAND CURVES

We've been looking at demand curves for individuals and for a very small market. In those graphs, the number of units measured along the horizontal axis is small, so the horizontal portions of the demand curves representing each unit are long enough to see clearly. This gives the demand curves a jagged appearance that resembles a staircase going downward. When the number of units measured along the horizontal axis is larger, the width of the horizontal portion representing each unit is smaller.

Figure 3.2 shows latte demand curves as they might look for a family, a neighborhood, and a city. The demand curves for the family and the neighborhood are jagged because the numbers of lattes demanded by these two groups are relatively small. On the graph for the city's demand, the horizontal axis measures thousands of lattes. With large quantities, the portion of the demand curve representing each unit is so narrow that its horizontal nature is imperceptible. The

> **change in demand**
> A shift in the entire demand curve, indicating a change in the quantity demanded at each price.

result is a demand curve that appears as a smooth line. Most of the markets we will examine in this book are large markets with smooth demand curves. Even in small markets, the demand curves for some goods appear smooth because the goods are available in many small units. For instance, you can purchase small fractions of a gallon of gasoline or a pound of coffee. This makes each unit's portion of the demand curve tiny and smooths out the demand curve.

CHANGES IN DEMAND VERSUS MOVEMENTS ALONG THE DEMAND CURVE

Recent studies suggest that coffee might help prevent memory loss, cavities, diabetes, and cancer. Do these potential health benefits make you willing to buy more lattes at each price? If so, you have experienced a *change in demand* for lattes. A **change in demand** shifts the entire demand curve, indicating a change in the quantity demanded at each price. An increase in demand is shown by a shift of the demand curve rightward. The rightward shift indicates that more lattes are demanded at each price.

Now suppose that caffeine is found to increase the risk of heart disease. This would decrease the amount that consumers are willing to pay for each latte, and decrease the quantity of lattes demanded at each price. The resulting decrease in demand is shown by a shift of the demand curve leftward.

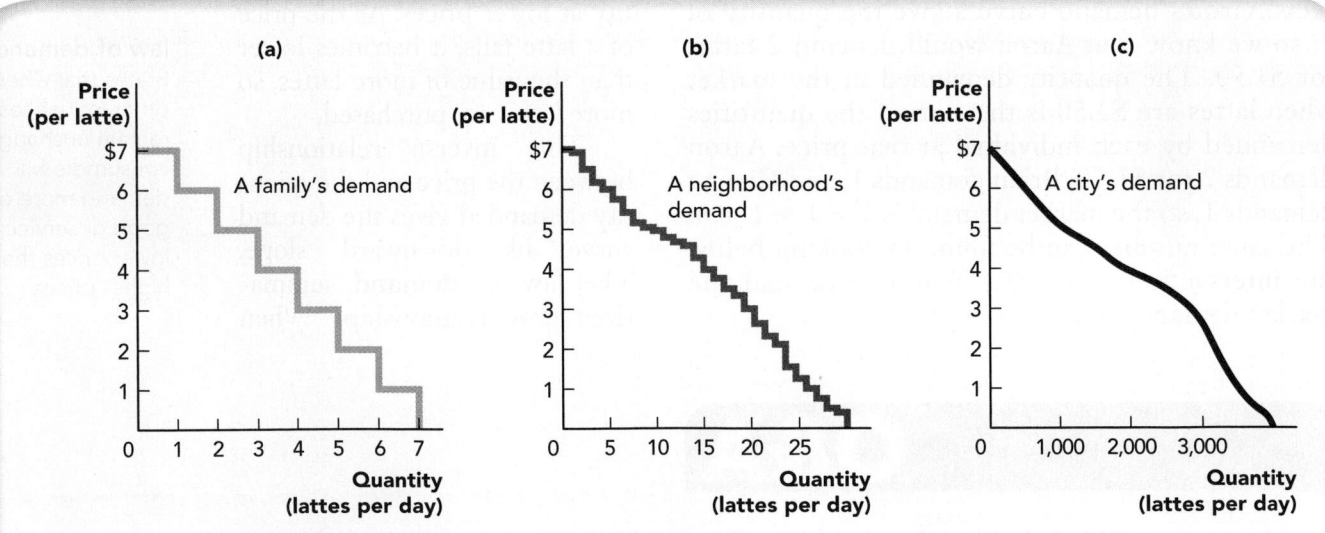

FIGURE 3.2 Jagged Versus Smooth Demand Curves

As the family's demand graph (a) shows, when the number of units measured along the horizontal axis of a demand graph is small, the horizontal portions of the demand curve representing each unit are long enough to see clearly. This gives the demand curve the jagged look of a staircase. When the number of units measured along the horizontal axis is larger, as in the neighborhood's demand graph (b), the width of each horizontal portion is smaller. When the number of units is large, as in the city's demand graph (c), the horizontal portions are so tiny that the demand curve appears smooth.

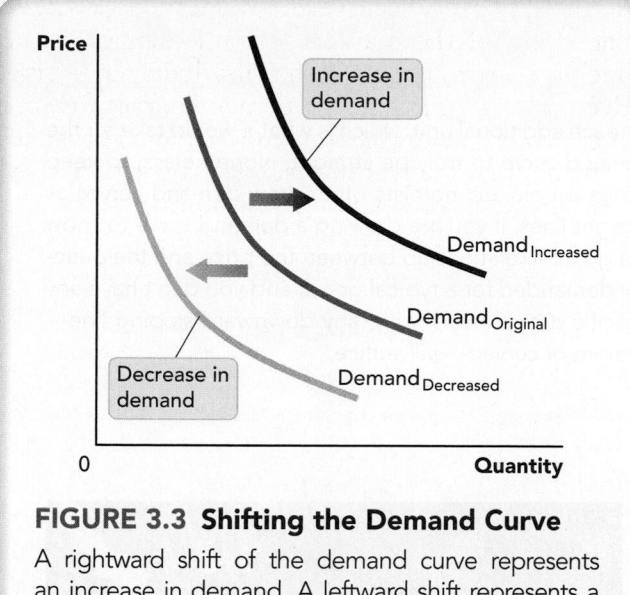

FIGURE 3.3 Shifting the Demand Curve

A rightward shift of the demand curve represents an increase in demand. A leftward shift represents a decrease in demand.

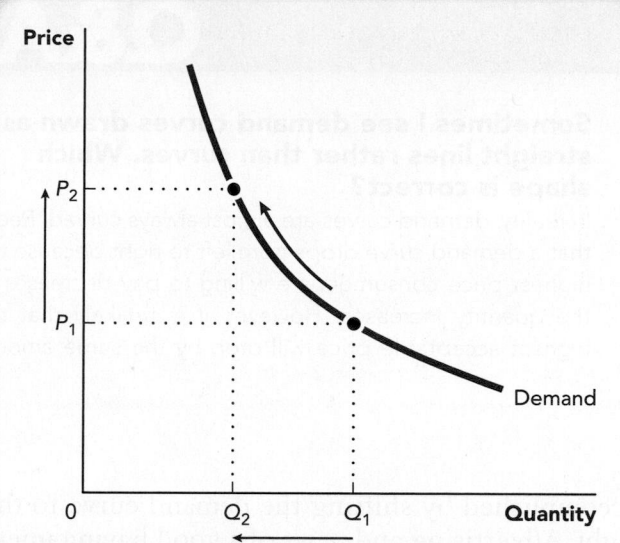

FIGURE 3.4 A Movement Along the Demand Curve

A change in the price causes a movement along the demand curve. For example, when the price increases from P_1 to P_2, the quantity demanded decreases from Q_1 to Q_2. A movement along the demand curve causes a change in the quantity demanded, but not a change in demand. In contrast, a change in demand would be illustrated by a shift of the demand curve.

Figure 3.3 illustrates an increase in demand and a decrease in demand. For convenience, we usually describe an increase in demand as a rightward shift, and a decrease in demand as a leftward shift. It can also be useful to think of demand curves as shifting up or down, as you will see in discussions of taxes and subsidies in later chapters.

Dunkin' Donuts sometimes offers 99-cent lattes in celebration of National Coffee Day on September 29. Customers respond to this price cut by purchasing more lattes. A change in the quantity demanded that is brought about by a price change does not qualify as a change in demand. Remember, a change in demand is synonymous with a shift of the demand curve. A change in the quantity demanded that results from a price change is shown by a **movement along the demand curve.** A price decrease leads to a movement downward and to the right along the demand curve. This causes the quantity demanded to increase, as in the case of the Dunkin' Donuts price cut. A price increase leads to a movement upward and to the left along the demand curve, as shown in Figure 3.4. A price (*P*) increase from P_1 to P_2 causes the quantity demanded (*Q*) to decrease from Q_1 to Q_2. Changes in the price of lattes do not shift the demand curve for lattes because the demand curve itself captures the relationship between the price and the quantity demanded. For this reason, when a price change causes a movement along the demand curve, the result is a change in the quantity

demanded but not a change (shift) in demand. You can remember the concept this way: It takes a change in something that isn't already measured on the axes of the graph to shift the demand curve.

> It takes a change in something that isn't already measured on the axes of the graph to shift the demand curve.

Demand Shifters

Starbucks spends over $100 million on advertising each year for one primary reason: The company wants to sell more coffee without lowering its price. That feat can only be

movement along the demand curve When a change in the price of a good causes a change in the quantity demanded.

Q&A

Sometimes I see demand curves drawn as straight lines rather than curves. Which shape is correct?

In reality, demand curves are almost always curved. Recall that a demand curve drops from left to right because the highest price consumers are willing to pay decreases as the quantity increases. However, it is unlikely that the highest acceptable price will drop by the same amount for each additional unit, which is what it would take for the demand curve to truly be straight. Nonetheless, to keep things simple, economists often draw demand curves as straight lines. If you are drawing a demand curve to show the general relationship between the price and the quantity demanded for a typical good, and you don't have any specific data to work with, any downward-sloping line—straight or curved—will suffice.

accomplished by shifting the demand curve to the right. Advertising and news of a good having unexpected benefits are among many influences that can shift the demand curve for the good. Both individual demand curves and market demand curves shift due to changes in:

- tastes
- expectations
- income
- the prices of related goods

Market demand curves also shift when there is a change in:

- the number of consumers

Let's take a closer look at these demand shifters.

TASTES

Demand is driven largely by what makes consumers happy. But what makes them happy can change. The early American colonists initially preferred tea over coffee. But then the British Tea Act of 1773 gave the British East India Company a virtual monopoly on tea exports to America. Resentment over the Tea Act famously caused colonists to board a British ship and dump its cargo of tea into Boston Harbor during the protest known as the Boston Tea Party. Resentment about tea also helped coffee become the beverage of choice in America. Like unjust legislation, advertising, research findings, media coverage, and fads all have powerful effects on tastes and preferences, which in turn shift demand curves for goods and services.

EXPECTATIONS

Changing expectations about the future affect demand curves in the present. If you come to expect that the price of coffee beans will increase tomorrow, you will have good reason to buy more beans today

Richard Levine/Alamy

▲ Are you thirsty? Effective advertising can shift your demand curve for coffee drinks.

before the price goes up. If you learn that a hurricane might hit tomorrow, you will want to purchase more bottled water today. Expectations of higher oil prices in the future boost the demand for fuel-efficient cars today. And expectations of lower future incomes, which might result from a dreary economic outlook and the threat of job losses, lead consumers to decrease their demand in the present and save more money to prepare for tough times ahead.

INCOME

With more income, consumers are willing to pay more for the things they enjoy. When Starbucks opened its first store in Seattle's Pike Place Market in 1971, the average income in the United States was about $3,500—the equivalent of about $21,000 in 2018 dollars after adjusting for inflation. By 2018, the average income had risen above $34,000. Rising incomes made it possible for more people to afford $4 lattes and helped spur an increase in the number of Starbucks stores in the United States to more than 13,000 in 2018. Starbucks coffee is considered a *normal good* because consumers buy more of it when their incomes increase. Upcoming

▲ Between 1971 and 2018, a roughly 50-percent increase in the average American's earnings (after adjusting for inflation) contributed to a rise in the demand for gourmet coffee.

chapters talk more about how income affects demand, and explore cases of *inferior goods*, which are goods that consumers buy less of when their incomes increase. For instance, as your income increases, you might demand less gas station coffee.

THE PRICES OF RELATED GOODS

For consumers who simply want a jolt of caffeine, cola and coffee are competing options. So if the price of coffee increases, some coffee drinkers might switch to cola. That substitution of cola for coffee will increase the demand for cola. Whenever an increase in the price of one good causes an increase in the demand for one or more other goods, the goods are considered **substitutes in consumption.** Likewise, when goods are substitutes in consumption, a decrease in the price of one causes a decrease in the demand for the other(s). For example, as the price of cell phone service has decreased, more people have cancelled their landline phone service. Other examples of substitutes in consumption include restaurant meals and home cooking, Apple iPads and Samsung Galaxy tablets, and taxi rides and Uber rides.

Two goods are **complements in consumption** if a decrease in the price of one causes an increase in the demand for the other. Consider triathlon bikes and entries into triathlon races. If you want to enter a triathlon, you must pay an entry fee and have a bike. In 2018 it cost more than $700 to enter an Ironman triathlon and there were about 65,000 entrants. If the entry fees decreased, more people would enter triathlons, and the demand for triathlon bikes would increase. The opposite is also true: If the entry fees increased, fewer people would enter triathlons and the demand for triathlon bikes would decrease. Other examples of complements

in consumption include coffee and cream, cell phones and cell phone cases, flashlights and batteries, and chili and hot sauce.

THE NUMBER OF CONSUMERS

The factors discussed so far affect both the demand of individuals and the overall market demand. Because market demand is the sum of every individual's demand, market demand also increases as consumers join the market and decreases as consumers leave the market. For example, if Cienna left the latte market, her demand would no longer be part of the market demand. Two fewer lattes would be demanded at prices below $3, and 1 fewer latte would be demanded at prices between $3 and $7. This would cause a decrease in market demand and a leftward shift of the market demand curve.

Consumer Surplus

When you shop, you seek goods that are worth more to you than the price you have to pay for them. If a latte is worth $6 to you and its price is $6, you could take it or leave it. But if you would be willing to pay $6 for a latte and its price is $3, that's an opportunity you wouldn't want to pass up. The net gain that makes purchases worthwhile—the difference between the most a consumer would be willing to pay for a good and the amount the consumer actually pays—is called **consumer surplus.**

Suppose the price of a latte is $3, as shown in Figure 3.5. Aaron would be willing to pay up to $6 for the first latte and $4 for the second latte. He won't buy the third latte because its $2 value to him is less than the $3 price. Each of the first 2 lattes provides Aaron with consumer surplus because the price is less than the most he would pay for them. On a graph, consumer surplus is found above the price line and below the demand curve. The shaded area of Figure 3.5 represents Aaron's consumer surplus. He receives $6 − $3 = $3 of consumer surplus from the first latte and $4 − $3 = $1 of consumer surplus from the second latte. His total consumer surplus is $3 + $1 = $4.

Now suppose the price rises to $5. Only the first latte is worth more than $5 to Aaron,

substitutes in consumption
Goods for which an increase in the price of one good causes an increase in the demand for the other good(s).

complements in consumption
Goods for which a decrease in the price of one good causes an increase in the demand for the other good(s).

consumer surplus
The difference between the most a consumer would be willing to pay for a good and the amount the consumer actually pays.

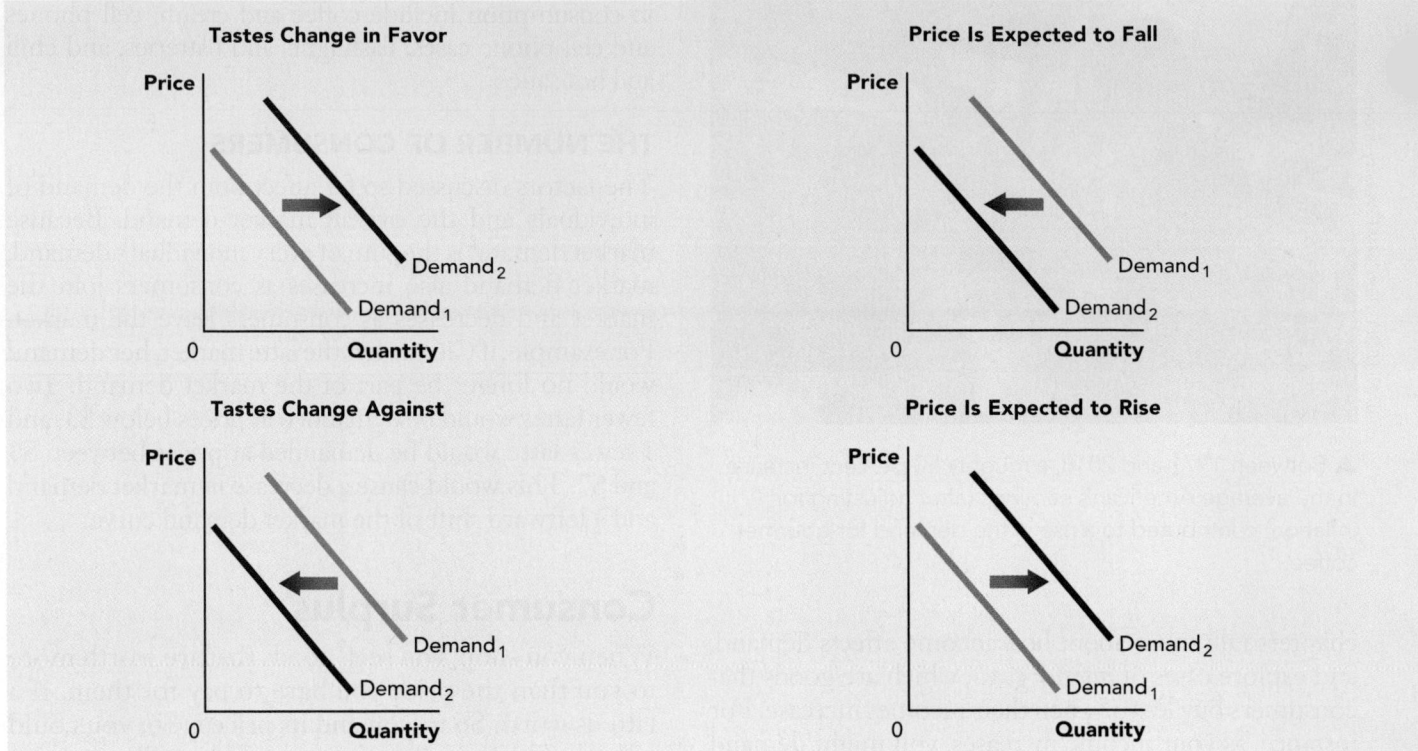

so he will buy 1 latte. With the smaller quantity demanded and the narrowed gap between the price and the value Aaron places on the first latte, the total consumer surplus falls to $6 − $5 = $1. The remaining consumer surplus is shown in dark blue in Figure 3.6. The light blue area shows the consumer surplus lost due to the price increase. A decrease in the price, as from $5 to $3, would have the opposite effect of increasing the consumer surplus by the amount shown in light blue.

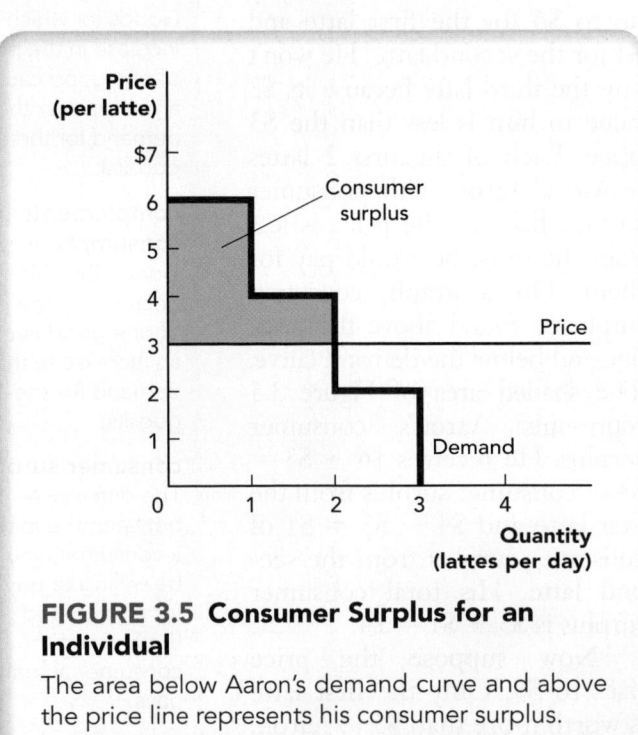

FIGURE 3.5 Consumer Surplus for an Individual

The area below Aaron's demand curve and above the price line represents his consumer surplus.

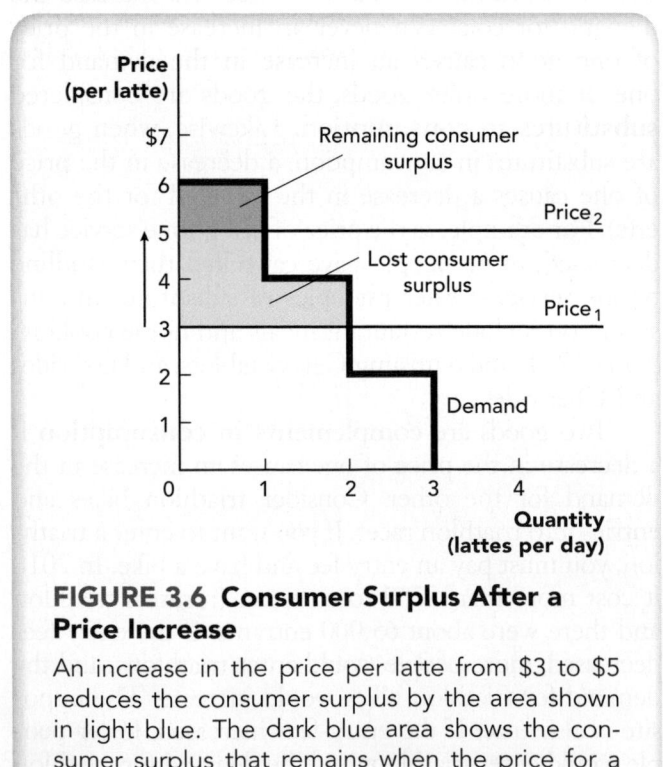

FIGURE 3.6 Consumer Surplus After a Price Increase

An increase in the price per latte from $3 to $5 reduces the consumer surplus by the area shown in light blue. The dark blue area shows the consumer surplus that remains when the price for a latte is $5.

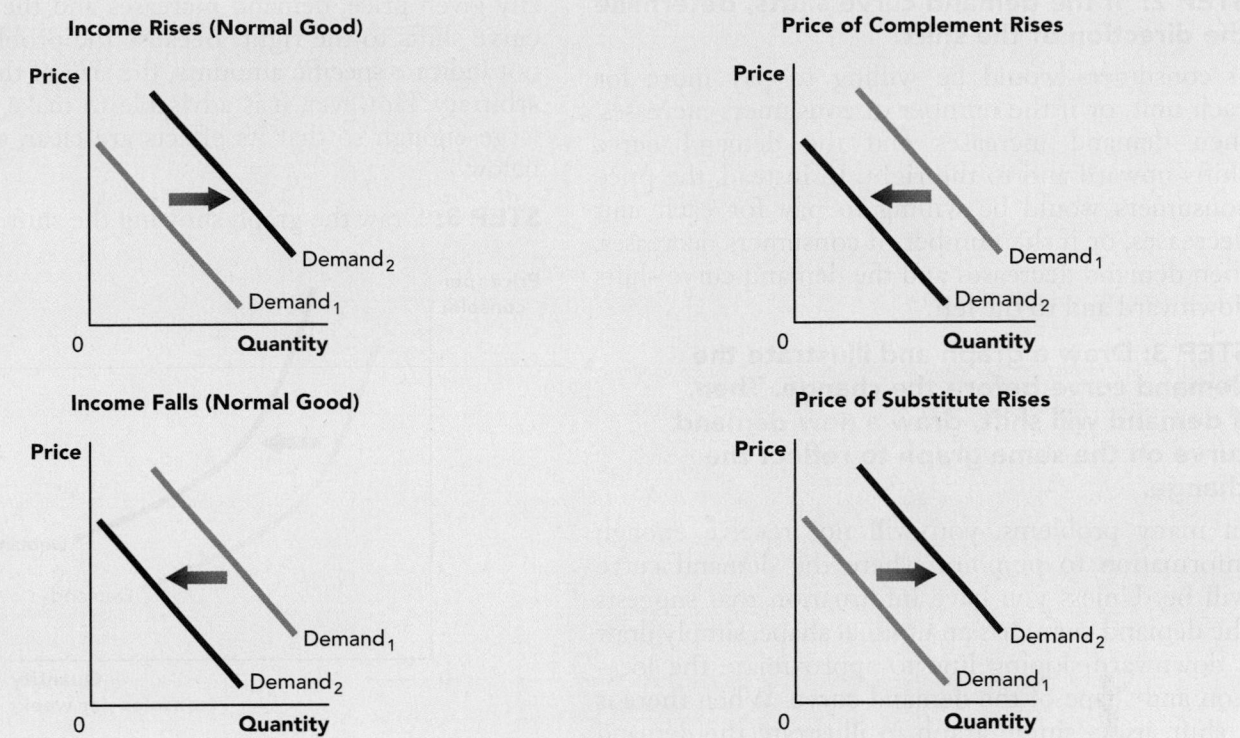

The blue area in Figure 3.7 shows the consumer surplus for the whole market when latte lovers Aaron, Brian, and Cienna can buy lattes for $3 each. In this case, a total of 5 lattes would be sold. Notice that the fifth latte does not provide any consumer surplus

FIGURE 3.7 Consumer Surplus in the Market

The consumer surplus for a market is found below the market demand curve and above the price line, as shown by the blue area on this graph.

because the purchaser of that latte, Cienna, receives $3 worth of marginal utility from it and pays $3 for it. The total consumer surplus in the market is found by adding the consumer surplus for each of the 5 lattes purchased: $4 + $3 + $2 + $1 + $0 = $10.

Steps to Solving Problems Involving Demand

Now that you've learned the underpinnings of demand, you are well-armed to tackle relevant problems. The following three steps will help you analyze the effects of a potential influence on demand.

STEP 1: Determine whether the influence shifts the demand curve.

Remember that a change in the price of a good does *not* shift the demand curve for that good. A price change only affects the quantity of the good demanded. If you can't remember the demand-curve shifters explained in the chapter, keep in mind that the demand curve is based on the value of marginal utility. Ask yourself whether the change you are considering affects the highest price consumers would be willing to pay for each unit of the good. If so, or if the change involves an increase in the number of consumers, the demand curve shifts.

STEP 2: If the demand curve shifts, determine the direction of the shift.

If consumers would be willing to pay more for each unit, or if the number of consumers increases, then demand increases and the demand curve shifts upward and to the right. If, instead, the price consumers would be willing to pay for each unit decreases, or if the number of consumers decreases, then demand decreases and the demand curve shifts downward and to the left.

STEP 3: Draw a graph and illustrate the demand curve before the change. Then, if demand will shift, draw a new demand curve on the same graph to reflect the change.

In many problems, you will not receive enough information to pinpoint where the demand curve will be. Unless you have information that suggests the demand curve has an unusual shape, simply draw a downward-sloping line to approximate the location and shape of the demand curve. When there is a shift, use a single graph to illustrate the demand curve before and after the shift. That will allow you to make comparisons between the old and new curves and to see the effects of the change.

Sample Problems

The following problems involve Sony PlayStation 4 (PS4) video game consoles. The games that console users play are purchased separately. The market for PS4 consoles is so large that the market demand curve is well illustrated by a smooth line. For each problem, we will follow the three steps outlined above to analyze the effect of the indicated change. The problems for review at the end of this chapter include similar problems for you to try on your own.

PROBLEM 1

The price of games for the PS4 console decreases.

STEP 1: Does the change in the price of games shift the demand curve for PS4 consoles? Yes! PS4 consoles and PS4 games are complements in consumption. The price decrease makes it less expensive to buy games to play on the PS4 console, and having more games increases the marginal utility received from owning a PS4. So if the price of PS4 games decreases, customers will be willing to pay more for a PS4 console, and more consoles will be purchased at any given price.

STEP 2: In which direction does demand shift? With customers demanding more PS4 consoles at

any given price, demand increases and the demand curve shifts to the right. Because the problem does not indicate specific amounts, the size of the shift is arbitrary. However, it is advisable to make the shift large enough so that its effects are clear, as shown below.

STEP 3: Draw the graph showing the shift.

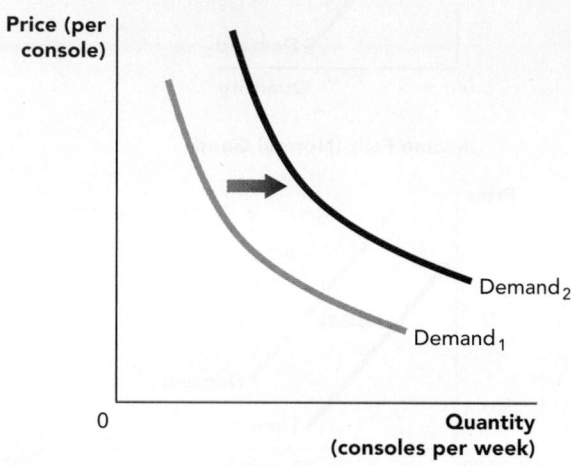

PROBLEM 2

The price of PS4 consoles decreases.

STEP 1: Does the change in the price of PS4 consoles shift the demand curve for PS4 consoles? No! A change in the price of PS4 consoles only causes a change in the quantity of PS4 consoles demanded, which is illustrated by a movement along the original demand curve.

STEP 2: Because there is no change in demand, there is no need to think about the direction of a shift.

STEP 3: Draw the graph with no shift, but with a movement along the demand curve to reflect the lower price of consoles.

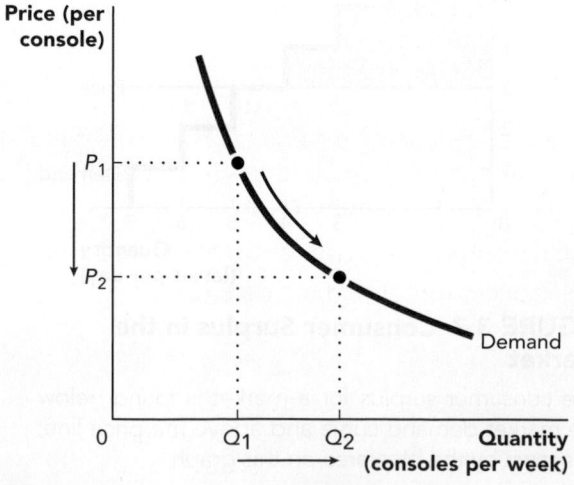

PROBLEM 3

The price of Xbox consoles, a competing product, decreases.

STEP 1: Does the change in the price of Xbox consoles shift the demand curve for PS4 consoles? Yes! Xbox consoles are a substitute in consumption for PS4 consoles. When the price of Xbox consoles decreases, some people who would have bought a PS4 console will buy an Xbox console instead.

STEP 2: In which direction does demand shift? The price decrease for Xbox consoles causes consumers to buy fewer PS4 consoles at any given price. So the demand for PS4 consoles decreases and the demand curve shifts to the left.

STEP 3: Draw the graph showing the shift.

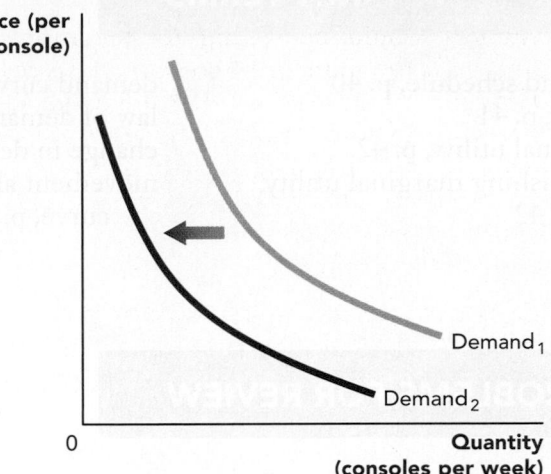

SUMMARY

When entrepreneurs like the owner of your local coffee shop decide which products to sell and what prices to charge, they consider what consumers like you want to buy and the prices you are willing to pay. That is, they look closely at demand. Demand also influences firms' decisions about the number of workers to hire. In these ways among others, demand is important to everyone in the economy.

The demand schedule indicates the quantity of a good or service that consumers would purchase at each price. The information in the demand schedule is determined by the additional benefit that consumers would receive from each unit of the good or service. That additional benefit is called marginal utility.

The demand curve is a graphical representation of the demand schedule. As people consume more of a good within a given period of time, they generally receive less and less additional benefit from one more unit. This diminishing marginal utility explains the downward slope of most demand curves.

If other influences on demand remain unchanged, the demand for a good will increase and the demand curve will shift to the right as the result of:

- a change in preferences in favor of the good
- an expectation of higher prices in the future

- an increase in income (for normal goods)
- a decrease in the price of complements in consumption
- an increase in the price of substitutes in consumption
- an increase in the number of consumers of the good

Conversely, demand will decrease and the demand curve will shift to the left if the opposite of any of these changes occurs. A change in the *price* of a good will not shift the demand curve for that good; it will only change the quantity demanded.

You wouldn't pay $3 for a cup of coffee that is only worth $2 to you. You seek purchases that provide you with a net gain, in that they are worth more to you than their price. That net gain is called consumer surplus. On a demand graph, consumer surplus is represented by the area below the demand curve and above the price line. When the price of a good falls, consumer surplus rises, and when the price of a good rises, consumer surplus falls. The prices of goods and services are determined by demand together with supply, which is the topic of the next chapter.

KEY TERMS

demand schedule, p. 40
utility, p. 41
marginal utility, p. 42
diminishing marginal utility,
  p. 42

demand curve, p. 42
law of demand, p. 43
change in demand, p. 44
movement along the demand
  curve, p. 45

substitutes in consumption,
  p. 47
complements in consumption,
  p. 47
consumer surplus, p. 47

PROBLEMS FOR REVIEW

1. Demand curves generally slope downward due to which of the following?
   a. lower prices for complements in consumption
   b. increases in personal income
   c. diminishing marginal utility
   d. diminishing marginal cost
   e. expectations of lower future prices

2. Suppose that after a successful advertising campaign, the quantity of lattes Brian would demand at each price (up to $7) increases by 1.
   a. Brian's pre-advertising demand schedule is provided in the accompanying table. Create a new table showing Brian's new demand schedule.
   b. On a correctly labeled graph, draw Brian's original demand curve. Then, using a different color, draw his new demand curve after the successful advertising campaign.

Price per Latte	Quantity Demanded by Brian
$7	0
6	0
5	1
4	1
3	1
2	1
1	2
0	2

3. Use the concept of diminishing marginal utility to explain why customers eventually stop drinking coffee, even at a café that provides free coffee refills.

For problems 4–9, draw a smooth, downward-sloping market demand curve for tea. Then show the effect of each of the indicated changes. Be sure to label the axes. Label the original demand curve Demand$_1$. If the demand curve shifts, label the new demand curve Demand$_2$.

4. Consumers expect the price of tea to increase significantly in the near future.

5. Consumers' incomes rise.

6. The price of coffee, a substitute for tea, decreases.

7. The price of tea increases.

8. New research suggests that tea drinkers catch fewer colds.

9. A British cruise ship docks in Boston and thousands of tea-loving tourists come ashore to buy T-shirts and tea.

10. Draw Brian's original demand curve for lattes, as you did in problem 2b.
    a. Use horizontal stripes to shade the area that represents Brian's consumer surplus when the price of lattes is $4 each.
    b. Use vertical stripes to shade the area that represents the increase in consumer surplus when the price falls from $4 to $2 per latte.

11. From which of your recent purchases did you receive the most consumer surplus?

12. Many public pools charge a single daily admission fee for an unlimited number of visits. Why do most people visit a pool only once in a day anyway? What does that indicate about consumers' daily demand curves for pool visits?

Supply

4

LEARNING OBJECTIVES
In this chapter, you will learn to:

1. Interpret a supply schedule
2. Work with graphical models of firm and market supply
3. Explain the relationship between supply and marginal cost
4. Identify factors that shift the supply curve
5. Discuss the importance of producer surplus

Vladimir Pisarenko/Shutterstock

Hairstylists create coifs, do 'dos, and even fashion a few mullets and Mohawks. They could serve more or fewer customers at the going rates, but they typically accept around 8 appointments each day. Why do they stop when the creation of another set of curls would bring in $50 or so? On the other hand, why do they do the 'dos they do when great books and beaches beckon? This chapter explains how sellers of goods and services decide what quantity to supply at each particular price.

Why Should I Care?

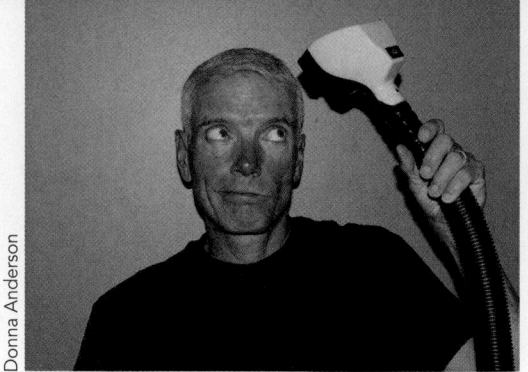

Donna Anderson

The supply of goods and services from firms is essential to life as we know it. If farmers supplied no food, you would have nothing to eat. If nurses supplied no care, some patients wouldn't survive. If hairstylists supplied no services, hair owners would be left to fend for themselves with scissors, clippers, and Flowbee vacuum trimming attachments like the one shown in the photo.

Perhaps you've already supplied services as a tutor, newspaper carrier, or barista. After graduation, you'll have more decisions to make about how much time to spend working at the going wage rate. If your career involves supplying goods, perhaps as the producer of a new brand of athletic shoes, you will also have to decide how many units to sell at the going price. Being familiar with the economics of supply will help you make those decisions, whether you're supplying shoes, news, or hairdos.

▲ Without an adequate supply of hairstyling services, you might pay a fortune for a mullet, or you might have to cut your own hair with a Flowbee (a vacuum attachment used to cut hair).

The Supply Schedule

Hairstylists supply services ranging from trims and colorings to waxes and foils. Let's consider a haircut with shampoo and blow dry that takes 30 minutes of a hairstylist's time. The quantity of haircuts a hairstylist would be willing to supply each day depends on the price paid for a haircut. Information on supply can be organized into a **supply schedule**, which indicates the quantity that would be supplied in a given period at various prices. A supply schedule does not indicate what stylists would most *like* to charge for each quantity.

Assuming hairstylists would like as much profit as possible, the ideal price would be infinity, but they aren't going to get it!

As with a demand schedule, a supply schedule can be expressed by numbers in a table or by a curve on a graph.

supply schedule
A table that indicates the quantity of a good or service that would be supplied in a given period at various prices.

For simplicity, assume that Devon, Eleanor, and Francis each own one of the only three hair salons in the local hairstyling market. The middle three columns of Table 4.1 are hypothetical Saturday afternoon supply schedules for the three firms. If he had to, Devon would accept $10 for a first haircut. If the price rose to $20, he would supply 2 haircuts that afternoon. He would provide 3 haircuts for $40 each and 4 for $60 each. Eleanor would not work for $10 or $20 per haircut, but she would provide 1 haircut if the price were $30 each and 2 if the price were $70 each. Francis requires at least $20 for his first haircut. He would provide 2 haircuts if the price were $50 each and 3 if he were paid $70 each.

For the purposes of this chapter, let's suppose that all hairstylists provide identical services. We'll also suppose that all hairstylists charge the same price. If one hairstylist tried to charge more than the others, his or her customers would switch to one of the other hairstylists who offered

Table 4.1 Firm Supply Schedules and the Market Supply Schedule for Haircuts

Price per Haircut	Quantity Supplied by Devon	Quantity Supplied by Eleanor	Quantity Supplied by Francis	Total Quantity Supplied by Market
$10	1	0	0	1
20	2	0	1	3
30	2	1	1	4
40	3	1	1	5
50	3	1	2	6
60	4	1	2	7
70	4	2	3	9

identical services at a lower price. In Chapter 9, we'll discuss what happens when a firm sells a good or service that differs from the offerings of other firms.

The *market supply schedule* indicates the total quantity that firms in the market would be willing to supply at various prices. It is found by summing the quantities that each of the individual firms would

▲ As the price paid for haircuts increases, the quantity of haircuts that hairstylists are willing to supply also increases.

Monkey Business Images/Shutterstock

supply at each price. At a price of $10, we know that Devon would supply 1 haircut, and no one else would supply any, so the market supply would be 1. For $20, Devon would supply 2 haircuts, Eleanor would not supply any, and Francis would supply 1, so the market supply would be 3. The other market supply values are determined in the same way. The last column of Table 4.1 shows the market supply schedule for haircuts.

The Supply Graph

The **supply curve** for a good or service illustrates the relationship between the price and the quantity that firms are willing to supply. Figure 4.1 shows the supply curves for Devon, Eleanor, Francis, and the market. The curves are visual representations of the supply schedules in Table 4.1. Suppose you wanted to know the quantity of haircuts each hairstylist and the market would supply at $45 each. As shown in Figure 4.1, you could find the quantities by drawing a horizontal dotted line with a height of $45 across the graphs. The quantity that would be supplied is shown directly below the point where the dotted line intersects each supply curve. This intersection occurs at a quantity of 3 for Devon, 1 for Eleanor, and 1 for Francis. The market would supply the sum of the quantities supplied by each of the individual firms: 3 + 1 + 1 = 5 at $45.

supply curve
A curve that illustrates the relationship between the price of a good or service and the quantity that firms are willing to supply.

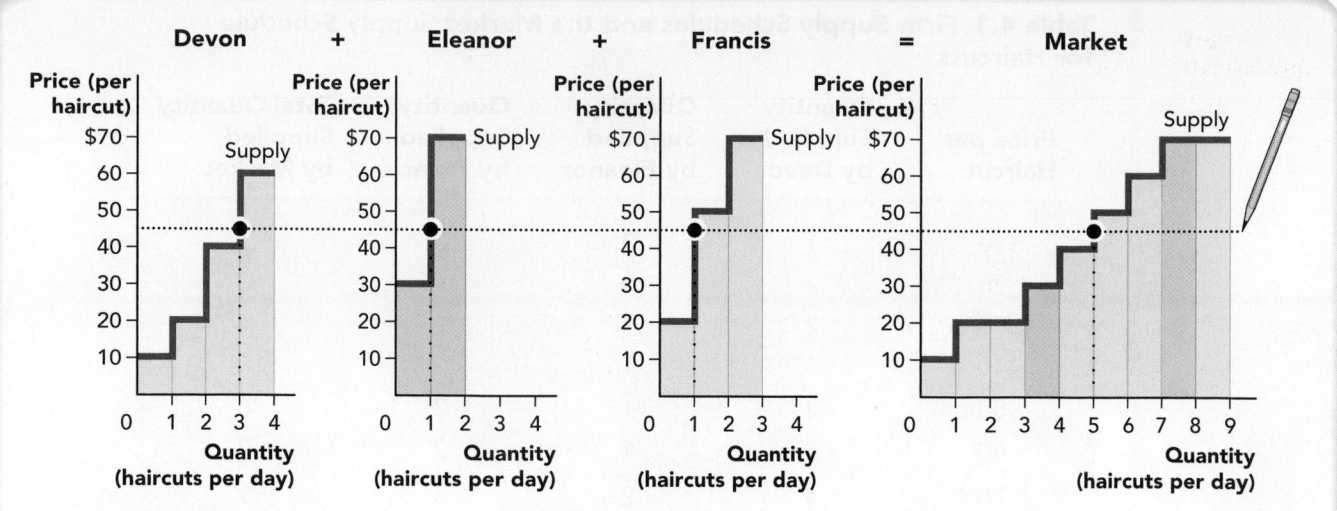

FIGURE 4.1 Firm Supply Curves and the Market Supply Curve

A firm's supply curve indicates the quantity the firm would supply within a given period at each price. The market supply curve is simply the summation of the supply curves for each of the firms in the market at each price.

THE RISING COST OF SUPPLYING ONE MORE

Like hairstylists, most firms are willing to supply higher quantities only at higher prices. Why? Because the cost of supplying each additional unit of a good or service tends to rise as more units are supplied. You learned in Chapter 3 that economists use the term *marginal* to mean "for one more." So the additional cost of supplying one more unit of a good or service is the **marginal cost.** The marginal cost typically rises as more units are produced, which means that a firm will only supply so much at a given price. Chapter 7 explains the details of why the marginal cost sometimes falls at first but eventually rises. For now, we consider a simple example of the rising cost of supplying one more.

Suppose Devon doesn't particularly like or dislike giving haircuts, so his decisions are based on the money he receives and the cost of providing his services. To begin with, we'll also suppose that the opportunity cost of Devon's time is his only significant cost of hairstyling. Cutting hair takes time that Devon could otherwise spend on activities he enjoys, such as gardening, weightlifting, and spending time with friends and family. Put yourself in Devon's shoes. What would motivate you to spend a half-hour giving someone a haircut? The payment you receive would need to equal or exceed the value of your best alternative use of that time.

marginal cost
The additional cost of supplying one more unit of a good or service.

Devon's refusal to give a haircut for less than $10 means alternative activities are worth at least $10 to him. Perhaps the first haircut causes him to miss a half-hour of gardening that he values at $10. In that case, the marginal cost of Devon's first haircut is the $10 opportunity cost of not being able to garden for that half-hour. If the price of a haircut were $10, Devon would be indifferent between gardening and giving a haircut. If the price of a haircut were $15, he would gladly supply the haircut because the price would exceed the opportunity cost of his time.

Devon's willingness to supply more haircuts only at higher prices is reasonable because as Devon provides more haircuts, he must give up increasingly valuable periods of his day. Figure 4.2 illustrates Devon's rising opportunity cost of time spent cutting hair. His first haircut would come out of his gardening time, which is less valuable to him than the exercise time he would give up if he gave a second haircut. This makes the opportunity cost of the second haircut higher than the opportunity cost of the first. Additional haircuts get in the way of increasingly valuable alternatives: time spent with friends, time spent with family, and so on. Due to the rising opportunity cost of time, which is the marginal cost of cutting hair, Devon will provide more haircuts only in exchange for higher prices. This explains the upward slope of the supply curve for haircuts.

At very low prices, a firm might minimize its losses by shutting down and not supplying anything. If it does produce output, the firm's supply curve is

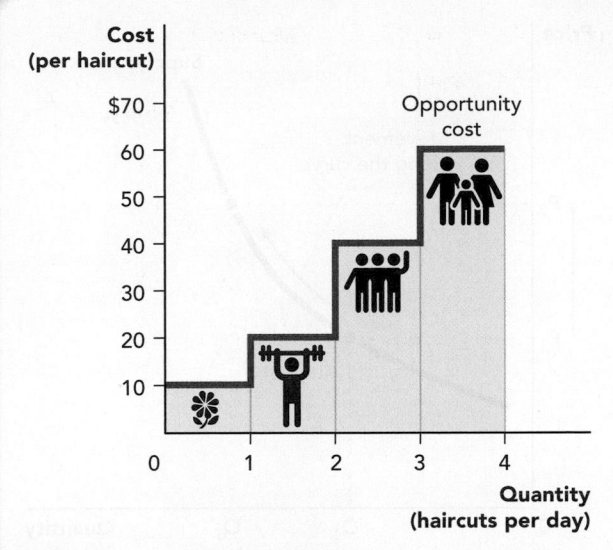

FIGURE 4.2 The Rising Opportunity Cost of Time Spent Giving Haircuts

As Devon spends more time cutting hair, he must give up increasingly valuable alternatives. The first haircut takes time he would have spent gardening. Giving a second haircut means he can't lift weights. The third and fourth haircuts take time he would have spent with friends and family.

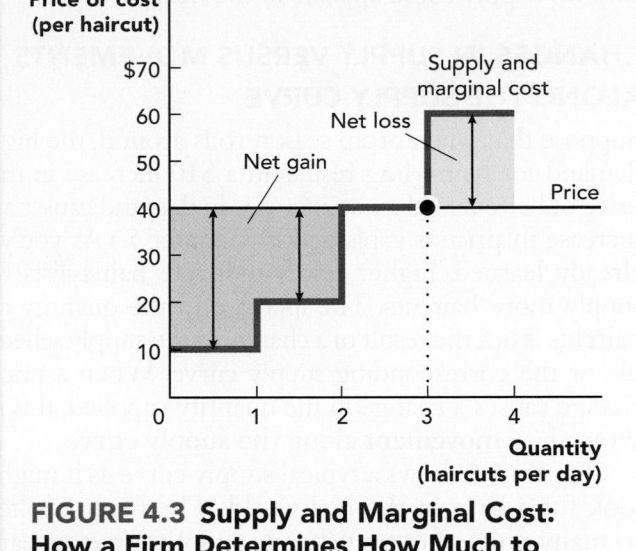

FIGURE 4.3 Supply and Marginal Cost: How a Firm Determines How Much to Produce

Devon receives a net gain from providing a haircut if his marginal cost is below the price the customer pays for it. Providing a haircut with a marginal cost above the price would result in a net loss. To avoid such losses, firms supply only those units for which the marginal cost is less than or equal to the price.

its marginal cost curve, which shows the additional cost of providing each unit. Figure 4.3 shows why supply is based on marginal cost. The sale of a haircut for which the additional (marginal) cost is below the price provides a *net gain* for the firm that adds to the firm's profit or subtracts from the firm's losses. The amount of the net gain is equal to the difference between the marginal cost and the price. The sale of any unit for which the marginal cost exceeds the price results in a *net loss* equal to the difference between the marginal cost and the price.

Devon decides how many haircuts to supply by pursuing net gains and avoiding net losses. Let's examine Devon's decision of how many haircuts to supply if the price is $40 each. The first cut has a marginal cost of $10, so with a price of $40, Devon will supply that haircut for a net gain of $40 − $10 = $30. He will supply the second haircut for a net gain of $40 − $20 = $20. He is indifferent between providing the third haircut or not because its marginal cost of $40 exactly equals the price. For simplicity, we will assume that firms will supply a unit for which the price equals the marginal cost.

If Devon supplied a fourth haircut for $40, his marginal cost of $60 would exceed the price by $60 − $40 = $20. In order to avoid net losses such as this,

firms will not supply units for which the marginal cost exceeds the price. This is why Devon stops after providing 3 haircuts. Higher prices may lead firms to supply more units. For example, if the price of haircuts rises to $65, this will exceed Devon's $60 marginal cost of providing the fourth haircut. So Devon will provide the fourth haircut to receive a net gain of $65 − $60 = $5. This direct relationship between the price and the quantity supplied is summarized by the **law of supply:** Under the *ceteris paribus* assumption that other influences remain unchanged, firms will supply a larger quantity of a good or service at higher prices than at lower prices.

The law of supply implies that supply curves rise from left to right, which is usually the case. The supply curves we've seen so far climb upward and have horizontal and vertical segments. Along those "curves," horizontal segments represent the marginal cost of each unit and vertical segments show the rise in the marginal cost as more units are produced. Like demand curves, supply curves appear smooth on a graph that represents such a large number of units that the horizontal segment

law of supply
When other influences remain unchanged, firms will supply a larger quantity of a good or service at higher prices than at lower prices.

for each unit is insignificantly small. An example of a smooth supply curve appears in the next section.

CHANGES IN SUPPLY VERSUS MOVEMENTS ALONG THE SUPPLY CURVE

Suppose that when prom season rolls around, the high demand for hairstyling results in a $10 increase in the price of haircuts. (How an increase in demand causes an increase in price is explained in Chapter 5.) As you've already learned, higher prices motivate hairstylists to supply more haircuts. The increase in the quantity of haircuts is not the result of a change in the supply schedule or the corresponding supply curve. When a price change causes a change in the quantity supplied, this is shown by a **movement along the supply curve.**

Figure 4.4 shows a typical supply curve as it might look for a firm in the real world. The firm supplies so many units of output that its supply curve appears smooth. A price increase leads a firm to operate at a higher point on its existing supply curve, and therefore to supply a larger quantity of its good or service. For instance, a higher price makes a hairstylist willing to work more hours and cut more hair, but this results from a movement along the supply curve, not from changes in the shape or position of the supply curve.

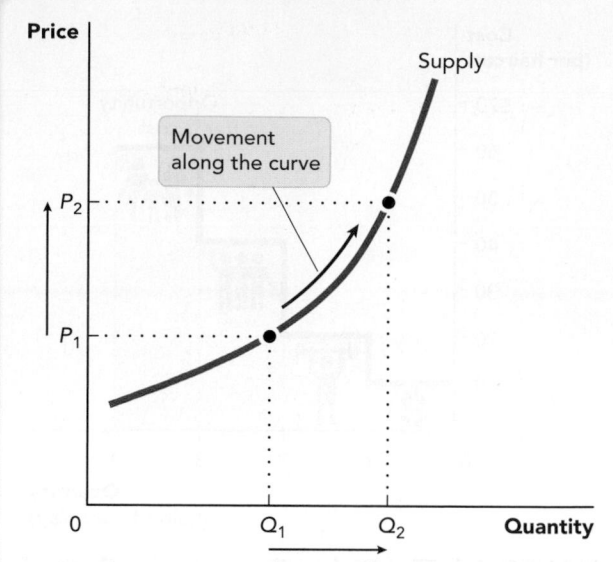

FIGURE 4.4 A Movement Along the Supply Curve

A change in the price (*P*) causes a movement along the supply curve. For example, when the price increases from P_1 to P_2, the quantity supplied increases from Q_1 to Q_2.

If the supply curve itself shifts, the quantity supplied changes at each price, which is called a **change in supply.** A rightward shift of the supply curve represents an increase in supply, showing that more units will be supplied at each price. (An increase in supply is sometimes described as a downward shift because when supply increases, firms will accept a lower price for each unit.) A leftward shift of the supply curve represents a decrease in supply, showing that

movement along the supply curve
A change in the quantity supplied that is caused by a change in the price of the good or service.

change in supply
A shift of the supply curve, indicating that there is a change in the quantity supplied at each price.

> When a price change causes a change in the quantity supplied, this is a *movement along the supply curve.*

fewer units will be supplied at each price. (A decrease in supply is sometimes described as an upward shift of the supply curve because when supply decreases, firms require a higher price for each unit.) Figure 4.5 illustrates an increase in supply and a decrease in supply.

Q&A

Stores sometimes offer lower prices when consumers buy a larger quantity. Does that contradict the law of supply?

Volume discounts—that is, discounts for buying a larger quantity of a product—are common, but they do not contradict the law of supply. The supply schedule indicates the *most* a firm would be willing to supply at a given price. When a tire store offers to sell 1 tire for $150 or 4 tires for $125 each, it is not saying that it will sell *at most* 1 tire for $150 and *at most* 4 tires for $125 each. In fact,

the store would happily sell 4 tires for $150 each instead of $125 each. Beyond that, the store would probably be willing to sell even more tires for $150 each than it would for $125 each. Because this pricing policy does not indicate the largest quantity the firm would supply for either $125 or for $150, it does not reveal the shape of the supply curve. Rather, the volume discount shows that the firm recognizes that consumers' *demand* curves are downward sloping, and that buyers will purchase more tires at the lower price.

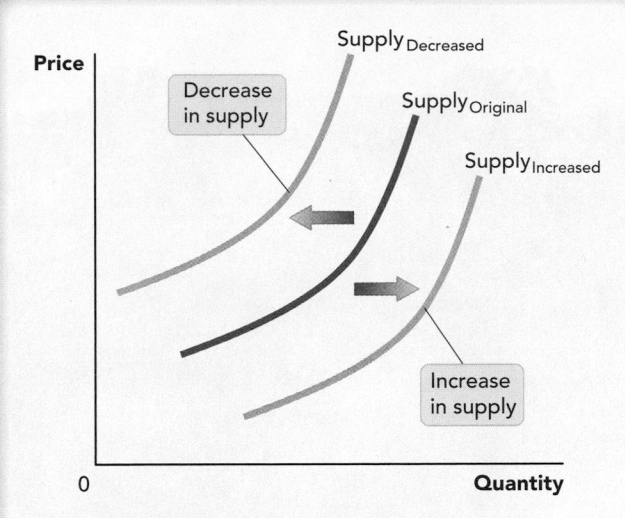

FIGURE 4.5 Shifts in the Supply Curve
A leftward shift of the supply curve represents a decrease in supply. A rightward shift represents an increase in supply.

Supply Shifters

Several types of changes cause the supply curve to shift. For example, let's make our discussion of haircutting costs more realistic by considering the costs of styling gel, disinfectant chemicals, shampoo, talcum powder, and other items that might be used while cutting hair. If these inputs become more expensive, hairstylists will reduce the number of haircuts they are willing to supply at each price. So the supply of haircuts will decrease and the supply curve will shift to the left. More generally, a firm's supply curve can shift as a result of changes in

- input costs
- expectations
- nature or the weather
- the prices of related goods or services

The *market* supply curve can shift as a result of any of the above changes, and due to a change in

- the number of firms

The rest of this section explores the details of these supply shifters.

INPUT COSTS

To produce most goods and services, firms must pay for inputs—such as electricity for hair dryers in salons, checkout clerks for grocery stores, aluminum for soda-pop cans, and lumber for home construction. New discoveries and new production methods can alter input costs. For example, the discovery of new sources of bauxite ore, from which aluminum is made, would lower the cost of aluminum. When the costs of inputs change, supply changes. Lower input costs shift supply curves to the right, because when production becomes less expensive, firms will supply more units at any given price.

Technology, which is the method of creating a good or service from inputs, has a direct influence on input costs. For instance, the development of sawmill technology that allows boards to be cut faster and with less waste has reduced the cost of producing lumber. The use of automated self-checkout lines has reduced the cost of labor at grocery stores. And electric clippers save barbers time by allowing them to cut hair much faster than they could with scissors alone. When technology lowers the marginal cost for firms, supply increases and the firms' supply curves shift to the right.

Input costs can also go up. Wars, environmental problems, government regulations, and worker shortages are among the causes of higher input costs. A war that disrupted the supply of bauxite ore from its least expensive sources would increase the cost of making aluminum. A widespread infestation of timber beetles would make it more difficult and expensive to obtain logs, which are inputs for lumber production. The U.S. Occupational Safety and Health Administration requires grocery stores to pay for training to teach employees how to avoid injuries. And a shortage of hairdressers, as occurred in Australia in 2015, makes it necessary for hair salons to pay higher wages in order to attract enough workers. Higher input costs shift supply curves to the left, because when it becomes more costly to produce a good or service, firms will supply fewer units at any given price.

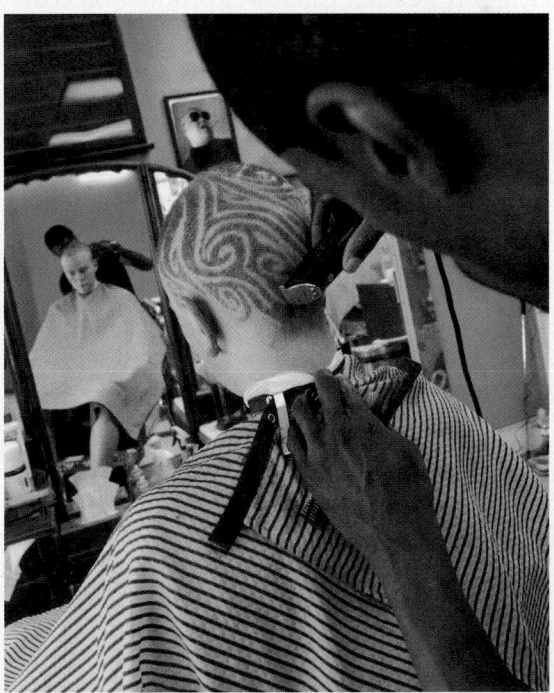

▲ Electric clippers are a form of technology that lowers the cost of hairstyling. Without them, it would take more time to provide a haircut, and the supply of haircuts would shift to the left.

EXPECTATIONS

Unlike perishable goods such as bananas, and services such as hairstyling, goods such as lumber and cans of soda-pop can be stored over time. For storable goods, the seller has a choice between offering the good for sale now or later. A lumber company that expects prices to rise in the near future will want to put off at least some of its sales until after the prices go up. Firms can do this by holding goods in *inventory*, or temporary storage, until the time is ripe for selling them. When expectations of higher prices cause firms to hold more goods in inventory, today's supply curve shifts to the left. The opposite is true if firms expect prices to fall in the near future: they will be eager to sell more of their goods now. For example, when lumber prices are expected to fall, the supply curve for lumber shifts to the right.

NATURAL DISASTERS AND WEATHER

Natural disasters and bad weather can increase production costs and decrease supply. For instance, a drought forces tree farmers to spend more time and money irrigating their trees. Because this increases the cost of producing each tree, farmers are not willing to supply as many trees for each price. The result is a decrease in the supply of trees and a leftward shift of the tree supply curve. Similarly, natural disasters can reduce the supply of some goods and services. When Hurricane Harvey struck in 2017, it shut down oil refineries in Texas. The result was a leftward shift of the oil supply curve. The opposite is also true: particularly good weather can lower production costs and

Rigucci/Shutterstock.com

▲ During a drought, tree farmers must spend more time and money irrigating their crops.

increase supply, shifting the supply curve to the right. For example, when ample rain in 2016 led to bumper crops of wheat in Kansas, the result was a rightward shift of the wheat supply curve.

PRICES OF RELATED GOODS AND SERVICES

Hairstylists can use their skills and facilities to cut hair, dye hair, perm hair, and perform a variety of other services. Haircuts, dye jobs, and perms are **substitutes in production** because the inputs used to provide each of

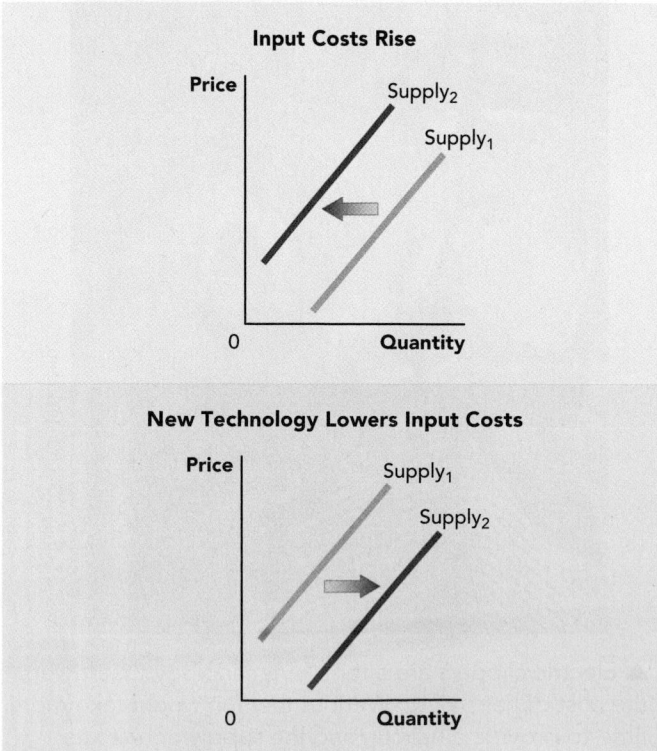

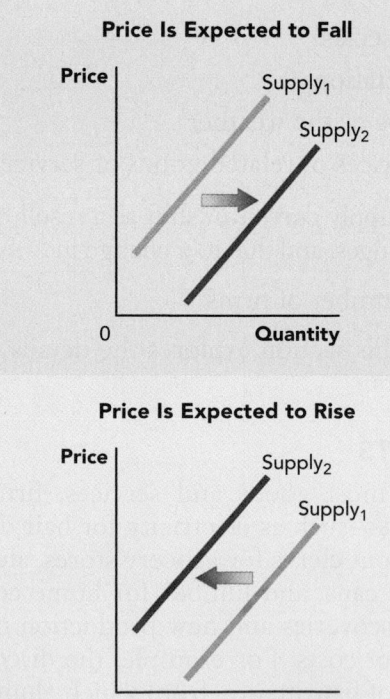

these services could otherwise be used to provide more of the others. Part of the opportunity cost of giving a haircut is that it takes time the hairstylist could otherwise spend dying hair. If dye jobs become more popular and their price rises, stylists will want to supply fewer haircuts because they can earn more money dying hair.

Paper and lumber are substitutes in production because a log can be used to produce either paper or lumber. Other substitutes in production include cheese and ice cream (alternative uses for milk) and corn ethanol and corn syrup (alternative uses for corn). When an increase in demand causes the price of one of these goods or services to increase, the supply of its substitute decreases because more inputs are devoted to the product with the elevated price. The opposite is also true: the supply of a good increases when the price of its substitute in production decreases.

Goods or services are **complements in production** if they are produced together using the same inputs. For example, fresh milk separates into cream and skim milk. When more skim milk is made, more cream is made as a byproduct. So if high prices boost the production of skim milk, the supply of cream will increase. The production of beer creates grain byproducts that can be fed to animals, so an increase in beer production leads to an increase in the supply of animal feed. Other complements in production include leather and beef, chicken breasts and chicken drumsticks, and oil and natural gas. When an increase in demand causes the price of one of these goods to increase, the supply of its complement will increase. The opposite is also true: when a decrease in demand causes the price of one of these goods to fall,

Macmillan Learning

▲ This machine separates raw milk into cream and skim milk. Because they are produced together using the same resources, these two goods are complements in production.

the supply of its complement will also fall.

THE NUMBER OF FIRMS

The factors discussed so far shift both the supply curves of individual firms and market supply curves. If the number of firms in a market changes, this, too, will shift the market supply curve. Suppose a new hairstylist named Gustavo opens a fourth salon, which competes with those operated by Devon, Eleanor, and Francis. We know that the

substitutes in production
Goods or services for which the inputs used to provide each of the goods or services could otherwise be used to provide more of the other(s).

complements in production
Goods or services produced together using the same inputs.

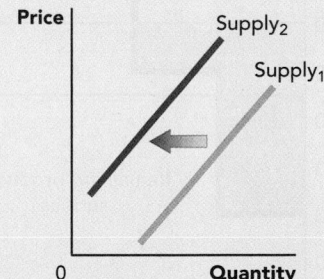

Natural Disaster Slows Production

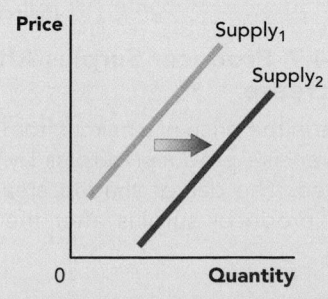

Good Weather Boosts Production

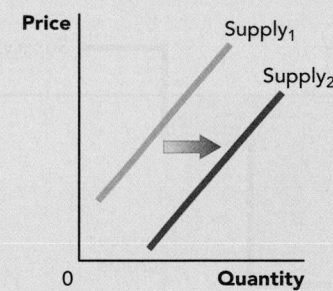

Price of Complement in Production Rises

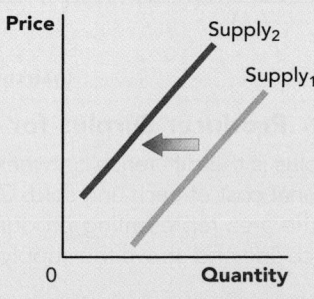

Price of Substitute in Production Rises

market supply curve for haircuts is found by adding up the quantities supplied by the individual salons at each price. With a new salon adding to the haircuts supplied by the other salons, the market supply curve shifts to the right. For example, at a price of $45, our original salons would supply a total of 5 haircuts. If Gustavo is willing to supply 2 haircuts for $45, the quantity supplied in the market is now 5 + 2 = 7 haircuts at that price. Just as an increase in the number of firms increases the market supply, a decrease in the number of firms decreases the market supply.

Producer Surplus

Like all hairstylists, Francis won't provide a haircut if the price is below the additional cost of giving that haircut. He would prefer for the price to be far above his marginal cost. Any amount by which the price exceeds the marginal cost of each unit sold provides a net gain called **producer surplus.** Suppose the price of a haircut is $60, as shown in Figure 4.6. Francis has a $20 marginal cost of supplying a first haircut and a $50 marginal cost of supplying a second haircut. Each of the 2 haircuts provides Francis with producer surplus because the price exceeds the marginal cost. Francis will stop after 2 haircuts because the $70 marginal cost of supplying a third haircut exceeds the $60 price.

> **producer surplus**
> Any amount by which the price exceeds the marginal cost of each unit sold.

On a graph, producer surplus is found below the price line and above the supply curve. Figure 4.6 shows Francis's producer surplus as the shaded area. He receives $60 – $20 = $40 of producer surplus from the first haircut and $60 – $50 = $10 of producer surplus from the second haircut. His total producer surplus is therefore $40 + $10 = $50.

Now suppose the price drops to $45. Only the first haircut has a marginal cost at or below $45, so Francis will supply 1 haircut. The total producer surplus falls to $45 – $20 = $25 as shown by the darker shaded area in Figure 4.7. The lighter shaded area shows the producer surplus lost due to the price decrease. An increase in the price, as from $45 to $60, would have the opposite effect of increasing the producer surplus by the amount shown by the lighter shaded area.

The shaded area in Figure 4.8 shows the producer surplus for the entire market when 3 salons are selling haircuts for $60 each. Seven haircuts are sold at this price. Notice that the seventh haircut does not provide any producer surplus because it has a marginal cost of $60 and the price is $60. The total producer surplus in the market is found by adding the producer surplus for each of the seven haircuts sold: $50 + $40 + $40 + $30 + $20 + $10 + $0 = $190.

Producer surplus is not the same thing as *profit*. Profit is the firm's net gain after subtracting *all* of its costs from the money it takes in. Producer surplus is found by subtracting only the marginal cost of each

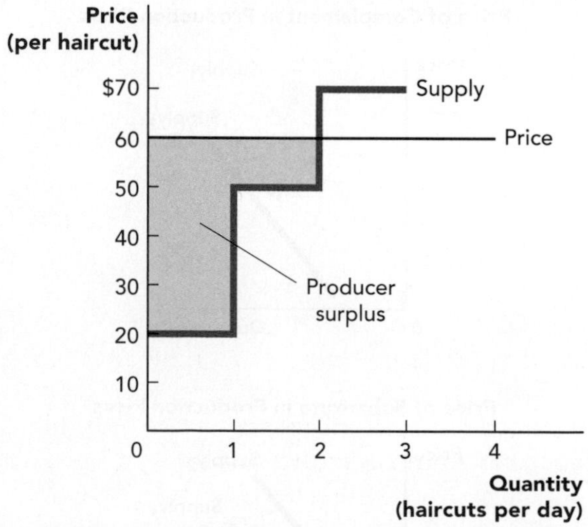

FIGURE 4.6 Producer Surplus for a Firm

Producer surplus is the difference between the price and the marginal cost of each unit sold. On a graph you will find the area representing producer surplus below the price line and above the supply curve.

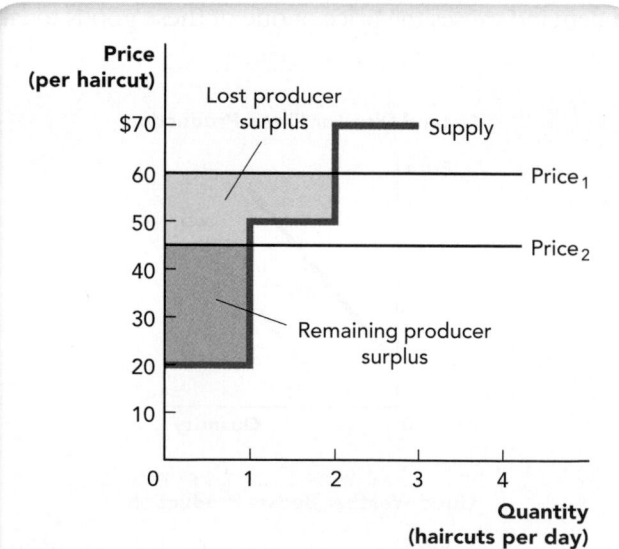

FIGURE 4.7 Producer Surplus After a Price Decrease

A decrease in the price of a haircut from $60 to $45 reduces Francis's producer surplus by the lighter shaded area. The darker shaded area shows his remaining producer surplus after the price falls to $45.

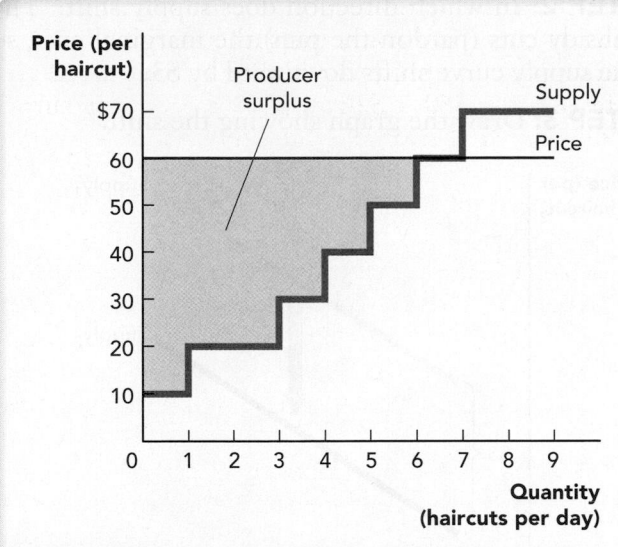

FIGURE 4.8 Producer Surplus in the Market

Like the producer surplus for a firm, the producer surplus for a market is found below the price line and above the supply curve, as shown by the shaded area on this graph.

unit from the money the firm takes in. Recall that the marginal cost for a hair salon is just the cost of things like the hairstylist's time, styling gel, and shampoo that the salon spends more on when providing another haircut. A hair salon does not spend more money on rent, advertising, or insurance when providing another haircut, so these types of costs aren't part of the marginal cost. After subtracting the marginal cost of each haircut and all the other costs, if a salon has money left over from customer payments, it has earned a profit.

Steps to Solving Problems Involving Supply

The following steps will help you analyze potential influences on supply and illustrate the effects of those changes on graphs.

STEP 1: Determine whether the influence shifts the supply curve.

Remember that a change in the price of a good does not shift the supply curve for that good. The only cost changes that shift the supply curve are those that change the marginal cost. There is no supply shift as a result of changes in rent, the cost of equipment, or taxes that don't depend on the quantity sold. Unless there is a change in the cost of providing each additional unit, the marginal cost has not changed. An increase in the annual license fee for hairstylists, for example, will increase a

hairstylist's costs, but not the marginal cost of supplying, say, 6 haircuts instead of 5.

STEP 2: If the supply curve shifts, determine whether it shifts leftward (and upward) to indicate a decrease in supply, or rightward (and downward) to indicate an increase in supply.

An increase in marginal cost or an expectation that the price of the good will increase in the near future shifts the firm's supply curve leftward and upward. A decrease in marginal cost, or an expectation that the price of the good will decrease in the near future, shifts the firm's supply curve rightward and downward. The market supply curve shifts whenever firms' supply curves shift, and in the same direction. The market supply curve also shifts leftward when the number of firms decreases and rightward when the number of firms increases.

STEP 3: Draw a graph and illustrate the supply curve before the change. Then, if supply shifts, draw a new supply curve on the existing graph to show the changes.

In many problems, you will work with abstract supply curves like the ones shown in Figures 4.4 and 4.5. These curves illustrate relative changes rather than providing exact numbers. Unless you have specific information about the shape or location of a supply curve, simply draw an upward-sloping line to represent supply. When there is a shift, draw the shifted supply curve on the same graph as the original supply curve so that you can easily compare the two curves and the shift's effects on the relationship between the price and the quantity supplied.

Sample Problems

For problems 1–3, begin by drawing a graph with a barber's upward-sloping supply curve for haircuts. Assume the supply curve is a straight line for simplicity. On the same graph, illustrate the effect, if any, of the indicated change.

PROBLEM 1
Due to a lice epidemic, a barber is forced to use one-time-use hygienic wraps to protect customers' clothing from hair, rather than the re-usable cloth wraps that might transfer lice from one customer to the next. Each one-time-use wrap costs $1.

STEP 1: Does the change shift the supply curve? Yes! The cost of each additional haircut now costs $1 more, so the marginal cost of each haircut rises by $1.

STEP 2: In which direction does supply shift? The $1 increase in marginal cost causes a decrease in supply. Specifically, the supply curve shifts upward by $1.

STEP 3: Draw the graph showing the shift.

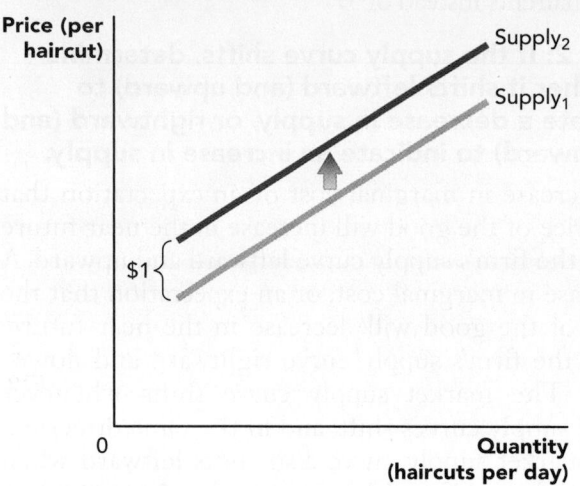

PROBLEM 2

The price of haircutting scissors increases by $10 per pair.

STEP 1: Does the change shift the supply curve? No! Although the barber will have to pay $10 more the next time he buys scissors, the purchase does not affect the cost of cutting one more person's hair. For example, if the barber provides 6 haircuts rather than 5 haircuts, the additional cost of the sixth haircut does not increase due to the higher price of scissors.

STEP 2: Because there is no change in supply, there is no need to think about the direction of a shift.

STEP 3: Draw the graph with no shift in supply.

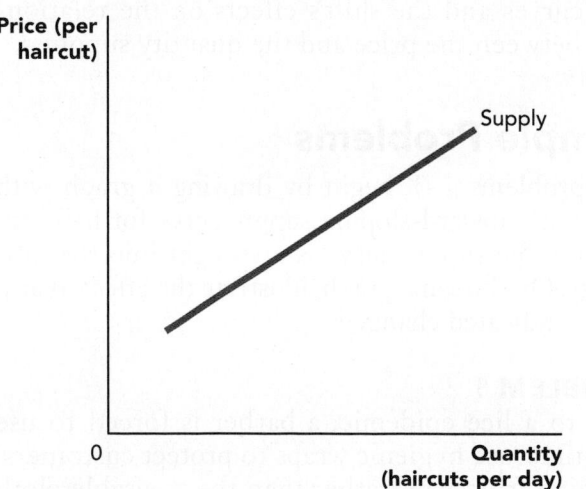

PROBLEM 3

To promote better grooming, the government subsidizes haircuts by giving $3 to barbers for each haircut they provide.

STEP 1: Does the change shift the supply curve? Yes! The haircut subsidy for barbers decreases the marginal cost of providing a haircut by $3.

STEP 2: In which direction does supply shift? The subsidy cuts (pardon the pun) the marginal cost, so the supply curve shifts downward by $3.

STEP 3: Draw the graph showing the shift.

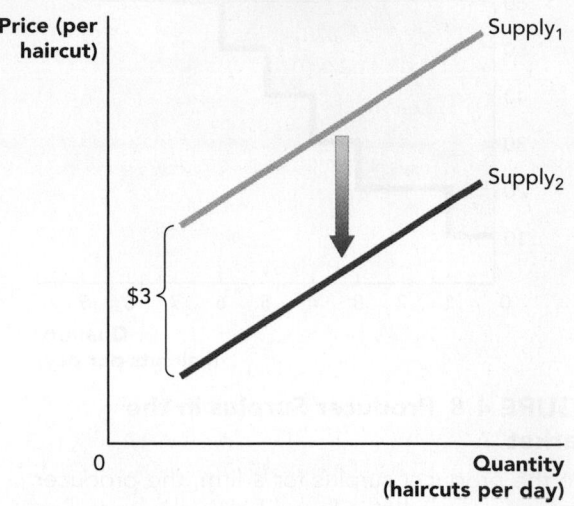

PROBLEM 4

Draw a supply curve for the haircut market and illustrate the effect of a new barbershop opening up in town.

STEP 1: Does the change shift the market supply curve? Yes! The number of firms has increased with the entry of the new barbershop.

STEP 2: In which direction does supply shift? The market supply curve is found by adding the quantity of haircuts the new shop would supply at each price to the number that existing shops would supply. Although we don't have the specifics on the size of this shift, we know that the market supply curve shifts to the right.

STEP 3: Draw the graph showing the increase in supply.

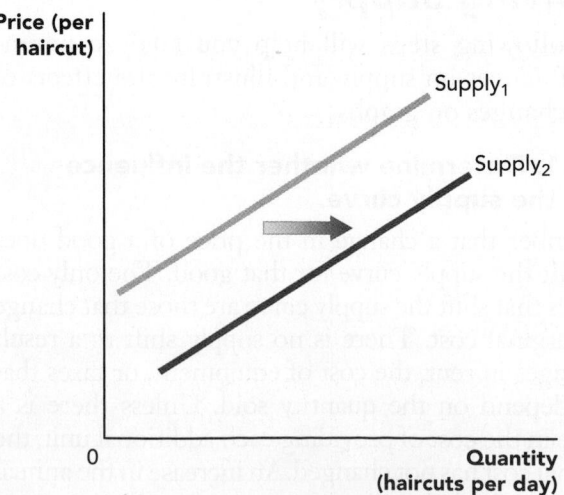

As you might have read on bumper stickers, "If you like food, thank a farmer," and "If you can read this, thank a teacher." Farms and schools are among the many types of firms that improve our standard of living by supplying valued goods and services. The price of a good or service helps determine the quantity supplied—higher prices motivate firms to supply larger quantities. The market supply is found by summing the quantities supplied by each of the individual firms at each price. A supply schedule shows how many units will be supplied at various prices, and can be in the form of a table or a supply curve on a graph.

The basis for supply schedules is the marginal cost, the cost of supplying each additional unit of the good or service. Rising opportunity costs are among the reasons the marginal cost of most goods and services eventually rises as more units are produced. Supply curves generally slope upward because firms will supply more only if the price rises enough to cover the higher additional cost of making more.

A firm's supply curve shifts due to changes in input costs, expectations about future prices, nature, the weather, or the prices of related goods or services. When the additional cost of making each unit of a good rises for any reason, or firms expect the price of the good to be higher in the future, the supply curve shifts leftward and upward. When the additional cost of making each unit of a good decreases for any reason or firms expect the price of the good to be lower in the future, the supply curve shifts rightward and downward. The market supply increases when the existing firms' supply increases and when the number of firms increases. Likewise, the market supply decreases when the existing firms' supply decreases and when the number of firms decreases.

Producer surplus is the difference between the price paid for each unit of a good and the marginal cost of providing each unit. Producer surplus is different from profit, which is the net gain after subtracting all costs from the money a firm takes in. Expenditures on machinery, advertising, and rent are examples of costs that are not part of the cost of supplying additional units, but must be subtracted to determine a firm's profit or loss. The next chapter brings market supply and market demand together to explain how prices are determined and how markets respond to changes in the marketplace.

KEY TERMS

supply schedule, p. 54
supply curve, p. 55
marginal cost, p. 56
law of supply, p. 57

movement along the supply
    curve, p. 58
change in supply, p. 58
substitutes in production, p. 61

complements in production,
    p. 61
producer surplus, p. 62

PROBLEMS FOR REVIEW

1. Supply curves generally slope upward due to the rise in which of the following?
   a. marginal utility
   b. marginal cost
   c. rent cost
   d. advertising cost
   e. demand

2. Suppose that Devon's landlord starts charging a $5 fee for each haircut Devon provides, and that nothing else changes.

   a. Make a table showing Devon's new marginal cost for each of the first 4 haircuts. You can determine Devon's original marginal cost for each haircut by looking at the height of his supply curve in Figure 4.3.
   b. Make a table showing Devon's new supply schedule; include quantities for each of the prices listed in Table 4.1.
   c. Draw Devon's original supply curve and his new supply curve after he must pay his landlord $5 per haircut.

For problems 3–6, draw a smooth, upward-sloping supply curve for a firm selling soap. Then show the effect of each of the indicated changes on the graph. Label the original supply curve "Supply₁." If the supply curve shifts, label the new supply curve "Supply₂."

3. The cost of lye, an ingredient in soap, decreases.

4. Soap makers expect the price of soap to be much higher next month.

5. The price of soap rises due to an increase in demand.

6. Price increases due to an increase in demand for a substitute in production: moisturizing cream that contains the same oils used to make soap.

7. Draw a smooth, upward-sloping curve to represent supply in the entire soap market and label it "Supply₁." Suppose that because firms in the soap market are experiencing losses, some shut down. Draw a new market supply curve on the same graph as the old one, showing the general effect of the decrease in the number of firms, and label it "Supply₂."

8. At a price of $18 for a haircut, Devon's supply curve indicates that he would supply 1 haircut. However, if he supplied 2 haircuts for $18 each, he would take in a total of $36. His only costs for providing 2 haircuts would be the $10 marginal cost of the first haircut and the $20 marginal cost of the second haircut, for a total of $30. Explain why Devon would not provide 2 haircuts even though his receipts of $36 would exceed his total cost of $30.

9. Draw Francis's supply curve as shown in the chapter and indicate the following:
   a. The producer surplus when the price is $40 per haircut, shaded with horizontal stripes.
   b. The increase in producer surplus when the price rises from $40 to $60 per haircut, shaded with vertical stripes.

10. Suppose people in your area hire college students to do yard work.
   a. Make a table that indicates the lowest hourly wage that you would accept to provide the first, second, third, fourth, and fifth hour of yard work tomorrow evening between 5 p.m. and 10 p.m. Take into account the other things that you could do tomorrow evening.
   b. Explain any differences between the least you would accept for the first hour of yard work and the least you would accept for the fifth hour of yard work.
   c. Draw your supply curve for yard work.
   d. What is one change in this situation that would shift your supply curve? In which direction would this change shift your supply curve?

Market Equilibrium

5

LEARNING OBJECTIVES

In this chapter, you will learn to:

1. Explain how a market reaches its equilibrium price and quantity

2. Discuss the effects of price ceilings and price floors

3. Show how shifts in supply and demand affect a market's equilibrium

4. Solve problems involving market equilibrium

Before tire rubber meets the road, it meets someone like Anthony Charnley, the owner of Anthony's Tire Store in Paso Robles, California. Anthony is one of about 18,000 tire dealers in the United States who collectively sell more than $20 billion worth of tires annually. On the demand side of this market are the owners of more than 250 million cars. Thanks to the workings of the tire market, long lines of customers seldom form at shops like Anthony's Tire Store, but tire shops are rarely without customers, either. The reason is that the quantity of tires demanded is approximately equal to the quantity supplied. This chapter explains how market prices bring these quantities into balance. It also introduces the implications of market outcomes for policymakers, sellers like Anthony Charnley, and buyers like you.

Why Should I Care?

In the markets for many of the things you buy, the model of supply and demand explains the prices you pay and the quantities that firms produce. **Although scarcity prevents you from having all the vacations, ice cream, and digital gadgetry you would like for free, markets accomplish a remarkable feat: they establish prices at which everyone who wants to buy a good or service at the going price can find a willing seller.** The model of supply and demand offers insight into the availability of everything from pop music to life-saving pharmaceuticals. The model also explains why water is cheap, diamonds are expensive, and the price of oil jumps up and down. Whether or not you jump up and down for diamonds, you can celebrate the fact that water costs less than diamonds.

Putting Supply and Demand Together

As in the markets for lattes, haircuts, and most other things, the demand curve for tires slopes downward and the supply curve for tires slopes upward. Figure 5.1 shows the supply curve and the demand curve for a hypothetical tire market in which all tires are identical. Combining the two curves on one graph allows us to compare the quantity that consumers would demand with the quantity that firms would supply at each price. Balance between the quantity demanded and the quantity supplied is achieved at the **equilibrium point,** which is where the supply curve and the demand curve intersect.

The price that brings the market to the equilibrium point is called the **equilibrium price.** To find the equilibrium price, look leftward from the equilibrium point to the vertical axis, which measures the price. The equilibrium price is $100 in the

equilibrium point
The point on a graph where the supply curve and the demand curve intersect.

equilibrium price
The price that brings the market to the equilibrium point.

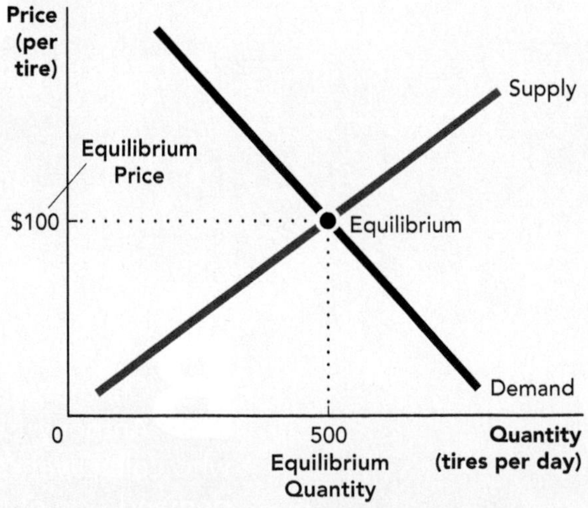

FIGURE 5.1 Market Equilibrium

The equilibrium point lies at the intersection of the supply curve and the demand curve. Only there does the quantity demanded equal the quantity supplied. Determine the equilibrium price by looking on the vertical (price) axis directly to the left of the equilibrium point. Determine the equilibrium quantity by looking on the horizontal (quantity) axis directly below the equilibrium point.

tire market illustrated in Figure 5.1. The quantity that is both demanded and supplied at the equilibrium price is called the **equilibrium quantity**. To find the equilibrium quantity, look on the horizontal axis, which measures the quantity, directly below the equilibrium point. In Figure 5.1, the equilibrium quantity is 500 tires.

We can expect markets to gravitate toward their equilibrium points.

We can expect markets to gravitate toward their equilibrium points. To see why, suppose the price per tire were only $40. Figure 5.2 shows that consumers would demand 725 tires but that firms would supply only 200. There would be a shortage of 725 − 200 = 525 tires in the market, and long lines of customers would form outside tire stores. Figure 5.2 shows the shortage as the horizontal distance between the supply curve and the demand curve at a price of $40.

What do you suppose tire dealer Anthony Charnley would do if people wanted to buy many more tires than he was willing to sell at the current price? If you're thinking he would raise the price, you have good

instincts! The shortage created by a $40 price would lead tire dealers to increase their price until customers no longer lined up ready to purchase more tires than the dealers wanted to supply. Notice in Figure 5.2 that, as the price rises, the horizontal gap between the supply curve and the demand curve narrows. At the equilibrium price of $100, the supply curve intersects the demand curve, and the shortage is eliminated because now the quantity demanded equals the quantity supplied.

Now suppose the price per tire were $140. Figure 5.3 shows that for $140, dealers would be willing to provide 700 tires, but customers would demand only 350. The result would be a surplus of 700 − 350 = 350 tires. This surplus is shown on the graph by the horizontal distance between the demand curve and the supply curve at a price of $140. You can probably guess what the dealers would do as excess tires piled up in storerooms—yes, reduce their price. Perform a Google search for "overstock sale" and you'll see this practice in action—retailers lowering their prices on everything from aircraft to Ziploc bags because of surpluses. As the price of tires decreases, the quantity demanded would increase and the quantity supplied would decrease until the surplus was eliminated at a price of $100.

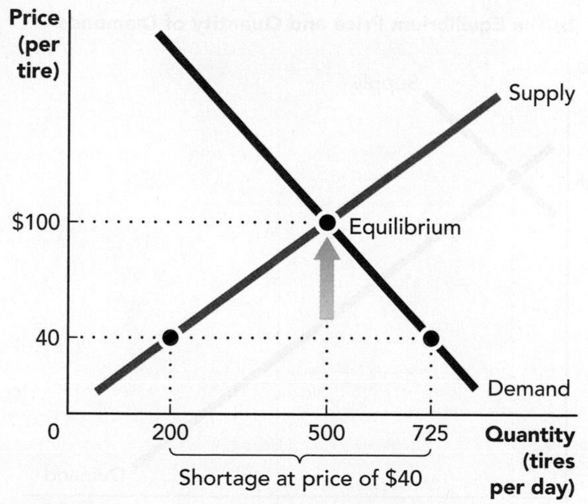

> **equilibrium quantity**
> The quantity that is both demanded and supplied at the equilibrium price.

FIGURE 5.2 How a Price Below the Equilibrium Price Leads to a Shortage

At a price below the equilibrium price, such as $40, the quantity of tires demanded exceeds the quantity supplied. This shortage prompts tire dealers to raise their prices. They will continue to do so until the equilibrium price is achieved.

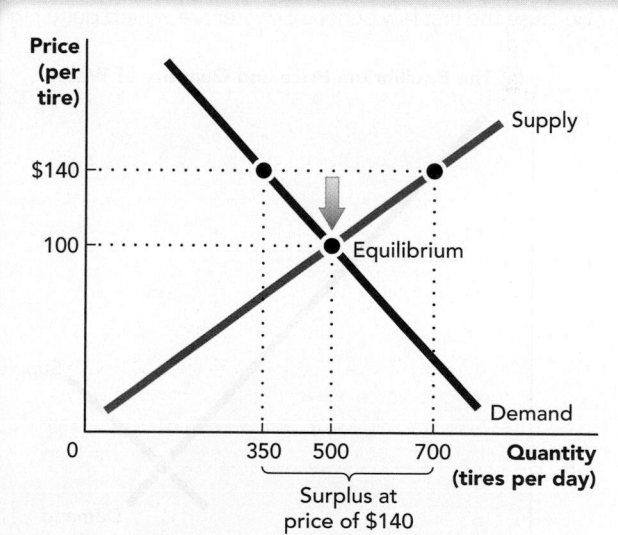

FIGURE 5.3 How a Price Above the Equilibrium Price Leads to a Surplus

At a price above the equilibrium price, such as $140, the quantity supplied exceeds the quantity demanded. The surplus prompts tire dealers to lower their price until the equilibrium price is reached, and the quantity of tires supplied equals the quantity demanded.

▲ When tire shops have a surplus of tires, they tend to lower their prices. This helps the price reach the equilibrium price.

The price charged in the tire market, which we will call the *market price* for tires, is pushed to the equilibrium price by these natural responses to shortages and surpluses. Once the equilibrium price is achieved, the quantity demanded equals the quantity supplied, so there is no further push toward higher or lower prices *unless* there is a change in supply or demand. Knowing that markets will gravitate to their equilibrium point, we can track what happens to the equilibrium price and quantity to discover the effects of a change in supply or demand. And by studying the equilibriums in the markets for different goods, we can find out why some prices are high and others are low. The Q&A box uses the equilibrium concept to explain prices that would otherwise seem quite strange.

Q&A

Why are some things that we can't live without so cheap, while some things that no one needs are so expensive?

It is curious that water, which is essential to every consumer, is practically free. On the other hand, diamonds, which no one needs in order to survive, are very expensive. Figure 5.4 illustrates why this and related paradoxes occur. Panel (a) shows the demand curve for water, which begins very high because the first few ounces of water are valued quite highly.

If water were in short supply, its price would be high as well. Instead, the supply of water is so large in most places that it brings the equilibrium price down to nearly 0.

Customers wouldn't pay as much for their first diamond as they would for their first cup of water that enables them to live. The supply of diamonds, however, is more limited than the supply of water. Thus, as panel (b) shows, it is that relatively small supply of diamonds that results in an equilibrium price that is relatively high.

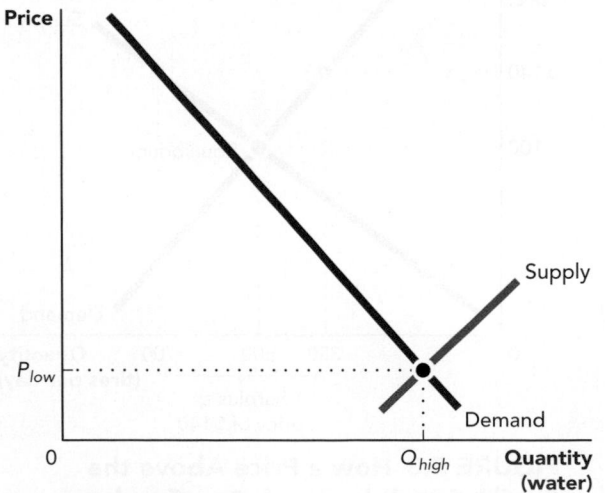

(a) The Equilibrium Price and Quantity of Water

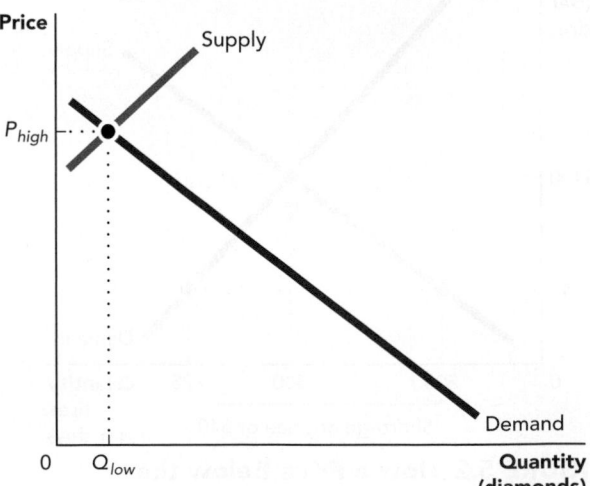

(b) The Equilibrium Price and Quantity of Diamonds

FIGURE 5.4 The Water–Diamond Paradox

Customers would pay a very high price for the first few ounces of water because water is essential to life. But the large supply of water brings the equilibrium price of water down to nearly 0. Customers don't need diamonds and would not pay as much for their first diamond as for their first cup of water, but the relatively small supply of diamonds results in a relatively high equilibrium price.

Price Controls

The market equilibrium determines the price for a good or service in the absence of intervention. Sometimes, however, governments control prices by putting upper or lower limits on them. These *price controls* have their benefits, but as you'll discover in this section, they also create problems of their own.

PRICE CEILINGS

A **price ceiling** is an artificial upper limit on the price of a good or service. The governments of Argentina, Russia, China, and France are among those that have capped prices on bread or rice in attempts to help the poor. In the United States, price ceilings aimed at curbing inflation have included caps on wages and food prices in the 1940s, and caps on oil prices in the 1970s. President Richard Nixon imposed a more general freeze on wages and prices in 1971. And millions of Americans live in apartments and mobile home parks whose rents are controlled by the government.

To have any effect on the price consumers pay, a price ceiling must be set below the equilibrium price in a market. A price ceiling set above the equilibrium price has no effect because firms don't want to charge more than the equilibrium price anyway! Recall that a price above the equilibrium price causes a surplus and leads firms to lower their price. For example, a price ceiling of $120 in the market for tires shown in Figure 5.5 would not affect tire sellers because they prefer the lower equilibrium price of $100.

We've seen that when the price set by firms is below the equilibrium price, a shortage results. A price ceiling set below the equilibrium price has the same effect: it drives the quantity demanded above the quantity supplied. But when a price ceiling is imposed, firms cannot raise their price to eliminate the shortage. Figure 5.5 shows that a price ceiling of $60 in the tire market would prevent firms from raising the price to the $100 equilibrium price.

Other than creating shortages, what's wrong with artificially low prices that result from price ceilings? Let's look into some of the problems they cause.

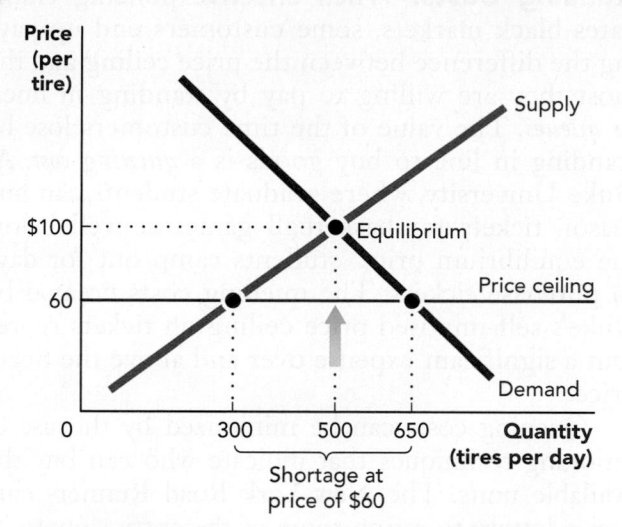

FIGURE 5.5 How a Price Ceiling Creates a Shortage

A price ceiling set below the equilibrium price causes the quantity demanded to exceed the quantity supplied, and firms cannot raise their price to eliminate the resulting shortage.

Black Markets. As Figure 5.5 shows, with a price ceiling of $60, firms are willing to supply only 300 tires. But consumers are willing to pay more than $60 for the first 649 tires. We know this because the demand curve lies above $60 for the first 649 tires. The willingness of customers to pay more than the going price can lead some sellers to charge prices above the price ceiling in an illegal market known as a **black market.** Black markets tend to emerge when there are price ceilings, and when the sale of particular goods or services is prohibited. For instance, black markets are common when sports teams cap their ticket prices below the equilibrium level so that students and others with limited incomes can attend games. At the Olympics, black-market scalpers sometimes sell tickets for 10 times their original price. To reduce this problem during the 2016 Olympics in Rio de Janeiro, the government of Brazil imposed scalping fines as high as 100 times the original ticket price.

Visualize a house below the equilibrium point to remember where a price ceiling should be.

price ceiling
An artificial upper limit on the price of a good or service.

black market
An illegal market.

Queuing Costs. When effective policing eliminates black markets, some customers end up paying the difference between the price ceiling and the most they are willing to pay by standing in lines, or *queues*. The value of the time customers lose by standing in line to buy goods is a *queuing cost*. At Duke University, where graduate students can buy season tickets for basketball games at well below the equilibrium price, students camp out for days to purchase tickets. The queuing costs created by Duke's self-imposed price ceiling on tickets represent a significant expense over and above the ticket price.

Queuing costs can be minimized by the use of rationing techniques that indicate who can buy the available units. The New York Road Runners club uses a lottery to ration some of the entry slots to its popular marathon. During World Wars I and II, many goods were in short supply, so the government distributed *rationing coupons*. The government gave out only enough rationing coupons to purchase the available supplies of the goods. When the U.S. government set a price ceiling on gasoline in 1979, several states rationed gasoline. People with even-numbered license plates could purchase gasoline only on even-numbered days, and people with odd-numbered license plates could purchase gasoline only on odd-numbered days.

price floor
An artificial lower bound on the price of a good or service.

deadweight loss
The loss of consumer or producer surplus caused by an inefficient quantity of output.

Inferior Quality. The excess demand that results from artificially low prices destroys the incentives for firms to maintain the quality of their products. For example, price ceilings for apartments in New York City and elsewhere lead landlords to cut back on their maintenance expenditures. And when the price of bread was capped in France, residents complained that bakers turned out doughy blobs that hardly rivaled the crusty baguettes they were used to.

Industry Decline. High prices motivate firms to produce higher quantities. Price ceilings do the opposite—they motivate firms to produce lower quantities. Malaysia discontinued a price ceiling on cement in 2008 because the ceiling curbed cement production and slowed development projects. Economists Rexford Santerre and John Vernon estimate that if price controls had been placed on pharmaceuticals between 1981 and 2000, 198 fewer drugs would have been introduced on the U.S. market.

PRICE FLOORS

A **price floor** is an artificial lower bound on the price of a good or service. Governments impose price floors to assist workers or industries. The minimum wage laws discussed in Chapter 11 are price floors on labor that are designed to assist low-income workers. Figure 5.6 illustrates the influence of a price floor in the tire market. To have any effect, a price floor must be set above the equilibrium price. If the price floor for tires were set below the equilibrium, say at $90, it wouldn't make any difference because tire dealers would

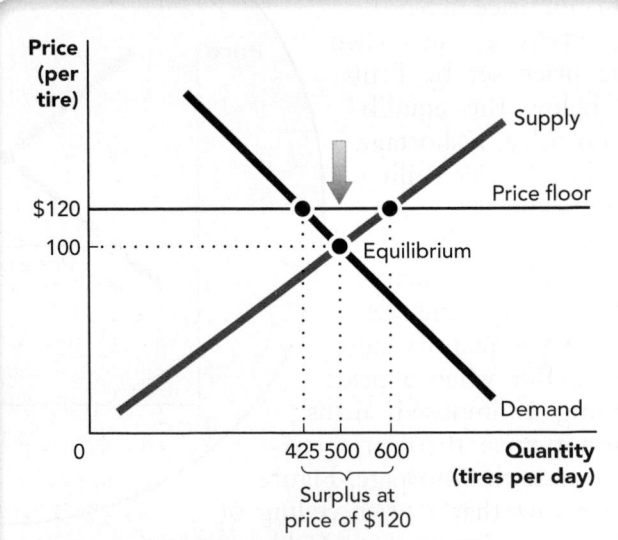

FIGURE 5.6 How a Price Floor Creates a Surplus

A price floor set above the equilibrium price causes the quantity supplied to exceed the quantity demanded, and firms cannot lower their price to eliminate the resulting surplus.

▲ During World Wars I and II, citizens could buy certain goods only if they had rationing coupons for them. By restricting the number of coupons given out, the government limited queuing costs.

ClassicStock/Alamy stock photo

charge more than that—$100—anyway. A price floor set above the equilibrium price *would* make a difference, though. A price floor of $120 would lift the price above the $100 that would otherwise be charged for tires. However, consumers would only purchase 425 tires for $120, whereas tire dealers would supply 600 tires. The price floor would thus create a surplus of tires.

Since 1949, the Dairy Price Support Program in the United States has set price floors for milk and other dairy products. Unlike minimum wage laws and other policies that simply stipulate minimum prices, the dairy program props up prices with a standing offer made by the government to purchase dairy products from farmers at the designated minimum prices. The government purchases the surplus milk, butter, and cheese that exists due to the price floors and donates the products to nutrition programs, Indian reservations, and the National School Lunch Program.

Indonesian producers recently set a price floor for tire-grade rubber. We can visualize the inefficiencies caused by this and other price controls by looking at what happens to consumer surplus and producer surplus as the result of a price floor. Panel (a) of Figure 5.7 illustrates the market for rubber in the absence of price controls. The equilibrium price is $1.00 and the equilibrium quantity is 3,500 kilograms. Recall from Chapter 3 that the area above the price and below the demand curve represents consumer surplus. Chapter 4 explained that the area below the price and above the supply curve represents producer surplus.

Panel (b) shows how a price floor of $1.45 per kilogram (kg) of rubber would reduce the quantity demanded to 2,000 kg per day. In this case, the consumer and producer surplus from the units of rubber beyond 2,000 kg would be lost because those units would not be purchased for $1.45. The yellow triangle in panel (b) represents the loss of consumer and producer surplus from the 3,500 − 2,000 = 1,500 kg that would be purchased at the equilibrium price of $1.00, but not for the price floor of $1.45. We use the term **deadweight loss** to describe a loss of consumer or producer surplus caused by an inefficient quantity of output, such as the 2,000 kg of rubber sold with the price floor.

Panel (c) shows that the same inefficiently low quantity of 2,000 kg per day would result from a price ceiling of $0.70 per kg. With the price ceiling, it is the quantity supplied that would be reduced to 2,000 kg per day, preventing consumers from buying any more than that quantity. Again, the consumer and producer surplus from units of rubber beyond 2,000 kg would be lost. The deadweight loss caused by the $0.70 price ceiling would be the same as that

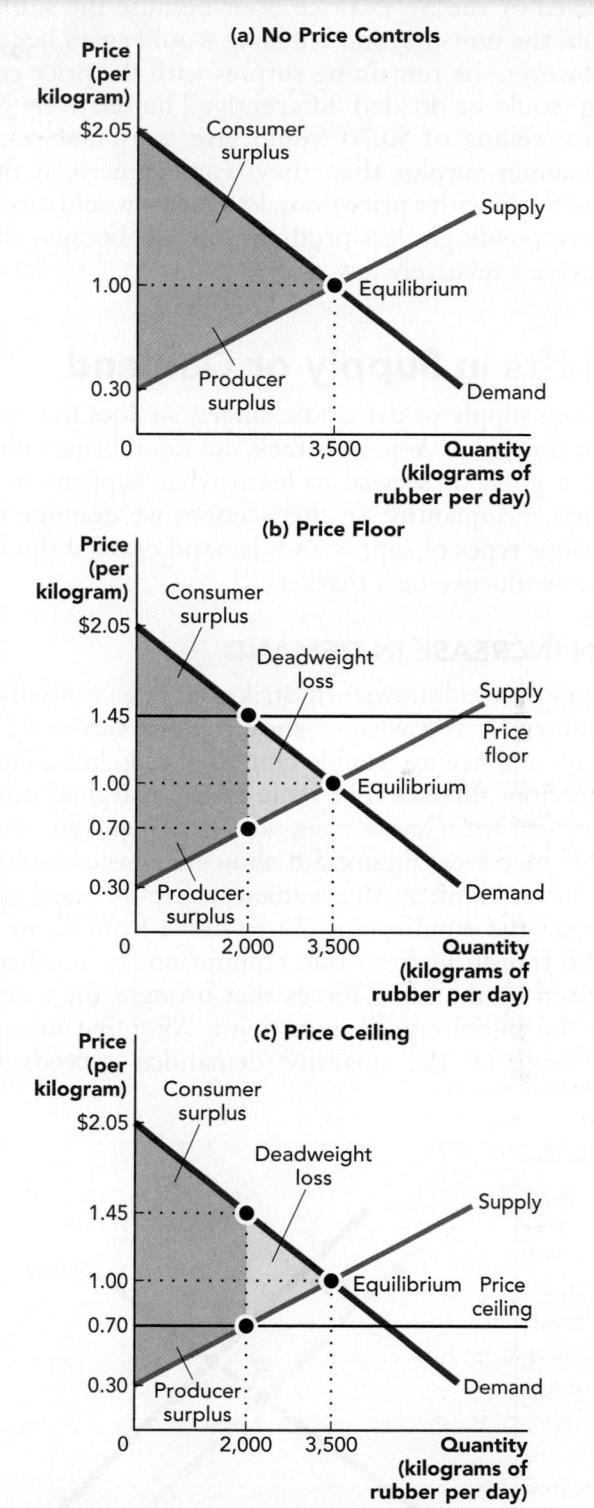

FIGURE 5.7 Deadweight Loss Caused by Price Controls

Panel (a) shows the consumer and producer surplus in a rubber market with no price controls. Panel (b) shows how a price floor causes a loss of consumer and producer surplus known as deadweight loss. The price ceiling in panel (c) causes the same deadweight loss as the price floor in panel (b), but the distribution of surplus between consumers and producers is different.

caused by the $1.45 price floor because the surplus from the units beyond 2,000 kg would again be lost. However, the remaining surplus with the price ceiling would be divided differently: The relatively low price ceiling of $0.70 would give consumers more consumer surplus than they would receive if they paid $1.45 with a price floor. Producers would receive correspondingly less producer surplus because they receive a relatively low price.

Shifts in Supply or Demand

When supply or demand changes, so does the equilibrium point. You can track the equilibrium point for a good or service to learn what happens to its price and quantity. In this section, we examine the various types of supply and demand curve shifts and their influence on a market.

AN INCREASE IN DEMAND

Suppose a bad snowstorm strikes large sections of the country. Drivers without snow tires are careening off roads and having trouble climbing steep hills. These situations increase the value of the marginal utility received from snow tires, so the demand for snow tires increases. Figure 5.8 shows how the resulting rightward shift in the demand curve for snow tires causes the equilibrium (E) to move from E_1 to E_2. The transition from one equilibrium to another is driven by the same forces that brought the market to the initial equilibrium point. After the increase in demand, the quantity demanded exceeds the

quantity supplied at the original equilibrium price of $100 per tire. The resulting shortage leads firms to charge a higher price. As the price rises, the quantity supplied rises and the quantity demanded falls, until a new equilibrium is reached at a price of $120 per tire and a quantity of 600 tires.

A DECREASE IN DEMAND

A product called Fix-a-Flat allows drivers to temporarily repair flat tires by spraying a can of sealant and air into the tires. Suppose that a new-and-improved formula for Fix-a-Flat repairs punctured tires permanently so the tires don't have to be replaced at all. This will result in a decrease in the demand for tires. Figure 5.9 shows how a decrease in tire demand moves the equilibrium from E_1 to E_2. Initially, the decrease in demand causes a surplus of tires at the original price of $100. Firms respond by charging less for tires. As the price falls in the tire market, the quantity demanded rises and the quantity supplied falls until equilibrium is reached at a price of $80 per tire and a quantity of 400 tires.

AN INCREASE IN SUPPLY

Toyo Tire & Rubber Company has used innovative technology to revolutionize the tire manufacturing process. Toyo's factory in Georgia uses robots and automated production systems to increase tire quality and decrease labor costs. Other tire manufacturers have adopted similar cost-saving technology. Lower costs have made tire companies willing to supply more tires at each price, so the market supply curve

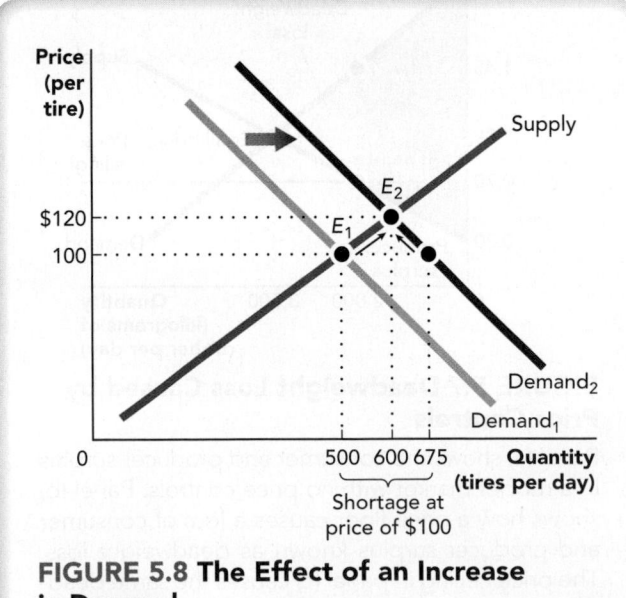

FIGURE 5.8 The Effect of an Increase in Demand

An increase in demand causes both the equilibrium price and the equilibrium quantity to increase.

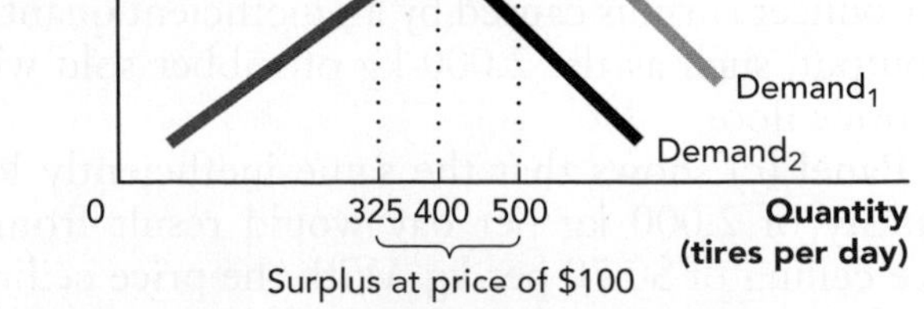

FIGURE 5.9 The Effect of a Decrease in Demand

A decrease in demand causes both the equilibrium price and the equilibrium quantity to decrease.

▲ Improved technology can lower the cost of making tires and shift the supply curve for tires to the right.

for tires has shifted to the right. As Figure 5.10 shows, the increase in supply moves the equilibrium from E_1 to E_2. After an initial surplus at the original equilibrium price of $100 per tire, the market forces already discussed result in a lower equilibrium price and a higher equilibrium quantity of tires in the market.

A DECREASE IN SUPPLY

An **import tariff** is a tax on goods or services purchased from another country. The United States normally collects a 4 percent import tariff on tires imported from China. From 2009 until 2012, President Barack Obama raised the tariff on tires to as much as 35 percent. The higher tariff increased the cost of imported tires and, by reducing foreign competition, made it possible for U.S. tire makers to charge more for their tires as well. Suppose the

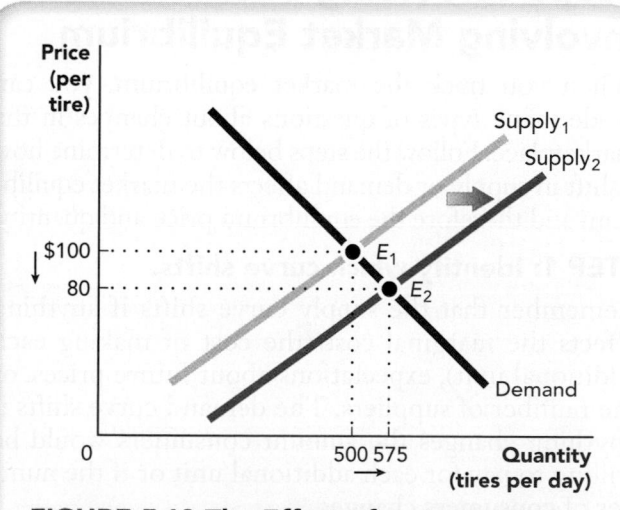

FIGURE 5.10 The Effect of an Increase in Supply

An increase in supply causes the equilibrium price to decrease and the equilibrium quantity to increase.

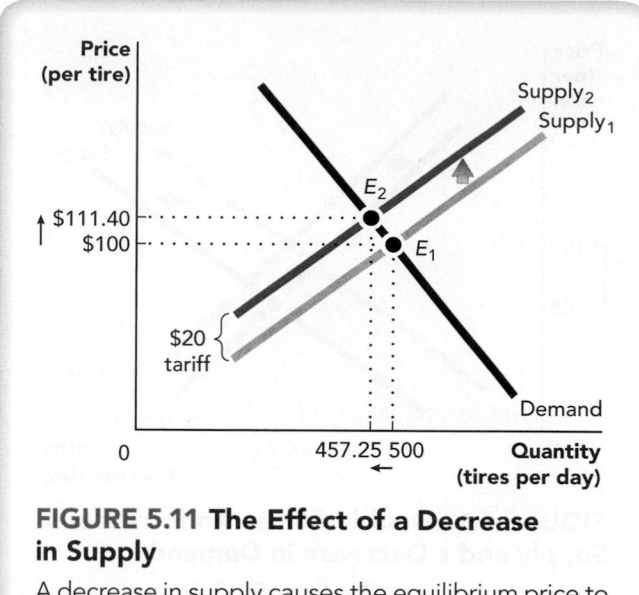

FIGURE 5.11 The Effect of a Decrease in Supply

A decrease in supply causes the equilibrium price to increase and the equilibrium quantity to decrease.

new tariff increased by $20 the amount that U.S. tire stores paid for each tire. Figure 5.11 shows the effect of a $20 increase in the stores' cost of each tire, which shifts the tire supply curve up by $20. As you learned in Chapter 4, a supply curve that shifts upward or to the left represents a decrease in supply. When supply decreases in this case, the equilibrium moves from E_1 to E_2, so there is a higher equilibrium price and a lower equilibrium quantity of tires in the market.

WHEN BOTH THE SUPPLY CURVE AND THE DEMAND CURVE SHIFT

When both curves shift at once, the effect on either the equilibrium price or the equilibrium quantity is clear, but the effect on the other measure depends on the relative size of the shifts. Starting at equilibrium point E_1 in Figure 5.12, if supply increases and demand decreases, the new equilibrium point will lie somewhere in the shaded area. Both the increase in supply and the decrease in demand lower the equilibrium price, so the effect on price is clearly downward. However, the increase in supply pushes the equilibrium quantity higher and the decrease in demand pushes the equilibrium quantity lower. The overall effect on the equilibrium quantity will depend on the relative sizes of the shifts.

Figure 5.12 illustrates a case in which the decrease in demand is small relative to the increase in supply. At the resulting equilibrium point E_2, we see that the price decrease is accompanied by a net increase in the quantity. If the decrease in demand had been large relative to the increase in supply, the equilibrium quantity would instead have decreased.

import tariff
A tax on goods or services purchased from another country.

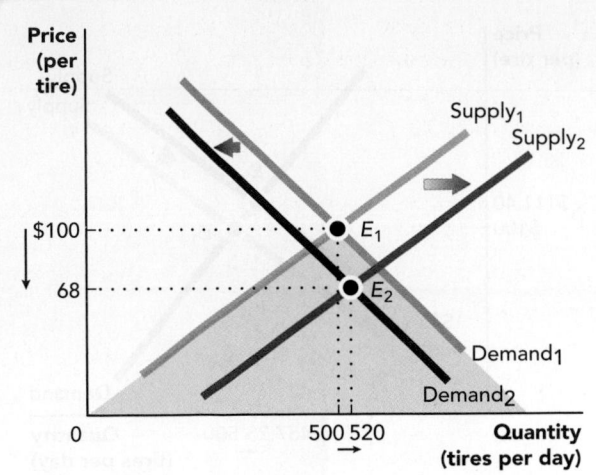

FIGURE 5.12 Double Shifts: An Increase in Supply and a Decrease in Demand

Starting from an equilibrium at E_1, if supply increases and demand decreases, the new equilibrium point will lie somewhere in the shaded area. The equilibrium price will definitely decrease because both shifts push the price lower. What happens to the equilibrium quantity will depend on the relative sizes of the shifts. In the case shown, the supply shift is larger than the demand shift, so the quantity is larger at the new equilibrium point E_2.

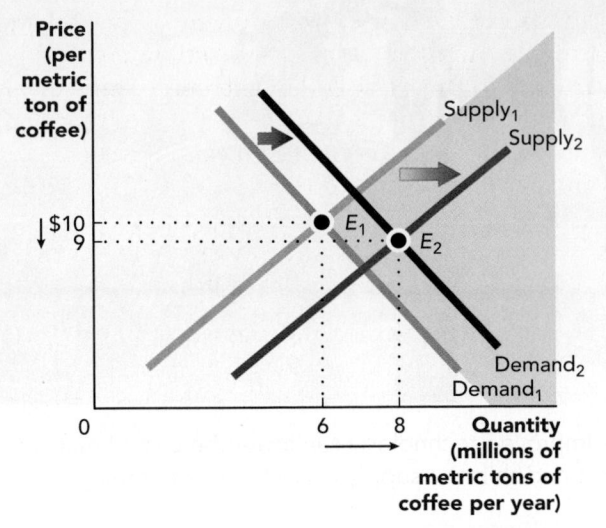

FIGURE 5.13 An Increase in Both Supply and Demand

When both supply and demand increase, the new equilibrium will lie somewhere in the shaded area. The equilibrium quantity will certainly increase because both shifts push the quantity higher. However, the equilibrium price might increase or decrease, depending on the relative sizes of the shifts. In the particular case shown, the increase in supply is larger than the increase in demand, so the price is lower at the new equilibrium E_2.

In the coffee market, the popularity of espresso cafés has increased the demand for coffee beans. If that were the end of the story, the resulting rightward shift of the demand curve would increase both the equilibrium quantity and the equilibrium price of coffee beans. However, there has also been a large increase in the number of farms that produce coffee beans. This increase in supply alone would increase the equilibrium quantity but decrease the equilibrium price. Together, the increased popularity of espresso cafés and the increase in the number of farms that produce coffee beans clearly increase the equilibrium quantity.

But what about the equilibrium price, since the increase in supply decreases it and the increase in demand increases it? The answer is that the equilibrium price could increase or decrease, depending on which shift is larger. Starting at E_1 in Figure 5.13, the new equilibrium point will lie somewhere in the shaded area. Over the past 20 years, growth in the global supply of coffee beans has outpaced growth in demand. When supply increases by more than demand, the equilibrium price falls, as exemplified by equilibrium E_2 in Figure 5.13.

Similar ambiguities arise from every type of double shift. Beware—double shifts are rare and usually require two separate influences: one that affects supply and another that affects demand.

It is a common mistake for students to shift both curves as the result of a change that really affects only one curve.

Steps to Solving Problems Involving Market Equilibrium

When you track the market equilibrium, you can tackle many types of questions about changes in the marketplace. Follow the steps below to determine how a shift in supply or demand affects the market equilibrium and therefore the equilibrium price and quantity.

STEP 1: Identify which curve shifts.

Remember that the supply curve shifts if anything affects the marginal cost (the cost of making each additional unit), expectations about future prices, or the number of suppliers. The demand curve shifts if anything changes the amount consumers would be willing to pay for each additional unit or if the number of consumers changes.

STEP 2: Identify the direction of any shifts.

The supply curve shifts upward and to the left (supply decreases) when the marginal cost increases, the expected future price rises, or the number of firms decreases. The opposite of any of these changes increases supply and shifts the supply curve downward and to the right. A demand curve shifts upward and to the right (demand increases) if the amount that consumers are willing to pay for each unit increases or if the number of consumers increases. A decrease in the amount that consumers are willing to pay or in the number of consumers decreases demand and shifts the demand curve downward and to the left.

STEP 3: Draw a graph of supply and demand and label the initial equilibrium price and quantity. Then, on the same graph, illustrate any shift and label the new equilibrium price and quantity.

By comparing the new equilibrium price and quantity to the initial equilibrium price and quantity, you can see how the change affects the market.

Sample Problem

Suppose a news story reveals that worn tires make driving much more dangerous than people had thought because worn tires lose traction on slick surfaces. On a graph, show how this news story is likely to affect the equilibrium price and quantity of new tires in the short run.

STEP 1: Which curve shifts? The news story does not affect the cost of making tires, and new tire stores can't open in the short run, so supply does not shift. The news does affect the amount that consumers are willing to pay for new tires, so the demand curve shifts.

STEP 2: In which direction is the shift? The story increases the amount that consumers are willing to pay for new tires, so the demand curve shifts upward and to the right.

STEP 3: Draw a graph and illustrate the effect of the shift on the equilibrium price and quantity.

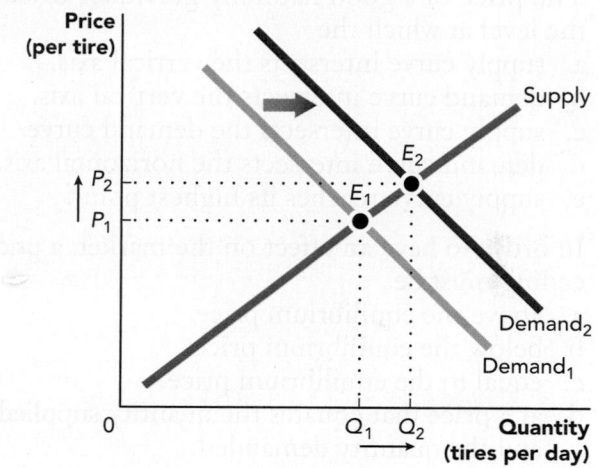

SUMMARY

In the market for any good or service, the quantity supplied equals the quantity demanded at the equilibrium price. If the price in a market is initially set above or below the equilibrium price, it won't remain at that level for long. If the price is set above the equilibrium price, a surplus of the good leads firms to charge less. A price set below the equilibrium price causes a shortage that leads firms to charge more.

Price ceilings and price floors are artificial limits on prices that are established by government or institutional policies. When a price ceiling keeps the price of a good or service below the equilibrium price, persistent shortages can bring about illegal black markets, industry decline, inferior quality, and queuing costs (because customers must stand in line to make purchases). When a price floor keeps

the price of a good or service above the equilibrium price, a surplus results because sellers will provide a larger quantity than buyers desire at that price.

To learn what happens to the price and quantity of a good as market conditions change, keep your eye on the equilibrium point. When only demand increases or decreases, the equilibrium price and quantity change in the same direction as demand. When only supply increases or decreases, the equilibrium quantity moves in the same direction as supply, but the equilibrium price moves in the opposite direction from supply. When both supply and demand shift, the effect on either the equilibrium price or the equilibrium quantity is clear, but the effect on the other measure depends on the relative sizes of the shifts.

KEY TERMS

equilibrium point, p. 68
equilibrium price, p. 68
equilibrium quantity, p. 69

price ceiling, p. 71
black market, p. 71
price floor, p. 72

deadweight loss, p. 73
import tariff, p. 75

PROBLEMS FOR REVIEW

1. The price of a good naturally gravitates toward the level at which the
   a. supply curve intersects the vertical axis.
   b. demand curve intersects the vertical axis.
   c. supply curve intersects the demand curve.
   d. demand curve intersects the horizontal axis.
   e. supply curve reaches its highest point.

2. In order to have an effect on the market, a price ceiling must be
   a. above the equilibrium price.
   b. below the equilibrium price.
   c. equal to the equilibrium price.
   d. at a price that equates the quantity supplied and the quantity demanded.
   e. None of the above

3. Redraw the graph shown here and label each of the following:

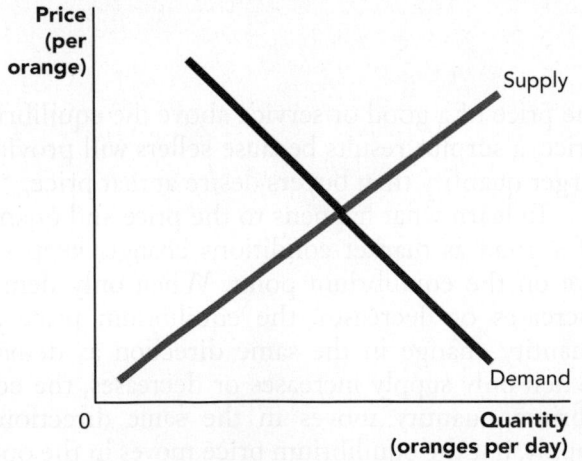

a. The equilibrium point
b. The equilibrium price and quantity
c. The level of a price floor that would alter the price charged in the market.
d. The horizontal distance that represents the surplus of oranges at the price floor you drew for part c.

4. What is a benefit of price ceilings? Identify four unintended consequences of price ceilings.

5. Given the pros and cons of price ceilings, if it were your decision, would you impose a price ceiling on the rent for apartments in New York City? Why or why not?

6. Draw a supply and demand graph for the mountain bike market, which has an upward-sloping supply curve and a downward-sloping demand curve. Label the equilibrium price and quantity P_1 and Q_1, respectively. Show how a successful advertising campaign featuring grinning teens speeding down idyllic wooded trails would affect the equilibrium price and quantity of mountain bikes; label the new equilibrium price and quantity P_2 and Q_2, respectively. Explain the reasoning behind any shifts in the curves.

7. Draw a supply and demand graph for computer memory chips that shows an upward-sloping supply curve and a downward-sloping demand curve. Label the equilibrium price and quantity P_1 and Q_1, respectively. Show how a design breakthrough that decreased the manufacturing cost of chips would affect the equilibrium price and quantity; label the new equilibrium price and quantity P_2 and Q_2, respectively. Explain the reasoning behind any shifts in the curves.

8. Almost half of U.S. telephone customers still use traditional "landline" telephone service, which transmits calls through wires. Draw a supply and demand graph for landline telephone service with an upward-sloping supply curve and a downward-sloping demand curve. Label the equilibrium price and quantity P_1 and Q_1, respectively. For many consumers, cell-phone service can substitute for landline telephone service. Show how a decrease in the price of cell-phone service would affect the equilibrium price

and quantity in the landline service market; label the new equilibrium price and quantity P_2 and Q_2, respectively. Explain the reasoning behind any shifts in the curves.

9. Draw a supply and demand graph for chocolate-chip scones, which have an upward-sloping supply curve and a downward-sloping demand curve. Label the equilibrium price and quantity P_1 and Q_1, respectively. Suppose the price of chocolate chips increases, and at the same time, new research comes out touting the health benefits of chocolate. Shade the area on your graph that represents all the points where the new equilibrium could lie. Explain what we know and what we don't know about the new equilibrium price and quantity.

10. Use the information in the table provided to draw the supply and demand curves for beef jerky and answer the following questions.

Price (per ounce)	Quantity Demanded (ounces)	Quantity Supplied (ounces)
$1	50	5
2	40	10
3	30	15
4	20	20
5	10	25
6	0	30

a. What is the equilibrium price?
b. What is the equilibrium quantity?
c. If a price ceiling of $2 were imposed in this market

i. how many ounces of beef jerky would be supplied?
ii. how many ounces of beef jerky would be demanded?

d. Suppose that there is no price ceiling, but the quantity of beef jerky demanded at each price falls to half the original quantity. Draw the new demand curve on your graph. What is the new equilibrium price and quantity?

11. Draw a supply and demand graph for the college-education market, which has an upward-sloping supply curve and a downward-sloping demand curve. Consider tuition to be the price of a college education. Label the equilibrium price and quantity P_1 and Q_1, respectively. For simplicity, assume that the education provided at each college is the same.

a. Shade and label the areas on your graph that represent consumer surplus and the producer surplus in this market.
b. Suppose the government imposes a price ceiling on college tuition. Use a horizontal line to indicate the level of a price ceiling that would make a difference in this market.
c. Use vertical and horizontal stripes to indicate the area on your graph that represents the deadweight loss caused by the price ceiling.
d. Use vertical stripes to indicate the area on your graph that represents the consumer surplus after the price ceiling is in place.
e. Use horizontal stripes to indicate the area on your graph that represents the producer surplus after the price ceiling is in place.
f. Do all students benefit from a price ceiling on college tuition? Why or why not?
g. Other than deadweight loss, what is another problem that could be caused by a price ceiling in the college-education market?

Elasticity

Christopher Woods

Christopher Woods sells handcrafted guitars in his shop near Chattanooga, Tennessee. He makes guitars for legendary bands, such as Motley Crue, but most of his customers are less famous and less rich. Although they love the sound of Christopher's guitars, his customers also want to hear about his prices and discounts. As he is picking his prices, Christopher must be tuned into trends in personal income, too. When his customers' incomes rise or fall, so do sales of his pricier guitars. During the last recession, sales of his high-end guitars took a slide. And when the prices of amplifiers and other electric guitar accessories rise, he notices a drop in guitar sales. So even though his passion is building fine instruments, ignorance of economics would leave Christopher Woods hanging by a string.

Why Should I Care?

This chapter is about the effects of changes in prices and income. **When you sell something, the profit-maximizing price depends on how customers respond to high and low prices.** When a store raises the price of something you typically buy, there are ways to avoid paying the higher price, such as being open to substitutes and giving yourself time to shop around for better deals. How people respond to price changes may also be important to you as a community member or a policy maker. For example, most states use lotteries to help fund public programs. If you love music, you might propose that the price of lottery tickets be increased by 5 percent to fund a community music program. However, the success of this strategy would depend on how consumers respond to higher lottery ticket prices. If consumers bought the same number of tickets, revenues would increase by 5 percent. But if the price increase caused a 5 percent decrease in ticket sales, the increase in revenues from the lottery would be 0. This chapter will help you make wise decisions and avoid pitfalls as a seller, a shopper, and a music lover, among other things.

The Price Elasticity of Demand

We can anticipate that when Christopher Woods lowers the price of his guitars, he will sell more guitars than he did before. But the effect a lower price will have on his sales and profits depends on how sensitive customers are to price changes. If Christopher can lower his price a little and sell a lot more guitars, that's an attractive change. If a large price decrease would lead to only a small increase in the quantity demanded, that's not the path to more profit. The **price elasticity of demand** measures consumers' sensitivity to price changes. It is a valuable indicator of just what will happen to the quantity demanded and to sales revenues as the price of a good or service fluctuates. To calculate the price elasticity of demand, use the following ratio:

> **price elasticity of demand**
> A measure of consumers' sensitivity to price changes.

$$\text{price elasticity of demand} = \frac{\text{percentage change in quantity demanded}}{\text{percentage change in price}}$$

The simplest way to calculate the percentage change is to divide the change (the new value minus the old value) by the old value. So you can calculate the price elasticity of demand as:

$$\text{price elasticity of demand} = \frac{\dfrac{\text{new quantity} - \text{old quantity}}{\text{old quantity}}}{\dfrac{\text{new price} - \text{old price}}{\text{old price}}}$$

Applying this formula, the price elasticity of demand between points A and B in Figure 6.1 is

$$\text{price elasticity} \atop \text{of demand} = \dfrac{\dfrac{5-6}{6}}{\dfrac{10-8}{8}} = \dfrac{\dfrac{-1}{6}}{\dfrac{2}{8}} = \dfrac{\dfrac{1}{6}}{\dfrac{1}{4}} = -\dfrac{2}{3}$$

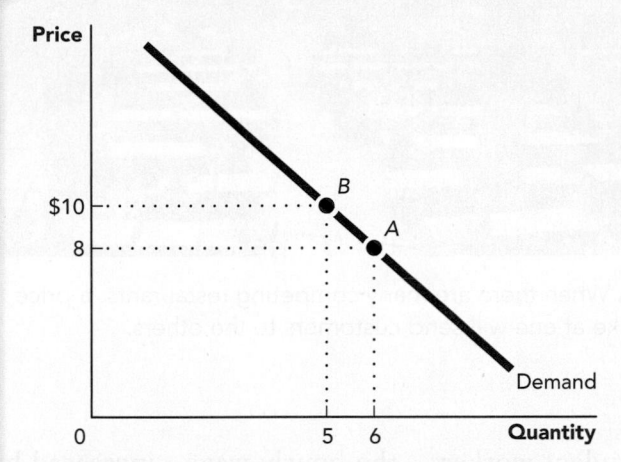

FIGURE 6.1 Finding the Price Elasticity of Demand

To find the price elasticity of demand, divide the percentage change in the quantity by the percentage change in the price.

Table 6.1 The Price Elasticities of Demand for Food Items

Food	Price Elasticity
Grapes	1.180
Tomatoes	0.622
Beef	0.621
Cheese	0.247
Butter	0.243
Apples	0.190
Coffee and tea	0.176
Eggs	0.110
Lettuce	0.090
Sugar	0.037
Margarine	0.009

Source: Economic Research Service; U.S. Department of Agriculture.

Along a downward-sloping demand curve there is an inverse relationship between the price and the quantity demanded. That is, a price *increase* leads to a *decrease* in the quantity demanded, and a price *decrease* leads to an *increase* in the quantity demanded. Because either the percentage change in quantity or the percentage change in price is always negative, and the other is positive, the price elasticity of demand is always negative. To keep things simple, it is common to omit the negative sign. For example, a price elasticity of demand stated as "1.2" implies an actual price elasticity of demand of −1.2. We adopt that convention in this textbook and state all price elasticities of demand as positive values.

Table 6.1 shows the price elasticities of demand for many types of food. If the price elasticity of demand for a good is relatively large, we know that a change in the price of that good causes a relatively large change in the quantity demanded. For example, if the price of each of the foods in Table 6.1 increased by 1 percent, the quantity of grapes demanded would decrease by the largest percentage (1.180 percent) because grapes have the largest price elasticity of demand. Likewise, the quantity of margarine demanded would decrease by the smallest percentage (0.009 percent). Next,

you'll learn more about how to interpret values of the price elasticity of demand.

ELASTIC, INELASTIC, AND UNIT-ELASTIC DEMAND

When consumers' response to a price change is a relatively small change in the quantity demanded, the price elasticity of demand is less than 1 and demand is considered **inelastic.** For example, demand tends to be inelastic for goods that must be purchased in a hurry. You are not likely to shop around for the best price if you need emergency medical care. And you're not likely to be sensitive to a price change when buying a textbook at the last minute. Demand is similarly inelastic for goods such as pencils that don't cost very much to begin with, because a price increase of 20 or 30 percent would amount to only a few cents. Demand is also inelastic when consumers have little choice but to purchase a good. That is the case for a good that becomes a necessity, such as a car needed to commute to work; a good to which customers are addicted, such as cigarettes; and a good with few substitutes, such as food at a ballpark concession stand.

If consumers' response to a price change is a relatively large change in the quantity demanded, then the price elasticity of demand is greater than 1,

inelastic demand
When the price elasticity of demand for a product is less than 1.

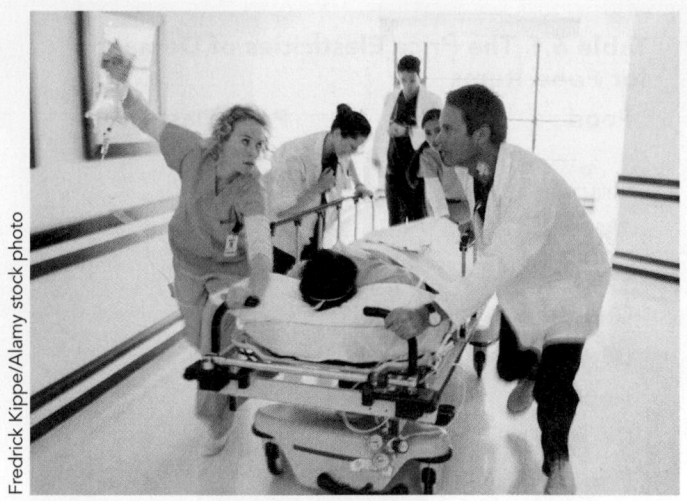

▲ When you need goods or services in a hurry, your demand is likely to be inelastic.

▲ When there are many competing restaurants, a price hike at one will send customers to the others.

and demand is considered **elastic.** Demand is typically elastic for expensive goods and services that are not necessities, such as fancy cars and exotic vacations. If you're considering a cruise and the price rises substantially, you might stay at home for a "staycation" instead. Demand is elastic for goods with many substitutes, such as hamburgers sold in a large food court. When a dozen restaurants share one location, a price hike at one restaurant sends customers to neighboring restaurants for cheaper alternatives. The demand for a good also tends to be more elastic when consumers have more time in which to make a purchase. Given enough time, consumers can find more ways to use products that have become less expensive, and they can find cheaper substitutes for products that have become more expensive. For instance, when the price of sugar increased due to government price supports in the United States, consumers initially had few options. Over time, however, consumers found inexpensive substitutes, including corn syrup and artificial sweeteners.

If a price change leads to a proportional change in the quantity demanded, then the price elasticity of demand is 1, and demand is considered **unit elastic.** For example, if a 10 percent increase in the price of airline tickets led to a 10 percent decrease in the number of tickets purchased, demand would be unit elastic. Consider, too, a college with a fixed budget to spend on student workers. If the price of

student workers—the hourly wage—increased by 10 percent, the college would respond by hiring 10 percent fewer workers.

In summary, demand is likely to be inelastic for goods that:

- **require only a small fraction of consumers' income**, such as pencils, newspapers, and bubble gum
- **are necessary**, such as medical treatments and required textbooks
- **have few substitutes**, such as gasoline and computer operating systems
- **are addictive**, such as tobacco and alcohol
- **must be purchased quickly**, such as car repairs and funeral arrangements

Demand is likely to be elastic for goods that:

- **require a large portion of consumers' income**, such as homes and country club memberships
- **are luxury items**, such as name-brand watches and designer clothing
- **have many substitutes**, such as Burger King hamburgers and Nike-brand soccer balls
- **can be purchased after a longer period** of thought about various alternatives, such as hairstyling services and running shoes

Table 6.2 summarizes the classification of demand as inelastic, elastic, or unit elastic, depending on whether the price elasticity of demand is between 0 and 1, more than 1, or exactly 1.

elastic demand
When the price elasticity of demand is greater than 1.

unit-elastic demand
When the price elasticity of demand is 1.

Table 6.2 Inelastic, Elastic, and Unit-Elastic Demand: A Summary

Type of Demand	Meaning	Example	Price Elasticity of Demand
Inelastic	Demand is not very sensitive to price changes	Emergency medical care	Less than 1.0
Elastic	Demand is very sensitive to price changes	Burger King hamburgers	Greater than 1.0
Unit-elastic	Demand is proportionately sensitive to price changes	Goods purchased on a strict budget, such as music downloads purchased with a $20 iTunes gift card	Equal to 1.0

TOTAL REVENUE AND THE PRICE ELASTICITY OF DEMAND

Total revenue is the total amount a firm receives from selling a good. Total revenue is easily found by multiplying the price of the good by the quantity sold. If Christopher Woods charges $100 per guitar and sells 20 guitars in a day, his total revenue is $100 × 20 = $2,000. Christopher knows that higher prices will decrease the quantity of guitars demanded, but how higher prices affect total revenue depends on the price elasticity of demand. If consumers' sensitivity to price changes makes demand elastic, then a price increase leads to a decrease in total revenue. This happens because the percentage increase in the price is smaller than the percentage decrease in the quantity the firm can sell. For example, suppose a

▲ When demand is elastic, a price change has a relatively large effect on the quantity demanded. This means that stores will receive less revenue if they increase their prices and more revenue if they decrease their prices.

Bruce yuanyue Bi/Alamy

20 percent price increase—from $100 to $120 per guitar—results in a 60 percent drop in Christopher's sales, from 20 to 8 guitars per day. The price elasticity of demand is 60% ÷ 20% = 3, and Christopher's total revenue falls from $2,000 to $960 per day as a result of the price increase. In panel (a) of Figure 6.2, the crosshatched area represents the total revenue at the $100 starting price and the green area represents the reduced total revenue at the $120 price. If Christopher has many competitors, it is likely that the demand for his guitars is indeed elastic and a price increase would reduce his total revenue.

> If consumers' sensitivity to price changes makes demand elastic, then a price increase leads to a decrease in total revenue.

Now suppose Christopher's sister, Robin, is the only guitar dealer in a remote town, and the only alternative to purchasing a guitar from her is to drive to a distant city to buy it. The lack of competition makes the demand for Robin's guitars inelastic, so a price increase results in a less-than-proportional decrease in the quantity demanded. Because there is a relatively small response to the higher price, total revenue increases. For example, suppose a 20 percent price increase—from

total revenue
The total amount that a firm receives from selling a good.

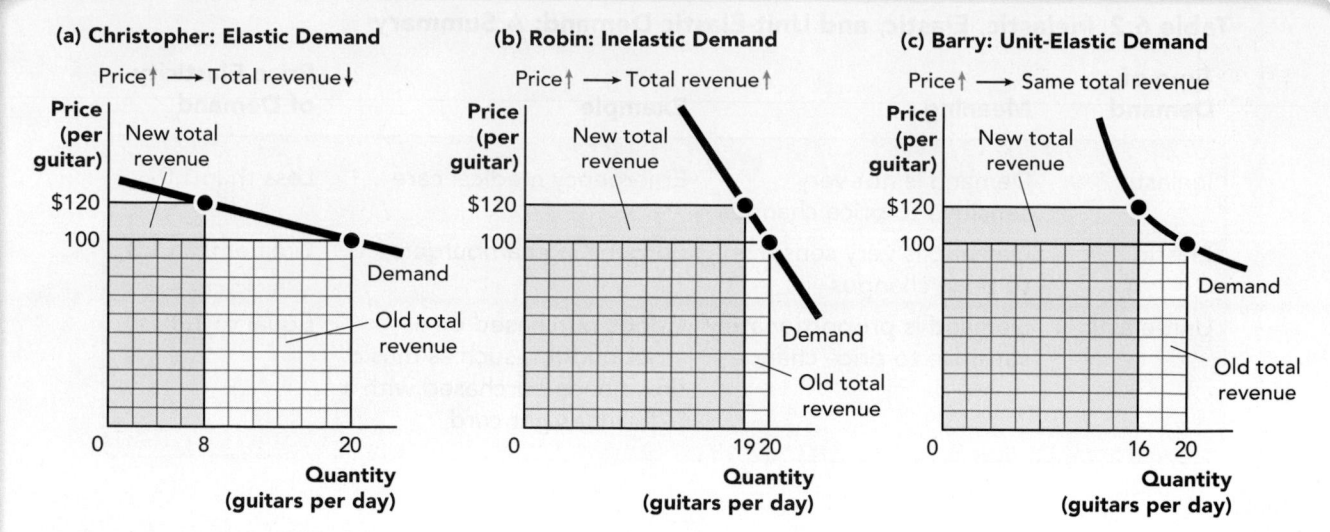

FIGURE 6.2 How Total Revenue Changes Depending on the Price Elasticity of Demand

(a) If demand is elastic, a price increase causes total revenue to decrease because the percentage decrease in the quantity is larger than the percentage increase in the price. **(b)** If demand is inelastic, a price increase causes total revenue to increase because the percentage increase in the price is larger than the percentage decrease in the quantity. **(c)** If demand is unit elastic, a price increase leads to no change in total revenue because the quantity decreases in proportion to the price increase.

$100 to $120—results in a 5 percent drop in Robin's sales, from 20 to 19 guitars. The price elasticity of demand is 5% ÷ 20% = 0.25, and Robin's total revenue increases from $2,000 to $2,280 as a result of the price increase. Panel (b) of Figure 6.2 illustrates this scenario.

Imagine that Christopher and Robin's brother, Barry, sells guitars in a third town where the demand for his guitars is unit elastic. If Barry raises the price of his guitars by 20 percent, the quantity demanded decreases by 20 percent—from 20 guitars to 16—so he ends up with the same total revenue. A price decrease likewise has no effect on his total revenue because the quantity demanded increases by the same percentage as the price decrease. Panel (c) of Figure 6.2 illustrates this scenario.[1]

Profit is the difference between total revenue and *total cost*—the sum of all the firm's costs. You have learned that when demand is inelastic, a price increase causes the quantity demanded to decrease but brings in more total revenue. With lower

quantities come lower production costs—it costs less to make less. And the combination of more total revenue and lower costs assures the firm more profit. So a firm facing inelastic demand should raise its price. A firm facing unit-elastic demand should also raise its price because its total revenue will remain unchanged but its costs will fall, so the firm's profit will increase. In contrast, when demand is elastic, a price increase results in a lower quantity demanded and less total revenue. The lower quantity again reduces costs, but the effect on profit is uncertain. The decrease in total revenue may or may not exceed the decrease in cost. How exactly firms find the profit-maximizing price and quantity is explained in Chapter 8.

PERFECTLY INELASTIC DEMAND

If consumers demand the same quantity of a good regardless of the price, the demand curve is vertical at the desired quantity. A vertical demand curve

---

[1]Based on the simple formula we used for a percentage change, the total revenue does change slightly. However, that would not be the case using the *midpoint formula*, with which a percentage change is found by dividing the change by the average of the beginning and ending values. When the beginning and ending values are far apart, the average of those values provides a compromise between using one value or the other as the numerator in the percentage-change calculation. Applying the midpoint formula, a 20 percent increase in price would come from an increase from $90 to $110: The $20 change divided by the $100 average equals 0.20. A 20 percent decrease in quantity would come from a decrease from 22 to 18: The change of 4 divided by the average of 20 equals 0.20. The initial total revenue would be $90 × 22 = $1,980. The total revenue after the price change would be $110 × 18 = $1,980.

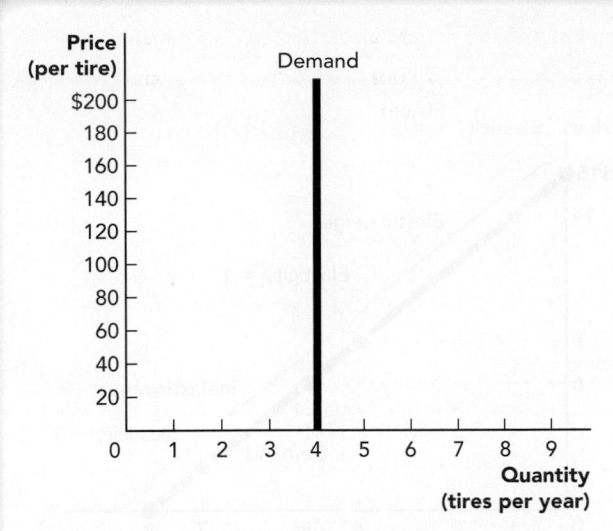

FIGURE 6.3 Perfectly Inelastic Demand

A vertical demand curve indicates that consumers demand the same quantity regardless of the price. In that case, demand is perfectly inelastic.

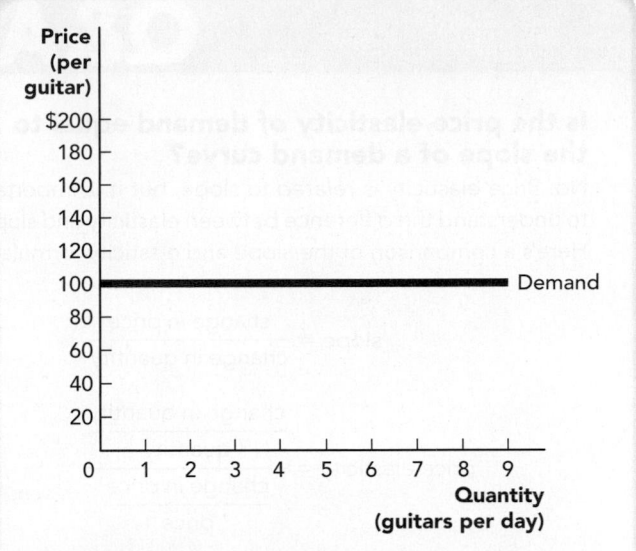

FIGURE 6.4 Perfectly Elastic Demand

A horizontal demand curve indicates that demand is perfectly elastic. Facing the perfectly elastic demand curve shown here, a firm can sell any quantity of guitars for $100 each. However, even the slightest increase in price would cause the quantity demanded to fall to 0.

represents **perfectly inelastic demand.** Although it is unlikely that an entire market would have perfectly inelastic demand, it is quite possible for individuals to have such demand. Figure 6.3 illustrates Penelope's perfectly inelastic demand curve for snow tires as a result of moving to Alaska and needing snow tires to get to work in the winter. She needs four tires, and price fluctuations within an affordable range will not change the quantity of snow tires she demands. Remembering that the price elasticity of demand is the percentage change in quantity divided by the percentage change in price, it is straightforward to identify the elasticity in this case. The percentage change in quantity is 0, and 0 divided by any percentage change in price gives us an elasticity of 0. Penelope's demand for life-saving surgery would be similar: if she needed one surgery, she would demand one surgery regardless of the price. Realistically, the quantity demanded would fall to 0 in each of these cases if the price grew so high that the consumer absolutely could not afford the purchase.

PERFECTLY ELASTIC DEMAND

A horizontal demand curve indicates **perfectly elastic demand.** Figure 6.4 shows a perfectly elastic demand curve for Christopher's guitars. With this demand, Christopher could sell any number of guitars for $100 each. But any price increase would cause the quantity demanded to fall to 0. This is

because the price elasticity of demand is infinite—the percentage change in the quantity demanded is infinite for any percentage increase in the price. This degree of sensitivity to price changes may seem improbable, but many firms do face demand that approximates perfect elasticity. If Get a Grip Guitars were one of 150 quite similar guitar stores in a big city, it might be that Christopher could sell his desired quantity at the going price; but, if he raised his price by any significant amount, he would lose virtually all his business to competitors selling the same guitars for less. There would be no reason to charge less than $100 because he can sell as much as he wants for that price.

As another example, there are thousands of sellers of identical agricultural products. Farmers can sell all the cabbages they want at the equilibrium price in the cabbage market. But if one farmer tried to charge a nickel more per head, grocers would buy their cabbage from one of the thousands of other farmers charging less for the same thing.

perfectly inelastic demand
When consumers demand the same quantity of a good regardless of the price.

perfectly elastic demand
When any price increase causes the quantity demanded of a good to fall to 0.

Q&A

Is the price elasticity of demand equal to the slope of a demand curve?

No. Price elasticity is *related* to slope, but it is important to understand the difference between elasticity and slope. Here's a comparison of the slope and elasticity formulas:

$$slope = \frac{change\ in\ price}{change\ in\ quantity}$$

$$price\ elasticity = \frac{\dfrac{change\ in\ quantity}{quantity}}{\dfrac{change\ in\ price}{price}}$$

Be careful not to confuse these formulas. Along a straight, downward-sloping demand curve like the one shown in Figure 6.5, the slope does not change at all; it is −2 everywhere on this line. Yet the price elasticity varies from infinity to 0. This is because quantity and price are part of the elasticity formula, and these values change as you move along the line. At the left end of the demand curve, the price is high and the quantity is low. A price change from $16 to $14 leads to an infinitely large percentage change in quantity from 0 to 1, making the price elasticity of demand infinite. In the very middle of the demand curve, the price elasticity of demand is 1. A 25 percent price change from $8 to $6 leads to a 25 percent change in quantity from 4 to 5. At the right end of the demand curve, the price is low and the quantity is high. An infinitely large percentage change in price from $0 to $2 results in a 12.5 percent decrease in quantity from 8 to 7.

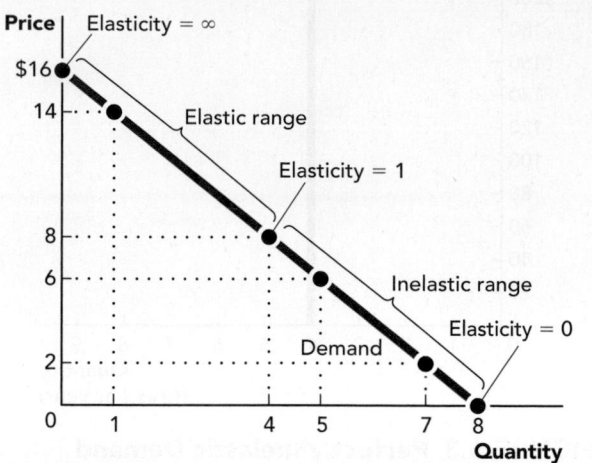

FIGURE 6.5 Elasticity Along a Straight, Downward-Sloping Demand Curve

Along a straight, downward-sloping demand curve, the price elasticity of demand ranges from infinity at the extreme left to 0 at the extreme right. In the middle of the curve, demand is unit elastic with an elasticity value of 1.

Any percentage over infinity is 0, so the price elasticity of demand is 0 at the right end of the demand curve.

Although they are not the same, the concepts of elasticity and slope are connected. For example, a demand curve with a shallow slope at a particular point has a higher price elasticity than a demand curve with a steep slope at the same point. Don't let this connection fool you into thinking that the slope of a demand curve is its elasticity.

---

price elasticity of supply
A measure of how responsive firms are to changes in the price of the good they are selling.

The Price Elasticity of Supply

The **price elasticity of supply** measures how responsive firms are to changes in the price of the good they are selling. The higher the price elasticity of supply, the more the quantity supplied increases in response to a price increase. The calculation is the same as for the price elasticity of demand except that the quantity supplied replaces the quantity demanded in the elasticity formula:

$$price\ elasticity\ of\ supply = \frac{percentage\ change\ in\ quantity\ supplied}{percentage\ change\ in\ price}$$

The price elasticity of supply depends on the cost of supplying additional units of a good. If the supply is fixed, as with the number of seats in a stadium, offices in the Empire State Building, and Taylor Swifts who can be signed to recording contracts, the quantity supplied is the same whether the price is $10 or $10,000,000. In this case, the supply curve is vertical at the available quantity. That means the percentage change in quantity is 0 for any price change, making supply perfectly inelastic. As with demand, supply typically becomes more price elastic over time. In the long run, stadiums can be enlarged and buildings can be expanded. This changes the price elasticity of supply for seats and offices from 0 to some positive number. Cloning possibilities aside, the supply of Taylor Swifts will remain perfectly inelastic.

▲ In the short run, the price elasticity of supply for office space is 0, because it takes time to build new buildings. In the long run, sufficiently high prices can bring about more offices, so the price elasticity of supply becomes positive. Whatever the price, you can't hire a second Taylor Swift, which makes her price elasticity of supply 0 even in the long run.

A perfectly elastic supply curve is horizontal, indicating that an unlimited quantity of the good or service would be supplied at a particular price, but a lower price would cause the quantity supplied to fall to 0. Consider a country with millions of unskilled workers who supply labor if the price for labor—the wage—exceeds the value of their time spent working at home and growing food for their own consumption. If the value of a typical worker's time at home is $0.99 an hour, millions of workers could be hired for $1.00 an hour. But any decrease in the wage would cause the quantity of labor supplied to fall to virtually 0. In this scenario, which resembles the situation in many developing countries, the supply of labor is perfectly elastic.

The Cross-Price Elasticity of Demand

Recall from Chapter 3 that when a decrease in the price of one good makes consumers want to buy more of another good, we call these goods *complements in consumption*. For example, when guitar prices drop and people buy more guitars, they also buy more sheet music. Other examples of complements in consumption include peanut butter and jelly, travel and luggage, and tea and sugar.

You also learned that when a decrease in the price of one good leads to a decrease in the demand for another good, we call these goods *substitutes in consumption*. For example, when car prices drop and more consumers buy cars, the demand for bus services drops. Other substitutes in consumption

▲ Coffee and tea are substitutes. If the price of one increases, demand for the other increases. Coffee and cream are complements. If the price of one increases, demand for the other decreases.

include burgers and hot dogs, cable TV and satellite TV, and coffee and tea.

A slight variation on the elasticity measures you have learned indicates whether pairs of goods are complements or substitutes. The **cross-price elasticity of demand** measures how the price of one good affects the quantity demanded of another good. The formula is very similar to the formula for the price elasticity of demand: It is the percentage change in the quantity demanded of one good (Good A) divided by the percentage change in the price of another good (Good B):

$$\text{cross-price elasticity of demand} = \frac{\text{percentage change in quantity of Good A demanded}}{\text{percentage change in price of Good B}}$$

Unlike the price elasticity of demand, the cross-price elasticity of demand can be positive or negative. The sign on the elasticity indicates whether the goods are complements or substitutes. If an increase in the price of one good causes a decrease in the demand for another, the cross-price elasticity of demand is negative and the goods are complements. Suppose the price of guitars increases by 10 percent, and because fewer guitars are purchased at the higher price, 3 percent less sheet music is sold. That makes the cross-price elasticity of demand between guitars and sheet music −3% ÷ 10% = −0.3. This negative value for the cross-price elasticity confirms that guitars and sheet music are complements.

> **cross-price elasticity of demand**
> A measure of how the price of one good affects the quantity demanded of another good.

Table 6.3 Substitutes and Complements: A Summary

Relationship	Meaning	Example	Cross-Price Elasticity Value
Substitutes	An increase in the price of one leads to an increase in demand for the other.	Fender-brand guitars and Gibson-brand guitars	Positive
Complements	An increase in the price of one leads to a decrease in demand for the other.	Guitars and guitar strings	Negative

If an increase in the price of one good causes an increase in the demand for another good, the cross-price elasticity of demand is positive and the goods are substitutes. Suppose a 10 percent increase in the price of new guitars results in a 20 percent increase in the demand for repairs on old guitars. The cross-price elasticity of demand between guitars and guitar repairs is then 20% ÷ 10% = 2. This is a positive number because new guitars and guitar repairs are substitutes. Table 6.3 summarizes the categorization of substitutes and complements on the basis of cross-price elasticity.

Income Elasticity of Demand

If a pay raise at work would lead you to buy more steaks, fancy coffee, foreign cars, fresh fruit, and designer clothing, these goods are *normal goods* for you. A **normal good** is one that you buy more of as your income increases. An **inferior good** is one that you buy less of as your income increases. The same good may be normal for some people and inferior for others—you might buy more T-shirts when your income increases and your parents might buy fewer. For many people, inferior goods include hamburgers, gas station coffee, used cars, canned fruit, and discount-store clothing. As they earn more income, people buy fewer of these items and buy more normal goods—for example, fewer hamburgers and more steaks.

The **income elasticity of demand** measures how changes

▲ Because fresh fruit is more expensive than canned fruit, many people buy more fresh fruit when their income is high than when their income is low. For these people, fresh fruit is a normal good and canned fruit an inferior good.

BW Folsom/Shutterstock.com

in income affect the demand for a good. The formula for income elasticity is the same as for price elasticity except that each incidence of the word *price* is replaced by the word *income*:

$$\text{income elasticity of demand} = \frac{\text{percentage change in quantity demanded}}{\text{percentage change in income}}$$

A negative income elasticity indicates that a good is inferior. A positive income elasticity indicates that a good is normal. Normal goods can be further categorized as *necessities* or *luxuries*. A **necessity** is a good with an income elasticity between 0 and 1. People buy more of necessities—such as basic food

normal good
A good you buy more of as your income increases.

inferior good
A good you buy less of as your income increases.

income elasticity of demand
A measure of how changes in income affect the demand for a good.

necessity
A good with an income elasticity between 0 and 1.

Table 6.4 Types of Goods as Determined by Income Elasticity: A Summary

Type of Good	Meaning	Examples	Income Elasticity Value
Inferior	Less is purchased when income increases	Used cars, staycations, gas station coffee	Negative
Normal	More is purchased as income increases	New cars, cruises, premium coffee	Positive
Necessity	Purchases increase less than in proportion to income	Basic food, clothing, medical care	Between 0 and 1.0
Luxury	Purchases increase more than in proportion to income	Restaurant meals, airline tickets	Greater than 1.0

and clothing—as their income increases, but purchases of these items increase less than in proportion to income. A **luxury** is a good with an income elasticity greater than 1. As income increases, purchases of luxuries such as restaurant meals and airline tickets increase more than in proportion to income. Table 6.4 summarizes the categorization of goods as normal, inferior, necessities, or luxuries based on their income elasticity of demand.

An understanding of income elasticity is important to business managers who must decide which products to promote when the economy is strong and when it is not. During tough economic times, fast-food chains put more emphasis on their value menus, which feature inferior goods such as simple hot dogs and hamburgers. And clothing stores tend to promote necessities such as socks and belts rather than luxury goods such as tuxedos. Table 6.5 shows the income elasticities of a variety of food products.

Table 6.5 The Income Elasticity of Demand for Food Items

Food	Income Elasticity
Apples	−0.362
Margarine	−0.336
Sugar	0.006
Eggs	0.287
Lettuce	0.372
Beef	0.392
Cheese	0.418
Butter	0.539
Grapes	0.561
Coffee and tea	0.818
Tomatoes	0.918

Sources: Economic Research Service; U.S. Department of Agriculture.

Apply What You've Learned: Elasticity and Taxes

For a sampling of elasticity's relevance to economic policy, let's examine how the price elasticity of demand and the price elasticity of supply affect the burden of taxes. Governments at all levels collect taxes to pay for the goods and services they provide, such as public schools, roads, disease control, police, firefighters, and the national parks. **Tax incidence** is the way the burden of a tax is divided among the affected parties. In this section, you will see that for taxes on goods and services, tax incidence does not depend on whether the buyer or the seller pays the tax. Instead, it depends on the elasticities of supply and demand.

luxury
A good with an income elasticity greater than 1.

tax incidence
The way the burden of a tax is divided among the affected parties.

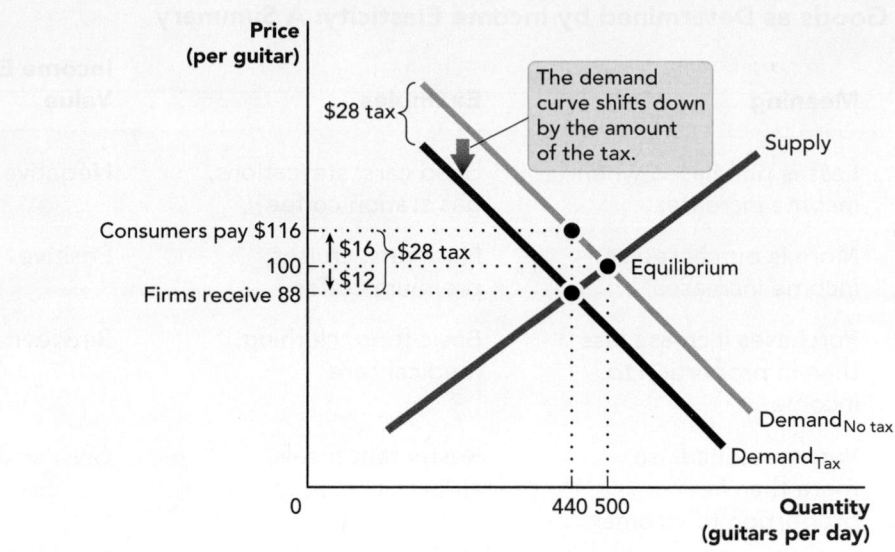

FIGURE 6.6 The Effects of a Tax on Consumers

When the government collects a tax from consumers, the amount that consumers are willing to pay firms for each unit of the good being taxed decreases by the amount of the tax. This shifts the demand curve down by the amount of the tax.

Goods and services can be subject to several types of taxes. A **sales tax** applies to a wide variety of goods and services. It is usually collected from the buyers as a percentage of the sale price. If you buy a $150 guitar that is subject to a 6 percent sales tax, you pay a tax of 6 percent of $150, which is $9, on top of the $150 price. So your total payment to the seller is $159. The seller then delivers your $9 tax payment to the government and keeps the $150.

An **excise tax** is a tax on a particular good or service. The extra taxes imposed on alcohol and cigarettes are examples of excise taxes. In most cases, an excise tax is a *per-unit tax*—a set amount collected by the government for each unit sold. For example, the state government of Tennessee collects a per-unit excise tax from tire sellers. Although excise taxes are typically the sellers' responsibility, the taxes can be passed on to consumers in the form of higher prices. In some cases, excise taxes are collected directly from buyers, like a sales tax. Indiana is one of several states that hold consumers responsible for paying a per-unit excise tax on guitars.

To see why tax incidence doesn't depend on who actually pays the tax, let's compare the effects of two taxes: a $28 excise tax on guitars paid by consumers, and an identical tax paid

by sellers. If it is collected from consumers, the tax affects the prices that consumers are willing to pay. Suppose that the light purple line in Figure 6.6 is the guitar demand curve without a tax. As always, the height of the demand curve above each unit represents the most a consumer is willing to pay for that unit. A tax doesn't change the amount a consumer is willing to pay, but when the consumer must pay a tax, the price the consumer is willing to pay in addition to the tax decreases. For example, a consumer who would pay at most $200 for the fifth guitar would now pay a price up to $172 for it, because that price plus the $28 tax brings the total payment to $200. Likewise, for each unit, the highest price a consumer would pay to the firm goes down by $28. So the tax shifts the demand curve facing firms down by the amount of the tax, as shown by the dark purple demand curve.

At the initial equilibrium, the price is $100 and consumers purchase 500 guitars. After the demand curve shifts, the market reaches a new equilibrium quantity of 440 guitars. Firms receive a price of $88 per guitar; this price does not include the tax, which they must send to the government. Consumers pay the $88 price plus the $28 tax, for a total of $116. Notice that the total amount consumers pay has increased by less than the $28 tax amount. The lower equilibrium price prevents the amount paid by consumers from increasing by the full amount of the tax, and places part of the burden of the sales

sales tax
A tax applied to a wide variety of goods and services.

excise tax
A tax on a particular good or service.

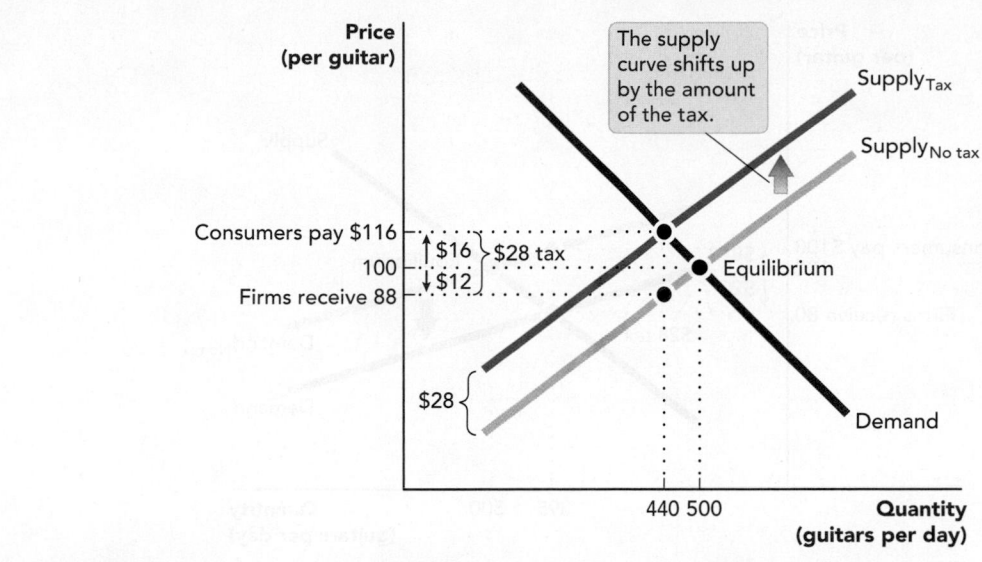

FIGURE 6.7 The Effects of a Tax on Firms

When the government collects a tax from firms, the amount that firms must receive for each unit of the good increases by the amount of the tax. This shifts the supply curve up by the amount of the tax.

tax on sellers of the good. The important lesson is that regardless of who is responsible for paying a tax, the burden of a tax is usually divided in some way between buyers who pay more due to the tax and sellers who receive less.

Now suppose the $28 guitar tax is paid by guitar stores. In this case, the tax doesn't affect the demand curve because consumers aren't responsible for paying the tax. But that doesn't mean the tax won't affect consumers. The tax on firms increases the marginal cost of providing each guitar by $28. If Christopher Woods is willing to provide a fifth guitar for $50, and he must pay a $28 tax for each guitar, he will not accept a price of $50 for that guitar. He needs to be able to keep a minimum of $50 for the fifth guitar. If he must pay $28 to the government, he will provide the fifth guitar for no less than $50 + $28 = $78. That way, after paying the tax, he has $50 to keep. Because firms will require an additional $28 for each guitar, the guitar tax shifts the supply curve for guitars up by $28, as shown in Figure 6.7. After the supply curve shifts, the equilibrium quantity is 440. Consumers share the tax burden by paying a price of $116 to firms. After paying the $28 tax, the firms keep $88.

You can see from Figures 6.6 and 6.7 that the amount consumers pay, the amount firms keep, and the equilibrium quantity are all the same, regardless of whether the per-unit tax is imposed on consumers or firms. If tax incidence does not depend on

who is responsible for a tax, what determines how the burden of the tax is divided? The price elasticities of supply and demand do. Figure 6.8 shows the same guitar-market equilibrium as in Figures 6.6 and 6.7, except that demand is more elastic than before. As a result, some of the tax burden is shifted from consumers to firms. With the more elastic demand curve, consumers pay $108 per unit instead of $116, and firms receive $80 per unit instead of $88. In contrast, if supply becomes more elastic, more of the tax burden is shifted to the consumers. Try drawing several graphs with supply and demand curves that are steeper or flatter than the ones shown here and examine how tax incidence changes.

Steps to Solving Elasticity Problems

Follow these steps if you are asked to calculate and interpret an elasticity value.

STEP 1: Identify which type of elasticity is relevant.

If the type of elasticity you need to calculate is not indicated in the question, you can deduce it from the goal of the calculation.

- To determine whether the demand for a good is elastic, unit elastic, or inelastic, calculate the price elasticity of demand.

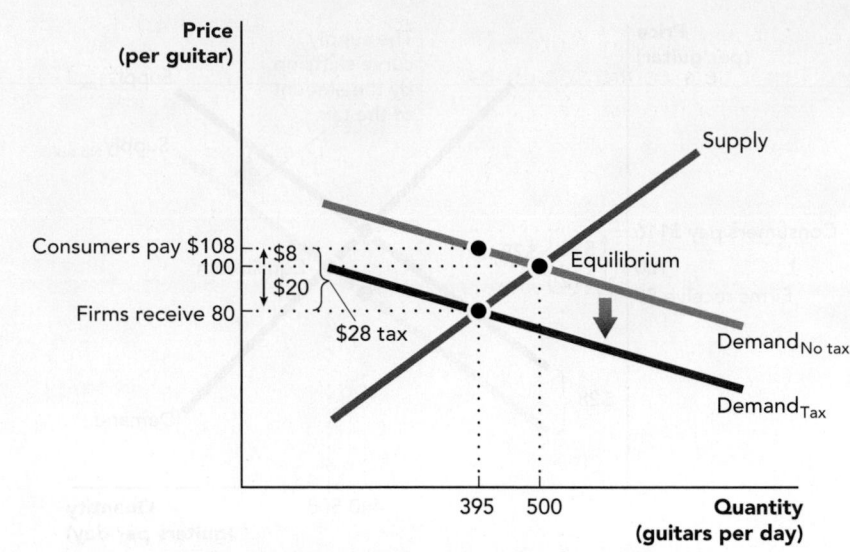

FIGURE 6.8 Tax Incidence: What Does and Doesn't Matter

Tax-incidence—that is, who bears the burden of a tax—does not depend on who is responsible for paying the tax. Instead, it depends on the price elasticities of supply and demand. Comparing this figure to Figure 6.6, you can see that an increase in the price elasticity of demand causes a decrease in the tax burden for consumers and an increase in the tax burden for firms.

- To determine whether the supply of a good is elastic, unit elastic, or inelastic, calculate the price elasticity of supply.
- To determine whether two goods are substitutes or complements, calculate the cross-price elasticity of demand.
- To determine whether a good is normal or inferior, calculate the income elasticity of demand.

STEP 2: Plug the appropriate values into the elasticity formula and solve for the elasticity.

$$\text{price elasticity of demand} = \frac{\text{percentage change in quantity demanded}}{\text{percentage change in price}}$$

$$\text{price elasticity of supply} = \frac{\text{percentage change in quantity supplied}}{\text{percentage change in price}}$$

$$\text{cross-price elasticity of demand} = \frac{\text{percentage change in quantity of Good A demanded}}{\text{percentage change in price of Good B}}$$

$$\text{income elasticity of demand} = \frac{\text{percentage change in quantity demanded}}{\text{percentage change in income}}$$

STEP 3: Interpret the results.

These number lines summarize the interpretation of elasticity values.

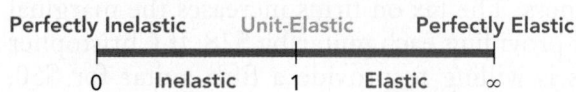

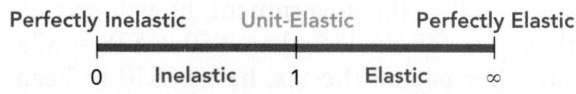

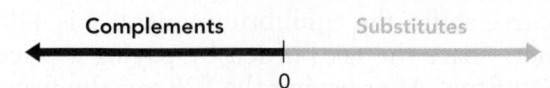

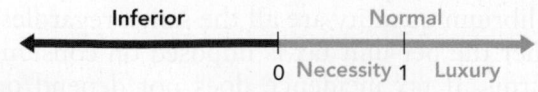

Sample Problem

Suppose you own a guitar store. A nearby store sells drum sets. Guitars and drum sets could be substitutes or complements. That is, a drop in drum-set prices might cause a decrease in guitar sales because people buy drum sets instead of guitars. Or, a drop in drum-set prices might lead to the creation of more bands that need guitarists. When the price of a drum set drops from $400 to $300, daily drum-set sales increase from 10 to 11, and daily guitar sales increase from 20 to 21. Calculate the type of elasticity that indicates whether guitars and drum sets are substitutes or complements and interpret your finding.

STEP 1: Identify which type of elasticity is relevant. It is the cross-price elasticity of demand that indicates whether goods are substitutes or complements, so that is the relevant type of elasticity. You also have enough information to calculate the price elasticity of demand for drum sets, but that is not what this question is asking for.

STEP 2: Plug the appropriate values into the elasticity formula and solve for the elasticity.

$$\text{cross-price elasticity of demand} = \frac{\text{percentage change in the quantity of guitars demanded}}{\text{percentage change in the price of a drum set}}$$

$$= \frac{\dfrac{21 - 20}{20}}{\dfrac{300 - 400}{400}} = \frac{.05}{-.25} = -.2$$

STEP 3: Interpret the results. The cross-price elasticity of demand is negative, so guitars and drum sets are complements.

Cross-Price Elasticity of Demand

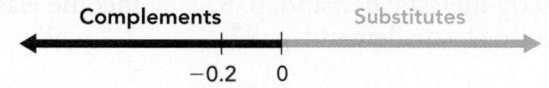

Complements — Substitutes

−0.2   0

SUMMARY

The price elasticity of demand indicates how sensitive consumers are to price changes. If this measure is greater than 1 (in absolute value—that is, without the negative sign), demand is elastic. This means consumers respond to price changes with more than proportional changes in the quantity demanded. If the price elasticity of demand is less than 1, demand is inelastic. This means that the quantity demanded changes less than in proportion to price changes. If the price elasticity is equal to 1, demand is unit elastic, and the quantity demanded changes in proportion to price changes.

Managers facing inelastic demand can increase their profits (or decrease their losses) by raising their prices: Their revenues will rise, and at the same time, their costs will fall because fewer units will be sold. Likewise, managers facing unit-elastic demand can gain financially by raising their prices: Their revenues will remain unchanged, but their costs will fall. When demand is elastic, a price increase leads to lower revenues and lower costs for firms, so the effect of a price increase on profits depends on which falls by more: revenues or costs.

The elasticity formula can be modified to find the price elasticity of supply, the cross-price elasticity of demand, and the income elasticity of demand. The price elasticity of supply measures the responsiveness of the quantity supplied to price changes. The supply of a product is elastic if its elasticity is greater than 1 and inelastic if its elasticity is less than 1. The cross-price elasticity of demand measures how the demand for one good is affected by the price of another good. If the cross-price elasticity of demand is positive, the goods are substitutes. For example, submarine sandwiches and pizza are substitutes. If the cross-price elasticity of demand is negative, the goods are complements. Cola and pizza are examples of complements.

The income elasticity of demand measures how changes in income affect the demand for a good. Goods are categorized as inferior or normal depending on whether their income elasticity of demand is negative or positive. Inferior goods, such as gas station coffee and used cars, have negative income elasticities. Normal goods, such as gourmet coffee and new cars, have positive income elasticities. Normal goods are classified as necessities or luxuries depending on whether their income elasticity is less than or greater than 1.

A sales tax is a tax that applies to a wide variety of goods and services, usually collected from buyers as a percentage of the sale price. An excise tax is a tax on a particular good or service, usually collected from sellers as a set amount for each unit sold. The burden of either type of tax is not determined by who is directly responsible for paying the tax. Rather, the burden is determined by the price elasticity of demand and supply. For example, when the price elasticity of demand is low, consumers are relatively unresponsive to price changes, and firms pass more of a tax on to consumers in the form of higher prices.

KEY TERMS

price elasticity of demand, p. 82
inelastic demand, p. 83
elastic demand, p. 84
unit-elastic demand, p. 84
total revenue, p. 85
perfectly inelastic demand, p. 87
perfectly elastic demand, p. 87

price elasticity of supply, p. 88
cross-price elasticity of demand, p. 89
normal good, p. 90
inferior good, p. 90
income elasticity of demand, p. 90

necessity, p. 90
luxury, p. 91
tax incidence, p. 91
sales tax, p. 92
excise tax, p. 92

PROBLEMS FOR REVIEW

1. Suppose the demand for acoustic (non-electric) guitars is unit elastic. If Christopher Woods increases the price he charges for acoustic guitars, assuming that the price elasticity of demand does not change, what will happen to his total revenue? Explain your answer.

2. How would you expect the elasticity of demand for each of the following products to compare with the price elasticity of demand for standard car tires? Explain your answer.
   a. Snow tires (not necessary, but handy on snowy days)
   b. School bus tires (purchased with tax dollars on a fixed schedule)
   c. Bicycle tires (which require a smaller portion of a consumer's income than car tires)
   d. Tires made by the most reputable company (more of a luxury than a necessity)

3. For each of the following scenarios, draw a graph that shows how an increase in supply will affect the equilibrium price and quantity.
   a. Demand is perfectly inelastic and supply is upward sloping.

   b. Demand is perfectly elastic and supply is upward sloping.
   c. Demand is downward sloping and supply is perfectly inelastic.

4. Suppose a 15 percent increase in the price of hot dogs sold at gas stations would lead to a 20 percent decrease in the quantity of hot dogs purchased at gas stations. What is the price elasticity of demand for hot dogs sold at gas stations?

5. Suppose that your friend's income increases from $25,000 to $50,000, and, as a result, the quantity of energy drinks she purchases increases from 4 per week to 10 per week. What is your friend's income elasticity of demand for energy drinks?

6. Suppose the price of an ad on a typical news website falls from $1,000 to $800, and, as a result, the quantity of ads on news websites rises by 10 percent and the quantity of ads in newspapers falls by 3 percent.
   a. What type of elasticity can tell you whether ads in newspapers and ads on news websites are complements or substitutes?
   b. Calculate the elasticity you chose in part (a) and interpret your results.

7. Provide an example not mentioned in the chapter of each of the following types of goods:
   a. A normal good
   b. An inferior good
   c. Two goods that are substitutes
   d. Two goods that are complements
   e. A luxury good
   f. A good that is a necessity

   For each type of good listed above:
   i. Indicate the type of elasticity you could use to verify that a good falls into that category.
   ii. Indicate the range of values for the indicated type of elasticity that would place the good into that category.

8. True or False: The slope of a demand curve at any particular point is equal to the price elasticity of demand at that point. Explain your answer.

9. Draw an upward-sloping supply curve and a downward-sloping demand curve for the tire market. Label the equilibrium price and quantity as P_1 and Q_1. Now suppose the government imposes a tax on consumers of $5 per new tire to help pay for the disposal of old tires. Indicate how the curves on the graph will change as a result of the tax. Label the new equilibrium quantity Q_2, the new amount that consumers pay per tire (including the tax) as P_C, and the price that firms receive (not including the tax) as P_F.

10. The demand for some pharmaceutical drugs is quite inelastic because customers need the drugs to survive. This has made it possible for some drug companies to charge more than $1,000 for a daily dose of medicine. In your opinion, is it acceptable for drug companies to charge the most that consumers are willing to pay for some drugs? Does your answer depend on whether the drug companies use their profits to fund research into new drugs? Explain one pro and one con of placing a price ceiling on drug prices.

Consumer Behavior

Jessie Walker/Media bakery

7

A student's room without posters is like a flower without petals. Each poster is the result of many choices about how best to use space, time, and money. As a consumer you decide which poster will go above your bed and which one will greet you as you walk in the door. You decide whether to go to the poster fair and how long to shop for the poster of your dreams. And you decide whether to spend more money to get posters of better quality or larger size, or to spend that money on other things you desire. So many choices, so little guidance—until now. This chapter explains how to maximize your happiness with a given amount of money.

Why Should I Care?

David Levene/eyevine/Redux

There's a science to buying art, among other goods and services. **Whether you're gracing a dorm room with movie posters or adorning a mansion with Vincent Van Gogh's masterpieces, every purchase you make comes at the expense of something else: the best alternative use of that money.** You can't spend the same $20 on both a poster and a restaurant meal; you have to make a choice. Whether you're deciding between posters and meals, computers and dance classes, or clothing and smartphone apps, your happiness can increase with an understanding of the economics of consumer behavior.

▲ It is always better to have more utils, but these subjective units of happiness have no precise interpretation. Even if two people both say they receive 100 utils from this poster of musician Ed Sheeran, that doesn't mean it makes them both equally happy.

Utility Maximization

In Chapter 3 you learned that *utility* means happiness or satisfaction. Your ultimate goal as a consumer is to get as much utility as possible out of the money you have to spend. Your level of utility depends on your preferences and your success in attaining whatever makes you happy. Because different consumers are likely to receive different levels of utility from the same goods and services, we see different choices among consumers about how to spend the same amount of money. With $50 to spend at the college bookstore, perhaps your roommate would buy an Ed Sheeran poster and two boxes of PowerBars, whereas you might prefer a sweatshirt and a Charles Dickens novel.

We can talk about a consumer's level of utility in terms of the number of *utils* the individual receives. Utils are a subjective measure of happiness with no standard interpretation. It is always better to have more utils, but because happiness, or utility, means different things to different people, it is not appropriate to compare utility among individuals. For example, it is safe to say that your professor prefers to have 101 utils rather than 100 utils. But even if you and your professor each say you receive 100 utils from the same poster, that doesn't mean the poster gives each of you the same amount of happiness. What you describe as 100 utils of happiness may be very different from what your professor describes that way. Yet important conclusions can be drawn from comparisons of utility levels for a particular person, and from the values that individuals place on the utility they receive from goods and services.

Marginal Utility and Total Utility

Recall that marginal utility is the additional utility received from one more unit of a good or service. You've also learned about *diminishing marginal utility*—the decrease in the benefit you receive from an additional unit of a good or service as you consume more of it. Posters and restaurant meals provide examples of diminishing marginal utility. The first poster you buy for your room gives you something to look at other than bare walls; the fifth poster adds variety; the fiftieth just covers up an existing poster. Likewise, the first restaurant meal you eat in a day satisfies hunger pains that a fifth meal does not, and you wouldn't want to consider a fiftieth meal.

The **total utility** from a good or service is the combined utility an individual receives from all of

total utility
The combined utility an individual receives from all the units consumed.

Table 7.1 Marginal Utility and Total Utility

Posters	Marginal Utility	Total Utility
1	55	55
2	50	105
3	40	145
4	20	165
5	−5	160

the units consumed. Don't be confused by the difference between total utility and marginal utility, or by the fact that these two measures of happiness tend to go in opposite directions. Table 7.1 shows the hypothetical levels of total utility and marginal utility that a student named Ed receives from purchasing various quantities of posters. When Ed has just one poster, his total utility and his marginal utility are the same, because the 55 utils he receives from that poster are both his additional utility from that poster and his total utility from posters (because he has no other posters).

The second poster increases Ed's total utility from 55 to 105, because his marginal utility from the second poster is 50, and 55 + 50 = 105. Like the second poster, the third and fourth posters each add less to Ed's total utility than the poster before, so Ed receives diminishing marginal utility from posters. But the marginal utility from these posters is still positive, so Ed's total utility continues to grow (see Figure 7.1). However, the marginal utility from the fifth poster is negative, perhaps because there's nowhere for that poster to go in Ed's room except on a window, which makes things worse. The negative marginal utility from the fifth poster causes his total utility to decrease.

The height of the total utility curve indicates the cumulative amount of utility received from all the posters up to the quantity shown on the horizontal axis. For example, with four posters, the total utility is the sum of the utility received from the first four posters: 55 + 50 + 40 + 20 = 165. The height of the marginal utility curve indicates the additional utility received from each particular poster. So the marginal utility at a quantity of four posters is just the 20 utils received from the fourth poster. The total utility curve always rises when marginal utility is positive and falls when marginal utility is negative.

To better understand the difference between total values and marginal values, imagine you are scooping ice cream from a carton into a bowl. As you near the bottom of the carton, each scoop may contain less ice cream than the previous scoop, but

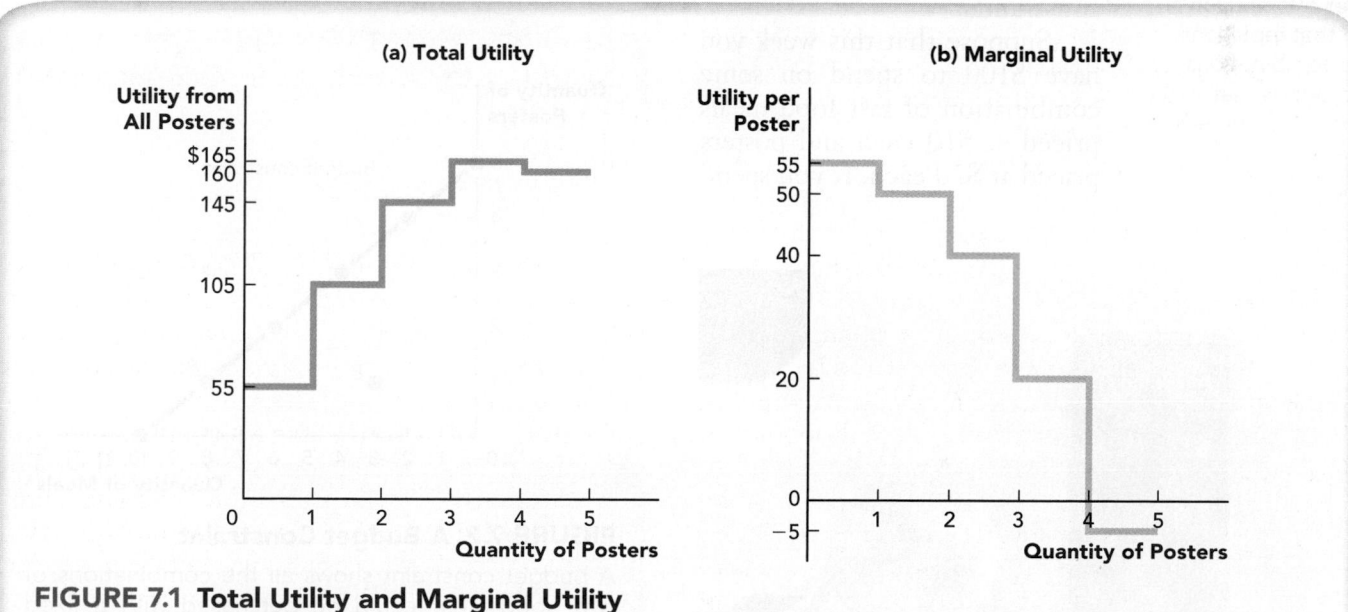

FIGURE 7.1 Total Utility and Marginal Utility

The total utility Ed receives from each quantity of posters shown in panel (a) is found by adding up the marginal utility shown in panel (b) for every poster up to that quantity. As long as Ed's marginal utility is positive, his total utility continues to rise. When Ed's marginal utility becomes negative after the fourth poster, his total utility begins to fall.

Q&A

If I get more utility out of my first poster than out of my second or third, shouldn't I consume just one poster and maximize my marginal utility?
It is easy to confuse marginal utility—the utility received from one more unit—with total utility, the sum of the marginal utility received from every unit consumed. Your goal is to maximize your total utility, not your marginal utility. If you maximized your marginal utility and stopped after one poster, you would miss out on potential gains from additional posters. If the marginal utility you receive from additional posters is worth more to you than the price of the posters, you would benefit from buying them, even if they don't add as much to your total utility as the first poster.

the mound of ice cream in your bowl keeps growing until the last scoop is empty. Marginal utility diminishes like the amount of ice cream in each scoop, but as long as there is some marginal utility, total utility grows like the mound of ice cream in the bowl.

Budget Constraints

You face constraints in your pursuit of happiness. There is only so much time, so much ice cream, so much wall space for posters, and so much money in your budget for restaurant meals, posters, ice cream, and everything else. In this section, we'll examine the budget constraints that bind your consumption decisions. Economists use similar models to study all sorts of constraints.

budget constraint
The set of points on a graph that represents all the combinations of two goods that exhaust a consumer's budget.

Suppose that this week you have $100 to spend on some combination of fast-food meals priced at $10 each and posters priced at $20 each. If you spend all your money on fast-food meals, you can buy 10 meals, because $10 \times \$10 = \$100$. But suppose you want to buy some posters as well. Because the price of a poster is twice the price of a meal, you must give up 2 meals for every poster. If you buy 1 poster, you will have $\$100 - \$20 = \$80$ left to buy 8 meals. If you buy 2 posters, you will have $60 left to buy 6 meals, and so on. The largest number of posters you could buy is 5, because $5 \times \$20 = \$100$.

We can use points on a graph to illustrate combinations of meals and posters. For example, point *A* represents the purchase of 8 meals and 1 poster. If we draw a line through all the points that exhaust your budget, we have a graphical depiction of your **budget constraint**. Each point along the budget constraint in Figure 7.2 represents a combination of

▲ Marginal utility is like ice cream: as long as you can scoop any up, it adds to the total.

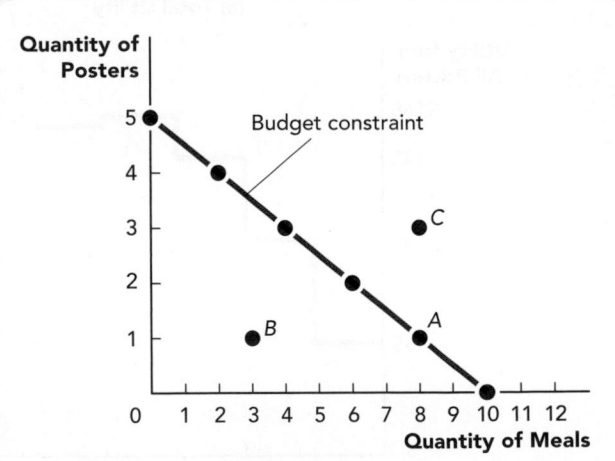

FIGURE 7.2 A Budget Constraint
A budget constraint shows all the combinations of two goods that could be purchased with a fixed budget. If you have $100 to spend on $10 fast-food meals and $20 posters, you could buy 10 meals, 5 posters, or any mix of these goods represented by a point along the budget constraint.

a quantity of meals and a quantity of posters with a total cost of $100.

Points on your budget constraint show the combinations of goods you could afford if you spend your entire budget. Points below your budget constraint show combinations that would leave some of your budget unspent. For example, if you purchased 3 meals and 1 poster, as shown by point *B* in Figure 7.2, you would spend (3 × $10) + (1 × $20) = $50, which is only half of your $100 budget. Consumption at a point above your budget constraint would require more money than you have available to spend. For example, to purchase 8 meals and 3 posters, as shown by point *C*, you would need ($8 × $10) + (3 × $20) = $140, which is over your $100 budget.

An increase in your budget shifts the budget constraint outward, showing that you can afford more posters and/or meals. Suppose your budget increased to $120. You could then purchase up to 12 restaurant meals, up to 6 posters, or any combination of posters and meals shown on or below the dark purple budget constraint in Figure 7.3. Likewise, a decrease in your budget to $80 would shift your budget constraint inward, as represented by the light purple line in the figure. In every case, your budget constraint indicates options from which you can choose. The next section explains how to make that choice so as to gain as much utility as possible.

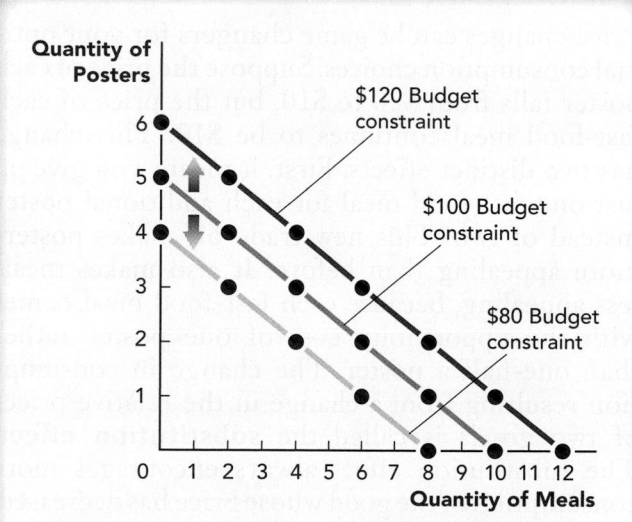

FIGURE 7.3 Shifting a Budget Constraint
An increase in your budget shifts your budget constraint outward. A decrease in your budget shifts your budget constraint inward.

The Optimal Consumption Rule

Utility maximization is all about getting the most bang for your buck—you want each dollar to bring as much satisfaction as possible. If the marginal utility you receive per dollar spent is higher for some goods than for others, it only makes sense to buy more of whatever gives you the most marginal utility per dollar and less of whatever gives you the least marginal utility per dollar.

Suppose you are considering a purchase of 3 posters and 4 fast-food meals at the prices of $20 and $10, respectively. Assume that your marginal utility from the third poster would be 40 and your marginal utility from the fourth fast-food meal would be 30. This is one way to spend your $100, but it is not the way that maximizes your happiness. Although your marginal utility from posters would be one-third higher than your marginal utility from meals, a poster costs *twice* as much as a meal. Rather than spending $20 on a third poster that would give you 40 utils, you could instead buy 2 more meals—your fifth and sixth in total—for $10 each. Suppose the first additional meal would give you 28 utils and the second additional meal would give you 25 utils. These two meals would add 53 utils to your total utility, which is more than the 40 utils you would lose by giving up the poster.

▲ Money can't buy everything, but it can buy this poster about what money can't buy. So should you buy the poster? Only if your marginal utility per dollar spent on the poster would be as high as or higher than your marginal utility per dollar spent on other goods.

The lesson here is that it isn't just the marginal utility you receive that matters, but the marginal utility you receive *per dollar spent*.

To maximize your utility with a fixed amount of money, follow the **optimal consumption rule** by selecting purchases that equalize the marginal utility you receive per dollar you spend on each good. If you purchase only posters and fast-food meals, the optimal consumption rule is satisfied when your entire budget is spent and

$$\frac{\text{marginal utility}_{\text{meals}}}{\text{price}_{\text{meals}}} = \frac{\text{marginal utility}_{\text{posters}}}{\text{price}_{\text{posters}}}$$

To maximize your utility . . . equalize the marginal utility you receive per dollar spent on each good.

Let's apply the optimal consumption rule to the proposed purchase of 3 posters and 4 fast-food meals. The posters give you $40 \div \$20 = 2$ utils per dollar and the meals give you $30 \div \$10 = 3$ utils per dollar. Figure 7.4 shows that you are not maximizing your utility in this case because you receive more utils per dollar from meals than from posters. You could become happier by shifting some of your money to the purchase of meals, which currently provide more additional utility per dollar than posters.

As you purchase more meals and fewer posters, diminishing marginal utility will cause the marginal utility of meals to fall and the marginal utility of posters to rise. This reallocation of the available funds should continue until the marginal utility per dollar of each good is the same. Consider a purchase of 2 posters and 6 fast-food meals. We know from Table 7.1 that your marginal utility from the second poster is 50, so your marginal utility per dollar spent on the second poster is $50 \div \$20 = 2.5$. This equals your marginal utility per dollar spent on the sixth meal: $25 \div \$10 = 2.5$. Because you have spent your budget for these goods and your marginal utility per dollar spent on each good is the same, this

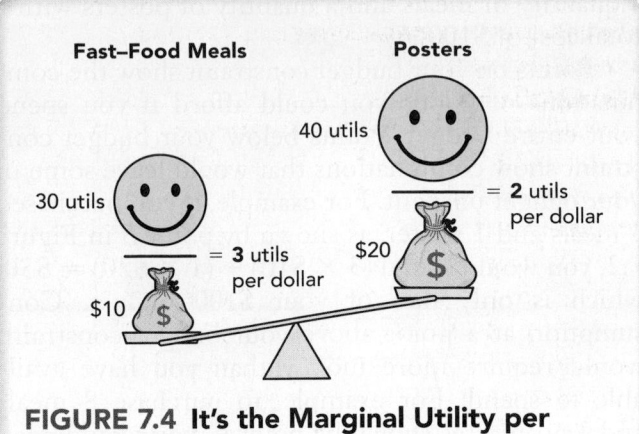

FIGURE 7.4 It's the Marginal Utility per Dollar That Matters

The good that gives you the most marginal utility isn't necessarily the good that gives you the most marginal utility per dollar.

combination satisfies the optimal consumption rule: You have maximized your utility given your budget constraint. By giving up 40 utils from the third poster, you gained 53 utils from the fifth and sixth meals, for a net gain of 13 utils. Of course, you don't really count the utils you receive, but a wise consumer will make the purchase that provides the most bang per buck.

The Substitution Effect and the Income Effect

Price changes can be game changers for your optimal consumption choices. Suppose the price of each poster falls from $20 to $10, but the price of each fast-food meal continues to be $10. This change has two distinct effects. First, it means you give up just one fast-food meal for each additional poster instead of two. This new trade-off makes posters more appealing than before. It also makes meals less appealing, because each fast-food meal comes with the opportunity cost of one poster rather than one-half a poster. The change in consumption resulting from a change in the relative prices of two goods is called the **substitution effect**. The substitution effect always encourages more consumption of the good whose price has decreased.

The second effect comes from the expansion of your purchasing power that has resulted from the new, lower price of posters. The price drop makes you feel richer because you can now afford some combinations of posters and fast-food meals you couldn't have afforded before: You can now buy

optimal consumption rule
States that you should select purchases that equalize the marginal utility you receive per dollar you spend on each good.

substitution effect
The change in consumption resulting from a change in the relative prices of two goods.

Cafe Terrace, Place du Forum, Arles, 1888 (oil on canvas)/Gogh, Vincent van (1853–INFORMATION & ARCHIVES/Rijksmuseum Kroller-Muller, Otterlo, Netherlands/Bridgeman Images

▲ When the price of a normal good such as posters of Vincent Van Gogh's artwork drops, consumers buy more of the good for two reasons. One is the *substitution effect:* Buyers switch away from other goods due to the change in relative prices. The other reason is the *income effect:* Buyers feel richer because they can purchase more with the same amount of money.

more posters, more meals, or more of both! The change in consumption resulting from the change in the purchasing power of a consumer's income after a price change is called the **income effect**. For normal goods, the income effect leads to more consumption when your purchasing power increases and less consumption when your purchasing power decreases.

The total effect of a price change is a combination of the substitution effect and the income effect. The two effects reinforce each other for a normal good in that they both decrease the quantity demanded when the price increases, and increase the quantity demanded when the price decreases.

The story is different for inferior goods. Recall that consumers buy less of an inferior good, such as low-quality hamburgers, when they feel richer. For an inferior good, the income effect leads to less consumption when your purchasing power increases and more consumption when your purchasing power decreases. When the price of an

inferior good decreases, the substitution effect and the income effect work in opposite directions. The substitution effect leads to an increase in the quantity demanded, but the income effect drives people away from the inferior good. The net effect of a price decrease for an inferior good is theoretically ambiguous. In practice, the substitution effect tends to be larger than the income effect, so a price decrease still leads to an increase in the quantity demanded. Likewise, a price increase for an inferior good generally leads to a decrease in the quantity demanded.

Lessons from Behavioral Economics

Economists generally assume that people act in their best interests, but some of their interests are not what you might expect, and sometimes consumers make mistakes. **Behavioral economics** is the study of how economic decision making is influenced by the limits of the human mind. Behavioral economists mine data on consumers' choices to unearth the desires and faults of the human mind. This section examines some of their findings.

CONSUMERS WANT BALANCE

Just as a balanced diet is healthy for your body, your mind likes balance, too. After spending an hour staring at posters on the wall, you'd probably rather spend the next hour doing something else, like going out for dinner at Taco Bell. If you ate at Taco Bell for lunch, however, you'd probably rather have some pizza or a burger for dinner. The appeal of balanced consumption follows from the law of diminishing marginal utility—even if Taco Bell is your favorite restaurant, you can have too much of a good thing. Sooner or later, a meal from almost any other restaurant will provide more satisfaction than yet another burrito supreme.

The interest in balance explains why people don't always have the same hairdos, wear the same clothes, or travel to the same vacation destinations. Firms are therefore wise to reinvent themselves on occasion. For example, a restaurant that adds new menu items allows customers to avoid the boredom of repetition without sending them across the street to a competing restaurant. Hence, we occasionally see

income effect
The change in consumption resulting from the change in the purchasing power of a consumer's income after a price change.

behavioral economics
The study of how economic decision making is influenced by the limits of the human mind.

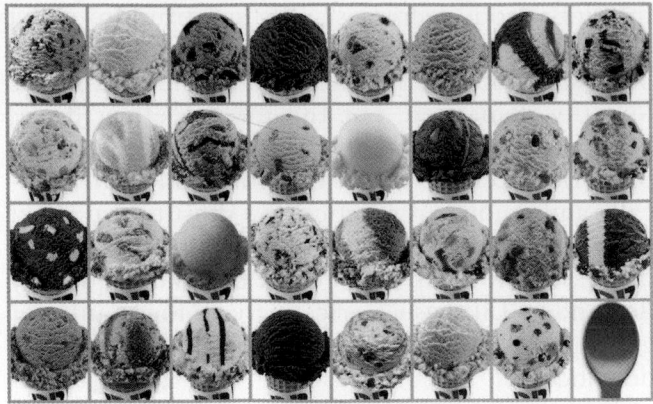

▲ Baskin-Robbins has introduced over 1,000 flavors since 1945. That many choices would confuse customers and exceed the space constraints in stores. How many choices do customers want? Baskin-Robbins decided the sweet spot for flavor choices is around 31, so the company only offers about that many at one time.

McRibs on the McDonald's menu, new flavors at Baskin-Robbins, new crusts at Pizza Hut, and new lattes at Starbucks.

CONSUMERS WANT SOME OPTIONS, BUT NOT TOO MANY

Consumers like stores and restaurants that offer a variety of choices, both because consumers like to try something new once in a while, and because options make it possible to more closely match each individual's preferences. However, it's possible for consumers to be confused by too many options, just as it's possible for them to feel restricted by too few.

Psychologists Sheena Iyengar and Mark Lepper conducted several experiments to gauge the effects of a limited and an extensive selection. In one of their experiments, they offered grocery store shoppers various samples from a selection of either 6 or 24 types of jams and then tracked the number of shoppers who purchased jam. Almost 30 percent of shoppers who were offered 6 jams purchased one of them. In contrast, only 3 percent of shoppers who were offered a selection of 24 jams made a purchase.

In a second experiment, Iyengar and Lepper gave students in a college class the opportunity to write an extra-credit paper for which the professors suggested either 6 topics or 30 topics to choose from. Of the students who were offered 6 choices, 74 percent wrote an extra-credit paper, whereas only 60 percent of the students who were offered 30 choices wrote the paper.

The appeal of having a manageable number of choices helps explain why car companies offer several but not an overwhelming number of component packages for new cars, why cable television companies

▲ There are 221,184 different ways to have a Whopper your way, but consumers prefer fewer choices, so Burger King lists only a few of them on its menu.

offer several but not many options for bundles of channels, and why the Burger King menu lists only a few of the 221,184 ways to customize a Whopper.

CONSUMERS WANT FAIRNESS

In a famous experiment that has been replicated many times over the past 30 years, economists Werner Guth, Rolf Schmittberger, and Bernd Schwarze set out to see how fairness affects people's decisions about money. They created an *ultimatum game* with two players: Player 1 and Player 2. Player 1 divides an amount of money, say $10, between herself and Player 2. After the division is made, Player 2 can either accept the proposed division or reject it, in which case neither player receives anything. If money were the only interest, Player 1 would offer Player 2 the smallest possible amount of money—no more than a penny—and Player 2 would accept it because something is better than nothing.

In practice, Player 1 typically offers Player 2 between $2.50 and $5.00. The sizable offers mean that Player 1 is either interested in fairness or thinks Player 2 might sacrifice his or her share of the money to punish Player 1 for making an unfair offer. (Recall that when an offer is rejected, neither player gets any money.) Many low offers are, in fact, rejected. Some players reject low offers out of revenge: They would rather receive absolutely nothing so the player who made the low offer doesn't get anything either.

To see how interested consumers are in fairness, apart from concerns of revenge, economists Daniel Kahneman, Jack Knetsch, and Richard Thaler developed the *dictator game*. In the dictator game, Player 1 can choose any division, and Player 2 has no choice but to accept it. Thus, Player 1 can keep all the money with no risk. Even so, the average Player 1 gives Player 2 about 20 percent of the money to be divided. The lesson is that the drivers of human behavior go beyond money: Altruism, equity,

▲ Money isn't everything. Altruism, equity, reciprocity, guilt, and fairness also affect what people buy and how much they are willing to pay for products. For example, many consumers pay more than necessary for fair-trade products like this soccer ball to help ensure that the workers who manufacture them receive fair wages.

reciprocity, guilt, and fairness, among other ethical considerations, also affect people's decision making.

The ethical component of consumer behavior has motivated firms to find new ways to serve communities, workers, and ecosystems. Consumers worldwide spend over $5 billion annually on *fair-trade* products that have relatively high prices but provide higher wages to workers in developing nations. Walmart is experimenting with biodegradable plastic packaging, and Subaru advertises its policy of sending no waste to landfills. The outdoor clothing–maker Patagonia has found success selling pricey but environmentally friendly products, including clothes made of organic cotton, to reduce the use of chemical pesticides, herbicides, and fertilizers.

CONSUMERS MAKE MISTAKES

Bounded rationality refers to the limits on optimal decision making that result from people's limited cognitive skills, information, or time. You can probably think of times when you felt unqualified, inadequately informed, or too rushed to make the best decisions. Bounded rationality can cause several types of mistakes, including:

- *Excessive optimism:* More than half of all new businesses fail within five years, which may indicate that entrepreneurs are excessively optimistic that they will succeed. Similarly, many criminals are irrationally optimistic that they won't get caught when they commit crimes.

- *Inaccurate risk assessments:* People tend to underestimate the risks of common but unpublicized events such as work-related accidents, and overestimate the risk of uncommon but dramatic or highly publicized events such as airplane crashes, earthquakes, and murders.

- *Susceptibility to framing:* The way a price or product is presented, or *framed*, can affect consumers' decisions. For example, sellers often charge a price that ends with "99," such as $19.99. Why? Because they know that buyers tend to focus more on the dollars than on the cents in a price. By charging $19.99, the sellers appear to be offering a significantly better deal than if they charged $20.00.

Happiness is also hindered by **bounded willpower**, that is, limits on our self-control that prevent us from achieving difficult but worthwhile goals. For example, bounded willpower can lead us to spend too much, eat too much, earn too little, do too little homework, and spend too little time at the gym. Bounded willpower may explain why more than one-third of American consumers have credit card debt that exceeds their savings.

bounded rationality
The limits on optimal decision making that result from people's limited cognitive skills, information, or time.

bounded willpower
The limits on self-control that prevent people from achieving difficult but worthwhile goals.

SUMMARY

In the pursuit of happiness, it is important to focus on the right objective. You should not seek to maximize marginal utility—that is just the benefit from one more unit of a good or service. Instead, try to maximize the *total* utility you receive from any given expenditure.

Points on your budget constraint show the combinations of goods you could buy if you spent exactly the amount of money you have budgeted for those goods. Points above your budget constraint represent combinations of the goods you cannot afford. Points below your budget constraint represent combinations that would leave some of your budget unspent.

Whatever your budget constraint, there is a strategy to help you get as much happiness as possible from your money: Buy more of whatever gives you the most marginal utility per dollar spent. If buying more of that good would put you over your budget, buy less of whatever gives you the least marginal utility per dollar. As you purchase more of a good, the marginal utility received from that good falls. This makes other goods relatively attractive and helps to even out the marginal utility you receive per dollar spent on all goods. Follow this strategy until your budget is spent and your marginal utility per dollar is the same for everything you buy. In practice, consumers don't actually count the number of utils they receive as they apply this winning strategy, but wise shoppers do buy the goods that provide the most bang per buck.

When a price changes, the best combination of goods to buy also changes. The effects of a price change can be separated into the substitution effect and the income effect. The substitution effect results from the change in the price of one good relative to the price of another good. For example, the substitution effect of a price decrease causes more consumption of the good that has become relatively less expensive and less consumption of the good that has become relatively more expensive. The income effect results from the change in the purchasing power of a consumer's income after a price change. A decrease in the price of one good raises the purchasing power of a consumer's income, making it possible to purchase more of either or both goods. After a price drop, the income effect results in more consumption of normal goods like meals at fancy restaurants, and less consumption of inferior goods like fast-food meals.

Behavioral economics is the study of how economic decision making is influenced by the limits of the human mind. Consumers desire plenty of options to choose from. That's why Baskin-Robbins offers a selection of 31 ice cream flavors. However, research suggests that too many choices can be overwhelming to consumers, which is one of the reasons why Baskin-Robbins doesn't offer more of their 1,000-plus flavors at any one time. Altruism, equity, reciprocity, guilt, and fairness also affect what people buy and how much they are willing to pay for products.

The limits on optimal decision making caused by imperfect intelligence or imperfect information are called bounded rationality. The consequences of bounded rationality include excessive optimism, inaccurate risk assessments, and irrational responses to the way prices or products are presented, or framed. Bounded willpower describes the limits on determination that prevent consumers from achieving difficult but worthwhile goals. Bounded willpower causes some people to spend too much, earn too little, procrastinate, overeat, lose control of their emotions, or do too little homework. Nice job having the willpower to finish this chapter!

KEY TERMS

total utility, p. 100
budget constraint, p. 102
optimal consumption rule, p. 104

substitution effect, p. 104
income effect, p. 105
behavioral economics, p. 105

bounded rationality, p. 107
bounded willpower, p. 107

PROBLEMS FOR REVIEW

1. This chapter explains that consumers prefer balance in their consumption of goods and services. Provide an example of how the desire for balance affects your own consumption behavior.

2. Suppose you and your neighbor indicate that you each receive 1,000 utils per month from the neighborhood park. Explain why this doesn't mean that you each receive the same amount of happiness from the park.

3. Explain whether the following statement is true, false, or uncertain: When marginal utility is decreasing, total utility is decreasing.

4. Insert the missing values for the marginal utility and the total utility received from smoothies:

Smoothies	Marginal Utility	Total Utility
1	100	100
2	95	
3		280
4	50	
5		340
6	−30	

5. Suppose this weekend you're going to the sporting goods store to spend a $75 gift certificate on some combination of $15 soccer balls and $5 pairs of socks. Draw your budget constraint, with the quantity of pairs of socks shown on the horizontal axis and the quantity of soccer balls shown on the vertical axis. Draw dotted lines to both axes from each point to indicate the quantity of each good represented by each point on your budget constraint.

6. On your graph for problem 5, draw the new budget constraint that results if the price of soccer balls increases to $25 and the price of socks remains $5 per pair. Shade the area on your graph that represents all the combinations of the two goods that you could afford after the price change.

7. Suppose that at your currently weekly consumption levels, your marginal utility from bagels is 100 and your marginal utility from oranges is 75. The price per bagel is $1.00 and the price per orange is $0.50. Next week, if all prices and your budget for bagels and oranges remain the same, you should consume

a. the same quantity of each good.
b. more bagels and fewer oranges.
c. more oranges and fewer bagels.

Explain your answer.

8. Gas prices typically end with 9/10 of a cent. If a price of 2.49\frac{9}{10}$ per gallon seems better to consumers than a price of $2.50 per gallon, this is most likely the result of

a. gasoline being an inferior good.
b. a desire for balance.
c. a desire for fairness.
d. bounded rationality.
e. bounded willpower.

9. This chapter explains three things that behavioral economists have determined that consumers want: (1) balance, (2) some options, but not too many, and (3) fairness. Which of these things leads consumers to spend more money than necessary to purchase a particular good or to win a particular game? Provide two examples, one of them from your own experience.

10. Does your decision making resemble the optimal consumption rule? Is there any way you could change your spending to receive more bang per buck?

Production Costs

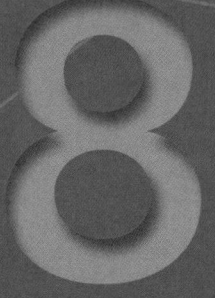

8

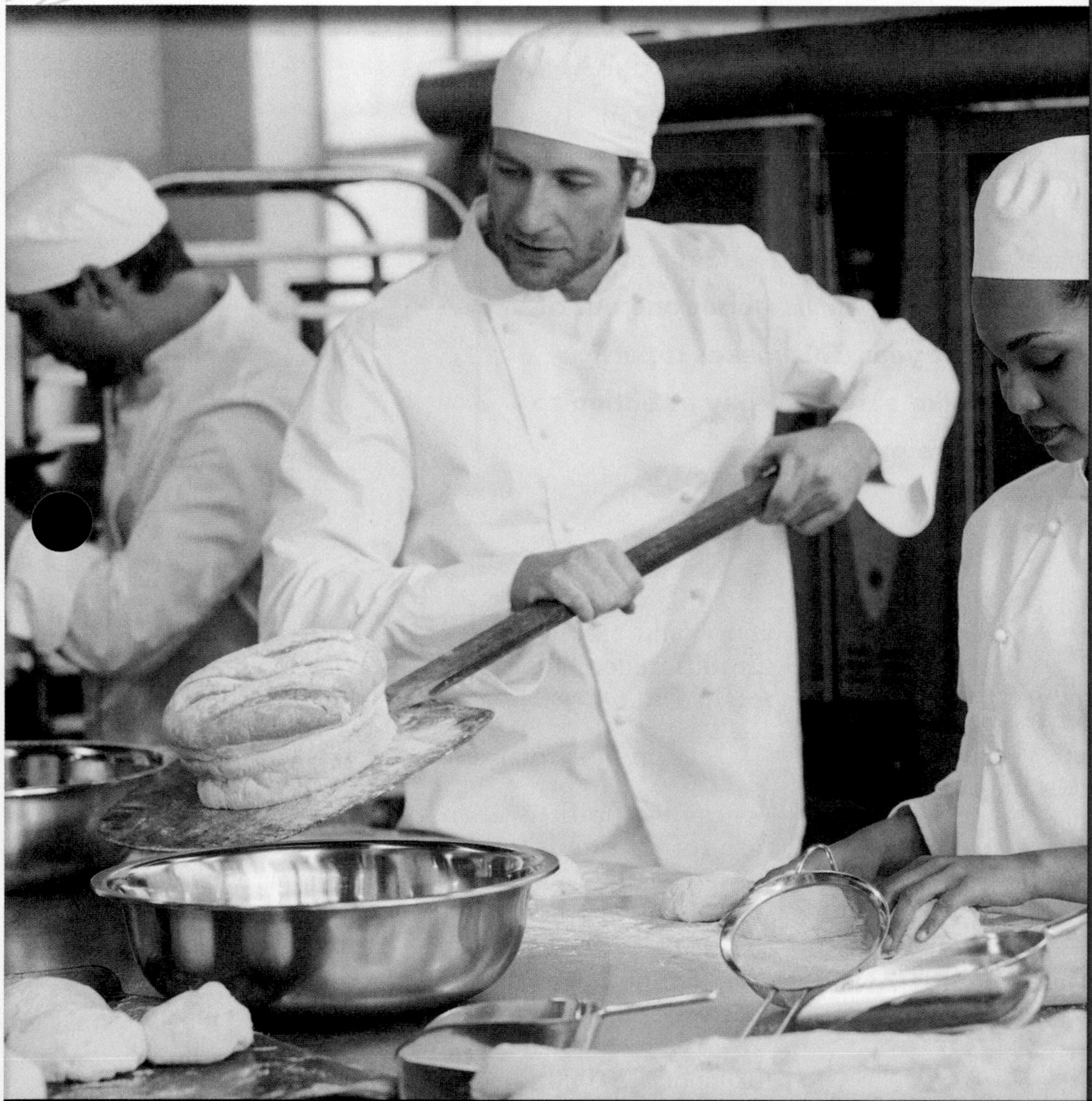

wavebreakmedia/Shutterstock.com

LEARNING OBJECTIVES

In this chapter, you will learn to:

1. Explain the difference between accounting profit and economic profit
2. Interpret a production function
3. Identify the cost-minimizing combination of inputs
4. Define the various types of costs faced by firms
5. Discuss the sources of economies of scale

There are nearly 9,000 bakeries in the United States. Before shoppers spend $33 billion each year on bread, cakes, and cookies, bakeries spend billions of their own dollars on bakers, ovens, stores, advertising, electricity, flour, sugar, butter—and let's not forget chocolate chips! When a bakery doesn't watch its costs carefully, customers can suffer from high prices, or worse, employees can lose their jobs and a community can lose its best source of goodies. This chapter explains how bakery owners and other entrepreneurs can examine the productivity and costs of inputs such as bakers and ovens.

Why Should I Care?

When you eat baked goods or anything else, your weight gain is the difference between the calories you take in and the calories you expend. Likewise, if you ever open a bakery or any other business, your profit will be the difference between the dollars you take in and the dollars you spend. So as bakery owners knead their bread dough, they must also be mindful of another type of "dough"—the type they spend on things like mixing machines and yeast. If the owners spend more than they earn, they lose money. Losses that persist in the long run mean no more dough of either type because the bakery fails. **About one out of every four new eateries fails in its first year. This makes it particularly important for business owners, like eaters, to pay attention to what they're taking in and what they're expending.**

Profit Maximization

Firms don't seek to maximize the total amount of money they receive from customers, because that's not what the owners get to keep. When you buy a birthday cake, the bakery uses most of your payment to cover its costs. What the owners keep, and therefore what they seek to maximize, is profit. In this section, you'll learn two common ways to calculate profit.

ACCOUNTING PROFIT AND ECONOMIC PROFIT

Imagine you've purchased an ocean-side storefront in Hawaii, where you're thinking of opening your own bakery, the Island Bakery. To keep the Island Bakery operating in the long term, your total revenue from the sale of baked goods would have to at least equal your total cost. Ideally,

you would earn a large profit. A firm's **profit** is the difference between its total revenue and its total cost:

$$\text{profit} = \text{total revenue} - \text{total cost}$$

A negative profit is a *loss*. Although the formula for profit is simple, one common way of using the formula could cause you to make the wrong decision about whether to open the business, as we'll see next.

Suppose you estimate that each year you would receive $260,000 in total revenue from sales in your bakery. Your annual costs would include $100,000 for labor, $70,000 for ingredients, and $25,000 for equipment rental. These are examples of **explicit costs**, which are costs that involve actual payments of money. Accountants use only explicit costs when calculating a firm's profit, so a firm's **accounting profit** is its total revenue minus its total explicit cost:

$$\text{accounting profit} = \text{total revenue} - \text{total explicit cost}$$

profit
Total revenue minus total cost.

explicit costs
Costs that involve actual payments of money.

accounting profit
Total revenue minus total explicit cost.

Assuming your revenue and cost estimates for the Island Bakery are correct, your accounting profit per year would be:

accounting profit = $260,000 in sales revenue
                       − $100,000 for labor
                       − $70,000 for ingredients
                       − $25,000 for equipment
                         rental
                       ――――――――――――――――――――
                       = $65,000

Should you proceed to open the Island Bakery on the basis of this information? No. The best decision-making requires full information on *all* costs and benefits, some of which haven't been considered yet.

Even though you own the building where the Island Bakery would reside, your use of it creates a cost—the opportunity cost of not being able to rent the building to someone else. And if you use your time and energy to run the Island Bakery, you face the opportunity cost of not being able to work in your next-best alternative job. These opportunity costs are examples of **implicit costs**, which are costs that do not involve a direct outlay of money. Note that some opportunity costs are not implicit costs: There is an opportunity cost of spending money, too, because you forego the opportunity to spend that money on something else.

When economists calculate profit, they consider both explicit costs and implicit costs. You should, too, before you decide to open a new bakery.

▲ One opportunity cost of opening your own bakery is that you forego the income you could earn working for someone else.

Dave Anderson

Economic profit is total revenue minus total cost, with total cost including both types of cost:

economic profit = total revenue − (total explicit cost + total implicit cost)

Suppose that if you didn't open your own bakery, your highest-paying alternative opportunity would be to manage the nearby Honolulu Cookie Company location for $40,000 per year. And if you didn't open your bakery, you could rent out your ocean-side storefront to someone else for $60,000 a year. Your implicit cost of opening the Island Bakery would therefore be $40,000 + $60,000 = $100,000 per year. Thus, your economic profit would be:

economic profit = $260,000 in total revenue
                     − $100,000 for labor
                     − $70,000 for ingredients
                     − $25,000 for equipment rental
                     − $60,000 for the opportunity
                       cost of using the building
                     − $40,000 for the opportunity
                       cost of your time
                     ――――――――――――――――――――――
                     = − $35,000

Once you include the implicit costs in your calculation, it becomes clear that you would lose $35,000 each year by opening the Island Bakery. You can earn the most money by managing the Honolulu Cookie Company.

Some opportunity costs are not implicit costs: There is an opportunity cost of spending money, too.

Did you have your heart set on running your own bakery? Remember that *all* costs and benefits should be factored in when making decisions. This includes the value of any satisfaction you would receive from owning your own business. If the joy of owning the Island Bakery would be worth more to you than the $35,000 decrease in your annual income, go for it.

implicit costs
Costs that do not involve a direct outlay of money.

economic profit
Total revenue minus total cost, with total cost including both total explicit cost and total implicit cost.

▲ The production function for your bakery shows how many loaves of bread you can produce with various quantities of bakers.

The Production Function

How many loaves of bread will bakeries make? And with what inputs? The decisions that maximize the profits of bakeries and other firms depend on the demand for goods, the costs of inputs, and the productivity of those inputs.

Suppose you decide to dive into the bakery business. Before the sun comes up on your bakery, you must decide how many loaves of bread to bake and what inputs to use in that process. Readily available information on the costs of hiring workers and renting ovens will influence your decisions, as will the prices at which you can sell baked goods. However, in order to determine the profit-maximizing quantity of loaves to bake and the cost-minimizing quantity of each input to hire, you need to know the *productivity* of inputs. An input's productivity is on display in a **production function**, which shows the relationship between the quantity of that input a firm uses and the quantity of output the firm can produce as a result.

To keep things simple, let's assume your bakery has only two inputs: ovens and labor. We can place these inputs into

production function
A relationship showing the quantity of each input that a firm uses and the quantity of output that the firm can produce as a result.

long run
The time period during which the quantities of all inputs can be changed.

short run
The time period during which the quantity of at least one input cannot be changed.

fixed input
An input whose quantity cannot be varied in the short run.

variable input
An input whose quantity can be varied in the short run.

useful categories by considering how quickly you could change the quantities of ovens and labor you employ. The **long run** describes the time period in which the quantities of all inputs can be changed. In the long run, the number of ovens and workers can be adjusted to accommodate different output levels at the lowest possible cost.

The **short run** describes the time period during which the quantity of at least one input cannot change. The quantity of output can be adjusted in the short run, but a firm's production costs will not be minimized if there is too much or too little of one or more inputs. There is no particular period after which the short run becomes the long run; the length of the short run depends on the situation. If it would take six months to expand your bakery and install new ovens, or to get out of a rental agreement in order to decrease the number of ovens, then the short run for you lasts six months.

FIXED INPUTS AND VARIABLE INPUTS

An input such as ovens is considered a **fixed input** because its quantity cannot be varied in the short run. Buildings and most other forms of capital are fixed inputs. Labor is a **variable input** because its quantity *can* be varied in the short run. Depending on the number of customers in your bakery on a particular day, you can ask workers to put in some overtime or go home early. If necessary, you can hire or fire workers fairly quickly as well. Since the long run is defined as the period in which all inputs are variable, there are no fixed inputs in the long run.

▲ In the short run, the quantity of at least one input cannot change. In a bakery, the quantity of labor, ingredients, and other variable inputs can change in the short run, but the quantity of fixed inputs such as bread ovens can only change in the long run.

MARGINAL PRODUCT

If there were only one worker in the Island Bakery, that worker would have to do it all: wash the floors, mix the dough, take customers' orders, place orders for supplies, and so on. Her talents would be spread more thinly than her crêpes, and she wouldn't become particularly good at any one task. With a second worker in the bakery, one worker could concentrate on the kitchen, mixing and baking and washing floors, while the other was focused on serving customers and ordering supplies. By specializing, the two workers could develop more expertise in their roles, and the two of them might accomplish more than twice as much as one worker could.

To inform hiring decisions, it is useful to measure the contribution of each unit of an input such as labor. The **marginal product** of an input is the increase in output gained from an additional unit of that input, leaving the quantities of other inputs unchanged. For example, the *marginal product of labor* is the increase in output gained from an additional unit of labor. In our bakery story, we will measure units of labor in terms of the number of workers hired each day. Labor units can also be measured in terms of the number of hours that employees work. In the long run, when the amount of capital can be varied, changes in the number of ovens will affect output as well. The increase in output gained from an additional unit of capital, holding the amount of labor unchanged, is called the *marginal product of capital*. First, we'll examine changes in the amount of labor in the short run when the amount of capital is fixed.

Table 8.1 The Island Bakery's Total Output and Marginal Product of Labor per Day

Workers	Total Output (loaves per day)	Marginal Product of Labor (loaves per day)
1	30	30
2	70	40
3	105	35
4	130	25
5	140	10

The first column of Table 8.1 shows options for the number of workers the Island Bakery can hire per day. The second column shows the total number of loaves that can be produced with 1, 2, 3, 4, and 5 workers. The third column shows the marginal product of labor for each worker. With only one worker, the total output and the marginal product of labor are both 30, because the 30 loaves produced by that one worker are all the output there is. With two workers, the total output is 70, which is an increase of 40 loaves over the total output with one worker. So the second worker has a marginal product of 40. Likewise, for the 3rd, 4th, and 5th workers, the marginal product is the change in the total product when each worker is added.

DIMINISHING MARGINAL PRODUCT

We've seen that the second worker contributed more to total output than the first worker. That resulted from opportunities for specialization that existed with two workers doing different tasks but not with just one worker doing everything. As more workers are added to the bakery staff, however, there are fewer new opportunities for specialization and growing problems with congestion and redundancy. As mentioned, the size of the bakery and the number of ovens is fixed in the short run, so with more workers there is less work space for each worker, and at some point a line will form to use the ovens. For these reasons, as Table 8.1 shows, the marginal product of labor drops from 40 for the second worker to 35; 25, and 10 for the third, fourth, and fifth workers, respectively.

Hero Images/Getty Images

▲ A single worker who has to do everything is unlikely to get particularly good at any one task. As a few more workers are hired, the benefits of specialization may allow each to add more to output than the one before. Eventually, however, redundancy and congestion cause the contributions of additional workers to fall.

marginal product
The increase in output gained from an additional unit of an input, leaving the quantities of other inputs unchanged.

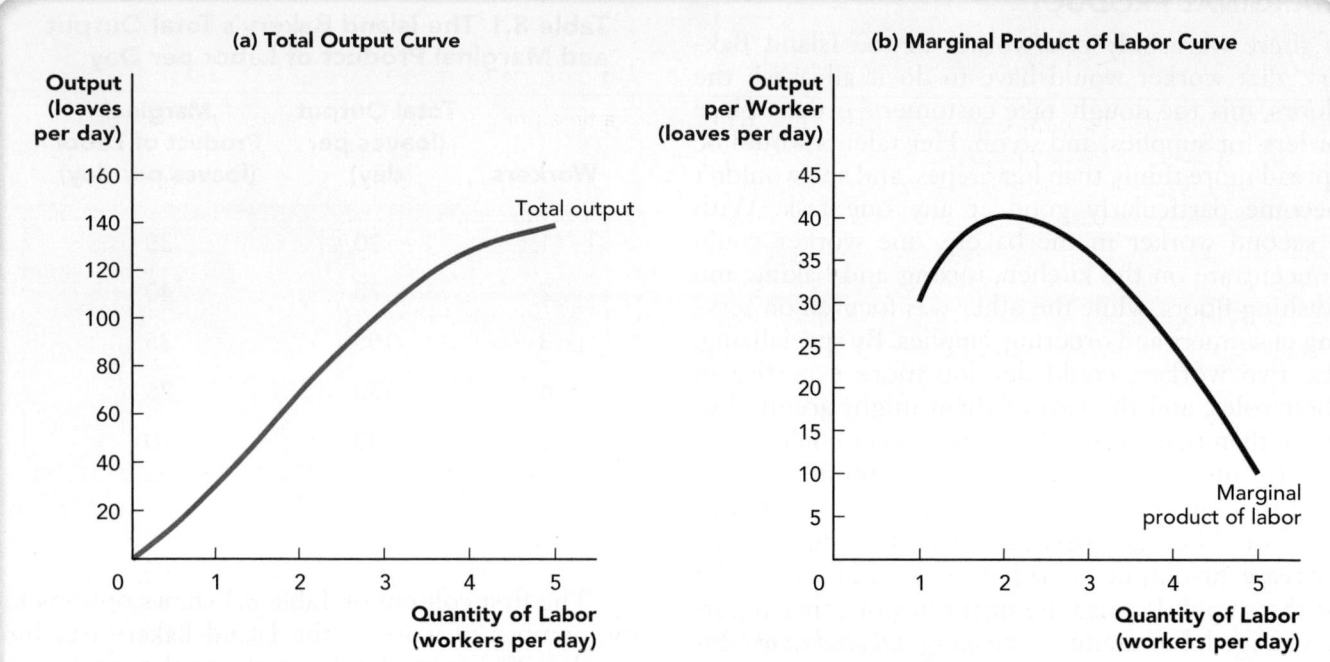

FIGURE 8.1 Island Bakery's Total Output and Marginal Product of Labor Curves
The marginal product of labor is the addition to total output made by each successive unit of labor. Even as the marginal product decreases, the total output increases as long as the marginal product is positive.

Figure 8.1 illustrates the information in Table 8.1. Panel (a) shows the total output for the first five workers at the Island Bakery. The total output increases for all five workers because the contribution of each worker is positive, even when it is smaller than the contribution of the previous worker. For instance, the fifth worker's marginal product of 10 units is smaller than the fourth worker's marginal product of 25 units, but these are both positive contributions that increase the total output. Only if a worker's marginal product were negative, perhaps because the worker got in the way and distracted other workers with jokes and idle conversation, would the total output decrease.

Panel (b) of Figure 8.1 shows the marginal product of the first five workers. Here we can clearly see the drop in the marginal product of labor that begins with the third worker. This drop is consistent with the **law of diminishing returns**, which states that as more of a variable input such as labor is added to a fixed input such as ovens, the marginal product of the variable input eventually declines. This is described as a "law" because the congestion and redundancy that occur as more workers are added to a bakery also occur in most other production settings. Just try adding more professors to a classroom or more bags of fertilizer to a garden—before long, the next one won't contribute as much to total output as the previous one.

law of diminishing returns
A "law" stating that as more of a variable input such as labor is added to a fixed input such as ovens, the marginal product of the variable input eventually declines.

Billy Hustace/Getty Images

▲ Even if too many bakers don't spoil the batter, they will certainly run out of things to do and get in each other's way. This causes the marginal product of labor to decrease.

Is it realistic to talk about buying fractions of units of inputs or goods?

In many cases it is possible to buy part of a unit of an input or a good. Workers don't have to be employed full-time. They can work half-time, overtime, or various other amounts of time. Rental companies offer similarly flexible options for the duration of rentals, making it possible for firms to rent buildings, equipment, or land for a fraction of a time period. Likewise, goods such as flour, gasoline, and cheese are infinitely divisible. Even bread can be purchased in many portion sizes. There's nothing better than a demi-baguette (a half loaf of French bread) with a fraction of a pound of sharp cheddar cheese. As discussed in Chapter 3, the divisibility of goods and inputs makes it appropriate to use smooth curves like the ones shown in this chapter to depict cost and productivity levels.

The Cost-Minimizing Combination of Inputs

Bread can be made using various combinations of capital and labor. At one extreme, bread can be made almost entirely with capital: Bread machines can mix, knead, and bake bread that goes untouched by human hands until it is eaten. At the other extreme, bread can be made almost entirely by hand. The cost-minimizing combination of inputs depends on the productivity of each input relative to its cost. The cost of a unit of labor is the **wage**. The cost of a unit of capital is the **rental rate** that must be paid each period to rent the building or equipment used for production. As discussed in the Island Bakery example, even if a firm owns its building or other capital,

the rental rate still applies: The rental rate is the opportunity cost of using capital, because if a firm didn't use its capital, it could rent it out to someone else.

In Chapter 7, you learned that consumers maximize their utility by getting as much as possible out of each dollar spent. Firms can minimize their costs the same way. Suppose the wage rate paid by the Island Bakery is $12.50 per hour. If hiring another hour of labor would increase the bakery's bread production by 25 loaves, then the marginal product of labor is 25, and you would receive $25 \div \$12.50 = 2$ loaves per dollar spent on another hour of labor.

The other option is to rent more capital, which in our story is represented by the ovens. Suppose the rental rate of ovens is $20 per hour. If renting an oven for another hour would increase the bakery's production by 50 loaves, then the marginal product of capital is 50, and you would receive $50 \div \$20 = 2.5$ loaves per dollar spent on capital. In this case, you should rent more ovens and hire less labor because capital's marginal product per dollar (2.5) exceeds labor's marginal product per dollar (2). Making this type of adjustment to get more output per dollar spent on inputs will decrease the cost of making any given amount of output. More generally, a firm can lower its cost by hiring more of the input with the highest marginal product per dollar and less of the input with the lowest marginal product per dollar.

Due to diminishing returns, the marginal product of capital will decrease as you use more capital, and the marginal product of labor will increase as you use less labor. Continue to adjust the quantities of each input until the marginal product per dollar spent on capital and labor is the same. You will then have the cost-minimizing combination of inputs. That is, the cost of producing any

▲ Bread can be made using many different combinations of capital and labor. For example, a bread machine can mix, knead, and bake a loaf of bread that human hands have never touched, or human hands can do almost all the work. To find the cost-minimizing combination of inputs, a firm should hire more of whichever input adds the most bread per dollar. This process continues until the desired quantity of bread can be made and each input adds the same amount of bread per buck.

Ken James/Bloomberg via Getty Images

wage
The cost of a unit of labor.

rental rate
The cost of a unit of capital.

amount of output is minimized when the marginal product per dollar spent on each input is the same, so the condition for cost minimization for a given output level is:

$$\frac{\text{marginal product of capital}}{\text{rental rate}} = \frac{\text{marginal product of labor}}{\text{wage}}$$

The same condition applies for any number of inputs. Notice that the trick to minimizing your costs as an entrepreneur is the same as the trick to maximizing your utility as a consumer: focus on getting the most bang per buck.

A Closer Look at Costs

Costs matter—a lot—to bakeries and to other firms. You've already seen that the supply curve is based on the cost of producing each unit, and that a firm's profit cannot be determined without having information on costs. Some firms decide to close their doors forever because the costs are too high relative to the prices they can charge for their products. This section sifts through the key ingredients of some critical types of costs and explains their relevance to firms.

FIXED COST AND VARIABLE COST

Suppose the Island Bakery is a smashing success and you frequently find yourself with a long line of bread customers. You will want to increase your production of bread, but remember that you have a fixed input—you can't change the number of ovens in the short run. The amount you spend on ovens therefore remains the same in the short run, regardless of the quantity of output, which makes the cost of ovens your *fixed cost*. That is, a firm's **fixed cost** is the cost of its fixed inputs.

To bake more bread in the short run, you will need to increase your use of variable inputs. For instance, you can hire more bakers, or have your existing bakers work more hours each day. That might not be the least expensive way to make more bread in the long run, but it will allow you to bake more bread with your existing ovens. If you increase your output in the short run by increasing your quantity of labor, your expenditure on labor is your *variable cost*. A firm's **variable cost** is the cost of all variable inputs, such as labor, the use of which is varied in the short run to change the quantity of output. A firm's **total cost** equals its fixed cost plus its variable cost:

$$\text{total cost} = \text{fixed cost} + \text{variable cost}$$

AVERAGE TOTAL COST

Once you know the Island Bakery's total cost, you can determine the cost, on average, of making a loaf of bread. This value, the **average total cost**, is found by dividing the firm's total cost by the quantity of output:

$$\text{average total cost} = \frac{\text{total cost}}{\text{quantity of output}}$$

For example, if it costs \$100 to make 40 loaves of bread, the average total cost is \$100 ÷ 40 = \$2.50. The average total cost is an important benchmark for a firm because if the average total cost of making a loaf of bread is below the price paid for the bread, the Island Bakery will earn a profit.

MARGINAL COST

You've learned that the marginal cost of making bread is the change in the firm's total cost when another loaf is made:

$$\text{marginal cost} = \frac{\text{change in the total cost}}{\text{change in the quantity of output}}$$

To better understand how marginal cost changes as more output is made, recall what happens to the marginal product of labor as more labor is hired. The marginal product of labor typically increases for the first few workers due to specialization, but then decreases due to redundancy and congestion. As the marginal product of labor increases, it takes less additional labor to produce another unit of output, so the marginal cost decreases. And as the marginal product of labor decreases, it takes a larger increase in the quantity of labor to produce another unit of output. This larger increase in the quantity of labor results in a larger increase in the total cost, so the marginal cost increases. Thus, the marginal cost decreases and increases as the marginal product of labor increases and decreases.

fixed cost
The cost of fixed inputs such as capital, the quantity of which cannot be varied in the short run.

variable cost
The cost of variable inputs such as labor, the quantity of which can be varied in the short run to change the quantity of output.

total cost
The fixed cost plus the variable cost.

average total cost
Total cost divided by the quantity of output.

Table 8.2 Love Loaves' Bread Production Costs

(1) Loaves	(2) Fixed Cost	(3) Variable Cost	(4) Total Cost	(5) Average Total Cost	(6) Marginal Cost
0	$10.00	$0.00	$10.00	—	—
1	10.00	8.20	18.20	$18.20	$8.20
2	10.00	12.20	22.20	11.10	4.00
3	10.00	13.70	23.70	7.90	1.50
4	10.00	14.80	24.80	6.20	1.10
5	10.00	16.80	26.80	5.36	2.00
6	10.00	20.00	30.00	5.00	3.20
7	10.00	25.00	35.00	5.00	5.00
8	10.00	32.80	42.80	5.35	7.80
9	10.00	44.00	54.00	6.00	11.20
10	10.00	59.00	69.00	6.90	15.00

SUMMARIZING COSTS WITH TABLES AND CURVES

Love Loaves, which operates out of a garden shed in Wolvercote, England, may be the smallest bakery in the world. We'll use the small scale of Love Loaves to take a simplified look at some specific costs. Table 8.2 lists hypothetical costs for the first 10 loaves of bread produced by Love Loaves in a day. The daily rental rate for Love Loaves' oven and shed is $10.00, so, as shown in the second column of the table, $10.00 is the firm's fixed cost regardless of the number of loaves produced.

The third column shows the variable cost of labor and ingredients. Unlike the fixed cost, the variable cost increases as more loaves are made because it takes more labor and ingredients to make more bread. The total cost in the fourth column is the sum of the fixed cost of $10.00 and the variable cost, which varies with the quantity of loaves. For instance, for two loaves, the variable cost is $12.20, so the total cost is $10.00 + $12.20 = $22.20. Here's a trick: A firm's total cost when the quantity of output is 0 tells you the firm's fixed cost, because the fixed cost is the only cost when no output is produced.

The fifth column shows the average total cost, which you just learned is the total cost divided by the quantity of output. The marginal cost for a particular unit, as shown in the last column, is the change in the total cost when that unit is made.

It is also the change in the variable cost when that unit is made. For instance, when the fifth unit is made, the total cost increases by $2.00 from $24.80 to $26.80. The variable cost also increases by $2.00 from $14.80 to $16.80. So the marginal cost of the fifth unit is $2.00.

Figure 8.2 shows the total cost curve, the variable cost curve, and the fixed cost curve for Love Loaves. The fixed cost curve has a constant height of $10.00 because that is what Love Loaves must pay to rent its oven and building in the short run, regardless of how many loaves the firm produces. The variable cost curve rises as more money is spent on labor and ingredients to make more bread. The total cost curve has the height of the fixed cost curve plus the height of the variable cost curve. Because the difference between the total cost curve and the variable cost curve is always the fixed cost of $10.00, these two curves are separated by that amount for every quantity.

Figure 8.3 shows the marginal cost curve and the average total cost curve for Love Loaves. The marginal cost curve crosses the average total cost curve at the lowest point on the average total cost curve. To see why, think about what happens to your average quiz grade after you take one more quiz. If the grade on the additional quiz is below your average, your average decreases. If your grade on the additional quiz is above your average, your average rises.

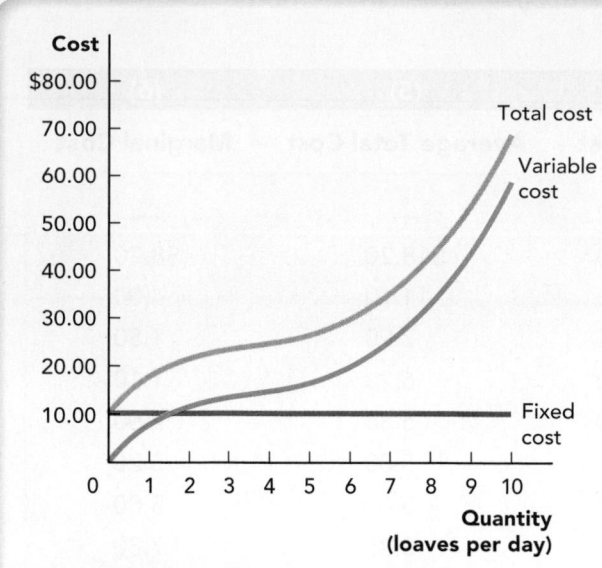

FIGURE 8.2 Love Loaves' Total Cost, Variable Cost, and Fixed Cost Curves

The fixed cost curve remains at a height of $10 because the fixed cost stays the same for every quantity. As the firm spends more on labor and other variable inputs to make more output, the variable cost curve rises. The total cost curve has the height of the fixed cost curve and the variable cost curve combined.

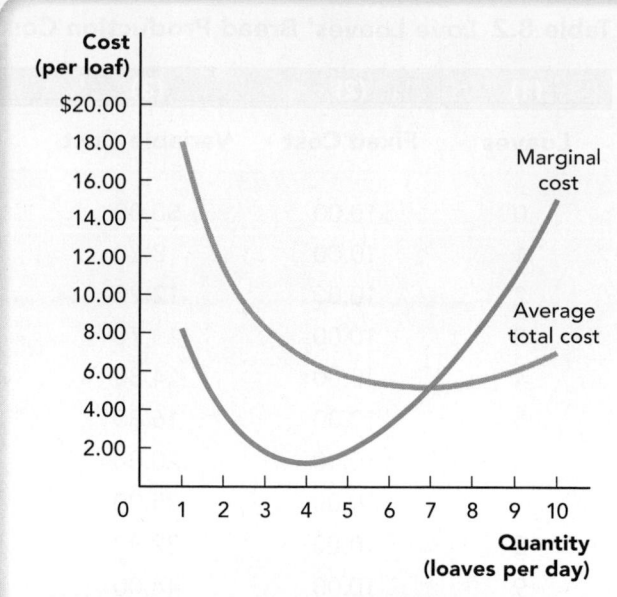

FIGURE 8.3 Love Loaves' Marginal Cost and Average Total Cost Curves

The average total cost curve always falls when the marginal cost curve is below it, and rises when the marginal cost curve is above it. The two curves intersect at the minimum point of the average total cost curve. At this point, the marginal cost goes from pulling down the average total cost to pulling it back up.

The same relationship holds for the marginal cost and average total cost. If the cost of one more unit—the marginal cost—is below the average total cost, the average total cost decreases. And if the marginal cost is above the average total cost, the average total cost rises. It follows that the marginal cost curve and the average total cost curve always intersect at the minimum point of the average total cost curve. This lowest point on the average total cost curve is where the marginal cost goes from pulling down the average total cost to pulling it back up.

You can see this relationship in Figure 8.3. The intersection of the two curves at a quantity of 7 shows where the marginal cost equals the average total cost. At quantities below 7, the average total cost decreases because the marginal cost is below it, pulling it down. At quantities above 7, the marginal cost pulls up the average total cost, just as a good quiz score pulls up your average score.

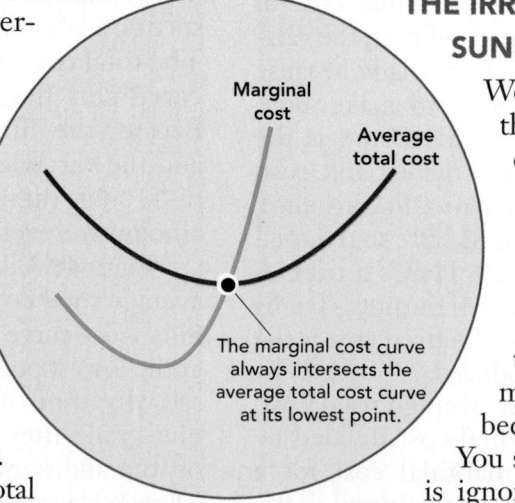

The marginal cost curve always intersects the average total cost curve at its lowest point.

THE IRRELEVANCE OF SUNK COSTS

We've seen several types of cost that matter a lot. There are also costs that should be ignored after they are incurred. Suppose you spent $10 on a loaf of great-looking cinnamon swirl bread, but by the time you got around to eating it, it was too stale to give you any enjoyment. Would you eat it anyway because you paid so much for it? You shouldn't! The best thing to do is ignore the expenditure completely

▲ Would you eat stale cinnamon swirl bread just because it was expensive? You shouldn't. The money you've already spent is a sunk cost that should be ignored.

▲ By making large quantities of bread, the Bimbo bakery group is able to spread some of its costs over millions of loaves of bread, thereby lowering its average total cost.

and pitch the bread. The $10 is a **sunk cost**, meaning it is already paid and you can't get it back. As you weigh the costs and benefits of a decision, only consider the costs that aren't sunk. Before buying a loaf of bread, the $10 isn't sunk, and you should buy the bread if it's worth at least $10 to you. After you own the bread, the additional cost of eating it is $0. If you'd get a penny or more worth of enjoyment out of it, eat it. If it gives you any displeasure, feed it to the dog.

Like consumers, firms should ignore sunk costs. Suppose that, as the owner of the Island Bakery, you spent $1,000 to recruit and train a new baker—but he turns out to be unreliable. If another baker is available who would do a better job, don't feel obligated to retain the unreliable baker just because you spent a lot of money on him. The costs of recruiting and training are sunk costs that you won't get back no matter what. Similarly, if you spend a lot of money developing a new product that doesn't appeal to customers, disregard the sunk development cost when deciding whether to discontinue the product.

Economies and Diseconomies of Scale

The Bimbo bakery group makes bread at a lower average total cost than Love Loaves does. How does Bimbo achieve a lower cost per unit? Part

of the difference involves the use of different ingredients. A lot of the difference comes from the cost advantages of producing large quantities. The Bimbo bakery group makes many millions of loaves of bread each year; Love Loaves makes a few thousand. Whenever an expense such as the cost of rent, insurance, administrative staff, or advertising can be spread across more units of output, the firm's average total cost decreases. In addition, large firms are often able to negotiate lower input prices from suppliers because the large firms purchase the products in bulk. Imagine the amount of flour purchased by Bimbo each year to make its $13 billion worth of bakery products!

Economies of scale exist when an increase in output results in a decrease in the average total cost a firm faces in the long run, which you'll recall is when all inputs can be varied. Figure 8.4 shows what the long-run average total cost for a bakery might look like. The downward slope of the curve for the first 10 million loaves indicates that economies of scale exist for quantities up to 10 million. Economies of scale eventually end for most firms—for this firm they end after the 10-millionth loaf. Sometimes economies of scale

sunk cost
A cost that has already been paid and cannot be recovered.

economies of scale
Economies that exist when an increase in output results in a decrease in the average total cost a firm faces in the long run.

end because a firm grows so large that it needs expensive new buildings and new levels of management. Growing firms also find it increasingly difficult to monitor the quality of their output and to motivate their employees to work hard.

Where economies of scale end, the firm has reached its **minimum efficient scale**, which is the smallest quantity at which the firm's long-run average total cost is minimized. In Figure 8.4, the long-run average total cost curve slopes upward immediately after reaching its minimum efficient scale of 10 million loaves. However, in some cases the long-run average total cost remains at its minimum over a range of output levels and then increases. The rising long-run average total cost indicates that as output increases, costs grow more than in proportion to output. When a firm's long-run average total cost rises with its output level, we say that the firm is experiencing **diseconomies of scale**.

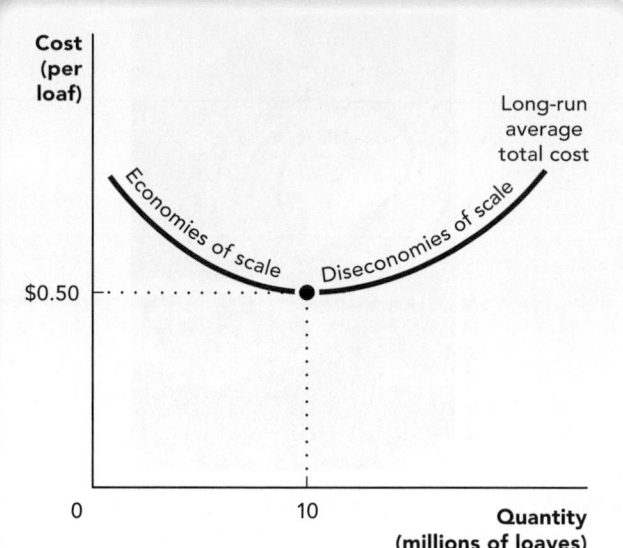

FIGURE 8.4 Economies and Diseconomies of Scale
Economies of scale exist if a firm's long-run average total cost decreases as output increases. This graph is for a hypothetical bakery that experiences economies of scale up to a quantity of 10 million loaves per year. After that point, the firm experiences diseconomies of scale.

SUMMARY

At the end of the day, bakery owners receive the satisfaction of a job well done and the profit they've earned on their cookies and buns. A firm's accounting profit is the difference between its total revenue and its total explicit cost—the cost of things like labor, flour, rent, and advertising that the firm actually pays money for. A firm's economic profit is the difference between its total revenue and its total cost. The firm's total cost includes both explicit costs and implicit costs, which are costs that aren't paid directly, such as the opportunity cost of using capital that could otherwise be rented to someone else.

A firm that wants to be around for a while must pay attention to the costs of inputs and the way the amount of output varies with the quantity of each input. The production function indicates the relationship between inputs and output. In the short run, the quantities of some inputs, such as a bakery's ovens, are fixed, and the costs of these inputs make up a firm's fixed cost. Other inputs can vary in quantity in the short run, such as bakers and flour. The costs of these inputs make up a firm's variable cost. In the long run, all inputs are variable.

As more of a variable input such as bakers is added to a fixed amount of space and ovens, congestion and redundancy eventually cause each new baker to contribute less than the previous baker. The result is diminishing returns, meaning that the marginal product of labor eventually decreases as more labor is hired. (There are diminishing returns from other inputs as well.) The total output, however, continues to rise even as the marginal product decreases. The exception would be if a firm were foolish enough to hire inputs with a negative marginal product. If another worker would have nothing to do and would hinder the work of others, then the marginal product of that worker would be negative and the total output would decrease if that worker were hired.

To minimize production costs, a firm should use more of whatever input increases output by the most per dollar spent, and use less of whatever input increases output the least per dollar spent, until the marginal product per dollar spent is equal for the two inputs. For example, if the number of additional loaves produced per dollar spent is higher for mixers than for baking trays, more mixers and fewer baking trays should be rented. As this shift in inputs occurs, the marginal product of mixers will decrease and the marginal product of baking trays will increase. The shift in inputs should stop when the marginal product per dollar spent on each input is equal, and there are sufficient inputs to produce the desired quantity of output.

The average total cost is the average cost of producing a unit of output, found by dividing the total cost by the quantity of output. A firm can earn profit if the average total cost is below the price of output. The average total cost falls when the cost of making one more unit—the marginal cost—is below it and rises when the marginal cost is above it. The average total cost curve and the marginal cost curve intersect at the lowest point on the average total cost curve.

No matter how much you've spent on something, if you can't return it and get your money back, its cost is sunk. You should ignore sunk costs when making decisions. Suppose you spent $6,000 on a used delivery truck for the Island Bakery and the truck subsequently stopped running. If the cost of repairing it is $1,200 and you'd only get $700 worth of additional use out of it, let the truck rust in peace.

Economies of scale exist when an increase in output results in a decrease in the average total cost in the long run. Economies of scale are achieved by spreading the cost of inputs such as rent and insurance over a growing quantity of output. Diseconomies of scale result when an increase in output causes an increase in the average total cost in the long run.

KEY TERMS

profit, p. 112
explicit costs, p. 112
accounting profit, p. 112
implicit costs, p. 113
economic profit, p. 113
production function, p. 114
long run, p. 114
short run, p. 114

fixed input, p. 114
variable input, p. 114
marginal product, p. 115
law of diminishing
   returns, p. 116
wage, p. 117
rental rate, p. 117
fixed cost, p. 118

variable cost, p. 118
total cost, p. 118
average total cost, p. 118
sunk cost, p. 121
economies of scale, p. 121
minimum efficient
   scale, p. 122
diseconomies of scale, p. 122

PROBLEMS FOR REVIEW

1. Identify at least 2 fixed inputs and 2 variable inputs in this picture.

wavebreakmedia/Shutterstock.com

2. Ben plays the bassoon in an orchestra for an annual salary of $60,000. He is considering the possibility of quitting his job as a musician and opening Ben's Bagel Shop instead. Ben estimates that the bagel shop would sell $190,000 worth of bagels per year and incur the following annual costs:

$70,000 for workers (other than himself)
$45,000 for ingredients
$15,000 for building rental
$5,000 for equipment rental

Assume that Ben's estimates are correct.

a. Calculate the annual accounting profit for Ben's Bagel Shop.
b. Calculate the annual economic profit for Ben's Bagel Shop.
c. If Ben's goal is to earn as much money as possible, should Ben open the bagel shop?

3. The following table provides information on the daily productivity of robots at the Island Bakery.

Robots	Marginal Product (loaves)	Total Output (loaves)
1	100	
2		220
3	110	
4		420
5	60	

a. Fill in the missing values for the marginal product of robots and the total output per day.
b. Draw the marginal product curve for robots.
c. Why does the marginal product of inputs such as robots eventually fall as more units are added?

4. The following table provides cost information for the first 5 loaves of bread produced by the Island Bakery. Fill in the missing values.

Loaves	Fixed Cost	Variable Cost	Total Cost	Average Total Cost	Marginal Cost
0	$25.00			$ ∞	—
1					$5.00
2					4.00
3					2.00
4					4.00
5					7.50

5. Use the information in the table from problem 4 to draw the marginal cost curve and the average total cost curve for the first 5 loaves made by the Island Bakery. If you were to continue these curves for larger quantities of loaves, what can you say about where the two curves would cross?

6. Suppose that, with your current use of inputs, the marginal product of labor is 100, the marginal product of capital is 12, the wage is $25, and the rental rate is $2. Could your firm lower its costs by adjusting the use of inputs? If so, how?

7. Suppose your family chooses to stay in an expensive hotel because it offers free breakfast. The next morning you notice a lovely bakery across the street that serves more appealing breakfasts. Your parents argue that the family should eat at the hotel because they have already spent so much to stay there. Explain what should and should not be considered when making this decision.

8. Is the following statement true or false? The marginal cost curve is downward sloping whenever the average total cost curve is downward sloping. Explain your answer.

9. Is the following statement true or false? Diseconomies of scale exist throughout the range of output for which the marginal cost is rising. Explain your answer.

10. Identify whether each of the following is an implicit cost or an explicit cost:
    a. The income you could earn if you weren't in college
    b. The money you pay for college tuition
    c. The money you could earn renting your car to someone else
    d. The taxes you pay when you buy food at a restaurant

11. Describe a real-life situation in which you have observed the diminishing marginal product of an input such as labor.

Perfect Competition

9

Chris Bennett/Farm Press

LEARNING OBJECTIVES

In this chapter, you will learn to:

1. Characterize a perfectly competitive market

2. Show how the entry and exit of firms affect profits in a perfectly competitive market

3. Explain how a firm decides whether to shut down its operations

4. Discuss the efficiency of perfectly competitive markets

Windfall Farms in California is one of about 18,600 cotton farms in the United States. When the farm's cotton is ready for market, owners Frank Williams and Mark Fickett don't spend a lot of time haggling over its selling price. Windfall Farms is a small part of the large cotton market, and the market price is established by a combination of the supply and the demand of thousands of sellers and buyers. When Williams and Fickett bring their harvest to a cotton merchant, the price they receive is established by those many buyers and sellers. The ample availability of competitors willing to sell at the market price prevents any one farmer from successfully charging a higher price. This is good for buyers, who pay lower prices as a result of the intense competition.

Why Should I Care?

Cotton accounts for 39 percent of the fibers used around the world to make fabric. It is probably in your clothing and bedding. It also makes up 75 percent of the paper money in your wallet. Like oil, which accounts for 37 percent of world energy use, cotton is a key commodity in international trade. But the differences between oil and cotton are, well, black and white. For one, there are only a few large oil companies, whereas cotton is grown on tens of thousands of farms in the United States and countless others overseas. The next chapter tells the story of the oil market, with its small number of large competitors. In this chapter, we dive into cotton and discuss the influence of its many competing producers. **You will discover how competition provides a check on the price of goods such as the food you eat and the cotton you're in contact with one way or another almost 24 hours a day.**

▲ Cotton dries us, clothes us, and wraps us as we sleep. It is competition that makes this comforting fabric so affordable.

How Competition Affects Markets

People have long heralded the virtues of competition among firms. Back in 1776, Scottish economist Adam Smith wrote that "the freer and more general the competition," the greater the benefits of markets. The U.S. Federal Trade Commission was established in 1914 to promote competition and it carries on that mission today. To see what all the fuss is about, consider what competition means to the cotton-jeans industry. To begin with, competition leads to higher-quality products. With competitors breathing down their necks, manufacturers toil to produce jeans that are stronger, softer, less likely to shrink, and more stylish. Competition also lowers prices. If one firm charged a price well above the average cost of making jeans, a competing firm would offer a lower price and capture the high-priced firm's share of the market.

Competition spurs innovation as well. In 1794, as the U.S. cotton industry was struggling to compete with cotton producers elsewhere, Eli Whitney invented the cotton gin, a machine that cut the cost of removing seeds from cotton fibers. With this invention, many once-struggling U.S. cotton farms began to prosper. Competition also leads to efficiency. In fact, the model of supply and demand that you've studied so far in this book—the one that results in firms producing every unit of output that provides a benefit at least as large as its cost—only applies to markets with lots of competition.

In the next chapter, you'll see that in monopolies and other types of markets that lack competition, the price rises and the quantity of output falls below the efficient level. Higher quality and quantity, more innovation and efficiency, and lower prices are the fruits of competition that so excited Adam Smith and others. Let's now unlock the secrets to competition—the goal of goals in the world of economics.

▲ Motivated by intense competition in the international cotton market, Eli Whitney invented the cotton gin in 1794.

Most economies have *market structures* with varying degrees of competition, as shown in Table 9.1. At one extreme are *monopolies*, with only one firm. As the only provider of long-distance passenger rail service in the United States, Amtrak is an example of a monopoly. A *duopoly* is a market dominated by two firms, such as Coke and Pepsi in the cola market. The oil market is an *oligopoly* because it is dominated by a small number of large firms. A *monopolistically competitive market* has many firms that sell products that

are similar but not identical, such as different types of fast food or clothing. This chapter focuses on *perfectly competitive markets*, which are at the opposite extreme from monopolies. A **perfectly competitive market** is one in which:

- There are many buyers and sellers
- Every firm sells the same standardized product
- Buyers and sellers have full information about the product and its price
- It is easy for firms to enter and exit the market

No market is perfectly competitive in every respect, but many markets come close to being perfectly competitive. Examples include the markets for agricultural goods such as wheat, carrots, and cotton; the markets for corporate stocks; and the markets for hot dogs and similar goods sold by street vendors. Let's examine the significance of each of the characteristics of perfect competition.

MANY BUYERS AND SELLERS

There's no magic number of firms that makes a market perfectly competitive, but let's consider the effect of growth in the number of firms with an example from childhood. As a kid you

> **perfectly competitive market**
> A market in which (1) there are many buyers and sellers; (2) every firm sells the same standardized product; (3) buyers and sellers have full information about the product and its price; and (4) it is easy for firms to enter and exit the market.

Table 9.1 Market Structures

Perfect Competition (cotton)	Monopolistic Competition (fast food)	Oligopoly (oil)	Duopoly (cola)	Monopoly (passenger rail)
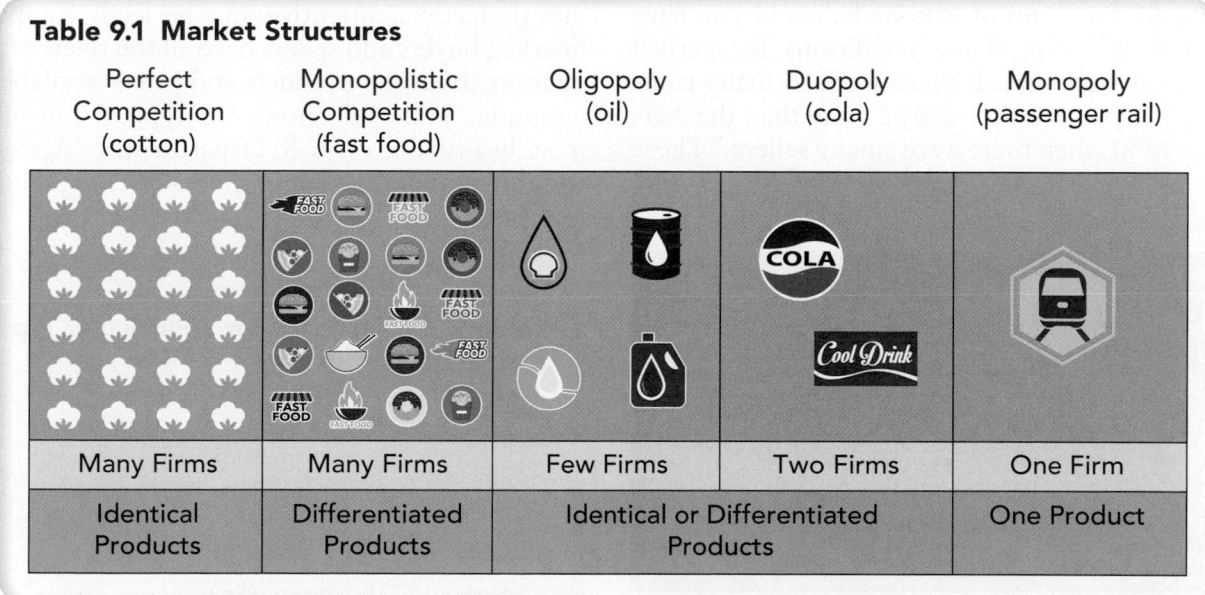				
Many Firms	Many Firms	Few Firms	Two Firms	One Firm
Identical Products	Differentiated Products	Identical or Differentiated Products		One Product

▲ Perhaps you experienced competition as a young entrepreneur selling lemonade. If the kids across the street charged less for their lemonade, you were forced to drop your price.

might have set up a lemonade stand at the end of your driveway. Suppose your average total cost per cup of lemonade was $1 and you sold each cup for $2, for an average profit of $1 per cup. As the only lemonade seller around on a hot day, you might have made some sales at that price. But what if the kid across the street had opened a lemonade stand and charged $1.50 per cup? You would have been out of business if you hadn't lowered your price.

Now suppose that even more kids in your neighborhood saw the profits being made in the lemonade business and opened stands of their own. Further undercutting would have sent the price plummeting toward $1. If every kid in the neighborhood were charging $1 for a cup of lemonade, could you have charged $1.05? Not if the conditions for perfect competition were met. If there were so many competitors that you couldn't charge more than the market price of $1, then there were "many sellers." There

▲ It takes a lot of farmers to feed a country, and a lot of farmers make for a lot of competition.

are many sellers of most agricultural crops, including corn, rice, wheat, and cotton. Having many sellers is a necessary condition for perfect competition, but that alone won't keep prices in check.

A STANDARDIZED PRODUCT

Now suppose you're charging $2 per cup of lemonade and the neighbor kids open their competing stands and charge $1.50 per cup. However, they are selling lemonade made from powder whereas your lemonade is fresh-squeezed. The product being sold is *not* standardized: Their powdered lemonade is not a perfect substitute for your fresh-squeezed lemonade. As a result, you might be able to keep selling your lemonade for $2. In a perfectly competitive market, the many firms sell identical products, so there is no reason to pay more to one firm than to another. In the cotton market, different grades and variations of cotton make the competition less than perfect. Nonetheless, the many sellers of common types of cotton allow the cotton market to closely approximate a perfectly competitive market.

FULL INFORMATION

What if you and a competitor were selling the same lemonade, but the competitor was located at the end of a cul-de-sac where only a few people knew to find her? As long as potential customers had incomplete information about her existence and her prices, you would have an easier time selling the same type of lemonade at a higher price. You might instead get away with selling inferior lemonade for the same price she charges. In those scenarios, the market is not perfectly competitive. In a perfectly competitive market, buyers and sellers have all the relevant information about the products and prices available. For example, Table 9.2 shows the type of information readily available on U.S. Department of Agriculture websites about the various grades of cotton and their prices.

Table 9.2 Daily Price for a Particular Type and Grade of Cotton

75.61

Average spot price in U.S. cents per pound for Upland cotton (color 41, leaf 4, staple 34)

As of: Thursday, February 1, 2018

Source: USDA Market News

EASY ENTRY AND EXIT FOR FIRMS

Remember when the kids in your neighborhood saw you making a profit in the lemonade market and opened their own stands? That was possible because it's easy to set up a lemonade stand. Then, as more kids entered the lemonade market, the price dropped. This example illustrates how the entry of new firms chasing profit moderates prices in perfectly competitive markets. The ability of competing firms to easily enter the market is critical to this process. Farming is a relatively easy business to enter on a small scale—seeds and soil are not terribly expensive and many people have gardens of their own. But imagine trying to enter the auto industry or the nuclear power industry. Because entry is far from easy in those industries, the markets for their products are far less competitive.

REALITY CHECK

In the real world, perfection is an ideal but seldom a reality. This applies to the notion of perfectly competitive markets as well. Although products made by thousands of firms are generally not identical, in many industries the products are very similar. Likewise, there are typically some imperfections in information and some costs for firms to enter or exit a market. Even so, the model of perfect competition is useful as a guide for what to expect when the imperfections of the competition in a market are minor.

A model that incorporated the many imperfections of most real markets would be complex and difficult to work with. Although the simplifications in the model of perfect competition are sometimes a stretch, a clear view of a simplified situation can be more instructive than an incomprehensible view of reality.

Prices and Profits in Perfectly Competitive Markets

Although a competitive market hosts thousands of firms, activity in the market can be studied with two graphs: one for the market as a whole and one for a representative firm that resembles each of the other firms in the market. In this section, we'll look at both types of graphs and see how they are connected.

FIRMS AS PRICE TAKERS

Cotton is produced across the American south, including in 59 of Alabama's 67 counties. When a farmer in Montgomery County, Alabama, wants to sell her cotton, she takes it to a cotton merchant such as Weil Brothers Cotton Incorporated, where she

Ashok Saxena/Alamy stock photo

▲ Firms in the competitive cotton market are price-takers: Rather than setting their own prices, the firms take the price established by supply and demand in the broader market for cotton.

will learn the going price for cotton that day. In a perfectly competitive market, the price is determined by the market's equilibrium, found at the intersection of the market supply curve and the market demand curve as shown in panel (a) of Figure 9.1.

Each individual farmer in the cotton market represents such a small part of that market that he or she can't influence the market price. Instead, each firm in a perfectly competitive market is a **price taker,** meaning that the firm takes the market equilibrium price as given. Suppose the equilibrium price is $1 per pound of cotton, as shown in Figure 9.1. Then the quantity demanded for $1 per pound equals the quantity supplied for that price. If one farmer tried to charge a bit more than $1 per pound, the buyer would refuse to pay the elevated price, knowing that many other farmers will sell their cotton for $1 per pound. There is also no reason for a farmer to sell cotton for less than the market price, because consumers buy every unit of cotton that farmers are willing to supply at the market price.

DEMAND AND MARGINAL REVENUE

Each firm in a perfectly competitive market can sell as much as it wants at the market equilibrium price, but can sell none at a higher price. Panel (b) of Figure 9.1 illustrates this situation with a demand curve for a representative cotton farm that is horizontal at the market price of $1. At prices above $1, the firm has no demand, so the demand curve does not appear anywhere above

> **price-taker**
> A firm that takes the market equilibrium price as given.

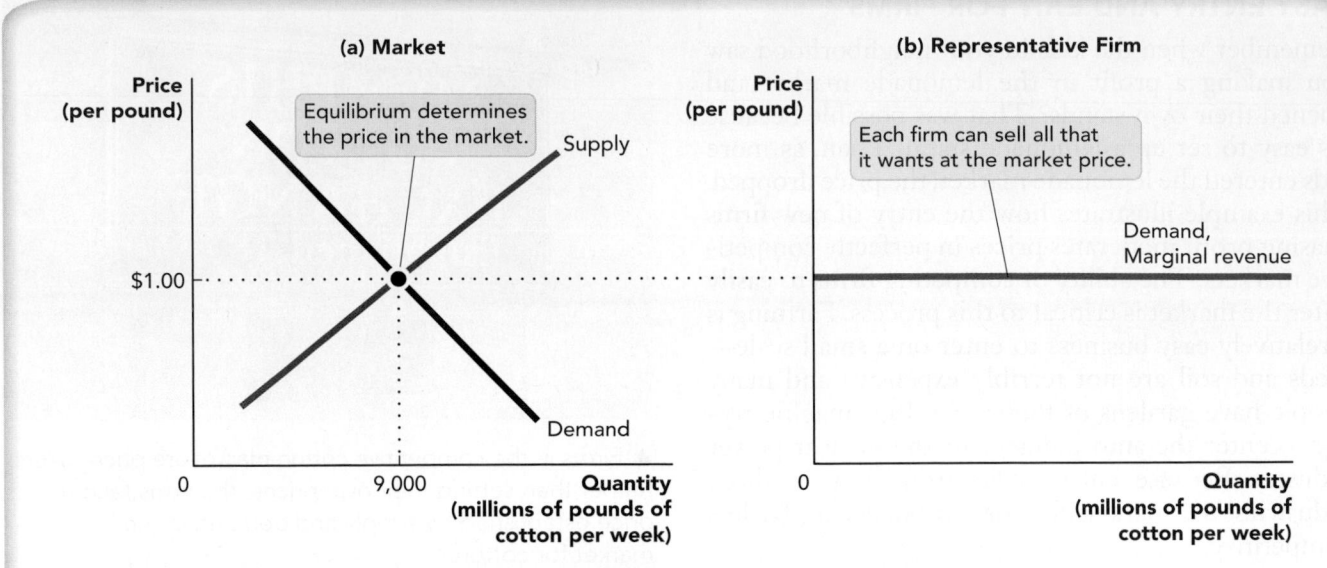

FIGURE 9.1 A Perfectly Competitive Market and a Representative Firm

As panel (a) shows, the price in a perfectly competitive market is established by the market equilibrium. Panel (b) shows that a firm in a perfectly competitive market can sell as much as it wants at the market equilibrium price, but none at a higher price. The firm's demand curve is therefore horizontal at the market price. Because each unit is sold for the market price of $1, that price is also the marginal revenue for each unit.

the height of $1. Although the firm could sell cotton for less than $1 per pound, it has no reason to because it can sell all that it wants for $1 per pound. That makes the demand below $1 irrelevant, so it is not drawn on the graph.

Because every pound of cotton is sold for $1, the additional revenue a farmer receives for selling another unit—the marginal revenue—is also $1 for each pound of cotton. Thus, the firm's marginal revenue curve for cotton is horizontal at $1 and coincides with the demand curve. When a market is not perfectly competitive, neither the demand curve nor the marginal revenue curve is horizontal, so don't think of horizontal lines as being the norm in all market structures.

Profit Maximization

Profit isn't everything. In Chapter 2, we discussed nonprofit firms that have goals other than profit. There are also for-profit firms that sacrifice profit for the prestige of serving a larger share of the market or for the pleasure of making the best product possible. In a perfectly competitive market, however, these alternative goals are improbable because no firm serves a large share of the market and all goods are identical. So we will assume that firms seek to maximize profit.

CHOOSING THE OPTIMAL QUANTITY OF OUTPUT

To find the quantity that brings in as much profit as possible, or minimizes losses, a firm should follow the same strategy that guides an individual's decisions about *how much* to buy, eat, sleep, or do anything else: Increase the quantity until the additional benefit of any more would fall below the additional cost.

For a firm deciding how much to produce, the additional benefit comes in the form of marginal revenue, and the additional cost is the marginal cost of making the good. So, the firm should produce more units until the marginal revenue from another unit would fall below the marginal cost. You'll find this profit-maximizing or loss-minimizing quantity where the marginal revenue equals the marginal cost. Since the marginal revenue for a perfectly competitive firm equals the price, we can also say that the optimal quantity is found where the price equals the marginal cost. The exception is when the firm is losing so much money that it should shut down completely to minimize its losses, an option discussed later in this chapter.

Figure 9.2 shows the marginal revenue and marginal cost curves for a cotton farm in a perfectly competitive market. For the first 600,000 pounds

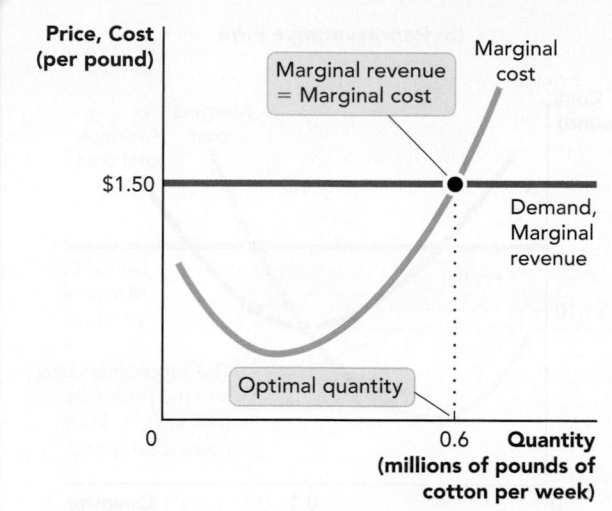

FIGURE 9.2 The Optimal Quantity of Output

A firm will maximize its profit or minimize its loss by producing the quantity at which the marginal revenue equals the marginal cost. The only exception is when a firm is losing so much money that it would be better off if it shut down completely.

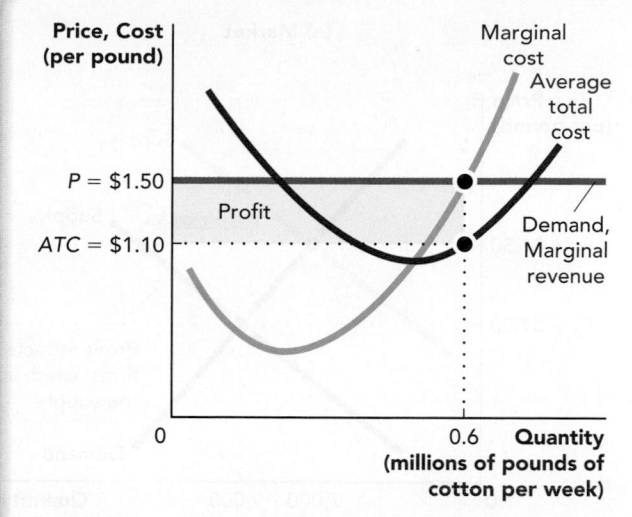

FIGURE 9.3 The Profit Rectangle

The firm's short-run profit is shown by the green rectangle. Its width is the quantity sold and its height is the price minus the average total cost at the quantity sold.

of cotton, the price of $1.50 per pound exceeds the marginal cost of production. So the farm will add to its profit, or subtract from its loss, by producing each of the first 600,000 pounds of cotton. For example, if the 100,000th pound of cotton costs $0.80 to produce and sells for $1.50, that pound will add $0.70 to the farm's profit. However, each pound of cotton beyond the 600,000th pound costs more than the selling price of $1.50 to produce, so producing those units would subtract from the farm's profit, or add to its loss. For example, if the 700,000th pound costs $1.75 to produce and sells for $1.50, the farm would lose $0.25 on the sale of that pound. The farm should therefore produce 600,000 pounds of cotton and no more.

PROFIT OR LOSS IN THE SHORT RUN

We know how to find the optimal quantity of output, but what will the firm's profit or loss be? We can identify the profit or loss as a rectangle on a graph like Figure 9.2 if we add the average total cost curve. Figure 9.3 shows the profit for a cotton farm if the market price is $1.50. The width of the rectangle is the horizontal distance from 0 to the quantity sold. The height of the rectangle is the vertical distance between the average total cost curve at the quantity sold and the price.

Recall that the average total cost curve shows the average cost of producing each unit, depending on the quantity produced. Figure 9.3 shows that at the profit-maximizing quantity of 600,000 pounds of cotton, the average total cost per pound is $1.10. Because the price (*P*) of $1.50 exceeds the average total cost (*ATC*) of $1.10 at this level of output, the farmer earns a profit.

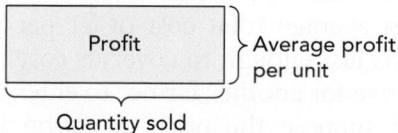

The profit rectangle's height—the price minus the average total cost—indicates the average profit per unit. So when the quantity produced is 600,000 pounds, the average profit per pound is $1.50 − $1.10 = $0.40. The area of the rectangle represents the profit from selling all 600,000 pounds. To find the amount of that profit, we simply multiply the rectangle's width (the quantity sold, 600,000), by its height (the average profit per unit of $0.40):

$$\text{profit} = \frac{600,000}{\text{pounds}} \times \frac{\$0.40 \text{ average}}{\text{profit per unit}} = \$240,000$$

Firms in a perfectly competitive market can earn profit in the short run. However, in the long run, new firms have time to enter the market in

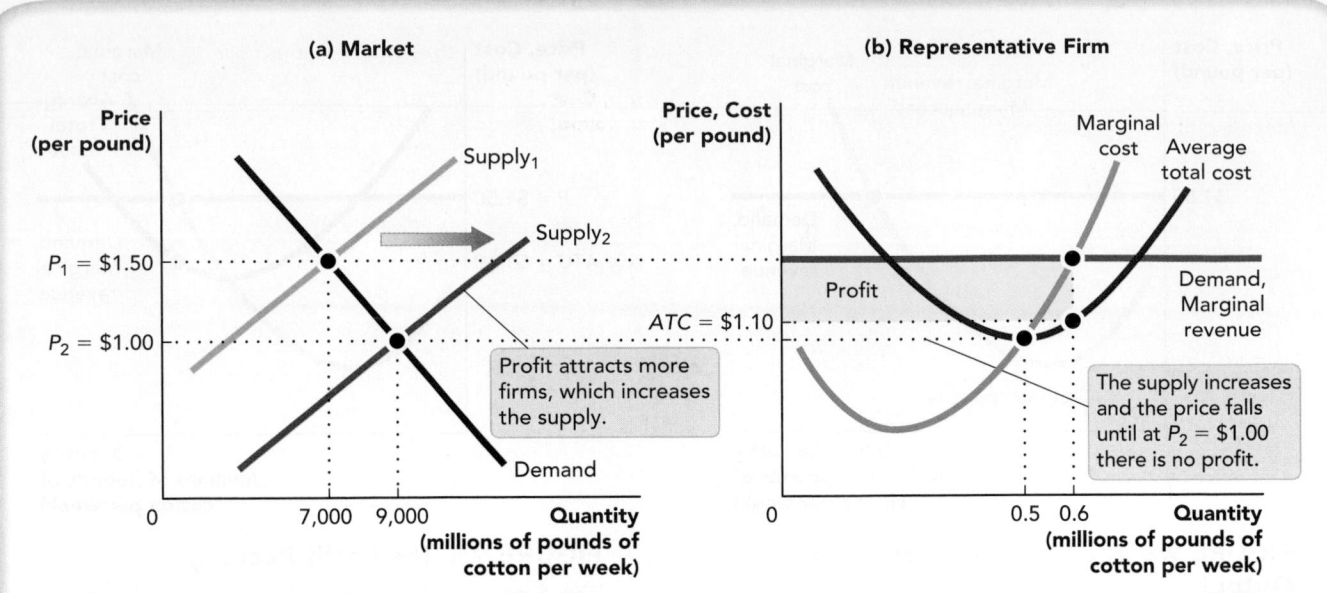

(a) Market

(b) Representative Firm

FIGURE 9.4 A Perfectly Competitive Market with Profit in the Short Run

If existing firms earn a profit, as shown in panel (b), new firms will enter the market seeking a share of the profit. The entry of new firms shifts the supply curve to the right, as shown in panel (a), and decreases the market price until the price equals the minimum average total cost of $1 and profit is eliminated.

pursuit of that profit. For example, profit in the cotton market—as shown in panel (b) of Figure 9.4—attracts more farmers who in turn grow more cotton. The increase in the number of cotton farms shifts the market supply curve for cotton to the right, as shown in panel (a), and reduces the market price. The number of farms grows until the lure of profit is eliminated. When the market price falls to the level of the farms' minimum average total cost of $1 per pound, each farm earns just enough to cover its costs, and there is no incentive for another farmer to enter the market.

Now, suppose the price of cotton is below the average total cost, as shown in Figure 9.5. In this case, the area of the rectangle in panel (b) represents the firm's loss. The height of the rectangle is the average loss per unit, and the width of the rectangle is the number of units sold. Suppose 400,000 (or 0.4 million) units are sold for $0.80 each, and the average total cost per unit at this quantity of output is $1.05. The width of the rectangle is 400,000 and the height of the rectangle is the average loss per unit, which is $1.05 − $0.80 = $0.25. The area of the rectangle is the firm's loss, which is 400,000 × $0.25 = $100,000.

If cotton farms experience large or persistent losses, some farms will shut down. The decrease in the number of

long-run equilibrium
A situation in which no firm has an incentive to enter or exit the market.

farms shifts the market supply curve to the left, as shown in panel (a) of Figure 9.5, and increases the market price of cotton. The exit of farms and the resulting rise in the price of cotton continues until the remaining farms no longer experience losses. When the market price rises to the level of the farm's minimum average total cost of $1 per pound, each farm can cover its costs and there is no incentive for additional farmers to leave the market.

LONG-RUN EQUILIBRIUM

You've seen that the existence of profits eventually draws more firms to enter a market, which drives the market price downward and lowers the profits of every firm. Conversely, the existence of losses causes some firms to exit a market over time, which raises the market price and lowers the losses of the remaining firms. In the long run, after firms have had time to come and go in response to market conditions, the profits and losses are eliminated.

Figure 9.6 shows the **long-run equilibrium**, in which no firm has an incentive to enter or exit the market because each firm earns zero profit. When the representative firm produces its optimal quantity of a half-million pounds in this long-run

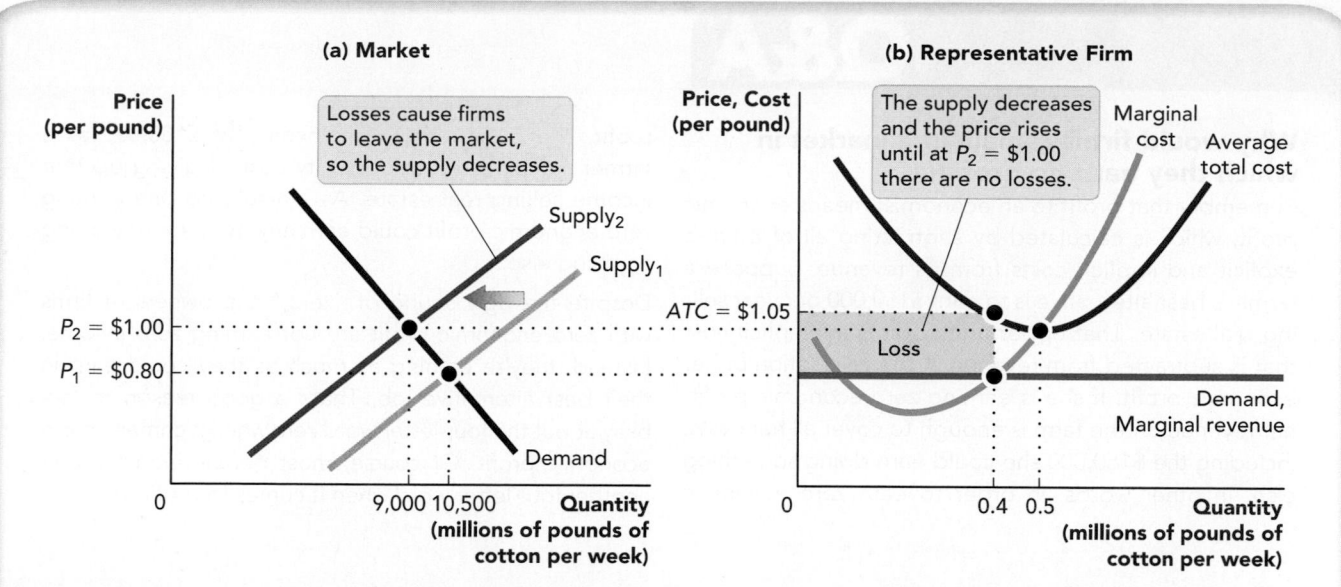

FIGURE 9.5 A Perfectly Competitive Market with Losses in the Short Run

If firms in a perfectly competitive market experience losses, some firms will exit the market. The exit of firms shifts the supply curve to the left and increases the market price until the price equals the minimum average total cost of $1 and the losses are eliminated.

equilibrium, the market price of $1 equals the firm's average total cost of $1, so the height of the profit or loss rectangle is 0. Mind you, this is zero *economic* profit, meaning that every associated explicit and implicit cost of the firm is covered. The Q&A box on the next page explains why firms find an economic profit of 0 to be acceptable.

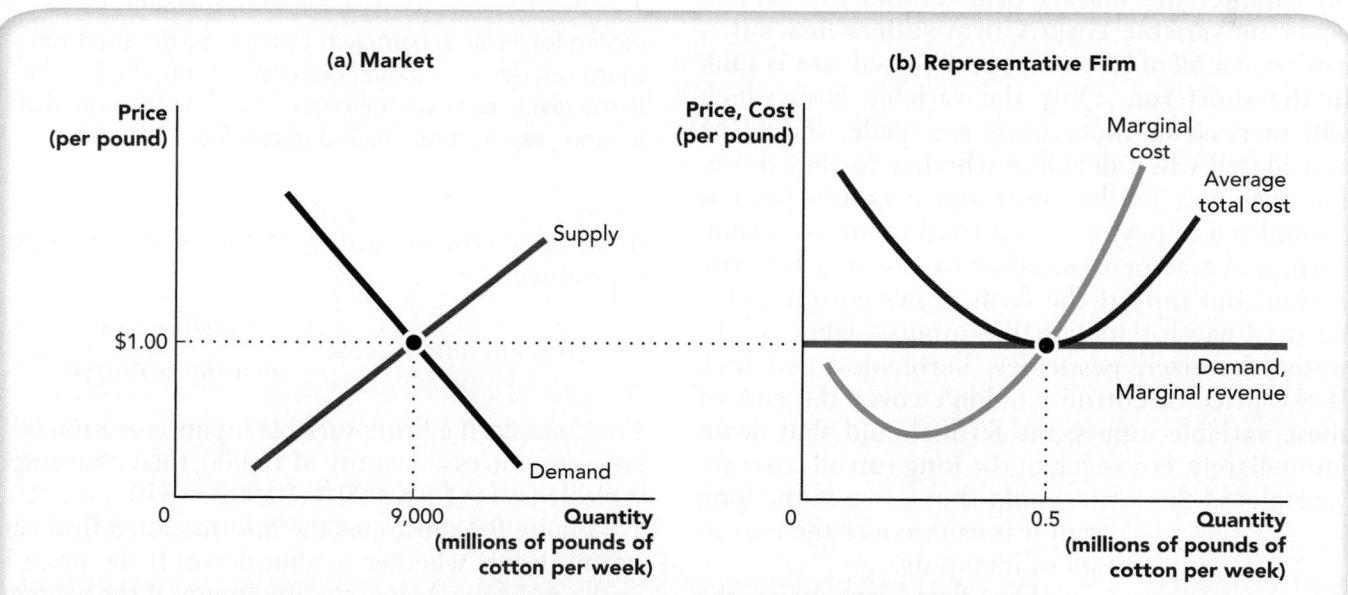

FIGURE 9.6 A Perfectly Competitive Market in Long-Run Equilibrium

As firms enter the market to seek profits, or exit the market to escape losses, a perfectly competitive market will eventually reach a long-run equilibrium that has firms earning zero profit.

Q&A

Why would firms remain in a market in which they earn no profit?

Remember that profit to an economist means *economic profit*, which is calculated by subtracting all of a firm's explicit and implicit costs from its revenue. Suppose a farmer's best alternative is to earn $150,000 per year selling real estate. That opportunity cost is an implicit cost that is subtracted from revenue in the calculation of her economic profit. If she is earning zero economic profit, her revenue on the farm is enough to cover all her costs, including the $150,000 she could earn doing something else. In other words, in order to earn zero economic profit, she must receive an income of $150,000 as a farmer to cover the opportunity cost of giving up that income selling real estate. As a result, no one earning zero economic profit could earn any more money doing anything else.

Despite the ugly sound of "zero," the owners of firms with zero economic profit are not earning zero income. Instead, they're earning as much as they could earn in their best alternative job. That's a good reason to feel okay about the four-letter word *zero* when it comes before economic profit. Of course, most people would prefer another four-letter word when it comes to profit: *more*.

> No one earning zero economic profit could earn any more money doing anything else.

The Shutdown Decision

To be or not to be in business? That is the question. The decision to shut down a firm hinges on whether the market price allows the firm to cover its variable cost. A firm suffers losses if it can't cover *all* of its costs, but the fixed cost is sunk in the short run. Only the variable cost, which will increase as more units are made, should be considered when deciding whether to shut down. For instance, in the short run a cotton farm is committed to paying for its fixed inputs—its land, barn, and tractors—whether or not it grows any cotton. But only if the farm grows cotton will it need to pay for its variable inputs—labor, seeds, water, fertilizer, pesticides, herbicides, and fuel. If the price of cotton wouldn't cover the cost of these variable inputs, the farm should shut down immediately. However, in the long run all costs are variable, so the farm should shut down in the long run if it can't cover the cost of *all* of its inputs.

The firm can make the shutdown decision simple by comparing the market price of its product to the *average variable cost* of producing it. The firm's **average variable cost** is

Chris Bennett/Farm Press

▲ In the short run, a cotton farm has committed to paying for its land, barn, and tractors. So the short-run shutdown decision should depend only on whether the farm's revenues cover the cost of its *variable* inputs such as labor, seeds, fertilizer, and tractor fuel.

average variable cost
A firm's variable cost divided by the quantity of its output.

its variable cost divided by the quantity of output it produces:

$$\text{average variable cost} = \frac{\text{variable cost}}{\text{quantity of output}}$$

For example, if a firm's variable inputs cost $100,000 and it produces a quantity of 10,000, then its average variable cost is $100,000 ÷ 10,000 = $10.

Figure 9.7 illustrates the information a firm can use to decide whether to shut down. If the price is in the red zone, below the minimum of the average variable cost curve at point *A*, the firm should shut down immediately. This is because the firm is receiving less revenue for each unit than it is spending on average for just the variable inputs; in other words, the firm is losing money on each and every unit. The

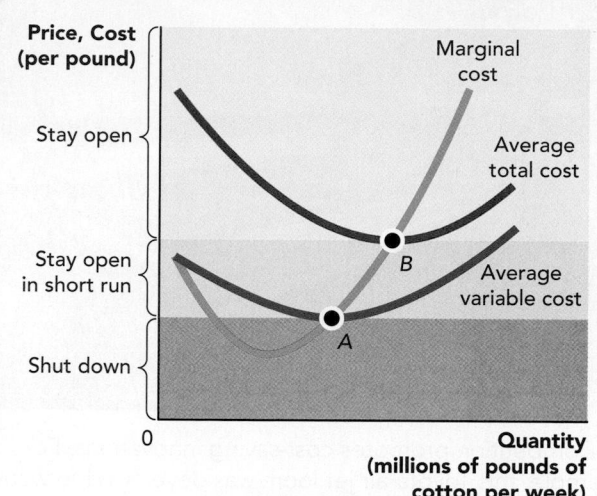

FIGURE 9.7 The Shutdown Decision

A firm should shut down immediately if the market price is in the red zone because the cost of the variable inputs needed to stay open exceeds the firm's revenue. If the market price is in the yellow zone, all the firm's variable cost is covered, along with some of its fixed cost. The firm should stay open in the short run to pay off some of its fixed cost rather than shutting down and covering none of the fixed cost. If the market price remains in the yellow zone in the long run, the firm should shut down. The firm should stay open if the market price is in the green zone because the firm will earn profit.

more units it produces, the more money it loses, so it is best for the firm to produce zero units.

Now suppose the price is in the yellow zone below the minimum of the average variable cost curve at point *B*, but above the minimum of the average variable cost curve at point *A*. In the yellow zone the firm is incurring losses, but the price exceeds the average variable cost. This means that the firm is able to cover its entire variable cost as well as some of its fixed cost. It is better to stay open and cover some of the fixed cost than to shut down and cover none of the fixed cost. Thus, the firm should stay open in the short run.

However, if the price remains in the yellow zone in the long run, the firm should shut down. The decision is different in the long run because only then can the firm get out of costs that are fixed in the short run, such as rental agreements for buildings and equipment, and eliminate its losses. If the price is in the green zone above the minimum of the average total cost curve at point *B*, the firm is making profit and should stay open both in the short run and in the long run.

What if the price is *exactly* equal to the average variable cost in the short run? In that case, the firm is indifferent between staying open and shutting down,

so it might as well use a coin-flip to make the decision. The firm is covering all of its variable cost, so it doesn't lose more money by staying open. But the firm is covering none of its fixed cost, so it isn't chipping away at that cost by being open. In reality, the firm's decision would probably rest on expectations about whether the price will increase or decrease in the near future. In economic analysis, the general convention is to assume that the firm will operate in the short run when the price equals the average variable cost. Likewise, we assume that the firm will operate in the long run when the price equals the average total cost.

THE FIRM'S SUPPLY CURVE

Knowing how a firm chooses what quantity to supply, and how it decides when to operate and when to shut down, we can identify the firm's supply curve. In the green zone, where the market price exceeds the minimum of the average total cost, the firm will produce in the short run and in the long run. The profit-maximizing quantity is found where the market price equals the marginal cost, so the firm's supply curve coincides with the marginal cost curve, as shown by the solid red line in the green zone of Figure 9.8.

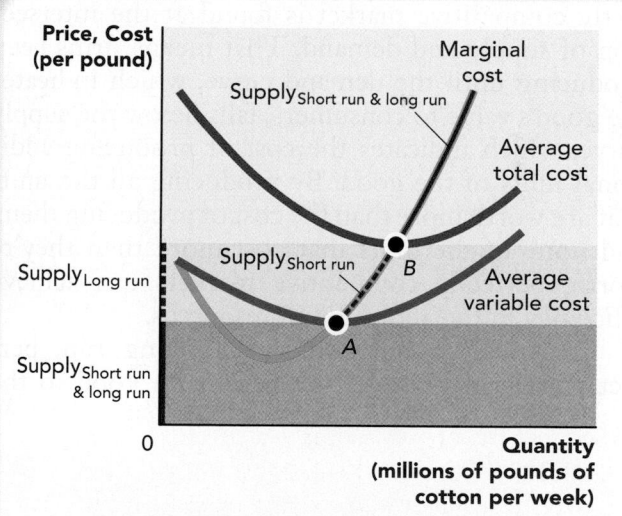

FIGURE 9.8 The Firm's Supply Curve

If the market price is in the green zone, the firm sells the quantity at which the price equals the marginal cost, so the firm's supply curve is the marginal cost curve. If the market price is in the yellow zone, the firm will operate in the short run but not in the long run, so the firm's supply curve is the marginal cost curve in the short run and the vertical axis (where the quantity is 0) in the long run. If the market price is in the red zone, the firm will shut down immediately, so the firm's supply curve coincides with the vertical axis both in the short run and in the long run.

In the yellow zone, where the market price exceeds the minimum of the average variable cost but not the minimum of the average total cost, supply differs in the short run and in the long run. The firm will operate in the yellow zone in the short run. This allows the firm to cover all of its variable cost and some of its fixed cost. Because the loss-minimizing quantity is found where the market price equals the marginal cost, the short-run supply curve in the yellow zone is the marginal cost curve, as shown in Figure 9.8 by the dashed red line labeled "Supply$_{Short\ run}$." In the long run, the firm will not operate in the yellow zone, so the firm's long-run supply curve is the red dashed line along the vertical axis where the quantity is 0.

We know that the firm will not operate in the red zone in Figure 9.8, where considerable losses result from a market price below the minimum of the average variable cost. Since the quantity supplied is 0 in that price range, the short-run and long-run supply curve in the red zone is illustrated by the solid red line along the vertical axis where the quantity is 0.

The Efficiency of Perfect Competition

You've learned that the quantity of output in a perfectly competitive market is found at the intersection of supply and demand. That means firms keep producing until the demand curve, which indicates the good's value to consumers, falls below the supply curve, which indicates the cost of producing additional units of the good. By producing all the units that are worth more than the cost of producing them, and none of the units that cost more than they're worth, perfectly competitive markets can achieve efficiency in the allocation of resources.

You've also seen that, in the long run, perfect competition drives the price of a good to the

▲ Competition promotes cost-saving innovations. For example, this Toyota air jet loom was developed to weave "the highest quality fabric at the lowest possible cost."

Steve Vidler/Newscom/Photoshot Images

minimum average total cost of producing the good. Firms that don't employ the inputs and methods that minimize their production costs are driven out of business by firms that can charge lower prices and attract more customers because they do minimize their costs. These incentives for cost minimization help firms in perfectly competitive markets achieve efficiency in production.

Motivated by competition, innovations such as the cotton gin, air jet looms, and biological enzymes for low-cost denim abrasion have lowered the cost of producing cotton clothing. The lower costs associated with new production processes allow some firms to earn profit, at least in the short run. In the long run, competitors may be able to replicate the cost-saving processes. However, if a firm can use patents, control over resources, or other barriers to prevent competitors from adopting the superior methods, the firm can establish a monopoly and earn profit even in the long run, as explained in the next chapter.

SUMMARY

A perfectly competitive market is characterized by many buyers and sellers, a standardized product, full information about the product and its price, and easy entry and exit by firms. Competition is cherished by consumers because it keeps prices in check and motivates producers to improve the quality of their goods and services.

The firms in a perfectly competitive market are so small relative to the market that they cannot independently influence the market price. Instead, they are price-takers, meaning that they take the market equilibrium price as given. Each firm can sell all the output it wants at the market price, but it will lose its customers to competing firms if it tries to raise its price. This makes the demand curve for a firm horizontal at the market price. Since every unit is sold for the same price, that price is also the marginal revenue for each unit.

If the market price is high enough for firms to earn a profit, more firms will enter the market. This increases the market supply and decreases the market price until all firms are earning zero profit. If the market price is low enough to cause firms to experience losses, some firms will exit the market. This decreases the market supply and increases the market price until all remaining firms are earning zero profit. Due to these responses to profits and losses, the long-run equilibrium in a perfectly competitive market has firms earning zero profit. It is acceptable for a firm to earn zero profit: Remember that the profit we are discussing is economic profit that takes into account opportunity costs, so no one earning zero economic profit could make more money doing anything else.

In the short run, the supply curve for a firm in a perfectly competitive market is the marginal cost curve above the minimum point of the average variable cost curve. Because its fixed cost is sunk in the short run, a firm will continue to operate in the short run despite losses as long as it is covering its variable cost. Anything earned in excess of the variable cost can go toward paying the firm's fixed cost. If the price is below the minimum average variable cost in the short run, the firm will shut down. Otherwise, it would lose money on every unit it produced, and the more units it produced, the more money it would lose. In the range of prices that causes the firm to shut down, the firm's supply curve lies along the vertical axis where the quantity is 0. In the long run, all inputs are variable, and the firm will shut down if the price is below the minimum of the average total cost curve.

Firms in a perfectly competitive market can achieve efficiency in allocation because they produce every unit that is worth more to consumers than the cost of production, and none of the units that cost more to produce than they are worth. Perfect competition also motivates firms to employ the inputs and methods that minimize their production costs for a given quantity of output, which in turn leads to efficiency in production. The next chapter explains why a lack of competition can cause inefficiency and raise the prices you pay at the store.

KEY TERMS

perfectly competitive market, p. 127

price-taker, p. 129

long-run equilibrium, p. 132

average variable cost, p. 134

PROBLEMS FOR REVIEW

1. Which of the following is *not* a characteristic of a perfectly competitive market?
   a. There are many buyers and sellers.
   b. The firms sell differentiated products.
   c. Firms are price-takers.
   d. Buyers and sellers have full information about the product and its price.
   e. It is easy for firms to enter and exit the market.

2. Assume that peaches are grown in a perfectly competitive market and that peach farms have cost curves that look like those in this chapter. Draw a graph for a peach farm that earns a profit. Label the axes, as well as the curves for demand, marginal revenue, average total cost, and marginal cost. Label the price of peaches "*P*" and the quantity of peaches the farm will produce "*Q*." Shade and label the farm's profit.

3. Suppose firms in a perfectly competitive market incur losses in the short run. Explain how this market will reach a long-run equilibrium. Illustrate your answer with side-by-side graphs of the market and a representative firm.

4. Suppose firms in a perfectly competitive market earn profits in the short run. Explain how this market will reach a long-run equilibrium. Illustrate your answer with side-by-side graphs of the market and a representative firm.

5. True, false, or uncertain: Unlike the marginal revenue curves for firms in other market structures, the marginal revenue curve for a perfectly competitive firm is horizontal. Explain your answer.

6. True, false, or uncertain: After some firms leave a market in which they were experiencing losses, the remaining firms will produce the same quantity of output as before the other firms left. Explain your answer using side-by-side graphs of the market and a representative firm.

7. Suppose Cotton Acres Farm earns revenue of $550,000 per year. Cotton Acres faces an annual variable cost of $300,000 and an annual fixed cost of $150,000. Is the cotton market in long-run equilibrium? How can you tell?

8. Suppose you start a peach farm and find yourself earning zero economic profit. Explain why that is not a good reason to shut the farm down.

9. True, false, or uncertain: A firm maximizes its profit by producing the quantity at which the marginal cost is as far below the price as possible. Explain your answer.

10. True, false, or uncertain: A firm will stay open in the short run even though it is incurring losses. Explain your answer.

11. What characteristics does the hamburger market in your area share with a perfectly competitive industry? What conditions for perfect competition does it violate?

12. Identify one example of a market not discussed in this chapter that closely resembles a perfectly competitive market.

Market Power

10

Dave Anderson

Perfect competition isn't the only game in town. There may be more cotton farms than you can shake a stick at, but you can count the number of U.S. sneaker producers on your toes. The same goes for producers of cars, cell phones, word processing software, steel, pharmaceuticals, and refrigerators. There are more than a few producers of oil, but a small number of large firms dominate the market. ExxonMobil and Chevron are the major players in the United States. At the international level, six of the ten largest companies in the world are oil companies. That makes for a lot of power in the energy business.

Why Should I Care?

Powerful sellers can drive prices higher and output levels lower. That makes it harder to be a buyer. If you've ever bought food at a ballpark or an airport, you've seen how prices are high when competitors are few. In some situations, a lack of competition works in consumers' favor. No pharmaceutical company would risk the hundreds of millions of dollars it takes to experiment with new cures if competition would quickly eliminate the reward of profit. And no one would want hundreds of electric companies building power plants and running their own sets of electrical wires throughout the same town. In this chapter, you will learn about market power and explore government policies that support market power when it is desirable. Chapter 12 explains policies that limit market power when it is undesirable.

▲ When competition is imperfect, one firm can charge more than another without losing all of its customers.

Sources of Market Power

There is no market power in a perfectly competitive market, with its many identical firms selling the same good or service. Recall that firms in a perfectly competitive market are price-takers—they can't sell anything if they charge more than the market price. In contrast, a firm has **market power** if it has influence over the price it charges. You've probably seen one gas station charge a higher price than another. A gas station that can charge a higher price has some market power, perhaps because its competitors can't match its services, reputation, or location. In this section, we take a closer look at this sort of imperfect competition and the sources of market power: legal barriers to entry, control of resources, strategic barriers, and economies of scale.

LEGAL BARRIERS TO ENTRY

Profit is an effective lure for producers. If society wants more of something that requires innovation—be it hip-hop music, cures for diseases, art, or computer operating systems—producers can be encouraged by opportunities for market power. The government provides firms with market power by granting patents, copyrights, and trademarks.

A **patent** is a grant of the right to be the only seller of an invention for a designated period of time. When a company holds a patent on an invention in the United States, competing firms are legally barred from selling the same good or service for 20 years. The availability of patent protection gives firms an incentive to innovate. ExxonMobil holds hundreds of patents on inventions, such as a paste that helps to disperse oil spills and surveying methods that help to reveal underground oil reservoirs. Pharmaceutical companies spend, on average, more than $1 billion to develop and test each successful new drug. Expenditures of that magnitude would not be made if patents did not make profits possible by protecting the developers of new products from competition for a period of time.

A **copyright** gives the creator of an original work the exclusive right to sell that work. Songs, writings, artwork, software, architecture, movies, and photographs are all examples of works protected

---

market power
A firm's ability to influence the price consumers pay for its good.

patent
A grant of the right to be the only seller of an invention for a designated period of time.

copyright
A legal right given to the creator of an original work to be the only seller of that work.

by copyrights. Copyrights generally last for the creator's lifetime plus 70 years. This means that if you take the time to author a great smartphone app or novel, you are rewarded with market power because others cannot legally copy it and sell it without your permission for a very long time.

A **trademark** is a word, phrase, symbol, or design that distinguishes the products of one firm from those of its competitors. The registration of a trademark with the U.S. Patent and Trademark office can provide exclusive rights for an unlimited period of time, although paperwork updates are required. The Starbucks mermaid logo and the stitching on the back pocket of Levi's jeans are examples of trademarks.

The owners of trademarks guard them closely. Unless you work at McDonald's, don't even think about beginning the name of a product with "Mc." Smokes R Us and Adults R Us are among the business startups that have tried unsuccessfully to use the "'R' Us" trademark owned by Toys 'R' Us. After Toys 'R' Us decided to close its stores in 2018, online retailers circled like vultures, waiting to jump at the opportunity to buy the familiar Toys 'R' Us trademark and the market power it conveyed.

▲ Under Armour owns the exclusive rights to its logo, which distinguishes its sportswear from competing products.

CONTROL OF RESOURCES

Exclusive control of a productive resource also conveys market power. The Organization of Petroleum Exporting Countries (OPEC) controls most of the world's most abundant oil reserves, which enables the organization to influence prices in the oil market. Justin Bieber has market power as well, because he controls the unique and valuable human resource that is himself. The rechargeable battery in your cell phone is made of lithium, the world supply of which is largely controlled by four providers. One of them, a mining company known as SQM, holds the rights to extract lithium from an ancient lake bed in Chile that holds more than one-quarter of the world's known lithium supply.

STRATEGIC BARRIERS

Market power can come from firms' illegal strategies to limit competition from their rivals. In 1909, the U.S. Department of Justice sued the Standard Oil Company for unfair methods of competition, including "local price cutting at the points where necessary to suppress competition, . . . espionage of the business of competitors, [and] the operation of bogus independent companies [that give the false appearance of competition]." More recently, Walmart and other major U.S. retailers have been accused of *predatory pricing*—the practice of temporarily lowering prices below the firm's own costs to drive competitors out of business. And the radio giant Clear Channel was accused of trying to monopolize the concert industry by threatening to only play music by bands that signed up with its concert promotion company, Live Nation. Chapter 12 discusses laws that prohibit practices such as these.

ECONOMIES OF SCALE

You learned in Chapter 8 that a firm experiences *economies of scale* if an increase in output causes a decrease in the average total cost in the long run. When economies of scale exist, a small number of large firms can produce at a lower cost per unit than a large number of small firms can. This is true for oil refineries because the roughly $500 million cost of building a refinery can only be justified if that cost can be spread across a large volume of output. As more gallons of oil are refined to produce gasoline, the cost of storage tanks, technicians, piping systems, and processing equipment is divided among more units of output, and the average total cost per gallon of gasoline decreases as a result.

In some markets, a consequence of economies of scale is that the optimal number of firms is one. Consider a firm that treats wastewater from homes and businesses so that the water can safely be released back into the environment. It costs tens of millions of dollars to build a water treatment plant and run water pipelines underground to homes and businesses. It would be prohibitively expensive for many water treatment plants to construct pipelines and compete for customers in the same small town. Yet a single water treatment plant can divide the high startup costs across such a large volume of output that the average total

trademark
A word, phrase, symbol, or design that distinguishes the products of one firm from those of its competitors.

Richard B. Levine/Avalon.red/Photoshot

Dave Anderson

▲ Perfect competition isn't feasible in the oil-refinery market. Due to economies of scale, the average total cost per gallon of gasoline is much lower if there are just a few large refineries in the market.

cost becomes affordable. High startup costs and the economies of scale that result are characteristic of a **natural monopoly,** a market in which the long-run average total cost for a single firm decreases for every increase in output the market could reasonably desire.

Once there is one water treatment plant, one bus company, one telephone company, one power company, one hospital, or one high school in a small town, competitors are unlikely to enter because there are too few customers to support two firms with high startup costs. The laws that restrict market power are relaxed for natural monopolies so that firms can take advantage of the critical economies of scale. To prevent firms from taking advantage of their market power and charging unduly high prices, governments often require natural monopolies to charge prices that approximate their average total costs. That way they don't lose money, but they don't earn economic profit either. The next section explains the characteristics of monopolies formed by any of the sources of market power we have discussed.

natural monopoly
A market in which the long-run average total cost for a single firm decreases for every increase in output the market could reasonably desire.

monopoly
A market with only one firm.

Monopolies

At the extreme of market power is a **monopoly**—a market with only one firm. The sole firm in a monopoly is called a *monopolist.* Customers can't switch to a competitor if a monopolist raises its price. Yet a monopolist

must be careful not to set its price too high. After all, monopolies aren't exempt from the law of demand: As a product's price goes up, the quantity demanded by consumers goes down. Next, you will learn how monopolists find the profit-maximizing quantity and price and how economists identify the inefficiency that can result from market power.

A MONOPOLIST'S PROFIT-MAXIMIZING QUANTITY AND PRICE

Jerry's is the only gas station in Caliente, Nevada. The gasoline market in Caliente is an example of a *local monopoly,* because although other stations sell gasoline in distant cities, Jerry's is the only gas station serving the local market. As the only firm in the market, a monopolist faces the entire downward-sloping market demand curve. Figure 10.1 shows how the monopolists' demand curve differs from the demand curve faced by a firm in a perfectly competitive market, and how the firm's revenue differs as a result. Panel (a) shows the horizontal demand curve for the perfectly competitive firm. Because the firm can sell as much as it wants at the market price, the additional revenue the firm receives for selling each unit—the marginal revenue—is simply the price. For example, suppose the firm begins at point *A*, selling 5 gallons of gasoline for $3.90 per gallon. The yellow rectangle represents the firm's total revenue of 5 × $3.90 = $19.50. If the firm decides to move to point *B* and sell 6 gallons for $3.90 per gallon, the firm's total revenue becomes 6 × $3.90 = $23.40. The firm's marginal revenue is $23.40 − $19.50 = $3.90, which is the price of the good, as shown by the green rectangle.

Panel (b) in Figure 10.1 shows the downward-sloping demand curve for Jerry's gas station. Starting at any point on a downward-sloping demand curve,

Andrew Palochko

▲ Monopolies are common in towns the size of Caliente, Nevada, because these towns are too small to support multiple gas stations, grocery stores, and beauty salons.

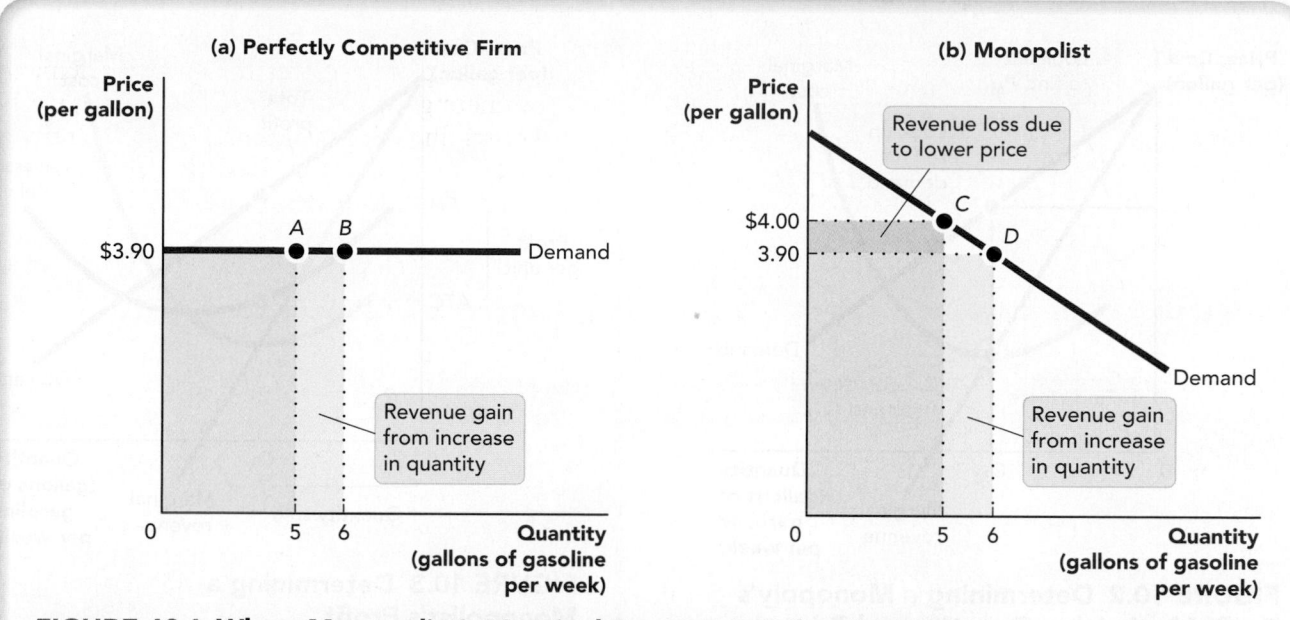

FIGURE 10.1 Why a Monopolist's Marginal Revenue Is Below Its Price
A perfectly competitive firm can sell as much as it wants at the market price, so the marginal revenue received from selling another unit equals the price. A monopolist must lower its price to sell more units, so the firm's marginal revenue is the new price minus the losses from lowering the price on units that could have been sold at a higher price.

the monopolist can sell more units only by lowering its price. So the additional revenue from selling another unit isn't simply the new, lower price that is received for that unit. The price cut causes the firm to receive less revenue from the sale of other units. As a result, the marginal revenue is the new price *minus* the decrease in revenue from units that could have been sold at a higher price.

Suppose Jerry's is operating at point C in Figure 10.1, panel (b), selling 5 gallons per week at a price of $4.00 per gallon. If Jerry's wants to sell another gallon, it must lower its price to $3.90 per gallon, as shown by point D. Jerry's receives $3.90 for the 6th gallon, as represented by the green rectangle. However, the marginal revenue is less than $3.90, because the $0.10 price drop causes Jerry's to lose $5 \times \$0.10 = \$0.50$ in revenue on the first 5 gallons it could have sold to customers at the higher price of $4.00 per gallon. The loss is shown by the orange rectangle in Figure 10.1, panel (b). The marginal revenue for the 11th gallon is therefore $\$3.90 - \$0.50 = \$3.40$.

You can also find the marginal revenue by calculating the change in the firm's total revenue when one more unit is sold. When Jerry's sells 5 units for $4.00, the total revenue is $5 \times \$4.00 = \$20.00$, as shown by the yellow and orange rectangles in panel (b)

of Figure 10.1. When Jerry's sells 6 units for $3.90, the total revenue is $6 \times \$3.90 = \$23.40$, as shown by the yellow and green rectangles. So the sale of the 6th unit increases Jerry's total revenue by $\$23.40 - \$20.00 = \$3.40$.

A monopolist's cost curves typically have the same general shape as those of perfectly competitive firms. Figure 10.2 shows the hypothetical marginal cost curve for Jerry's. Like every type of firm, a monopolist maximizes its profit (or minimizes its loss) by choosing the quantity that equates the firm's marginal revenue and marginal cost. In Figure 10.2, the monopolist's profit-maximizing quantity, Q_M, is found on the horizontal axis directly below the intersection of the firm's marginal revenue and marginal cost curves.

We have already seen that a monopolist's marginal revenue is less than its price. Since the price is found on the demand curve, it follows that the marginal revenue curve must lie below the demand curve. To be precise, when the demand curve is a straight line, the marginal revenue curve lies halfway between the demand curve and the vertical axis, as shown in Figure 10.2. Notice also that the marginal revenue curve eventually falls below the horizontal axis, indicating that the marginal revenue becomes negative. This occurs when the price at which

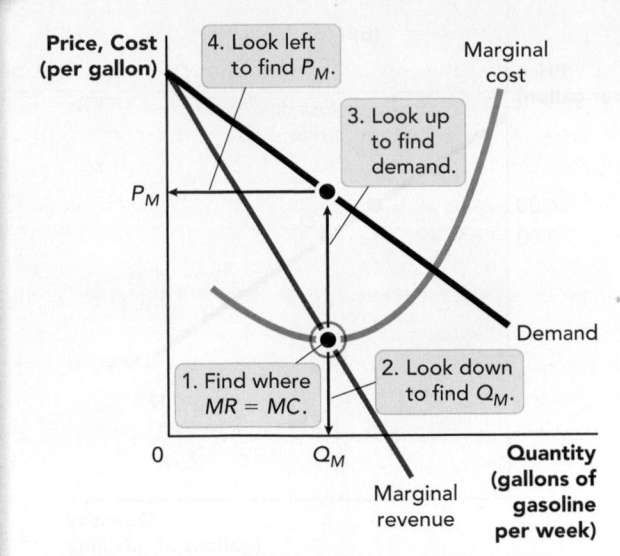

FIGURE 10.2 Determining a Monopoly's Profit-Maximizing Quantity and Price

Like every other type of firm, a monopolist finds its profit-maximizing quantity, Q_M, on the horizontal axis directly below the intersection of the marginal revenue (MR) curve and the marginal cost (MC) curve. The highest price the monopolist can charge for Q_M is found at the height of the demand curve above Q_M.

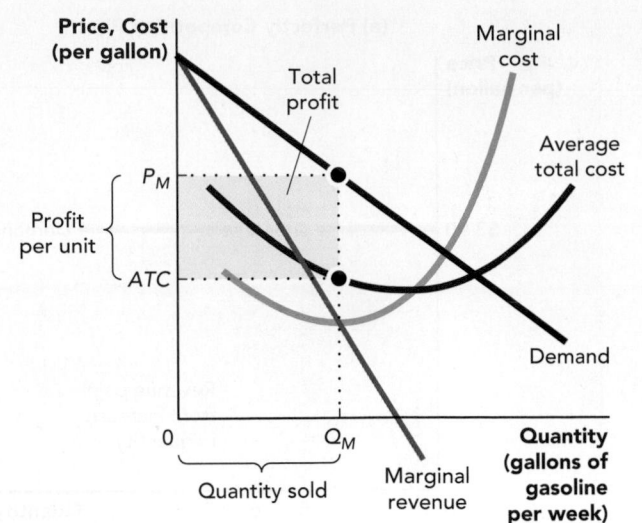

FIGURE 10.3 Determining a Monopolist's Profit

The monopolist's total profit is shown by the green rectangle. To find the total profit, first determine the profit per unit (indicated by the height of the rectangle) and then multiply it by the quantity sold (indicated by the width of the rectangle).

another unit can be sold is less than the loss from the price cut needed to sell another unit.

When selecting its price, the firm looks to the demand curve for guidance, because the height of the demand curve indicates the highest price the firm can charge for each particular quantity. To find the most it can charge for Q_M units, the monopolist can follow a line straight up from Q_M to the demand curve, and then left to the price axis. There we see that Q_M units can be sold for at most P_M. So to maximize its profit, Jerry's will sell Q_M units for a price of P_M.

How much profit does the monopolist make by selecting the profit-maximizing quantity and price? The answer depends on the firm's average total cost (ATC) per unit for this quantity of output. To find the total profit, first subtract the average total cost per unit from the price per unit, which gives you the profit per unit:

$$\text{profit per unit} = P_M - ATC$$

Second, multiply the profit per unit by the quantity sold:

$$\text{total profit} = \text{profit per unit} \times \text{quantity sold}$$

The green rectangle in Figure 10.3 shows the total profit earned by selling the profit-maximizing quantity

of output. We know this because the rectangle's height is the profit per unit and its width is the quantity of units sold, so the area of the rectangle—height × width—is equivalent to the formula for total profit.

EFFICIENCY AND MARKET POWER

The allocation of resources is efficient from a societal standpoint if each good is produced until the price (P) consumers are willing to pay for another unit equals the marginal cost (MC) of providing that unit:

At the efficient quantity for society, $P = MC$.

Unfortunately, the quantity that is best for society is not the quantity that maximizes profit for a monopolist. In Figure 10.4, Q_S is the efficient quantity for society. This quantity would be demanded if the price were P_S. The profit-maximizing quantity is Q_M. Because the demand curve is above the marginal cost curve at Q_M, we know that consumers are willing to pay more for additional units than the cost of making them. So by restricting the quantity to Q_M and charging P_M, from the standpoint of society, the monopolist allocates too few resources to the production of the good:

For a monopoly, $P > MC$.

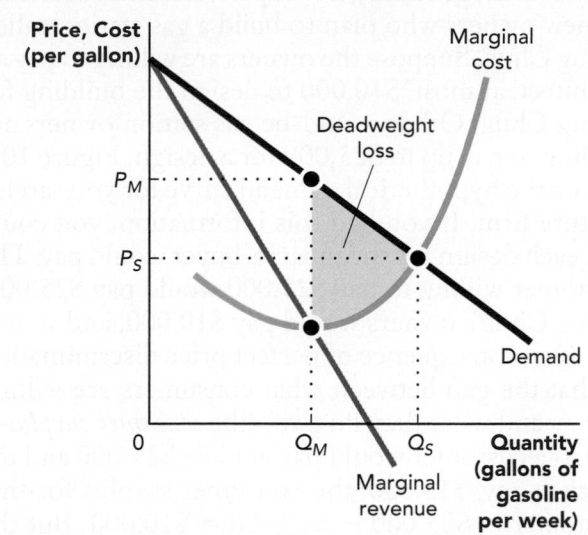

FIGURE 10.4 Deadweight Loss Caused by a Monopoly

Relative to a perfectly competitive market, a monopolist charges a higher price and sells less output than a perfectly competitive market with the same costs. By restricting the output to Q_M, the monopolist causes a deadweight loss for society. That loss is equal to the net gains that could be achieved if the socially optimal quantity, Q_S, were produced.

Recall from earlier chapters that economists use the term *deadweight loss* to describe the loss to society that results when resources aren't allocated efficiently. We can measure the deadweight loss caused when a monopolist produces less than the socially optimal quantity of output. If another gallon of gasoline would be worth $3.50 to consumers and could be produced for $2.50, society misses out on a net gain of $3.50 − $2.50 = $1.00 if that unit is not produced. Each unit provides a benefit shown by the height of the demand curve above that unit and comes at a cost shown by the height of the marginal cost curve above that unit. The units between Q_M and Q_S would be worth more to consumers than the cost of their production. So when a monopolist produces only Q_M, the shaded area that lies below the demand curve and above the marginal cost curve between Q_M and Q_S represents the resulting deadweight loss. Some monopolies do not create a deadweight loss, as we'll see next.

PRICE DISCRIMINATION

It is common for every customer to pay the same price when buying the same good from the same firm. At Jerry's, everyone pays the price per gallon posted on the big sign out front. But when a firm practices **price discrimination,** the same good is sold to different customers at different prices. If you've ever flown in a plane, it's very possible that the people sitting around you paid a different price for their tickets than you did. Colleges practice price discrimination by offering selected students scholarships or other types of discounts on their tuition. And when you receive a student discount on a movie ticket, the theater is practicing price discrimination.

With price discrimination, firms pursue higher profits by charging higher prices to those customers who are willing to pay the most. Many students and senior citizens have limited incomes, so higher movie ticket prices would cause them to buy disproportionately fewer tickets. In other words, customers in these price-sensitive groups typically exhibit a relatively elastic demand for movie tickets. Price discrimination allows firms to charge customers with inelastic demand a higher price without losing customers with elastic demand who will only pay a lower price.

To price-discriminate, a firm must be able to:

1. Influence the price rather than being a price-taker; that is, the firm must have some market power
2. Identify those customers whose demand is relatively elastic
3. Prevent the resale of the good from one group to another

Movie theaters can check IDs to verify whether a person is a student or a senior citizen, and can print color-coded tickets to prevent the resale of discounted tickets. Airlines have ways to price-discriminate between customers with varying price elasticities as well. The demand for tickets by business travelers is relatively inelastic because they must be in certain places at certain times for business meetings—and in most cases, their employers are paying for their tickets. Vacation travelers are more price-sensitive because they must pay for their own tickets and typically have many options for when, where, and how to travel. Conveniently for the airlines, business travelers tend to want to be home on weekends, and vacation travelers generally prefer to travel on weekends. So the airlines can earn more revenue from business travelers by charging higher prices for trips that don't include a Saturday-night stay.

Grocery stores price-discriminate by making coupons available in newspapers and on websites. Price-sensitive customers with an elastic demand for groceries will take the time to cut out or print the coupons and bring them to the store to receive lower prices. Customers who care less about grocery prices are less likely to

price discrimination
When the same good is sold to different customers at different prices.

bother with the coupons. So coupons allow grocery stores to sell the same goods at different prices to different customers who self-select themselves according to their elasticities of demand.

In the extreme case of **perfect price discrimination,** each customer is charged the highest price he or she is willing to pay. Suppose you're an architect who designs gas stations and you have market power because there aren't a lot of people with your knack for the proper placement of large gas pumps and small restrooms. Since you negotiate the price of a design separately with each customer, you can charge higher prices to customers with bigger budgets, if, that is, you can identify the big spenders. Sellers of big-ticket items such as cars and homes sometimes do this by asking customers questions about their jobs, neighborhoods, previous purchases, and—to be more direct—budgets. When you buy a car, you're likely to hear the question, "How much would you like to spend?" Of course, you'd *like* to spend zero. What the salesperson is really trying to ask is, "What is the most you're willing to pay?"

True story: Like Caliente, the town of Chugwater, Wyoming, used to have just one gas station: Horton's Corner. After an SUV ran into Horton's Corner, a fire broke out and burned the gas station to the ground. The property has since been sold to new owners who plan to build a gas station called Chug Chug. Suppose the owners are willing to pay an architect, at most, $10,000 to design the building for Chug Chug. Other would-be gas station owners are willing to pay up to $25,000 for a design. Figure 10.5 shows the hypothetical demand curve for your architecture firm. If you had this information, you could sell each design for the most its buyer would pay. The customer willing to pay $25,000 would pay $25,000, Chug Chug's owners would pay $10,000, and so on.

One consequence of perfect price discrimination is that the gap between what consumers are willing to pay and what they do pay—the *consumer surplus*—is 0. If a customer would pay at most $25,000 and the price is, say, $15,000, the consumer surplus for that customer is $25,000 − $15,000 = $10,000. But the same customer receives no consumer surplus if the price she must pay is $25,000.

Another repercussion of perfect price discrimination is that the price of each unit is equivalent to the marginal revenue for that unit. This is true because a perfect price discriminator doesn't need to lower the price of other units to sell more. When your architectural firm sells the 20th design for $15,000, it doesn't need to lower its price on the first 19 designs that command a higher price, so the marginal revenue from the 20th design is the entire price of $15,000. This has important implications. Earlier

perfect price discrimination
When each customer is charged the highest price he or she is willing to pay.

Q&A

How exactly do perfect price discriminators determine the highest price that customers are willing to pay? And how can a customer avoid paying too much?

When you go to negotiate the price of a good or service, it's wise not to wear expensive clothing or arrive in a fancy car. Sellers pick up clues about how much money you are willing and able to spend from what you wear and what you drive. They may ask probing questions about where you live and what you do for a living, and they typically inquire about how much you can afford. Your responses to these questions may help them zero in on the amount you're willing to pay, especially if you divulge information about your budget and your level of interest.

Your use of modern technology can be even more revealing. When you surf the web, shop online, swipe your loyalty cards, or make purchases with credit cards, you leave a trail of information that exposes your tastes and spending habits. Data sets holding that information, sometimes referred to as *big data*, make it easier for sellers to learn more about your willingness to pay, even if they've never met you.

The travel website Priceline.com uses yet another tactic: It asks buyers to identify the amounts they would be willing to pay for big-ticket items such as flights, cars, and vacation packages. Knowing what buyers would pay and what sellers would accept, Priceline.com makes it possible for sellers to collect high prices from big spenders while also accepting lower prices from customers with tight budgets—as long as the prices aren't too low.

When dealing with a seller who would like to price-discriminate, your best strategy is to appear to have a tight budget, even if you don't. Wear your oldest jeans and your cheapest watch to the negotiating table so that you don't look like someone with money to burn. If you're desperate for the product, let that be your secret. And if you must reply to a question about what you'd be willing to pay, reveal nothing but your best estimate of the lowest acceptable offer.

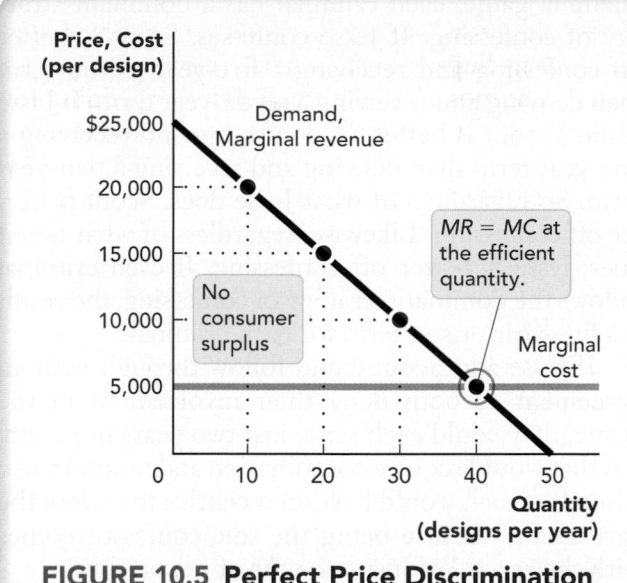

Price, Cost (per design)

Demand, Marginal revenue

MR = MC at the efficient quantity.

No consumer surplus

Marginal cost

Quantity (designs per year)

FIGURE 10.5 Perfect Price Discrimination

A firm that practices perfect price discrimination charges each customer the most that customer would be willing to pay. This eliminates consumer surplus but results in an efficient quantity of output.

rvlsoft/Alamy

▲ The market for cars is dominated by a small number of firms, which makes it an oligopoly. Each firm is large enough relative to the market to allow its business strategies to affect other firms. For example, if General Motors lowered its prices significantly, Ford would suffer a decrease in demand.

in this chapter, you learned that from the standpoint of society, resources are allocated efficiently if the *price* equals the marginal cost. Your firm maximizes its profit by producing the quantity at which the *marginal revenue* equals the marginal cost. But the marginal revenue *is* the price when your firm practices perfect price discrimination. So, when your marginal revenue equals your marginal cost of $5,000 at a quantity of 40 units, your price also equals your marginal cost. That is, you maximize your profit by producing the efficient quantity for society.

Oligopolies

In between the extremes of perfect competition and monopoly are two market structures that are more moderate and more common: *oligopoly* and *monopolistic competition*. An **oligopoly** is a market dominated by a small number of firms. The U.S. markets for cell phones, automobiles, textbooks, and movies are oligopolies, as is the market for gasoline in any mid-sized town. Each firm in an oligopoly is called an *oligopolist*. There is competition in an oligopoly, but not enough to prevent that firm from having some market power. For example, some oligopolists are able to charge more for cell phones than others because in the cell phone oligopoly, there are not hundreds of firms selling exactly the same product.

A **duopoly** is an oligopoly dominated by two firms, such as Microsoft and Apple in the market for computer operating systems, Coke and Pepsi in the cola market, and Airbus and Boeing in the airplane market.

GAMES OLIGOPOLISTS PLAY

Unlike perfectly competitive firms, oligopolists are interdependent, in that there are so few firms that the business strategies of each firm can affect the other firms. For instance, a successful advertising campaign by Delta Airlines can affect Southwest Airlines' ticket sales, and a price cut by ExxonMobil can hurt BP's gasoline sales. Economists analyze the strategies of oligopolists using the tools of **game theory,** which is the study of behavior among players whose decisions are interdependent.

The classic game of interdependence, the *prisoner's dilemma*, is described in the context of two criminals. The lessons learned from the prisoner's dilemma apply to law-abiding oligopolists and college students, too. Suppose two criminals, Jesse and Scout, have been apprehended after robbing a gas station. The evidence against them is weak. The police have

oligopoly
A market dominated by a small number of firms.

duopoly
An oligopoly dominated by two firms.

game theory
The study of behavior among players whose decisions are interdependent.

placed the criminals in separate interrogation rooms, where each must independently decide whether to confess to the crime or deny any involvement.

A *payoff matrix* shows all the possible outcomes for each player in a game, and how the outcome depends on each player's strategy. The payoff matrix in Figure 10.6 indicates the number of years Jesse and Scout will spend in prison, depending on each criminal's strategy to confess or deny participation in the robbery. The outcome lies in the left column of the payoff matrix if Jesse's strategy is to confess and in the right column if Jesse's strategy is to deny participation. Similarly, the outcome lies in the top row of the payoff matrix if Scout's strategy is to confess and in the bottom row if Scout's strategy is to deny participation.

Within each box, Scout's outcome is on the left in red and Jesse's outcome is on the right in blue. If both criminals confess, they will each spend five years in prison. If they both deny involvement, since the evidence is weak, they will each receive a relatively light prison term of two years. But if one confesses and the other denies, the confessor will receive a very light one-year sentence as gratitude for allowing the police to break the case. In contrast, the criminal who does not confess and is known to be a lying denier will spend a long seven years behind bars.

A player has a **dominant strategy** if the same strategy is best regardless of what the other player does. In the prisoner's

dilemma game, each criminal has a dominant strategy of confessing. If Jesse confesses, Scout is better off confessing and receiving a five-year prison term than denying and receiving a seven-year term. If Jesse denies, Scout is better off confessing and receiving a one-year term than denying and receiving a two-year term. So regardless of what Jesse does, Scout is better off confessing. Likewise, regardless of what Scout does, Jesse is better off confessing. If each criminal follows the dominant strategy of confessing, the result is a five-year prison term for each criminal.

If Jesse and Scout could follow through with an agreement to both deny their involvement in the crime, they could each serve just two years in prison, but that would require coordination and mutual trust. Also, they each would have an incentive to violate the agreement, because being the sole confessor comes with the reward of just one year of prison time.

As oligopolists decide whether to cut prices, advertise more, offer new services, or improve quality, situations that resemble the prisoner's dilemma are common. Suppose Chevron and BP are each trying to decide whether to charge low prices or high prices for gasoline. Figure 10.7 shows the companies' hypothetical profits per day in millions of dollars, depending on the pricing strategies they adopt. Let's consider how BP's payoff from each possible strategy relates to Chevron's selected strategy. If Chevron charges a low price, BP will earn $10 million if it charges a low price and $5 million if it charges a high price (due to the loss of customers to Chevron). So a

dominant strategy
A strategy that is best regardless of what the other player does.

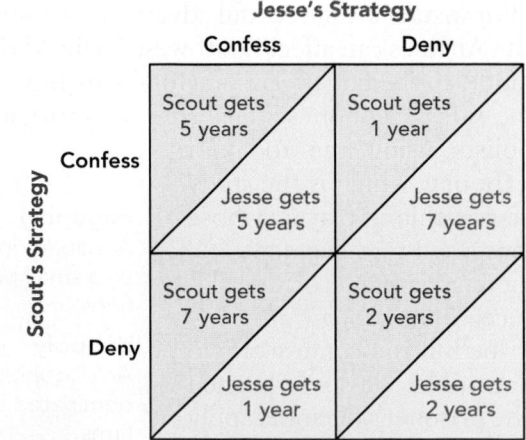

FIGURE 10.6 A Prisoner's Dilemma
The incentives in a prisoner's dilemma lead to an outcome that, for both players, is inferior to the outcome that would result from cooperative strategies.

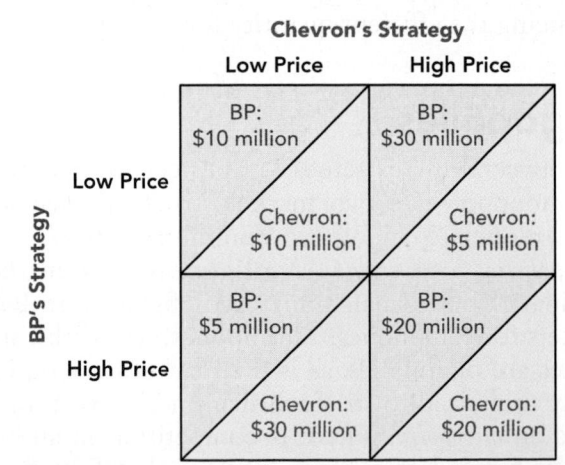

FIGURE 10.7 Game Theory for Oil Companies
Although the dominant strategy for each firm is to charge a low price, their profits will increase if they can coordinate their actions and both charge a high price.

low price is better for BP in this scenario. If Chevron charges a high price, BP will earn $30 million if it charges a low price (by picking up many of Chevron's customers), or $20 million if it charges a high price. So a low price is again better for BP.

Because BP is better off charging a low price regardless of what Chevron does, charging a low price is a dominant strategy for BP. For the same reasons, charging a low price is a dominant strategy for Chevron. If they each follow the dominant strategy of charging a low price, each will earn $10 million. Yet if they can coordinate their actions and both charge a high price, their profits double.

Perhaps you've felt the forces of a prisoner's dilemma yourself. For instance, if no one dressed up for job interviews, all the candidates could wear more comfortable clothing and save money on interview attire. But the dominant strategy is to dress up, because if other job candidates dress up, you will look relatively bad in casual clothing; and if other candidates dress down, you can stand out by dressing up. Countries face prisoner's dilemmas, too. For example, if other countries have the latest weapon systems, your country also wants to have those systems for national security. And if other countries don't have the latest weapon systems, your country wants to have them in order to get the upper hand. So the dominant strategy for each country is to invest in the latest weapon systems. But it would be cheaper and arguably safer for no one to have these systems than for everyone to have them.

The repetition of games broadens the possible strategies to include responses to the other player's strategy in the previous round. For example, with a *tit-for-tat strategy* you begin by cooperating with your opponent, and then adopt the same strategy the other player chose last time. Following a tit-for-tat strategy, BP would charge a high price if Chevron charged a high price last time, and a low price if Chevron charged a low price last time. BP's tit-for-tat strategy would encourage Chevron to cooperate and charge a high price to avoid the punishment of BP charging a low price in the next round.

The tit-for-tat strategy is more forgiving than the *grim trigger strategy*. Following the grim trigger strategy, BP would begin by cooperating (by charging a high price), but if Chevron undercuts BP and charges a low price even once, BP will charge a low price in every subsequent round. If it is announced or anticipated beforehand, the grim trigger strategy can be a strong deterrent to noncooperation, but it closes the door to reconciliation.

To avoid price wars, some oligopolists sidestep price competition and instead compete in other areas such as service or location. Oligopolists can also seek better outcomes through collusion. However, many forms of collusion are illegal. For example, several prominent colleges were accused of colluding on student financial aid packages in the 1990s. To avoid problems with the law, some firms engage in **tacit collusion,** meaning that they follow the same strategy without discussing it—as part of an unstated or implied agreement. For instance, some oligopolists coordinate their pricing strategies by following the lead of one firm that serves as a *price leader.* The biggest gas station in town might become a price leader for others in the area. The automakers and the airlines are also prone to follow the strategies of price leaders.

CARTELS

Oligopolists would like to earn profits like a monopolist. Although it is illegal in the United States, in some other places oligopolists can try to band together and form a *cartel* that acts like a monopolist. A **cartel** is a group of producers that conspires to restrict the quantity of output and increase their profits. For example, OPEC is a cartel made up of oil producers from 13 countries. When the members of OPEC abide by their agreement to restrict the amount of oil they supply to the market, they can charge the price a monopolist would charge, maximize their combined profit, and divide that profit among the members. Sometimes the agreement works well, as it did in 1973, when OPEC successfully restricted the supply of oil and sent oil prices through the roof.

tacit collusion
When firms follow the same strategy without discussing it—as part of an unstated or implied agreement.

cartel
A group of producers that conspires to restrict the quantity of output and increase their profits.

▲ At this OPEC meeting, the oil ministers discussed lower output targets for 2018. If the members of a cartel can agree to restrict output, they can act like a monopolist and share the resulting profits. But incentives to cheat on the agreement and sell a bit more on the side can cause cartels to fail.

Unfortunately for cartels, and fortunately for their customers, a cartel's members have an incentive to cheat on their agreement. You've seen that the profit-maximizing price for a monopolist is above its marginal cost, which means that additional units could be sold for a price below the profit-maximizing price but above the cost of making those units. When the incentive to cheat leads many cartel members to secretly increase their production, the cartel cannot maintain the monopoly level of output, and prices and profits tumble downward. This can cause the collapse of the cartel's plan to operate like a monopoly.

Monopolistic Competition

Some big cities have so many gas stations that each represents only a small part of the market. The same is true for restaurants, fitness centers, beauty salons, and gift shops. In these markets, as in perfectly competitive markets, the large number of firms removes the interdependence among firms that exists in oligopolies. The effect of any one firm's pricing strategy on other firms is too small to consider. But these firms hold some market power because their locations, products, and levels of customer service can differ. For example, there are a lot of cafés in Seattle, but the convenience, ambiance, lattés, and service are better in some cafés than in others, so some cafés can charge a higher price than others. **Monopolistic competition** exists in such a market when three conditions are met:

1. Firms can easily enter or exit the market.
2. There are many firms competing in the market.
3. The firms and their products are *not* identical.

These conditions give a monopolistically competitive market a mixed bag of characteristics from other market structures. Because the products sold by the firms in a monopolistically competitive market are differentiated, the firms face downward-sloping demand curves like the firms in oligopolies and monopolies. Figure 10.8 shows the graph for a monopolistically competitive firm in the long run. The downward-sloping demand curve makes it resemble the graph for a monopoly. A key difference is the absence of profit, which a monopolist can earn even in the long run. Like a monopolist, a monopolistically competitive firm produces less

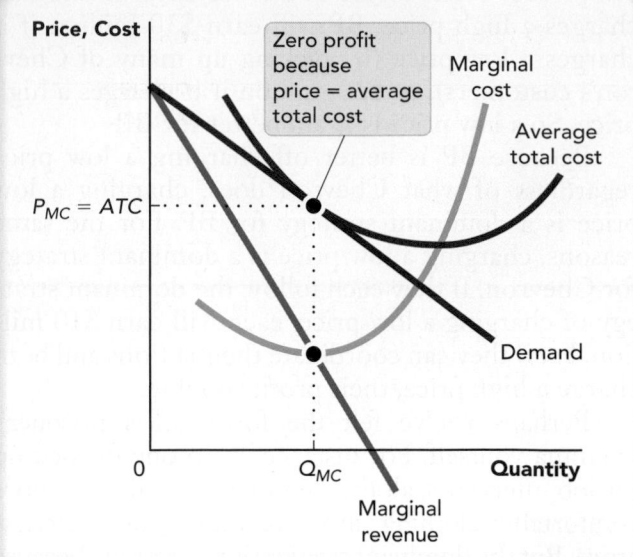

FIGURE 10.8 A Monopolistically Competitive Firm in the Long Run

Profits will attract new firms into a monopolistically competitive market. In the long run, the entry of new competitors drives down the demand for products from the existing firms until each firm earns zero economic profit.

than the socially optimal quantity of output. The ease of entering a monopolistically competitive market means that any economic profit will attract new competitors. In the long run, competition drives down each firm's demand until the price equals the average total cost. As a result, firms in a monopolistically competitive market earn zero economic profit in the long run, which is also the case in a perfectly competitive market.

To increase their market power, firms in monopolistically competitive markets try to offer superior quality and service, and invest in advertising to emphasize the differences between their products and their competitors' products. This is called *product differentiation*. For example, Jimmy John's sandwich shops offer home delivery, which many of its

monopolistic competition
Competition that exists in a market under three conditions: (1) Firms can easily enter or exit the market; (2) there are many firms competing in the market; and (3) the firms and their products are not identical.

Source: Burger King

▲ Firms in monopolistically competitive markets try to increase their market power by emphasizing the differences between their product and the products of their competitors.

Table 10.1 Market Structures

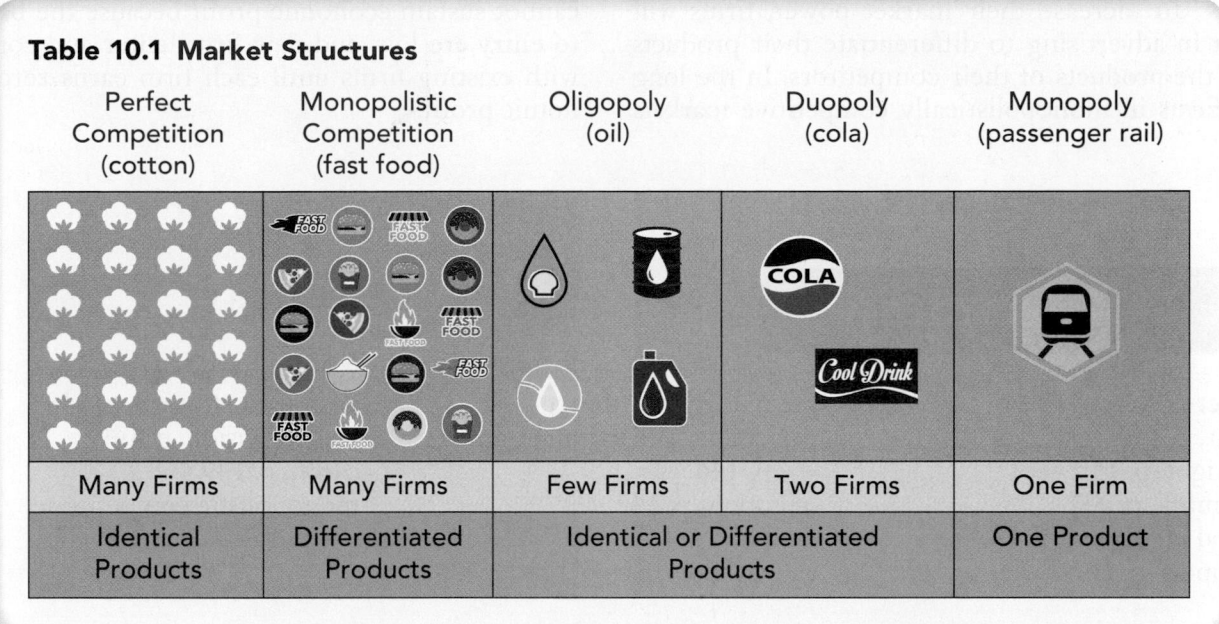

Perfect Competition (cotton)	Monopolistic Competition (fast food)	Oligopoly (oil)	Duopoly (cola)	Monopoly (passenger rail)
Many Firms	Many Firms	Few Firms	Two Firms	One Firm
Identical Products	Differentiated Products	Identical or Differentiated Products		One Product

competitors don't provide. And Burger King won't let you forget that all hamburgers are not created equal. The next time you drive down a highway, notice how many of the billboards are for products sold in monopolistically competitive markets. Among the many competitors in those markets, you have little reason to choose a particular firm unless it can convince you that its product is better than the rest.

Table 10.1 repeats the summary of market structures from Chapter 9. The next chapter applies some of what you've learned about market structures to the markets for labor and other factors of production.

SUMMARY

Market power gives a firm some say in pricing its product. Market power can be achieved through legal barriers that prevent competitors from entering the market, such as patents, copyrights, and trademarks. Some firms pursue market power by charging prices below their own costs to drive other competitors out of business. A firm that controls the resources needed for its product enjoys market power, as does a firm with startup costs that are so high that it is impractical for several firms to serve the same market.

A market with only one firm is a monopoly. To maximize profit, a monopolist will charge a higher price and produce less output than a perfectly competitive market facing the same costs. This makes the output level for a monopoly inefficiently low and creates a net loss for society called a deadweight loss. The exception is when a monopolist is a perfect price discriminator, meaning that each customer is charged a price equal to the most he or she would be willing to pay. In that case, the monopolist produces the efficient quantity but provides no consumer surplus.

In between monopoly and perfect competition in the range of market power fall the market structures of oligopoly and monopolistic competition. An oligopoly is a market with a small number of interdependent firms. Oligopolists can increase their earnings if they are able to coordinate their actions. Sometimes this is achieved with tacit collusion, such as the unstated agreement to take pricing cues from a firm that acts as a price leader. Although it is not legal in the United States, firms in some other countries can join together as a cartel—an entity that makes pricing and output decisions like a monopoly does. Oligopolists that do not collude may fall victim to a prisoner's dilemma, in which case selfish, uncoordinated behavior leads to an inferior outcome for each firm.

In a monopolistically competitive market, many firms sell similar but not identical products. There are so many firms that each has little effect on the others. To increase their market power, firms will invest in advertising to differentiate their products from the products of their competitors. In the long run, firms in monopolistically competitive markets cannot sustain economic profit because the barriers to entry are low, and new firms enter and compete with existing firms until each firm earns zero economic profit.

KEY TERMS

market power, p. 140
patent, p. 140
copyright, p. 140
trademark, p. 141
natural monopoly, p. 142
monopoly, p. 142

price discrimination, p. 145
perfect price discrimination,
　p. 146
oligopoly, p. 147
duopoly, p. 147
game theory, p. 147

dominant strategy, p. 148
tacit collusion, p. 149
cartel, p. 149
monopolistic competition,
　p. 150

PROBLEMS FOR REVIEW

1. For which of the following types of firms does the marginal revenue equal the price? (Choose all that apply.)
   a. A firm in a perfectly competitive market
   b. A monopolist that charges all customers the same price
   c. A perfect price discriminator

2. What three conditions are required for price discrimination? Describe a situation not mentioned in the book in which you have seen customers paying different prices for the same good or service.

3. Suppose a patent makes you the only seller of a new cold remedy. Draw a graph for your monopoly, assuming it resembles a typical monopoly. Include the curves for demand, marginal revenue, marginal cost, and average total cost. Shade and label the areas that represent profit and deadweight loss. Label the profit-maximizing price and quantity as P_M and Q_M.

4. Suppose the patent held by the monopoly in problem 3 expires and many competitors enter the market. Which of the following will be eliminated in the long run due to monopolistic competition?
   a. Deadweight loss
   b. Profit
   c. The separation of the marginal revenue curve and the demand curve

Draw a new graph for your firm as it might look in the long run. Label the profit-maximizing price and quantity as P_{MC} and Q_{MC}.

5. The following table shows a firm's output, fixed cost, marginal costs, and marginal revenue. Do the values in this table indicate that the firm is a monopolist or part of a perfectly competitive market? How can you tell?

Loaves	Fixed Cost	Marginal Cost	Marginal Revenue
1	$25.00	$5.00	$9.50
2	25.00	4.00	9.50
3	25.00	2.00	9.50
4	25.00	4.00	9.50
5	25.00	7.50	9.50
6	25.00	10.50	9.50

6. True, false, or uncertain: In a perfectly competitive market, firms are interdependent, and economists use game theory to analyze the firms' behavior. Explain your answer.

7. In the case of a prisoner's dilemma, the outcome when each player adopts its dominant strategy is

worse than the outcome that could be achieved with cooperation. The following payoff matrix shows the hypothetical daily profit in millions of dollars for Citgo and Shell, depending on each firm's decision about whether to advertise or not.

a. What is the dominant strategy, if any, for each firm?
b. Would this game be appropriately described as a prisoner's dilemma? Why or why not?

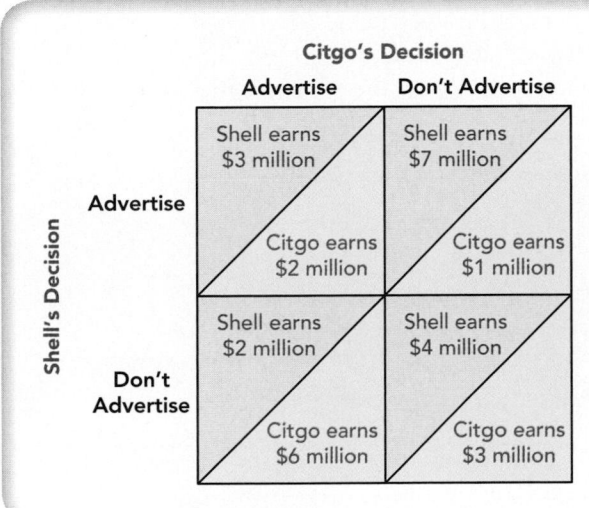

8. In which market structures do firms enjoy some degree of market power?

9. What is the source of market power for each of the following producers?
   a. author Stephen King
   b. cable television provider Spectrum
   c. Perrier water producer Nestlé, which owns the Perrier spring

10. There are many competing laundromats in Cleveland, but some will wash and fold your clothes for you, some provide free beverages, and some offer Wi-Fi. Which market structure characterizes the laundromat market of Cleveland?

11. Given that monopolies create deadweight loss, why does the government grant patents and copyrights that give firms monopoly power?

12. Identify one monopolistically competitive market that was not mentioned in this chapter. Discuss how firms in that market try to differentiate their products and encourage consumers to be loyal to their brands.

Factor Markets

11

Terry Harris/Alamy stockphoto

LEARNING OBJECTIVES

In this chapter, you will learn to:

1. Explain the derived demand for factors of production

2. Discuss the shape and shifters of labor supply curves

3. Determine how changes in the labor market affect the equilibrium wage and quantity of labor

4. Identify the reasons wages differ across workers, and discuss the policies used to address income inequality

5. Compare and contrast the market for land with the market for labor

Jeep tours take customers to America's most scenic spots, from the summit of Hawaii's Mauna Kea volcano to the rim of the Grand Canyon in Arizona. The companies that sell these tours must make purchases of their own: They buy factors of production—goods and services used to produce other goods and services. Entrepreneurs, like Greg Pieper of San Juan Scenic Jeep Tours, hire guides, booking agents, and mechanics and purchase fleets of commercial jeeps. The entrepreneurs also buy or rent property for their ticket offices and jeep storage. This chapter travels through the territory where firms find the inputs for the goods and services they produce: the factor markets.

Why Should I Care?

Recall from Chapter 2 that the factors of production fall into four general categories: land, labor, capital, and entrepreneurship. This chapter explains the workings of factor markets by examining the factor market you may soon enter (if you haven't already): the labor market. Decisions made by the buyers and sellers of the factors of production—such as you when you become a worker—determine wages and other factor payments. These decisions in turn influence the prices of all goods and services. The factor markets also hold important clues about how you can earn a high income. And if you are interested in policies that address income inequality, you will discover some of the pros and cons of various policies by studying factor markets. **This chapter will give you a better understanding of factor markets that affect you as a buyer of goods, a seller of labor, a voter on economic policy, and a potential future employer.**

The Derived Demand for Factors of Production

If you're up for a thrill, try a jeep tour along Hell's Revenge Trail in Utah or Black Bear Pass in Colorado. To provide those thrills, tour companies need jeeps, guides, booking agents, trails, and entrepreneurs to bring together the various factors of production. The quantities of these factors that jeep tour companies employ depend on the demand for jeep tours. When the demand for jeep tours increases, the demand for these factors increases. Because the demand for a factor is derived from the demand for whatever the factor produces, factor demand is referred to as a **derived demand.** In this section, we investigate the demand for the factors of production, using labor as an example.

derived demand
Demand for a factor that is derived from the demand for whatever the factor produces.

▲ The demand for jeep tour guides is derived from the demand for jeep tours. If consumers buy more jeep tours, the firms that sell them will demand more guides.

A FIRM'S LABOR DEMAND

You know that the demand for a good is determined by the largest amount consumers would be willing to pay for each unit of that good. Factor demand is no different. A firm's demand for labor is determined by the most a firm would be willing to pay for each unit of labor. How much would a firm pay for the services of one more worker for one hour? The firm would pay no more than the amount that worker would contribute to the firm's hourly revenue.

Recall that the additional output produced when one more unit of a factor of production is hired is called the *marginal product* of that factor. So the extra output produced by one more worker is the *marginal product of labor*. If hiring a second worker allows a jeep tour company to provide jeep tours to 6 more customers per hour, the marginal product of labor for the second worker is 6. However, for hiring decisions, the firm doesn't just want to know how much another worker would contribute to its output; it wants to know how much the worker would contribute to its revenue. The contribution one more worker would make to a firm's revenue is called the **marginal revenue product (MRP)** of that worker. So, if the marginal revenue earned from each customer is $15 per hour, the marginal revenue product of the second worker is the 6 additional customers she makes possible, multiplied by the $15 marginal revenue per hour from each customer— that is, 6 × $15 = $90.

More generally,

$$\frac{\text{marginal revenue}}{\text{product}} = \frac{\text{marginal}}{\text{product}} \times \frac{\text{marginal}}{\text{revenue}}$$

The table that accompanies Figure 11.1 shows how the marginal revenue product is found for the first seven guides hired per hour by a jeep tour company. To find the marginal revenue product, first determine the marginal product of each worker, which is each worker's contribution to total output. Recall the law of diminishing returns, explained in Chapter 8: The marginal product of workers eventually falls as more workers are hired, due to the limited amounts of capital, land, and other inputs available for each worker's use. In the case of jeep tours, each newly hired guide contributes fewer tours than the previous guide because increasingly crowded jeeps and trails make fewer tours possible. To determine the marginal revenue product for a guide, we multiply the guide's marginal product of labor by the marginal revenue per jeep tour.

A firm's labor demand curve is equivalent to its marginal revenue product curve. We can expect the labor demand curve to have the familiar downward slope of other demand curves because, as more workers are hired, one or both of the elements of the marginal revenue product—the marginal product and the marginal revenue—will fall. Why? The marginal product will fall due to diminishing returns.

Quantity of Labor (workers)	Total Output	Marginal Product × of Labor	Marginal = Revenue	Marginal Revenue Product
1	7	7	$15	$105
2	13	6	15	90
3	18	5	15	75
4	22	4	15	60
5	25	3	15	45
6	27	2	15	30
7	28	1	15	15

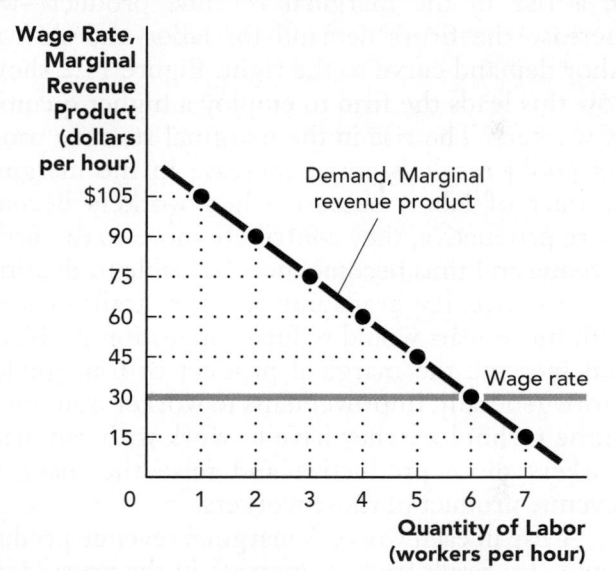

FIGURE 11.1 A Firm's Hiring Decision
A firm's demand for labor is determined by its marginal revenue product of labor. A firm will hire more workers until the wage paid for another worker would exceed the marginal revenue product of labor.

And you learned in Chapter 10 that if the market is not perfectly competitive, the marginal revenue falls as output increases—which is what happens when more workers are hired. With the marginal product falling and the marginal revenue either falling or remaining the same, the marginal revenue product will fall. So, the demand curve for labor slopes downward, as shown in Figure 11.1.

marginal revenue product (MRP)
The contribution one more worker would make to a firm's revenue.

A firm will hire more workers until the next worker hired would contribute more to the firm's cost than to its revenue. Suppose the jeep tour company pays its guides an hourly wage of $30. In Figure 11.1, we see that the first few guides are a bargain. For instance, the second guide provides a marginal revenue product of $90 per hour and is paid $30 per hour. However, because the sixth guide contributes just $30 to revenue per hour and is paid $30 per hour, the firm should stop hiring after the sixth guide. The firm wouldn't want to pay $30 per hour to hire the seventh worker, who adds only $15 to hourly revenue. So the optimal quantity of labor is found where the cost of an additional worker—the hourly wage in this case—equals the marginal revenue product.

An increase in the value of each worker—that is, a rise in the marginal revenue product—will increase the firm's demand for labor and shift its labor demand curve to the right. Figure 11.2 shows how this leads the firm to employ a higher quantity of workers. The rise in the marginal revenue product could result from an increase in the marginal product of labor, because when workers become more productive, they contribute more to the firm's revenue and thus become more valuable to the firm. For instance, the availability of more trails or jeeps with more seats would reduce congestion problems and increase the marginal product of tour guides. More generally, improvements in worker training or in the technology they have to work with can make workers more productive and raise the marginal revenue product of those workers.

A rise in each worker's marginal revenue product could also result from an increase in the price of the good or service the workers produce, which in turn increases the firm's marginal revenue. Conversely, a decrease in the marginal product of labor, or in the price of the good or service (and thus in the marginal revenue), will decrease the firm's marginal revenue product and shift the firm's labor demand curve to the left. Figure 11.2 shows how a leftward shift in the labor demand curve leads the firm to employ fewer workers.

A MARKET'S LABOR DEMAND

The market demand for labor depends on:

- the marginal revenue product of labor for firms in the market
- the number of firms in the market

When changes in the marginal revenue product shift firms' demand curves for labor, the market

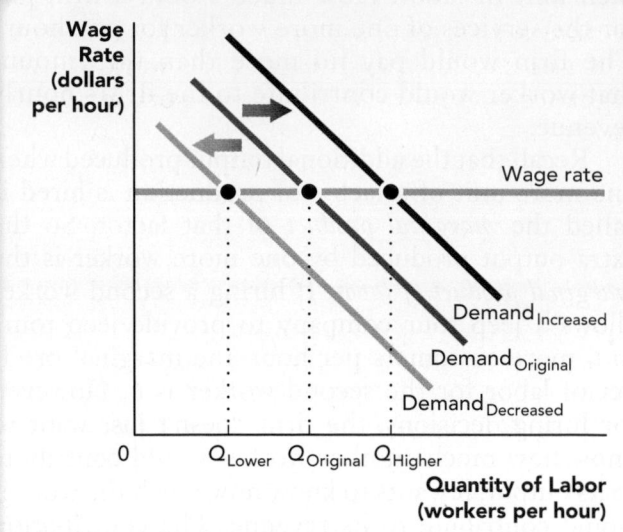

FIGURE 11.2 Shifts in a Firm's Labor Demand Curve

When the marginal revenue product of each worker rises, the labor demand curve shifts to the right and the firm hires more workers. When the marginal revenue product of each worker falls, the labor demand curve shifts to the left and the firm hires fewer workers.

demand curve for labor shifts in the same direction. The market demand curve for labor also increases as the number of firms increases, and it decreases as the number of firms decreases. For example, the number of retail stores in the United States is 1.1 million and growing. As more and more stores open, the demand for retail managers and salespeople increases. So, if you look on a job-search website such as Monster.com, you're likely to find thousands of job openings in retail management and retail sales.

The Supply of Labor

You face a trade-off between income and free time: The more you work, the more income you have, but the less time you have available for your studies and leisure. And the more you work, the more valuable are the activities you must give up to do so. You can work a little in the time you would normally spend goofing off—time with minimal value. If you worked all day, however, you would have no time to devote to your education, family, friends, favorite hobbies, and other top priorities. These unavoidable trade-offs shape the supply of labor.

AN INDIVIDUAL'S LABOR SUPPLY

Because the opportunity cost of an hour of work increases as you spend more time working, you might accept a low hourly wage to work for a brief period, but you wouldn't work for many hours unless you received a higher wage. This gives your labor supply curve an upward slope. Figure 11.3 shows your hypothetical daily labor supply curve. Suppose that for an hourly wage of $8, you would give up your least productive hour of leisure each day—time you would otherwise spend goofing off—and work instead. If your wage were $13 an hour, you would also be willing to spend less time on sports and hobbies, and work for a total of two hours per day. For $18 an hour, you would also be willing to get up earlier and minimize the time you spend on social media, freeing up a total of three hours per day.

If your opportunity cost of working decreases or the importance to you of earning income increases, your labor supply curve will shift to the right. For example, your opportunity cost of working will decrease when you finish school, because you won't have to forego your education in order to work a lot of hours. The opportunity cost of working can also change due to demographic changes such as urbanization. In 1810, 90 percent of American families lived on farms, where all family members completed critical chores. Today, more than 80 percent of American families live in urban areas, where the work people do at home is less critical to their livelihoods. So the opportunity cost of working for a firm is lower, and city dwellers are willing to supply more labor to the workforce as a result.

A MARKET'S LABOR SUPPLY

Chapter 4 explained that you find the market supply curve for a good by adding up the quantity supplied by each firm at each price. Likewise, you find the market supply curve for labor by adding up the quantity of labor supplied by each worker at each wage. So the market labor supply curve shifts when:

- the supply curves of individual workers shift
- the number of workers changes

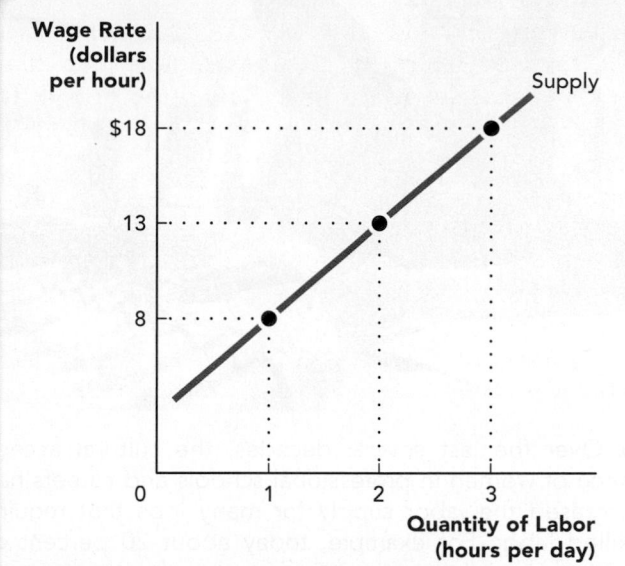

FIGURE 11.3 An Individual's Labor Supply Curve

Because the opportunity cost of time spent working rises as people work more, workers are typically willing to spend more time working for a high wage than for a low wage. As a result, most people have an upward-sloping labor supply curve.

The number of workers can change due to changes in birth or death rates, *emigration* (people going to live in other countries), *immigration* (people arriving from other countries to stay), and changes in demographics such as age and education levels. Moreover, urbanization and cultural changes can affect both the willingness of individual workers to supply more labor and the overall number of workers in the labor force. For example, cultural changes have affected women's supply of labor over the past century. It has become increasingly acceptable for women to work outside the home, and time-saving inventions such as machines that wash clothes and dishes have freed up more time for many women. Those advances, along with improved access to formal education, have dramatically increased the supply of female engineers, lawyers, doctors, and other professionals. And an increase in the average age of

All work involves trade-offs. More work means more income but less leisure.

Income   Leisure

▲ Over the last several decades, the cultural acceptance of women in professional schools and careers has increased the labor supply for many jobs that require skilled labor. For example, today about 20 percent of engineers are women.

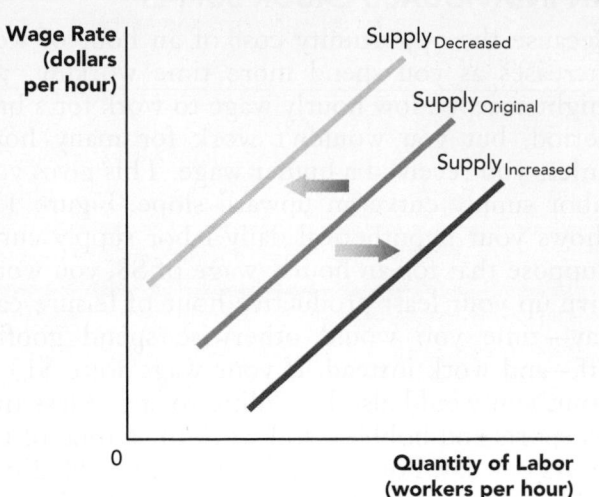

FIGURE 11.4 Shifts in the Market Labor Supply Curve

The market labor supply curve shifts to the right when new workers enter the workforce, and when existing workers are willing to supply more labor for any given wage. The market labor supply curve shifts to the left when some workers leave the workforce, and when existing workers will not supply as much labor for any given wage.

childbearing, in part the result of improved access to education, has decreased the opportunity cost of work for young women who would otherwise have children to care for at home. For these and related reasons, the percentage of working-age women who participate in the workforce increased from 34 percent in 1950 to 57 percent in 2018.

The market labor supply curve shifts to the right when existing workers increase their supply of labor or when new workers enter the labor market. For instance, at graduation time, many young people make themselves available for full-time jobs, so the supply of labor increases. When workers decrease their supply of labor or some workers leave the labor market, the market labor supply curve shifts to the left. For example, during a long recession, some workers drop out of the workforce because they are discouraged by the dim prospects of finding a job, so the labor supply decreases. Figure 11.4 illustrates these shifts in the market labor supply curve.

Equilibrium in the Labor Market

A perfectly competitive labor market behaves much like a perfectly competitive product market. The market equilibrium determines the quantity of labor hired and the price of labor—the *wage rate*. Figure 11.5 shows a labor market that is initially in equilibrium at point E_1, with a wage rate of $9 per hour and firms hiring 10,000 workers per hour. Just as in the product markets discussed in Chapter 5, shifts in the supply curve or the demand curve

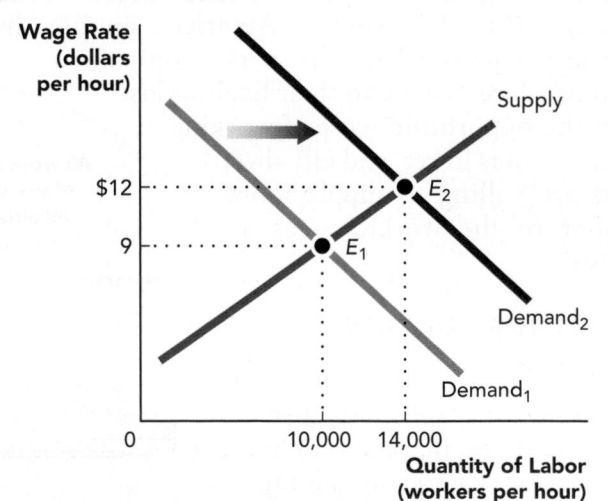

FIGURE 11.5 Equilibrium in the Labor Market

Equilibrium in the labor market determines the wage rate and the quantity of labor hired. Shifts in the supply curve or the demand curve change the equilibrium, and thus the wage rate and the quantity of labor hired. For example, an increase in the demand for labor increases both the wage rate and the quantity of labor hired.

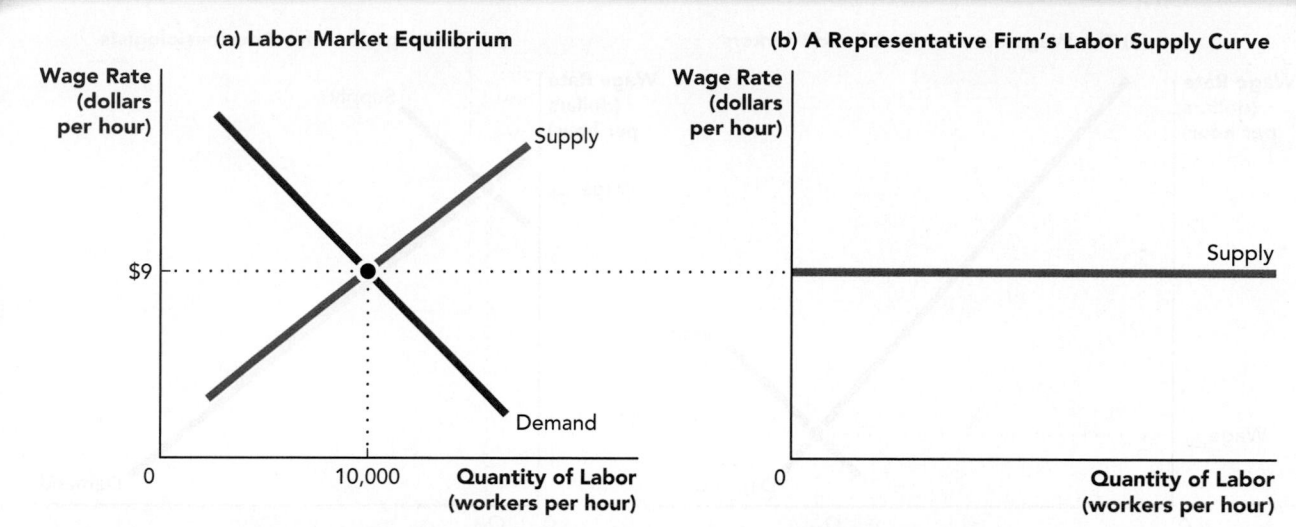

FIGURE 11.6 Labor Market Equilibrium and a Firm's Labor Supply Curve

Each firm in a perfectly competitive labor market is so small relative to the market that it can hire as much labor as it wants at the wage rate determined by the market equilibrium, which is shown in panel (a) at the intersection of the market labor supply curve and the market labor demand curve. This means that the firm's labor supply curve is horizontal at the equilibrium wage, as shown in panel (b).

change the location of the equilibrium point. For example, if the demand curve shifts to the right as shown in Figure 11.5, the new equilibrium point is E_2. The equilibrium wage rate rises to $12 per hour, and the equilibrium quantity of labor rises to 14,000 workers per hour.

Recall that a firm in a perfectly competitive product market is a price taker, meaning that the firm is so small relative to the market that it must take the market price as given. A firm in a perfectly competitive labor market is a *wage taker*—it is too small to independently influence the wage rate, but it can hire all the labor it wants at the market wage rate. The graphs in Figure 11.6 illustrate this situation. Panel (a) shows a labor market in equilibrium. Panel (b) shows how the firm faces a labor supply curve that is horizontal at the market equilibrium wage rate.

Why Wage Rates Differ

Our knowledge that the wage rate in a perfectly competitive labor market is established at the equilibrium of supply and demand will help us understand why wages are high in some labor markets and low in others. In labor markets with a large supply of workers relative to the demand, the equilibrium wage rate is relatively low. The market for

workers in fast-food restaurants is an example. The U.S. fast-food industry requires more than 3 million employees to cook and serve its burgers and fries, but there is an ample supply of workers because almost every member of the workforce qualifies for these jobs. This relatively large supply of workers brings the average wage for fast-food jobs down to $9.03 per hour. Panel (a) of Figure 11.7 shows how the abundant supply of fast-food workers results in a low equilibrium wage.

In markets with a small supply of workers relative to the demand, the equilibrium wage rate is relatively high. The market for anesthesiologists is an example. Almost everyone who undergoes surgery needs an anesthesiologist to administer medications that reduce pain. The supply of anesthesiologists is relatively low due to the long and expensive training these jobs require, the long hours anesthesiologists work, and the stress of work that can be a matter of life or death for a patient. As a result, anesthesiologists earn about $111.94 per hour—one of the highest wage rates in the United States. Panel (b) of Figure 11.7 on the next page shows how the limited supply of anesthesiologists allows them to earn a high equilibrium wage.

It is clear that if you want to earn a high wage, it helps to choose a career with a high demand for labor relative to the supply. The example of

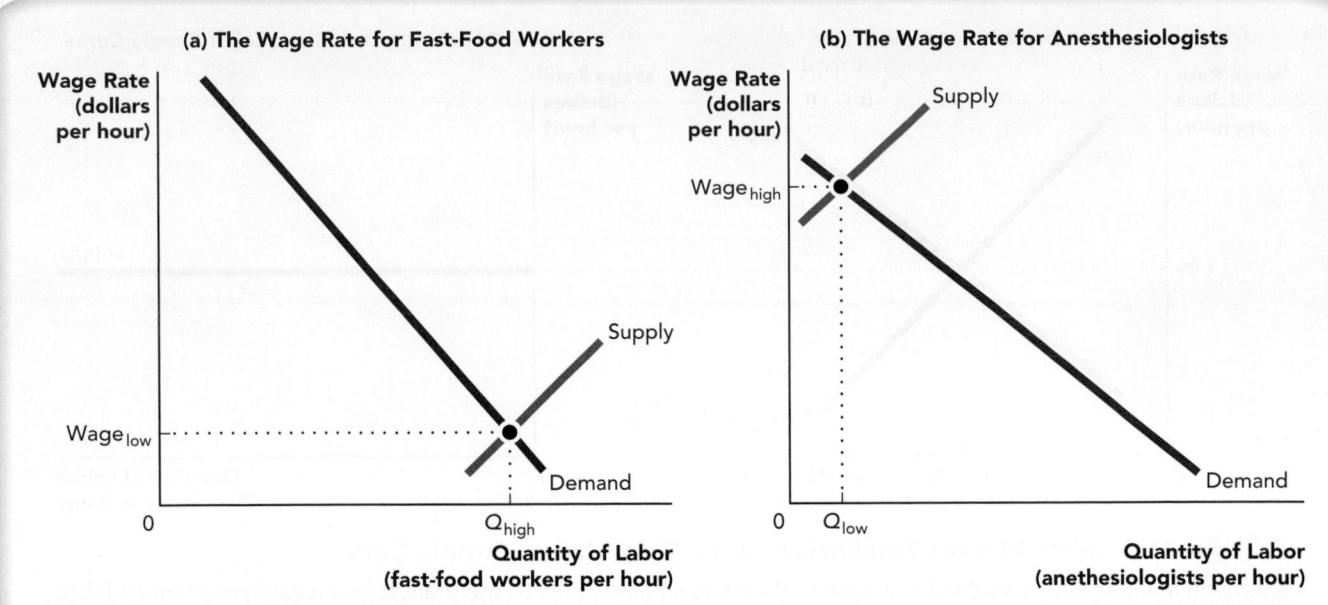

FIGURE 11.7 Why Fast-Food Workers Earn Less Than Anesthesiologists
The wage rate is low in markets with a large labor supply relative to the labor demand, as shown in panel (a). High wages result from a small labor supply relative to the labor demand, as shown in panel (b).

fast-food workers shows that high demand alone is not enough to guarantee a high wage. A low supply of workers alone is not enough either. For instance, there are fewer than 14,000 shampooers in the United States, but they aren't in great demand because most people shampoo their own hair. The relatively low demand causes professional shampooers to earn even less than fast-food workers: an average of $8.94 per hour.

compensating wage differential
A wage premium that compensates for the exceptional burdens of a job.

> If you want to earn a high wage, it helps to choose a career with a high demand for labor relative to the supply.

COMPENSATING WAGE DIFFERENTIALS

The labor supply in some markets is low because the associated jobs are

- dangerous, as in bridge painting
- dirty, as in mining
- difficult, as in aerospace engineering

Workers in jobs with these characteristics generally earn more than workers in markets with a similar labor demand but a more desirable work environment that attracts a larger labor supply. A wage premium that compensates for the exceptional burdens of a particular job is called a **compensating wage differential**. For example, while the average hourly wage in the United States is $22, the average wage

KARL MONDON/Newscom/Tribune News Service/SAN FRANCISCO/CA/USA

▲ Compensating wage differentials reward those workers who perform dangerous, dirty, or difficult jobs.

is $28 for bridge painters, $25 for mining machine operators, and $50 for aerospace engineers.

In some other labor markets, the supply is high because the jobs are cleaner, safer, easier, or in other ways more appealing. For instance, many people would enjoy working outside in a beautiful natural setting, so there is an ample supply of park rangers. As a result, the average hourly wage rate for park rangers ($18) is low relative to the wage rates for jobs with similar qualifications in a less desirable workplace.

EMPLOYMENT DISCRIMINATION

When prejudice takes precedence over profit, discrimination can lower the demand for workers in targeted groups, regardless of their productivity. Firms that do not discriminate are better poised for success because they draw from a larger pool of potential employees and can select the candidates who are best suited for the jobs, without regard for the personal characteristics that form the bases for discrimination. Discrimination can also occur at a profit-maximizing firm as a result of prejudice on the part of the firm's customers. For example, a hair salon whose potential customers prefer to have their hair styled by women has an incentive to discriminate against male hairstylists in order to maximize profit. Whether the source of prejudice is the firm or its customers, discrimination decreases the demand for workers in the targeted group, and thus can lower the wage rates those workers receive.

Discrimination continues despite state and federal laws that forbid most forms of discrimination on the basis of race, sex, pregnancy, religion, national origin, disability, military status, and age. For instance, a recent study by Sonia Ghumman and Ann Marie Ryan found that women who wore Muslim headscarves during job interviews in the United States were relatively unlikely to advance in the hiring process. And in 2015, the U.S. Supreme Court ruled that clothing retailer Abercrombie and Fitch wrongfully rejected the job application of Muslim teenager Samantha Elauf because of her headscarf, even though she did not explicitly state that she was wearing the headscarf for religious reasons.

In some cases, however, discrimination is legal. Title VII of the Civil Rights Act of 1964 allows employers to discriminate on the basis of religion, sex, or national origin when the characteristic is a *bona fide occupational qualification (BFOQ)*, meaning that it is "reasonably necessary to the normal operation of that particular business or enterprise." For example, a Catholic church can legally discriminate against non-Catholic applicants when hiring Catholic priests. The Age and Discrimination Employment Act extends this BFOQ exception to discrimination on the basis of age. For instance, the Federal Aviation Administration legally requires airline pilots to retire at the age of 65. Employment discrimination on the basis of height, weight, and appearance is also legal in most states, and studies find that the average wage is higher for workers who are tall, slender, or attractive.[1]

The Distribution of Income

Differing wage rates contribute to a wide divergence in incomes among families in the United States, and an even wider income gap between typical families in rich countries and poor countries. The World Bank reports that more than 1.2 billion people around the world live on less than $1.25 per day. The width of each stripe in Figure 11.8 shows the share of income

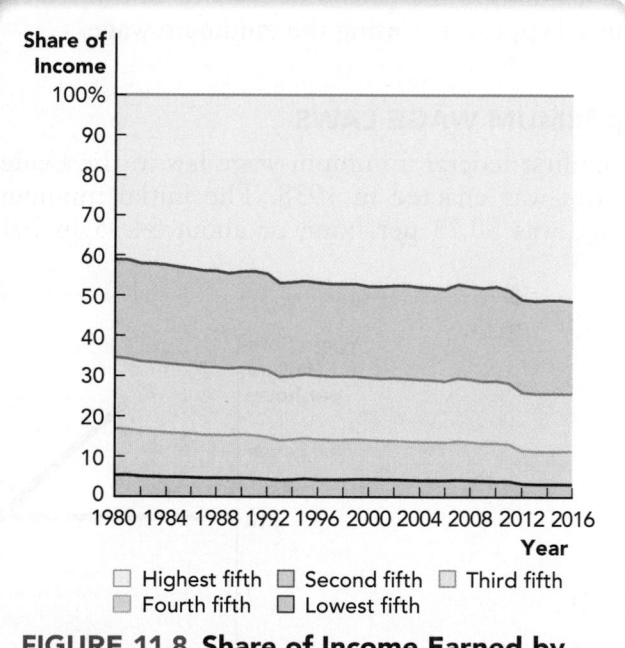

FIGURE 11.8 Share of Income Earned by U.S. Households

The width of each stripe in this graph represents the share of income earned by 20 percent of U.S. households since 1980. The green stripe represents the earnings of the richest 20 percent; the reddish stripe represents the earnings of the poorest 20 percent.

---

[1] For a summary of this research, visit www.stlouisfed.org/publications/regional-economist/april-2005/so-much-for-that-merit-raise-the-link-between-wages-and-appearance.

earned by 20 percent of U.S. households, from the richest at the top to the poorest at the bottom. Between 1980 and 2016, the percentage of income earned by the poorest 20 percent of families decreased from 5.3 percent to 3.1 percent. Over the same period, the percentage of income earned by the richest 20 percent of families increased from 41.1 percent to 51.5 percent.

How much income inequality is "acceptable"? How should the government help the poor? These questions stir up controversy because policies that reduce income inequality involve trade-offs. On the one hand, an even distribution of income would achieve equality, but people would have little reason to work hard, innovate, or take risks with a business if everyone received the same income. On the other hand, *severe* income inequality leads to problems that include extreme poverty, disease, depression, and crime—all of which make the quality of life worse for everyone in an economy, rich or poor. Although there is disagreement over the acceptable level of inequality, we can use the tools of economics to inform debates about how to address the problem. Next, we'll examine the pros and cons of one often-discussed approach: raising the minimum wage.

MINIMUM WAGE LAWS

The first federal minimum wage law in the United States was enacted in 1938. The initial minimum wage was $0.25 per hour, or about $4.35 in 2018

dollars after adjusting for inflation. The inflation-adjusted minimum wage reached a peak of about $11.25 in 1968, and was $7.25 in 2018. More than half of all U.S. states and the District of Columbia have their own minimum wages that exceed the federal minimum wage. The effects of a minimum wage depend on the shapes of the supply and demand curves for labor. Figure 11.9 shows a labor market with relatively elastic supply and demand at the equilibrium point. With no minimum wage, the market wage is $7 and the quantity of labor hired is 1,500 workers per hour.

When a minimum wage of $10 is imposed, it acts as a price floor by preventing firms from paying their workers a lower wage rate. The quantity of labor supplied for $10 per hour is 2,000 workers, but the quantity of labor demanded is just 1,100 workers. The difference, 900 workers, is the quantity of unemployed labor. Some of these 900 workers would have been employed at the $7 market wage, and some were attracted to the labor market by the higher $10 wage. So the minimum wage produces mixed results. The 1,100 workers who receive $10 per hour are better off than they would have been without the minimum wage because their wage rate increased by $3 per hour. The $1,500 − 1,100 = 400$ workers who are unemployed, but who would have been employed without the minimum wage, are worse off. And the $2,000 − 1,500 = 500$ workers who desire

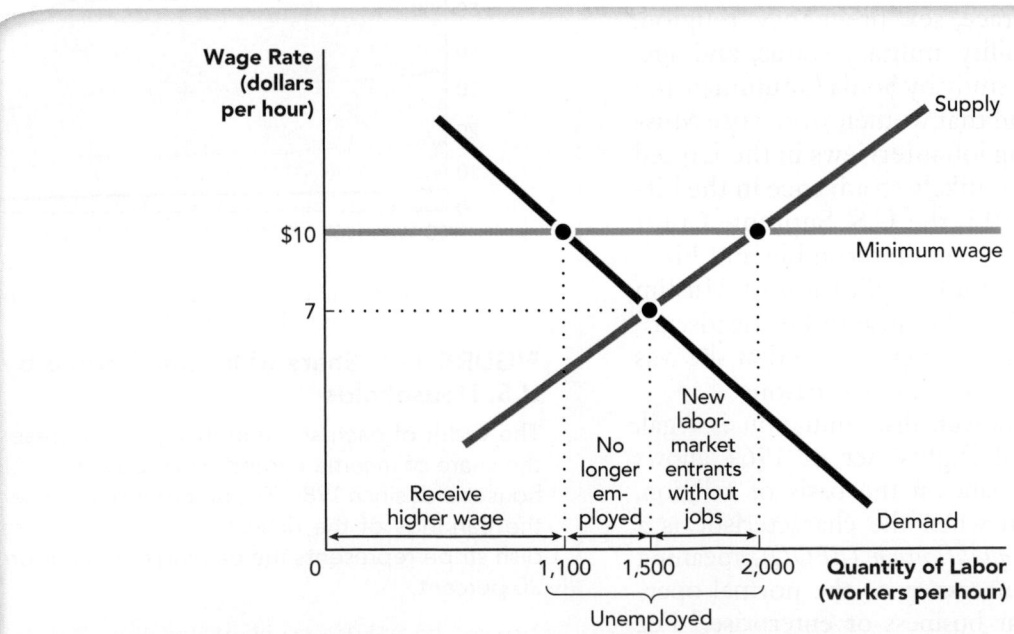

FIGURE 11.9 A Labor Market with a Minimum Wage

A minimum wage set above the equilibrium wage rate increases the earnings of the workers who receive the minimum wage. A minimum wage can also result in unemployment by causing some people to lose their jobs and by leading more people to enter the labor market because they would like to work for the new, higher wage rate.

▲ McDonald's is experimenting with self-service kiosks. Machines that are good substitutes for workers cause the demand for labor to be relatively elastic.

The number of workers that a minimum wage sends into each category—better off, worse off, and desirous of work—depends on the elasticities of the labor supply curve and the labor demand curve. The elasticity of the labor demand curve, in turn, depends on the timeframe and the options available to the firms. In the long run, firms have the opportunity to implement labor-saving capital if it is available, so the demand for labor will be relatively elastic if workers can easily be replaced by machines. If good substitutes for workers are unavailable or expensive, the demand for labor will be relatively inelastic. If the same number of workers will be hired with or without a minimum wage, the demand for labor is perfectly inelastic. For instance, if McDonald's needs five workers to cover each shift and the company doesn't hire more than five workers to begin with, it will not be able to hire fewer workers as the result of a minimum wage.

Economists David Card and Alan Krueger found that when New Jersey increased its minimum wage by about 19 percent, there was no significant decrease in employment in the state's fast-food industry. This could be explained by a relatively inelastic labor demand curve. Figure 11.10 shows that when the labor demand curve is relatively inelastic, employers will hire almost as many workers at the minimum wage as at the equilibrium wage.

employment for $10 per hour but wouldn't want to work for $7 per hour are unemployed, although they wouldn't have been employed without the minimum wage, either.

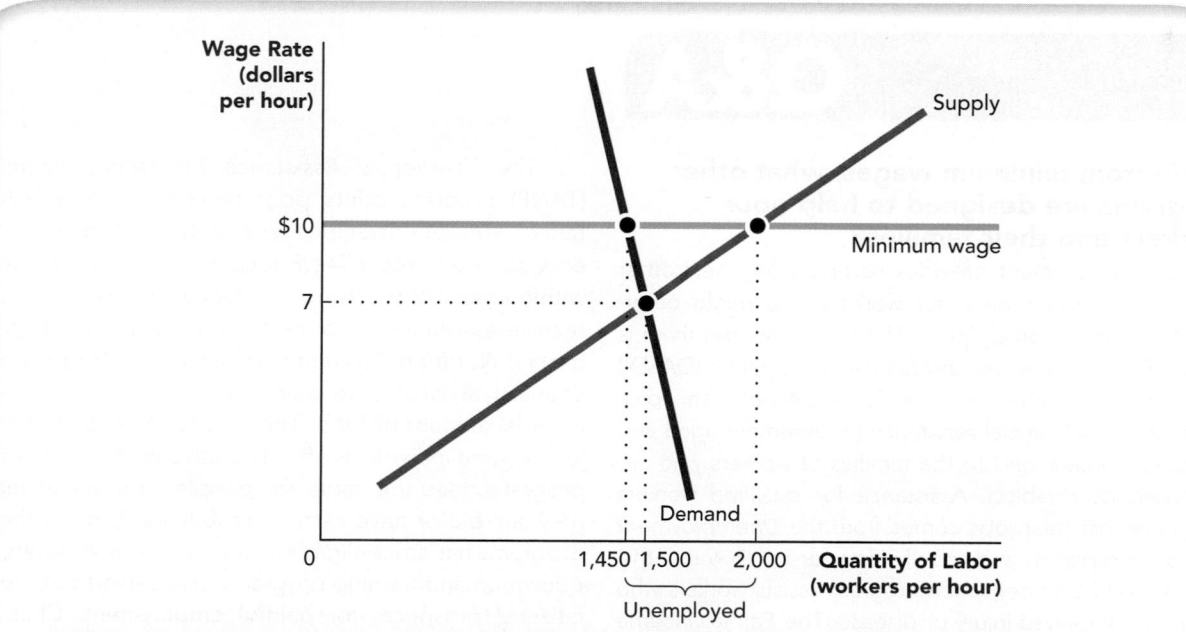

FIGURE 11.10 Relatively Inelastic Demand for Labor and a Minimum Wage

The decrease in the quantity of labor demanded as a result of a minimum wage depends on the elasticity of the labor demand curve. If the demand for labor is inelastic, the drop in employment will be small relative to the wage increase. Even so, there can be a significant increase in unemployment due to the larger number of workers who would like to supply labor at the higher wage.

The minimum wage in Figure 11.10 results in only 50 fewer workers being hired. Recall that 400 fewer workers were hired as a result of the minimum wage shown in Figure 11.9 because the demand for labor was relatively *elastic*.

When the demand for labor is relatively inelastic or perfectly inelastic, the minimum wage still creates unemployment, but this is mostly or entirely due to a larger number of workers wanting to supply labor at the higher wage. When few workers lose their jobs, the direct financial burden of the minimum wage falls primarily on the firms that pay the higher wage. However, like any increase in production costs, firms will pass some of the burden on to consumers in the form of higher prices.

The pros and cons of wages that are above the equilibrium wage don't always come from minimum wage laws. *Labor unions* are organizations formed to empower workers as they negotiate for better working conditions, job security, fringe benefits, and wages. Union action was on display in 2016 when about 40,000 unionized employees of Verizon refused to work until the company agreed to pay higher wages. After six weeks of negotiations, Verizon and the union members agreed on a 10.9% wage increase over four years. When a union successfully negotiates a higher wage for its members,

▲ Workers around the country have rallied for higher minimum wages and more unions, both of which have pros and cons.

the workers who receive the higher wage are better off. But, as usual, there are winners and losers. The firm will earn less profit, the customers may pay higher prices, and the firm may hire fewer workers at the higher wage. Unions often address the risk of layoffs with clauses in their agreements. The final agreement at Verizon stipulated that 1,400 additional employees would be hired.

Q&A

Aside from minimum wages, what other programs are designed to help poor workers and their families?

The U.S. government provides several safety nets other than the minimum wage for workers who might otherwise become extremely poor. The largest among them is the *Old-Age, Survivors, and Disability Insurance* (OASDI) program, often referred to as *Social Security*. This program provides financial assistance to retirement-aged and disabled workers, and to the families of workers who are deceased or disabled. Assistance for qualified workers who have lost their jobs comes from the *Unemployment Insurance* program and usually lasts for up to 6 months. The *Workers Compensation* program assists workers who have a work-related injury or disease. The *Earned Income Tax Credit* (EITC) reduces tax payments, or provides tax refunds, for many low-to-moderate-income workers with children and for many low-income workers without children.

The *Temporary Assistance for Needy Families* (TANF) program offers poor families financial assistance, work opportunities, and child care so that parents can work. Most TANF recipients must go to work within 2 years of receiving assistance, and no family can receive assistance for more than 5 years. The *Supplemental Nutrition Assistance Program* (SNAP) provides financial assistance to help poor people purchase a minimal amount of food. The *Medicaid* program helps low-income individuals afford health care; the *Medicare* program does the same for people who are at least 65 years old or have certain disabilities. Each of these programs has strict eligibility requirements. A variety of education and training programs also serve to improve citizens' prospects for gainful employment. Chapter 18 discusses the related topic of programs to help the poor in developing countries.

Markets for Other Factors

The markets for land and capital work very much like the market for labor. The demand for each factor is determined by the marginal revenue product of that factor, and the price of each factor is established by the equilibrium of supply and demand in the market for that factor. One difference between the two markets has to do with the supply curves for factors. Because it is not so easy to increase the quantity of land, for example, the supply curve for land is less elastic than the supply curve for labor. Yet, as the price of land increases, the quantity of land offered for sale does increase. This is usually because land that has not been on the market is put up for sale due to an increase in land prices. Sometimes land that has been unsuitable for productive uses can be repurposed when the price of land increases, such as when irrigation systems turn deserts into crop land, and when bulldozers turn rugged land into flat land. In some cases, land is actually created where there had been water. Hundreds of new islands have been created off the coast of the United Arab Emirates,

▲ When the price of land rises, the quantity of land supplied can increase in several ways. In some cases, exemplified by these new islands in the United Arab Emirates, new land is actually created where there had been water.

and thousands of acres have been added to New York City by expanding its shoreline. And then there are the plans of firms such as SpaceX to allow humans to make use of the land on Mars . . .

SUMMARY

If your firm offered guided rafting trips along the Colorado River, you would hire more guides and rent more rafts as customers demanded more raft trips per day. That makes the demand for the factors of production a *derived demand*—the demand is derived from the demand for the goods or services produced using the factors of production. The demand curve for a factor is equivalent to the marginal revenue product curve for the factor. The marginal revenue product is found by multiplying the marginal product of the factor by the marginal revenue received from selling whatever the factor produced. For the river-rafting guides, the marginal revenue product of each guide is found by multiplying the number of additional passengers that guide made possible by the additional revenue received from each passenger. The marginal revenue product of a guide is the amount that the guide contributes to the firm's total revenue, and therefore it is the most the firm would pay to hire the guide.

Due to the diminishing marginal product of most factors, the demand curve for a factor of production generally takes the familiar downward slope of demand curves for goods and services. Firms hire more units of a factor of production until the

marginal revenue product of another unit would fall below the cost of another unit.

The supply curve for most factors of production is upward sloping. This is the result of the generally increasing cost of providing additional units of a factor. For labor, the increasing cost comes primarily from the increasing opportunity costs people experience when they commit more time to work. The market labor supply curve shifts when the supply curves of individual workers shift or the number of workers changes. The number of workers can fluctuate due to changes in birth or death rates, emigration, immigration, and changes in demographics such as citizens' ages and education levels. Urbanization and cultural changes can affect both the willingness of individual workers to supply more labor and the overall number of workers in the labor force.

Like the price of a good in a perfectly competitive product market, the price of a factor in a perfectly competitive factor market is determined by the equilibrium of supply and demand for the factor. A single firm hiring in a perfectly competitive factor market is so small relative to the market that it can hire as much of the factor as it wants at the market price. This means that the firm faces a horizontal factor supply curve.

Factor payments such as the wages paid to workers are higher in markets with a high demand for the factor relative to the supply of the factor. For instance, a stellar baseball player earns a high wage because the popularity of the best players places a high demand on a few star performers. In other markets, the demand for labor can be relatively low due to low demand for the product the workers produce, low worker productivity, or discrimination. The supply of labor is relatively low for jobs that are dangerous, dirty, or difficult; accordingly, workers in those jobs receive compensating wage differentials that elevate their wages above those paid for safer, cleaner, and easier jobs.

Differing wage rates contribute to a wide divergence in family incomes across the United States, and an even wider income gap between typical families in rich countries and poor countries. The share of income received by the richest 20 percent of U.S. families is 6 times that of the poorest 20 percent of families. Safety nets for poor workers and their families include government programs that provide food, financial assistance, and health care, along with education and training so that workers can improve their employment prospects. Federal and state laws have also established minimum wage rates. The workers who receive minimum wages are made better off by these laws, but minimum wage laws can cause unemployment—so, as usual, there are trade-offs.

The markets for land and capital work very much like the market for labor. The demand for each factor is determined by the marginal revenue product of that factor, and the price of each factor is established by the equilibrium of supply and demand in the market for that factor. A difference is that the supply curve for land is less elastic than the supply curve for labor due to the relative difficulty of increasing the supply of land.

KEY TERMS

derived demand,
    p. 156

marginal revenue product (MRP),
    p. 157

compensating wage differential,
    p. 162

PROBLEMS FOR REVIEW

1. Using a separate graph for each change, show the effects of the following changes on the market labor demand curve. (*Hint:* The change might cause a shift in, or movement along, the market labor demand curve. You do not need to draw any other curves.)
   a. an increase in the wage rate
   b. an increase in the price of the good that the workers produce
   c. a decrease in the marginal product of labor
   d. a decrease in the number of firms

2. Fill in the missing numbers in the following table.

Quantity of Labor (workers)	Total Output	Marginal Product of Labor	Marginal Revenue	Marginal Revenue Product
1	22	22	$2	
2	45		2	
3		20	2	
4	80		2	
5		10	2	

If the wage rate is $25, how many workers should the firm hire?

3. Using a separate graph for each change, show the effects of the following changes on the market labor supply curve.

   a. a decrease in the wage rate
   b. an increase in the opportunity cost of time spent working
   c. a decrease in the marginal product of labor
   d. an increase in the number of workers

4. For 30 years, the Ringling Brothers' and Barnum and Bailey Circus operated Clown College. Suppose the tuition for Clown College doubles, making it more difficult to obtain clown qualifications. What will happen to each of the following?

   a. the market labor supply curve for clowns
   b. the market labor demand curve for clowns
   c. the equilibrium wage rate for clowns
   d. the equilibrium quantity of clowns hired

5. Suppose the demand for hammocks increases. What will happen to each of the following in the market for hammock makers?

   a. the market labor supply curve
   b. the market labor demand curve
   c. the equilibrium wage rate
   d. the equilibrium quantity of workers hired

6. Suppose a shop called Buy the Sea Shore sells seashells in a perfectly competitive shell market and hires labor from a perfectly competitive labor market. Draw the labor demand curve and the labor supply curve for Buy the Sea Shore, assuming these curves have their usual shapes. Then show how a decrease in the supply of labor *in the market* will affect your graph. Label the quantity of labor hired before and after the labor supply decreases as L_1 and L_2 respectively.

7. Draw a graph for a labor market with a perfectly inelastic (vertical) labor demand curve and an upward-sloping labor supply curve. Label the equilibrium quantity of labor L_e and the equilibrium wage rate W_e. Draw a dotted line at the level of a minimum wage rate set above the equilibrium wage rate. Label the minimum wage W_m and the quantity of labor supplied at the minimum wage L_m. Label the distance along the horizontal axis that represents unemployment.

8. Workers in each of the following occupations earn more than the average wage. Indicate characteristics of each occupation that might lead to high wages by causing the demand for labor to be relatively high or the supply of labor to be relatively low.

   a. firefighting
   b. rocket science
   c. television broadcasting
   d. farming

9. Describe one situation not mentioned in the chapter in which discrimination in the hiring process would:

   a. conflict with a firm's profit maximization
   b. be acceptable due to a bona fide occupational qualification (BFOQ)

10. What is one pro and one con of a minimum wage? Do you believe that raising the minimum wage would be an appropriate way to decrease income inequality? Why or why not?

11. Advances in automation and robotics have eliminated some jobs. Examples include cashiers replaced by self-checkout lanes and manufacturing workers replaced by robotic arms. At the same time, those technological advances have created new jobs for engineers, software developers, and other workers who build, sell, and support the new systems. What incentives are there for workers to obtain the levels of education required to fill these new jobs? Do you believe these incentives are adequate? Explain one new government policy or program you would implement to encourage more workers to obtain the education and training needed to fill high-tech jobs.

Market Failure and Government Failure

12

ArtFamily/Shutterstock

When you're immunized against chickenpox or the flu, other people benefit because you don't contract these diseases and pass them along. When deciding how many vaccinations to get, do you consider the benefits other people receive from your vaccinations? If not, you might get too few vaccinations and too much flu, from a societal point of view.

Purchasing and wearing "I-♥-Immunizations" T-shirts affects other people as well. On one hand, the message could encourage more people to get vaccinated, which means they are less likely to spread disease to others. On the other hand, unless the T-shirts are made with organic cotton, the purchase of more T-shirts can lead to more use of the potentially dangerous pesticides, herbicides, and fertilizers that are often applied to cotton crops. If you and the 7 billion other cotton consumers on the planet don't factor these effects into your decisions, the result is an inefficiently large number of T-shirts.

Why Should I Care?

When markets fail to allocate resources efficiently, the result can be too little of things you probably appreciate, such as education, immunizations, and police protection, and too much of things you probably don't want a lot of, such as trash, toxins, and traffic. The good news is that government policies can sometimes provide remedies for market failure. The bad news is that government policies can also fail. **A better understanding of how and when markets don't function as they should, and when government efforts to thwart market failure are likely to flop, can lead to less failure and more fixes.**

Market Failure: Sources and Remedies

Under the right conditions, markets provide incentives for consumers and firms to allocate resources efficiently. The conditions are right for efficiency when: (1) Firms are perfectly competitive; (2) consumers and firms have all the information that is relevant to their decisions in the marketplace; (3) consumers can't use any goods or services without paying for them; and (4) there are no **externalities,** which are side effects felt by people other than those causing the effects. Examples of such side effects include the benefits from immunizations and the damage caused by pollution.

Unfortunately, the real world is an imperfect place where those conditions are hard to meet. When markets do not allocate resources efficiently, the result is called **market failure.** Markets can also fail to achieve fair or *equitable* outcomes, which consumers strongly desire, as discussed in Chapter 8. In this section, you will learn about the sources of market failure and the available remedies.

externalities
Side effects felt by people other than those causing the effects.

market failure
When markets do not allocate resources efficiently.

positive externalities
Desirable effects felt by people who were not involved in the decisions that created those effects.

Allen Creative/Steve Allen/Alamy stockphoto

▲ The reasons for market failure include spillover effects called *externalities* that are felt by people who were not involved in the decisions that created those effects. For example, the decision to drive causes the externalities of road congestion and pollution.

POSITIVE EXTERNALITIES

Positive externalities are desirable effects felt by people uninvolved in the decisions that created those effects. By reducing the spread of disease, immunizations create positive externalities. Well-educated people create positive externalities by passing on knowledge to people around them and by making informed decisions as voters and community members. So by going to college,

Dave Anderson

▲ Planting flowers creates the positive externality of beauty for passersby. Because the people deciding how many flowers to plant don't receive all the benefits of their decisions, they are unlikely to plant the quantity that is best for society.

you are a source of positive externalities. Other sources of positive externalities include bakeries that send sweet smells into the air, homeowners who plant beautiful gardens enjoyed by passersby, and bloggers who post valuable information online for free.

By going to college, you are a source of positive externalities.

When analyzing the effects of externalities, it is helpful to break them down and consider the external benefit or cost of each unit of a good. The increase in the external benefit created by the purchase of one more unit of a good is called the **marginal external benefit.** If each flu vaccination is worth $10 to people other than the purchaser—because the vaccination cuts the risk of them catching the flu from the purchaser—the marginal external benefit of each flu vaccination is $10.

Of course, the purchaser also benefits from the vaccination. The purchaser's benefit from one more unit of a good is called the **marginal private benefit.** The **marginal social benefit** is the additional benefit for everyone affected by the purchase of one more unit, so it equals the marginal private benefit plus the marginal external benefit:

marginal social benefit = marginal private benefit
+ marginal external benefit

Suppose the 50th buyer of a flu vaccination gets $25 worth of benefit and that, again, other people get $10 worth of benefit from each flu vaccination. That means the 50th flu vaccination provides a marginal private benefit of $25, a marginal external benefit of $10, and a marginal social benefit of $25 + $10 = $35. Likewise, the marginal social benefit of every other recipient's flu vaccination exceeds the marginal private benefit by the $10 marginal external benefit. Figure 12.1 illustrates how the $10 marginal external benefit lifts the marginal social benefit curve up above the marginal private benefit curve by $10.

A firm's cost of providing one more flu vaccination is called the **marginal private cost.** In the next section, you'll learn how the *marginal social cost*

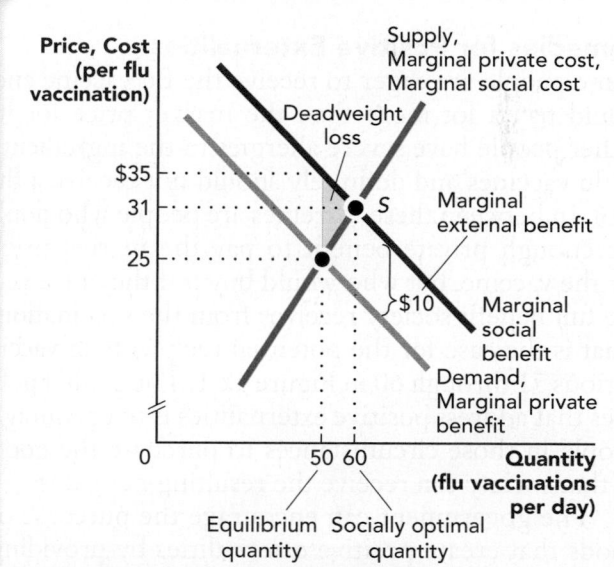

FIGURE 12.1 A Positive Externality Results in a Deadweight Loss

When a good such as flu vaccinations creates positive externalities, each unit of the good provides a benefit to *society* that isn't received by the buyers or sellers of the good. Consequently, the quantity purchased is less than the best quantity for society, and the result is a deadweight loss.

exceeds the marginal private cost when there are negative externalities. However, in this example vaccinations create only positive externalities, so there is no difference between those two costs.

Earlier chapters explained that the supply and demand curves for a good are based on the good's marginal cost and marginal benefit. Now that we have distinguished between "private" and "social" benefits and costs, we should clarify that a good's marginal private cost and marginal private benefit are the bases for supply and demand. Figure 12.1 shows the market equilibrium at the intersection of the supply (marginal private cost) curve and the demand (marginal private benefit) curve. The equilibrium price is $25, and the equilibrium quantity is 50 vaccinations. However, because only 50 vaccinations are received, society misses out on the net gain—the difference between the marginal social benefit and the marginal social cost—that the next 10 vaccinations would have provided. This results in a deadweight loss, which is represented by the yellow area between the marginal social benefit curve and the marginal social cost curve over the range from 50 to 60 vaccinations.

The *socially optimal quantity* that would eliminate the deadweight loss is 60. The socially optimal quantity is found on the quantity axis below point *S*, where the marginal social cost curve and the marginal social benefit curve intersect.

Remedies for Positive Externalities

Some people are eager to receive the flu vaccine and would pay a lot more than the market price for it. Other people have severe allergies to the ingredients in flu vaccines and definitely should not receive a flu shot. In between these extremes are people who don't see enough private benefit to pay the market price for the vaccine, but who would buy it if they received the full benefit society receives from the vaccination. That is the case for the potential recipients of vaccinations 51 through 60 in Figure 12.1. The goal of policies that address positive externalities is to encourage people in those circumstances to purchase the good so that society can receive the resulting net gains.

The government can encourage the purchase of goods that create positive externalities by providing payments called *subsidies* to buyers or sellers. If each recipient of a flu vaccination gets a $10 subsidy from the government, the buyers *internalize*, or feel personally, the full benefit of their decision and do what is best for society. That is, by setting the subsidy equal to the marginal external benefit of the vaccine, consumers receive the amount that separates the marginal private benefit and the marginal social benefit. This effectively shifts the marginal private benefit (demand) curve up to equal the marginal social benefit curve. The new demand curve coincides with the marginal social benefit curve in Figure 12.1 and intersects the supply curve at a quantity of 60. The fortunate result is that consumers buy every vaccination that provides a social benefit that exceeds its social cost.

Suppose that, without a subsidy, your marginal private benefit of getting vaccinated is $23. In this case, you would *not* pay the market price of $25 for a flu vaccination that's worth only $23 to you, even though it's worth $23 + $10 = $33 to society. By increasing demand, the subsidy creates a new equilibrium at point *S* in Figure 12.1. The new equilibrium price is $31. However, after receiving the $10 subsidy, the portion of that $31 that you actually pay is only $31 − $10 = $21. You *would* pay $21 for a vaccination you value at $23, so the subsidy motivates you to do what's best for society.

Chapter 6 explained that the effect of a tax is the same whether it's collected from the buyer or the seller. Likewise, the effect of a subsidy is the same whether it's given to buyers or sellers. Either way, a subsidy equal to the marginal external benefit will close the gap between the marginal social benefit and the marginal social cost, yielding the socially optimal quantity. Subsidies are used in efforts to achieve efficiency in the markets for education, vaccinations, solar panels, and tree seedlings, among other goods and services. Regretfully, there is not yet a subsidy given to sweet-smelling bakeries.

A second way to deal with positive externalities is for the government to require a certain amount of the good or service that creates the externalities.

▲ Because trees create the positive externalities of beauty and clean air, private incentives don't lead consumers to buy the best quantity of trees for society. As a remedy for this, some local governments subsidize citizens' tree purchases by paying part of the price of each tree.

Andy Katz/Pacific Press/LightRocket via Getty Images

Every state requires at least some vaccinations, with varying exceptions based on a person's medical conditions, religious beliefs, and philosophical disagreements. Every state also requires students to receive a certain amount of education. If policy makers succeed in requiring the socially optimal quantity of these goods and services, the result can be an efficient allocation of resources. However, a lot of information is required to find the socially optimal quantity: The government needs accurate estimates of the marginal private benefit and the marginal private cost, in addition to the marginal external benefit. In contrast, the subsidy solution only requires the government to estimate the marginal external benefit. With the correct subsidy in place, what buyers and sellers know about their own private benefits and costs will guide the equilibrium to the socially optimal quantity.

NEGATIVE EXTERNALITIES

Your high school probably had a rule against wearing T-shirts decorated with obscenities. The buyers of such T-shirts presumably like them, but some other people are offended by them. An offensive T-shirt creates **negative externalities,** which are undesirable effects felt by people who were not involved in the decisions that created those effects.

The production and transportation of T-shirts and most other goods also creates negative externalities. For example, the extraction and processing of raw materials such as oil, which is used to make polyester fabric, adversely affect wildlife and cause the release of toxic chemicals. The combustion of each gallon of gasoline or diesel fuel causes the release of between 18 and 22 pounds of carbon dioxide, a greenhouse gas that contributes to global warming. More than 95 percent of transportation in the United States is powered by fossil fuels. Diesel fuel, gasoline, and coal power the tractors in the cotton fields, the trucks that bring cotton to market, the factories that make cotton fabric and T-shirts, the freighters that carry T-shirts across the oceans, the trains and trucks that haul the shirts to stores, and the cars that carry shoppers to the mall to buy them. Negative externalities are the aftermath of all of these activities.

The fact that producing or using certain goods imposes costs on society doesn't mean that none of those goods should be made. It is efficient to produce T-shirts, even offensive ones, as long as the marginal cost to society of doing so is less than the marginal benefit to society. The trouble with negative externalities is that they raise the cost paid by society above the cost paid by decision makers. The amount

by which one more unit increases the external cost is called the **marginal external cost.** The full cost to society of making another unit, the **marginal social cost,** is the sum of the marginal private cost and the marginal external cost:

$$\text{marginal social cost} = \text{marginal private cost} \\ + \text{marginal external cost}$$

Suppose the marginal external cost of each T-shirt is \$2. Figure 12.2 shows how the marginal external cost causes the marginal social cost to exceed the marginal private cost. The market equilibrium at the intersection of the supply and demand curves determines the equilibrium price of \$15 and the equilibrium quantity of 100. So the market produces a quantity that differs from the socially optimal quantity of 80, found at the intersection of the marginal social cost curve and the marginal social benefit curve at point *S*.

negative externalities
Undesirable effects felt by people who were not involved in the decisions that created those effects.

marginal external cost
The amount by which one more unit increases the external cost.

marginal social cost
The sum of the marginal private cost and the marginal external cost.

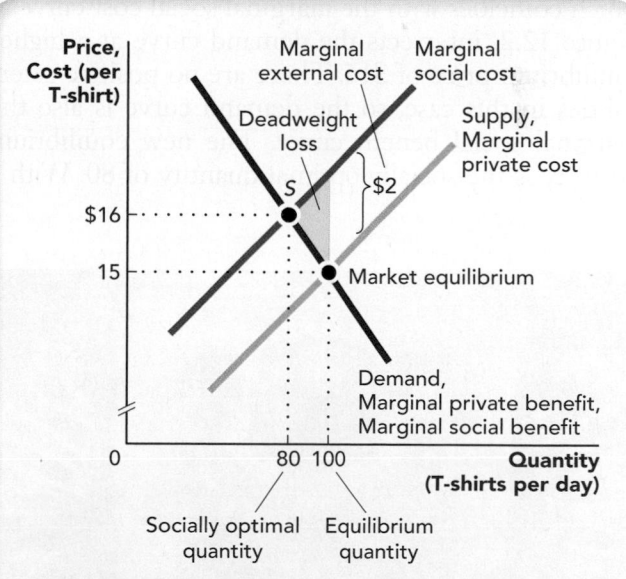

FIGURE 12.2 A Negative Externality Results in a Deadweight Loss

When there are negative externalities, each unit of the good imposes a marginal external cost on society that isn't paid by either the buyers or the sellers of the good. As a result, too much of the good is consumed.

The first 80 T-shirts provide a marginal social benefit that equals or exceeds the marginal social cost, so they should be produced despite the associated $2 marginal external cost. Each T-shirt beyond 80 imposes a cost on society that exceeds the benefit it provides, as indicated by the marginal social cost curve being above the marginal social benefit curve for those units. The yellow area between the two curves labeled deadweight loss shows the net loss to society as a result of producing 100 T-shirts instead of the socially optimal 80.

Remedies for Negative Externalities

The first few T-shirts provide value that far exceeds their cost. Your most valued T-shirts might be the ones from your first 5K race, your favorite concert, and your favorite sports team. But then there's the T-shirt you bought on your rained-out beach vacation because you were bored and it was cheap. Society is worse off from the existence of any such shirts, for which the cost to you and to the rest of society exceeds the benefit to you.

One solution is to have firms pay the full cost of what they produce, including the marginal external cost. This can be done by imposing an excise tax on the good equal to the marginal external cost—$2 in our T-shirt story. From the consumers' point of view, the $2 tax shifts the supply curve up by $2 to equal the marginal social cost curve. The new supply curve, which coincides with the marginal social cost curve in Figure 12.2, intersects the demand curve at a higher equilibrium price of $16. There are no positive externalities in this case, so the demand curve is also the marginal social benefit curve. The new equilibrium quantity is the socially optimal quantity of 80. With a $2 excise tax in place for T-shirts, you would still purchase your favorites, but not the ones that are worth less to you than the cost to society. Excise taxes like this already exist for many goods that cause negative externalities, including alcohol, cigarettes, and gasoline.

Regulation is a second solution for negative externalities. For example, in the United States (among other countries), the government limits the amount of sulfur dioxide power plants can emit and the number of fish that can be caught in certain waterways. The government estimates the socially optimal quantity and limits output to that quantity. As with government requirements for the purchase of goods and services such as vaccines that create positive externalities, if the government correctly identifies the socially optimal quantity, limits can achieve an efficient allocation of resources. But to set appropriate limits, the government needs good estimates of the marginal private benefit and the marginal private cost, along with the marginal external cost. The tax solution only requires the government to estimate the marginal external cost because, as we have seen, an excise tax equal to the marginal external cost provides the needed incentive for consumers to purchase the socially optimal quantity.

In some cases, policy makers decide they do have enough information to set limits. In extreme cases, policy makers estimate that even the first unit has a marginal social cost that exceeds the marginal social benefit. The optimal quantity of these products is 0. This is why there are laws that forbid, for example, the sale of deadly drugs such as heroin and cocaine, the manufacture of paint and gasoline containing lead (which is toxic), and the sale of products made from the bodies of endangered animals.

IMPERFECT INFORMATION

Even if everything else about a market is ideal, a lack of information can cause market failure. If firms don't have good information on consumer demand, they won't respond to the needs and wants of society. If consumers don't know what goods and services are available or where to find the best prices, they won't be able to make choices that maximize their happiness. And if consumers aren't fully aware of the benefits of a good or service, the demand for it will be too low. For example, consumers who don't know the health benefits of avocados don't buy as many of them as they should. And researchers have found that the best way to increase school attendance in Africa—better than bribes of food, money, or medical care—is to spread information about how education improves people's lives.

Dave Anderson

▲ Some T-shirts are worth their weight in gold to their owners. But, as the result of negative externalities in the production process, some T-shirts cost society more than they are worth.

How exactly does the government put limits on things such as pollution and fishing?

In some cases, a specific limit is imposed on each source of negative externalities, such as a limit of 100 tons of sulfur dioxide emissions per factory per year, or a catch limit of 1,000 fish per boat per day. Relatively new *cap-and-trade* approaches provide more flexibility and better incentives for the firms being regulated. For instance, coal-fired power plants in the United States now receive *tradable emissions permits* that allow them to emit a certain amount of sulfur dioxide each year. If a power plant can reduce its emissions enough that it doesn't need all its tradable emissions permits, it can then sell its extra permits to another power plant that has greater difficulty reducing its emissions, perhaps because it is older and has less effective filtration systems. This gives every power plant an incentive to reduce emissions when it is reasonably inexpensive to do so, because every reduction means either the plant can sell more permits, or it doesn't have to buy as many permits. Similar systems with permits called *individual transferable quotas* are in place in some commercial fisheries.

Asymmetric information exists when either the buyer or the seller has more information than the other party. Sellers often have more insight about their products than buyers. If a seller convinces buyers that a product is better than it really is, the demand for it will be inappropriately high. Perhaps you know people who thought they were buying a deluxe vacation at a reasonable price, only to find that they paid too much for a lousy hotel on a crummy beach.

The asymmetric information problem of **adverse selection** involves one party taking advantage of information the other party lacks when the second party is deciding what to buy or sell. For instance, people who face particularly high risks of health problems are more likely to buy health insurance. If insurance companies can't identify high-risk customers, they can't charge prices that reflect the risks buyers pose.

Economist George Akerlof points out that when the sellers of used cars know more about their cars than potential buyers, adverse selection can fill the

> **asymmetric information**
> When either the buyer or the seller has more information than the other party.
>
> **adverse selection**
> When one party takes advantage of information the other party lacks when the second party is deciding what to buy or sell.

Cartoon Resource/Shutterstock.com

"I'm looking to dramatically increase my insurance coverage."

◀ Like this man preparing to jump over a line of cars on his motorcycle, you know more about your insurance needs than your insurance company does. Asymmetric information such as this can lead to adverse selection and cause market failure if insurers charge prices that don't account for the risks their customers take.

used-car market with "lemons"—cars that have major flaws. Suppose a good used car is worth $20,000 and a lemon of a used car is worth $10,000. Buyers are unwilling to pay $20,000 for a used car that might only be worth $10,000. Because imperfect information makes it necessary for sellers to charge a price below the value of a good used car, the owners of good used cars are dissuaded from selling them. But buyers will pay $10,000 for a used car, and maybe more if they think the car might be a good one. So lemon owners are content to sell their cars, and lemons dominate the market.

Imperfect information also causes problems with the risks insurance customers take. Smartphones can cost more than $1,000 to replace, but you can buy insurance that lowers the replacement cost considerably. Would you be as careful with a smartphone if you didn't have insurance as if you did? **Moral hazard** is the problem of people taking more risks when they are insured against the consequences. Because insurance companies can't monitor how carefully their customers treat their smartphones, the companies have difficulty charging higher prices to customers who throw their phones around, bring them to the beach, or leave them in unlocked cars.

moral hazard
The problem of people taking more risks when they are insured against the consequences.

copayment
A fixed amount of money that someone with insurance must pay each time the individual incurs a cost covered by the insurance.

coinsurance
When the insured pay some percentage of the costs incurred.

deductible
The amount that insurance customers must pay before their insurance starts covering costs.

Moral hazard is a problem with many forms of insurance, including health insurance, fire insurance, and theft insurance, which leads people to take more risks with the security of their valuables. It is also a problem for firms that have insurance or receive government protection. For example, when the U.S. government protected financial institutions such as Bear Stearns from bankruptcy during the Great Recession, economists noted that if financial institutions expect the government to bail them out when they make bad investments, the financial institutions might take excessive risks.

Remedies for Imperfect Information

Insurance companies have developed several useful approaches to asymmetric information problems. Health insurance companies try to separate more and less healthy customers by offering differing levels of coverage at different prices. The Affordable Care Act in the United States offers four levels of coverage: bronze, silver, gold, and platinum. People with healthy lifestyles will find the smaller amounts of coverage under the bronze plan desirable and will be charged a lower price. People who know they are unhealthy will reveal themselves by selecting greater amounts of coverage under the silver, gold, or platinum plans and will be charged a higher price.

Life insurance companies typically require new customers to get a checkup to make sure they don't have preexisting conditions that threaten their lives. Car insurance companies use information on driver age, gender, participation in drivers' education classes, grades in school, and car type (among other things) to price new policies according to likely costs. Over time, there are further price adjustments based on each driver's experience with accidents, speeding tickets, and related incidents.

Another line of defense against moral hazard involves *copayments*, *coinsurance*, and *deductibles* that require the insured to bear some of the burden of risk taking. A **copayment** is a fixed amount of money that someone with insurance must pay each time the individual incurs a cost covered by the insurance. For instance, your medical insurance might have you pay $15 each time you buy a prescription medication. With **coinsurance**, the insured pay some percentage of the costs incurred. For example, patients with the original Medicare medical insurance pay 20 percent of the cost of their treatment. A **deductible** is an amount that insurance customers must pay before their insurance starts covering costs. For instance, in 2018 a patient with Medicare hospital insurance had to pay the first $1,340 of his or

▲ Because insurance companies have incomplete information on their customers' behaviors, the insurers can't always raise prices for those customers who take high risks. This causes the moral hazard problem of excessive risk taking by the insured.

AlexandrBognat/Getty Images

her hospital bills before the insurance would cover any costs. Copayments, coinsurance, and deductibles might make some people think twice before taking up smoking or riding a bike without a helmet.

Modern technology also provides some remedies for information problems. For example, sardine fishermen in India used to unintentionally supply some cities with so many fish that prices plummeted and fishermen had to discard large quantities of sardines. What the fishermen didn't know was that sardines sold for much higher prices in neighboring cities. Today, the fishermen have cell phones that enable them to check prices in many cities and bring their fish to wherever the need is greatest. Economist Robert Jenson found that after cell phones became widely used by the Indian fishermen, sardine prices became more consistent, the fishermen earned more profit, and fewer fish were wasted.

The Internet contains so much information on virtually everything that it has been called the *information superhighway*. Although information on the Internet is far from perfect, it contributes much to the efficiency of markets. Websites like Amazon, craigslist, eBay, and Zillow help bring together buyers and sellers who wouldn't otherwise find each other. Online reviews from Angie's List, Yelp, TripAdvisor, the Better Business Bureau, and Consumer Reports help consumers better understand the quality of what they're buying. And myth-busting websites such as Snopes.com try to set the facts straight on topics steeped in misinformation.

That said, it is important to remember that most information on the Internet doesn't go through the extensive fact-checking process common among publishers of the best newspapers, journals, and books. Unfortunately, misinformation travels across the information superhighway as fast as facts do—maybe even faster. For instance, websites that feature reviews struggle to keep sellers from posting glowing reviews of their own goods and services. Even so, the proliferation of credible websites provides unquestionable benefits to information seekers.

Advances in data collection are changing the world of marketing. To gather information about their customers, many sellers use credit card numbers, names, email addresses, and store loyalty card information to track their customers' purchases. If a woman buys a pregnancy test and then prenatal vitamins, the store knows to start sending her coupons for diapers and baby food. Even more information is revealed by online browsing and shopping. Your clicks reveal your favorite styles,

Source: ebay

▲ Are you looking for something unusual? Auction websites like eBay and online retailers like Amazon match buyers and sellers who wouldn't otherwise find each other. And online reviews help buyers understand what they're getting. Unfortunately, the Internet also facilitates the spread of *misinformation* because the fact-checking procedures of many websites are insufficient.

sports, and cereals, and sellers are likely to follow up with ads for related products.

Because information remains so important, costly, and incomplete, the government tries to ensure that consumers have the information they need to make good buying decisions. For example, the Federal Trade Commission requires the disclosure of any compensation that reviewers receive for product endorsements, including "clicks" and "likes" on social media. To reveal information on food safety, restaurants in most states must post their food-safety scores for customers to see. To foster competition in the travel market, hotels in most European countries must post their room rates outside their front doors where passersby can easily find them. To help ensure a satisfactory level of expertise among specialized service providers, states require teachers, sports agents, electricians, accountants, doctors, and lawyers, among other professionals, to obtain a license in their field. And a variety of government agencies

Table 12.1 Federal Government Agencies and the Information They Provide

Agency	Information Provided
Consumer Financial Protection Bureau (CFPB)	Information about how to avoid deceptive practices by financial firms, pay for college, own a home, and plan for retirement.
Consumer Product Safety Commission (CPSC)	Safety education and information on recalls, regulations, product testing, and the latest research on product safety.
Federal Trade Commission (FTC)	Alerts about consumer fraud, education on the rights and responsibilities of consumers and firms, and tips on how to avoid scams.
Food and Drug Administration (FDA)	Research-based information to help consumers maintain and improve their health with medicines and foods.
Occupational Safety and Health Administration (OSHA)	Education and training on workplace safety to help workers and firms create safe and healthy work environments.

Sherman Antitrust Act
Legislation that restricts anticompetitive behavior by firms, such as the consolidation of several companies under the control of one business enterprise known as a *trust*.

work to promote the information available to consumers, workers, and firms. Table 12.1 lists several federal government agencies and the types of information they provide to consumers and firms.

IMPERFECT COMPETITION

The real-world flu-vaccine market has only a small number of firms, which makes the competition in this market imperfect. The same problem exists for goods ranging from breakfast cereal to sleep medicine—the many products you see on the store shelves are made by a small number of firms. For example, Kellogg's, Post, General Mills, and Quaker Oats make most of the cereals you'll find in a typical grocery store. This means the market for these products isn't perfectly competitive and that the firms have some market power.

You learned in Chapter 10 that imperfectly competitive firms charge a price above the marginal cost and produce less than the socially optimal quantity. So, as with positive and negative externalities, the

Recall that imperfect competition leads to a deadweight loss.

result of imperfect competition is a deadweight loss. This loss to society and the associated high prices and low quantities involved have troubled economists for hundreds of years. Next, we'll discuss legislation enacted to limit these pitfalls.

Remedies for Imperfect Competition

The first federal law to limit market power was preceded by problems with imperfect competition in the oil market that bubbled up more than a century ago. In 1890, Standard Oil of Ohio controlled almost 90 percent of the oil refined in the United States. That same year, Congress passed the **Sherman Antitrust Act,** legislation that restricts anticompetitive behavior by firms, such as Standard Oil's consolidation of several companies under the control of one business enterprise known as a *trust*. The Act's author, Senator John Sherman, wrote that the Act's purpose is "to protect the consumers by preventing arrangements designed . . . to advance the cost of goods to the consumer." In other words, he didn't want you to have to pay unnecessarily high prices due to market power. The Act's immediate effect on Standard Oil was to reduce the firm's market power by dividing it into 34 independent companies. Exxon-Mobil, ConocoPhillips, and Chevron are some of the companies that descended from the split-up of Standard Oil.

In 1914, Congress passed the **Clayton Antitrust Act** to deter anticompetitive practices the Sherman Act failed to address. The Clayton Act prohibits the following actions (not in all situations, but when they would substantially decrease competition in a market):

- The same person sitting on the boards of directors of competing firms
- Price discrimination (discussed in Chapter 10)
- Mergers and acquisitions that turn multiple firms into one
- Exclusive trade agreements between firms

The Clayton Act covers several types of anticompetitive trade agreements. An **exclusive dealing agreement** prevents a buyer from making purchases from the competitors of a particular seller. For example, the case of *United States v. Dentsply International, Inc.*, established that under the Clayton Act, a manufacturer of artificial teeth could not prevent its dental-dealer customers from carrying competing brands of teeth. A **tying agreement** requires a buyer to purchase a second product from the seller. For instance, the case of *Eastman Kodak Company v. Image Technical Services, Inc.* established that Kodak could not require buyers of its copy-machine parts to purchase its repair services as well. In 1914, Congress also created the Federal Trade Commission, which helps to police anticompetitive practices such as corporate mergers and acquisitions, and keeps consumers informed.

PUBLIC GOODS

When a tornado rips through Oklahoma City, the area's $4.5 million system of 181 tornado sirens alerts citizens to take cover. Roughly 20,000 tornado sirens stand at the ready across the United States, but these outdoor sirens weren't purchased by private individuals. Let's consider why. To begin with, a tornado siren is a *non-rival good*. More than one person can use the same unit of a **non-rival good** at the same time. If a siren alerts your neighbor, you will be alerted as well. On the other hand, a T-shirt is a *rival good*, because while your neighbor wears it, you cannot. A tornado siren is also *non-excludable*. When a **non-excludable good** is in use by one person, there is no way to exclude others from using it. A good such as a tornado siren that is both non-rival and non-excludable is called a **public good.** Other public goods include streetlights, fire departments, disease control efforts, fireworks displays, crime prevention, health and safety inspections, and military protection. Goods such as T-shirts, gasoline, and candy bars that are rival and excludable are called **private goods.**

When a tornado is approaching, warning sirens save lives. Yet people don't go to the store and buy this type of public alert system for themselves. If someone else in your neighborhood

▲ Because free riders can be protected by tornado sirens without having to pay for them, too few of these public goods would be purchased if they were provided in a private market.

Clayton Antitrust Act Legislation that prohibits anticompetitive actions such as price discrimination, mergers, and exclusive trade agreements between firms when such actions would substantially decrease competition in a market.

exclusive dealing agreement An agreement that prevents a buyer from making purchases from the competitors of a seller.

tying agreement An agreement that requires a buyer to purchase a second product from the seller.

non-rival good A good the same unit of which can be used by more than one person at the same time.

non-excludable good A good others can't be excluded from using.

public good A good that is both non-rival and non-excludable.

private goods Goods that are rival and excludable.

bought a tornado siren, you would be able to *free ride* on that purchase. To **free ride** is to enjoy the benefits of a good without paying for it. The opportunity to free ride makes everyone in the neighborhood reluctant to spend their money on a siren, so if private individuals were the only ones buying sirens, there would be too few. Likewise, people would buy too few streetlights, fireworks displays, and police cars if they thought they might be able to free ride on the purchases of others. The underallocation of resources for public goods such as these makes public goods a source of market failure.

Remedies for Free-Rider Problems

You may have noticed that all the public goods we have mentioned are sometimes or always provided by the government and funded with tax revenues. By requiring most citizens to pay taxes to help provide goods and services with widespread benefits, free riding is limited. This solution is implemented at every level of government. For example, the federal government provides military protection and the centers for disease control. State governments provide prisons and enforce health and safety standards. City and county governments provide fire departments and streetlights. Similarly, many neighborhood associations require residents to pay dues that are used to purchase flowerbeds, security cameras, playgrounds, and other public goods.

INEQUITY

Chapter 1 introduced the three fundamental economic questions, the last of which asks: For whom should goods be produced? Market economies distribute goods to the people who are willing and able to pay the highest prices for them. In some cases, the people who can pay the highest prices are not those with the most to gain from a good. And sometimes markets distribute income and goods in ways that are less than fair. For example, markets provide no income to a worker who was laid off during a recession or was incapacitated by a work-related injury. It is a normative question whether it is fair for that person to have nothing. When inequities do exist, there are ways to address them, but the solutions involve trade-offs.

free ride
To enjoy the benefits of a good without paying for it.

government failure
When governments implement policies that allocate resources inefficiently.

Remedies for Inequity

Governments typically address equity goals by collecting taxes disproportionally from rich citizens and using tax revenues to fund programs for underprivileged citizens. For instance, high-income workers pay a larger percentage of their income in U.S. federal income taxes than low-income workers. Revenues from these and other taxes fund programs designed to improve equity, such as Social Security, Medicare, Medicaid, unemployment insurance, and Temporary Aid to Needy Families (TANF). Previous chapters explained minimum wage policies and antidiscrimination laws that were also established with the goal of equity.

Conflicts between equity and efficiency complicate policy decisions. For example, valuable programs that promote equity are funded by taxes that cause inefficiency. You have seen how sales taxes cause deadweight losses by deterring sales that would otherwise benefit consumers and firms. Minimum wages similarly reduce the number of workers hired below the efficient level, and income taxes reduce the incentive to work. These sources of inefficiency weigh against the equity improvements that come from better educational opportunities, health care systems, and job training programs. The normative decisions of which programs to fund are generally left to policy makers and voters, but economists can provide useful information to decision makers by measuring the costs and the benefits of particular programs.

Government Failure: Sources and Remedies

Solutions to market failure often involve government policies, but governments can fail, too. When governments implement policies that allocate resources inefficiently, the result is **government failure.** The sources of government failure include:

- *Imperfect information.* Some information that would help the government make better decisions is prohibitively expensive or impossible to obtain.
- *Conflicting perspectives and goals.* Disagreements among government policy makers and their constituents lead to conflicts that use up time, energy, and money.
- *Bureaucratic inefficiencies.* The organization of a government requires paperwork, administrative work, and communications that take time and money away from more productive activities.

This section explores these and related sources of government failure. Note that corruption is another source of inefficiency in both governments and firms, as discussed in Chapter 18.

IMPERFECT INFORMATION

In their pursuit of efficiency, policy makers face a challenging wish list of information. When choosing the size of a tax or subsidy to remedy an externality problem, such as a tax on gasoline or a subsidy for tree seedlings, policy makers must estimate the size of the externality. When setting caps on various types of pollution, policy makers must estimate the private costs and benefits of the ability to pollute, as well as the external costs of pollution, in order to find the best quantity for society. When setting a price that will allow a natural monopoly to cover its

costs, policy makers must estimate the monopoly's average total cost. And when determining the optimal quantity of a public good to provide, policy makers must estimate the benefits to everyone who uses the good. Miscalculations can lead to taxes, subsidies, limits, and public good purchases of the wrong size, and thus to misallocated resources.

The government hires thousands of scientists, economists, and other experts to help find the information needed for policy making. But information-seeking is expensive, and research methods, the availability of data, and the interpretation of the results are all imperfect. Consider some of the existing research on the external cost of gasoline use in automobiles. Economists Winston Harrington, Ian Parry, and Margaret Walls estimate the external cost to be about $3 per gallon. The International Center for Technology Assessment estimates the external cost to be between $7 and $20. So it is unclear what excise tax per gallon of gasoline would bring the cost of gasoline up to its full cost to society. As of 2018, the national excise tax per gallon of gasoline was $0.184, and the average state and local tax was $0.310, for a total of $0.494 per gallon. So if the true marginal external cost is anywhere in the range of these existing estimates, there is government failure and overconsumption. This failure stems partly from imperfect information, and partly from the types of problems we discuss next.

CONFLICTING PERSPECTIVES AND GOALS

Students of the martial art of aikido are taught not to confront an attacker head on, because collisions drain energy and provide no forward progress. When government officials use their energy in direct opposition to each other, energy can be similarly wasted, along with time and money. Special interest groups—students, retirees, various industries, educators, environmentalists, and so on—also spend large amounts of time, energy, and money to shift government policies in their favor. Moderate disagreements aren't necessarily a problem—an adversary can raise important issues and make policy makers rethink flawed initiatives. And governmental bodies can make progress with a spirit of compromise. But more serious conflicts can lead to stagnation and government failure.

The trade-offs necessary in the world of economics confound matters of policy making and create tension between people with differing objectives. For example, policy makers face a trade-off between the objectives of low inflation and low unemployment in an economy. Why? Because the policies that

▲ Some people feel the government is too big. Other people would like the government to do more to address existing problems.

Jeff Malet/Jeff Malet Photography/Washington DC United States of America/Newscom

Alex Menendez/AP Images

decrease inflation tend to increase unemployment, whereas the policies that decrease unemployment tend to raise inflation. This forces policy makers to choose between the two objectives.

Even when the best objective is clear, the best way to achieve it may not be. During a recession, there is general consensus that the policy objective should be job creation. But there is inevitably disagreement over how best to accomplish that. Some people believe the government should increase its spending to create jobs during a recession. Others believe the government should loosen health and environmental regulations or lower taxes in hopes of creating jobs. So a lot of time, energy, and money are spent arguing about the means to the end.

BUREAUCRATIC INEFFICIENCIES

As the size of a government grows, so does the difficulty of organizing the government's operations and putting the right people in touch with each other to accomplish the government's goals. There are individuals or groups, such as members of Congress or government agencies, who would benefit from exchanges of information. For instance, in order for the many crime-prevention agencies to have full information, there must be communications between the Federal Bureau of Investigation; the Central Intelligence Agency; the Transportation Safety Administration; the National Security Agency; the Secret Service; and federal, state, and local police departments. The number of communications required to exchange information between multiple groups, or parties, grows exponentially as the number of parties grows.

Figure 12.3 shows that with 2 parties, only 1 communication is needed. With 4 parties, 6 communications are needed. With 8 parties, 28 communications are needed. This is indicative of the growing cost of communications and other interactions as a government, or any other organization, grows. The rapid growth in communication costs doesn't necessarily mean there is inefficiency, but it does make it increasingly difficult for the additional benefits of growth to exceed the additional costs.

Economists use the term **transaction costs** to describe the costs of completing a transaction, such as negotiating a policy or purchasing a good, not including the price of the good itself. Transaction costs include

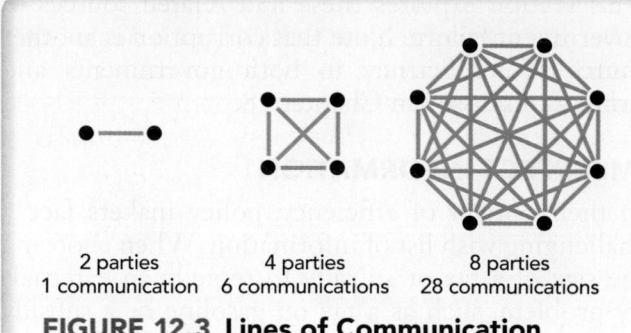

FIGURE 12.3 Lines of Communication
The flow of ideas and information becomes complicated as governments grow. The number of communications needed for each party to share information with every other party grows faster than the number of parties involved.

transaction costs
The costs of completing a transaction, such as negotiating a policy or purchasing a good, not including the price of the good itself (e.g., the costs of any necessary information gathering, communications, and transportation).

the costs of any necessary information gathering, communications, and transportation. If you buy a house, the transaction costs include the time you spend meeting with inspectors, lawyers, and bankers, as well as the fees you pay them.

For a government, transaction costs stem from the politics of lawmaking, the struggles to monitor and enforce compliance with the laws, the red tape of documenting government transactions, and the challenge of educating the nation's citizens, among other burdens. As a government grows, transaction costs grow. You have probably gotten a taste of the transaction costs of paying taxes, passing legislation, and resolving disputes. The Taxpayer Advocate Service estimates that U.S. taxpayers spend 6.1 billion hours a year preparing their taxes. That's a lot of time that cannot be spent making T-shirts or receiving immunizations!

Remedies for Government Failure
The tools of economics can't resolve every political debate, but unbiased cost-benefit analysis and a focus on efficiency are steps in the right direction. The government should invest in more information-gathering, pursue more goals, and cut bureaucratic hurdles until the marginal benefit of these actions equals their marginal cost. The best specific approaches to questionable government programs are less clear due to the trade-offs involved. The targets for government reform, including paperwork requirements, regulations, taxes, and government expenditures, exist for a purpose. The difficult question is whether their purpose justifies their expense. Cost-benefit comparisons become

muddled in the political arena as politicians, corporations, and special-interest groups bring competing agendas and conflicting information to the table.

An important lesson from economics is that even a large benefit does not justify the existence of a program, and even a large cost does not justify the elimination of a program. Rather, programs should live or die on the basis of a careful comparison of all the associated benefits and all the associated costs. For example, the state government of Colorado spends more than any other state on fire prevention, but that large expense is justified by the even larger benefits of fighting fires in a state that is vulnerable to devastating forest fires. One recent fire that did get out of control burned 14,280 acres of forest and destroyed 509 homes.

SUMMARY

Market outcomes are efficient under ideal conditions, but the real world is less than ideal. Externalities, imperfect information, imperfect competition, and free-rider problems stand in the way of market efficiency. If you've ever driven behind a slow, smelly truck, or if you've ever been awed by a neighbor's flower display, you've experienced externalities. Markets overprovide goods that create negative externalities and underprovide goods that create positive externalities. Similarly, buyers with inadequate information about a product may buy too much of it or too little.

Information is also important to firms. For example, health insurance companies with limited information about the health of their customers may charge the wrong price for their policies. Markets also fail when imperfect competition leads to inefficiently high prices and low quantities. And because public goods are non-rival and non-excludable, free riders hope to benefit from what others purchase, which results in too few private purchases of public goods.

There are policy approaches to each of the sources of market failure. To promote the use of goods and services that create positive externalities, the government can provide subsidies or require a certain minimum amount of use, as is the case for education and vaccines. To reduce the use of goods and services that create negative externalities, the government can impose taxes or limit quantities, as is the case for fish caught in some bodies of water. Government agencies such as the Consumer Product Safety Commission help consumers make informed decisions. When asymmetric information makes insurance companies vulnerable to customers who are particularly expensive to insure, insurance companies can require copayments, coinsurance, and deductibles. Life insurance companies typically require new customers to get checkups to make sure they don't have preexisting conditions that could threaten their lives.

Antitrust legislation, including the Sherman Antitrust Act and the Clayton Antitrust Act, targets anticompetitive behavior by firms. With the backing of these laws, the Federal Trade Commission scrutinizes business mergers, acquisitions, pricing practices, and other behavior that could harm consumers. To deter the free-rider problems associated with public goods, the government uses tax revenues to purchase goods and services such as fighter jets, streetlights, and safety inspections.

Even efficient markets can distribute income and goods in unfair ways. One common way to address inequities is to collect taxes disproportionately from the rich and fund programs that serve underprivileged citizens. But trade-offs between equity and efficiency complicate decision making. For example, the tax collections used to fund programs that promote equity can lead to inefficiently low levels of consumption or employment.

Like markets, governments can fail. Governments face imperfect information as they try to determine socially optimal amounts of taxes, subsidies, regulations, and public goods. The optimal size and scope of government is hard to pin down because people have differing priorities and diverse perspectives on the role of government. Conflicting goals and the influence of special-interest groups put lawmakers at odds with one another, which diverts time and money away from forward progress. Additional inefficiencies result from excessive administrative chores and paperwork, among other sources of transaction costs. Although the tools of economics can't resolve every political debate, unbiased cost-benefit analysis is a step in the right direction.

KEY TERMS

externalities, p. 172
market failure, p. 172
positive externalities, p. 172
marginal external benefit, p. 173
marginal private benefit, p. 173
marginal social benefit, p. 173
marginal private cost, p. 173
negative externalities, p. 175
marginal external cost, p. 175
marginal social cost, p. 175

asymmetric information, p. 177
adverse selection, p. 177
moral hazard, p. 178
copayment, p. 178
coinsurance, p. 178
deductible, p. 178
Sherman Antitrust Act, p. 180
Clayton Antitrust Act, p. 181
exclusive dealing agreement,
    p. 181

tying agreement, p. 181
non-rival good, p. 181
non-excludable good, p. 181
public good, p. 181
private goods, p. 181
free ride, p. 182
government failure, p. 182
transaction costs, p. 184

PROBLEMS FOR REVIEW

1. True, false, or uncertain? Perfectly competitive markets allocate resources efficiently. Explain your answer.

2. Identify whether each of the following statements refers to a problem caused by a positive externality, a negative externality, imperfect information, imperfect competition, a public good, or none of the above:

   a. Society would be better off if more people wore smiley-face T-shirts, which brighten the moods of the people who see them.

   b. People pay too much for Lame-brand T-shirts because consumers don't realize the shirts will fall apart after three weeks.

   c. Too few people pitch in to purchase bat houses that attract mosquito-eating bats to their neighborhood. Instead, residents hope to benefit from mosquito eradication efforts paid for by others.

   d. People buy too many *I ♥ New York* T-shirts because the market price doesn't include the pollution costs of making and shipping the shirts.

   e. The only grocery store in a small town charges more than $7 for a quart of orange juice.

3. Identify the source of market failure addressed by each of the following remedies:

   a. Copayments made by insurance customers
   b. Antitrust legislation

   c. The pre-purchase of mechanical checkups for used cars
   d. Subsidies
   e. The Federal Trade Commission
   f. Cap-and-trade programs
   g. Public education

4. Suppose the strings of holiday lights used to decorate yards are produced in a perfectly competitive market and that each string purchased creates a positive externality of $1 due to its visual appeal to neighbors.

   a. Draw a hypothetical graph for the holiday light market with an upward-sloping supply curve and a downward-sloping demand curve. Label the following:

      i.   marginal private cost curve
      ii. marginal social cost curve
      iii. marginal private benefit curve
      iv. marginal social benefit curve
      v.   market price
      vi. equilibrium quantity
      vii. socially optimal quantity

   b. Explain how the graph would change if all holiday lights were strung indoors where neighbors couldn't see them.

5. The *Urban Dictionary* defines *second-hand rap* as the "phenomenon created when some idiot with a loud car stereo believes the entire community would like to have their own music, conversations, or inner peace drowned out by . . .

the sound of a car being vibrated apart." Suppose loud car stereos are produced in a perfectly competitive market and that each stereo creates a negative externality of $50.

a. Draw a hypothetical graph for this market with an upward-sloping supply curve and a downward-sloping demand curve. Label the following:

   i.   marginal private cost curve
   ii. marginal social cost curve
   iii. marginal private benefit curve
   iv. marginal social benefit curve
   v.   market price
   vi. equilibrium quantity
   vii.socially optimal quantity

b. Describe two specific remedies that could bring about the socially optimal quantity of loud car stereos.

6. The government of Jefferson County, Colorado, purchases forests and preserves them as "green space" so the surrounding communities can enjoy views of the natural landscape. These views are non-rival and non-excludable.

a. Would a private market for green space bring about the efficient amount of green space, too much green space, or too little green space? Explain your answer.

b. Identify a public good not mentioned in the chapter and explain who provides it and how it is paid for.

7. Policy making to remedy market failure requires the government to estimate values such as marginal private costs, marginal private benefits, marginal external costs, and marginal external benefits. Indicate which of these values must be estimated correctly in order to allocate resources efficiently using each of the following approaches.

a. Taxes used to correct for a negative externality

b. Subsidies used to correct for a positive externality

c. A government provision of public goods that does not cause externalities

d. Limits on the quantity of a private good that causes negative externalities

8. To check for conflicting agendas among your friends, ask five of them which policy option they would vote for in each of the following categories of government spending:

a. Increase / Decrease / Make no change in spending on the military.

b. Increase / Decrease / Make no change in spending on public education.

c. Increase / Decrease / Make no change in subsidies for solar power.

How would you expect an economist to recommend that these policy decisions be made?

9. Excessive paperwork requirements can be a source of government failure.

a. Identify a paperwork task that you must complete for school, work, or the government.

b. What is the benefit of the paperwork?

c. Do you think the administrators who demand the paperwork consider the transaction costs when deciding how much paperwork to require?

d. Do you think the marginal benefit of completing the paperwork exceeds the marginal cost?

e. Why do you suppose the volume of paperwork sometimes becomes inefficiently large?

10. Explain an activity not mentioned in this chapter that occurs where you live and causes a positive or negative externality. Why does the activity cause market failure? In your opinion, what is the best remedy for this market failure?

11. Explain a specific situation in which equity and efficiency are conflicting goals. In the situation you described, would you be willing to sacrifice some efficiency to gain more equity? Why or why not?

Measuring an Economy's Performance

13

Simon Annable/Shutterstock.com

LEARNING OBJECTIVES

In this chapter, you will learn to:

1. Interpret and critique several measures of economic progress
2. Discuss the difference between nominal values and real values
3. Describe the effects of inflation
4. Explain how price levels are measured
5. Identify and explain the various types of unemployment

A rising tide lifts all boats. A rising economy has a similar effect, lifting sales, wages, profits, investments, charitable donations, tax revenues, and people's spirits. Ship captains who understand the tides gain foresight for navigating the seas. Benefits likewise go to those who correctly interpret macroeconomic indicators and chart the economy's course toward economic growth, stable prices, and full employment. In this chapter, we sail into macroeconomics. You will learn about measures of the big economic picture, including economy-wide levels of prices, output, and unemployment. On the basis of these measures, managers hire or fire, consumers spend or save, employees take time off or work overtime, politicians are voted in or out, and policy makers turn the rudder of economic policy toward recovery or restraint.

Why Should I Care?

The daily news delivers a deluge of numbers about the pulse of the economy. Why does economic performance make headlines? Because the economy is like the mom in the Tracy Bird song, "When Mama Ain't Happy, Ain't Nobody Happy." When the economy is suffering, almost everyone suffers, and many workers earn less or lose their jobs entirely. With less income, households make fewer purchases. With the drop in consumer spending, business owners see their sales and profits dwindle. As the economy tumbles downward, so do prices in the stock market. Stocks traded on the New York Stock Exchange and the NASDAQ stock exchange represent over $10 trillion worth of investments. As the value of these investments falls, so does the wealth of the owners of these investments, including families, colleges, hospitals, churches, and people investing money to fund their retirement. In short, **the health of the economy matters not just to workers and firms, but to students, retirees, and virtually everyone in between.**

Measures of Economic Progress

While traveling in a car you have a number of goals: You want to make steady forward progress, you want to be comfortable, and you want to avoid a crash. Your success in achieving some of these goals is easy to measure. For example, your speedometer provides objective data on your rate of forward progress. In contrast, your comfort is subjective. Passengers in the same car might report differing levels of comfort because they have different interests and priorities. Perhaps you have disagreed with fellow passengers about the ideal temperature, window height, or radio volume in a car. On the other hand, your speedometer reading is a relatively straightforward, if imperfect, measure of how your trip is going.

Policy makers at the steering wheel of the economy want steady economic progress, comfortable lives for citizens, and the avoidance of stock market

Alexander Davidyuk/Shutterstock.com

▲ In complex situations, it is common to emphasize objective, easy-to-quantify measures of how things are going. For a car trip, speed is such a measure. For the economy, the standard of living is a popular focus.

crashes. Economic goals, like driving goals, are measured with varying levels of difficulty. It is relatively easy to measure advancements in the standard of living, which Chapter 1 described as a measure of the material wealth available to help people live comfortably. Economists use readily available measures of production and income to track the standard of living, as discussed in this section. It is harder to quantify the **quality of life,** which is a broader measure of the comfort and satisfaction that citizens enjoy. The quality of life comes partly from the standard of living, but also from more subjective sources of happiness such as health, recreation, the quality of the environment, freedom, security, and a good family life.

Even though it is only one part of the quality of life, the standard of living receives a lot of attention because: (1) It is relatively easy to calculate; (2) it is an objective measure; and (3) it is a key contributor to the quality of life. This section highlights the most common measure of the standard of living: the *gross domestic product*. The next section describes shortcomings of focusing on the gross domestic product and explains alternative yardsticks for measuring the well-being of society.

GROSS DOMESTIC PRODUCT

Increases in a country's standard of living come from increases in the production of goods and services, as measured by the country's *gross domestic product*. **Gross domestic product (GDP)** is the total value of all *final goods and services* produced within a country in a given time period, typically a year. **Final goods and services** are those purchased by their ultimate consumer rather than by a firm for use in producing something else. **Intermediate goods** are purchased by firms and either become part of another good or are used up in the production of a good. The rubber used to make tires and the engines that go into cars are examples of intermediate goods.

Expenditures on intermediate goods are not counted in GDP until they are included in the value of a completed product, like a car. The value of the rubber and the engine is part of the value of the car. So, to count the value of the intermediate goods and then count the value of the final good containing the intermediate goods would be to double-count the value of the intermediate goods. Spending on used goods isn't counted either, because the value of used goods was included in GDP when those goods were sold for the first time.

How GDP Is Calculated. The U.S. GDP is calculated by the Bureau of Economic Analysis (BEA), an agency of the U.S. Department of Commerce. The BEA adds up the spending on final goods and services in the economy, which is divided into four categories:

- **Consumption spending by households.** Most spending in the United States is on three types of consumer goods and services:
  - *Durable goods*, which are goods that are expected to last three or more years, such as cars, TVs, and hot air balloons
  - *Nondurable goods*, which are goods that are either expected to last less than three years, such as magazines and socks, or can be used only once by consumers, such as cheeseburgers and oil
  - Services, such as health care, education, sports and entertainment

- **Investment spending by firms.** The investment component of GDP includes business spending on equipment, machinery, and other capital. It also includes the value of newly constructed businesses and homes, and the value of goods produced and held in inventories for future sale. As for purchases of stocks and bonds and deposits of money into banks, even though they may be referred to as investments, they are not included in GDP because they do not represent production.

- **Government spending on goods and services.** This includes spending by federal, state, and local governments on public schools, streets, parks, prisons, and the military. This does not include spending on interest payments, Social Security benefits, unemployment benefits, or other transfers of money from the government to individuals or firms for which no good or service is received by the government in exchange.

quality of life
A broader measure of citizens' comfort and satisfaction that comes partly from the standard of living, but also from more subjective sources of happiness such as health, recreation, environmental quality, freedom, security, and family life.

gross domestic product (GDP)
The total value of all final goods and services produced within a country in a given time period, typically a year.

final goods and services
Goods and services purchased by their ultimate consumer rather than by a firm for use in producing something else.

intermediate goods
Goods purchased by firms that either become part of another good or are used up in the production of a good.

- **Net exports (exports minus imports). Exports** are goods or services *sold to* foreign buyers. Exports are included in GDP because they represent domestic production. **Imports** are goods or services *purchased from* foreign firms. Because imports are not produced domestically, they are not counted in U.S. GDP. The value of U.S. net exports has been negative in every year since 1980, which means that each year consumers in the United States spend more on imports than other countries spend on U.S. exports.

GDP figures are used widely by government agencies and private corporations to get a read on the direction the economy is taking. The nation's central bank, the Federal Reserve, uses GDP as a gauge of how the economy is performing and as a basis for policy decisions. The president and Congress use it to plan the federal budget. Stock traders use it as an indicator of economic activity. And the Central Intelligence Agency (CIA) uses the inflation-adjusted GDP per person as a benchmark for the standard of living in countries around the world.

Nominal Versus Real Values

Head Balloons charges $23,190 for its smallest hot air balloon. This and all prices listed by sellers are *nominal prices*, which means they are the prices customers actually pay. More generally, a **nominal value** is the actual amount paid or received. Price tags indicate nominal prices. The wages specified in employment contracts are *nominal wages*. The interest rates listed on bank kiosks are *nominal interest rates*. And when the newspaper publishes the value of goods and services produced in the economy recently, that's a nominal value as well.

▲ Hot air balloons need burners to heat the air inside the balloons. If the value of the burner were included in GDP calculations when it was sold to the balloon maker, and again when the balloon package was sold to the final customer, that burner's value would be counted twice. To avoid this type of double counting, GDP calculations include only the value of *final goods and services* purchased by their ultimate consumers.

davelogan/E+/Getty Images

exports
Goods or services sold to foreign buyers.

imports
Goods or services purchased from foreign firms.

nominal value
The actual amount paid or received for a good or service.

purchasing power
The value of an amount of money expressed in terms of what one could buy with it.

The trouble with nominal values arises when comparisons are made over time. Consider McDonald's, which sold roughly $7.5 million worth of hamburgers between 1948 and 1955. Today, McDonald's sells about $7.5 million worth of hamburgers *every day*. Does McDonald's sell as many burgers every day as it did between the years 1948 and 1955? No. In the earlier time period, McDonald's sold hamburgers for 15 cents, so the $7.5 million came from the sale of 50 million hamburgers. Now a hamburger at McDonald's sells for about $1. That means the $7.5 million now comes from the daily sale of only 7.5 million hamburgers, not 50 million. The change in the nominal price of burgers from 15 cents to $1 made the nominal sales figure grow faster than McDonald's actual growth in hamburger sales.

Now consider a job that paid an annual salary of $15,000 in 1955. Back then, a worker could purchase 100,000 hamburgers with that money. If, in 2019, the salary for the same job were $50,000, the nominal salary would have increased by $35,000. But the **purchasing power** of the salary—what one could buy with it—would have actually *fallen* considerably. The $50,000 salary would buy only 50,000 hamburgers in 2019, half as many as the $15,000 salary would

New York Daily News Archive/Getty Images

▲ The prices of McDonald's hamburgers, among other goods and services, get inflated over time.

have bought in 1955. Nominal values are therefore misleading when used as measures of growth in production or purchasing power.

Like a helium balloon, prices and nominal wages rise with inflation. **Inflation** is an increase in the general price level of goods and services. And just as inflating a balloon makes it look bigger but doesn't add to the amount of latex material that makes up the balloon, a rise in nominal wages due to inflation doesn't add to the purchasing power of your earnings—your earnings simply look bigger. Suppose you earned $8 an hour when the price of hamburgers was $1. You could purchase 8 hamburgers with your hourly earnings. If inflation doubled both your wage rate and the price of a hamburger, your earnings would look bigger, but your new $16 wage would still buy only 8 hamburgers at the new price of $2.

The opposite of inflation is **deflation**, a general *decrease* in the prices of goods and services. Deflation is less common than inflation, although Japan and several European countries have experienced falling prices in recent years. Later in the chapter you'll learn how inflation and deflation are measured. The next chapter discusses the *causes* of inflation and deflation.

Economists adjust nominal values to account for inflation. A **real value** is a nominal value adjusted to remove the effects of inflation. An increase in your hourly wage from $8 to $16 is clearly an increase in your nominal wage because the amount you actually receive has gone up. If inflation prevents you from buying more goods and services with your higher wage, as in the preceding hamburger example, your *real* wage has not changed. Looking at real values instead of nominal values helps avoid confusion about whether changing dollar amounts represent changing purchasing power. That is, only if your real wage

increases can you buy more burgers. In this chapter, you will learn how to find real values using a *price index*.

GDP can be measured in real or nominal terms. An increase in real GDP indicates that production has increased. An increase in nominal GDP could mean that production has increased *or* that prices have increased, or both. Suppose nominal GDP in the United States increased from $20 trillion in one year to $24 trillion in the next year, an increase of 20 percent. If inflation raised prices by 20 percent over the same year, the entire increase in the value of production would be explained by the higher prices. In other words, the same amount of goods and services that sold for $20 trillion in the first year would sell for $24 trillion in the second year. Real GDP would remain unchanged as illustrated by the top set of balloons in Figure 13.1.

If the price level remained the same from one year to the next, a 20 percent increase in nominal GDP over that period could only be explained by a 20 percent increase in the level of production. Because the increase in the dollar value of the output would come entirely from the increase in output, nominal GDP and real GDP would both increase by the same percentage (20 percent in this case), as shown by the middle set of balloons.

It is more common for both prices and production to increase from one year to the next. Suppose real GDP increased by 20 percent, and over the same year, the price level increased by 10 percent. At the old price level, the value of the output would have increased by 20 percent from $20 trillion to $24 trillion. But at the higher price level, the new output has a 10 percent higher dollar value of $26.4 trillion. So the increase in nominal GDP from $20 trillion to $26.4 trillion

inflation
An increase in the general price level of goods and services.

deflation
A decrease in the general price level of goods and services.

real value
A nominal value adjusted to remove the effects of inflation.

Both a change in production and a change in prices affect nominal GDP, whereas only a change in production affects real GDP.

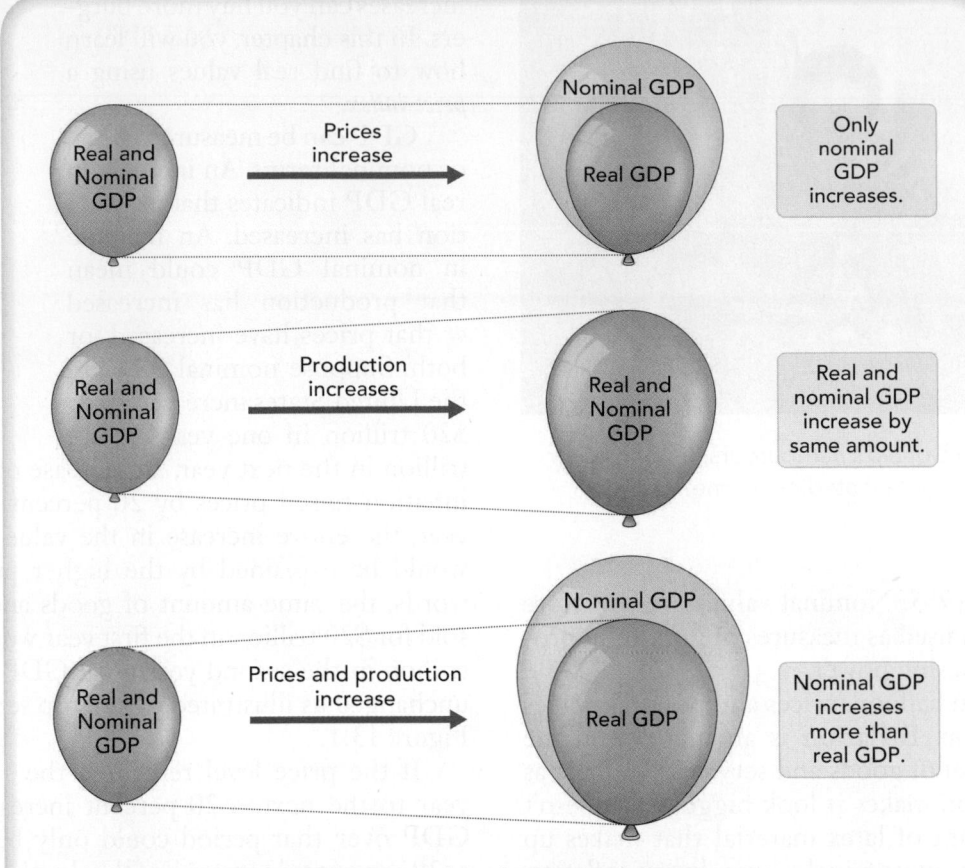

FIGURE 13.1 Increases in Real and Nominal GDP

The top set of balloons shows that an increase in the price level causes an increase in nominal GDP but no change in real GDP. The middle set of balloons shows that an increase in production causes real GDP and nominal GDP to increase by the same proportion. The bottom set of balloons shows that an increase in both the price level and production result is an increase in real GDP and an even larger increase in nominal GDP.

business cycle
The alternation between expansions and contractions in the economy's level of output.

peak
The transition from an expansion to a contraction in the economy.

trough
The transition from a contraction to an expansion in the economy.

comes partly from an increase in production and partly from an increase in prices. This is illustrated by the bottom set of balloons, which shows that if prices and production both increase, nominal GDP increases by even more than real GDP. Keep in mind why: Both a change in production and a change in prices affect nominal GDP, whereas only a change in production affects real GDP. Since inflation causes nominal GDP to change even when production has

remained the same, comparisons in production levels over time should be made using real GDP rather than nominal GDP.

GDP AND THE BUSINESS CYCLE

Real gross domestic product has its ups and downs. The **business cycle** is the alternation between expansions and contractions in the economy's level of output. As shown in Figure 13.2, the transition from an expansion to a contraction creates a **peak.** The transition from a contraction to an expansion creates a **trough.** A prolonged contraction is sometimes called a *recession*. In the United States, the National Bureau of Economic Research (NBER) determines whether a contraction is considered a

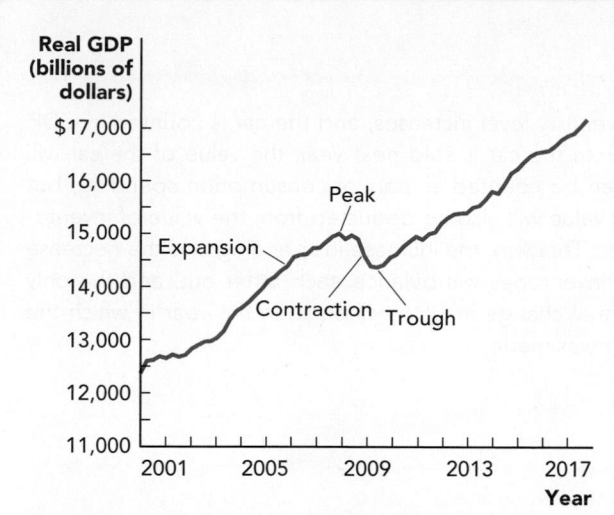

FIGURE 13.2 The Business Cycle

The economy's output expands and contracts over time. The high points of this *business cycle* are called *peaks;* the low points are called *troughs.*

Source: Bureau of Economic Analysis.

recession. According to the NBER, a **recession** is "a significant decline in economic activity spread across the economy, lasting more than a few months."

A very deep contraction is called a **depression,** which is loosely defined as a 10 percent or more

decrease in output over the period of a year. The United States experienced a depression from 1929 until 1933, with a nearly 33 percent decline in output, and again from 1937 until 1938, when output declined by 18.2 percent. In contrast, a time of great expansion in economic activity is called a **boom.** Booms have no narrow definition, but they are marked by a general contentment with the pace of economic growth.

The importance of real GDP is heightened by its relation to many goals beyond productivity. The value of output approximates the value of income because most earnings come from the sales of goods and services. Changes in real GDP correspond with changes in employment, because it generally takes more workers to make more output. If real GDP increases faster than the population, there is an increase in **real GDP per capita,** which is real GDP divided by the number of people in the population.

Table 13.1 shows the GDP, GDP per capita, and unemployment rate for an

recession
A significant decline in economic activity spread across the economy, lasting more than a few months.

depression
An economic downturn loosely defined as a 10 percent or more decrease in output over the period of a year.

boom
A time of great expansion in economic activity.

real GDP per capita
Real GDP divided by the number of people in the population.

Table 13.1 An International Comparison of 2017 GDP, GDP per Capita, and the Unemployment Rate (Adjusted for differences in the purchasing power of currencies in each country)

Country	GDP ($ billions)	GDP per Capita	Unemployment Rate
China	$23,120	$16,600	4.0%
United States	19,360	59,500	4.4
India	9,447	7,200	8.8
Brazil	3,219	15,500	13.1
France	2,826	43,600	9.5
Mexico	2,406	19,500	3.6
Canada	1,764	48,100	6.5
Argentina	912	20,700	8.1
South Africa	757	13,400	27.6
Greece	300	27,800	22.3

Source: The World Factbook.

If a good is made this year and sold next year, when is it included in GDP?

Suppose the Ford Motor Company makes a car in December of this year and doesn't sell it until January of next year. The car should be included in this year's GDP, and the Bureau of Economic Analysis has a way to make that happen. The BEA collects data on changes in firms' inventories of goods. So when Ford makes a car, its inventory level increases, and the car is counted in GDP. When the car is sold next year, the value of the car will then be counted as part of consumption spending, but its value will also be deducted from the value of inventories. That way, the increase in spending and the decrease in inventories will balance each other out, and the only actual change in GDP will occur in the year in which the car was made.

assortment of countries in 2017.[1] The distinction between GDP and GDP per capita (GDP per person) is an important one to make when comparing the standard of living in different countries. For example, China and the United States have similar GDP levels, but China's population is more than 4 times that of the United States, so China has a relatively low GDP per capita. The higher GDP per capita in the United States indicates a higher standard of living, in that citizens on average receive more income and can purchase more goods and services. Figure 13.3 shows the general increase of real GDP per capita in the United States since 1960.

GDP AND THE QUALITY OF LIFE

GDP is a useful measure of the standard of living, but it does not capture many of the broader elements of the quality of life. For that reason, although policy makers and the media seem to herald GDP growth as a uniformly splendid event, increases in GDP may or may not indicate improvements in the well-being of society. Chapter 18 explains that, depending on the distribution of income, the benefits of GDP growth might only be enjoyed by a small fraction of the population. And when increases in the quality of products aren't reflected in prices, the quality of life can increase even when GDP doesn't. For example, a few years ago a $400 watch was little more than a status symbol that could tell you the time and date. Today, a watch that represents the same $400 addition to GDP can connect you to the Internet, tell you how many miles you've run, unlock the door to your hotel room, and help you find the nearest

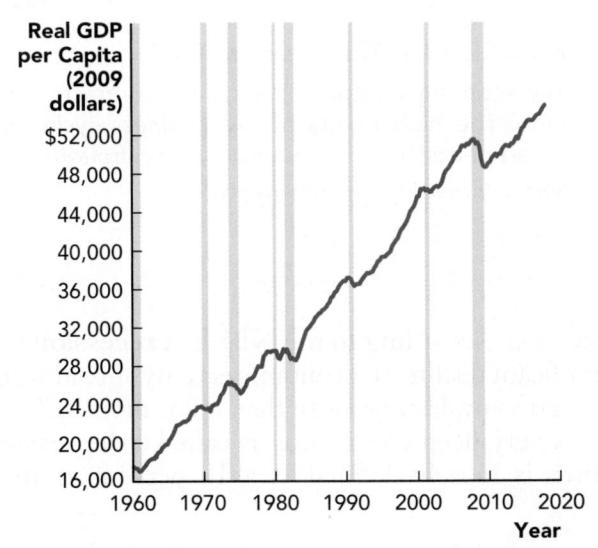

FIGURE 13.3 Real GDP per Capita in the United States

Real GDP per capita is found by dividing a country's real GDP by the size of its population. When real GDP per capita rises, the standard of living rises because the average citizen receives more income and there are more goods and services available to purchase. The shaded areas in the graph indicate recessions.

Source: Federal Reserve Bank of St. Louis.

Chipotle. This section explains more ways in which GDP is an imperfect measure of the quality of life, and details alternative approaches that may better serve that purpose.

---

[1]Because we are looking at a single year, there is no need to adjust for inflation in order to distinguish real values from nominal values. These figures are, however, adjusted for differences in the purchasing power of the currencies used in these countries.

▲ Not long ago, a $400 watch was little more than a status symbol that could tell you the time and date. Now a $400 watch will connect you to the world. When quality improvements bring consumers more satisfaction for the same price, there is no corresponding increase in GDP.

▲ At some point, balloon-making machines wear out. Expenditures to replace machines such as this one are included in GDP, but the expenditures merely keep the amount of capital at its current level; they do not represent an increase in the availability of goods or services.

Expenditures That Increase When Society Is Worse Off.

Some goods and services are purchased to address problems that are making society worse off, such as crime, natural disasters, disease, pollution, and war. In a typical year, for example, about $550 billion of the U.S. GDP is spent on police, prisons, security systems, and other purchases that would be unnecessary if crime did not exist. If the crime problem worsens, this component of GDP will increase, but society will be worse off.

GDP increased in 2017 when hurricanes Harvey and Irma caused more than $100 billion worth of damage in the southern United States. The extraordinary expenditures on emergency medical care, home repairs, and community recovery efforts indicated growing problems with tropical storms, not growth in the availability of goods and services for consumers to enjoy. Such recovery expenditures can be subtracted from GDP to obtain a more accurate measure of social well-being, but usually they are not.

GDP also includes spending to replace worn-out equipment, machines, and buildings. Economists use the term **capital depreciation** to describe the wear on capital during the production process. Expenditures to replace worn-out machines are similar to expenditures to fix problems with crime and pollution. Although such spending is part of GDP, it does not represent an increase in the availability of goods and services that make society better off.

Suppose that after making $1,000,000 worth of balloons, a balloon-making firm must replace $20,000 worth of machinery. GDP would increase by $1,020,000, but the net gain for society would just be the $1,000,000 worth of balloons. The $20,000 worth of new balloon-making machines would merely bring the value of the firm's capital back to its starting point. The U.S. government publishes *net national product* (NNP) figures that are calculated as GDP minus the value of capital depreciation. NNP is a better measure of the quality of life than GDP because NNP indicates the *increase* in the availability of goods and services, but it does not account for the other problems with GDP discussed in this section.

Desirable Goods and Services That Aren't Part of GDP.

We've seen that GDP increases even when we purchase goods and services in response to growing problems. There are also many goods and services that improve our social well-being but are not included in GDP. For instance, the load of laundry you washed last week—along with all unpaid housework, gardening, childcare, and do-it-yourself home improvements—are not included in GDP. Likewise, the volunteer work performed at churches, food banks, nursing homes, schools, and elsewhere is not part of GDP. Yet the same services *are* counted in GDP when they are performed by paid professionals and reported to the government.

Also not included is the estimated $1 trillion worth of production each year in what's called the *underground economy* of the United States. Production in the underground

capital depreciation
Wear on capital during the production process that depletes the capital's value.

▲ The effect of real GDP growth on leisure time and environmental quality depends on how that growth is carried out. For example, if real GDP growth comes from new uses of robots and other forms of technology, the leisure time workers enjoy may stay the same or increase.

economy is not reported to the government and thus cannot be counted as part of GDP. For example, someone who grows marijuana illegally and sells it is part of the underground economy, as are a waiter who doesn't report all of his tips and a roofer who gets paid in cash and doesn't report the income. A better measure of the quality of life would include estimates of the value of all *nonmarket* goods and services such as these.

Last but not least among factors omitted from GDP is leisure time. Real GDP would be higher if everyone worked all the time, but then we would have no time to enjoy the additional output. As elated as workers might be about weekends, days off, and the prospect of early retirement, the value of leisure time doesn't find its way into GDP calculations. Increases in real GDP may or may not involve decreases in leisure time, depending on how they are achieved. For instance, improvements in computers, transportation systems, and robotics have made it possible for workers to make more output in less time. In fact, between 1900 and 2018, the average workweek in the U.S. manufacturing sector decreased from 53 hours to 41 hours, even as real GDP per capita increased considerably. An ideal measure of the quality of life would capture this and other changes in the value of leisure time.

MEASURES OF THE QUALITY OF LIFE

Economists have proposed several alternatives to GDP as broader measures of the quality of life. Examples include:

- The Genuine Progress Indicator (GPI)
- The Human Development Index (HDI)
- Net National Welfare (NNW)
- The Index of Sustainable Economic Welfare (ISEW)

Most of these measures are found by starting with GDP, adding omitted expenditures that make society better off, and subtracting expenditures that grow in response to growing problems. For example, the calculation for Net National Welfare is:

NNW = GDP + nonmarket output − externality costs − pollution abatement and cleanup costs − capital depreciation (including natural capital such as forests and oil reserves)

Some of the measures start from scratch. For instance, the ISEW formula begins with the values of personal consumption and household labor, adds the values of beneficial public expenditures on things like health and highways, and subtracts the costs of environmental degradation, auto accidents, and other problems.

After skimming out the undesirable elements of GDP and adding in desirables not captured in GDP, most alternative measures have diverged from GDP over the past several decades. For example, the path of the Genuine Progress Indicator in Figure 13.4 shows that for 20 years starting in 1977, GPI per

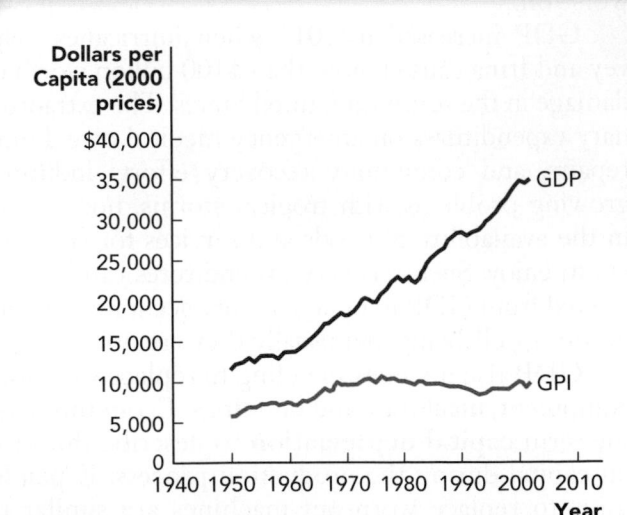

FIGURE 13.4 Comparing the GDP and the GPI

Per-capita values for the Genuine Progress Indicator have followed a downward trend since 1977, even as GDP per capita has increased.

Source: rprogress.org.

capita followed a mostly downward trend, even as GDP per capita rose dramatically. This means that the elements of GDP that are removed in the GPI calculation, such as expenditures on crime and disease that society would rather avoid, make up a substantial portion of GDP growth. Although the Genuine Progress Indicator is not currently calculated at the national level, many U.S. states use it to more accurately track the quality of life.

Inflation

In 1998, it cost about $1.50 to buy a slice of cheese pizza in New York City. In 2018, the average price for a slice was about $3.00. Inflation, which you'll recall is an increase in the general price level of goods and services, is the primary reason prices aren't what they used to be. If all prices and everyone's income increased at the same rate, inflation would be a minor nuisance. For instance, suppose a worker earned $6 per hour in 1998. At that time, she could buy 4 pizza slices for $1.50 each with her hourly wage. If her wage doubled to $12 per hour between 1998 and 2018, and if over the same period the price of pizza doubled to $3.00, she could again buy 4 pizza slices with her hourly wage (4 slices for $3.00 each cost $12). The amount of pizza she could purchase with her hourly earnings remains unchanged.

So what's all the fuss about inflation? Unfortunately, the real story of inflation isn't so simple. Rising prices create both winners and losers. Inflation hurts people whose incomes don't increase when prices increase, because their incomes won't buy as much at the higher prices. For instance, if a worker continued to earn $6 per hour while the price of pizza slices doubled from $1.50 to $3.00, an hour's pay would only be enough to buy 2 slices of pizza rather than 4. Employment contracts typically keep wages the same for a year or more, and many households receive the same payments each month from retirement funds or other fixed-income investments.

The winners when there is inflation are those who owe a fixed amount of money, perhaps to pay back school loans or fulfill long-term rental contracts. Inflation makes the amount owed less valuable because it will buy less stuff. Suppose you owe someone $200 and that the price of a balloon ride is $50. You owe enough money to buy 4 balloon rides. If prices double before you repay your loan, the price of a balloon ride will become $100 and the real value of your $200 payment will be cut in half. Why? Because you will only have to pay back enough money to buy 2 balloon rides instead of 4. By contrast, the money lender will be worse off than if the inflation hadn't occurred. Rather than collecting enough money for 4 balloon rides, the lender will receive enough for only 2 balloon rides.

Inflation also imposes two types of transaction costs. **Menu costs** are the costs to firms of updating price lists to keep up with inflation. The classic example is the cost of reprinting restaurant menus after inflation causes prices to change. Similarly, many stores have signs, price tags, and computer programs that must be updated whenever prices change.

Shoe-leather costs are the costs individuals incur in their efforts to minimize inflation's erosive effects on the value of their money. When prices are rising rapidly, people try to limit the effects of inflation by holding as little cash as possible. Instead, they invest their money in assets that will hold their value, such as real estate or gold, or they deposit their money in bank accounts that pay interest. However, holding less cash means making more frequent trips to the bank or ATM to make withdrawals. Those extra trips wear down the soles of shoes, which is why these transaction costs are symbolically referred to as shoe-leather costs. The valuable time spent on these banking transactions creates an even larger burden.

In 2018, Venezuela experienced an inflation rate that sometimes exceeded 5 percent per day. When Brazil faced high inflation rates in the 1990s, there were stories of grocery store

> **menu costs**
> The costs to firms of updating price lists to keep up with inflation.
>
> **shoe-leather costs**
> The costs individuals incur in their efforts to minimize inflation's erosive effects on the value of their money.

▲ Inflation erodes the purchasing power of cash. When the inflation rate is high, consumers hold less cash and try to protect the value of their money by keeping more of it in bank accounts that pay interest. But that increases the *shoe-leather costs* of making trips to the ATM when cash is needed.

Mint Images Limited/Alamy

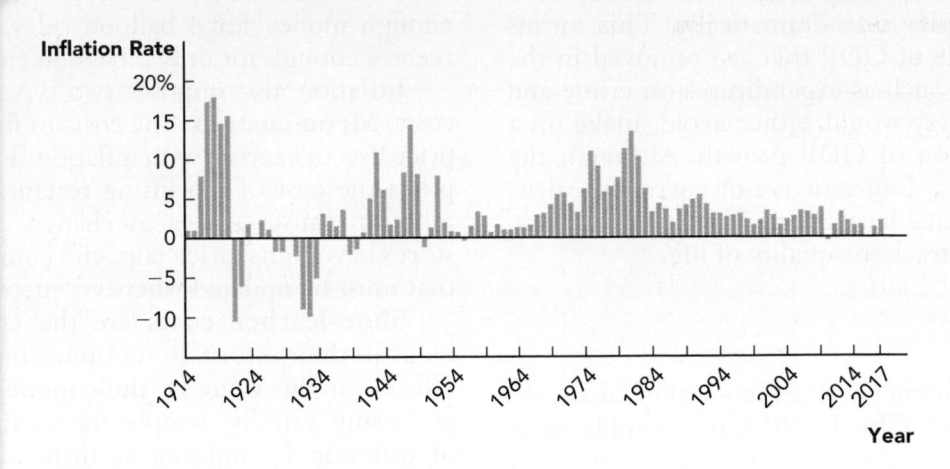

Inflation Rate

FIGURE 13.5 U.S. Inflation Rates

At different times over the past century, the United States has experienced double-digit inflation and deflation.

Source: Bureau of Labor Statistics.

hyperinflation
A period character-ized by very high rates of inflation.

Consumer Price Index (CPI)
A measure of vari-ation in the overall price level of goods and services pur-chased by typical consumers.

clerks constantly going through the aisles putting stickers with higher prices on the goods, and shoppers running ahead of the clerks to avoid paying the new, higher prices. That created a double whammy of menu costs for the stores and shoe-leather costs for the shoppers.

Figure 13.5 shows the annual U.S. inflation rate for the past century. Even rates of 2 or 3 percent are enough to require restaurants to print new menus now and then, and the occasional double-digit rates certainly caused some wear on shoe soles. Other countries have endured very high rates of infla-tion, known as **hyperinflation.** This includes the occasional 50-plus-percent *galloping infla-tion* experienced in Argentina, Brazil, Venezuela, Yugoslavia, and elsewhere over the past 30 years. In November of 2008, Zimbabwe experienced one of the worst bouts with inflation ever, when prices doubled nearly every day. Galloping inflation in Germany in the 1920s made the purchasing power of money so low that it was used as wallpaper and to make kites. When people needed wheelbarrows to cart around enough money to pay their bills, there were tales of thieves stealing the wheelbar-rows but leaving the money behind.

▲ Inflation in Germany during the 1920s made the purchasing power of money so low that children made kites out of money.

The Consumer Price Index

To keep track of inflation, the U.S. government cal-culates the **Consumer Price Index (CPI)**, a mea-sure of variation in the overall price level of goods and services purchased by typical consumers. The CPI is the most widely used price index.[2] To cal-culate it, each month the Bureau of Labor Statis-tics collects prices on a representative "basket" of about 80,000 goods and services that fall into more than 200 categories, such as breakfast cereals, men's

---

[2]Other price indexes used for related purposes include the *GDP Deflator* and the *Producer Price Index.*

shirts, and college tuition. The prices are collected from about 23,000 firms in 87 urban areas. Sales and excise taxes are included; income taxes and the prices of investments such as stocks and bonds are not. The CPI value for a particular month is found by dividing the cost of the basket in that month by the cost of the basket in an arbitrarily chosen *base period* (currently 1982–1984), and multiplying by 100. For example, if the basket cost $3 million this month and $1 million in the base period, then the CPI for this month is ($3 million ÷ $1 million) × 100 = 300.

Because it is an important measure of the cost of living, the CPI is used to update all sorts of prices and payments, including apartment rents, Social Security benefits, and child support payments. The growth rate of the CPI between one year and the next indicates the inflation rate over that period. For example, the CPI was 237.8 in May of 2015 and 240.2 in May of 2016. By plugging these numbers into a simple formula, you can discover the growth rate in the CPI, and thus the inflation rate, between those years. The general formula for the inflation rate between two years, Year 1 and Year 2, is

$$\text{inflation rate} = [(\text{CPI}_{\text{Year 2}} \div \text{CPI}_{\text{Year 1}}) - 1] \times 100$$

The inflation rate between 2015 and 2016 is

$$\begin{aligned}\text{inflation rate} &= [(\text{CPI}_{2016} \div \text{CPI}_{2015}) - 1] \times 100\\ &= [(240.2 \div 237.8) - 1] \times 100\\ &= 1.01\%\end{aligned}$$

So there was 1.01 percent inflation over the period.

We can use CPI figures to find real values by adjusting nominal values for inflation. Perhaps you've seen old signs advertising Pepsi for 5¢. That was really the price in 1940, but was it a great deal? The CPI holds the answer. We can adjust the price in one year, Year 1, to reflect the price level in another year, Year 2. To indicate that we've made an adjustment to the Year-2 price level, we say that the price is in "Year-2 dollars." The formula for finding the real price is

$$\begin{aligned}\frac{\text{real price in}}{\text{Year-2 dollars}} &= \text{nominal price in Year 1}\\ &\times (\text{CPI}_{\text{Year 2}} \div \text{CPI}_{\text{Year 1}})\end{aligned}$$

With this formula we can adjust prices, incomes, and other values for the effects of inflation. As we have seen, this is important when we compare values across years. It is common to adjust all values to reflect the price level in the current year, although values can be adjusted to any year's price levels. Let's use this formula to adjust the 1940 price of Pepsi to its 2017 equivalent. The CPI in 1940 was 14.0;

Pepsi sold for 5¢ in 1940, which sounds like a great deal—until you adjust for inflation and see that 5¢ then is equivalent to 88¢ now.

in 2017, it was 245.1. To adjust the 5¢ price for the inflation between 1940 and 2017, we multiply 5¢ by the CPI in 2017, divided by the CPI in 1940:

$$\$0.05 \times (\text{CPI}_{2017} \div \text{CPI}_{1940}) = \$0.05 \times (245.1 \div 14.0) = \$0.88$$

So a 5¢ price in 1940 wasn't a great bargain—it was equivalent to an 88¢ price in 2017.

Unemployment

The standard of living for most citizens may rise and fall over the course of the business cycle, but for those workers who become unemployed, income hits rock-bottom. Unemployment also takes emotions to rock-bottom. As unemployment rates climb, so do poverty, alcoholism, crime, and suicide rates. These are among the reasons why economists keep a close watch on the measures of unemployment to be discussed in this section. Policies to limit unemployment are discussed in Chapters 15 and 17.

THE UNEMPLOYMENT RATE

Being unemployed is more than a matter of not being employed. To be considered unemployed, you must be willing and able to work, and actively seeking work. In other words, you must be part of the **labor force,** which is made up of everyone who is

- aged 16 or older
- not on active military duty
- not institutionalized (such as in prison or in a nursing home)
- employed or has engaged in job-search activities in the past four weeks

> **labor force**
> Everyone who is aged 16 or older, not on active military duty, not institutionalized, and employed or recently looked for a job.

The **unemployment rate** is the percentage of the labor force that is unemployed. You can find the unemployment rate by dividing the number of unemployed people by the number of people in the labor force and multiplying by 100:

$$\text{unemployment rate} = \frac{\text{unemployed}}{\text{labor force}} \times 100$$

unemployment rate
The percentage of the labor force that is unemployed.

discouraged workers
People who are willing and able to work and have looked for a job in the past year, but who have not looked for a job in the past four weeks because they have given up on finding a job.

underemployed workers
People who are working fewer hours than they want or are overqualified for their positions.

For example, during the worst of the Great Recession of 2007–2009, there were 154.0 million people in the U.S. labor force and 15.7 million of them were unemployed. The unemployment rate was therefore $(15.7 \div 154.0) \times 100 = 10.2\%$.

Each month, the U.S. Bureau of Labor Statistics (BLS) estimates the unemployment rate in the United States using data from surveys on the employment status of about 110,000 people in 60,000 households. Figure 13.6 shows the U.S. unemployment rate since 1928. By far, the worst unemployment problems came during and after the Great Depression in the 1930s, when double-digit unemployment persisted for a decade.

The official unemployment rate does not account for

discouraged workers who have given up on finding a job. The U.S. BLS defines **discouraged workers** as those who are willing and able to work and have looked for a job in the past year, but who have not looked for a job in the past four weeks. According to recent estimates, the inclusion of discouraged workers in the labor force would increase the unemployment rate by about one-half of a percentage point.

Unemployment rates also fail to capture the problem of **underemployed workers**—those who are working fewer hours than desired or who are overqualified for their positions. Part-time workers who would prefer to work full time are underemployed, as are college graduates who deliver pizza. In 2018, the BLS estimated that more than 3 percent of the labor force worked part time but desired full-time work. The BLS does not estimate the number of college graduates delivering pizza or any other type of overqualified worker.

There are also problems that skew the reported unemployment rate *upward*. Workers who don't report their employment to the government are considered unemployed in the BLS unemployment rate calculations. These workers include drug dealers, prostitutes, and others working illegally, as well as people in legal jobs who work for unreported cash payments to avoid paying taxes. Economists Richard Cebula and Edgar Feige estimate that $2 trillion worth of income in the United States goes unreported each year. On a broader scale, the

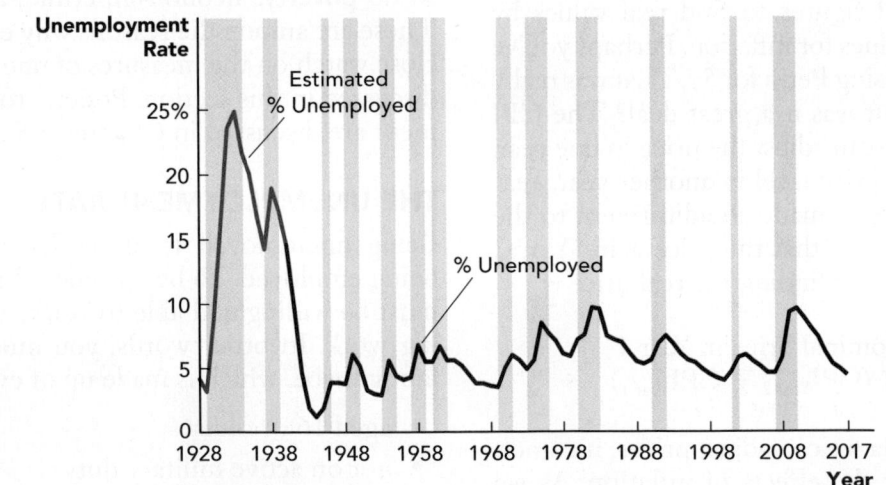

FIGURE 13.6 Historical U.S. Unemployment Rates

Most of the variation in the unemployment rate comes from fluctuations in the business cycle. The highest unemployment rates are experienced during recessions and depressions, the periods of which are shaded in the graph.

Sources: Bureau of Labor Statistics, TheBalance.com, InfoPlease.com.

International Labor Organization estimates that 70 percent of workers in developing countries are not counted in the labor force.

TYPES OF UNEMPLOYMENT

There are several different types of unemployment, each with its own causes and effects. The type of unemployment a worker is experiencing affects the likely duration of the unemployment spell and the possible remedies. This section explains the most common types of unemployment.

Frictional unemployment is caused by the need for workers and employers to spend time searching for each other. Even when the economy is booming, it takes time for workers to find the jobs that best match their skills and interests, and for employers to find the workers who best suit their needs. Frictional unemployment tends not to last as long as other types of unemployment because it is only a matter of available workers finding available jobs. Job-search websites such as Monster.com help publicize the availability of workers and jobs across the country. Some amount of frictional unemployment is actually desirable. By taking time to shop around, workers find jobs that are more satisfying, better paying, and closer to home, and employers find workers who are more productive and dedicated.

Structural unemployment is caused by a mismatch between the skills workers have and the skills employers seek. Sometimes the problem is one of location—the workers don't live in areas of the country where their skills are needed. In other cases, there aren't enough jobs anywhere to employ all the workers with a particular skill. The U.S. trend away from manufacturing and toward services has left many manufacturing workers structurally unemployed because their skills differ from those needed in health care, education, finance, and other service industries. Professional football players who become too old to compete find themselves structurally unemployed if they haven't developed a second set of skills. Structural unemployment can also result from a change in technology. For example, as more people get their news online, more printing press operators find themselves unemployed. Structural unemployment tends to last longer than frictional unemployment due to the time it takes workers to develop new skills.

Cyclical unemployment is caused by contractions in the economy. During a contraction, firms produce less output, so they need fewer workers.

The result is an overall shortage of jobs in the economy. Many of the economic policies of central banks and governments are designed to minimize the size of contractions and the cyclical unemployment they create. Depending on how long it takes for the economy to recover, cyclical unemployment can last a few months or many years.

Seasonal unemployment is caused by a change in the need for workers due to a change in seasons. Ice cream just doesn't sell well in the wintertime, so many ice cream stands close or decrease their staffing until warm weather returns. Lifeguards and fruit harvesters are also likely to become unemployed in the winter. Ski instructors and furnace-repair specialists have a hard time finding work in the summer. Department stores and package-delivery companies hire extra workers during the holiday season, and inns in Vermont hire more staff during the fall when tourists flood in to watch the leaves change colors. When the season is over, these extra staff members must look for new jobs. All these seasonal fluctuations in hiring lead to

frictional unemployment Unemployment caused by the need for workers and employers to spend time searching for each other.

structural unemployment Unemployment caused by a mismatch between the skills workers have and the skills employers seek.

cyclical unemployment Unemployment caused by contractions in the economy.

seasonal unemployment Unemployment caused by a change in the need for workers due to a change in seasons.

Jeff Carpenter/Shutterstock

▲ Tourists flock to Vermont in the fall when the leaves change color. When the tourists return home, however, many workers in the tourism industry become seasonally unemployed.

seasonal unemployment. Table 13.2 summarizes the types of unemployment and their causes.

FULL EMPLOYMENT AND THE NATURAL RATE OF UNEMPLOYMENT

Some amount of unemployment is inevitable. There will always be frictional unemployment because there are always workers in between jobs and new workers entering the labor force who need time to search for new jobs. And there are always structurally unemployed workers who need retraining to keep up with the ever-changing mix of products and production processes. For these reasons, zero unemployment cannot be achieved. However, *full employment* is a real possibility. **Full employment** is the level of employment when there is no cyclical unemployment. The unemployment rate when there is full unemployment in the economy is called the **natural rate of unemployment.** Most economists agree that the natural rate of unemployment in the United States is in the neighborhood of 5 percent. Upcoming chapters will discuss economic policies designed to achieve full employment.

full employment
The level of employment when there is no cyclical unemployment.

natural rate of unemployment
The unemployment rate when there is full employment in the economy.

Table 13.2 Summary of Unemployment Types

Type of Unemployment	Cause
Frictional	The time it takes to match workers with jobs
Structural	A mismatch between the skills workers have and the skills employers need
Cyclical	A downturn in the economy
Seasonal	A change in staffing needs due to a change in seasons

SUMMARY

The gross domestic product (GDP) is the total value of all final goods and services produced in a country. GDP is a useful measure of the standard of living within an economy, but it is less appropriate as a measure of the quality of life. To more accurately measure the quality of life, economists have developed alternative measures such as the Genuine Progress Indicator (GPI) and Net National Welfare (NNW). The alternative measures typically omit expenditures on fixing problems such as environmental degradation, disease, and natural disasters; they do include the value of beneficial activities that are not counted in GDP calculations, such as unpaid work and the intangible benefits of leisure time, health, and education.

The amounts you actually pay or receive as prices, incomes, or interest rates are nominal values. These values generally change over time when there is inflation or deflation. Real values are adjusted to remove the effects of changes in the overall price level. To compare values between time periods, it is important to look at real values rather than nominal values.

Inflation raises the prices of goods and services across the economy. Inflation also raises wages, but it still hurts some people and helps others. For example, people with a fixed income are hurt by inflation because their income won't buy as much as it used to. People who owe a fixed amount of money are helped by inflation because it diminishes the purchasing power of the amount they must repay. Businesses face the menu costs of having to update prices on menus, tags, signs, and price lists to keep up with inflation. And to limit inflation's erosive effects on cash holdings, individuals incur the shoe-leather costs of holding less cash and having to make frequent trips to the bank.

The CPI captures the overall price level of about 80,000 goods and services purchased by typical consumers in urban areas across the United States. By plugging CPI values into simple formulas, you can calculate inflation rates and convert any nominal value into a real value.

The unemployment rate is the percentage of the labor force that is not working. To be considered part of the labor force, a worker must be willing and able to work, and actively seeking work. Frictional unemployment exists because it takes time for workers to search for jobs that match their skills and interests, as well as for employers to find workers who suit their needs. Structural unemployment is caused by a mismatch between the skills workers have and the skills employers seek. Cyclical unemployment is caused by an overall shortage of jobs due to an economic downturn. Seasonal unemployment is caused by a change in seasons that reduces the need for some types of workers. Since frictional and structural unemployment always exist, the unemployment rate never reaches 0. An achievable goal is full employment, which means there is no cyclical unemployment. The unemployment rate when full employment is achieved is called the natural rate of unemployment.

Unemployment figures do not account for discouraged workers who have given up on finding a job, nor for underemployed workers, who are overqualified for their positions or would like to work longer hours. The omission of these workers from unemployment rate calculations causes the official unemployment rate to understate the size of the unemployment problem. At the same time, workers who illegally do not report their employment to the government cause the unemployment rate to be higher than it would be if all work were reported.

KEY TERMS

quality of life, p. 191
gross domestic product (GDP), p. 191
final goods and services, p. 191
intermediate goods, p. 191
exports, p. 192
imports, p. 192
nominal value, p. 192
purchasing power, p. 192
inflation, p. 193
deflation, p. 193
real value, p. 193
business cycle, p. 194

peak, p. 194
trough, p. 194
recession, p. 195
depression, p. 195
boom, p. 195
real GDP per capita, p. 195
capital depreciation, p. 197
menu costs, p. 199
shoe-leather costs, p. 199
hyperinflation, p. 200
Consumer Price Index (CPI), p. 200
labor force, p. 201

unemployment rate, p. 202
discouraged workers, p. 202
underemployed workers, p. 202
frictional unemployment, p. 203
structural unemployment, p. 203
cyclical unemployment, p. 203
seasonal unemployment, p. 203
full employment, p. 204
natural rate of unemployment, p. 204

PROBLEMS FOR REVIEW

1. Which of the following contribute to the quality of life but not to the standard of living? (Circle all correct answers.)
   a. Socks
   b. Clean air
   c. Watermelons
   d. Leisure time
   e. Freedom

2. Identify each of the following as an intermediate good or a final good.
   a. A toothbrush
   b. Helium sold to a circus to fill balloons
   c. Glass sold to Samsung to make into cell-phone screens
   d. Flour sold by a restaurant supply company to Domino's Pizza
   e. Flour sold by a grocery store to your family

3. Consider a typical worker, an unemployed worker who got divorced and had heart-bypass surgery in the same year, and a blissful retiree. The typical worker produces about $110,000 worth of output each year. The litigation costs for a "lightly conflicted" divorce run about $50,000, and the health-care costs for heart-bypass surgery are about $100,000. The retiree could go back to work and earn a $115,000 annual salary, but she chooses to work in her garden and perform volunteer work instead.
   a. Which of these people causes GDP to go up by the largest amount?
   b. Which of these people do you think is the happiest?
   c. What is the blissful retiree's contribution to GDP?

4. The following table provides fictional 2018 data for the Island of Hot Air. What was the Island of Hot Air's GDP in that year?

Category	Value (millions of dollars)
Household spending	$200
Investment spending by firms	100
Government spending on goods and services	50
Exports	15
Imports	25
Transfers	20
Depreciation	5
Volunteer work	10

5. Suppose that in 2020, a store owner offers you an annual salary of $50,000 to work as a manager. The owner says the last manager, hired in 2010, was pleased to accept $50,000 as a starting salary. Is the owner's justification for the offer reasonable? Explain why or why not.

6. The federal minimum wage in 1981 was $3.35; in 2018, it was $7.25. Yet some people say the federal minimum wage in place in 2018 was lower than the federal minimum wage in 1981. On what basis could that be true?

7. Use the CPI values provided below to calculate the inflation rate between the given years.
   a. $CPI_{1973} = 44.4$; $CPI_{1974} = 49.3$
   b. $CPI_{2011} = 224.9$; $CPI_{2012} = 229.6$

8. In 2017, the CPI was 245.1 and a ticket to the Super Bowl cost $2,200. Use the following CPI values and the nominal Super Bowl ticket prices provided to calculate the real price of Super Bowl tickets in 1967, 1984, and 2015, expressed in 2017 dollars.
   a. $CPI_{1967} = 33.4$; ticket price = $12
   b. $CPI_{1984} = 103.9$; ticket price = $60
   c. $CPI_{2015} = 237.0$; ticket price = $800

9. Categorize each of the following people as being part of the labor force or not.
   a. Jesse, a new college graduate looking for her first job
   b. Lin, a 70-year-old practicing optometrist
   c. Greg, who is in prison and does not work
   d. Silvia, who was fired from her previous job and submitted her last job application two months ago
   e. Juan, who works part-time at the ballpark

10. Suppose 10,000 people live on the island of Yap. Its labor force is made up of 6,000 workers, 2,000 of whom are unemployed. Calculate the unemployment rate in Yap.

11. Indicate whether each of the following people causes the official unemployment rate to overestimate or underestimate the severity of the unemployment problem.
   a. John, who sells drugs illegally
   b. Trish, who tried for a year to find a job and then stopped looking, even though she would really like to work
   c. Reggie, who works part-time but would prefer to work full-time
   d. Ansel, who details cars for cash and doesn't report it to the government

12. Categorize each of the following people as being frictionally unemployed, structurally unemployed, cyclically unemployed, or seasonally unemployed.
   a. Chloe, who lost her job as a florist when a recession hit the economy
   b. Claire, who drives a Zamboni at an outdoor skating rink during the winter but can't find work during the summer
   c. Miguel, who quit a job in Kansas and is searching for a job in Kentucky
   d. Karena, who is trained in television repair but lacks the skills to work on modern "smart" TVs

Aggregate Demand and Aggregate Supply

14

LEARNING OBJECTIVES

In this chapter, you will learn to:

1. Explain the shape and shifters of the aggregate demand curve
2. Describe how the multiplier effect increases aggregate demand
3. Explain the shape and shifters of the short-run aggregate supply curve
4. Discuss how changes in the macroeconomic equilibrium affect the price level and real GDP
5. Illustrate economic growth using a long-run aggregate supply curve

Franck Fotos/Alamy Stock Photo

They say everything is big in Texas, from hats and steaks to cars and farms. You can think of macroeconomics as the Texas of economics. Macroeconomics covers such large-scale topics as gross domestic product, unemployment, and inflation. To analyze the big ideas in macroeconomics we super-size the supply and demand model to make it a model of the supply and demand of every good and service. We call this the model of *aggregate supply* and *aggregate demand*. With this model of the big economic picture we can explain the economy's big problems and analyze the effects of policies designed to achieve big economic goals.

Why Should I Care?

You've studied the importance of inflation, real gross domestic product (real GDP), and unemployment. This chapter discusses aggregate demand and aggregate supply, which are a big deal because together they determine an economy's levels of inflation, real GDP, and cyclical unemployment. Like a Texas Star weathervane that reveals the changing direction of the wind, the model of aggregate demand and aggregate supply reveals the direction of changes in prices and output. **We can manipulate this model to see how contemplated policy changes would affect inflation, real GDP, and unemployment.** Understanding the levels of the prices you pay, the output available for you to purchase, and the unemployment you contend with, without a grasp of aggregate demand and aggregate supply, would be like trying to catch a steer without a lasso.

▲ Discussions of aggregate demand lump all goods and services together into a single measure of the demand for everything purchased by consumers, firms, or governments, including exports but not imports.

Aggregate Demand

In this chapter, we examine a model of prices and output for the economy as a whole. The curves in this model are shaped by the decisions of buyers and sellers in the economy, which puts us in familiar territory because we have already modeled the buying and selling sides of particular product markets. The word *aggregate* describes something that is formed by combining many parts. Aggregate demand is formed by combining the many parts of demand for an economy's goods and services—the demand for everything purchased by consumers, firms, or governments, including exports demanded by consumers in other economies, but not imports of goods or services produced in other economies. While there are similarities between the demand for a particular good and the demand for all goods in the economy, there are also important differences, as you will learn next.

> **aggregate demand curve**
> A curve that shows the quantity of all final goods and services demanded in an economy at various price levels.

WHY THE AGGREGATE DEMAND CURVE SLOPES DOWNWARD

Recall from Chapter 13 that the price level is a measure of the prices of all goods and services. The **aggregate demand curve** shows the quantity of all final goods and services demanded at various price levels. Figure 14.1 compares the demand curve for hats in panel (a) with the aggregate demand curve in panel (b). The aggregate demand curve is downward sloping like the demand curve for hats, but notice that the axes on the graphs are different. The vertical axis on the aggregate demand graph measures the overall price level (PL) in the economy, not just the price of one good (P). And the horizontal axis on the aggregate demand graph measures real gross domestic product (Y)—the sum of all final goods and services produced in the economy, rather than the quantity of a single good (Q).

The negative slope of the aggregate demand curve indicates that as the price level in the economy increases, the overall quantity of final goods and services demanded decreases. But the explanation

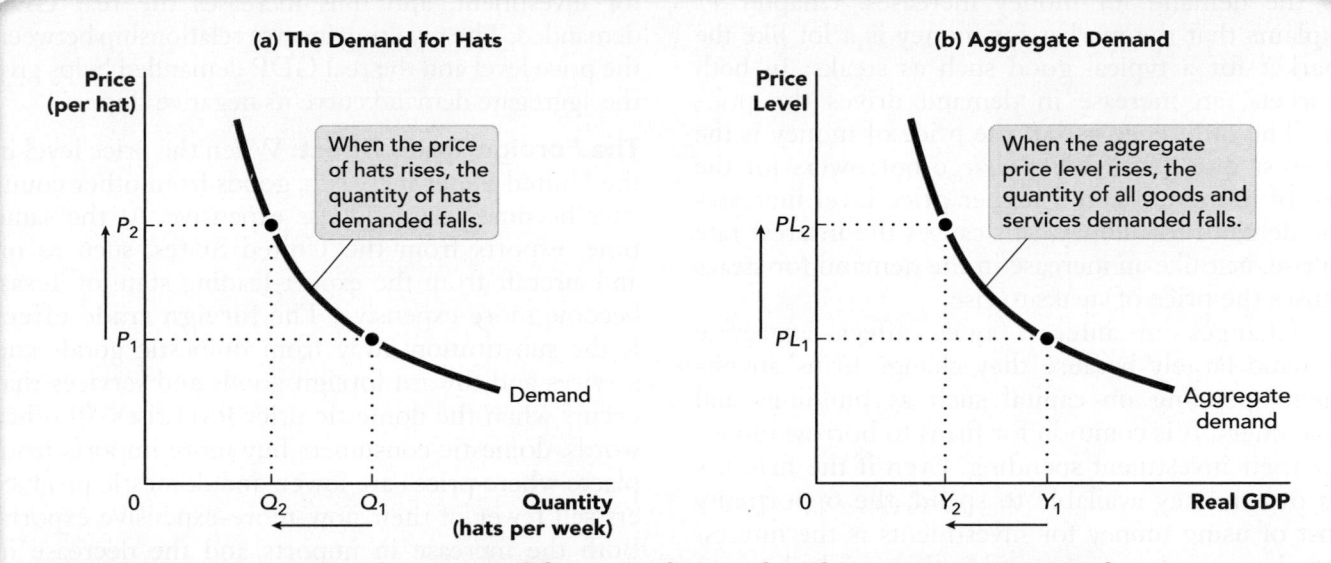

(a) The Demand for Hats

Price
(per hat)

P_2

P_1

When the price
of hats rises, the
quantity of hats
demanded falls.

Demand

0   Q_2 Q_1 Quantity
(hats per week)

(b) Aggregate Demand

Price
Level

PL_2

PL_1

When the aggregate
price level rises, the
quantity of all goods and
services demanded falls.

Aggregate
demand

0   Y_2 Y_1 Real GDP

FIGURE 14.1 Comparing the Demand for a Single Good with Aggregate Demand

The demand curve in panel (a) shows the relationship between the price of hats and the quantity of hats demanded. The aggregate demand curve in panel (b) shows the relationship between the overall price level in the economy and the quantity of all final goods and services demanded.

of the shape of the aggregate demand curve is different from the explanation of the demand curve's shape. When just the price of cowboy hats increases, there is a decrease in the quantity of cowboy hats demanded. Cowboys respond to higher hat prices by buying fewer hats and more of other goods whose prices have not increased, such as boots or steaks.

The story is different for aggregate demand. The negative slope of the aggregate demand curve is not the result of switching from one good to another to avoid buying a good with a new, higher price. When the overall price level in the economy changes, the prices of hats, boots, steaks, and everything else change by roughly the same proportion, so the price of one good relative to another remains about the same. However, there are three effects that *do* cause the aggregate demand curve to slope downward like the demand curve for hats: the *real wealth effect*, the *interest rate effect*, and the *foreign trade effect*. Next, you'll see how each of these effects causes an inverse relationship between the price level and the quantity of all goods demanded (that is, the real GDP demanded).

The Real Wealth Effect. As the price level increases, the money in your pocket and in your piggy bank will buy fewer goods and services. With your wealth losing value, you feel poorer, which is a good reason to curb your consumption. The **real wealth effect** is the decrease in the quantity of goods and services demanded as a result of a decrease in consumers' real wealth that is caused by

inflation. The size of the bite that inflation takes out of wealth depends on how the wealth is held. Like the prices of most goods and services, the prices of assets such as land and gold typically increase and decrease with the overall price level, so the value of wealth held in those assets may be shielded from the effects of inflation and deflation. Interest payments on many types of bank deposits are adjusted for inflation, which helps to maintain the real value of those deposits. But wealth held as cash or in non-interest-bearing accounts loses value with inflation. To summarize the real wealth effect:

Price level ↑ → The value of wealth ↓ →
    Consumers feel poorer →
    Consumption ↓ → Real GDP demanded ↓

Rather than being a substitution away from particular goods that have become more expensive, the real wealth effect can be seen as a substitution away from consumption in the present when the price level is high, and toward consumption in the future when the price level might be lower.

The Interest Rate Effect. As prices rise, consumers need more money to buy any given quantity of goods and services,

> **real wealth effect**
> The decrease in the quantity of goods and services demanded as a result of a decrease in consumers' real wealth that is caused by inflation.

so the demand for money increases. Chapter 17 explains that the market for money is a lot like the market for a typical good such as steaks: In both markets, an increase in demand drives the price up. The difference is that the price of money is the interest rate that lenders charge borrowers for the use of money. When a higher price level increases the demand for money, this causes the interest rate to rise, just like an increase in the demand for steaks causes the price of steaks to rise.

Changes in interest rates affect aggregate demand largely because they change firms' investment spending on capital such as buildings and machinery. It is common for firms to borrow money for their investment spending. Even if the firm has its own money available to spend, the opportunity cost of using money for investments is the interest rate, because the money could otherwise be lent out in exchange for interest payments. The **interest rate effect** is the decrease in investment that occurs when a rise in the price level causes an increase in the interest rate. For example, when higher prices raise the interest rate, it costs more to borrow money to build skyscrapers in Dallas, so fewer investments in new skyscrapers are made. Investment goods such as skyscrapers are among the final goods and services that comprise real GDP, so the drop in investment decreases the real GDP demanded.

To summarize how the interest rate effect works: An increase in the price level leads to an increase in the demand for money, which causes the interest rate to rise. The higher interest rate results in a decrease in investment, which lowers the real GDP demanded. Or more concisely:

Price level ↑ → Money demand ↑ → Interest rate ↑
→ Investment ↓ → Real GDP demanded ↓

interest rate effect
The decrease in investment that occurs when a rise in the price level causes an increase in the interest rate.

foreign trade effect
The substitution away from domestic goods and services and toward foreign goods and services that occurs when the domestic price level rises.

As we've discussed, a higher interest rate makes it less desirable to borrow money for investment. At the same time, a higher interest rate makes it more desirable to save money in an account that earns interest. So the interest rate effect of an increase in the price level is essentially a substitution away from borrowing and toward saving. The interest rate effect also works in reverse: A decrease in the price level decreases the demand for money, which decreases the interest rate. A lower interest rate makes it more desirable to borrow money

for investment, and thus increases the real GDP demanded. The resulting inverse relationship between the price level and the real GDP demanded helps give the aggregate demand curve its negative slope.

The Foreign Trade Effect. When the price level in the United States increases, goods from other countries become relatively less expensive. At the same time, exports from the United States, such as oil and aircraft from the export-leading state of Texas, become more expensive. The **foreign trade effect** is the substitution away from domestic goods and services and toward foreign goods and services that occurs when the domestic price level rises. In other words, domestic consumers buy more imports from places where prices are lower, and domestic producers sell fewer of their now-more-expensive exports. Both the increase in imports and the decrease in exports cause the real GDP demanded in the United States to fall. To summarize the foreign trade effect of an increase in the price level:

Domestic price level ↑ →
Imports become relatively inexpensive,
exports become relatively expensive →
Imports ↑ and Exports ↓ →
Real GDP demanded ↓

The opposite is also true: When the U.S. price level decreases, exports increase, imports decrease, and the real GDP demanded in the United States increases. So the foreign trade effect reinforces the negative relationship between the price level and the real GDP demanded.

Bill Cobb/SuperStock

▲ The relative price levels across countries affect the activities at ports, such as this one in Texas. When the price level in the United States rises, U.S. consumers import more goods from abroad and export fewer goods to other countries. The resulting net decrease in the demand for U.S. goods is called the *foreign trade effect.*

Together, the real wealth effect, the interest rate effect, and the foreign trade effect assure that the aggregate demand curve has a negative slope. Even though changes in the overall price level don't cause substitutions between goods, they do cause substitutions between present and future consumption, between borrowing and saving, and between domestic and foreign goods—all of which create an inverse relationship between the price level and the real GDP demanded.

FACTORS THAT SHIFT THE AGGREGATE DEMAND CURVE

Recall that GDP is made up of consumption (C), investment (I), government spending on goods and services (G), and net exports, which are exports (X) minus imports (M):

$$GDP = C + I + G + (X - M)$$

Almost anything that increases or decreases one of these elements of GDP will shift the aggregate demand curve to the right or to the left, respectively, as shown in Figure 14.2. An exception is a change in the price level, which causes a movement along the aggregate demand curve, rather than a shift, due to the effects explained in the previous section. This section explains the changes that shift aggregate demand.

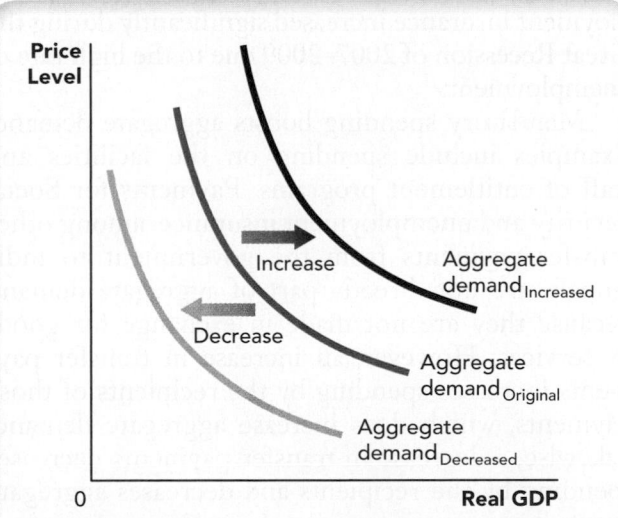

FIGURE 14.2 Shifts in Aggregate Demand
When anything other than a change in the price level increases consumption, investment, government spending on goods and services, or net exports, the aggregate demand curve shifts to the right. Conversely, when anything other than a change in the price level decreases consumption, investment, government spending on goods and services, or net exports, the aggregate demand curve shifts to the left.

Changes in Consumption. To grasp what increases consumption on a grand scale, think about what puts you in the mood to go shopping. If the price level in the economy remained unchanged but your income increased, you might be ready to upgrade your car. If the taxes on your income, property, or purchases decreased, you would have more money to spend and you might eat out more often. If changes in your nation's leadership, government policies, the prospects for peace, or anything else made you optimistic about increases in your future income or job security, you might feel more confident about refurnishing your home. And if an increase in the amount of money in circulation made it easier for you to earn or borrow money, you might find it easier to spend money on a new laptop computer. All of these changes encourage consumers to spend more money, and lead to an increase in aggregate demand. This increase is represented by a rightward shift in the aggregate demand curve. The opposite of any of these changes has the opposite effect of decreasing aggregate demand and shifting the aggregate demand curve to the left.

Changes in Investment Spending. Investment spending by firms is typically paid for with borrowed money for which the interest rate is the price. When the interest rate falls, investment becomes less expensive, which makes more investment projects profitable. So a decrease in the interest rate leads to more investment. Firms will also invest more if they become more optimistic about earning profits from their investments. This could occur if the firms expect improvements in the economy or the implementation of pro-business policies. If the taxes levied

▲ Consumption increases when people feel richer or become more optimistic about their future income levels, such as when they win a game show or get accepted to medical school.

Q&A

Increases in consumption, investment, and net exports were discussed as reasons for movements along the aggregate demand curve. Now they're being described as reasons for shifts in the curve. How can they cause both?

The earlier discussion of movements along the aggregate demand curve and the current discussion of shifts in the aggregate demand curve differ in regard to the root cause of the changes. The wealth effect, interest rate effect, and foreign trade effect are all caused by changes in the price level that result in changes in consumption, investment, and net exports. Because an aggregate demand curve shows the relationship between the price level and the real GDP demanded, the results of changes in the price level are built into the shape of the curve without any need for a shift. It is only when a change in consumption, investment, net exports, or government spending is caused by something other than a change in the price level that the aggregate demand curve shifts.

So when you're trying to figure out whether a change related to aggregate demand shifts the aggregate demand curve or causes a movement along it, ask yourself whether the cause was a change in the price level. If it was, the result will be a movement along the aggregate demand curve. If it wasn't, the result will be a shift in the aggregate demand curve.

---

on firms decrease, some of the money the firms no longer need to pay to the government may go toward investment spending. And if the money supply increases, it becomes easier for firms to borrow money, which leads to more investment spending. Each of these changes increases aggregate demand; the opposite of each of these changes decreases aggregate demand.

Changes in Government Spending. Government spending can be divided into three categories: *discretionary spending*, *mandatory spending*, and *net interest payments*.

Discretionary spending is authorized by annual appropriations acts. Examples of discretionary spending include spending on public schools, highways, the Federal Bureau of Investigation, and NASA's Mission Control Center in Houston, Texas. Discretionary spending can increase or decrease on an annual basis, depending on the decisions of policy makers. Increases in discretionary spending increase aggregate demand; decreases in discretionary spending decrease aggregate demand.

Mandatory spending is required by laws other than annual appropriations acts. Examples include spending on *entitlement programs* such as Social Security, Medicare, Medicaid, unemployment insurance, federal employee retirement and disability benefits, and the Supplemental Nutrition Assistance Program (SNAP). Spending on these programs changes when the associated laws change, or when the cost of funding eligible recipients changes. For example, spending on unemployment insurance increased significantly during the Great Recession of 2007–2009 due to the high rate of unemployment.

Mandatory spending boosts aggregate demand. Examples include spending on the facilities and staff of entitlement programs. Payments for Social Security and unemployment insurance, among other transfer payments from the government to individuals, are not directly part of aggregate demand because they are not made in exchange for goods or services. However, an increase in transfer payments increases spending by the recipients of those payments, which does increase aggregate demand. Likewise, a decrease in transfer payments decreases spending by the recipients and decreases aggregate demand.

Net interest spending is the government's interest payments on its debt, minus interest income the government receives. Government spending on interest payments is not part of aggregate demand because it is not spending on a good or service.

Changes in Net Exports. Net exports—exports minus imports—increase when a nation's exports increase or its imports decrease. For instance, when

discretionary spending Government spending authorized by annual appropriations acts.

mandatory spending Government spending required by laws other than annual appropriations acts.

net interest spending A government's interest payments on its debt, minus interest income the government receives.

Table 14.1 Changes That Increase Aggregate Demand

Consumption increases, which occurs when:
- Income or wealth increases
- Income taxes, sales taxes, or property taxes decrease
- Optimism increases about consumers' future income or job security
- The money supply increases

Investment increases, which occurs when:
- The interest rate decreases
- Firms become more optimistic about future profits
- Taxes on firms decrease
- The money supply increases

Government spending on goods and services increases, which occurs when:
- Policy changes require an increase in discretionary spending
- Mandatory spending on goods and services increases

Net exports increase, which occurs when:
- Foreign countries increase their imports (which are our exports)
- Domestic consumers decrease their imports

the economy of a U.S. trading partner such as Canada, Mexico, or China improves, that country is likely to import more U.S. machinery, electronics, aircraft, pharmaceutical drugs, and other goods and services. Those imports for the U.S. trading partner are exports from the United States. An increase in exports increases aggregate demand.

Looking at the flow of goods and services in the other direction, high import prices, trade restrictions, or changes in people's needs or desires can lead U.S. consumers to import fewer goods and services and to spend more domestically. Changes that increase exports or decrease imports will increase a country's net exports, which increases aggregate demand and shifts the country's aggregate demand curve to the right. A decrease in net exports has the opposite effect.

Table 14.1 summarizes the changes that increase a component of aggregate demand—consumption, investment, government spending, or net exports—and shift the aggregate demand curve to the right. The opposite of each of these changes decreases aggregate demand and shifts the aggregate demand curve to the left.

Table 14.2 The Spending Multiplier

Spent	Saved
$100.00	$20.00
$80.00	$16.00
$64.00	$12.80
$51.20	$10.24
...	...
$500.00	$100.00

Multiplier Effects and Aggregate Demand

Aggregate demand comes from spending. In turn, spending leads to more spending, which leads to more spending, and so on. Consider the Pierce Ranch in Texas, which consists of about 32,000 acres of pasture, rice, and row crops. Mexico is a major importer of U.S. rice. Suppose that out of every $100 the Pierce Ranch receives from the sale of its rice to Mexican grocers, the owners of the ranch save $20, which is 20 percent. The owners spend the remaining $80 on things like new harvesting equipment. Similarly, suppose the sellers of harvesting equipment save 20 percent of their $80 in revenue, which is $16. They spend the remaining $64 on things like welding helmets from the Texas Welders Supply Company. This process of sellers saving some of their revenues and spending the rest continues until there is no more money to be spent because the entire $100 of cash received from Mexico is held as savings. Table 14.2 illustrates this process. In the end, as the result of the initial $100 expenditure, $500 is spent and $100 is saved. The next section explains an easy way to find the total amount of new spending.

THE MARGINAL PROPENSITIES TO CONSUME AND SAVE

Behind this transformation of $100 of spending into $500 of spending are several economic factors you experience often. When you receive money, you might spend some of it and save some of it. The fraction of new income that is spent is called your **marginal propensity to consume (MPC)**. The fraction of new income that is saved is called your **marginal propensity to save (MPS)**. In a simple situation in which all income is either spent on consumption or saved, MPC + MPS = 1. So the portion of income that isn't spent is saved: MPS = 1 − MPC. In the rice example, the ranch and the farm equipment seller each had a marginal propensity to consume of 80 percent or 0.80, so their marginal propensity to save was 0.20 = 1 − 0.80.

THE SPENDING MULTIPLIER

The **spending multiplier** indicates the total amount of spending that results from each $1 "injected" into the economy by new spending. The formula for the spending multiplier is

$$\text{spending multiplier} = \frac{1}{1 - \text{MPC}} = \frac{1}{\text{MPS}}$$

This form of the multiplier is sometimes called the "simple" spending multiplier due to the simplifying assumption that all income is either spent or saved. In our discussion of the multiplier we also assume that the price level is constant. We'll get closer to reality later with the addition of taxes and imports. We'll also see that with an upward-sloping aggregate supply curve, increases in aggregate demand raise the price level, which reduces the multiplier effect.

In the rice example, the marginal propensity to save was 0.20, which made the spending multiplier $\frac{1}{0.20} = 5$. So, when Mexico injected $100 of cash into the U.S. economy with its purchase of rice, the total amount of new spending that resulted from the initial $100 purchase was $100 × 5 = $500. Altogether, the United States exports more than $250 billion worth of goods to Mexico annually. With the help of the multiplier effect, these exports have an even larger effect on aggregate demand.

---

marginal propensity to consume (MPC)
The fraction of new income that is spent.

marginal propensity to save (MPS)
The fraction of new income that is saved.

spending multiplier
The total amount of spending that results from each $1 injected into the economy by new spending.

leakage
In the context of the spending multiplier, this is something that takes money out of the cycle of spending and respending within the economy, such as saving, taxes, or imports.

LEAKAGES

The existence of income taxes makes the multiplier smaller. Like savings, taxes represent a **leakage** that takes money out of the multiplier process of spending and respending in the economy. The portion of income that consumers spend on domestic consumption is the portion that doesn't leak into savings, taxes, or a third type of leakage: imports. For example, if the engineers who designed a dam in the United States spent some of their income on sweaters imported from Norway, less money would be spent and respent in the United States than if the engineers had bought no imports.

An analogy will clarify the effect of leakages: Imagine the spending process as a bucket of money passed from buyers to sellers, who in turn become buyers, and so on. Along the way, some of the money leaks out of the bucket as savings, taxes, and spending on imports (see Figure 14.3). The smaller the leakages, the longer the bucket can be passed around to create more domestic spending before all the money leaks out. So, smaller leakages result in a larger multiplier effect.

FIGURE 14.3 The Leaky Bucket
Spending is the portion of income that doesn't leak into savings, taxes, or imports.

When the only leakage was savings, the multiplier was equivalent to $\frac{1}{MPS}$. With the added leakages of taxes and imports, the multiplier becomes $\frac{1}{leakages}$, with "leakages" being the fraction of each new dollar that is saved, taxed, or spent on imports. If 20 percent goes to savings, 15 percent goes to taxes, and 5 percent goes to imports, the multiplier is $\frac{1}{0.20 + 0.15 + 0.05} = 2.5$. As leakages grow, the multiplier shrinks, as we would expect from the leaky bucket analogy.

Short-Run Aggregate Supply

Just as aggregate demand is the demand of all goods and services in the economy, aggregate supply is the supply of all goods and services in the economy. The **short-run aggregate supply curve** shows the quantity of all final goods and services supplied in the short run at various price levels. Later in this chapter, you'll see how aggregate supply changes in the long run.

THE SHAPE OF THE SHORT-RUN AGGREGATE SUPPLY CURVE

Figure 14.4 shows the general shape of a short-run aggregate supply curve: It is flat at low levels of real GDP, it has an upward-sloping mid-section, and

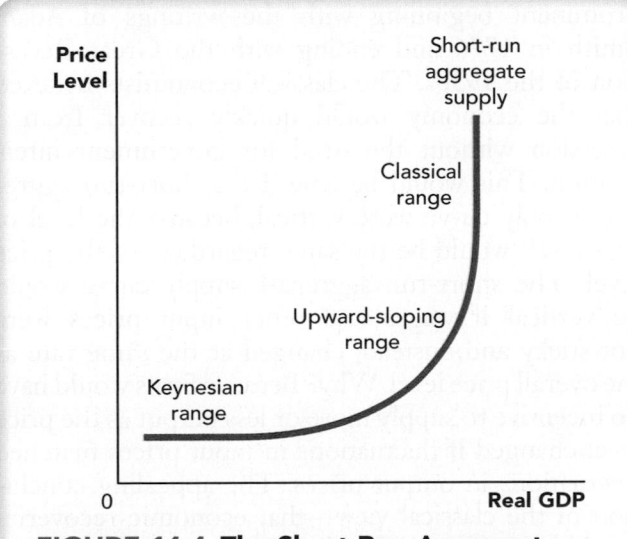

FIGURE 14.4 The Short-Run Aggregate Supply Curve

The short-run aggregate supply curve is horizontal in the Keynesian range, has an upward-sloping mid-section, and is vertical in the classical range.

it becomes steep at high levels of real GDP. This section explains the reasons for this shape and the implications for the workings of the economy.

The Keynesian Range. British economist John Maynard Keynes studied the economy during the Great Depression of the 1930s and concluded that, even with no increase in the price level, firms would be willing to supply more output in response to an increase in aggregate demand. In other words, in his view, the short-run aggregate supply curve was horizontal. That made particular sense during the Great Depression, when more than 20 percent of workers were unemployed and many other factors of production lay idle. Under those conditions, firms would have been content to increase their output to keep up with any increase in aggregate demand, even without the motivation of a higher price level. The same reasoning applies whenever a recession or depression leads to a very low level of real GDP, so the left end of the short-run aggregate supply curve resembles a horizontal line, as Figure 14.4 shows. The relatively flat section of the curve is referred to as the "Keynesian range" of the short-run aggregate supply curve.

The Upward-Sloping Range. The midsection of the short-run aggregate supply curve generally slopes upward like the supply curves for hats and steaks, but for a different reason. The positive slope of the short-run aggregate supply curve is caused by long-term contracts for workers and other factors of production. The employment contracts of many teachers, auto workers, and baseball players are negotiated just once every three years. Many other labor contracts are adjusted once a year for inflation and to provide employees with merit raises. Likewise, the contracts known as *leases* for capital and land are typically negotiated for a period of at least a year. This includes the leases for restaurant buildings, office copy machines, farms, and mining operations. Here, we'll discuss the wages received by labor, which are representative of the costs of all factors of production.

You've seen how important it is to distinguish between nominal and real values when considering monetary values over time. **Nominal wages** are the actual number of dollars workers receive as compensation. **Real wages** are wages adjusted for

short-run aggregate supply curve
A curve that shows the quantity of all final goods and services supplied in an economy in the short run at various price levels.

nominal wages
The actual number of dollars workers receive as compensation.

real wages
Wages adjusted for inflation to indicate their purchasing power.

inflation to indicate their purchasing power—that is, the quantity of goods and services the wages will buy. If the price level and nominal wages both increased by the same proportion—say, 10 percent—there would be no change in what workers could purchase with their nominal wages, so real wages would stay the same. But if the price level increased and nominal wages stayed the same, real wages would fall because workers would be unable to purchase as many goods and services at the higher prices as they could before prices rose. Simply put: Nominal wages go up and down with the dollar amounts workers receive. Real wages go up and down with the quantity of goods and services those wages will buy.

> Nominal wages go up and down with the dollar amounts workers receive. Real wages go up and down with the quantity of goods and services the wages will buy.

Economists use the term *sticky* to describe inflexible or hard-to-change values. Nominal wages that change only when contracts are renegotiated and not every time the price level changes are referred to as **sticky nominal wages.** Consider how sticky nominal wages affect the willingness of the owners of Riscky's Steakhouse to supply steaks. If the price level increased by 25 percent, as it did in Syria in 2017, a steak that used to cost $8 would now cost $10. But a waiter with a sticky nominal wage of $8 per hour due to a long-term contract would still receive $8 per hour. As a result, rather than an hour of labor costing as much as a steak, it would only cost as much as four-fifths of a steak. In other words, real wages would decrease. The lower real wage increases the profit earned from each steak and makes Riscky's Steakhouse willing to hire more workers and produce more output. Of course, a similar story can be told about every firm in the economy. With all firms willing to supply more when the price level increases, there is a positive relationship between the price level and short-run aggregate supply.

sticky nominal wages
Nominal wages that change only when contracts are renegotiated, not every time the price level changes.

▲ Wage contracts at restaurants and other businesses fix employees' wage rates for a year or more. As a result, it takes a long time for wages to adjust to changes in the price level.

philipus/Alamy Stock Photo

When the price level decreases, long-term wage contracts prevent nominal wages from falling as fast as the price level. The result is higher real wages. So firms respond to a decrease in the price level by hiring fewer workers and producing less output. For these reasons, whether the price level increases or decreases, sticky nominal wages give the midsection of the short-run aggregate supply curve an upward slope.

The Classical Range. The theories of a group of economists known as the *classical economists* were prominent beginning with the writings of Adam Smith in 1776 and ending with the Great Recession of the 1930s. The classical economists believed that the economy would quickly recover from a recession without the need for government intervention. This would be true if the short-run aggregate supply curve were vertical, because the level of real GDP would be the same regardless of the price level. The short-run aggregate supply curve would be vertical if wages and other input prices were not sticky and, instead, changed at the same rate as the overall price level. Why? Because firms would have no incentive to supply more or less output as the price level changed if fluctuations in input prices matched fluctuations in output prices. The appealing conclusion of the classical view—that economic recoveries would be swift and effortless on the part of the government—conflicted with the realities of the decade-long Great Depression. Even so, remnants of classical economic theory remain influential to this day.

Even with sticky wages, the short-run aggregate supply curve becomes vertical at the physical limit of the economy's productive capacity. At high levels of real GDP, the economy approaches its physical limit and the short-run aggregate supply curve becomes steep. The curve becomes vertical when the economy can't produce any more output regardless of the price level. The vertical section of the curve is known as the *classical range* of aggregate supply.

FACTORS THAT SHIFT THE SHORT-RUN AGGREGATE SUPPLY CURVE

The short-run aggregate supply curve shifts whenever producers are willing to supply more or less output for a reason other than a change in the price level. Figure 14.5 shows how an increase in aggregate supply is illustrated by a rightward shift in the aggregate supply curve, and how a decrease in aggregate supply is illustrated by a leftward shift in the aggregate supply curve. Like the supply curves for hats and steaks, the short-run aggregate supply curve shifts when production costs change.

The short-run aggregate supply curve becomes vertical when the economy reaches its productive capacity.

Consider the cost of a widely used input such as oil. An increase in the price of oil increases the cost of producing and transporting most goods. This lowers profits and the willingness of firms to supply goods at any particular price level. Similar shifts can result from changes in other input prices, business taxes, regulations, or productivity.

Input Prices. When the wage rate or the prices of other inputs decrease, lower costs give firms higher profits per unit and make firms willing to supply more output. This shifts the short-run aggregate supply curve to the right. An increase in input prices has the opposite effect: It raises costs, lowers profits, and shifts the short-run aggregate supply curve to the left. Input prices change as the result of changes in the demand or supply of the inputs. For example, the discovery of a new source of oil would increase the supply of oil and lower its price. And an expansion of the beef industry would increase the demand for corn and other grains used to make cattle feed and raise the prices of those inputs.

Business Taxes and Regulations. Riscky's Steakhouse pays a tax on its profit. If the corporate tax rate were to increase, the firm's after-tax profit would decrease, thereby cutting into the restaurant's incentive to sell food. A substantial increase in the corporate tax rate would affect other firms in similar ways, and the short-run aggregate supply curve would shift to the left. Conversely, a decrease in the corporate tax rate could increase firms' incentives to increase production and shift the short-run aggregate supply curve to the right.

Steakhouses also operate under regulations that require exhaust hoods over grills to vent dangerous fumes away from cooks and customers. The hoods cost tens of thousands of dollars. If the regulations changed and restaurants no longer were required to use the hoods, it would be less expensive to open a restaurant and supply grilled steaks.

Similarly, some manufacturing plants create toxic waste that can be released into nearby waterways at a low cost, but is more expensive to transport to safer disposal sites. If regulations changed and firms were allowed to release more toxins into the air and waterways, the short-run aggregate supply curve

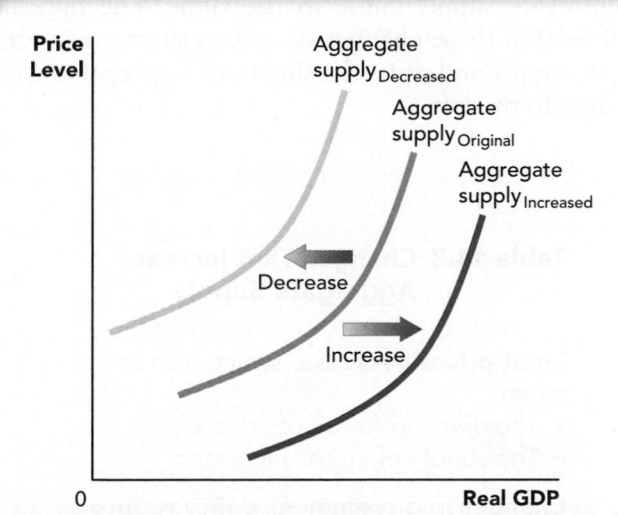

FIGURE 14.5 Shifts in the Short-Run Aggregate Supply Curve

Short-run aggregate supply increases and the short-run aggregate supply curve shifts to the right when input prices decrease, business taxes decrease, a change in regulations lowers the cost of production, or productivity increases. The opposite of any of these changes causes short-run aggregate supply to decrease and shifts the short-run aggregate supply curve to the left.

▲ New regulations that increase the costs of doing business, such as requirements that restaurants and other businesses vent toxic fumes away from workers and customers, shift the aggregate supply curve to the left.

▲ In 2016, massive wildfires near Fort McMurray, Canada, shut down the area's oil production. The loss of more than 1 million barrels of oil per day caused oil prices to rise, which increased the cost of producing and transporting many other goods and shifted the aggregate supply curve to the left.

would shift to the right. As you probably guessed, tighter regulations would shift the short-run aggregate supply curve to the left.

Changes in Productivity. You know that tech geeks are good for the economy, right? Technology and other improvements in production methods boost productivity. For example, the Texas Medical Association reports that the adoption of electronic medical records allows more patients to receive better treatment in less time. With electronic medical records there are no medical charts to misplace, no physical records that require storage space, no problems with illegible handwriting, and fewer issues with duplicated efforts and inaccurate information. More generally, after improvements in technology, education, or transportation systems in an economy, firms will supply more output at any given price level. The result is a rightward shift in the short-run aggregate supply curve. Decreases in productivity are less common, but wars, natural disasters, and disease are among the tragedies that could shift the short-run aggregate supply curve to the left.

When a change in aggregate supply is sudden and unexpected, it is described as a **supply shock.** Supply shocks can be positive or negative. For instance, if ideal temperatures and rainfall created an abundance of crops such as wheat and corn, which are inputs into thousands of goods, the resulting increase in aggregate supply would constitute a positive

supply shock
A sudden and unexpected change in aggregate supply.

supply shock. And if a war or fire disrupted supplies of oil and caused the prices of gasoline, heating oil, and related inputs to spike, this would cause a negative supply shock.

Table 14.3 summarizes the changes that increase short-run aggregate supply and shift the short-run aggregate supply curve to the right. The opposite of each of these changes decreases short-run aggregate supply and shifts the short-run aggregate supply curve to the left.

Table 14.3 Changes That Increase Aggregate Supply

Input prices decrease, which occurs when:
- The demand for inputs decreases
- The supply of inputs increases

Changes in government policy reduce production costs, which occurs when:
- Business taxes decrease
- Regulations that add to the cost of production are removed

Productivity increases, which occurs when:
- Technology improves
- Education improves
- Transportation systems improve

Macroeconomic Equilibrium

As illustrated in Figure 14.6, the intersection of the aggregate demand curve and the short-run aggregate supply curve determines the short-run **macroeconomic equilibrium** in the economy. What you've already learned about the market equilibrium for a good applies similarly to the macroeconomic equilibrium for the economy. It occurs at the price level that equates the quantity of output demanded and supplied. If the price level is above or below the equilibrium level, surpluses or shortages will cause adjustments in the price level until the equilibrium level is reached.

Just as shifts in supply and demand can change the equilibrium price and quantity of a good, shifts in aggregate supply and aggregate demand can change the price level and the real GDP in the economy. We say "can change" rather than "do change" because what changes depends on the shapes of the curves. Figure 14.7 shows that an increase in aggregate demand in the Keynesian range changes the macroeconomic equilibrium from point *A* to point *B*, which causes an increase in real GDP but no change in the price level.

Figure 14.8 shows an increase in aggregate demand in the classical range of the short-run aggregate

macroeconomic equilibrium
The state of the economy in which aggregate demand equals aggregate supply.

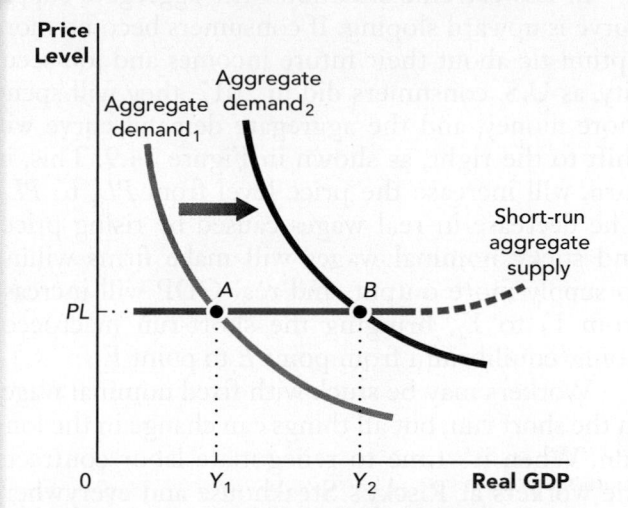

FIGURE 14.7 The Effect of a Shift in Aggregate Demand in the Keynesian Range of the Short-Run Aggregate Supply Curve

In the Keynesian range of the short-run aggregate supply curve, an increase in aggregate demand causes an increase in real GDP but does not affect the price level.

supply curve. The result is a change in the macroeconomic equilibrium from point *C* to point *D*, which merely increases the price level with no change in real GDP.

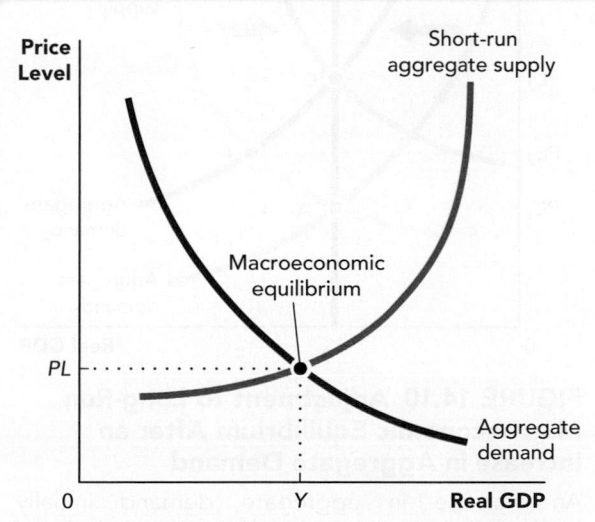

FIGURE 14.6 Macroeconomic Equilibrium

The intersection of the aggregate demand curve and the short-run aggregate supply curve establishes the macroeconomic equilibrium that determines the price level and real GDP in the economy.

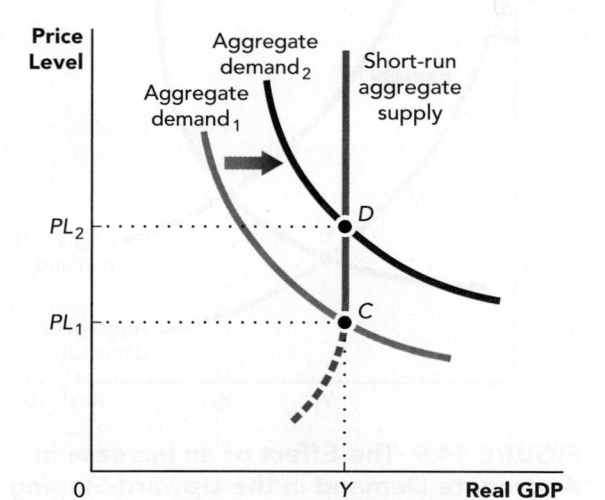

FIGURE 14.8 The Effect of a Shift in Aggregate Demand in the Classical Range of the Short-Run Aggregate Supply Curve

In the classical range, an increase in aggregate demand causes an increase in the price level but no change in real GDP.

In less extreme situations, the aggregate supply curve is upward sloping. If consumers become more optimistic about their future incomes and job security, as U.S. consumers did in 2017, they will spend more money, and the aggregate demand curve will shift to the right, as shown in Figure 14.9. This, in turn, will increase the price level from PL_1 to PL_2. The decrease in real wages caused by rising prices and sticky nominal wages will make firms willing to supply more output, and real GDP will increase from Y_1 to Y_2, bringing the short-run macroeconomic equilibrium from point E to point F.

Workers may be stuck with fixed nominal wages in the short run, but all things can change in the long run. When it's time to renegotiate labor contracts, the workers at Riscky's Steakhouse and everywhere else will demand higher nominal wages in response to both the higher price level and the increased demand for workers needed to make the new, higher quantity of output. Higher nominal wages will remedy the erosion in real wages caused by the higher price level, but they will also cut into the firms' profits. As wages

> **long-run aggregate supply curve**
> A curve that shows the relationship between real GDP and the price level in the long run.

and other input prices rise to match the higher price level, the quantity of output that firms will supply at any given price level decreases, and the short-run aggregate supply curve shifts to the left. This adjustment continues until the short-run aggregate supply curve intersects the aggregate demand curve at the same level of real GDP that was produced before the increase in aggregate demand, as shown by point C in Figure 14.10.

Points A and C are on the **long-run aggregate supply curve,** which shows the relationship between real GDP and the price level in the long run. Because points A and C are both at the same level of real GDP, the change in the price level had no effect on real GDP after the economy had time to adjust to the change in aggregate demand. This immunity of real GDP to changes in the price level makes the long-run aggregate supply curve vertical. You will learn more about the long-run aggregate supply curve in the next section.

Figure 14.11 shows how an economy adjusts in the long run after a decrease in aggregate demand moves the macroeconomic equilibrium from point A to point B.

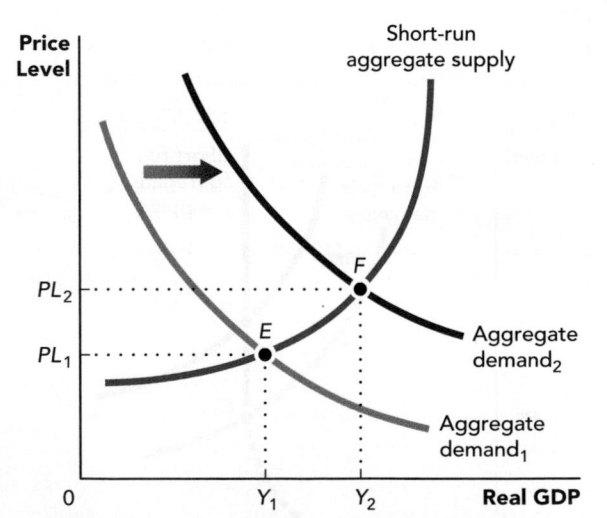

FIGURE 14.9 The Effect of an Increase in Aggregate Demand in the Upward-Sloping Section of the Short-Run Aggregate Supply Curve

In the common case of an upward-sloping short-run aggregate supply curve, an increase in aggregate demand will move the macroeconomic equilibrium from point E to point F. This will increase the equilibrium price level from PL_1 to PL_2 and increase the equilibrium real GDP from Y_1 to Y_2.

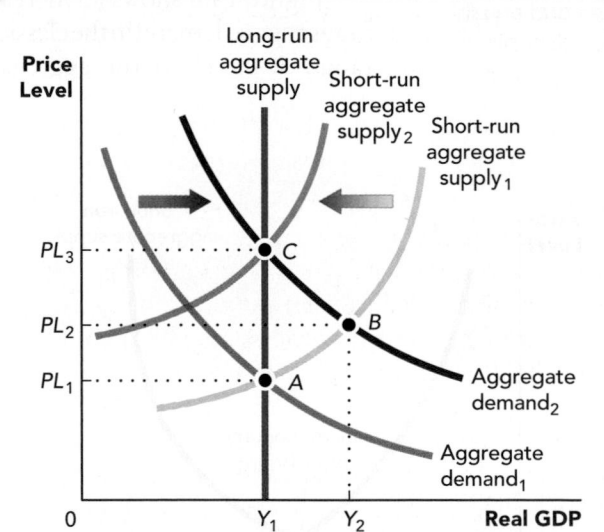

FIGURE 14.10 Adjustment to Long-Run Macroeconomic Equilibrium After an Increase in Aggregate Demand

An increase in aggregate demand initially increases both the price level and the level of output, moving the macroeconomic equilibrium from point A to point B. This puts upward pressure on input prices and decreases short-run aggregate supply. This adjustment continues until the short-run aggregate supply curve and the aggregate demand curve intersect at point C on the vertical long-run aggregate supply curve.

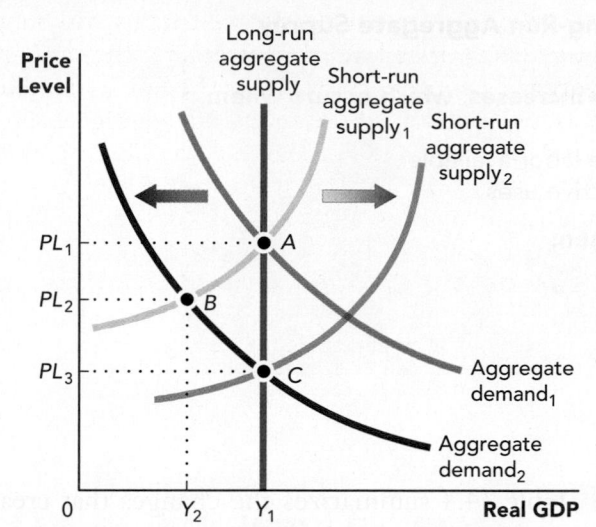

FIGURE 14.11 Adjustment to Long-Run Macroeconomic Equilibrium After a Decrease in Aggregate Demand

A decrease in aggregate demand initially decreases both the price level and the level of output, moving the macroeconomic equilibrium from point A to point B. This puts downward pressure on input prices and increases short-run aggregate supply. This adjustment continues until the short-run aggregate supply curve and the aggregate demand curve intersect at point C on the long-run aggregate supply curve.

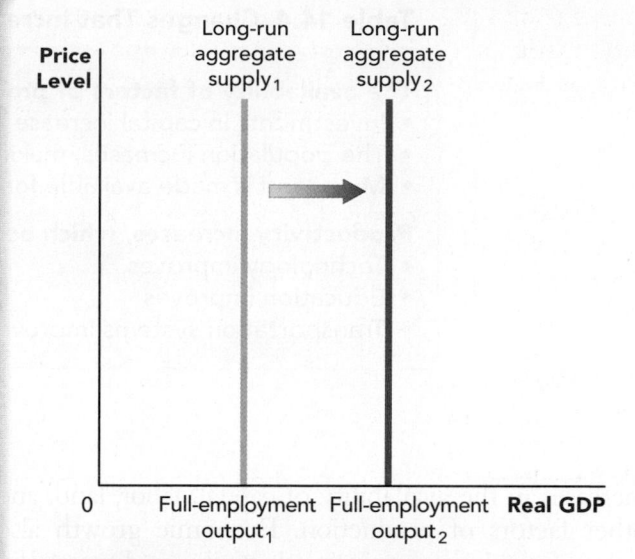

FIGURE 14.12 Illustrating Economic Growth with the Long-Run Aggregate Supply Curve

The long-run aggregate supply curve shifts to the right when economic growth increases the level of real GDP that the economy can sustain. The sources of economic growth include increases in the factors of production and increases in the productivity of those factors.

When labor contracts are renewed, the lower price level and the lower level of employment needed to make the reduced quantity of output lead to a decrease in nominal wages. As wages and other input prices fall, the quantity of output that firms will supply at any given price level increases, and the short-run aggregate supply curve shifts to the right. This adjustment continues until the short-run aggregate supply curve intersects the aggregate demand curve at the same level of real GDP that was produced before the decrease in aggregate demand, as shown by point C on the long-run aggregate supply curve in Figure 14.11.

Long-Run Aggregate Supply and Economic Growth

Figures 14.10 and 14.11 illustrated changes that affect the price level but have no effect on real GDP in the long run; they just cause movements along the vertical long-run aggregate supply curve. The long-run aggregate supply curve is located at the level of real GDP that can be produced with full employment, which is called **full-employment output,** or *potential output.*

Keep in mind that full employment is achieved when there is no cyclical unemployment; it does not mean that everyone in the labor force is working, because there is always frictional and structural unemployment. The economy is able to produce beyond the full employment output level in the short run by reducing frictional unemployment below its natural rate, but that can't last. The scarcity of workers at very low unemployment rates causes wage rates to rise. As we have seen, higher wages shift the short-run aggregate supply curve to the left until long-run equilibrium is reached at the full-employment output level.

Chapter 1 explained that an increase in output achieved by employing previously idle workers does not constitute economic growth. Likewise, an increase in output made possible by temporarily reducing frictional unemployment below its natural rate is not economic growth. Rather, economic growth is an increase in the level of real GDP that the economy can sustain—it is an increase in long-run aggregate supply. Economic growth can be illustrated by a rightward shift in the long-run aggregate supply curve, as shown in Figure 14.12. The sources of economic growth include

> **full-employment (or potential) output**
> The level of real GDP that can be produced with full employment.

Table 14.4 Changes That Increase Long-Run Aggregate Supply

The availability of factors of production increases, which occurs when:
- Investments in capital increase
- The population increases, making more labor available
- More land is made available for productive uses

Productivity increases, which occurs when:
- Technology improves
- Education improves
- Transportation systems improve

increases in the availability of capital, labor, land, and other factors of production. Economic growth also comes from increases in productivity, as discussed in the preceding section. In recent decades, real GDP has increased by about 2 to 3 percent per year in the United States.

Table 14.4 summarizes the changes that create economic growth and shift the long-run aggregate supply curve to the right. The opposite of each of these changes shifts the long-run aggregate supply curve to the left. Chapter 18 focuses on the goal of economic growth.

SUMMARY

All it takes is a graph of aggregate demand and aggregate supply to tell a story of inflation, production, employment, and economic growth. The aggregate demand curve shows the relationship between the price level and the quantity of final goods and services demanded in an economy. The aggregate demand curve is downward sloping, but not due to substitutions between goods like the ones that cause the demand curves for typical goods, such as steak and oil, to slope downward. When the price level in the economy rises, the prices of steak, oil, and most other goods rise, so changes in demand are not caused by changes in relative prices. Instead, the aggregate demand curve slopes downward because of the real wealth effect, the interest rate effect, and the foreign trade effect.

The real wealth effect is the decrease in the quantity of goods and services demanded as a result of a decrease in real wealth caused by inflation. The real wealth effect causes people to substitute away from consumption in the present when the price level is high, and toward consumption in the future when the price level might be lower.

The interest rate effect is the decrease in investment brought about when a rise in the price level increases the demand for money and causes an increase in the interest rate. The higher interest rate

causes people to substitute saving for borrowing because by saving they can earn the higher interest rate, whereas by borrowing they have to pay it.

The foreign trade effect is the decrease in net exports caused by a higher domestic price level. When domestic prices rise, consumers purchase fewer domestic goods and services and more foreign goods and services.

The aggregate demand curve shifts when there is a change in consumption, investment, government spending, or net exports not caused by a change in the price level.

Increases in spending pack more punch due to the multiplier effect. When new spending occurs, the seller typically spends some of the money received, as does the next seller, and so on. Some portion of that money continues to be respent until all the money leaks into savings. The total amount of spending that results from a new expenditure is found by multiplying the dollar amount of the new expenditure by the spending multiplier. The spending multiplier is found by dividing 1 by the portion of each dollar of income that is saved. When taxes and imports are involved, the spending multiplier is 1 divided by the portion of each dollar of income that leaks into savings, taxes, or imports.

The aggregate supply curve shows the quantity of final goods and services supplied at different price levels. Because long-term contracts cause wages and other input prices to increase more slowly than output prices, firms earn more from each unit when the price level increases. This gives them an incentive to supply more units. The positive relationship between the price level and aggregate supply causes the short-run aggregate supply curve to slope upward in its midsection. At low levels of real GDP, the short-run aggregate supply curve is horizontal. At the highest level of real GDP the economy could possibly produce, the short-run aggregate supply curve becomes vertical. The short-run aggregate supply curve shifts when there is a change in input prices, business taxes, regulations, or productivity.

The long-run aggregate supply curve is vertical at the output level that corresponds with full employment. The long-run aggregate supply curve shifts to the right when there is economic growth, which can come from increases in the availability of inputs or in the productivity of those inputs. For example, the increasing availability of capital and the advancements of technology have made more goods and services available across the economy, from high-speed automobile assembly lines that produce more cars to mechanical bulls that make it possible to ride a bull in a bar.

KEY TERMS

aggregate demand curve, p. 208
real wealth effect, p. 209
interest rate effect, p. 210
foreign trade effect, p. 210
discretionary spending, p. 212
mandatory spending, p. 212
net interest spending, p. 212
marginal propensity to consume
    (MPC), p. 214

marginal propensity to save
    (MPS), p. 214
spending multiplier, p. 214
leakage, p. 214
short-run aggregate supply curve,
    p. 215
nominal wages, p. 215
real wages, p. 215
sticky nominal wages, p. 216

supply shock, p. 218
macroeconomic equilibrium,
    p. 219
long-run aggregate supply curve,
    p. 220
full-employment (or potential)
    output, p. 221

PROBLEMS FOR REVIEW

1. True or false: The aggregate demand curve slopes downward because when the price level rises, consumers substitute one good for another. Explain your answer.

2. True or false: The short-run aggregate supply curve slopes upward because when the price level rises, sticky wages create incentives for firms to produce more output. Explain your answer.

3. Which of the following changes cause the aggregate demand curve to shift to the left? Choose all that apply.
   a. An increase in the price level
   b. A decrease in wealth
   c. An increase in exports
   d. A decrease in workers' optimism about job security
   e. An increase in the interest rate
   f. A decrease in government spending

4. Which of the following changes cause the short-run aggregate supply curve to shift to the right? Choose all that apply.
   a. An increase in the price level
   b. A decrease in input prices
   c. An increase in aggregate demand
   d. A decrease in business taxes
   e. An increase in productivity
   f. A decrease in the money supply

5. Calculate the spending multiplier in each of the following situations under the assumption that there are no taxes or imports:
   a. The MPS = 0.10
   b. The MPS = 0.05
   c. The MPC = 0.75
   d. Half of all new income is saved

6. Suppose the government spends $10 billion that it already has on hand to improve the nation's railway system. If the marginal propensity to consume is 0.80, what will the total increase in spending be after the multiplier process is complete?

7. The short-run aggregate supply curve can have three ranges: the Keynesian range, the upward-sloping range, and the classical range. In which range does an increase in aggregate demand cause each of the following?
   a. An increase in both the price level and real GDP
   b. An increase in the price level but not real GDP
   c. An increase in real GDP but not the price level.

8. The aggregate supply curve takes on a different shape in the long run.
   a. Draw a long-run aggregate supply curve and label it $LRAS_1$.
   b. What is the name for the level of output at which the long-run aggregate supply curve meets the horizontal axis?
   c. Explain why increases in the price level do not affect aggregate supply in the long run.
   d. On the same graph, show what happens to the long-run aggregate supply curve when productivity increases. Label the new curve $LRAS_2$.

9. Draw a graph of aggregate demand, short-run aggregate supply, and long-run aggregate supply. Label the curves and axes. Label the price level as PL_1 and the real GDP as Y_1.
   a. Show how the graph will change if the money supply decreases. Label the new price level as PL_2 and the new real GDP as Y_2.
   b. Show what happens in the long run to bring the equilibrium of aggregate demand and short-run aggregate supply back to a point on the long-run aggregate supply curve. Label the new price level as PL_3.
   c. Explain why the change that you drew for part (b) occurred.

10. Identify a possible cause of each of the following in the country where you live:
    a. A negative supply shock
    b. A positive supply shock
    c. A decrease in aggregate demand
    d. An increase in aggregate demand

11. Suppose you are the president of your country and are making a speech to the public about government efforts to boost the economy. How would you explain the way an increase in government spending can increase overall spending in the economy by more than the government's initial increase in spending?

Fiscal Policy

15

LEARNING OBJECTIVES

In this chapter, you will learn to:

1. Explain how government expenditures are funded

2. Compare and contrast the major schools of economic thought

3. Model the effects of expansionary and contractionary fiscal policies

4. Identify potential problems with the use of fiscal policy

5. Discuss the pros and cons of supply-side fiscal policy

Late in 2007, the U.S. economy plunged into the greatest recession since the Great Depression of the 1930s. One year into the Great Recession, real GDP had dropped by almost 4 percent. By 2009, the unemployment rate had reached 10 percent, leaving 15 million workers unemployed. The government deployed its weapon of *fiscal policy* against this monster of a recession. Fiscal policy is the use of government spending, taxes, and *transfer payments* (such as unemployment insurance and tuition grants) to help stabilize the economy. This chapter explains the strengths and vulnerabilities of this controversial category of economic policy.

Why Should I Care?

A recession's downward spiral inflicts pain on consumers, workers, business owners, and the broader community. Consumers and firms spend conservatively as a recession barrels along because they cannot predict the length or severity of their economic woes. Exports fizzle as the recession spreads to other countries around the world. Declining sales for firms translate into declining employment for workers, and could make it harder for you to find a job. Falling stock prices reduce the value of investments held by almost half of all American adults. And lower incomes make it harder for charities, churches, and governments to collect the money they need to offer services that may be important to you.

Fiscal policy offers a possible fix for a weak economy, but policy makers often differ on the best approach to take. At the height of the Great Recession, minority leader of the U.S. House of Representatives John Boehner remarked, "It's time for government to tighten their belts and show the American people that we 'get' it." Boehner's message was that the government should spend less money during the recession. In contrast, economist and Nobel laureate Paul Krugman responded to comments like Boehner's by saying, "Now is a time when the government should be spending more, not less. If we ignore this insight and cut government spending instead, the economy will shrink and unemployment will rise." This chapter will give you a new understanding of the economics underlying many such high-stakes debates over fiscal policy. In Chapter 17, you will learn how a nation's central bank can carry out *monetary policy*, another line of defense against recessions.

Government Expenditures and Taxes

fiscal policy
The use of government spending, taxes, and transfer payments to help stabilize the economy.

The influence of **fiscal policy** comes from government expenditures and taxes. Figure 15.1 breaks down the U.S. federal government's $3.98 trillion in expenditures in 2017. About two-thirds of the spending is *mandatory*, in that it pays for programs such as Social Security, Medicare, and Medicaid, which are required by existing laws. Less than one-third of the spending is *discretionary*, meaning that the amounts are chosen each year by Congress and the president. A majority of discretionary spending is allocated to

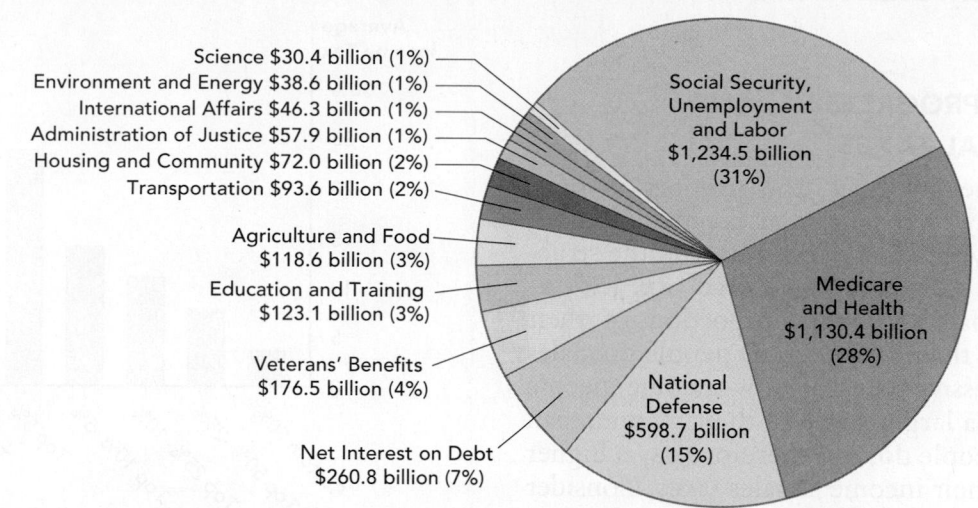

FIGURE 15.1 Spending by the U.S. Federal Government in 2017

The largest expenditures by the federal government are on Social Security, health care, and the military.

Source: Office of Management and Budget.

the military. Other areas of discretionary spending include education, veterans' benefits, transportation, energy, and the environment.

Figure 15.2 shows the major sources of the federal government's $3.32 trillion in revenue in 2017. Individual income taxes provide the largest share of revenue. The second-largest share comes

from the *payroll taxes* withheld from employees' paychecks to support Social Security, Medicare, unemployment insurance, and other government programs. Corporate income taxes are the other substantial source of federal government revenues. Sales taxes and excise taxes are major sources of revenue for state and local governments, but they

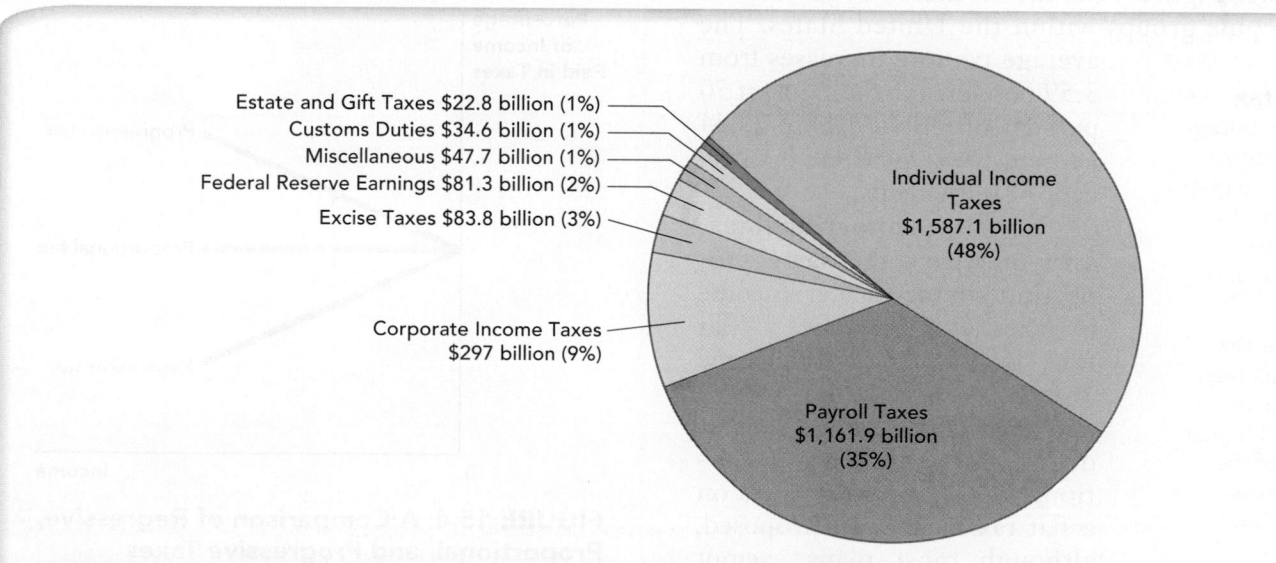

FIGURE 15.2 Sources of Federal Government Revenue in 2017

Individual income taxes are the largest source of revenues for the federal government, followed by payroll taxes and corporate income taxes.

Source: Office of Management and Budget.

provide relatively little revenue for the federal government.

REGRESSIVE, PROGRESSIVE, AND PROPORTIONAL TAXES

As your income increases, the proportion of it that you will pay for a particular tax may increase, decrease, or stay the same, depending on the structure of the tax. Under a **regressive tax,** low-income people pay a higher proportion of their income in taxes than high-income people do. Sales taxes are regressive because low-income people typically spend a larger share of their income than high-income people do, and therefore pay a higher proportion of their income as sales taxes. Consider a 5 percent sales tax. If Family A earns $10,000 each year and spends all of it, Family A pays $500 in sales taxes—5 percent of its income. If Family B earns $100,000 each year and spends $20,000 of it, Family B pays $1,000 in sales taxes. Although Family B's annual tax bill is twice that of Family A's, the $1,000 payment represents only 1 percent of Family B's income. The low-income family thus pays a higher *proportion* of its income in sales taxes than the high-income family does.

Under a **progressive tax,** high-income people pay a higher proportion of their income in taxes than low-income people do. Any tax for which the average tax rate increases as one's income increases is a progressive tax. The federal income tax is an example. Figure 15.3 shows the average tax rate for income groups within the United States. The average tax rate increases from 3.59 percent for the poorest 50 percent of individuals to 27.44 percent for the richest 0.1 percent of individuals.

Under a **proportional tax,** everyone pays the same proportion of his or her income in taxes. For instance, a "flat tax" that applied the same average tax rate to everyone and allowed no exemptions or deductions would be a proportional tax. Many variations on a flat tax have been proposed, although most plans exempt low-income individuals or provide a deduction based on family size, which makes the plans progressive rather than proportional. Figure 15.4 summarizes what happens to a

regressive tax
A tax system under which low-income people pay a higher proportion of their income in taxes than high-income people do.

progressive tax
A tax system under which high-income people pay a higher proportion of their income in taxes than low-income people do.

proportional tax
A tax system under which everyone pays the same proportion of their income in taxes.

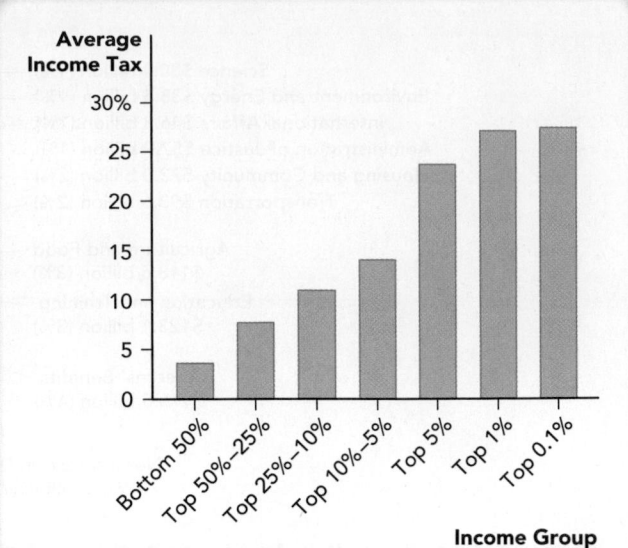

FIGURE 15.3 Average Tax Rates by Income Group, 2017

The U.S. federal income tax is progressive, meaning that high-income people generally pay a higher proportion of their income in taxes than low-income people do.

Source: Internal Revenue Service.

household's average tax rate as its income increases under regressive, proportional, and progressive taxes.

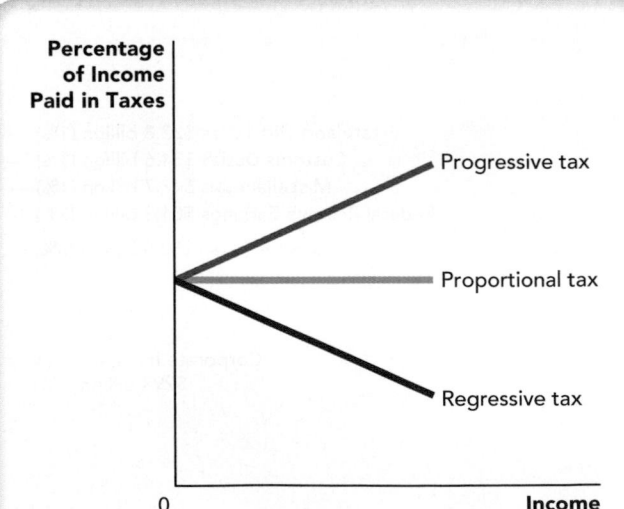

FIGURE 15.4 A Comparison of Regressive, Proportional, and Progressive Taxes

As a household's income increases, the proportion of that income paid for a particular tax will decrease, stay the same, or increase, depending on whether the tax is regressive, proportional, or progressive.

IMBALANCES IN THE BUDGET: SURPLUSES, DEFICITS, AND THE DEBT

Government revenues rarely match government expenditures. For a year in which revenues exceed expenditures, the government has a **budget surplus.** If expenditures exceed revenues, the government has a **budget deficit.** In 2000, the U.S. federal government took in $2.03 trillion and spent $1.79 trillion, which resulted in a budget surplus of $240 billion. In 2017, revenues were $3.32 trillion and expenditures were $3.98 trillion, which resulted in a budget deficit of $666 billion.

The federal **debt** is the accumulation of past budget deficits, minus past budget surpluses. Don't confuse an annual deficit with the accumulated debt. Each deficit adds to the existing debt. For example, at the beginning of 2016, the federal debt was $18.12 trillion, but the $1.42 trillion budget deficit in 2016 brought the debt up to $18.12 trillion + $1.42 trillion = $19.54 trillion by the end of 2016.

Figure 15.5 shows the federal debt as a percentage of GDP between 1940 and 2018. The growth in government spending during wars and recessions leads to large deficits that increase the debt. During recessions, lower levels of income and spending decrease tax revenues and further enlarge deficits. These effects explain the large increases in the debt during World War II in the mid-1940s and during the Great Recession of 2007–2009. A strong economy leads to more income and higher tax collections, which can generate a surplus and decrease the debt. That is exactly what happened in the late 1990s.

Governments try to avoid debt and the accompanying burden of interest payments. But, like individuals, governments sometimes decide to spend borrowed money because they believe their needs justify the expense. For governments, the needs can relate to national defense, natural disasters, economic crises, or crumbling roads and bridges, among other national priorities. The good news is that the burdens of debt are in some ways smaller for governments than for individuals. Governments with a long history of repaying their debts are able to pay lenders relatively low interest rates in exchange for the low risk of default. For example, the U.S. federal government has almost never defaulted on its loans, so the interest rates it pays are small relative to what the average individual pays. In addition, most governments are around for much longer than any individual, so the governments can spread the repayment of loans over relatively long periods of time. And governments have

budget surplus
The excess of government revenues over government expenditures over a given period, usually one year.

budget deficit
The excess of government expenditures over government revenues over a given period, usually one year.

debt
The accumulation of past budget deficits, minus past budget surpluses.

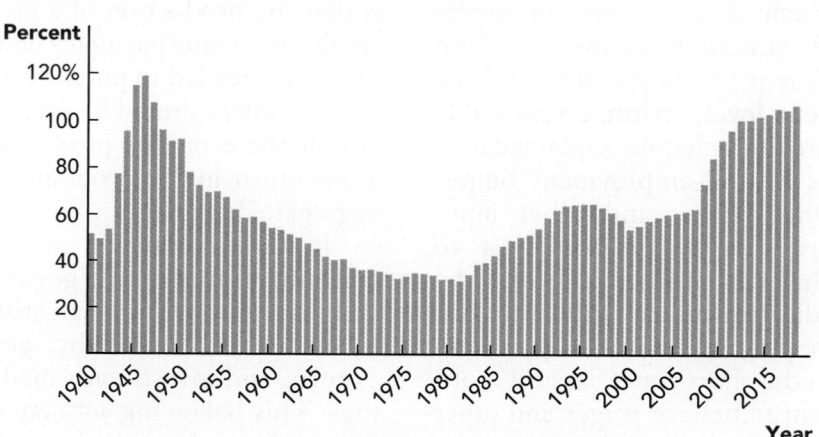

FIGURE 15.5 Federal Debt as a Percentage of GDP, 1940–2018
Periods of war or recession typically cause the government to spend more money than it collects in taxes. The result is a budget deficit that adds to the federal debt. When the economy is strong, tax collections can exceed government expenditures. This leads to a budget surplus that decreases the debt.
Source: Office of Management and Budget.

the unique ability to tax citizens to collect money for the repayment of loans. Individuals don't have this luxury. In light of these advantages, how appropriate is it for the government to borrow money to fund fiscal policies? There are several schools of thought about that issue, as we'll see next.

Schools of Economic Thought

Seventy-five years before the Great Recession, the Great Depression devastated the world economy. U.S. unemployment rates reached a staggering 24.9 percent. Waves of poverty and despair rippled across the globe. Because sinking economies inflict such pain, economists toil to improve their theories about how to keep economies afloat. When one popular theory fails a reality check, attention turns to alternative theories. This section introduces three long-established schools of economic thought, the influences of which are still felt in modern policy debates.

CLASSICAL THEORY

According to **classical theory,** fiscal policy is not needed to stabilize the economy. Adam Smith (1723–1790) is considered the father of classical economics. In 1776, Smith published *An Inquiry into the Nature and Causes of the Wealth of Nations,* which extolled the virtues of *free markets* with minimal government intervention. He believed that as long as monopoly power and immorality could be contained, free markets would yield the best outcome for society.

Classical economists argue that after a destabilizing event, such as a decrease in aggregate demand, self-adjustment mechanisms within the economy are sufficient to bring real GDP back to the full-employment level within a reasonable period of time. The previous chapter explained how the economy returns to full-employment output when wages and other input prices are able to adjust to changes in the price level. If the adjustments are swift, the economy returns to full employment in the short run. Classical economists believe wages and other prices are flexible enough to permit such a rapid self-adjustment and thus avoid the need for government assistance.

Artepics/age fotostock/Superstock

▲ Classical economist Adam Smith believed that, under the right conditions, natural adjustments in wages and prices would swiftly stabilize the economy without the assistance of fiscal policy.

classical theory
Economic theory rooted in the idea that the economy can stabilize itself.

Say's law
A theory that supply creates its own demand.

French businessman and economist Jean-Baptiste Say (1767–1832) reinforced the classical view that the economy can take care of itself. According to **Say's law,** supply creates its own demand. The idea is that the production of a given level of real GDP results in income payments equivalent to the amount of money needed to purchase that level of real GDP. So consumers should be prepared to demand all the output the economy produces and thereby prevent a downturn in the economy caused by insufficient aggregate demand.

If some income is not spent domestically by consumers, and instead goes toward taxes, imports, and savings, Say's law can still hold if that unspent income is balanced by government spending, exports, and investments made with borrowed savings. This balancing act may be assisted by market forces: According to classical theory, the interest rate will rise or fall to bring the amount of money demanded for investments into balance with the amount of money supplied as savings.

KEYNESIAN THEORY

Classical theory dominated economic thought from the mid-1700s until the early 1930s. When the Great Depression hit in 1929 and GDP languished below the full-employment output level year after year, it became evident that the self-adjustments touted by classical theorists could sometimes be a long time coming. The Great Depression turned the attention of policy makers to theories proposed by the English economist John Maynard Keynes (1883–1946) in his book *The General Theory of Employment, Interest and Money*. **Keynesian theory** suggests that government involvement is sometimes needed to stabilize the economy. Keynes argued that sticky wages and other rigidities in the economy prevent the swift self-adjustment that classical economists hope for. Keynes also did not believe that adjustments in the interest rate would be enough to equalize savings and investment. He argued that individuals sometimes have irrational desires to hold

cash. And he believed that the opportunities for investment, rather than the interest rate, are the primary driver of investment demand. All recent U.S. presidents have been sufficiently persuaded by Keynesian theory to actively address recessions with fiscal policy measures.

MONETARIST THEORY

Like classical theory, Keynesian theory came into question during an economic crisis. The inability of Keynesian policies to curtail high inflation and unemployment in the 1970s opened the door for the relatively new monetarist school of thought. **Monetarist theory** emphasizes limited growth in the money supply as a means of controlling inflation. Like classical economists, monetarists believe that the economy is inherently stable and that the government's involvement in the economy should be minor. They also favor *passive* economic policy, meaning that the government should not actively implement new policies in response to swings in the business cycle.

Milton Friedman (1912–2006) and Anna Schwartz (1915–2012) successfully promoted monetarism in their book *A Monetary History of the United States, 1867–1960*. Among the messages in the book was that "Inflation is always and everywhere a monetary phenomenon." In the 1970s, the United States experienced the combination of stagnating real GDP and inflation known as **stagflation**. Monetarists argued that this phenomenon could occur only if there were too much money in the economy. If the money supply were expanded at the rate of growth in real GDP, there would be no extra money in the economy to fuel inflation. Steady growth in the money supply would also reduce uncertainty about the effects that a central bank's more reactive monetary policy might have on the economy. Our nation's central bank, the Federal Reserve, adopted monetarist principles from 1979 until 1982 under the leadership of Paul Volcker. By limiting growth in the money supply over that period, the Federal Reserve successfully brought the U.S. inflation rate down from 13.5 percent to 6.2 percent.

▲ John Maynard Keynes advocated active government involvement to help the economy out of recessionary and inflationary periods. He argued that the economy's self-adjustment process is thwarted by inflexible wages and prices, as well as by inadequate incentives for investment.

Keynesian theory
Economic theory centered on the idea that government involvement is sometimes needed to stabilize the economy.

monetarist theory
Economic theory that emphasizes limited growth in the money supply as a means of controlling inflation.

stagflation
A combination of stagnating real GDP and inflation in an economy.

▲ Monetarists Milton Friedman and Anna Schwartz believed that the government should minimize its role in trying to fix the economy, and that the money supply should be increased at the rate of economic growth.

Surprising Consensus and Some Lingering Disagreement

At times, the adversarial relationship between members of the differing schools of thought has been intense. Milton Friedman engaged in frequent public debates with fellow Nobel laureate and Keynesian economist Paul Samuelson. Shortly before his death in 2009, Samuelson pointed to the Great Recession as evidence against Friedman's monetarist theories:

> Today we see how utterly mistaken was the Milton Friedman notion that a market system can regulate itself. . . . Everyone understands now, on the contrary, that there can be no solution without government. The Keynesian idea is once again accepted that fiscal policy and deficit spending has a major role to play in guiding a market economy.

But there were gems of wisdom, along with flaws, in each of the economic theories. With the passage of time came reality checks and research that narrowed the range of disagreement. Keynes himself appreciated the benefits of free markets touted by classical economists, while pointing out that classical theory included reasons for Keynesian-style oversight. Finding middle ground, he wrote:

> The modern classical theory has itself called attention to various conditions in which the free play of economic forces may need to be curbed or guided. But there will still remain a wide field for the exercise of private initiative and responsibility.

This section explains some of the many important areas of general consensus among modern economists and some continuing sources of discord.

As the predominant economic theories shifted from classical to Keynesian to monetarist and back to Keynesian, views on the effectiveness of fiscal policy flipped back and forth as well. Today, most economists agree that expansionary fiscal policy does shift the aggregate demand curve to the right. There is also consensus that problems with lags and politics (which are discussed in the next section) make fiscal policy undesirable as the primary tool for stabilizing the economy. However, when market forces and monetary policy can't resolve an economic crisis, most economists support the use of fiscal policy.

In the past, classical economists felt that fiscal policy was ineffective against unemployment problems.

▲ Most economists agree that expansionary fiscal policy such as the American Recovery and Reinvestment Act does shift the aggregate demand curve to the right.

Keynesian economists believed that fiscal policy could decrease the unemployment rate and keep it low for the long term. Monetarist economists argued that no policy could keep the unemployment rate below the natural rate of unemployment—roughly 5 percent—that corresponds with production at the full-employment level of output. Most economists now agree that fiscal and monetary policy can affect the unemployment rate in the short run but cannot keep unemployment below the natural rate in the long run.

Most economists now agree that fiscal and monetary policy can affect the unemployment rate in the short run but cannot keep unemployment below the natural rate in the long run.

Despite the consensus on many topics, some disagreements among economists persist. There are adherents to new versions of classical, Keynesian, and monetarist schools of thought, among others, and economists still debate the appropriate use of fiscal policy. For example, during the Great Recession, economists including Paul Krugman believed that the U.S. government's fiscal policy expenditures should have been much larger than those favored by policy makers and their economic advisors in Washington, D.C. Economists have also differed on the role the Federal Reserve should play in the economy. Should the Federal Reserve actively respond to fluctuations in the business cycle with policy changes? Should it focus on a target inflation rate such as 2 percent? Should the bank try to correct wide fluctuations in stock prices? Economists disagree. Chapter 17 explains the workings of the Federal Reserve and its options for monetary policy. The rest of this chapter explains how fiscal policy works when the decision is made to use it.

Types of Fiscal Policy

If you've ever played the Monster Hunter video game, you know that the best weapon for a battle depends on the type of monster you're trying to slay.

Likewise, the best fiscal policy for a battle against economic instability depends on the type of problem the government is trying to eliminate. In this section, you will learn how policy makers deploy expansionary fiscal policy to fight a recession and use contractionary fiscal policy to slow the economy down when it is overheated.

EXPANSIONARY FISCAL POLICY

When real GDP falls below the full-employment level in an economy, a **recessionary gap** exists between the actual level of output and the full-employment level of output. Figure 15.6 illustrates a recessionary gap between Y_1 and Y_2. Cyclical unemployment accompanies a recessionary gap because there are more than enough workers to produce the equilibrium level of output.

> **recessionary gap**
> The gap between the actual output level and the full-employment output level when an economy produces less than its full-employment level of output.

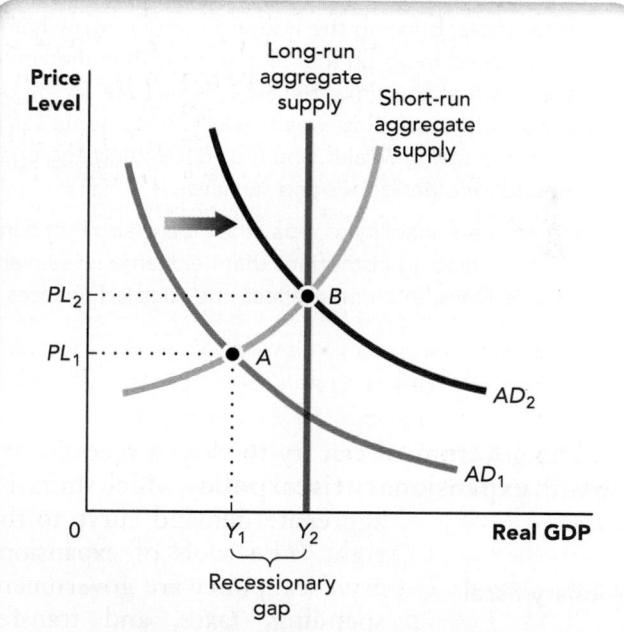

FIGURE 15.6 The Effects of Expansionary Fiscal Policy

At point A, real GDP is below the full-employment level of output, and a recessionary gap exists between the actual level of output (Y_1) and the full-employment level of output (Y_2). The government can use expansionary fiscal policy to shift the aggregate demand curve to the right and close the gap. This results in a new long-run equilibrium at point B.

Q&A

What caused the Great Recession?

The trouble began with a spike in oil prices in 2007. That spike shifted the aggregate supply curve to the left and made the economy vulnerable by increasing the costs of production and transportation. Then the *housing bubble* burst. A *bubble* is a rapid, unsustainable increase in the price of assets such as homes or stocks. Low interest rates, easy access to loans, and optimism about ever-rising housing prices increased the demand for homes between 2001 and 2007. This created a bubble in home prices.

As homes became overvalued, interest rates were also on the rise. Many homeowners had adjustable-rate mortgage loans for which the interest rates rose along with the interest rates for new loans. The result was a growing number of homeowners who couldn't make the payments on their home loans. Limited regulation of lending institutions as well as legislation enacted to improve access to loans contributed to the accumulation of high-risk home loans. Between 2007 and 2011, through a process called *foreclosure*, lenders took possession of more than 4 million homes that had unpaid loan payments and put them up for sale. Meanwhile, the demand for homes fell, as did home prices, bursting the housing bubble. Many homeowners owed more on their home loans than the homes were worth at the time. Because homes are an important part of households' wealth, decreasing home values led to decreasing wealth, and thus decreasing aggregate demand for other goods and services.

Homeowners' inability to repay their loans also hurt banks and other lending institutions that held large investments in home loans. In a ripple effect, the crippled finances of homeowners and lending institutions spread to everyone who relied on them as customers or lenders. The crisis spread even further when many of the lenders bundled their home loans and sold them to investors all over the world. The widening financial crisis lowered corporate profits, stock prices, and confidence in future prosperity. Many banks became reluctant to lend money, which made it harder for consumers and businesses to make large purchases. All these events and the resulting pessimism sent the economy spiraling downward into a recession that lasted for 18 months. For a colorful overview of the complicated investments and questionable regulations that preceded the Great Recession, watch the 2015 film *The Big Short*.

Andy Dean Photography/Shutterstock.com

▲ After a borrower misses several home-loan payments, the lender can use the process of foreclosure to take possession of the home and put it up for sale.

The government can try to close a recessionary gap with **expansionary fiscal policy**, which shifts the aggregate demand curve to the right. The tools of expansionary fiscal policy are government spending, taxes, and transfer payments. **Transfer payments** are government payments to individuals or firms for which no good or service is provided in return. Examples of transfer payments include Social Security benefits, payments as part of the Supplemental Nutrition Assistance Program (SNAP) that provides food aid for the poor, and Pell Grants for college students. To give the economy a boost, the government can:

- Increase government spending
- Increase transfer payments
- Decrease taxes

An increase in government spending has a direct effect on aggregate demand. An increase in transfer payments or a decrease in taxes has an indirect effect on aggregate demand by giving consumers more money, some of which is spent on consumption and thereby increases aggregate demand. However, people typically save some of the money they gain from transfer payments and lower taxes. So unless the marginal propensity to consume is 1

expansionary fiscal policy
Government policy that shifts the aggregate demand curve to the right.

transfer payments
Government payments to individuals or firms for which no good or service is provided in return.

(meaning all money gained is spent), an increase in government spending has a larger effect on aggregate demand than does an increase in transfer payments or a decrease in taxes of the same amount.

Figure 15.6 shows the effect of expansionary fiscal policy that successfully eliminates a recessionary gap. Starting with a short-run equilibrium at point A, some combination of an increase in government spending, an increase in transfer payments, and/or a decrease in taxes increases aggregate demand from AD_1 to AD_2. This results in a new long-run equilibrium at point B and brings real GDP to the full-employment output level of Y_2.

The U.S. Congress and President Barack Obama used expansionary fiscal policy during the Great Recession when they enacted the American Recovery and Reinvestment Act (ARRA). The Act authorized an estimated $831 billion in spending over a 10-year period and utilized all three tools of fiscal policy: increased government spending, increased transfers, and lower taxes. The roughly $550 billion increase in government spending included $53.6 billion to help schools avoid layoffs and modernize their buildings. Tax cuts that amounted to $288 billion included incentives such as an $8,000 tax credit for first-time home buyers. And the $82.2 billion in transfers authorized by the act included $40 billion in extended unemployment insurance benefits and $19.9 billion for the Supplemental Nutrition Assistance Program.

CONTRACTIONARY FISCAL POLICY

If you've ever eaten so much ice cream you felt sick, you know that too much of a good thing can be a bad thing. Too much growth in aggregate demand can be bad because it causes inflation and uncertainty about the price level. When the equilibrium real GDP rises above the full-employment level of output, an **inflationary gap** exists between the actual level of output and the full-employment level of output. Figure 15.7 illustrates an inflationary gap between Y_1 and Y_2. The government can respond to a harmful level of inflation with contractionary fiscal policy. To cool down the economy and close an inflationary gap, the government can:

- Decrease government spending
- Decrease transfer payments
- Increase taxes

Each of these policies has the effect of decreasing aggregate demand. A decrease in government

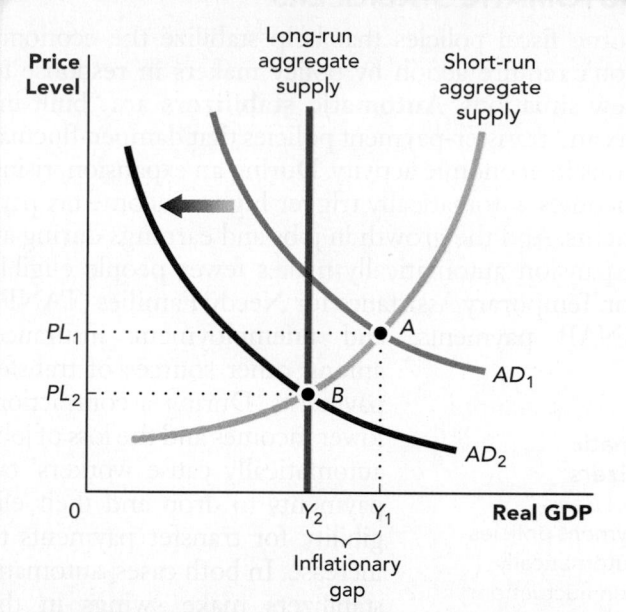

FIGURE 15.7 The Effects of Contractionary Fiscal Policy

When real GDP rises above the full-employment level of output, an inflationary gap exists between the actual level of output (Y_1) and the full-employment level of output (Y_2). The government can use contractionary fiscal policy to close the gap by shifting aggregate demand to the left from AD_1 to AD_2.

spending has the largest effect because if the government spends $1 less, the direct result is a $1 decrease in spending in the economy. With a decrease in transfer payments or an increase in taxes, some of the money that consumers lose would have been saved and not spent. If consumers save $0.25 out of each $1 they receive, a $1 decrease in transfer payments or a $1 increase in taxes will only decrease spending by $0.75.

Figure 15.7 shows the effect of contractionary fiscal policy that successfully eliminates an inflationary gap. Starting with a short-run equilibrium at point A, some combination of a decrease in government spending, a decrease in transfer payments, and/or an increase in taxes decreases aggregate demand from AD_1 to AD_2. This results in a new long-run equilibrium at point B, which corresponds with the full-employment output level of Y_2.

inflationary gap
The gap between the actual output level and the full-employment output level when an economy produces more than its full-employment level of output.

AUTOMATIC STABILIZERS

Some fiscal policies that help stabilize the economy don't require action by policy makers in response to new situations. **Automatic stabilizers** are "built-in" tax and transfer-payment policies that dampen fluctuations in economic activity. During an expansion, rising incomes automatically trigger higher income tax payments. And the growth in jobs and earnings during an expansion automatically makes fewer people eligible for Temporary Assistance for Needy Families (TANF), SNAP payments, and unemployment insurance, among other sources of transfer payments. During a contraction, lower incomes and the loss of jobs automatically cause workers' tax payments to drop and their eligibility for transfer payments to increase. In both cases, automatic stabilizers make swings in the business cycle smaller than they would otherwise be. One study found that automatic decreases in individual federal taxes alone offset as much as 8 percent of initial changes in real GDP.

> **automatic stabilizers**
> Tax and transfer-payment policies that automatically dampen fluctuations in economic activity.
>
> **recognition lag**
> The delay between the onset of a problem and the realization that it exists.

▲ When the economy contracts, automatic decreases in tax payments and increases in government transfers such as SNAP program payments help stabilize the economy.

Potential Problems with Fiscal Policy

Even when there is agreement that fiscal policy should be used, its implementation poses several potential problems. This section explains how fiscal policy can be hampered by timing issues, politics, and the crowding out of private spending.

TIMING

Automatic stabilizers kick in without any need for new legislation. That's a good thing because new policies developed in response to economic crises can be a long time coming. To begin with, it takes time for economic problems to be identified. The delay between the onset of a problem and the realization that it exists is called a **recognition lag.** The recognition of economic downturns that deserve attention is complicated by the fact that every big contraction starts with a small one that may or may not quickly reverse itself.

Economists study early warning signs called *leading indicators* to distinguish between a mild downswing and the beginning of an economic calamity. Table 15.1 shows the 10 measures of future economic strength included in the *Conference Board*

Table 15.1 Measures of Future Economic Strength

1. The average weekly hours worked by manufacturing workers
2. The average number of initial applications for unemployment insurance
3. Manufacturers' expenditures on new orders for consumer goods and materials
4. The speed of delivery of new merchandise from suppliers to vendors
5. Expenditures on new orders for capital goods unrelated to defense
6. The number of new building permits for residential buildings
7. The S&P 500 stock index
8. The nation's money supply adjusted for inflation
9. The difference between long-term and short-term interest rates
10. Average consumer expectations for business conditions

Source: The Conference Board.

Leading Economic Index, a popular index intended to forecast economic activity. For example, item #10 on the list is based on the *University of Michigan Index of Consumer Expectations,* which indicates the optimism with which consumers make spending decisions.

The number of new homes under construction is a leading indicator of larger trends in spending. The demand for new housing rises and falls depending on consumers' optimism and their willingness to spend money. The construction of homes also results in many other purchases, including new furniture, lighting, flooring, and major appliances. Despite these indicators, there is always uncertainty over what the future will bring.

Once there is sufficient agreement that looming economic problems warrant a fiscal policy response, policy makers must craft proposals and pass them through the legislative process. The delay between the recognition of a problem and the implementation of a solution is called the **implementation lag.** For example, during the Great Recession, 42 days passed between the Senate's introduction of the American Recovery and Reinvestment Act and the stroke of President Obama's pen to enact the law. Another 43 days went by before the first funds authorized by the act were released to help stimulate the economy.

After a policy is implemented, the **outside lag** causes a further delay between the policy change and the resulting effect on the economy. Consider the $96 billion worth of checks the U.S. government sent to citizens in 2008 to help stimulate the economy. Only about one-third of that money was spent within a year. Citizens saved the rest for future spending or used it to repay their debts. Any delay in spending holds up the desired effect of fiscal policy and increases the outside lag.

Recognition lags, implementation lags, and outside lags explain why new fiscal policies take effect slowly. When an economic crisis is likely to last for several years, fiscal policies may well improve conditions before the natural conclusion of the crisis. But a short-lived contraction in the economy may end before a fiscal-policy fix has its full effect on aggregate demand. If the economy has already started expanding before the fiscal policy takes effect, the late-acting fiscal policy can send the economy into an inflationary period.

POLITICS

Few things bring political drama to a head like battles over fiscal policy. In 2013, the federal government partially shut down for 16 days because the members of Congress disagreed about spending programs. The many

implementation lag
The delay between the recognition of a problem and the implementation of a solution.

outside lag
The delay between a policy change and its resulting effect on the economy.

▲ Changes in fiscal policy require some degree of agreement among the leaders of our government, which is easier said than done. For instance, Congressman John Lewis and President Donald Trump often don't see eye-to-eye on policy proposals.

sources of pressure on policy makers complicate fiscal policy decisions. Voters pressure policy makers to bring them more direct benefits from fiscal policy. This leads to the *pork barrel* politics of government representatives pushing for spending in their own local districts. Firms and special-interest groups exert pressure as well. According to the Center for Responsive Politics, special-interest groups hired almost 11,000 lobbyists in 2018 to sway policies in favor of interests ranging from the creative arts to national defense. Hoping to influence policy decisions, some individuals and firms donate large sums of money to politicians. Policy makers also have their own beliefs about what is best for society. These varied influences pull policy makers in many directions, some of which do not lead to economic efficiency.

CROWDING OUT

The U.S. government collected enough in taxes and other revenues to pay its expenses in only 13 of the 87 years between 1930 and 2018. In recent years, roughly 10 percent of government spending has been paid for with borrowed money. The resulting government debt has its own indirect influence on aggregate demand. As the government borrows more money, the demand for borrowed money increases, which drives up the price of money—the interest rate. The higher interest rate decreases, or "crowds out," private investment, which is a component of aggregate demand. This effect of more government spending causing less private investment is called **crowding out.**

In theory, investment demand could be so sensitive to increases in the interest rate that an increase in government spending could cause an equivalent decrease in private investment. In this situation, known as *complete crowding out*, an increase in government spending would have no effect on aggregate demand because each $1 of government spending would eliminate $1 of private investment. In practice, complete crowding out isn't likely to occur, although *partial* crowding out is a real possibility.

Figure 15.8 shows an economy facing a recessionary gap when the equilibrium is at point A. An increase in deficit-financed government spending shifts the aggregate demand curve from AD_1 to AD_2 to reach a new equilibrium at point B at

crowding out
The effect of more government spending causing less private investment.

supply-side fiscal policy
Fiscal policy that focuses on increasing aggregate supply to increase an economy's output and decrease the inflation rate.

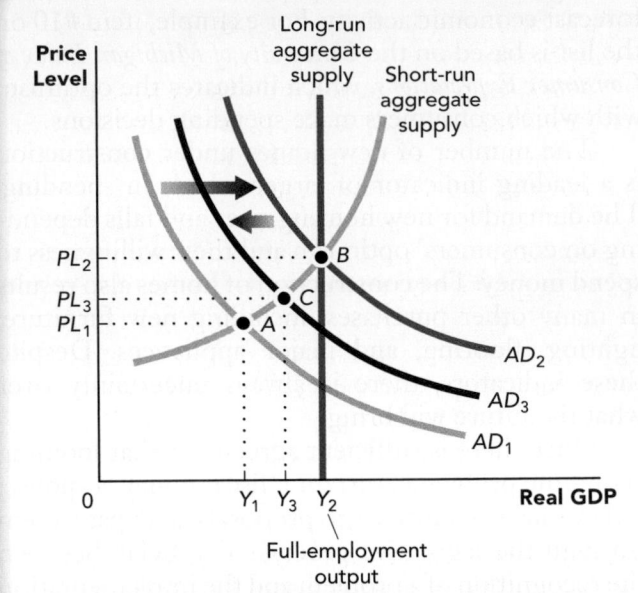

FIGURE 15.8 Partial Crowding Out

When the government borrows to pay for fiscal policy, the increased borrowing increases the demand for money and thus the interest rate. The higher interest rate decreases, or "crowds out," private investment, which is part of aggregate demand. As a result of crowding out, fiscal policy that would otherwise shift aggregate demand from AD_1 to AD_2 has a smaller net effect of shifting aggregate demand from AD_1 to AD_3.

full-employment output. However, due to partial crowding out, the aggregate demand curve shifts leftward from AD_2 to AD_3 and the resulting equilibrium is at point C, below full-employment output. After accounting for the crowding out, the net effect of this government spending is an increase in real GDP from Y_1 to Y_3. This is an improvement, but a recessionary gap remains in the short run, along with the associated cyclical unemployment.

Supply-Side Fiscal Policy

The policies discussed so far shift the aggregate demand curve and affect real GDP and the price level. Shifts in the aggregate supply curve also affect real GDP and the price level. **Supply-side fiscal policy** focuses on increasing aggregate supply to increase an economy's output and decrease the inflation rate. Supply-side approaches drew attention in the 1980s with support from President Ronald Reagan and economists such as Arthur

Laffer. This section explains popular approaches to supply-side policy and outlines their strengths and weaknesses.

Many supply-side economists seek to strengthen the incentives for individuals to work, and for firms to produce, by lowering the tax rates on income and profit. Cuts in income taxes raise workers' **disposable income,** which is the income they are able to spend or save after paying their taxes. When workers earn more disposable income for each hour of work, they are inclined to work more hours. Lower taxes on firms likewise allow the firms to keep more of the revenue they receive, thereby motivating them to increase their output and create jobs.

The downside of lower taxes is that the government relies on tax revenues for its operations, and we've seen that the U.S. federal government is deeply in debt. Arthur Laffer pointed out that a decrease in the income tax rate might increase or decrease tax revenues, depending on how much economic activity it generates. If a cut in the tax rate from, say, 40 percent to 30 percent motivated you to put in more work hours and earn $150,000 a year instead of $100,000, then your income tax payment would increase from $40,000 to $45,000. As shown in Figure 15.9, Laffer theorized that tax revenues would increase when a high tax rate was lowered, because high tax rates are a strong deterrent to work. Low tax rates are a weaker deterrent, so the decrease of an already low tax rate would not spur enough additional work to increase the tax revenues.

President Reagan signed the Economic Recovery Tax Act in 1981, lowering individual income tax rates by 23 percent. Unfortunately, the Office of Tax Analysis estimated that the act lowered federal

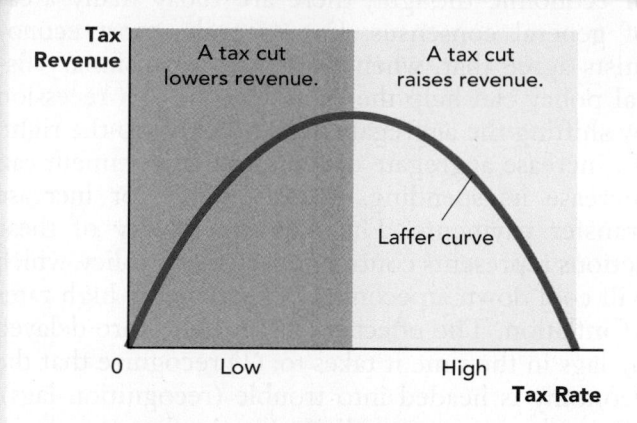

FIGURE 15.9 The Laffer Curve
Arthur Laffer pointed out that a decrease in the income tax rate might actually increase tax revenues if it gives workers an incentive to earn a lot more income. Unfortunately, a lower tax rate is only likely to yield more tax revenues if the initial tax rate is extremely high.

income tax revenues by 13 percent relative to the revenue that would have been collected if the act hadn't been passed. Tax cuts in 2001 also decreased inflation-adjusted tax revenues. So, in the United States, tax rates are sufficiently low to be on the left side of the Laffer Curve. Yet there is general consensus that individuals and firms are incentivized by lower taxes and that there are merits to the goals of supply-side economics.

> **disposable income**
> The income that remains for recipients to spend or save after they have paid their taxes.

SUMMARY

Fiscal policy is the government's use of spending, taxes, and transfer payments to stabilize the economy. If the government's tax revenues exceed its expenditures for the year, there is a budget surplus. If the government's expenditures exceed its tax revenues for the year, there is a budget deficit. The government's debt is the accumulation of past budget surpluses and deficits.

Prior to the Great Depression, policy makers were persuaded by classical economic theory to favor the hands-off approach of letting the economy correct itself. Then the Great Depression hit in 1929 and spread misery around the world for

more than a decade. With the economy on its knees, John Maynard Keynes and his followers advocated fiscal-policy responses to reinvigorate the economy. The popularity of Keynesian strategies waned in the 1970s when they failed to contain inflation rates, and a new, more passive strain of policy called monetarism gained prominence. Instead of actively responding to economic fluctuations, monetarists believe a nation's central bank should gradually increase the money supply on pace with a realistic level of economic growth.

Despite some sharply different opinions among economists who subscribe to the various schools of economic thought, there are today many areas of general consensus. For example, most economists agree that, when necessary, expansionary fiscal policy can help the economy out of a recession by shifting the aggregate demand curve to the right. To increase aggregate demand, the government can increase its spending, decrease taxes, or increase transfer payments. The opposite of any of these actions represents contractionary fiscal policy, which will cool down an economy experiencing high rates of inflation. The effects of fiscal policy are delayed by lags in the time it takes to: (1) recognize that the economy is headed into trouble (recognition lags); (2) implement new policies (implementation lags); and (3) see the new policies take effect on the economy (outside lags). Fiscal policy measures must also survive bloody political battles. And borrowing to pay for fiscal policy can increase interest rates and crowd out private spending.

Automatic stabilizers are "built-in" tax and transfer policies that help shorten the duration of recessions and periods of excessive inflation. During a contraction, lower incomes and the loss of jobs automatically cause workers' tax payments to drop and their eligibility for transfer payments to increase. The lower taxes and increased transfer payments help consumers continue the spending needed to revitalize the economy. During an expansion, rising incomes automatically trigger higher income tax payments and make fewer people eligible for transfer payments. The resulting decrease in disposable income has a dampening effect on consumer expenditures.

Supply-side fiscal policy focuses on increasing aggregate supply by implementing tax cuts that encourage production and employment. When tax rates are very high, tax cuts can encourage so much more production and income that tax revenues actually increase. That result is unlikely to occur today, however, given the relatively low tax rates in the United States. Nonetheless, most economists agree that the economic stimulus that can result from a tax cut is sometimes worth the resulting loss of tax revenues. There is also growing consensus among economists that fiscal policy is effective but slow, that monetary policy should be the first line of defense against economic instability, and that neither monetary policy nor fiscal policy can hold the unemployment rate below the natural rate of unemployment in the long run.

KEY TERMS

fiscal policy, p. 226
regressive tax, p. 228
progressive tax, p. 228
proportional tax, p. 228
budget surplus, p. 229
budget deficit, p. 229
debt, p. 229
classical theory, p. 230

Say's law, p. 230
Keynesian theory, p. 231
monetarist theory, p. 231
stagflation, p. 231
recessionary gap, p. 233
expansionary fiscal policy, p. 234
transfer payments, p. 234
inflationary gap, p. 235

automatic stabilizers, p. 236
recognition lag, p. 236
implementation lag, p. 237
outside lag, p. 237
crowding out, p. 238
supply-side fiscal policy, p. 238
disposable income, p. 239

PROBLEMS FOR REVIEW

1. True or false: Classical economists argue that the economy can correct itself quickly after a destabilizing event, such as a decrease in aggregate demand. Explain your answer.

2. True or false: Keynesian economists are opposed to the use of fiscal policy. Explain your answer.

3. True or false: Monetarist economists support the use of adjustments in the money supply to actively respond to swings in the business cycle. Explain your answer.

4. Which of the following are areas of general agreement among modern economists?
   a. To stabilize the economy, fiscal policy should be used prior to monetary policy.
   b. Expansionary fiscal policy increases aggregate demand.
   c. Various types of lags make passive monetary policy undesirable as a tool for stabilizing the economy.
   d. Fiscal and monetary policy can affect the unemployment rate in the short run.

5. Suppose the economy is experiencing a recessionary gap.
   a. Draw a graph showing aggregate demand, short-run aggregate supply, and long-run aggregate supply. Label both axes, all curves, and the recessionary gap. Label the actual output level as Y_1, the actual price level as PL_1, and the full-employment output level as Y_f.
   b. Explain one specific supply-side fiscal policy that could eliminate the recessionary gap.
   c. Show how the policy you explained in part b would change your graph if the policy were successful.

6. Suppose the economy is experiencing an inflationary gap.
   a. Draw a graph showing aggregate demand, short-run aggregate supply, and long-run aggregate supply. Label both axes, all curves, and the inflationary gap. Label the actual output level as Y_1, the actual price level as PL_1, and the full-employment output level as Y_f.
   b. Explain one specific contractionary fiscal policy that could eliminate the inflationary gap.
   c. Show how the policy you explained in part b would change your graph if the policy were successful.

7. Suppose the economy is experiencing a recessionary gap.
   a. Draw a graph showing aggregate demand, short-run aggregate supply, and long-run aggregate supply. Label both axes, all curves, and the recessionary gap. Label the actual

output level as Y_1, the actual price level as PL_1, and the full-employment output level as Y_f.
   b. Explain one specific expansionary fiscal policy that Keynesian economists might suggest to eliminate the recessionary gap.
   c. Show how the policy you explained in part b would change your graph if the policy were successful.

8. Suppose the economy develops an inflationary gap. Identify two automatic stabilizers that will help dampen the upswing in the economy.

9. Which of the following events is most likely to cause or contribute to each of the problems listed below in the context of fiscal policy?

   Events:
   a. a decline in interest rates
   b. government borrowing
   c. political squabbling
   d. a decrease in saving
   e. an increase in saving
   f. defunding of data collection for the *University of Michigan Index of Consumer Expectations*

   Problems:
   ___ crowding out
   ___ implementation lags
   ___ recognition lags
   ___ outside lags

10. If you were the president of your country and you felt that government spending must be cut, in which specific category of spending would you recommend the largest cuts be made? Discuss the costs and benefits of making cuts in that type of spending.

Money and Banking

16

Dave Anderson

Farmers National Bank sits on Main Street in the center of Danville, Kentucky. The bank has expanded into the building next to it, and into the building around the corner. On the opposite corner is another bank. Yet another bank is located on the corner on the other end of the block. The department store across the street closed, and its building remained empty for a decade, but Farmers National Bank added three local branches to meet the mounting demands of Danville's 16,349 residents. Farmers also opened seven branches in surrounding areas. What makes money and banks so important to economies large and small? This chapter opens the vault and shares the virtues of what's inside.

Why Should I Care?

Imagine an economy without money. To buy things, you would have to trade the goods and services you have for the goods and services you want. If you were a chicken farmer you would need to carry chickens with you on shopping trips and hope other sellers would accept them for payment. And if you sold washing machines or oak trees, you'd need a strong back.

Some say money is the root of all evil. Would the absence of money remove evil from the world? No. If there were no money, the same greed and disrespect that sparks evil would still exist. People would simply steal chickens instead of money, like foxes do in the animal kingdom that includes evil but not money. Goods and services would likewise become the currency for bribes, corruption, and deceit. **Money is not the root of evil so much as the seed of efficiency**, partly because it is a lot easier to carry around than an oak tree. In this chapter, you will learn the virtues of money, the functions of banks and similar institutions, and the process by which money is created out of thin air.

The Functions of Money

What has money done for you lately? What does it do for other participants in the economy? Most notably, money makes our lives easier by serving as a medium of exchange, a store of value, and a unit of account.

MEDIUM OF EXCHANGE

Do you want tickets to your favorite sport's championship competition? If so, you'll have to come up with something the ticket-seller wants. In the absence of money, you would have to *barter*. **Barter** is the exchange of goods and services for other goods and services. For barter to work, there must be a *double coincidence of wants:* The seller must have what the buyer wants, and the buyer must have what the seller wants. If the ticket-seller wants dental work or a trip to Spain, life could get complicated for you.

Fortunately, we have money available to serve as a **medium of exchange,** which is something that is widely accepted as payment for goods and services. The ticket-seller will take money, as will his dentist and his travel agent. The broad acceptance of money as a medium of exchange simplifies transactions throughout the economy. It also makes getting tickets to the championship competition a bit easier than pulling teeth.

STORE OF VALUE

Fish don't store well. Nor do peaches, ski lessons, roses, or concerts. Makers of anything perishable, temporary, or seasonal have particular reason to

▲ Peaches aren't a good store of value because they rot when kept over time. But farmers can sell their peaches in exchange for money, which can be used to make purchases far into the future.

▲ Dollars provide a standard unit of account with which to measure prices, wealth, and the benefits and costs of virtually everything.

appreciate money. As a **store of value,** money can be used to make purchases in the future. It may lose or gain value due to inflation or deflation, but after a year or so, a year-old dollar is likely to be worth a lot more than a year-old flounder. So fisherman, farmers, florists, and flutists can sell their goods or services when they please, and use the money they received from those sales to purchase goods and services long into the future.

UNIT OF ACCOUNT

In some stores, everything conveniently costs $1. In every store in the United States, everything costs some number of dollars and cents. Imagine the inconvenience of shopping in a store with no standard unit for prices. A can of cashews might cost one chicken, three lollipops, or 42 ounces of olive oil. Money simplifies things by serving as a **unit of account**—a standard measure for prices and economic comparisons.

Beyond using dollars to measure prices, wages, and wealth, economists also use dollars to express the value of things that may surprise you, including happiness, pain, and life itself. For instance, economists have found that, on average, Americans value the life of an unidentified individual at about $10 million. Policy makers can compare this amount to the cost of saving a life by passing safety regulations. For example, regulations that require airplane manufacturers to install emergency floor lighting in airplanes save lives at an estimated cost of $1.25 million each. Policy makers should find that a bargain. But policy makers may reconsider regulations that limit the levels of the herbicides *atrazine* and *alachlor* in drinking water at an estimated cost of $386 billion per life saved.

What Makes Something Money?

Money can be anything that is generally accepted in exchange for goods and services. That includes the bills and coins we call **currency,** as well as deposits in checking and savings accounts. In the past, beads, silk, shells, and spices have all served as money. In prisons, summer camps, and other places where currency is forbidden, cigarettes, chocolate, postage stamps, and coffee sometimes serve as money even today.

store of value
Something that can be used to make purchases in the future.

unit of account
A standard measure for prices and economic comparisons.

money
Anything that is generally accepted in exchange for goods and services.

currency
Bills and coins used as money.

▲ If you like to hold money in your pocket or purse, it's a good thing we don't use large doughnut-shaped rocks for money like they do on the island of Yap. Carrying that money around would be a real drag—literally. The Yapese realized that, too, and now they use U.S. dollars for small purchases.

THE IDEAL CHARACTERISTICS OF MONEY

Some things work better as money than others. Ideally, money is not only accepted for financial transactions, but is also durable, portable, uniform, in limited supply, and divisible into smaller units such as dollars and cents. To better understand why each of these characteristics is important, let's examine how something that lacks these characteristics—say, fish—would perform as money.

- Durable—Fish would rot in your piggy bank.

- Portable—Most fish wouldn't fit in your wallet.

- Uniform—Fish with the parasitic disease known as "ick" aren't the same as regular fish.

- In limited supply—A large money supply leads to high prices. Given the abundance of fish in the world, imagine how many fish it would take to buy a house.

- Divisible—Fish are divisible, but who wants the guts?

Modern currency exhibits these ideal characteristics to varying degrees. Coins are durable enough to last about 25 years. Bills are more portable, but a dollar bill only lasts about 18 months. U.S. currency is uniform aside from special editions. For example, as part of the U.S. Mint's 50 State Quarters Program, the Washington State quarter features a king salmon on one side. There are also limited supplies of all modern currencies. Governments and central banks carefully monitor the availability of currency and go to great lengths to prevent counterfeiters from adding to the money supply. For instance, look at any U.S. bill and you will find intricate details that make the bill hard to duplicate, such as tiny red and blue threads imbedded in the paper. Money is also divisible. You can take a $100 bill into a bank and exchange it for 10,000 pennies or for various other combinations of smaller bills or coins.

commodity money
Money that has value apart from its use as money.

Types of Money

Money has taken many forms over the ages. Some types have worked better than others. Colonists in Nova Scotia tried using fish as money. Police in Southern California reported recently that drug dealers are accepting Tide liquid detergent as money. This section explores several of the more successful types of money.

COMMODITY MONEY

More than 3,000 years ago, the Chinese used cowry shells as one of the first forms of money. Early Native Americans used strings of beads made from clam shells as money called *wampum*. Other early forms of money include animal skins, spices, tea, alcohol, and barley. These are all examples of **commodity money**—money that has value apart from its use

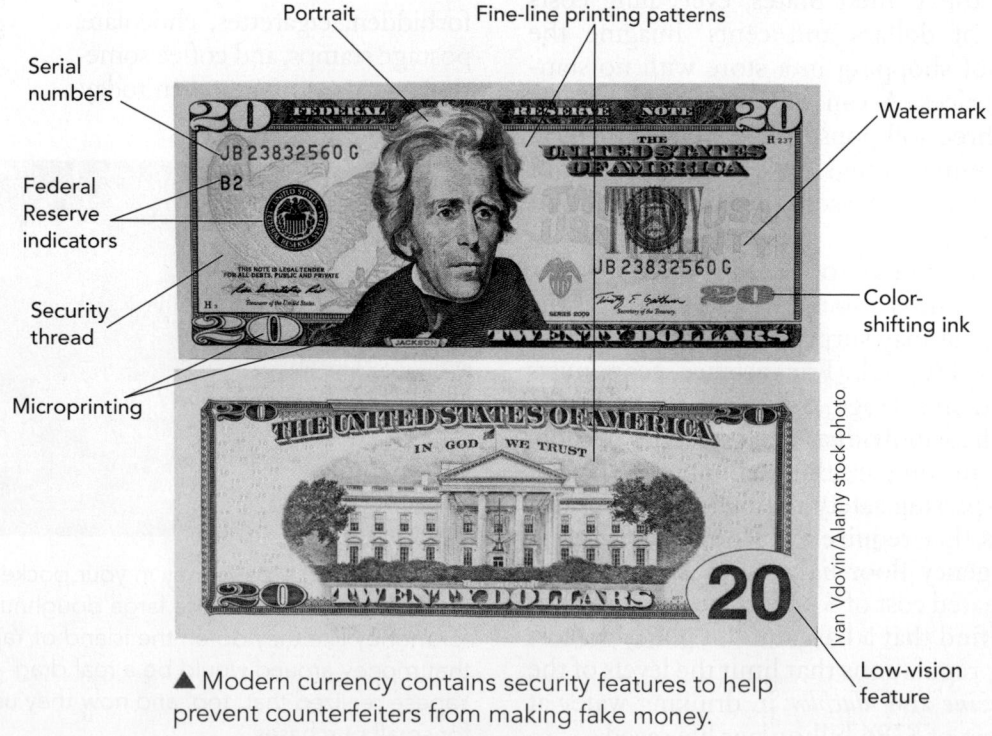

Serial numbers

Portrait

Fine-line printing patterns

Federal Reserve indicators

Watermark

Security thread

Color-shifting ink

Microprinting

Low-vision feature

Ivan Vdovin/Alamy stock photo

▲ Modern currency contains security features to help prevent counterfeiters from making fake money.

▲ When coins were made of precious metals, some users would clip the edges to extract some of the metal.

Nikreates/Alamy Stock Photo

▲ Between 1882 and 1933, gold certificates like this one (seen front and back) served as paper money in the United States. Each bill represented an ownership of gold and could be redeemed for gold coins.

PAUL J. RICHARDS/Getty Images

as money. The ability to use commodity money for other purposes makes it widely accepted.

The limited supplies of most commodities offer the added benefit of keeping the money supply from growing too rapidly and causing inflation. To see why an overly abundant form of money would cause inflation, imagine if grains of sand replaced dollar bills as money. People could easily become billionaires just by scooping up pails of sand. As a result, you might be willing to pay millions of grains of sand for a new pair of shoes. And you might accept no less than millions of grains of sand for an hour of your time as a worker. With an economy full of buyers like you who are willing to pay a lot more, and sellers like you who require much higher payments, the result would be inflation. That is, the aggregate demand and aggregate supply curves would shift upward and reach a new equilibrium at a higher price level.

Coins made from relatively rare materials such as silver and gold became popular forms of commodity money in Europe and parts of Asia more than 2,000 years ago. A problem with money made from precious metals, however, is that it tempts people to extract some of the metal from their coins before spending them. People clipped or shaved the edges of coins, or drilled holes in them to extract some of the metal before hammering the holes shut. They then melted down the extracted metal and sold it. These practices caused the coins to wither away. As a countermeasure, ridges or letters on the edges of coins make unnatural wear more noticeable.

PAPER MONEY AND THE GOLD STANDARD

The Chinese began to experiment with paper money more than 1,000 years ago. Paper money was far easier to produce and carry than commodity money, although the ease of production led to its own problems. Large amounts of money flooded the economy and caused inflation. After repeated problems with paper money, the Chinese ended their first experiment around 1455, but not before the Italian merchant and explorer Marco Polo and others brought the idea to Europe. By the nineteenth century, countries around the world were using paper money. Since the paper that served as money was itself worthless, the credibility of paper money was, well, thin.

Advanced monetary systems promoted trust in paper money by backing it with precious metals. In 1816, England was the first country to formally adopt a gold standard. Under a **gold standard,** the value of money is measured in terms of gold, and paper currency can be exchanged for an established amount of gold. The United States had a gold standard off and on between 1873 and 1971. A similar standard for silver existed in the United States off and on between 1785 and 1968.

By limiting the quantity of money to the quantity of gold available to back it, a gold standard deters the type of rapid increases in the money supply that can cause high rates of inflation. Unfortunately, there are times when the money supply should grow faster than the gold supply. For example, early in the Great Depression, a larger money supply would have curbed deflation problems, lowered interest rates, and made

gold standard
A monetary system in which the value of money is measured in terms of gold.

Coprid/Shutterstock.com

▲ Modern coins are made of inexpensive metals such as copper, manganese, nickel, and zinc. They are not commodity money due to the minimal value of the materials. Rather, they are *fiat money*, whose value comes from a government decree that they can be used to make purchases.

more money available for people to spend. Instead, the money supply was limited by the gold supply at the worst possible time. Problems with the supply of gold escalated when citizens began hoarding it as a safer alternative to investments in stocks and real estate. In 1933, four years into the Great Depression, President Franklin Delano Roosevelt took the United States off the gold standard. Similar problems with rigid gold supplies and fluctuating gold prices during the 1930s led countries around the world to also drop the gold standard and implement systems of *fiat money*.

FIAT MONEY

In 1971, with trust in U.S. currency strong, the U.S. government stopped backing its money with commodities and hasn't done so since. Today, all U.S. currency is **fiat money,** which has value because the government says it does. The coins in your pocket contain no silver or gold and, like modern bills, are backed only by faith in the government. Under the direction of the U.S. Department of Treasury, the U.S. Bureau of Engraving and Printing makes our "paper" money out of cotton and linen, and the U.S. Mint makes our coins out of copper, manganese, nickel, and zinc. The currency is distributed by the nation's central bank, the Federal Reserve (the focus of the next chapter).

> **fiat money**
> Money that has value because the government says it does.

NEW FORMS OF MONEY

The digital age has brought us digital books, songs, photos, and more recently, money. *Bitcoins* are a digital form of money invented

in 2008 and exchanged online by people around the world. Other examples of digital money include *Litecoin, Ethereum,* and *Zcash.* Each Bitcoin user has a virtual wallet on a computer or smartphone that holds digital representations of money. For a small fee, users can transfer Bitcoins anywhere in the world over the Internet. Bitcoins are not regulated by any government or bank.

The value of Bitcoins fluctuates with supply and demand. Unlike credit card transactions, Bitcoin transfers cannot be traced, which unfortunately makes them attractive to criminals. The FBI has found websites that sell illegal drugs and other contraband in exchange for Bitcoins.

As bodies of digital code, Bitcoins are durable, portable, uniform, and divisible. The supply of Bitcoins is limited by the software that allows new Bitcoins to be made. However, Bitcoins and most other digital money aren't backed by a commodity or by a government, so they aren't widely accepted by buyers and sellers. Because wide acceptance is critical to any form of money, developers of digital money systems are challenged to build confidence in their currency. If you are interested in learning more about how Bitcoins work, see the related graphic below.

WHAT ISN'T MONEY

A credit card is not money. Rather, it is used to initiate a loan of money. When you make a purchase with a credit card, the credit card company pays money to the seller. Later, you receive a bill from the credit card company, and eventually you must repay the money your credit card company paid to the seller.

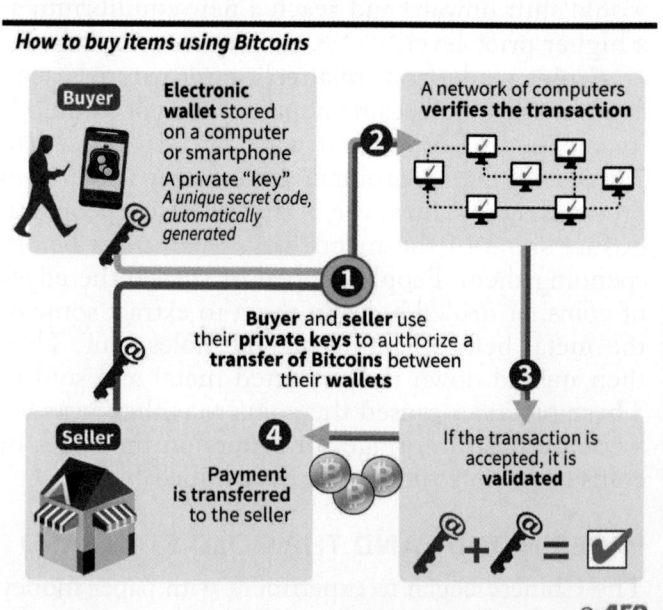

SOPHIE RAMIS, ALAIN BOMMENEL, GUSTAVO IZUS, WILLIAM ICKES AFP/Newscom ANELL

▲ Bitcoin is an unregulated digital currency used to make quick and anonymous online purchases or money transfers.

Q&A

Will digital alternatives replace cash entirely?
Credit cards have helped customers go cashless since the 1950s. Inexpensive credit card readers now allow most sellers to accept credit cards, including street vendors, taxi drivers, and even babysitters. Today, customers can make purchases with their smartphones and smartwatches using Google Wallet or Apple Pay. And with apps including Venmo, Paypal, and Square Cash, individuals can exchange money electronically. These advances and the growing popularity of electronic money might make it necessary for future editions of this textbook to explain what cash *was*.

Yet several benefits of cash will prolong or prevent its demise. The Federal Reserve estimates that two-thirds of all U.S. currency resides in foreign countries, where people hold it as a relatively stable alternative to their own currencies. Even within the United States, many people like to hold some cash because they fear security breaches within computer banking systems. For example, in 2014, more than $450 million worth of digital Bitcoins were allegedly stolen by computer hackers. Cash also comes in handy for tip jars, poker games, church collection plates, and garage sales. But with babysitters starting to accept electronic payments, can the poker club and the church treasurer be far behind?

Illustration/Kristin Hambridge and Shutterstock.com

▲ Cash is convenient when it's time to pay a cashier or contribute to the collection basket at church, but alternative methods of payment are gaining popularity.

You will also pay interest on the loan if you do not repay the full amount soon enough. Likewise, debit cards and checks are not money. Rather, you can use these items to initiate a transfer of money from your checking account to a seller's checking account. Apple Pay and similar payment systems for digital devices aren't money either. They allow you to make payments by providing access to your credit or debit card information electronically, saving you the trouble of digging for your card.

The Time Value of Money

Would you prefer to receive $10,000 now or in 10 years? You would probably prefer to have the money now because:

- Money received now can be invested to obtain even more in the future.
- You don't want to delay the gratification that money can buy.
- Anything could happen over 10 years. The source of the money could dry up, a change in your health could change your ability to enjoy purchases made with the money later on, inflation could ravage the money's purchasing power,

or zombies could take over the world. That is, something totally unforeseen could prevent you from receiving or enjoying your money.

The **time value of money** is the principal that it's better to have any given amount of money sooner rather than later. Even if you're patient and have no worries about what the future holds, you should choose to receive money ASAP. The opportunity to receive interest payments on bank deposits, or to earn returns on stocks, bonds, real estate, or other investments, makes it advantageous to get your money up front.

For example, money deposited in a savings account at your bank will be rewarded with interest payments from the bank. With the addition of those interest payments, the amount of money in your account will grow over time. Suppose you deposit $100 for a year and the interest rate is 5 percent. You will have $105 in your account at the end of the year. But if you didn't have $100 to deposit until the end of the year, you would miss out on those interest payments. As a result, you would only have $100 in the bank at the end of the year.

Because people prefer to receive money up front, 80 to

time value of money
The principal that it's better to have any given amount of money sooner rather than later.

The time value of money motivates most lottery winners to choose an upfront lump-sum payment of roughly half of their lottery earnings rather than opting for annual payments over several decades.

90 percent of lottery winners choose to take a lump-sum payment of roughly half of their lottery earnings immediately rather than annual payments over several decades. When it comes to paying bills, however, later is better than sooner: It is better to keep your money where it will earn returns for as long as possible, and pay the bills later—but not too late! Keep the time value of money in mind as you negotiate contracts, decide when to pay your income taxes, and contemplate other benefits and costs that will come in the future.

Measures of the Money Supply

The Federal Reserve monitors the money supply to make sure there is enough money in the economy to support the spending and lending that people desire, but not enough money to cause a high rate of inflation. The Federal Reserve doesn't track the candy bars and cigarettes that serve as money at summer camps and prisons, but it does track several versions of the money supply, including *M1* and *M2*.

M1

M1 is made up of the types of money that are easiest to spend, namely:

1. *Currency in circulation.* This is the currency held by individuals and firms. It does not include the currency held by the Federal Reserve or in bank vaults.
2. *Checkable deposits.* These are deposits that can

M1
The portion of the money supply that consists of currency in circulation, checkable deposits, and traveler's checks.

M2
The portion of the money supply that consists of M1 and "near money" that is harder to exchange for goods and services than cash or checkable deposits.

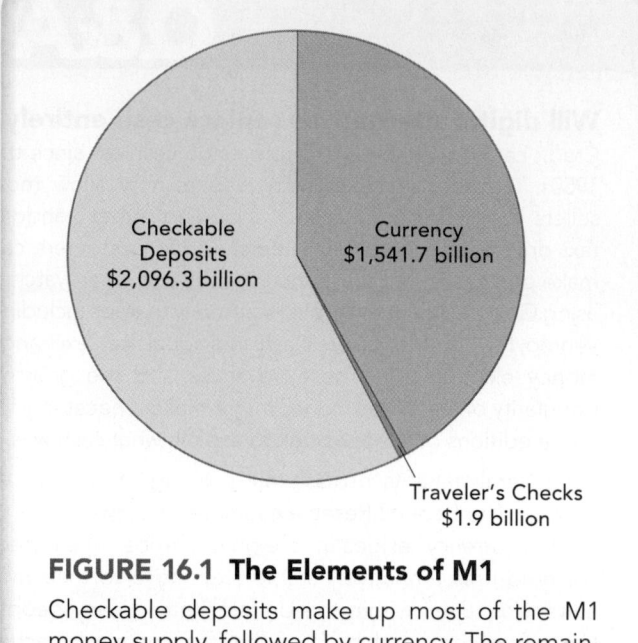

FIGURE 16.1 The Elements of M1
Checkable deposits make up most of the M1 money supply, followed by currency. The remaining component, traveler's checks, makes up only a tiny portion of M1.
Data from: Federal Reserve.

be withdrawn by writing checks. Checkable deposits include deposits in checking accounts, negotiable orders of withdrawal (NOW) accounts (checking accounts that pay interest), and share draft accounts at credit unions, which work like checking accounts at banks.

3. *Traveler's checks.* Some banks sell traveler's checks, which offer travelers an alternative to carrying cash. Traveler's checks are safer to travel with than cash because if they are lost or stolen, the company that sold the checks will refund the money to the person who purchased the traveler's checks. Unlike traveler's checks, the checks you write on your checking account do not constitute money—only the actual deposits in your checking account do.

Figure 16.1 shows the makeup of M1, which amounted to $3.6 trillion in 2018.

M2

M2 is made up of M1 plus several types of *near money* that are harder to exchange for goods and services than cash or checkable deposits. The additional steps involved in spending near money, such as making withdrawals or cashing in investments, make these types of money less *liquid*. M2 includes:

1. M1.

2. *Deposits in savings accounts.* You can make unlimited withdrawals from your savings accounts at an ATM or teller's window. Several other types of withdrawals from savings accounts, including automatic transfers and withdrawals made with debit cards, are limited to six per month. These limits make it harder to spend money in savings accounts than cash or money in checking accounts.

3. *Small time deposits* (under $100,000). *Certificates of deposit* (*CDs*) are an example of time deposits. CDs are similar to savings accounts, but the money must be deposited for a certain period of time and the interest rate is typically fixed. There is a penalty for withdrawing a time deposit prior to the stated maturity date.

4. *Retail money market mutual funds.* These are collections of investments in short-term debt securities. The securities include *U.S. Treasury bills* and *commercial paper,* which represent loans to the government and corporations, respectively. Retail money market mutual funds are open to any investor. Institutional money market mutual funds are designed primarily for institutional investors (banks, corporations, and pension plans) and are not part of M2.

In 2018, there was $13.9 trillion in the M2 money supply. Figure 16.2 shows the makeup of M2.

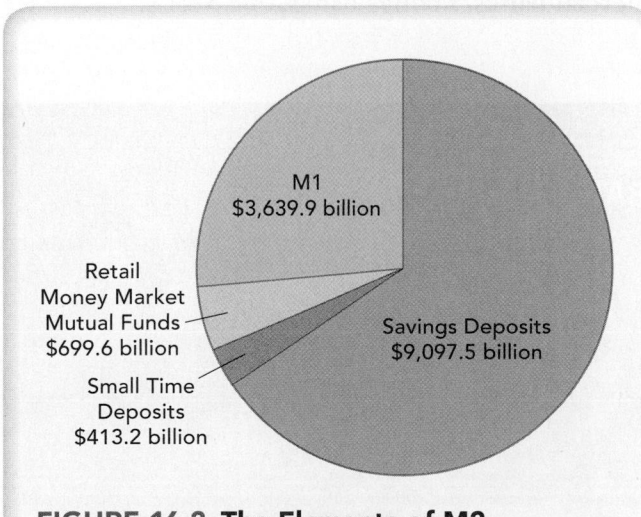

FIGURE 16.2 The Elements of M2

M2 is a broader measure of money than M1. M2 includes M1 and three less liquid forms of money: savings deposits, time deposits under $100,000, and retail money market mutual funds.

Banks and Thrifts

Communities large and small rely on banks and similar financial institutions to encourage saving and offer loans that support fledgling businesses and households. Many of the smallest communities that have little else have a bank. This section highlights the importance of these institutions, which grease the wheels of the economy.

THE ROLE OF COMMERCIAL BANKS IN THE ECONOMY

Farmers National Bank and the banks on Main Street in your town are **commercial banks,** which are primarily in the business of accepting deposits, making loans, and providing similar services to firms and the general public. In contrast, *investment banks* such as Goldman Sachs specialize in helping corporate customers raise money to expand their businesses, and do not take deposits. At a commercial bank, you can deposit your money into a checking account or a savings account where it can earn interest, or you can purchase a certificate of deposit that pays a higher rate of interest but ties up your money for a pre-set period of time.

Commercial banks are more than a safe place to hold money. Initially they offered loans only to firms, but commercial banks now provide a wide variety of loans to individuals as well. These include *consumer loans* for big purchases like boats and cars, *mortgage loans* for homes, and *home equity loans* that use the borrower's home as collateral for loans of many types. Since 1999, when Congress repealed two sections of the Glass-Steagall Act of 1933, commercial banks have also been able to sell insurance and stocks, among other investments.

RELATED FINANCIAL INSTITUTIONS

Commercial banks are no longer unique in the financial world. **Thrifts,** which include *credit unions, savings banks*, and *savings and loan associations*, now have much in common with commercial banks. **Credit unions** are not-for-profit financial cooperatives with the central mission of providing affordable loans for the working class. Credit unions are owned by their members,

commercial banks
Banks that are primarily in the business of accepting deposits, making loans, and providing similar services to firms and the general public.

thrifts
Bank-like institutions that include credit unions, savings banks, and savings and loan associations.

credit unions
Not-for-profit financial cooperatives with the central mission of providing affordable loans for the working class.

who are also their customers. The members share something in common, which might be that they work in the same industry, have ties to the same university, or live in the same community.

Credit unions began in Germany in the mid-nineteenth century. St. Mary's Cooperative Credit Association in Manchester, New Hampshire, which opened in 1908, was the first credit union in the United States. From the beginning, credit unions have taken deposits and loaned money at relatively low interest rates for members' short-term needs, such as paying bills. Mortgage loans, which allow people to purchase homes and repay the money over the course of 20 or 30 years, were not among the services initially offered by credit unions. But, like commercial banks, credit unions have broadened their scope in recent decades. Today, most credit unions provide mortgage loans, issue credit cards, and offer share draft accounts, which are equivalent to checking accounts.

Savings banks are banks established to help working-class families save money. They promote thrift by providing a safe place for individuals to make deposits and earn interest. When savings banks were introduced in the 1800s, they provided loans for the purchase of homes and other real estate. Today, in addition to savings accounts and mortgage loans, savings banks offer a wide array of services that include checking accounts, CDs, credit cards, and a variety of loans for businesses and consumers. Some savings banks are corporations owned by stockholders. Others are *mutual savings banks* owned by their depositors.

Savings and loan associations (S&Ls) are financial institutions with the primary focus of providing mortgage loans. Like savings banks, S&Ls originated in the 1800s and offered savings opportunities and loans to the working class. Regulations limited the services provided by S&Ls but allowed them to pay slightly higher interest rates than banks. In the late 1970s and 1980s, Congress loosened the regulations on S&Ls, among other financial institutions. The new policies removed limits on the interest rates paid by banks and thrifts and allowed thrifts to offer checking accounts. Now, S&Ls offer a full complement of financial services, including checking accounts, CDs, and loans for businesses and consumers. Some S&Ls are owned by their depositors; others have issued stock to raise funds, in which case the stockholders own the institution.

savings banks
Banks established to help working-class families save money.

savings and loan associations (S&Ls)
Financial institutions whose primary focus is to provide mortgage loans.

BANK AND THRIFT FAILURES

Banks and thrifts strive to protect your life savings, but what if they can't? Thousands of banks failed in 1933 under the strain of the Great Depression. The fear of losing money drove depositors to line up outside banks and withdraw what money they could from their accounts. Similar *bank runs* occurred more recently at failing banks in Greece, China, and the United States. Even a financially sound bank cannot accommodate withdrawals by many customers at the same time. Why? Because most of the deposits are lent out to other bank customers.

As the news spread during the Great Depression that banks were running out of money, widespread panic ensued. In the midst of the resulting bank runs of 1933, President Roosevelt declared a four-day bank holiday that closed all banks. This gave legislators time to respond to the crisis, and it gave depositors time to calm down and be reassured about their money.

The federal government quickly established the Federal Deposit Insurance Corporation (FDIC) to help rekindle trust in the banking system. The FDIC initially insured bank customers against the loss of deposits up to $5,000. Over the years, the amount insured grew and by 2018, depositors were insured for amounts up to $250,000 per eligible account. The National Credit Union Insurance Fund provides similar insurance for deposits in credit unions. The Federal Savings and Loan Insurance Corporation (FSLIC) insured deposits in S&Ls until 1989. Today, the FDIC insures commercial banks, savings banks, *and* S&Ls.

▲ Bank failures cause panic among depositors, who rush to withdraw their money before it is too late. When this happened in Greece in 2015, some banks required police protection.

▲ The 2007 collapse of Lehman Brothers—a large investment bank that had been in business for more than 150 years—sent the U.S. economy into a tailspin.

S&Ls were in crisis in the 1980s. The combination of a weak economy, bad loans that were unlikely to be repaid, corruption, and mismanagement caused about 750 out of the nation's 3,234 S&Ls to collapse. Although this had been the largest bank-related crisis since the Great Depression, deposit insurance prevented general panic among depositors. Other stakeholders were not so lucky, including borrowers, whose access to affordable loans became limited. At that point, the U.S. Congress feared a complete collapse of the S&L industry. To protect the health of the broader economy, the federal government created the *Resolution Trust Corporation* to buy bad loans from S&Ls to help keep the thrifts afloat. This prevented a larger economic catastrophe, but it cost the government an estimated $132 billion.

In 2008, the bankruptcy of an investment bank called Lehman Brothers caused the U.S. stock market to crash and started a domino effect that deepened the Great Recession. In response to the economy's plunge, Congress approved the Troubled Asset Relief Program (TARP) to administer up to $700 billion in loans and investments. TARP assisted struggling financial institutions, businesses, and homeowners who could not repay their mortgage loans. By 2018, a total of $439 billion of TARP funds had been spent, and the U.S. Treasury had recovered $443 billion as repayments or returns on TARP investments. You will learn more about policies related to the Great Recession in Chapter 17.

Money Creation

With the help of people like you, money can be created without a printer or a mint. This happens in our **fractional reserve banking system**, in which banks and thrifts can lend out all but a fraction of the money they receive as deposits. The deposits that banks have not loaned out are called **reserves.** The Federal Reserve System requires banks to retain a portion of their deposits as reserves to meet the withdrawal needs of their depositors. The percentage of total deposits that a bank cannot lend out is referred to as the **reserve requirement.** The reserves that cannot be lent out are called **required reserves.** The reserves that *can* be lent out are called **excess reserves.** The current reserve requirement for banks with deposits exceeding $115.1 million is 10 percent. So when you deposit a check for $100 in such a bank, $10 must be held as required reserves, leaving $90 as excess reserves that can be loaned out. This lending makes money creation possible.

The money-creation process begins with the availability of excess reserves. You create excess reserves when you deposit money in your bank. When the Federal Reserve wants to increase the money supply, it creates excess reserves by buying government securities such as U.S. Treasury bonds, bills, or notes from banks. This and other operations of the Federal Reserve are explained in detail in the next chapter. Suppose the Federal Reserve buys a Treasury bond from Farmers National Bank for $100. The $100 received from the Federal Reserve is not a deposit; it is owned by the bank, so the reserve requirement does not apply. Instead, the entire $100 constitutes excess reserves that the bank can lend out.

Let's see how $100 in excess reserves can increase the money supply by $1,000.

1. Suppose Alesia receives the $100 as a loan from Farmers National Bank and uses it to buy a cell phone from Basil. Basil deposits the $100 in his checking account at River Bank. Given the reserve requirement of 10 percent, River Bank must keep $10 of Basil's deposit on hand and can lend out $90.
2. River Bank lends $90 to Cal for fertilizer, which Cal buys from Denzel. Denzel deposits the $90 in his checking account at Extra Credit Union.

fractional reserve banking system
A banking system that allows banks and thrifts to lend out all but a fraction of the money they receive as deposits.

reserves
The deposits that banks have not loaned out.

reserve requirement
The percentage of total deposits that a bank cannot lend out.

required reserves
Reserves that cannot be lent out.

excess reserves
Reserves that can be lent out.

3. Extra Credit Union holds $9 as required reserves, and lends the other $81 of Denzel's deposit to Elizabeth.

4. At this point there is $271 in the money supply that didn't exist before the initial $100 loan: Basil's $100, Denzel's $90, and Elizabeth's $81.

5. The cycle of loans becoming deposits, which then become loans again, will continue until banks have no more excess reserves they can (or wish to) lend out.

Figure 16.3 illustrates the money creation process.

You can use the *money multiplier* to determine how much money could be created by any amount of excess reserves after the cycle of loans and deposits has ended. The **money multiplier** indicates the largest amount of money that can be created with each $1 of excess reserves. The money multiplier is found by dividing 1 by the reserve requirement:

$$\text{money multiplier} = \frac{1}{\text{reserve requirement}}$$

For example, if the reserve requirement is 10 percent, the money multiplier is $1 \div 0.10 = 10$. So each $1 of excess reserves can increase the money supply by up to $10.

Knowing the money multiplier and the amount of excess reserves, you can easily determine the potential increase in the money supply by multiplying the amount of excess reserves by the multiplier:

$$\text{potential increase in the money supply} = \text{excess reserves} \times \text{money multiplier}$$

In this example, the excess reserves are $100 and the multiplier is 10, so the potential increase in the money supply is $100 \times 10 = $1,000$. The actual increase in the money supply will be smaller than the potential increase if:

• individuals hold some of their money as cash rather than depositing it; or

• banks hold some of their excess reserves rather than lending them all out.

For instance, if you hold a dollar in your pocket rather than depositing it in your bank account, your bank cannot lend

money multiplier
A ratio that indicates the largest amount of money that can be created with each $1 of excess reserves.

The Federal Reserve buys a $100 Treasury bond from Farmers National Bank.

Farmers National Bank lends $100 to Alesia.

Alesia buys a cell phone from Basil for $100.

Basil deposits the $100 into his checking account at River Bank.

River Bank holds $10 as required reserves and lends $90 to Cal.

Cal spends the $90 on fertilizer purchased from Denzel.

Denzel deposits the $90 into his checking account at Extra Credit Union.

Extra Credit Union holds $9 as required reserves and lends $81 to Elizabeth.

This process continues until there are no more excess reserves.

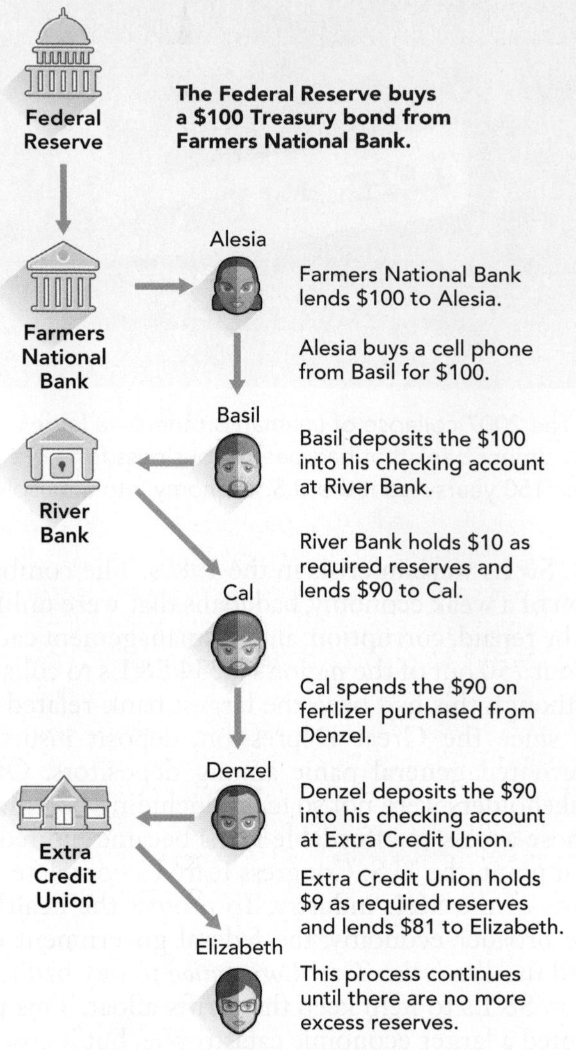

FIGURE 16.3 Money Creation
Banks and thrifts create money with excess reserves through a cycle of loans and deposits. In this example, $100 in excess reserves leads to loans of $100, $90, and $81, for a total of $271. With continuing loans and deposits, the money supply could increase by as much as $1,000.

any portion of that dollar to someone else. That limits the money creation process. Earlier we discussed the possibility that Google Wallet, Apple Pay, and other alternative spending methods will lead people away from holding cash. If that happens, more money will be deposited and more money will be lent out, so more money creation will take place.

SUMMARY

Money doesn't grow on trees, but without money, consumers would need to carry around trees, hens, appliances, or whatever else they produce to barter with. Money removes the need to barter by serving as a widely accepted medium of exchange. Money is also a store of value and a unit of account.

Ideally, money is durable, portable, uniform, in limited supply, and divisible. Modern currency exhibits these ideal characteristics to varying degrees. Commodity money takes its value from the non-money uses of the commodities. Precious metals, rare woods, shells, animal skins, spices, and cigarettes have all served as commodity money. Fiat money is not made from materials that are valuable for non-money uses, but has value because the government says it does. Paper money and coins made of inexpensive metals are examples of fiat money. New forms of money include digital money such as Bitcoins.

The saying that *time is money* suggests that the passage of time costs money. Indeed, time is money if there are missed opportunities for money to be deposited in an account that pays interest, or if the money could be invested elsewhere to earn worthwhile gains. The time value of money comes from these opportunities to benefit by getting money sooner rather than later.

The most common measures of the money supply are M1 and M2. M1 includes the most easy-to-spend, or *liquid*, forms of money, namely currency, checkable deposits, and traveler's checks. M2 includes everything in M1 plus deposits in savings accounts, time deposits under $100,000, and retail money market mutual funds. Money held by the Federal Reserve and in bank vaults is not in circulation and thus is not considered part of the money supply.

Commercial banks and thrifts encourage people to save by providing a relatively safe place to deposit money, and by paying interest on most types of deposits. These institutions also make loans to help people go to college, buy homes and cars, and start new businesses.

In a fractional reserve banking system, banks and thrifts can lend out all but a fraction of the money they receive as deposits. The money that *can* be lent out is referred to as excess reserves. By lending out their excess reserves, banks and thrifts effectively create money, because the same money deposited by one person becomes a loan to someone else.

KEY TERMS

barter, p. 244
medium of exchange, p. 244
store of value, p. 245
unit of account, p. 245
money, p. 245
currency, p. 245
commodity money, p. 246
gold standard, p. 247
fiat money, p. 248

time value of money, p. 249
M1, p. 250
M2, p. 250
commercial banks, p. 251
thrifts, p. 251
credit unions, p. 251
savings banks, p. 252
savings and loan associations
    (S&Ls), p. 252

fractional reserve banking system,
    p. 253
reserves, p. 253
reserve requirement, p. 253
required reserves, p. 253
excess reserves, p. 253
money multiplier, p. 254

PROBLEMS FOR REVIEW

1. For which of the ideal characteristics of money are coins clearly superior to bills? Explain your answer.

2. What aspect of the U.S. monetary system that is no longer in place limited the expansion of the money supply early in the Great Depression? Explain your answer.

3. True or false: A barter system would be as convenient as a money system if you happened to produce something easy to carry such as pencils. Explain your answer.

4. True or false: Modern U.S. currency can be exchanged for a set amount of silver or gold.

5. Write "M1" next to each of the following items that is part of the M1 money supply; write "M2" next to the items that are part of the M2 money supply.
   a. Currency in circulation
   b. Currency held by the Federal Reserve
   c. Checkable deposits
   d. Traveler's checks
   e. Deposits in savings accounts
   f. Time deposits under $100,000
   g. Retail money market mutual funds
   h. Stocks
   i. Credit cards

6. Suppose the Federal Reserve buys $4,000 worth of Treasury bonds from River Bank. Calculate the largest total increase in the money supply that could result if the reserve requirement is:
   a. 25%
   b. 20%

7. Indicate whether an increase in each of the following would increase or decrease the total amount of money created when the Federal Reserve adds money into the economy by purchasing Treasury bonds from a commercial bank.
   a. The amount of cash held by individuals
   b. The size of the Federal Reserve bond purchase
   c. The excess reserves held by banks
   d. The reserve requirement

8. True or false: Banks and thrifts started out as very similar financial institutions, but over time they became increasingly specialized. Explain your answer.

9. Suppose the highest return you can receive on your money is a 6 percent rate of interest from your bank. That interest is paid in one lump sum at the end of each year for amounts deposited for the entire year. Which of the following options would provide you with the most money one year from now? Which option would provide you with the least money one year from now?
   a. Receiving $100 today that you can deposit in your bank
   b. Receiving $104 one year from now
   c. Receiving $50 today that you can deposit, and $52 one year from now

10. Do you think that digital alternatives to cash will completely replace cash in the next decade? Why or why not?

Monetary Policy

Alex Wong/Getty Images

LEARNING OBJECTIVES

In this chapter, you will learn to:

1. Explain the fundamentals of the Federal Reserve System
2. Discuss the tools of monetary policy
3. Describe the strengths and limitations of monetary policy.
4. Show the effects of monetary policy using a model of the money market

In 2018, Jerome Powell replaced Janet Yellen as the chair of the Federal Reserve System. The Federal Reserve System, or *Fed*, is the central bank of the United States. Powell's impressive credentials include a degree from Princeton University, service as the Under Secretary of the U.S. Treasury, and membership on the Board of Governors of the Federal Reserve System for six years. Yet, as usual, Congress held lengthy and contentious confirmation hearings before approving the new chair of the Fed for a four-year, renewable term. In this chapter you will learn why Congress takes a great interest in who leads the Fed, and you will become familiar with the Fed's powerful policy making tools. By the end of the chapter, you will understand why Fed policy is so important that mere hints about policy decisions from the tone of Powell's voice can shake up the stock market.

Why Should I Care?

The Federal Reserve—not Congress or the president—has the sole authority to control the monetary policies of the United States. **The Fed influences the money supply, interest rates, and the availability of loans, including those you may have taken out to pay for your car, apartment, or education.** Although the leaders of the Fed are appointed by the president and require Congressional approval, the Fed operates as an autonomous unit with the authority to make its own decisions, free from political pressures.

In good economic times, the Fed can steadily expand the money supply to help keep the economy on course. In bad economic times, given the lags, limitations, and politics of fiscal policy, many people look to the Fed's monetary policy to turn the economy around. All of this gives the Fed and its policies well-recognized importance. For instance, Matthew Yglesias, *Slate Magazine*'s business and economics correspondent, described the Fed Chair as "the second-most important person in the government and one of the most important people in the whole world." To get an idea of the importance of the Federal Reserve itself, take a bill out of your wallet and look at the top line of text: Guess what organization receives top billing!

▲ U.S. bills are actually *Federal Reserve Notes* because they are issued at the discretion of the Federal Reserve. The $10 Federal Reserve Note features Alexander Hamilton, the first U.S. Secretary of the Treasury, who fought to establish a central bank for the United States.

The Federal Reserve System

Alexander Hamilton was the first Secretary of the U.S. Treasury. In 1790, Hamilton recommended that the U.S. Congress establish a central bank to manage the debts and finances of the newly formed United States. Hamilton's efforts led to experimentation with a central bank from 1791 until 1811. It took another century of bouts with economic instability, including several depressions, to convince many Americans that the nation needed an institution like the **Federal Reserve System**. Conservatives wanted an unregulated private banking system, but progressives wanted a government-owned banking system. Finally, in 1913, the two sides reached a compromise and passed the Federal Reserve Act. Under this act, banks remain privately owned, but the Federal Reserve System oversees and regulates them.

The nation was divided into 12 districts, each with a Federal Reserve Bank to oversee the commercial banks and similar financial institutions in that district. Figure 17.1 shows the 12 Federal Reserve districts and the location of each of the Federal Reserve Banks within the districts. Figure 17.2 illustrates the structure of the Federal Reserve System. The seven-member **Board of Governors**

Federal Reserve System
The central bank of the United States.

Board of Governors of the Federal Reserve
A seven-member board that manages the operations of the Federal Reserve.

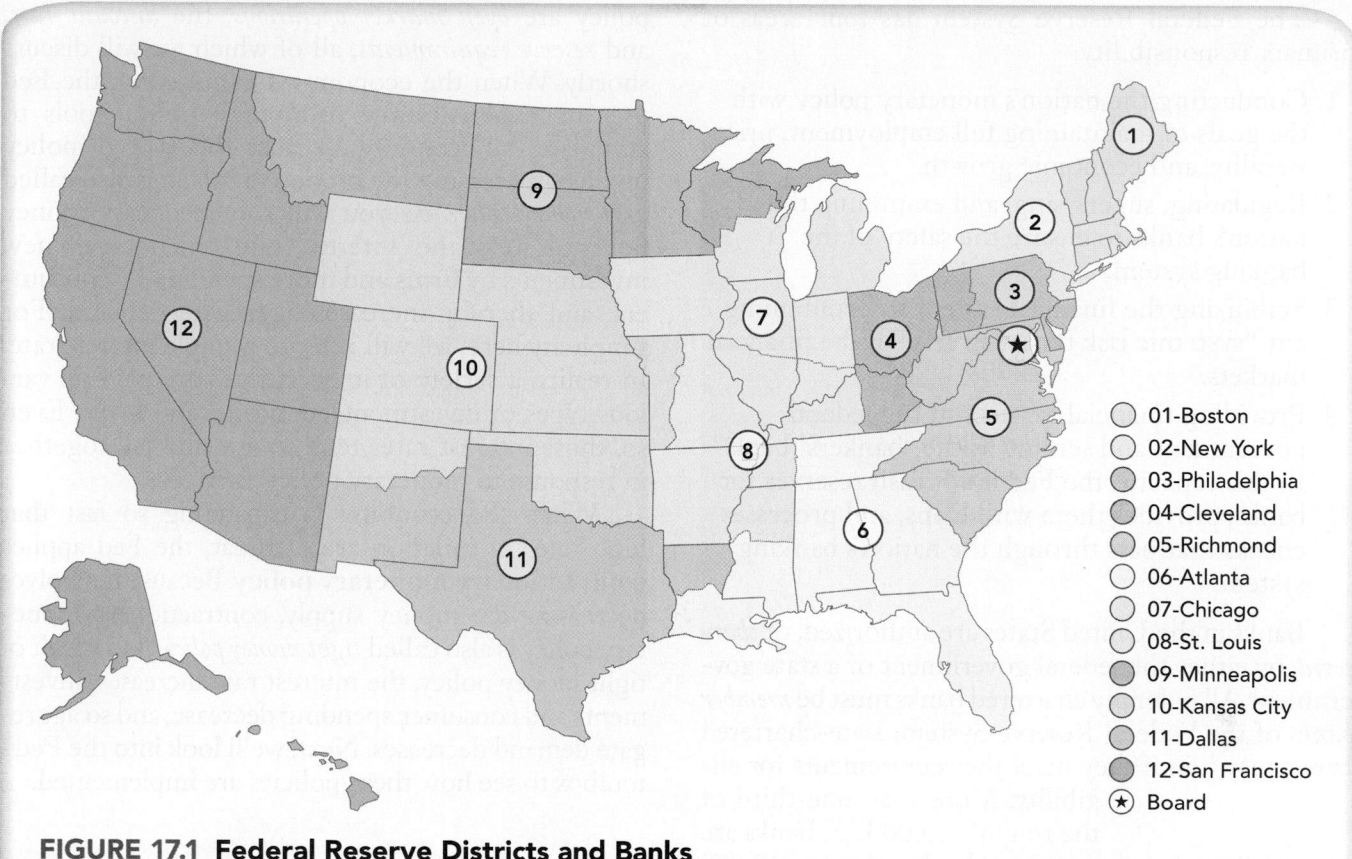

FIGURE 17.1 Federal Reserve Districts and Banks

The United States is divided into 12 Federal Reserve districts, each with a Federal Reserve Bank to serve and oversee the district's commercial banks and similar financial institutions.

Legend:
- 01-Boston
- 02-New York
- 03-Philadelphia
- 04-Cleveland
- 05-Richmond
- 06-Atlanta
- 07-Chicago
- 08-St. Louis
- 09-Minneapolis
- 10-Kansas City
- 11-Dallas
- 12-San Francisco
- ★ Board

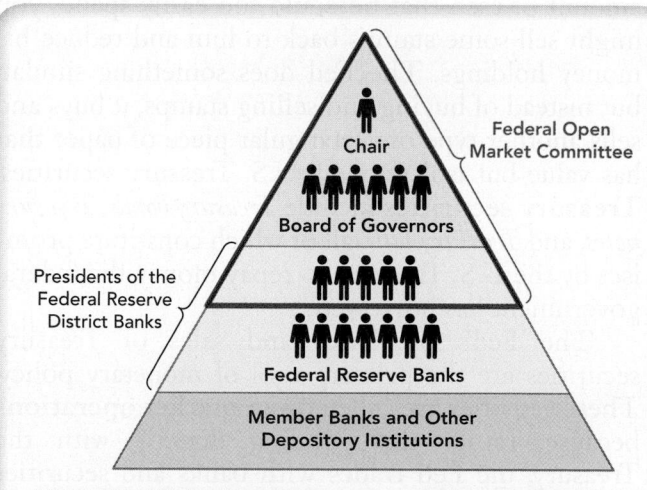

FIGURE 17.2 The Structure of the Federal Reserve System

The Chair and 6 other members of the Board of Governors oversee the Federal Reserve System. The Federal Open Market Committee, which is responsible for monetary-policy decisions, is made up of the Board of Governors, 5 district bank presidents, and 7 nonvoting participants.

manages the operations of the Fed. The Board members are appointed by the president of the United States and serve 14-year non-renewable terms. The Board helps craft monetary policies, oversees the Federal Reserve Banks, writes banking regulations, and supervises efforts to keep the nation's banks in compliance with the Fed's regulations.

The Banking Acts of 1933 and 1935 created the **Federal Open Market Committee (FOMC)**, which is the body within the Federal Reserve System ultimately responsible for making monetary-policy decisions. The Committee has 12 voting members and 7 non-voting participants. The voting members are the 7 members of the Board of Governors, the president of the Federal Reserve Bank of New York, and the presidents of 4 of the other 11 Federal Reserve district banks, who serve on a one-year, rotating basis.

Federal Open Market Committee (FOMC)
The body within the Federal Reserve System that is ultimately responsible for making monetary-policy decisions.

The Federal Reserve System has four areas of primary responsibility:

1. Conducting the nation's monetary policy with the goals of maintaining full employment, price stability, and economic growth.

2. Regulating, supervising, and examining the nation's banks to ensure the safety of the banking system.

3. Stabilizing the financial system and containing any "systemic risk that may arise in the financial markets."

4. Providing financial services to the federal government and serving as the "bankers' bank." In this capacity, the Fed holds cash reserves for banks, provides them with loans, and processes checks that pass through the nation's banking system.

Banks in the United States are authorized, or *chartered*, by either the federal government or a state government. All federally chartered banks must be *member banks* of the Federal Reserve System; state-chartered banks may join if they meet the requirements for eligibility. More than one-third of the roughly 5,000 U.S. banks are member banks. About 17,000 U.S. *depository institutions* offer checking accounts and other banking services but are not member banks. These depository institutions include credit unions, savings banks, savings and loan associations, and non-member commercial banks. Although they are not formally part of the Federal Reserve System, these institutions are subject to the Fed's regulations. They also have access to the financial services offered by the Federal Reserve Banks in their districts, which include check processing, electronic funds transfers, and currency distribution.

The Tools of Monetary Policy

The Fed uses **monetary policy** to manage the money supply and interest rates in efforts to stabilize the economy. The three traditional tools of monetary policy are *open market operations*, the *discount rate*, and *reserve requirements*, all of which we will discuss shortly. When the economy is contracting, the Fed uses its **expansionary monetary policy** tools to stimulate the economy. Because this type of policy involves increasing the money supply, it is also called *easy money policy*. As you will soon see, easy money policy lowers the interest rate, encourages new investments by firms and more spending by consumers, and thereby increases aggregate demand. For simplicity here, we will refer to a single interest rate. In reality, a variety of interest rates are paid on various types of investments, deposits, and loans. Even so, those interest rates tend to rise and fall together in response to monetary policy changes.

When the economy is expanding so fast that high rates of inflation are a threat, the Fed applies **contractionary monetary policy**. Because it involves decreasing the money supply, contractionary monetary policy is also called *tight money policy*. As a result of tight money policy, the interest rate increases, investments and consumer spending decrease, and so aggregate demand decreases. Next, we'll look into the Fed's toolbox to see how these policies are implemented.

OPEN MARKET OPERATIONS

Suppose you had a younger brother who didn't have enough money to buy some of his favorite things. You might decide to put some spending money in his pocket by buying part of his stamp collection. Later, if the holidays left him holding a large amount of cash that he could too easily spend, you might sell some stamps back to him and reduce his money holdings. The Fed does something similar, but instead of buying and selling stamps, it buys and sells another type of rectangular piece of paper that has value but isn't money: U.S. Treasury securities. **Treasury securities** include *Treasury bonds*, *Treasury notes*, and *Treasury bills*, all of which constitute promises by the U.S. Treasury to repay money the federal government has borrowed.

The Fed's purchases and sales of Treasury securities are the primary tool of monetary policy. These activities are called **open market operations** because, rather than dealing directly with the Treasury, the Fed trades with banks and securities broker-dealers in the "open market" for Treasury securities. When the FOMC determines that the economy is contracting and would benefit from more spending money, it instructs the Federal Reserve Bank of New York to buy Treasury securities. Figure 17.3 shows how this easy money policy of buying securities sends money that had not been

monetary policy
Policies the Federal Reserve uses to manage the money supply and interest rates in efforts to stabilize the economy.

expansionary monetary policy
Monetary policy designed to stimulate the economy.

contractionary monetary policy
Monetary policy designed to slow the economy down and fight inflation.

Treasury securities
Documents that constitute promises by the U.S. Treasury to repay money that the federal government has borrowed.

open market operations
The Fed's purchases and sales of Treasury securities.

When the Fed Buys Treasury Securities:
Money goes to banks in exchange for securities that are not money, so the money supply increases.

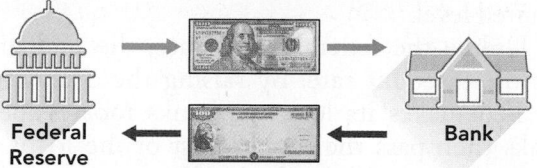

Federal Reserve → → Bank

When the Fed Sells Treasury Securities:
Money comes from banks in exchange for securities that are not money, so the money supply decreases.

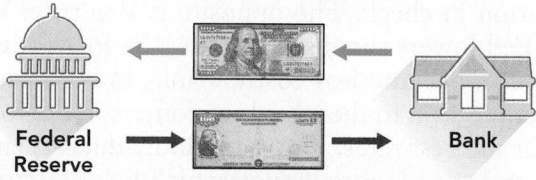

Federal Reserve → → Bank

FIGURE 17.3 Open Market Operations
When the Fed buys securities, it puts new money into the economy. In contrast, when the Fed sells securities, it takes money out of the economy. These *open market operations* are the Fed's primary tool for monetary policy.

▲ When the Federal Open Market Committee decides to buy or sell Treasuries, it is the people in this building, the Federal Reserve Bank of New York, who actually carry out the open market operations.

in circulation out into the economy in exchange for securities that, like postage stamps, have value but aren't money. By taking in something that is not money and sending out money, the Fed adds to the economy's money supply.

As the new money travels into the economy, its first stop is in the accounts of those who sold their Treasury securities to the Fed. Typically, the sellers are financial institutions with accounts at the Federal Reserve, so the Fed simply credits their accounts for the amounts of the purchases. The growth in the sellers' accounts creates excess reserves that can be lent out. This lending sets the money creation process in motion—the loans lead to deposits that lead to more loans, and so on, as explained in Chapter 16.

You know from earlier discussions of supply and demand that an increase in the supply of a good leads to a decrease in the price of the good. The same is true of an increase in the supply of money. The price paid to borrow money is the interest rate, so an increase in the money supply brought about by the Fed's purchase of Treasury securities causes interest rates in the economy to decrease. Lower interest rates make more loans for

everything from investments in business growth to college tuition payments worthwhile. These additional expenditures increase aggregate demand.

When the FOMC determines that the money supply is dangerously large and high rates of inflation are looming, it instructs the Federal Reserve Bank of New York to sell Treasury securities. With this tight money policy, the Fed sells Treasury securities, which do not constitute money, in exchange for money that had been in bank accounts. By taking in money and sending out something that is not money, the Fed reduces the economy's money supply. Banks then cannot make as many loans as before, and the money creation process is reversed, with a decrease in loans causing a decrease in deposits, and so on. This decrease in the money supply brought about by the Fed's sale of securities causes interest rates to rise. With higher interest rates, fewer loans for investment projects and other private expenditures are worthwhile. The resulting decrease in expenditures causes aggregate demand to decrease.

The Fed focuses on one particular interest rate as it conducts its monetary policy: the *federal funds rate*. The **federal funds rate** is the interest rate banks charge each other for short-term loans. The Fed does

federal funds rate
The interest rate that banks charge each other for short-term loans.

not choose the federal funds rate directly; rather, the supply of bank reserves relative to the demand for bank reserves determines the federal funds rate. However, the FOMC does set a *target rate*, or a target range of rates, for the federal funds rate. The Fed then guides the federal funds rate toward the target by increasing or decreasing the money supply, which increases or decreases the supply of reserves relative to the demand for reserves.

Changes in the federal funds rate cause changes in other interest rates as well. When banks have to pay a higher federal funds rate to borrow money from each other, they raise the interest rates on their loans to customers. And when it costs banks less to borrow money, they offer lower interest rates to customers.

The Fed's actions during the Great Recession illustrate the use of targets for the federal funds rate. Before the recession, in June of 2007, the Fed's target for the federal funds rate was 5.25 percent. The FOMC felt that this rate would allow the economy to grow at a desirable pace while preventing excessive inflation. When the economy showed signs of weakness, starting in September of 2007, the Fed lowered the target for the federal funds rate 10 times. In December of 2008, the target rate was down to between 0 and 0.25 percent. The Fed kept the target rate at that level until December of 2015 to help prevent another economic downturn.

A danger of having interest rates near 0 is that it limits the Fed's ability to stimulate the economy by lowering interest rates further. In 2015, looming economic problems and near-zero interest rates led some European central banks to set negative interest rates. Depositors actually had to *pay* interest to keep their money on deposit. To avoid paying interest, some depositors withdrew their money and stashed it elsewhere or spent it, but a surprising number of depositors kept their money in the banks. The FOMC has discussed the possibility of negative interest rates, but they have yet to try that experiment.

THE DISCOUNT RATE

The Fed's monetary policy toolbox also contains a more direct, but less used, tool designed to affect interest rates: the **discount rate**, which is the interest rate that Federal Reserve banks charge financial institutions for short-term loans. Banks typically use these loans to meet the Fed's requirement that they hold a fraction of their customers' deposits on reserve. If

discount rate
The interest rate that Federal Reserve Banks charge financial institutions for short-term loans.

the reserve requirement is 10 percent, and a bank has loaned out all but 7 percent of its deposits, the bank can borrow the equivalent of 3 percent of its deposits from a Federal Reserve Bank to bring its reserves up to the required level.

Unlike the federal funds rate, the Fed directly sets the discount rate. By raising the discount rate, the Fed makes its loans to banks more expensive. Banks then pass the higher cost of the loans on to their customers in the form of higher interest rates. The higher interest rates make it harder to justify loans for everything from new computer systems in doctors' offices to redecorating projects in your home. The resulting decrease in spending helps keep inflation in check. The opposite is also true: When the Fed lowers the discount rate, the loans it makes to banks become less costly. Banks in turn pass the lower costs on to their bank customers in the form of lower interest rates. Firms and individuals then borrow and spend more money, which helps stimulate a sluggish economy.

The Federal Reserve is described as the "lender of last resort" because it will lend money to qualifying institutions whose financial problems are so severe that other lenders turn them away. Banks with no other option can borrow money from their regional Federal Reserve Bank's lending facility, which is called the *discount window*. Financially healthy banking institutions also can use the discount window when they simply need brief, often overnight, loans.

During an economic crisis, the uncertain times can make consumers reluctant to spend money and banks reluctant to lend it. To invigorate the flow of money through the economy during a crisis, the Fed makes extra efforts to encourage banks to borrow at the discount window. For example, after the 9/11 attacks and during the Great Recession, the Fed offered special lending programs to banks, some of which are explained later in this chapter.

RESERVE REQUIREMENTS

Recall that the Federal Reserve sets reserve requirements that specify the percentage of deposits that banks must hold, either in their vaults or in their accounts at the Federal Reserve. The reserve requirement for most banks is 10 percent, which means that a bank with $300 million in deposits must hold $30 million as required reserves.

The previous chapter explained how the reserve requirement ties into the money creation process initiated by a Fed purchase of Treasury securities: If all money is deposited and banks hold no excess reserves, the total increase in the money supply is the initial

Digital Vision./Getty Images

▲ If the Fed decreases the reserve requirement, banks don't need to hold as much money, so they lend out more. This additional lending fuels the money creation process and increases the money supply.

increase divided by the reserve requirement. So if the reserve requirement is 10 percent and the Fed buys $50 million in Treasury securities, the total increase in the money supply under these conditions will be $50 million $\div$ 0.10 = $500 million. In other words, $50 million injected into the economy by the Fed will lead to a $500 million increase in the money supply.

When the Fed *raises* the reserve requirement, the money creation process is constrained because a smaller portion of each deposit can be loaned out. When the Fed *lowers* the reserve requirement, banks can lend out a larger share of their deposits, so even more money is created.

A bit of experimentation with the numbers reveals the considerable influence of the reserve requirement on the money creation process. Again, suppose the Fed increases the money supply by purchasing $50 million in Treasury securities and banks hold no excess reserves. But now assume that the reserve requirement is only 5 percent instead of 10 percent. In this case, the total increase in the money supply will be $50 million $\div$ 0.05 = $1 billion rather than $500 million. As another example, assume the reserve requirement is 25 percent. In this case, the total increase in the money supply as a result of the Fed purchasing $50 million in Treasury securities will be just $50 million $\div$ 0.25 = $200 million.

The ability to adjust the reserve requirement clearly gives the Fed considerable leverage for manipulating the money supply. Reserve requirements are such a valuable tool for stabilizing a banking system that they are adopted by more than 90 percent of the world's central banks. In practice, the Fed rarely changes the reserve requirement because it would be quite a burden for banks to have to adjust their policies and procedures in response to frequent changes. However, banks with small amounts of deposits are exempt from the reserve requirement, and banks with medium amounts of deposits face a relatively low 3 percent reserve requirement. Every year the Fed changes the amounts of deposits that qualify banks for these lower reserve requirements, which effectively changes the reserve requirements for some banks. Table 17.1 summarizes how the Fed can use its traditional tools to conduct expansionary or contractionary monetary policy.

Strengths and Limitations of Monetary Policy

A variety of factors can limit the success of Federal Reserve policies. As with fiscal policies, it takes time for the Fed to identify problems, select a monetary policy response, and implement that policy. However, because the FOMC is a much smaller and less politically charged group than Congress, it can respond relatively quickly. For example, even before the Great Recession officially became a recession in December of 2007, the Fed detected trouble and began implementing expansionary monetary policy. In August of 2007, the Fed lowered the discount rate, and in September of 2007, it increased the money supply enough to lower the federal funds rate by one-half percent.

Table 17.1 The Traditional Tools of Monetary Policy

Tool	Expansionary Monetary Policy	Contractionary Monetary Policy
Open market operations	Buy Treasury securities	Sell Treasury securities
Discount rate	Decrease	Increase
Reserve requirement	Decrease	Increase

Who pays for the Fed's operations?

The Fed earns its own operating income and is not funded by the federal government. As the owner of trillions of dollars' worth of Treasury securities, the Fed earns a great deal of interest, which in 2017 amounted to $113.6 billion.

The Fed also receives payments from depository institutions for check-processing services and loans. Altogether, the Fed actually earns more than it needs to pay its bills, and provides its profit—$80.2 billion in 2017—to the U.S. Treasury.

The speed and power of monetary policy are hindered by pessimism. Once a recession takes its toll, the entrenched uncertainty and lost confidence in the economy are hard to overcome. Even dramatically lower interest rates and an injection of massive amounts of money into the economy can be slow to turn things around. After hitting the depths of a recession, consumers aren't in the mood to spend money like they used to, banks are loath to lend, and firms are reluctant to hire new workers for fear that the crisis will continue. But history shows that, in most cases, patience has been rewarded with glimmers of renewed optimism and eventual recovery.

NEW MONETARY POLICY TOOLS FOR SEVERE PROBLEMS

The Great Recession motivated the inception of innovative new Fed programs. At the heart of the financial crisis was a *liquidity crisis*—a shortage of cash flowing through the economy—fueled by a shortage of loans. Because so many borrowers were defaulting on their home loans, banks were hesitant to lend what excess reserves they had to their customers or to other banks. Without adequate access to loans, many firms found it difficult to pay their workers and produce goods, which only worsened the recession.

To address the liquidity crisis, the Fed set up three temporary programs or *facilities* to improve the availability of loans. In December of 2007, the Fed established the Term Auction Facility (TAF), which allowed financially sound commercial banks and thrifts to borrow money at interest rates below the discount rate. To secure these short-term loans, the institutions had to put up **collateral**, which is an asset a borrower forfeits to a lender if the borrower doesn't repay the loan. The collateral could be any of a variety of financial assets, including bundles of mortgage loans called *mortgage-backed securities*. So many people were defaulting on their mortgage loans during that period that mortgage-backed securities were described as *toxic assets*. By accepting the toxic assets as collateral, the Fed was fulfilling its role as the lender of last resort to banks and thrifts. By 2010, all the loans made under the TAF had been repaid in full, with interest, in accordance with the terms of the facility.

Three months after establishing the Term Auction Facility, the Fed established the Term Securities Lending Facility (TSLF), which auctioned off 28-day loans of Treasury securities. The borrowers were *primary dealers*, which are major investment banks and securities firms authorized to deal directly with the Fed. HSBC Securities and Goldman, Sachs & Co. are examples of primary dealers. These borrowers, like borrowers at the TAF, were allowed to use high-risk mortgage-backed securities as collateral for their loans. This allowed primary dealers heavily invested in toxic assets to temporarily obtain low-risk Treasury securities that could in turn be used as collateral for the other types of loans that primary dealers use to fund their operations. The TSLF essentially provided a lender of last resort to primary lenders, who do not have access to the Fed's discount window. In all, the TSLF loaned out $2.3 trillion worth of Treasury securities.

That same month, the Fed established the Primary Dealer Credit Facility (PDCF) to help primary dealers lend out more money while still covering their reserve requirements. The PDCF lent money to primary dealers for one day at a time at the discount rate paid by the most financially sound financial institutions. Mortgage-backed securities were again accepted as collateral for the loans. A total of $8.95 trillion was loaned out through the PDCF. In 2010, after these programs had served their intended purposes, the Fed closed the TAF, the TSLF, and the PDCF because lenders had regained a reasonable amount of liquidity.

collateral
An asset a borrower forfeits to a lender if the borrower doesn't repay the loan.

THE QUANTITY THEORY OF MONEY

The website *WheresGeorge.com* tracks the lives of dollar bills by having people voluntarily report their bills' serial numbers, locations, and uses. A bill used today to tip a street musician in New York might be spent next month on guitar strings in Tennessee, and spent again a few weeks later at a McDonald's drive-through in North Carolina. Figure 17.4 shows the actual path of a particular dollar bill. Because the same money is typically spent several times over the course of a year, the money supply and the amount of money spent in a year differ. The **velocity of money** is the number of times the average unit of currency is spent in one year. In the United States, it is typical for a dollar to be spent six to eight times each year, although higher and lower velocities are not uncommon.

The relationship between the money supply (M), the velocity of money (V), the price level (P), and real GDP (Y) can be expressed as the **equation of exchange**, which is

$$MV = PY$$

The right side of the equation—the price level times real GDP—represents expenditures in the economy. For these expenditures to increase, there must be an increase in the left side of the equation—that is, an increase in either the money supply or the velocity of money, or both.

The equation of exchange is central to many discussions of monetary policy. Monetarists believe that the velocity of money and real GDP remain largely unchanged in the short run. If that is the case, an increase in the money supply merely causes a proportional increase in the price level. Monetarists refer to this idea as the **quantity theory of money**. From the equation of exchange, you can see that if V and Y are constant, an increase in M by, say, 5 percent must be balanced by a 5 percent increase in P. So monetarists believe that *discretionary monetary policy*—adjustments in the money supply in response to changes in the economy—will mostly just affect the price level in the economy. This supports the monetarists' claim that the optimal monetary policy is a slow, steady increase in the money supply, with no discretionary adjustments in response to economic contractions and expansions.

Critics of the quantity theory of money point out that there are periods when the velocity of money is quite stable and periods when it is not, so it is an oversimplification to treat V as a constant. These economists also argue that if prices are fairly stable or "sticky," as is sometimes the case, then an increase in the money supply—which is on the left side of the equation of exchange—is balanced by an increase in real GDP—which is on the right side of the equation. In other words, these economists argue that increasing the money supply *can* increase real GDP and not just the price level.

velocity of money
The number of times the average unit of currency is spent in one year.

equation of exchange
An equation that expresses the relationship between the money supply (M), the velocity of money (V), the price level (P), and real GDP (Y).

quantity theory of money
The theory that an increase in the money supply merely causes a proportional increase in the price level.

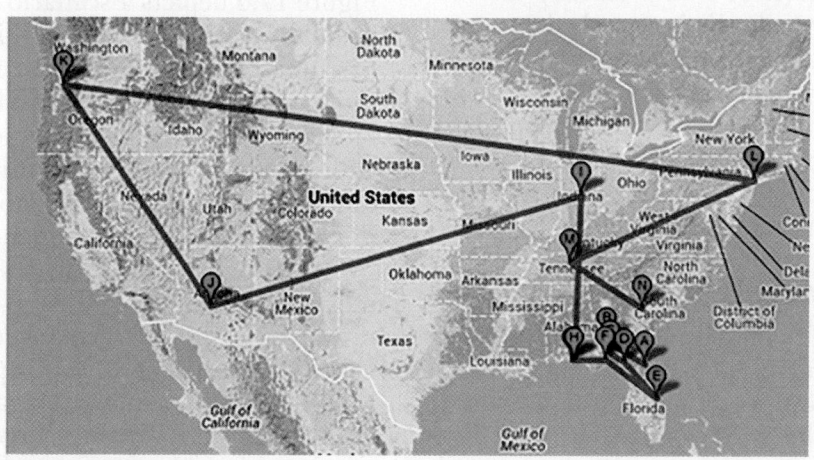

FIGURE 17.4 Where's George?

As WheresGeorge.com illustrates, a typical one dollar bill (with George Washington's face on it) is spent many times in many places. The *velocity of money* is the number of times a bill is spent on average in one year.

Given the prospect that discretionary monetary policy might influence real GDP, most economists agree that it is worth trying when an economy is in distress. For instance, during the Great Recession, the Fed resorted to a new monetary policy tool called *quantitative easing*. **Quantitative easing** is a substantial expansion of the money supply achieved with central bank purchases of securities from banks and other financial institutions. Quantitative easing differs from normal open market operations in that the scale of the purchases is larger and the purpose is not to achieve a targeted interest rate. Even when open market operations have brought interest rates down to nearly 0, it is hoped that a massive influx of money into the banking system will stimulate the economy by encouraging more loans and more spending.

The Fed conducted three rounds of quantitative easing between 2008 and 2014 by purchasing trillions of dollars' worth of Treasury bonds and mortgage-backed bonds. Although there was near consensus that the Fed needed to take action against the recession, it remains controversial whether the amount of quantitative easing was appropriate and whether the bond purchases achieved their desired purpose.

quantitative easing
A substantial expansion of the money supply achieved with central bank purchases of securities from banks and other financial institutions.

transactions demand
The demand for money used to make typical day-to-day purchases.

precautionary demand
The demand for money that can be used to cover unexpected expenses.

speculative demand
The demand for money used to take advantage of investment opportunities or avoid losses due to anticipated changes in the value of alternative investments.

The Market for Money

The tools of monetary policy take effect through the market for money. Money is demanded and supplied in a market with many similarities to the familiar markets for goods and services. You have already learned that the Fed controls the money supply using monetary policy. In this section, you will learn about the demand for money and how the combination of demand and supply determines interest rates in the economy.

MONEY DEMAND

If you hold money in your purse, pocket, or piggy bank, you won't earn interest on it like you would if it were in a savings account. And you won't earn a return on it like you typically would if it were invested in stocks, bonds, or real estate. So why hold money? Aside from

coin collecting and the opportunity to own a fabulous pair of cufflinks made from nickels, there are three primary reasons people hold money: to make transactions, as a precaution, and for speculative purposes:

- **Transactions demand** is the demand for money used to make typical day-to-day purchases. It would be terribly inconvenient to have to sell stocks or make a withdrawal from a savings account every time you wanted to buy a soft drink or a magazine.

- **Precautionary demand** is the demand for money that can be used to cover unexpected expenses. Many people like to keep some extra money stashed away for a "rainy day." You never know when you might need to pay for car repairs, a new furnace, or medical care.

- **Speculative demand** is the demand for money used to take advantage of investment opportunities or to avoid losses due to anticipated changes in the value of alternative investments. For example, if you think the value of stocks, bonds, real estate, or other investments is going to fall in the future, you might want to sell any such investments and hold more money instead.

Figure 17.5 shows the demand curve for money. The demand curve is downward sloping because people want to hold more money when the opportunity cost of holding money—the interest rate—is low than when it is high. When the interest rate is fairly high, say, 10 percent, people have a strong incentive to cut back on their money holdings and instead put money into accounts that pay interest. Figure 17.6 depicts a scenario in which people want to hold (or demand) $1.0 trillion at an interest rate of 10 percent. If the interest rate fell to 2 percent, the lower opportunity cost of holding money would increase the quantity of money demanded to $1.6 trillion. This inverse relationship between the interest rate and the quantity of money demanded results in a downward-sloping demand curve for money.

A change in the price of milkshakes causes a movement along the demand curve for milkshakes, rather than a shift in the demand curve for milkshakes. Likewise, the demand curve for money stays the same when the price of money—again, the interest rate—changes. But the demand curve shifts when a variety of other things change. Something that causes people to expect more "rainy days," such as an increase in well-publicized natural disasters, can cause a change in precautionary demand. Speculative demand changes when people become more optimistic or pessimistic

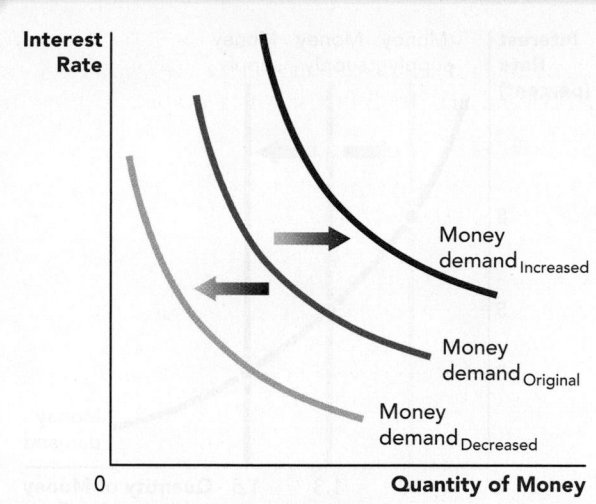

FIGURE 17.5 Money Demand

Lower interest rates decrease the opportunity cost of holding money and thereby increase the quantity of money demanded. This gives the money demand curve a downward slope. The demand curve shifts to the right when there is an increase in the transactions demand, the precautionary demand, or the speculative demand for money. The demand curve shifts to the left when any of these types of demand for money decreases.

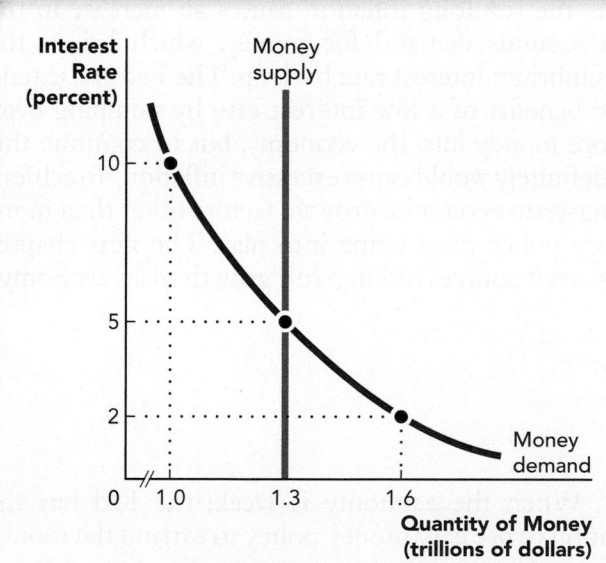

FIGURE 17.6 Equilibrium in the Market for Money

The money supply curve is vertical at the quantity of money chosen by the Fed. The intersection of the money supply curve and the money demand curve establishes the equilibrium interest rate.

about the future value of alternative investments. And changes in the overall price level, real GDP, technology, and institutions trigger changes in the transactions demand for money:

- *Changes in the price level.* When it takes more money to buy goods and services, the transactions demand for money increases because consumers need more money in their pockets to cover the new, higher prices.

- *Changes in real GDP.* An increase in real GDP means that people are buying more goods and services, which takes more money and increases the transactions demand for money. An increase in real GDP also means that workers are earning more money, and people tend to hold more money when they make more money.

- *Changes in technology.* After ATMs became popular, people started holding less money because they could easily visit an ATM if they ran out. The transactions demand for money also decreased as the use of credit cards and debit cards increased, making it possible to buy most things without holding money. Digital wallets such as *Google Pay* and related technological advances are likely to make it even easier to get by, and to buy, without a wallet full of cash.

- *Changes in institutions.* An example of an institutional change occurred in 1980 when new legislation made it possible for banks to pay interest on checking accounts. The change lowered the opportunity cost of holding money in checking accounts rather than in savings accounts of various types. Because money held in checkable deposits counts among the money demanded, the increase in checkable deposits represented an increase in the demand for money.

MONEY SUPPLY AND EQUILIBRIUM

The supply curve for money differs from the upward-sloping supply curves of most goods and services. The quantity of milkshakes that firms will supply increases as the price of milkshakes increases. In contrast, the supply of money is controlled by the Fed, which does not respond to changes in the interest rate the way firms respond to price changes. Instead, the Fed chooses the money supply that will establish the money market equilibrium at the Fed's targeted rate of interest. The money supply curve is thus vertical at the quantity of money chosen by the Fed, as shown in Figure 17.6. That is, if the money supply is $1.3 trillion, the money supply will be $1.3 trillion whether the interest rate is 10 percent or 2 percent.

As in other markets, the price of money—the interest rate—is determined by the equilibrium of supply and demand. For example, Figure 17.6 shows a situation in which the equilibrium quantity of money supplied and demanded in the economy is initially $1.3 trillion, and the equilibrium interest rate is 5 percent. Next, we'll see how monetary policy can change this equilibrium.

THE EFFECTS OF MONETARY POLICY

With monetary policy, the Fed can increase the money supply and shift the money supply curve to the right, or decrease the money supply and shift the money supply curve to the left. For example, with expansionary monetary policy the Fed could increase the money supply to $1.5 trillion. Figure 17.7 shows that this would bring the equilibrium interest rate down to 3 percent. A lower interest rate makes borrowing less expensive for many groups that can help the economy recover. These groups include entrepreneurs who want to start new ice cream shops, existing shoe companies that want to expand into the soccer cleat market, universities that want to build new residence halls, and families who want to buy new homes.

With contractionary monetary policy, the Fed could decrease the money supply to $1.1 trillion. Figure 17.7 shows that this shifts the money supply curve to the left and increases the equilibrium interest rate to 8 percent. This makes loans for investment projects and other purchases more expensive and helps to cool down an overheated economy.

While monetary policy can help the economy out of a recession, the effects of monetary policy are generally short-lived. You've seen how an increase in the money supply lowers the interest rate and increases aggregate demand. However, the higher aggregate

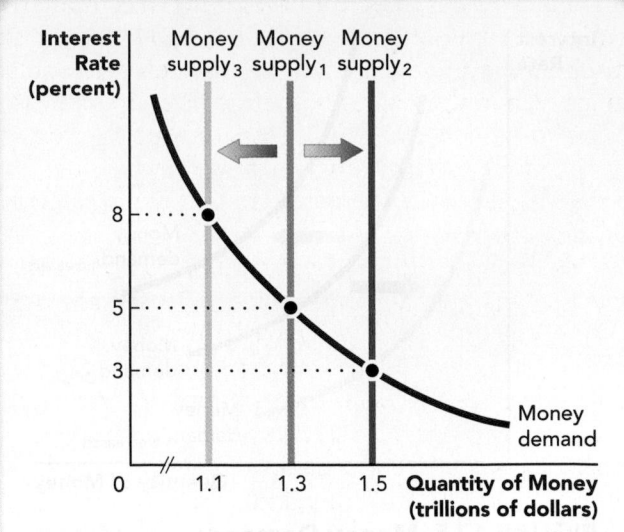

FIGURE 17.7 Expansionary and Contractionary Monetary Policy

Expansionary monetary policy increases the money supply and shifts the money supply curve to the right. This lowers the equilibrium interest rate. Contractionary monetary policy decreases the money supply and shifts the money supply curve to the left. This lowers the equilibrium interest rate.

demand pushes the price level upward. In the long run, the resulting inflation causes an increase in the transactions demand for money, which brings the equilibrium interest rate back up. The Fed can extend the benefits of a low interest rate by pumping even more money into the economy, but to continue this indefinitely would cause excessive inflation. To achieve long-term economic growth, factors other than monetary policy must come into play. The next chapter discusses sources of long-run growth in an economy.

SUMMARY

Monetary policy is conducted by a nation's central bank, which in the United States is the Federal Reserve System known as the Fed. The Fed is led by a chairperson, a Board of Governors that consists of seven members (including the Chair), and the presidents of the Federal Reserve's 12 district banks. In addition to promoting economic stability with monetary policy, the Fed oversees the nation's financial system and provides financial services to banks, thrifts, and the government.

When the economy is weak, the Fed has the option to use easy money policy to expand the money supply. Expansionary monetary policy lowers interest rates in the economy and encourages borrowing and spending, which increase aggregate demand. When there is a threat of high inflation, the Fed can use tight money policy to contract the money supply. Contractionary monetary policy increases interest rates in the economy, which discourages borrowing and spending and helps cool the economy down.

The Fed has three traditional tools for monetary policy: (1) open market operations; (2) changing the discount rate; and (3) changing the reserve requirement. When the Fed uses open market operations, it either buys or sells U.S. Treasury securities "on the open market," depending on whether the goal is to infuse money into the economy or take money out of the economy.

By lowering the discount rate, which is the interest rate the Federal Reserve charges financial institutions for short-term loans, the Fed makes it cheaper for banks to borrow money from its discount window. This, in turn, encourages banks to charge their customers lower interest rates and increase the availability of loans to individuals and firms. Raising the discount rate has the opposite effect of raising the interest rates that banks charge their customers and reducing the availability of loans.

The Fed can also raise or lower the reserve requirement. A higher reserve requirement lowers the amount of excess reserves that banks have to lend out, and contracts the money creation process initiated by the Fed's purchases of Treasury securities. A lower reserve requirement has the opposite effect: It increases the amount of money that banks can lend out and expands the money creation process. When a financial emergency strikes, the Fed sometimes takes additional steps to ease the pain. During the Great Recession, the Fed launched several new programs to quickly make more loans available to financial institutions.

As with the government's fiscal policies, the Fed's monetary policies can be delayed by the time it takes to identify problems and implement policy responses. However, because the FOMC is a much smaller and less politically charged group than Congress, it can respond relatively quickly. Once a recession takes its toll, the entrenched uncertainty and lost confidence in the economy are hard to overcome. Even dramatically lower interest rates and large injections of money into the economy can be slow to turn it around.

The velocity of money is the number of times per year that the average unit of currency is spent. Monetarists argue that the velocity of money and real GDP are stable in the short run. On the basis of that assumption, the quantity theory of money suggests that an increase in the money supply leads to a proportional increase in the price level in the economy—but not an increase in real GDP. So, monetarists do not favor expansionary monetary policy for the purpose of boosting real GDP. Instead, they recommend a slow and steady increase in the money supply.

Other economists point out that prices can be "sticky" and the velocity of money can fluctuate, so monetary policy has a less predictable effect on prices and can influence real GDP. Given the possibility that it could be helpful, most economists agree that a moderate amount of discretionary monetary policy is worth trying in times of economic crisis.

The market for money works much like the markets for goods and services. The price of money is the interest rate, because that is the opportunity cost of holding money that could otherwise be placed into a savings account that earns interest, or invested elsewhere to earn a similar rate of return. The money supply curve is vertical at the quantity of money chosen by the Federal Reserve.

Monetary policy can be effective in the short run when the economy needs a quick fix. However, the effects on real GDP generally don't last long. For instance, the increase in aggregate demand caused by expansionary monetary policy leads to inflation. When prices are higher, consumers demand more money to buy goods and services. This increase in the demand for money increases the interest rate. And the higher price level and interest rate put an end to the short-run benefits of expansionary monetary policy. The next chapter examines approaches to economic development designed to achieve long-lasting increases in an economy's productive capacity.

KEY TERMS

Federal Reserve System, p. 258
Board of Governors of the
    Federal Reserve, p. 258
Federal Open Market Committee
    (FOMC), p. 259
monetary policy, p. 260
expansionary monetary policy,
    p. 260

contractionary monetary policy,
    p. 260
Treasury securities, p. 260
open market operations, p. 260
federal funds rate, p. 261
discount rate, p. 262
collateral, p. 264
velocity of money, p. 265

equation of exchange, p. 265
quantity theory of money, p. 265
quantitative easing, p. 266
transactions demand, p. 266
precautionary demand, p. 266
speculative demand, p. 266

PROBLEMS FOR REVIEW

1. Which of the following is *not* among the primary responsibilities of the Fed?

   a. Conducting the nation's monetary policy with the goal of maintaining full employment, price stability, and economic growth

   b. Regulating, supervising, and examining the nation's banks

   c. Ensuring the velocity of money does not exceed the nation's rate of economic growth

   d. Maintaining the stability of the financial system

   e. Serving as a "bankers' bank"

2. Explain how open market operations can lead to an increase in aggregate demand. *Hint:* Your explanation should mention the role the interest rate plays in the sequence of events.

3. Which of the following constitutes easy money policy and is carried out directly by the Fed?

   a. The sale of Treasury securities

   b. A decrease in the federal funds rate

   c. A decrease in the discount rate

   d. An increase in the reserve requirement

4. Suppose the reserve requirement is 10 percent.

   a. If the Fed buys $10 billion worth of bonds from commercial banks, what is the largest possible increase in the money supply that could result from this open market operation?

   b. What accompanying change in the reserve requirement would double the largest possible increase in the money supply that could result from this open market operation?

5. True or false: During the Great Recession, the Fed increased the availability of loans by opening a facility that loaned money directly to individual consumers. Explain your answer.

6. Suppose the money supply increases by 8 percent.

   a. Given what monetarists believe about the equation of exchange, what do they predict will be the result of the increase?

   b. If prices and the velocity of money remain unchanged, what will be the result of the increase?

7. Explain two reasons why a person might hold money other than for day-to-day purchases.

8. Which of the following would not shift the money demand curve to the right?

   a. A decrease in the interest rate

   b. An increase in the price level

   c. An increase in real GDP

   d. A computer glitch that prevented ATMs from working for an indeterminate period of time.

9. Draw a graph showing the supply and demand curves for money and label the curves and axes. Show what would happen to the equilibrium interest rate and the equilibrium quantity of money if the Fed sold Treasury securities on the open market.

10. Suppose you are the Federal Reserve chairperson and you see the economy slipping into a recession. Which of the Federal Reserve's tools would you use first in efforts to stabilize the economy? Why would you prefer that particular tool?

Economic Growth and Development

18

Jon Arnold Images Ltd/Alamy Stock Photo

LEARNING OBJECTIVES

In this chapter, you will learn to:

1. Explain the primary goals and measures of economic development
2. Describe strategies for achieving economic growth
3. Identify major challenges facing developing countries
4. Discuss success stories and failures in economic development

Cruise ships docked in Jamaica take on clean drinking water from abundant limestone aquifers. Pristine beaches, bauxite mines, and sugarcane fields top a long list of the island nation's assets. Jamaican coffee is among the best in the world, as is its rum. And tourists flock to Jamaica to enjoy waterfalls and resorts. Despite having ample natural resources and an educated, energetic workforce, Jamaica is a relatively poor country. Jamaica's GDP per capita was $9,200 in 2017, compared with $59,500 in the United States. Like many countries, Jamaica is struggling to improve its citizens' standard of living and quality of life.

Why are some countries rich and other countries poor? Adam Smith raised that question in 1776 in his famous book, *An Inquiry into the Nature and Causes of the Wealth of Nations*. Economists continue to scratch their heads over the same puzzle today, motivated by a desire to help the 2.4 billion people on the planet who live on less than $2 a day. There are no easy answers, but in this chapter we'll examine how the pieces of the puzzle are coming together.

Why Should I Care?

Dave Anderson

Adam Smith put it this way: "No society can surely be flourishing and happy of which by far the greater part of the numbers are poor and miserable." Living in poverty doesn't just mean that people can't afford to buy new clothes or a car. Living in poverty is truly life-threatening. Malnutrition in poor countries claims the lives of more than 3 million children under the age of 5 each year. Even in the United States, more than 20 percent of everyone under the age of 18 lives in poverty. Economic development can bring better living conditions to people in desperate situations.

There are still more reasons to care about economic development. Crime and terrorism often make inroads in areas where good jobs and education systems are lacking. It is hard to expect high environmental standards in places where people barely have enough money to meet basic needs. And where medical systems are relatively primitive, deadly diseases are more likely to get out of control. All of these problems have global repercussions, so **when economic development helps others improve their quality of life, your quality of life stands to improve as well.**

▲ This restaurant in Jamaica appears primitive to us, but everything is relative. On average, incomes in the Democratic Republic of the Congo are one-half the incomes in North Korea, which are one-fifth the incomes in Jamaica, which are one-sixth the incomes in the United States, which are half the incomes in Qatar.

Measures of Economic Growth and Development

Political economist Thomas Malthus wrote that the cause of wealth and poverty is "the grand object of all enquiries" in his field. Indeed, with an estimated 842 million people going to bed hungry each night, and 3 million people dying every year from vaccine-preventable diseases, the determinants of wealth and poverty are pieces in a very important puzzle.

The long-term cure for poverty begins with **economic growth,** which is an increase in the productive capacity of an economy. Economic growth allows a country to increase its output and improve the standard of living of its citizens. Recall from Chapter 13 that economists use the real GDP per capita—that is, the output per person, adjusted for inflation—as a measure of a country's standard of living. In this chapter, we will discuss the benefits of economic growth in terms of increases in the real GDP per capita.

Keep in mind that economic growth is not synonymous with an increase in real GDP per capita. Real GDP per capita can increase for reasons other than economic growth, as when a country makes more productive use of its existing resources and technology. And if the population of a country grows at a faster rate than its real GDP, the country's real GDP per capita will fall. For example, if the population increases by 20 percent and the real GDP increases by

economic growth
An increase in the productive capacity of an economy.

10 percent, the real GDP per capita will fall because the growing output level is spread more thinly across the even more rapidly growing population.

The increases in income and output that accompany economic growth can lead to improvements in health care, education, job opportunities, transportation systems, and housing, among many other comforts and conveniences. Economic growth can also lead to pollution and environmental degradation. This makes it prudent for nations to adopt growth-related policies that actively promote beneficial types of growth while minimizing detrimental side effects. For instance, the government of Jamaica is confronting environmental problems with a detailed master plan for sustainable tourism development. China hopes to tame its smog problem by rapidly expanding its capacity to generate electricity from wind, water, and solar sources. And at a United Nations conference in 2015, nearly 200 countries pledged to attack global climate change. The plan includes $100 billion in assistance each year to help poor countries grow without causing excessive harm to the planet.

Economic development is a combination of economic growth and a broader set of non-material improvements in the quality of life. For example, an advancement in human rights could improve the quality of life in a country and thereby contribute to its economic development. However, this would not constitute economic growth unless it somehow increased the country's productive capacity. Michael Todaro, a pioneer in the field of economic development, describes it as "the process of improving the quality of all human lives" by increasing people's incomes, promoting human dignity, and expanding the range of goods and services available to consumers. Kofi Annan, the former Secretary General of the United Nations, said that a developed country is "one that allows all its citizens to enjoy a free and healthy life in a safe environment." Countries whose citizens experience a relatively low quality of life are referred to as **developing countries,** or *less developed countries*.

The *Human Development Index* (HDI) measures the progress of countries on the basis of their citizens' life expectancy, years of schooling, and income per capita. Table 18.1 shows the top 10 and bottom 10 countries according to this measure. In 2016, Norway had the highest HDI value—0.949—out of the 188 countries studied. The Central African Republic had the lowest HDI value, 0.352. The United States tied for tenth with an HDI value of 0.920.

The HDI is a broader measure of areas targeted for improvement than is the real GDP per capita. However, the two measures—HDI and GDP—tend to move together, as you can see in Figure 18.1 on

Table 18.1 The Most and Least Developed Countries According to the Human Development Index

Rank	Country	HDI
The Top 10 Countries		
1	Norway	0.949
2	Australia	0.939
2	Switzerland	0.939
4	Germany	0.926
5	Denmark	0.925
5	Singapore	0.925
7	Netherlands	0.924
8	Ireland	0.923
9	Iceland	0.921
10	Canada	0.920
10	United States	0.920
The Bottom 10 Countries		
179	Eritrea	0.420
179	Sierra Leone	0.420
181	Mozambique	0.418
181	South Sudan	0.418
183	Guinea	0.414
184	Burundi	0.404
185	Burkina Faso	0.402
186	Chad	0.396
187	Niger	0.353
188	Central African Republic	0.352

Data from United Nations Development Program, *Human Development Report, 2016.*

the next page. The bubbles in the graph represent countries. Larger bubbles represent countries with larger populations. Countries with low real GDP per capita values, such as Niger and the Democratic Republic of the Congo, have low HDI values. Countries with high real GDP per capita values, such as Norway and Australia, have high HDI values. The strong correlation between real GDP per capita and the Human Development Index

economic development
A combination of economic growth and a broader set of non-material improvements in the quality of life.

developing countries
Countries whose citizens experience a relatively low quality of life.

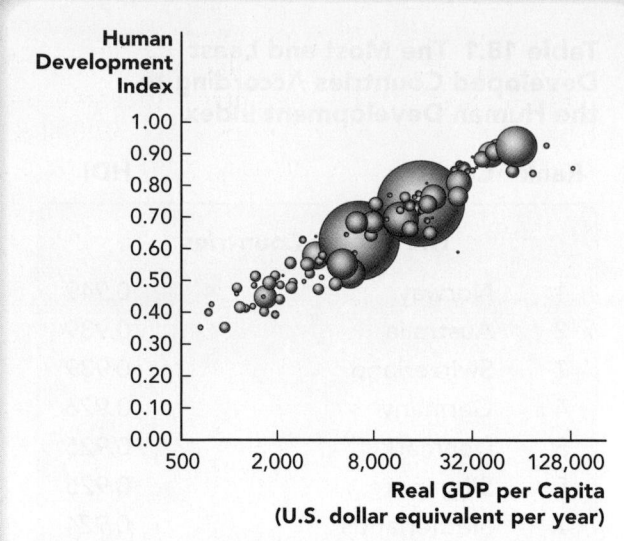

FIGURE 18.1 HDI and Real GDP per Capita

There is a strong correlation between a country's real GDP per capita and its Human Development Index value. This makes economic growth a valid goal for policy makers seeking much broader improvements in the quality of life.

Free Material from Gapminder.org; *Data sources:* United Nations Development Program; World Bank.

▲ The resilience of children is universal, but the gap between living conditions in developed and developing countries is wide. In the United States, there are 2.4 doctors per 1,000 citizens, and 7 out of 1,000 babies die in infancy. In Sierra Leone, there are 0.02 doctors per 1,000 citizens, and 114 out of 1,000 babies die in infancy.

makes economic growth a valid goal for those seeking improvements in much more than just real GDP per capita. Hans Rosling, a Swedish physician who has correlated the two measures, concludes: "If you want better health and education, fix economic growth."

GLOBAL COMPARISONS

The contrasts between developed countries and developing countries can be dramatic. Annual expenditures on education per primary-school student range from about $45 in the Central African Republic to about $13,000 in countries that include the United States. The number of doctors per 1,000 citizens ranges from less than 0.1 in Tanzania and Ethiopia to more than 6 in Greece and Cuba. Education and health care are among several factors that both influence economic growth and are influenced by it.

In Afghanistan, Mali, and Somalia, 1 in 10 infants dies before reaching the age of 1. In Jamaica, the infant mortality rate is 14 deaths per 1,000 births—twice the rate in the United States. There are just 1.8 hospital beds per 1,000 people in Jamaica, compared with 3.1 per 1,000 people in the United States. The unemployment rate in Jamaica is 14.3 percent, almost 3 times the unemployment rate in the United States. But although the average Jamaican earns just one-sixth the income

of the average American, billions of people around the world would be thrilled to earn as much as the average Jamaican. For example, North Koreans earn one-fifth of what Jamaicans earn, and the Congolese earn one-half of what North Koreans earn.

Workers are among the factors of production that support economic growth. Population growth increases the number of workers, but it also increases the number of mouths to feed. Many countries experience rapid population growth during the early stages of development because improvements in health care cause death rates to fall while birth rates remain high. Whether population growth boosts a country's real GDP per capita depends on its growth in output relative to its growth in population. And the growth in output depends on the supply of physical capital and the skills of workers, among other factors discussed in this chapter.

Like economic growth, population growth can be beneficial or problematic, depending on how it is handled. Population growth typically leads to the growth of cities, where large firms benefit from economies of scale and become centers for research and innovation. But without adequate planning and infrastructure, such *urbanization* can lead to problems with congestion, malnutrition, crime, pollution, and shortages of food and water.

Increases in GDP per capita may or may not increase the incomes of most citizens. How income is distributed within a country depends in part on the opportunities available for poorer citizens to advance their careers. Income distribution also depends on the education and training of the workforce, the progressivity of income taxes, and the structure of government transfer programs. Those seeking improvements in income distribution can track the **Gini coefficient**, a measure of income inequality that equals 0 if everyone in a country earns the same income, and equals 1 if the richest person earns all the income. The Gini coefficient for the United States is 0.450. Figure 18.2 shows Gini coefficients for countries around the world. The least developed countries generally have low Gini coefficients because almost everyone in those countries is similarly poor. For example, the Gini coefficient is 0.268 for Moldova and 0.321 for Bangladesh.

Moderately wealthy countries typically have more inequality and thus larger Gini coefficients. Although some people in these countries are rich, many people remain poor because the moderate overall levels of income limit the ability to fund education, training, and transfer programs for the poor. For example, the Gini coefficient is 0.497 for Brazil and 0.505 for Chile. In the wealthiest countries, it is relatively easy to fund programs that help the underprivileged out of poverty, so almost everyone is fairly well off. As a result, the Gini coefficient is 0.215 for Finland and 0.280 for Iceland.

The income and output available to countries as they consume, invest, and fund development programs is, indeed, all over the map. In Figure 18.3, the countries with the highest levels of GDP per capita are shown in dark blue. Citizens of the world's highest-earning country, Liechtenstein, enjoy a GDP per capita in excess of $139,000 per year. GDP per capita exceeds $65,000 per year in the 15 richest countries. The United States is the 20th-highest-earning country, with a GDP per capita of $59,500. In 91 countries, the GDP per capita is less than $10,000 per year. In Burundi, the Central African Republic, the Democratic Republic of the Congo, and Liberia, the GDP per capita is less than $1,000 per year.

We've seen how low the income levels are in some countries, but are improvements being made? And are income levels converging across countries over time? In Figure 18.4, we see that until the nineteenth century, the levels of real GDP per capita were similarly low in countries across the globe. Then, in the mid-1800s, industrialization boosted the income levels in Western Europe, the United States, and Australia. After the Great Depression of the 1930s and World War II in

Gini coefficient
A measure of income inequality that equals 0 if incomes in a country are equal, and equals 1 if the richest person earns all the income.

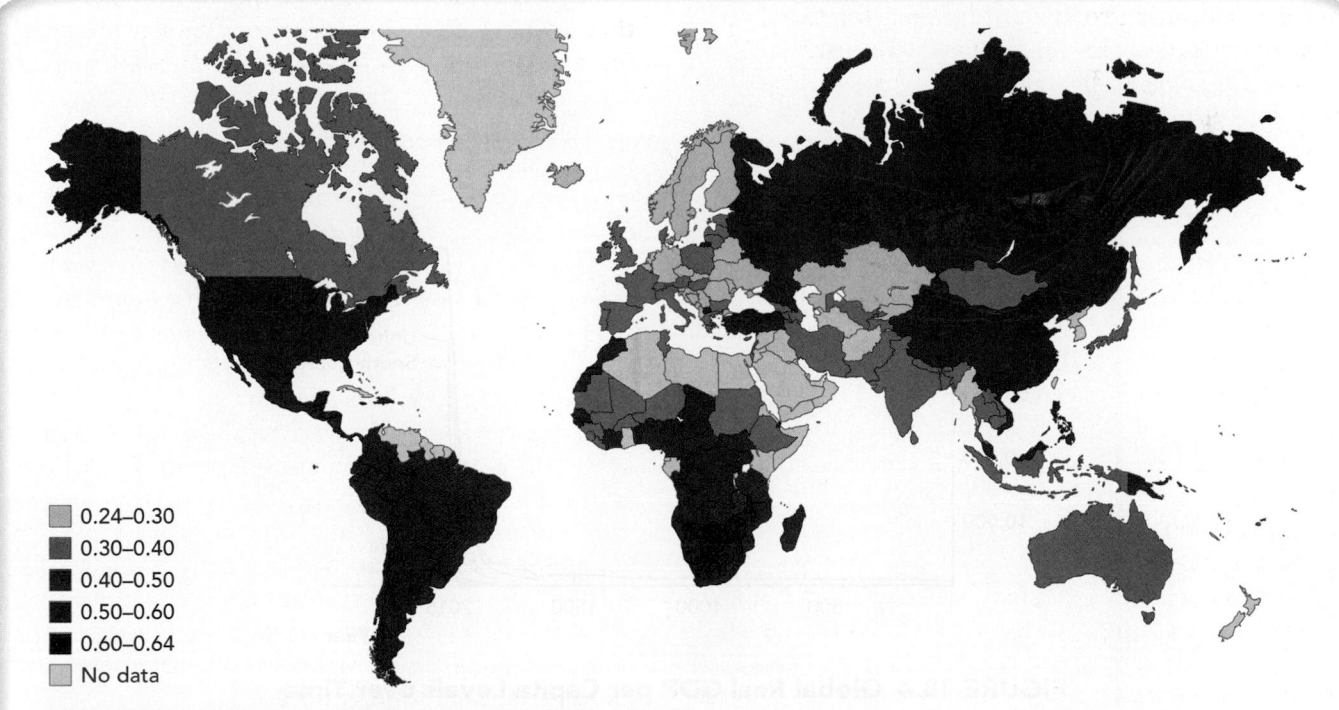

FIGURE 18.2 Gini Coefficients Around the World
People's incomes are the most similar in the most developed countries, where almost everyone earns a high income, and in the least developed countries, where almost everyone earns a low income.
Data from Central Intelligence Agency.

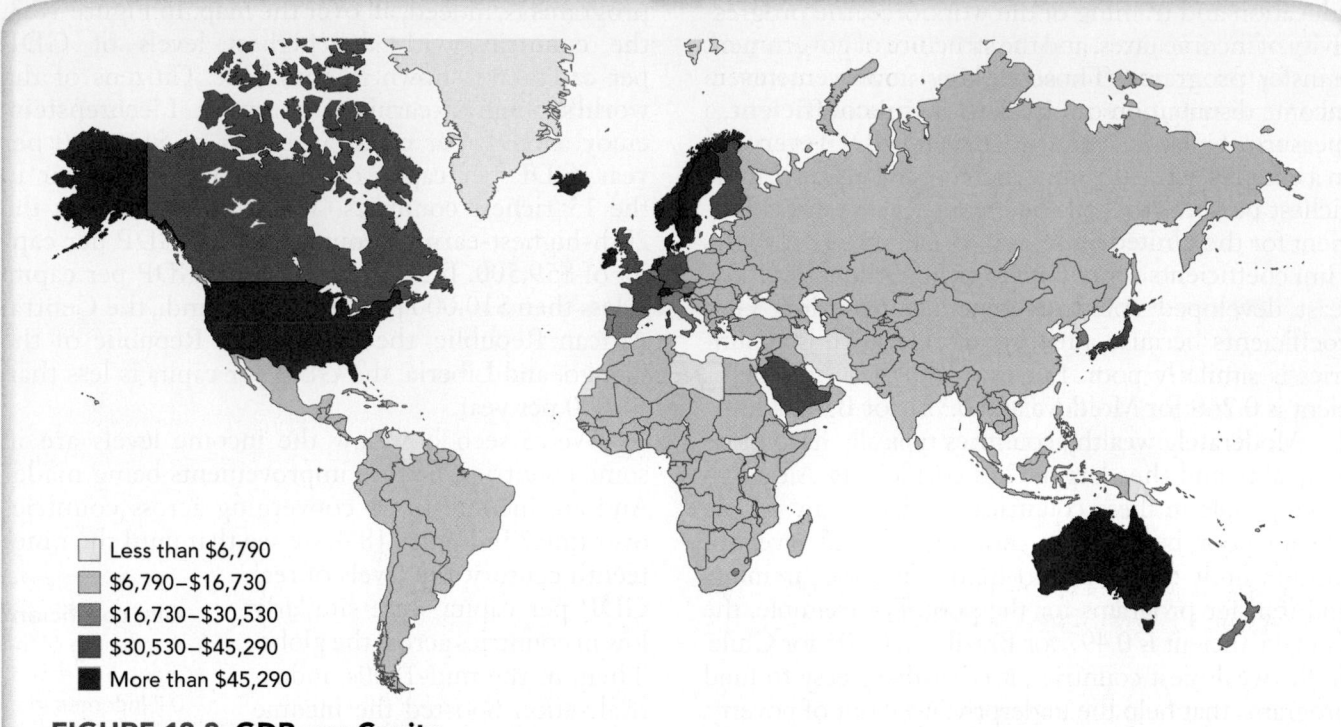

FIGURE 18.3 GDP per Capita

In Liechtenstein, the GDP per capita exceeds $139,000 per year. In the 15 richest countries, the GDP per capita exceeds $65,000 per year. In 91 countries, GDP per capita is less than $10,000 per year.

Data from World Bank.

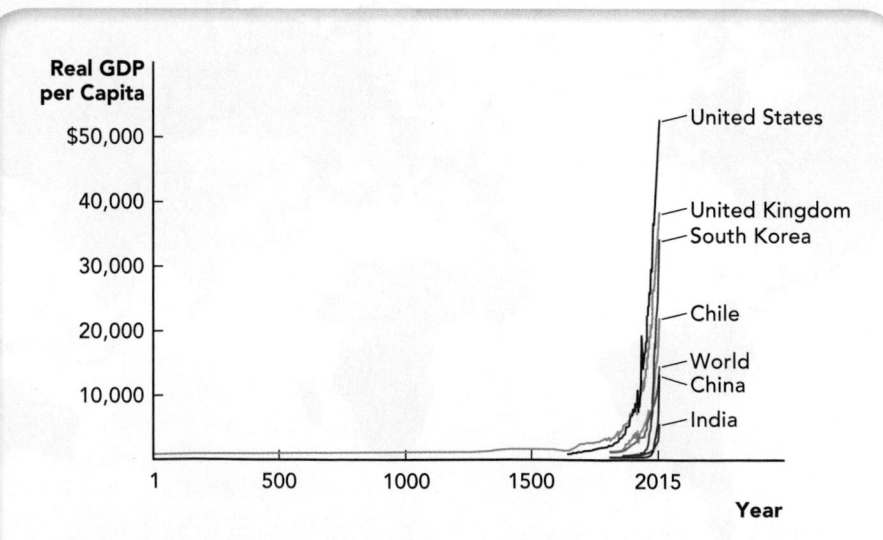

FIGURE 18.4 Global Real GDP per Capita Levels over Time

Levels of real GDP per capita were similar worldwide until about 200 years ago. Since then, most countries have experienced at least some economic growth, but at rates that have varied dramatically across regions of the globe.

Data source: Our World in Data.

the early 1940s, most countries enjoyed increased prosperity, with exceptions in Africa and parts of Asia. Differing rates of economic growth, however, led to widening gaps in the wealth of nations.

A comparison of more recent growth rates shows that some of the income gaps are starting to narrow. Table 18.2 shows the estimated average annual rate of growth in real GDP per capita between 2013 and 2017 for the 10 countries with the most rapidly increasing real GDP per capita and the 10 countries with the most rapidly decreasing real GDP per capita. Notice that most of the countries with rapidly growing real GDP per capita are shown in Figure 18.3 to have relatively low levels of GDP per

capita. Conversely, most of the countries with rapidly decreasing real GDP per capita are shown in Figure 18.3 to have high levels of GDP per capita. These cases of fast growth in poor countries and slow growth in rich countries indicate some convergence of income levels across countries. Unfortunately, convergence is not a general trend among countries with moderate levels of real GDP per capita. Later in this chapter, you will learn about barriers that have slowed the convergence of income levels.

ECONOMIC GROWTH AND THE PRODUCTION POSSIBILITIES FRONTIER

We can use the production possibilities frontier (PPF) to illustrate the difference between economic growth—an increase in a country's productive capacity—and a more productive use of existing resources. Recall from Chapter 1 that the PPF shows all the combinations of two goods that could be produced in a given time period using all available resources. If a country is producing less than it could, this is represented by a point inside the PPF, as shown by point *A* in Figure 18.5.

Table 18.2 Countries with the Fastest-Increasing and Fastest-Decreasing Levels of Real GDP per Capita, 2013–2017

Country	Growth Rate
Countries with Rapidly Increasing Real GDP per Capita	
Ireland	9.95%
Ethiopia	7.56
Nauru	7.51
China	6.33
Myanmar	6.23
Uzbekistan	6.19
India	5.94
Turkmenistan	5.90
Bangladesh	5.77
Lao P.D.R.	5.65
Countries with Rapidly Decreasing Real GDP per Capita	
Yemen	−12.62%
Venezuela	−10.85
Equatorial Guinea	−9.19
South Sudan	−8.72
Timor-Leste	−7.39
Qatar	−4.64
Suriname	−4.56
Macao SAR	−4.14
Libya	−3.63
Brunei Darussalam	−2.99

Source: International Monetary Fund.

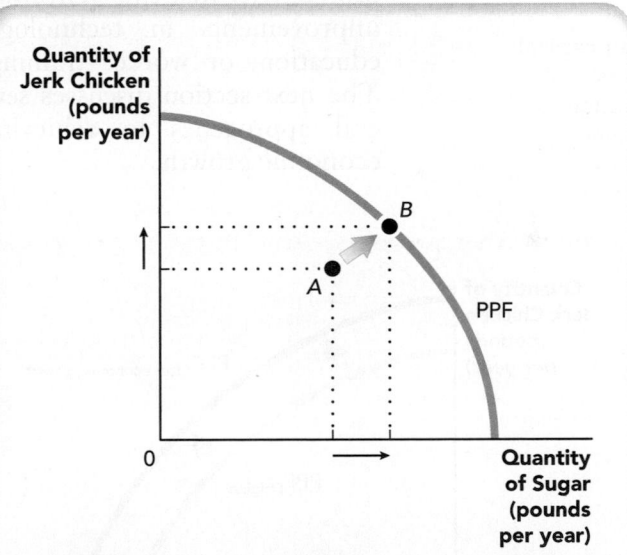

FIGURE 18.5 An Increase in Capacity Utilization

In the short run, increases in real GDP come from either using existing resources that had been idle or making more productive use of a country's resources using existing technology. These methods make it possible to produce more of some goods without producing less of others; the result, however, is an increase in capacity utilization rather than economic growth. This increase in capacity utilization is represented on the graph by a movement from a point inside the PPF, such as point *A*, to a point closer to or on the PPF, such as point *B*.

To keep things simple, suppose that Jamaica produces only two goods: (1) its famously spicy jerk chicken, and (2) sugar. By making better use of its available resources, Jamaica can make more jerk chicken, more sugar, or more of both without making less of either one. If Jamaica more fully utilizes its productive capacity, it can move from a point inside the PPF, such as point *A*, to a point closer to or on the PPF, such as point *B*. This can be achieved in the short run by using resources that had been idle, or by using existing technology to make more productive use of the same resources. Such an increase in real GDP—one that takes the economy closer to its productive capacity without increasing that capacity—is an increase in capacity utilization, not economic growth.

Economic growth increases the productive capacity of a country and shifts the PPF outward, as shown in Figure 18.6. This corresponds to an increase in the country's potential output and a rightward shift in its long-run aggregate supply curve. The sources of economic growth include increases in the availability of capital, labor, land, and other factors of production, as well as increases in productivity that can stem from improvements in technology, education, or worker training. The next section discusses several approaches to achieving economic growth.

human capital
Workers' skills, knowledge, and experience.

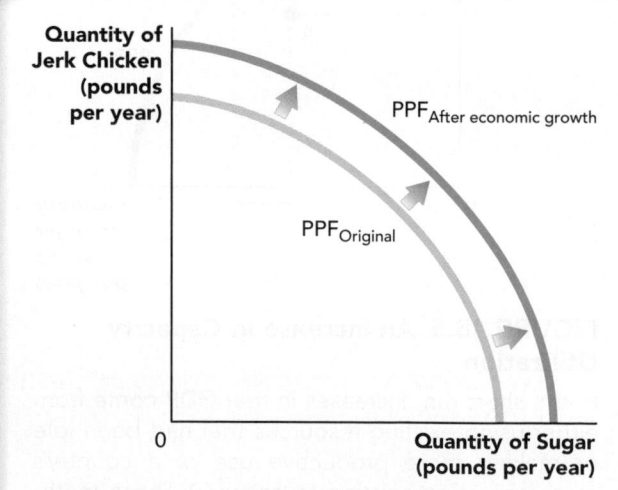

FIGURE 18.6 Economic Growth

In the long run, improvements in technology, the capabilities of workers, or the availability of factors of production can shift the PPF outward. This represents economic growth in the economy, rather than an increase in capacity utilization.

Strategies for Achieving Economic Growth

Economists study the characteristics of rich and poor countries in efforts to unlock the secret to prosperity. Their varying findings and interpretations have generated several broad schools of thought. Some schools emphasize the importance of workers' skills, knowledge, and experience, which collectively form **human capital**. Others focus on the type of capital we have discussed already—goods used to make other goods—which we'll refer to as *physical capital* here to distinguish it from human capital. Chapter 19 explains how international trade can help a country improve its finances and consume outside its production possibilities frontier. Additional strategies to promote economic growth involve monetary policy, research and development, foreign direct investment, and various types of loans.

MORE PHYSICAL CAPITAL

Physical capital is essential to productivity. Imagine trying to make jerk chicken without a grill, weave fabric without a loom, deliver lumber without a truck, or catch fish without a net. The *neoclassical growth model* of Nobel laureate and economist Robert Solow shows how developing countries might catch up to developed countries in terms of income per capita by acquiring more physical capital. In his model, Solow assumes that each country has the same technology, and that productivity differences among countries result from differing amounts of physical capital per worker, not from differing amounts of human capital.

The diminishing marginal product of capital makes capital more valuable in countries that have little of it. For example, the first computer in a country would have a big impact: It would be used to make the most critical calculations that, until that point, had been made by hand. The second computer would be used for the second-most-valued work. The thousandth computer might just be used for video games. The millionth computer might be a spare laptop for someone who already has a desktop computer.

Suppose you were a profit-maximizing investor in computers and that, as Solow assumed, productivity differences came from differences in physical capital. Given the higher return from one more computer in countries where many complex operations had yet to be automated, you would take new computers as they became available and put them to work in developing countries where the marginal productivity of

▲ In this classroom in Jamaica, the students outnumber the chairs and have no computers. Other things being equal, this means that new chairs and computers would contribute more to productivity in Jamaica than in other countries that already have a relative abundance of these types of capital.

computers was the highest. You and other investors would continue to do this until the developing countries caught up with the developed countries in terms of computer availability—that is, until every country had the same marginal productivity of computers.

The same incentives would exist for investors in all types of capital. So, if differing levels of physical capital were the source of unequal productivity levels to begin with, Solow's model suggests that productivity levels in different countries would converge as capital was allocated to the countries where it was the most productive. As we'll see next, flaws in Solow's assumptions weaken this balancing effect.

MORE HUMAN CAPITAL

Solow's neoclassical growth model applies to countries with similar human capital and technology but different amounts of physical capital. Unfortunately, rich and poor countries are not so similar. Real-world differences in human capital and technology across countries stand in the way of convergence. Another Nobel laureate, economist Robert Lucas, found that capital moves mostly among developed countries, rather than between developed and developing countries. This is partly because workers in developed countries have more human capital. The additional skills, education, and experience these workers have enable them to make better use of additional physical capital than workers in many developing countries could. The lesson here is that improvements in the levels of human capital in developing countries would help them attract more physical capital. And increases in either type of capital can lead to economic growth.

Lucas suggests that beneficial side effects from human capital can help make up for differences in the marginal product of capital between some developed and developing countries. Workers' skills, education, and experience rub off on other workers. One country may have twice the average education level of another, but by working with more knowledgeable people, the workers in the high-education country end up with *more than* twice the human capital. Lucas estimates that a 10 percent increase in the human capital of your co-workers will increase your own productivity by 3.6 percent.

Lucas also noted that despite the higher levels of human capital in developed countries, many developing countries, including Jamaica, do have a higher marginal product of physical capital than the United States, among other developed countries. So why isn't all the new capital flowing into places like Jamaica? Lucas concludes that there are impediments to the desired free flow of capital into developing countries. The owners of capital sometimes have inadequate information about the opportunities for investments in developing countries. Political instability in developing countries can create additional uncertainty about the return on investments made in those countries. And many developing countries impose high taxes, known as import tariffs, on capital coming from abroad. For example, India charges a 20 percent tariff on imported commercial vehicles. Developing countries can also be disadvantaged by low levels of technology, poor transportation systems, inadequate law enforcement, and limited supplies of land and other factors of production.

MORE MONEY

Money alone is not the missing piece for stimulating economic growth. The previous chapter explained that monetary policy is useful for helping the economy out of short-term dips in the business cycle, but increases in the money supply generally do not produce the type of sustainable increases in real GDP that constitute economic growth. More than a few countries have tried unsuccessfully to promote economic growth by expanding their money supplies. They've found that adding money to an economy with relatively few goods just leads to inflation. For instance, the government of Venezuela printed large sums of money in 2017 and 2018. Rather than increasing the standard of living, the result was inflation, estimated at 8,900 percent over a 12-month period. Hungary's inflation rate in 1946 reached 200 percent per day, so prices tripled every day!

▲ More money with which to buy the same goods just leads to inflation.

Chapter 17 explained how monetary policy could give the economy a temporary boost. Let's examine why, in the long run, increases in the money supply affect little beyond prices. Consider the Jamaican town of Port Royal, now a peaceful peninsula of coconut palms, but once a stomping ground for pirates including Edward "Blackbeard" Teach and Henry Morgan. For simplicity, suppose the town's residents are divided evenly among three occupations: farmers, fishers, and firewood collectors. Each farmer can harvest enough coconut milk to provide a day's beverages for three people. Each fisher can catch enough fish to feed three people for a day. And each firewood collector can collect enough firewood for one day's worth of cooking and heating fires for three people.

If there are no changes in productivity, the local options for the residents of Port Royal are essentially the same regardless of the money supply. With no money, each resident could trade two of the three units of the good he or she produces each day for one of each of the other goods. With two Jamaican dollars each, residents could pay $1 for each of the two goods they don't produce and earn $2 selling two units of what they do produce.

Now suppose the residents find Henry Morgan's buried treasure chest filled with Jamaican dollars, and they spread them throughout the community so that each resident has $2 million. If the only thing that changed is that they have more money, they could pay more for their daily rations—up to $1 million per unit of the goods they don't produce. But this would create nothing but inflation. Rather than printing piles of money or looking for buried treasure, countries should focus on improving their

research and development (R&D)
Work directed toward the creation or improvement of products or processes.

production levels and establishing international trade agreements with other countries that have differing specialties, as discussed further in Chapter 19.

MORE RESEARCH AND DEVELOPMENT

Advancements in technology allow more or better products to be made with a given amount of inputs. The most profitable companies in the world, including Samsung, Apple, Hewlett-Packard, and IBM, use cutting-edge technology to produce innovative products. Being on the cutting edge requires sizable investments in **research and development (R&D)**, which is work directed toward the creation or improvement of products or processes. Many types of R&D are tremendously expensive. The automaker Volkswagen and the technology firms Samsung, Intel, and Microsoft each spend more than $10 billion per year on R&D. The high cost of competing in these and other highly profitable industries is prohibitive for developing countries. The next section explains how international cooperation can help bring new technology and funds for R&D into developing countries.

MORE FOREIGN INVOLVEMENT

Foreign governments and nongovernmental organizations can assist developing countries in several ways. International organizations such as UNICEF and Save the Children provide food, wells for drinking water, medicine, and other goods and services that are in short supply. The World Bank is an international financial institution that supports development by providing funding and technical assistance to the poorest countries. The funding includes grants and low-interest loans that can help poor communities pay for schools, health care, family-planning assistance,

▲ About 1 percent of the U.S. federal budget goes to assist other counties with their economic development. In 2017, that included $12 million in financial aid for Jamaica and $220 million for Bangladesh.

natural resource management, and infrastructure, such as bridges and waste-disposal facilities.

The governments of developed countries also often provide loans or grants to developing countries. For example, in 2017 the U.S. government provided $12 million in financial aid to Jamaica and $177 million to Haiti. The success of this type of aid varies, depending on how well the aid is directed toward a country's greatest needs, how successfully the aid reaches the needy without being pilfered by corrupt intermediaries, and how sustainable the projects financed by the aid are after the temporary assistance ends. Aid often comes with conditions from the donors. For example, when the European Union provided $4.39 billion in aid for economic development in Mali in 2014, the money came with stipulations for democratic elections, peacekeeping operations, and other democratic and social reforms. In some cases, the country receiving the financial aid is required to use the money to purchase goods and services from the donor country.

Many corporations invest money abroad by purchasing stocks or bonds sold by firms and governments in other countries. Firms seeking a more active role abroad can engage in **foreign direct investment (FDI)**, which is investment to acquire a lasting interest in a firm operating in another country. FDI can be the purchase of a business in one country by an investor in another country, or the expansion of an existing business from one country into another.

Examples of FDI include U.S.-based Walmart's launch of stores in India, and the China Communications Construction Company's establishment of a headquarters in Jamaica. The government of Jamaica actively seeks FDI to infuse technology and related physical capital into its industrial sector. FDI is controversial, however, because it gives foreign corporations influence over domestic firms and because most of the profits are sent back to the countries the corporations call home. That is particularly true in the case of *banana republics*, as explained in the Q&A box that follows. Where assistance ends and exploitation begins is a matter of debate.

MORE DOMESTIC LOANS

When entrepreneurs contemplate borrowing money to invest in a new or growing business, the interest rates they must pay for loans can tip the scale for or against an investment project. In 2017, the *prime interest rate* charged for the lowest-risk business loans in the United States was 4.0 percent. In Jamaica, that rate was 16.6 percent; in Zimbabwe, it was 20.0 percent; and in Ghana, it was 31.8 percent. These rates reflect the high demand for loans in developing countries relative to the supply of loans. Low savings rates limit the

foreign direct investment (FDI)
An investment made to acquire a lasting interest in a firm operating in another country.

Q&A

What is a "banana republic"?

A *banana republic* is generally a small, impoverished country whose economy is largely dependent on foreign investment and the production of a single good, such as bananas. For instance, in 1899, Americans Minor Keith and Andrew Preston formed the United Fruit Company (UFCO) in Central America. The core operations in UFCO's fruit empire were banana farms and fruit transportation systems in Guatemala. UFCO was wildly successful and soon controlled Guatemala's telegraph lines, mail delivery to the United States, and all shipments in and out of the country's major port, Puerto Barrios. UFCO created jobs, built schools, and sometimes paid decent wages, but large portions of its profits left Guatemala, and the country remained poor. UFCO later changed its name to United Brands and, in the 1970s, sold its land holdings in Guatemala to the Del Monte Corporation. Countries that resemble banana republics today, and their primary exports, include Botswana (diamonds), Ghana (cocoa), Honduras (bananas and coffee), and Zambia (copper).

▲ The poor in Guatemala still live in homes with wood stoves and dirt floors.

amount of money available to be lent out, and the interest rates charged reflect the added uncertainty of loan repayment in unstable economies.

Most new businesses everywhere start out small. Amazon, Apple, Disney, Google, Harley Davidson, and Hewlett-Packard are among the businesses that started out in a garage. The trouble with the high interest rates in developing countries is that they make it much harder for successful new businesses to grow. Few entrepreneurs can afford to borrow enough money at an interest rate of 17 percent, let alone 32 percent, to expand out of a garage or makeshift shack into a facility with ample room for growth.

One remedy for high interest rates is **microcredit,** which is the extension of small loans to impoverished borrowers. The typical microcredit recipient would be ineligible for traditional loans due to a lack of collateral, steady employment, or a documented credit history. Founded in Bangladesh in 1983, the *Grameen Bank* is among the earliest and most successful microcredit organizations. The Grameen Bank requires no collateral for its loans to needy citizens—mostly women—who vow to use the money to improve the quality of their lives. For example, a woman might receive a small loan to purchase a sewing machine for a new dressmaking business. Because each branch of the Grameen Bank lends to local villagers, lenders know borrowers relatively well, which helps them select deserving loan recipients and motivates the repayment of loans. Each borrower is grouped with four other citizens who do not help repay the loan, but provide peer pressure for the repayment of the loan. Thanks to the success of this system, nearly 99 percent of Grameen Bank loans are repaid.

In both developing and developed countries, many fledgling entrepreneurs have difficulty obtaining loans. One solution is *crowdfunding*, a form of microcredit that funds projects by pooling small amounts of money from large numbers of people. Prospective funding recipients typically post written descriptions of their projects on crowdfunding websites, sometimes accompanied by videos. There are three types of crowdfunding, each with a different type of incentive for potential contributors like you to pitch in some money:

- *Donation crowdfunding.* On donation crowd-funding websites such as Kickstarter.com and RocketHub.com, people seeking funding for their projects list rewards for donors. Examples of the rewards include a thank-you note, a signed copy of a book whose publication is

▲ Microcredit programs such as the Grameen Bank and crowdfunding sites like Kickstarter.com are helping entrepreneurs who would otherwise be unable to get loans to launch their businesses.

Web Pix/Alamy Stock Photo

being funded, or the ability to name your own beer made by a brewery that is being funded. The rewards grow with the size of the donation, but because the rewards are generally small, the primary incentive to donate is a desire to support the projects.

- *Debt crowdfunding.* Investors in the projects listed on debt crowdfunding websites such as Upstart.com and FundingCircle.com expect to receive their money back with interest. There are risks involved, because in some cases the borrower defaults on the loan and the lender gets little or no money back. Some debt crowdfunding websites, such as Kiva.org, are dedicated to lending to people in developing countries. These sites do not charge interest on their loans, nor do the investors receive interest payments.

- *Equity crowdfunding.* Websites such as CircleUp.com and Wefunder.com give investors the opportunity to become part-owners of a business or other project. If the project is successful, the value of that partial ownership could grow substantially. If the project fails, the investment could become worthless.

Challenges for Developing Countries

Developing countries must clear several hurdles as they implement strategies for economic growth. These include crime and corruption, unfortunate geography, weak institutions, and unfit leadership.

microcredit
The extension of small loans to impoverished borrowers.

This section sketches out the problems and some possible cures.

CRIME AND CORRUPTION

Foreign investors are dissuaded by high crime rates, which create safety concerns and necessitate added costs for security. High-crime countries also struggle to attract tourists, whose spending can support progress in places endowed with little more than natural beauty. Jamaica's murder rate of around 40 per 100,000 per year may be one reason some people travel farther and spend more money to go to Hawaii instead, where the murder rate is around 2 per 100,000 per year.

Corruption is the abuse of power by dishonest business leaders or politicians who, for example, steal money earmarked for development projects or demand bribes from people who want to do business in the country. In many developing countries, the need to pay bribes to obtain business licenses and construction permits increases the cost of starting new businesses. Multinational corporations are reluctant to operate in countries where crime and corruption cast doubt on the safety of their investments.

In some cases, governments seize the assets of foreign companies or take control of large parts of international firms. Over the past decade, for instance, Venezuela's government has taken over the assets of companies in the telecommunications, steel, banking, and oil industries. Some of the companies received fair compensation, although the takeovers led to lawsuits from ConocoPhillips and Exxon Mobil.

Transparency International, a nongovernmental organization based in Germany, created the *Corruption Perceptions Index* to measure the corruption problem in 180 countries. The index scores are based on the perceptions of independent experts. Table 18.3 lists the 10 countries with the best and worst corruption scores in 2017. New Zealand and Denmark set the standard for excellence; South Sudan and Somalia reportedly have the largest problems with corruption. The United States ranks sixteenth with a score of 75.

GEOGRAPHY

It has been said that the three things most important to success in business are location, location, and location. A restaurant that would flourish along an interstate highway would fail a mile down a side road that few cars travel. Location is important to growth and development on a larger scale, too. Unfortunately, many less

▲ The Jamaican non-profit organization National Integrity Action posts billboards like this one to remind people that corruption deters investments and slows economic growth.

Table 18.3 Transparency International's Corruption Perceptions Index

Rank	Country	Index Score
The Best 10 Countries		
1	New Zealand	89
2	Denmark	88
3	Finland	85
3	Norway	85
3	Switzerland	85
6	Singapore	84
6	Sweden	84
8	Canada	82
8	Luxembourg	82
8	Netherlands	82
The Worst 10 Countries		
171	Equatorial Guinea	17
171	Guinea-Bissau	17
171	North Korea	17
171	Libya	17
175	Sudan	16
175	Yemen	16
177	Afghanistan	15
178	Syria	14
179	South Sudan	12
180	Somalia	9

Dave Anderson

▲ Location matters. Most developing countries are in the tropical zone, where extreme heat, disease, and political instability made early industrialization untenable. Yet geographical challenges can be overcome. Places with little else but sand can attract tourists whose money can buy almost anything.

developed countries are located where few firms travel. Opening an industrial park in the rain forest would be like opening a Hardee's fast-food restaurant on a side road—business would be much too slow.

Although the fertile heartland of the United States and the oilfields of Norway provide those countries with advantages not found in Jamaica or Rwanda, an abundance of natural resources is neither necessary nor sufficient for economic growth. Globalization extends trade, transportation, and communications around the world. This helps countries with even the smallest advantage in producing a few goods or services to trade for almost anything made anywhere else. Japan and Singapore are examples of export-oriented countries that have used trade to overcome their natural-resource constraints and become wealthy.

The small size of many countries isn't necessarily a detriment to economic growth, either. Although many of the world's poorest countries are small, such as Haiti and Liberia, so are many of the richest countries, such as Luxembourg, Qatar, Japan, and Singapore. A country's disadvantageous location or small size is more than a speed bump on the road to economic growth, but other factors turn out to be more important to a country's potential for development.

WEAK INSTITUTIONS

India is among the countries whose economic development is impeded by weak institutions. In this context, the term *institutions* refers to the laws, customs, and practices of a country. One such problem in

India is weak contract enforcement. Suppose a group of doctors signs a contract with a construction company to build a new medical clinic. The doctors want to be able to rely on that contract as they hire staff members, purchase equipment, and make plans for the new clinic. If contracts are not well enforced due to the laws, customs, and practices in the country, the doctors—among other people trying to start new ventures—face additional risks and uncertainty. In many countries with this problem of weak contract enforcement, entrepreneurs may need to pay bribes and prepare costly back-up plans.

Economic development is also hampered by weak enforcement of property rights. If someone else can seize the property you have purchased for your business, you will not want to invest your time and money in developing that property. The same issue arises for creative work, which is known as *intellectual property:* You would not want to spend your time and money creating artwork, books, songs, photographs, films, or related works in places where weak institutions might not protect your intellectual property.

UNFIT LEADERSHIP

A national leader's skills, intelligence, integrity, charisma, and goals can make or break that nation's economic development efforts. Leaders in developing countries can steer the gains from economic growth and international aid toward investments in human and physical capital, or into the pockets of corrupt officials. How valuable is a capable leader? Consider the corporate world in which the 50 highest paid U.S. executives earn more than $15 million a year. In 2017, the CEO of Nike earned $47.6 million and the CEO of Starbucks earned $21.8 million. Not every high salary is deserved, but CEO salaries reflect the undeniable importance of the person at the top. In countries, as in corporations, leaders set the tone, establish the priorities, and orchestrate the policies for progress.

Most new businesses fail, and most countries are not wealthy, but the best leaders can turn things around. It took the guidance of CEO Howard Schultz to turn around Starbucks, which went from closing 600 stores in 2008 to opening 2,254 new stores in 2017. And it took the perseverance of President Sir Quett Ketumile Joni Masire to lead Botswana through democratization and three decades of rapid economic growth at the end of the last century. For troubled countries, a change in leadership provides an immediate change in outlook and is often a first step for countries seeking reform.

Progress in Economic Development

No single strength guarantees a country's prosperity and no single weakness spells inevitable doom. Many countries successfully use their limited strengths to overcome a variety of weaknesses. We have seen that the real GDP per capita in most countries has risen substantially over the past century. Levels of health and education are rising almost everywhere as well. Since 1950, the average life expectancy at birth for the world's citizens has increased from less than 50 years to almost 70 years. The Human Development Index is also rising steadily for all regions of the world. Since 1980, the global HDI has risen from 0.56 to more than 0.70, indicating meaningful improvements in health, education, and income levels.

There are many economic development success stories. For instance, the Bahamas overcame the challenge of tropical geography and became one of the wealthiest Caribbean countries by combining the strengths of capable leaders, strong banking institutions, and infrastructure support for the country's enormous tourism industry. Hong Kong, Singapore, South Korea, and Taiwan were developing countries 50 years ago. They have since transformed their economies into engines of growth by providing high levels of education for their citizens, developing their industrial sectors, and engaging heavily in international trade.

Sadly, there are also stories of failure. Many countries in Africa and elsewhere struggle with seemingly insurmountable weaknesses, such as the common triple threat of corrupt leaders, weak institutions, and limited infrastructure. Jamaica, in the Caribbean, is among many countries whose great potential is stymied by plodding economic growth and crushing government debt. Economists join the global community in confronting the tough questions and seeking solutions. Hopefully, with improved understanding of the problems and increased awareness of possible solutions, advancements will come to those countries as well.

SUMMARY

Even the most affluent countries would benefit from better transportation systems, improved sources of energy and water, and advancements in medical cures, among other goods and services. In the poorest countries, billions of people live with inadequate food and shelter. By making better use of existing resources, a country can increase its production of some goods without making less of anything. This is an increase in capacity utilization, represented graphically by a movement from a point within a country's production possibilities frontier to a point closer to or on the frontier. With economic growth, the productive capacity of the economy increases, shifting the production possibilities frontier outward.

Economic development is a combination of economic growth and a broader set of improvements in the quality of life. There is compelling evidence that health, literacy, and other nonmaterial aspects of the quality of life improve with economic growth, which makes well-planned economic growth a valid focus. The Human Development Index (HDI) provides a broader measure of economic development based on citizens' life expectancy, years of schooling, and income per capita. The Gini coefficient indicates how evenly income is distributed among citizens in a country.

Common strategies to achieve economic growth and development involve infusions of physical capital, human capital, research and development, and money. Many developing countries face the challenges of crime and corruption, undesirable geographical locations, weak institutions, and unfit leaders. Other things being equal, the low levels of physical capital in developing countries would make new additions of physical capital particularly valuable. Relatively high returns would attract investments in physical capital and help close the gaps of productivity and income between countries. But differences in human capital, infrastructure, crime, institutions, and leadership mean that physical capital isn't necessarily more productive where it is relatively scarce. In developing countries where physical capital *is* relatively productive, political instability and trade barriers can thwart the convergence of physical capital levels and thus productivity levels.

Monetary policy and international aid may provide short-term improvements, but seldom translate into long-term solutions. Foreign direct investment (FDI) can help a developing country build its industrial sector, although most of the resulting profit is sent back to the foreign firm's home country. There is no simple answer to the question of how to improve the quality of life for people in the poorest countries. Yet, little by little, for the world as a whole, technology is improving, life expectancies and literacy rates are increasing, and real GDP per capita is rising. Economists are piecing together the puzzle of how best to spread the growing prosperity by creating new opportunities in developing countries.

KEY TERMS

economic growth, p. 272
economic development, p. 273
developing countries, p. 273

Gini coefficient, p. 275
human capital, p. 278
research and development (R&D), p. 280

foreign direct investment (FDI), p. 281
microcredit, p. 282

PROBLEMS FOR REVIEW

1. A graph illustrating the general relationship between the wealth of a country and the size of the Gini coefficient would look like which of the following? (*Hint:* This chapter doesn't contain such a graph, but it discusses the relationship and provides examples.)
   a. A smile
   b. A frown
   c. A horizontal line
   d. A vertical line
   e. An upward-sloping line

   Explain why the graph has the shape that it does.

2. By reducing its unemployment rate, Sierra Leone was able to produce more diamonds and more dried fish without making less of anything. Use a PPF graph to illustrate the change that occurred in this scenario.

3. After investing in new mining equipment and roads, Jamaica was able to increase its production of coffee and bauxite. Use a PPF graph to illustrate the change that occurred in this scenario. (*Hint:* The graph for this problem should look different from the graph for the previous problem.)

4. Research at Abdou Moumouni University (AMU) in Niger has been hampered by a lack of adequate computer systems. Suppose Mondelez International, Inc., the maker of Oreo cookies and Ritz crackers, wants to invest in a new computer network for one university that is looking into healthy and delicious substitutes for fat. Scholars at both your school and AMU are working on the project. Under what assumptions would Mondelez be better off investing in a computer network at AMU rather than at your school? How does this question relate to the issue of convergence according to the Solow growth model?

5. Suppose that a country's HDI value increased and its real GDP per capita decreased in the same year. What could cause the HDI to increase despite a decrease in real GDP per capita? Is it common to see the HDI and real GDP per capita move in opposite directions? Explain your answer.

6. True or false: An increase in the money supply is among the most effective ways to promote economic growth. Explain your answer.

7. Which of the following is an example of foreign direct investment?
   a. You buy bonds sold by the government of Belize.
   b. You buy stock in BP, a British company.
   c. You buy a cheese factory in Wisconsin.
   d. You buy a winery in France.

8. Give two reasons why microcredit is often the only hope for entrepreneurs in developing nations who need loans.

9. According to Robert Lucas, how can your roommate's investment in human capital make *you* more productive?

10. Volcanic activity is slowly forming new islands in the Pacific Ocean. Suppose you will become the president of one such island, Loihi. When above water, Loihi will have a small population of people on it and a large population of fish surrounding it. Identify three specific elements of the strategy you will adopt to improve the quality of life for the people on the island.

International Trade and Finance

19

Layne Kennedy/Getty Images

LEARNING OBJECTIVES

In this chapter, you will learn to:

1. Explain the benefits of an open economy

2. Calculate the balance of trade and describe its implications

3. Discuss common barriers to trade and their repercussions

4. Use a model of the foreign exchange market to explain how exchange rates are determined

The Bobblemaker company makes thousands of custom bobblehead dolls each year in Shenzhen, China. Bobblemaker makes customized cake-top dolls for weddings, as well as bobblehead angel dolls, Zeus dolls, and everything in between. Each doll ordered in the United States is created from the clays of Asia and travels thousands of miles before wiggling and jiggling in the States. Thanks to international trade, you could have a bobblehead version of your economics professor made and delivered to your door in less time than it takes to get a passport. Personalized bobblehead dolls are among the many items gained through international trade that can enrich your life, but that are not made anywhere near your home.

Why Should I Care?

You can buy a pair of jeans made in the United States for about $150. If you paid less for yours, you can bet they were acquired through international trade. The coffee that wakes you and the chocolate you bake into your favorite cookies come from trees in distant lands. The shoes, dishes, televisions, and tools you buy are probably made on the other side of the globe. International trade is to thank for most of the products we eat, wear, and work with.

Fortunately, U.S. customers aren't doing all the buying. People in other countries buy trillions of dollars' worth of U.S. oil, cars, aircraft, computers, chemicals, movies, and college educations, among other goods and services. **By specializing in what the United States can make at a relatively low cost, and trading for what other countries can make at a lower cost, buyers and sellers in the United States and abroad can all be made better off.** This chapter explains the pros and cons of international trade, the flows of money between countries, and the exchange rates that affect what you pay for a bobblehead doll.

▲ With a closed economy we wouldn't have the chocolate for chocolate chip cookies.

The Benefits of an Open Economy

A country that trades with other countries has an **open economy.** If there were a country that did not engage in international trade, it would have a **closed economy.** The self-sufficiency of a closed economy sounds appealing. It's natural for the citizens of a country to say, "We can make food, clothing, and almost everything we need. Why should we buy these goods and services from other countries and send our money overseas?" Yet it turns out that much can be gained from trade. Even Nigeria and Brazil—the two countries that trade the least, relative to the sizes of their economies—import billions of dollars' worth of goods each year. This section explains the benefits of trade that make it hard to resist.

open economy
An economy that engages in international trade.

closed economy
An economy that does not engage in international trade.

COMPARATIVE ADVANTAGE

When you go to McDonald's, it's not because you can't make a hamburger yourself. You are willing to pay $1 for a McDonald's hamburger because you would spend more than $1 worth of time and money on the shopping and cooking required to make your own hamburger. But McDonald's specializes in making hamburgers and has developed efficient systems of production, so McDonald's spends less than $1 worth of time and money making a hamburger. It is because the opportunity cost of making a hamburger is greater for you than it is for McDonald's that you both benefit from the exchange of your $1 for a McDonald's hamburger. Similar differences in opportunity costs among countries make international trade beneficial for trading partners.

Suppose the United States and China use their resources to make bobblehead dolls and baseball bats. The opportunity cost of making a doll is measured in terms of the number of baseball bats that cannot be made with the available resources because the doll is made instead. The United States and China have different opportunity costs of making a doll, but for simplicity, assume the opportunity cost within each country remains the same as more dolls are made. This makes each country's production possibilities frontier (PPF) a straight line, as shown for the United States in Figure 19.1.

The PPF represents every combination of bats and dolls that could be made per year using all of the country's resources. Point *A* in Figure 19.1 shows that if the United States used all of its resources to make bats, it could make 20 million bats per year. Point *E* shows that if the United States instead used all of its resources to make dolls, it could make 10 million dolls per year.

Each time the number of dolls the United States produces in a year increases by 1, the number of bats that can be made decreases by 2, so the opportunity cost of producing a doll in the United States is two bats. The PPF for the United States is a straight line with a slope of −2 because, moving from left to right along the PPF, the height of the line falls by a quantity

of two bats for each additional doll. For example, moving from point *C* to point *D*, the quantity of dolls increases from 5 million to 6 million, an increase of 1 million, and the quantity of bats decreases from 10 million to 8 million, a decrease of 2 million.

We can find the opportunity cost of each bat by looking at the same graph. Moving upward along the PPF, we see that each time the number of bats increases by 1, the number of dolls decreases by half a doll for each additional bat. For example, moving from point *C* to point *B*, the quantity of bats increases by 1 million and the quantity of dolls decreases by half a million. The opportunity cost of each bat is thus half a doll.

If one country can make a good at a lower opportunity cost than another country, the country with the lower opportunity cost has a **comparative advantage** over the country with the higher opportunity cost of producing that good. Suppose Chinese producers are particularly skilled at making dolls such that their opportunity cost of making each doll is only one bat. Figure 19.2 shows the PPF for China, which is a straight line with a slope of −1 because one million fewer bats can be made when the quantity of dolls increases by

comparative advantage
The ability to make a good at a lower opportunity cost than another country.

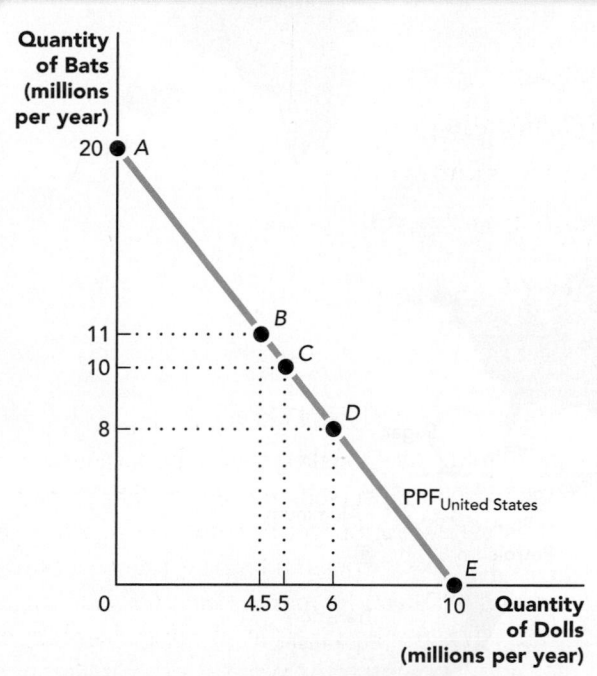

FIGURE 19.1 The Production Possibilities Frontier for the United States
Suppose the United States starts at point C. If the country wants to produce 1 million more dolls, it has to move along the PPF to point D, where 2 million fewer bats can be made. This indicates that the opportunity cost of making each doll is two bats. If, instead, the United States wants to produce 1 million more bats, it has to move along the PPF from point C to point B, where half a million fewer dolls can be made. So the opportunity cost of making each bat is one-half of a doll.

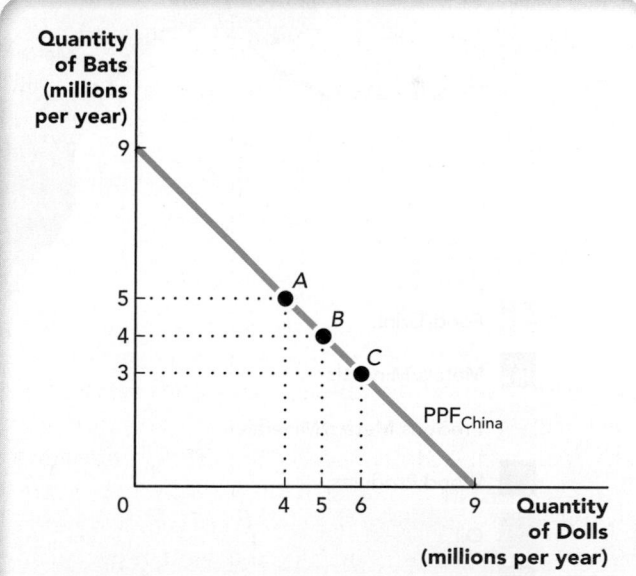

FIGURE 19.2 The Production Possibilities Frontier for China
Suppose China starts at point B. To make another 1 million dolls, it must move along its PPF to point C and make 1 million fewer baseball bats. The opportunity cost of each doll is therefore one bat. Going in the other direction along the PPF, if China moves from point B to point A, it can make 1 million more bats but must give up 1 million dolls. So each bat has an opportunity cost of one doll.

one million. For example, a movement from point *A* to point *B* increases the production of dolls by 1 million, from 4 million to 5 million, but decreases the production of bats by 1 million, from 5 million to 4 million.

China enjoys a comparative advantage over the United States when it comes to making dolls because China's opportunity cost of one bat per doll is less than the U.S.'s opportunity cost of two bats per doll. On the other hand, when it comes to making bats, the United States has a comparative advantage because the opportunity cost of making a bat in the United States is one-half of a doll, which is less than China's opportunity cost of one doll per bat. Table 19.1 summarizes the opportunity costs for each country.

absolute advantage
A country's ability to make more of a good than another country using a given quantity of resources.

Table 19.1 The Opportunity Costs of Bat and Doll Production in the United States and China

	Opportunity Cost per Bat	Opportunity Cost per Doll
United States	1/2 Doll	2 Bats
China	1 Doll	1 Bat

ABSOLUTE ADVANTAGE

A country has an **absolute advantage** over another country in the production of a good if it can make

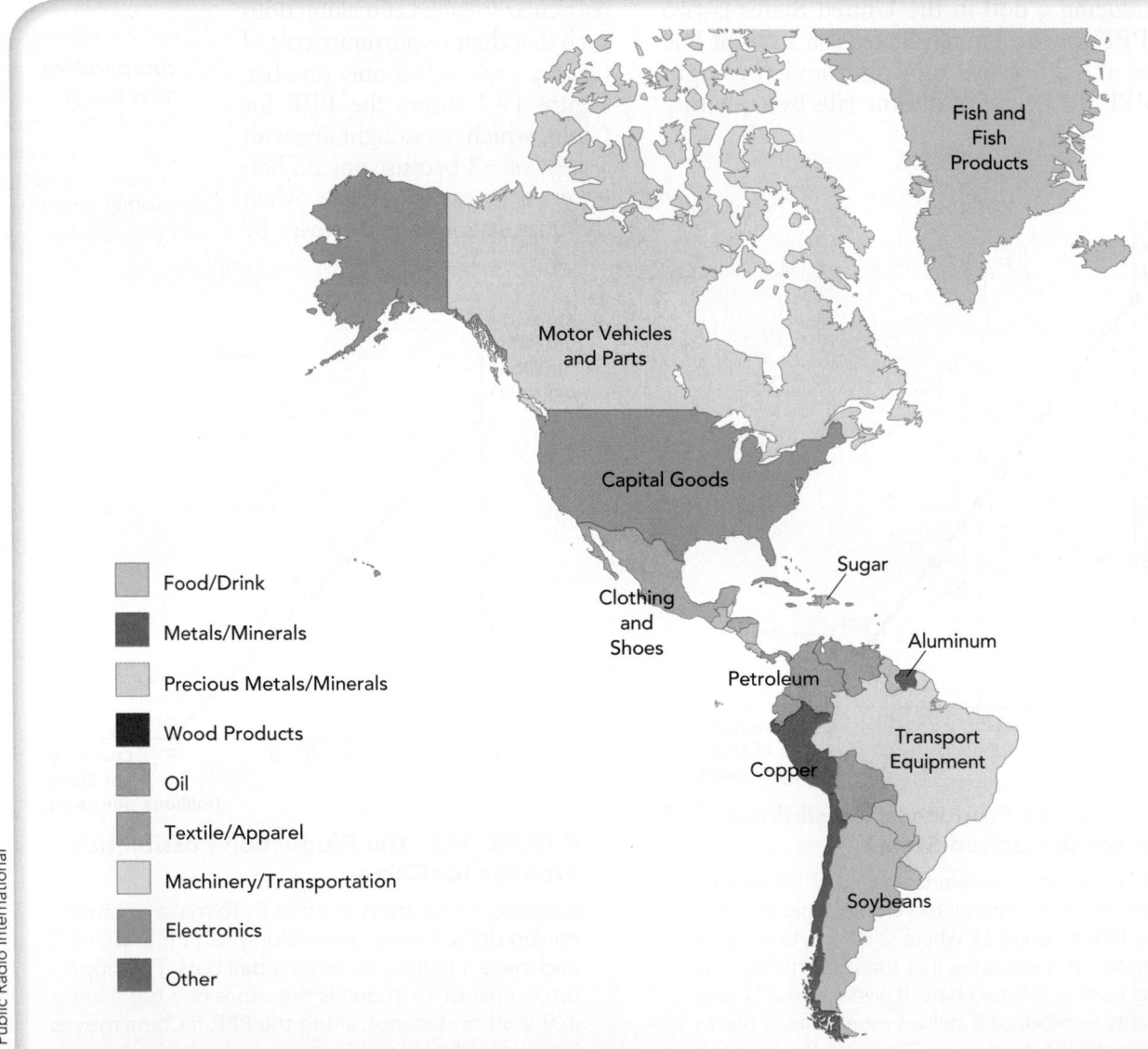

Legend:
- Food/Drink
- Metals/Minerals
- Precious Metals/Minerals
- Wood Products
- Oil
- Textile/Apparel
- Machinery/Transportation
- Electronics
- Other

Map labels: Fish and Fish Products, Motor Vehicles and Parts, Capital Goods, Clothing and Shoes, Sugar, Aluminum, Petroleum, Transport Equipment, Copper, Soybeans

Public Radio International

FIGURE 19.3 Countries' Highest Valued Exports

Countries specialize according to their comparative advantages. This map shows the good, or category of goods, that various countries gain the most revenue from exporting.

more of that good than the other country, using a given quantity of resources. We see from Figures 19.1 and 19.2 that the United States can make more dolls and more bats than China. The United States could make at most 10 million dolls, whereas China could make at most 9 million. Making only bats, the United States could make 20 million, whereas China could make 9 million. So, assuming the countries have the same resources to work with, the United States has an absolute advantage over China in the production of both dolls and bats.

A country with an absolute advantage does not necessarily have a comparative advantage. For example, suppose Jamaica can make up to 5 million dolls or up to 5 million bats. China has an absolute advantage over Jamaica in the production of both goods because China can make more—up to 9 million—of either good. But

both countries have the same opportunity cost of one doll per bat and one bat per doll, so there is no comparative advantage for China or Jamaica in the production of either good.

MUTUALLY BENEFICIAL TRADE

Mutually beneficial trade can occur between two countries whenever either country has a comparative advantage in producing something. This section shows that this is true even if one particular country has an absolute advantage in making every good. Countries generally export the goods they have a comparative advantage in making, and import the goods other countries have a comparative advantage in making. Figure 19.3 shows the good, or category of goods, that various countries gain the most revenues from exporting.

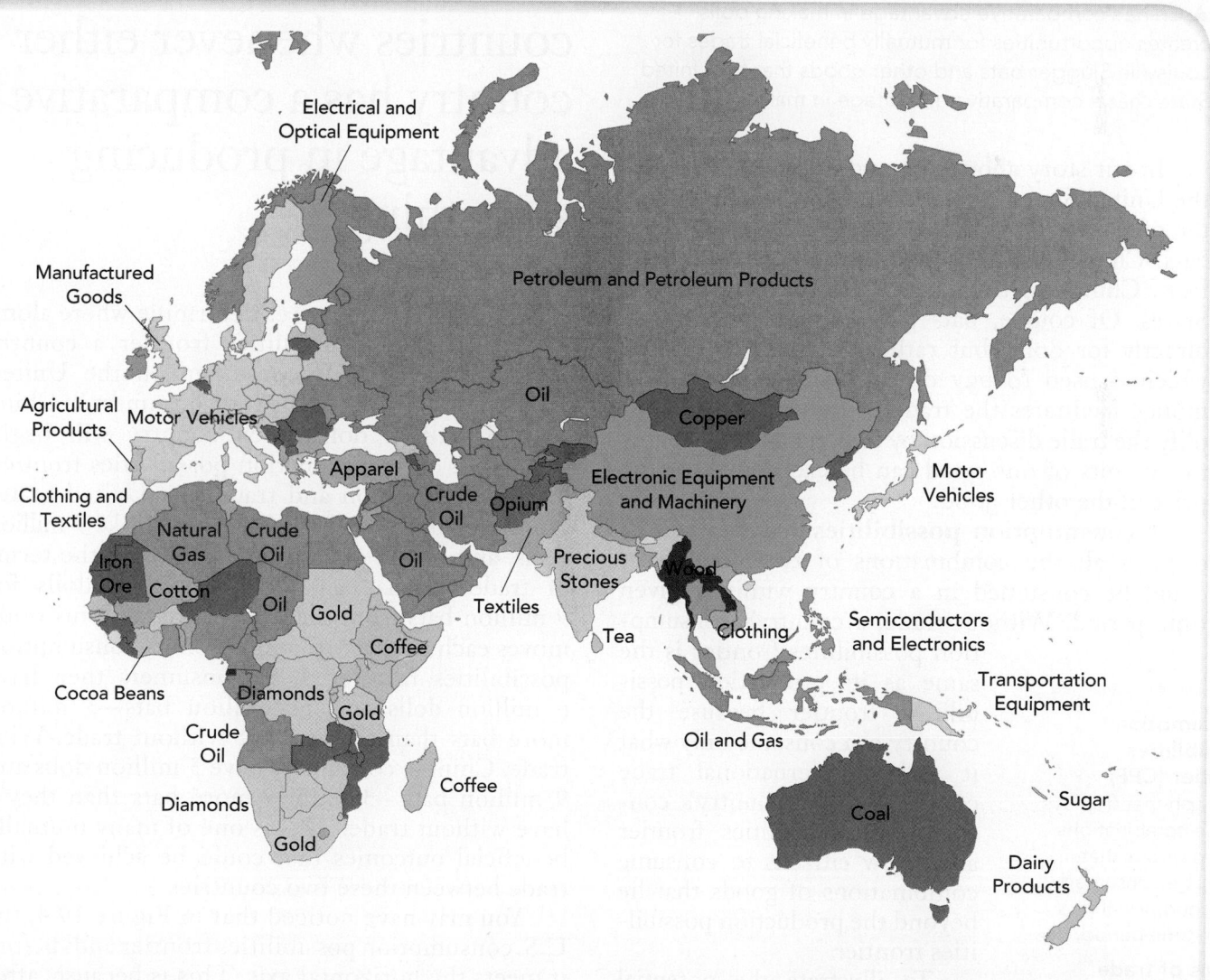

Ed Reinke/AP Images

▲ China's comparative advantage in making dolls creates opportunities for mutually beneficial trades for Louisville Slugger bats and other goods that the United States has a comparative advantage in making.

In our story about bats and dolls, we'll see that the United States and China can both be made better off if the United States specializes in making bats, China specializes in making dolls, and dolls from China are traded for bats from the United States. Of course, bats generally are not traded directly for dolls, but rather are sold for money, which is used to buy dolls. Although the use of money facilitates the trade of goods, we can simplify the trade discussion by looking directly at how many units of one good can be exchanged for the price of the other good.

A **consumption possibilities frontier (CPF)** displays all the combinations of two goods that could be consumed in a country within a given time period. Without trade, a country's consumption possibilities frontier is the same as its production possibilities frontier because the country can consume only what it makes. International trade can expand the country's consumption possibilities frontier and allow citizens to consume combinations of goods that lie beyond the production possibilities frontier.

To illustrate the potential gains from trade, Figure 19.4 shows hypothetical consumption possibilities frontiers for the

consumption possibilities frontier (CPF)
A graph that displays all the combinations of two goods that could be consumed in a country within a given time period.

terms of trade
The rate at which one good is exchanged for another.

United States and China, along with their production possibilities frontiers. Let's assume that each country specializes completely in making one of the two products and that there are no trade barriers (such as tariffs or quotas) that hamper their trade. The slope of each country's CPF depends on the **terms of trade,** which establish the rate at which one good is exchanged for another. In this example, we'll assume that one doll trades for 1.5 bats. The actual terms of trade depend on supply and demand, currency exchange rates (as discussed later in this chapter), and, in some cases, negotiations over the terms of trade.

Mutually beneficial trade can occur between two countries whenever either country has a comparative advantage in producing something.

Consumer preferences determine where along its consumption possibilities frontier a country actually consumes. If consumers in the United States want 6 million dolls and consumers in China want 3 million dolls, each country will begin at point *A* on its production possibilities frontier. With specialization and trade, the United States can make 20 million bats, China can make 9 million dolls, and (given our assumption about the terms of trade) China can trade 6 million dolls for 9 million bats from the United States. This trade moves each country to point *B* on its consumption possibilities frontier. U.S. consumers then have 6 million dolls and 11 million bats—3 million more bats than they'd have without trade. With trade, Chinese consumers have 3 million dolls and 9 million bats—3 million more bats than they'd have without trade. This is one of many mutually beneficial outcomes that could be achieved with trade between these two countries.

You may have noticed that in Figure 19.4, the U.S. consumption possibilities frontier ends before it meets the horizontal axis. This is because, after trading 13.5 million bats for 9 million dolls, the United States would have all the dolls that China could make, and no additional trades could occur.

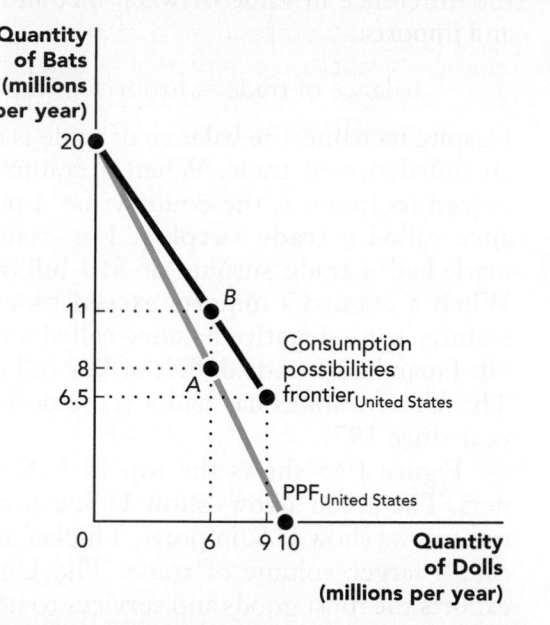
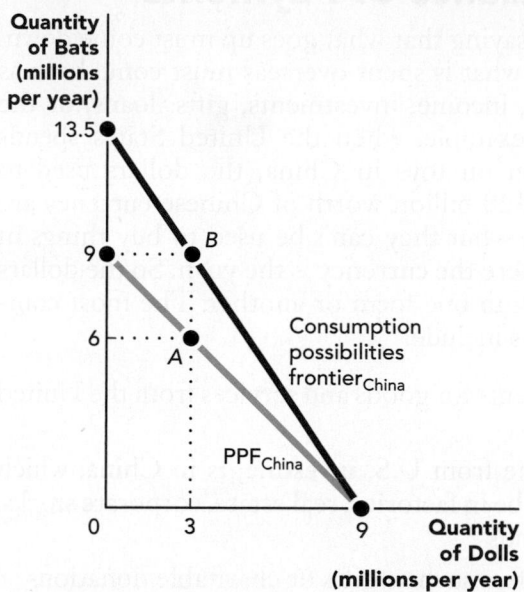

FIGURE 19.4 How Trade Creates a Consumption Possibilities Frontier Beyond Each Country's Production Possibilities Frontier

Specialization according to comparative advantage allows trading partners to consume along consumption possibilities frontiers that exceed their production possibilities frontiers. Suppose that point A in each panel indicates the quantities of dolls and bats each country would produce and consume with no trade. Point B in each panel shows one of the many preferable consumption bundles made possible by specialization and trade.

What terms of trade would make both sides better off from trade?

Suppose you would like to find the mutually beneficial terms of trade for bobblehead dolls that are exchanged for bats. First, look at each country's opportunity cost of making a doll in terms of the number of bats it must give up. We know that the country with the lowest opportunity cost has a comparative advantage in making dolls and can benefit by exporting dolls in exchange for bats made by the other country. Any terms of trade between the opportunity cost of the exporting country and the opportunity cost of the importing country will make both countries better off than they would be without trade.

Again, suppose that the opportunity cost of producing one doll is two bats in the United States and one bat in China. Because China's opportunity cost of producing a doll is lower, it should export dolls and the United States should export bats. As the table to the right indicates, any terms of trade between one and two bats per doll makes both countries better off. Suppose the United States

trades 1.25 bats per doll from China. These terms are better for the United States than the opportunity cost of 2 bats per doll that it faces without trade. Meanwhile, China gets 1.25 bats per doll, which is an improvement over its opportunity cost of 1 bat per doll without trade.

Mutually Beneficial Terms of Trade	
	Opportunity Cost per Doll
China	1 bat
United States	2 bats
Mutually Beneficial Terms of Trade	Between 1 and 2 bats per doll

The Balance of Payments

There's a saying that what goes up must come down. Similarly, what is spent overseas must come back as purchases, income, investments, gifts, loans, or the like. For example, when the United States spends $20 billion on toys in China, the dollars used to purchase $20 billion worth of Chinese currency are put to use—but they can't be used to buy things in China, where the currency is the yuan. So the dollars come back in one form or another. The most common forms include:

- Payments for goods and services from the United States
- Income from U.S. investments in China, which could be in factories, real estate, corporate stocks, or bonds
- Transfers such as gifts or charitable donations
- Chinese investments in U.S. real estate, corporate stocks, bonds, or government securities

A country's **balance of payments accounts** summarize its transactions with other countries over a specified time period. These international transactions include trade in goods and services, receipts and payments of income, investments in stocks and bonds, and foreign direct investment (as explained in Chapter 18). Although the overall value of expenditures and receipts must balance, surpluses in some areas can make up for deficits in other areas. For instance, Americans buy more goods from the Chinese than the Chinese buy from Americans, but the Chinese buy a lot of U.S. Treasury securities and thereby lend our government more money than Americans lend in China. In 2018, the Chinese owned about $1.2 trillion worth of U.S. Treasury securities. The purchase of these bonds sent $1.2 trillion back to the United States to balance $1.2 trillion of the spending by U.S. consumers on goods imported from China.

THE BALANCE OF TRADE

The largest component of the balance of payments is the **balance of trade,** which is the difference in value between a country's exports and imports:

balance of trade = exports − imports

Despite its name, the balance of trade is more often an imbalance of trade. When a country's exports exceed its imports, the country has a positive balance called a **trade surplus.** For example, Denmark had a trade surplus of $10 billion in 2017. When a country's imports exceed its exports, the country has a negative balance called a **trade deficit.** Japan had a trade deficit of $27 billion in 2017. The United States has had a trade deficit in every year since 1975.

Figure 19.5 shows the top 15 U.S. trade partners. The green arrows show U.S. exports, and the red arrows show U.S. imports. Thicker arrows indicate a larger volume of trade. The United States exports the most goods and services to its neighbors in Canada and Mexico and imports the most from China.

Table 19.2 breaks down the balance of trade for the United States. Although services are the largest sector in the U.S. economy, they make up a minority of U.S. exports. Many types of services are difficult to export, but the U.S. does sell legal services, military services, college educations, and travel services (such as airline tickets) to citizens of other countries. In the service category, the value of U.S. exports exceeded the value of U.S. imports in 2017, giving the United States a trade surplus in services. In the larger goods category, the value of U.S. imports such as clothing and toys from China exceeded the value of U.S exports such as industrial machines and aircraft, giving the United States a trade deficit in goods. Overall, the United States had a trade deficit of $568 billion, the largest trade deficit in the world.

balance of payments accounts A summary of a nation's transactions with other countries over a specified time period.

balance of trade The difference in value between a country's exports and imports.

trade surplus The surplus that exists when a country's exports exceed its imports.

trade deficit A deficit that exists when a country's imports exceed its exports.

Table 19.2 U.S. Balance of Trade, 2017

Category	Exports	Imports	Surplus
	(in billions of dollars)		
Goods	$1,551	$2,362	−$811
Services	781	538	243
Total	2,332	2,900	−568

Data source: Bureau of Economic Analysis.

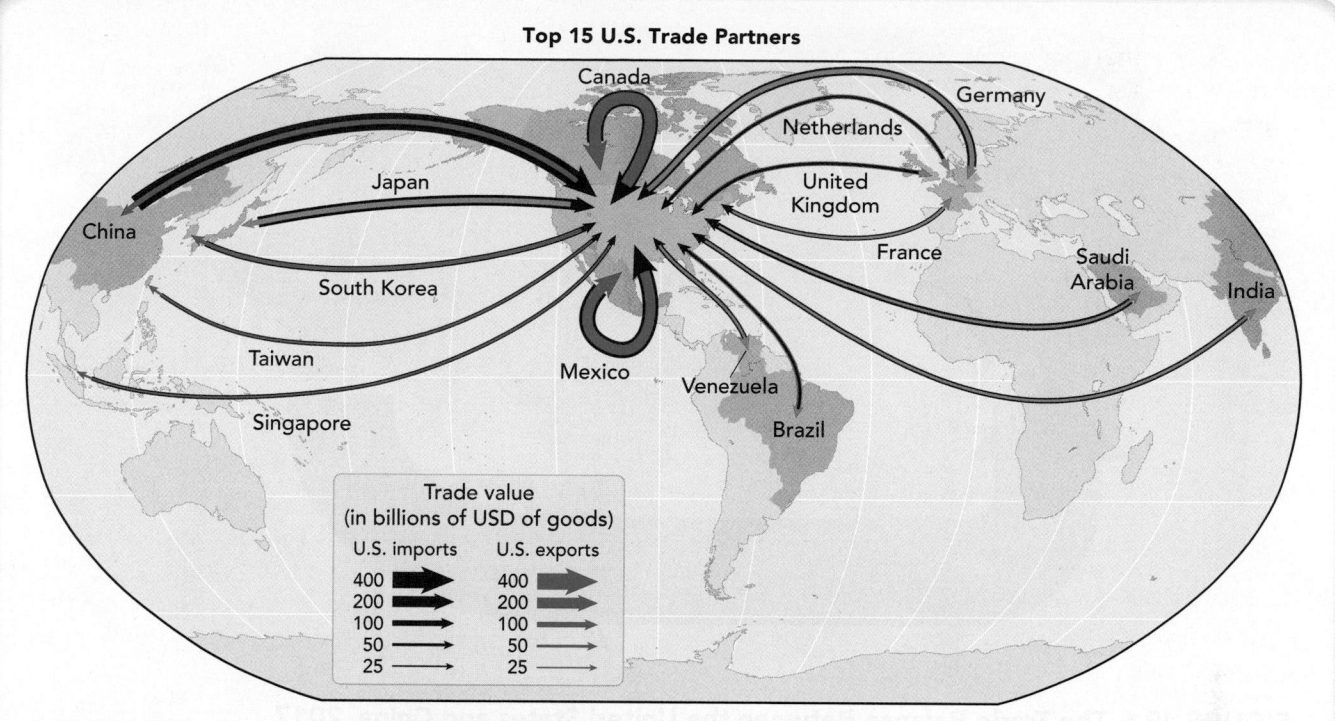

Top 15 U.S. Trade Partners

Trade value
(in billions of USD of goods)

U.S. imports	U.S. exports
400	400
200	200
100	100
50	50
25	25

FIGURE 19.5 The Top 15 U.S. Trading Partners

Canada and Mexico are the biggest customers for U.S. exports. The United States imports the most from China and Canada. The United States' largest trade surplus is with the Netherlands, and its largest trade deficit is with China.

Data source: International Trade Administration/U.S. Census Bureau.

TRADE DEFICITS

Trade deficits are common in the Americas, Africa, and Eastern Europe. There are several reasons for the large and persistent U.S. trade deficits. Except for during recessions, the strong U.S. economy has given consumers enough income to purchase large quantities of goods from overseas, and the relatively low prices in developing countries make their exports especially attractive. Meanwhile, U.S. prices are relatively high, and the citizens of developing countries are relatively poor, which makes it difficult for them to purchase as much from the United States as Americans buy from them. The growing variety and improving quality of goods available from abroad adds to the U.S. appetite for imports. Figure 19.6 shows the balance of trade between the U.S. and China in 2017. China is also among the countries that have made their exports more affordable by depressing the exchange rates for their currencies, as explained later in this chapter.

There are pros and cons to a trade deficit. In the short run, a trade deficit gives U.S. consumers a higher standard of living because more goods and services enter the country as imports than U.S. firms are sending abroad as exports. Sooner or later, this benefit

has its costs. For every dollar by which imports exceed exports, there is a compensating imbalance somewhere else in the balance of payments. It might be that foreign consumers are increasing their ownership of U.S. real estate or firms. For example, a Chinese company called Qingdao Haier paid General Electric $5.4 billion for its appliances division in 2016. And in 2008, the InBev company based in Belgium paid $52 billion for the Anheuser-Busch company, the brewer of roughly half of America's beer. The compensating imbalance might also be a net increase in the foreign ownership of U.S. debt in the form of Treasury securities. When that is the case, the net gain in goods and services Americans purchase this year results in a net loss in goods and services that they can purchase when the debt to foreigners is repaid later.

Barriers to Trade

Every country now has an open economy, but some economies are more open than others. Figure 19.7 shows that imports as a percentage of GDP vary widely across countries. Several factors affect a county's decisions about what and how much to trade. As you have learned, specialization and trade

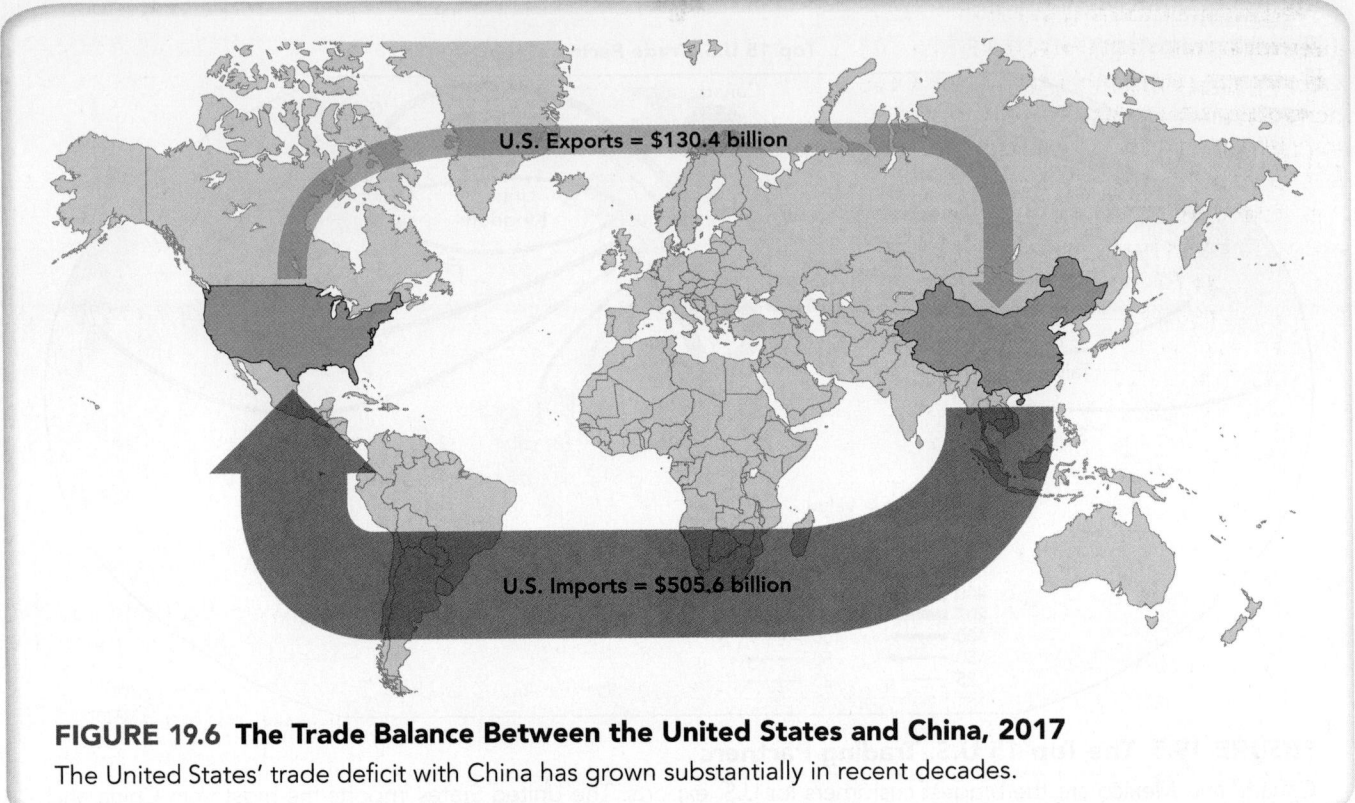

FIGURE 19.6 The Trade Balance Between the United States and China, 2017
The United States' trade deficit with China has grown substantially in recent decades.

can increase the quantities of goods and services consumed in each of the participating countries. However, the gains from trade may not be well understood, and trade can have its obstacles. For instance, high transportation costs complicate trade for countries with primitive transportation systems and countries that specialize in heavy, inexpensive goods—such as bricks, drinking water, watermelons,

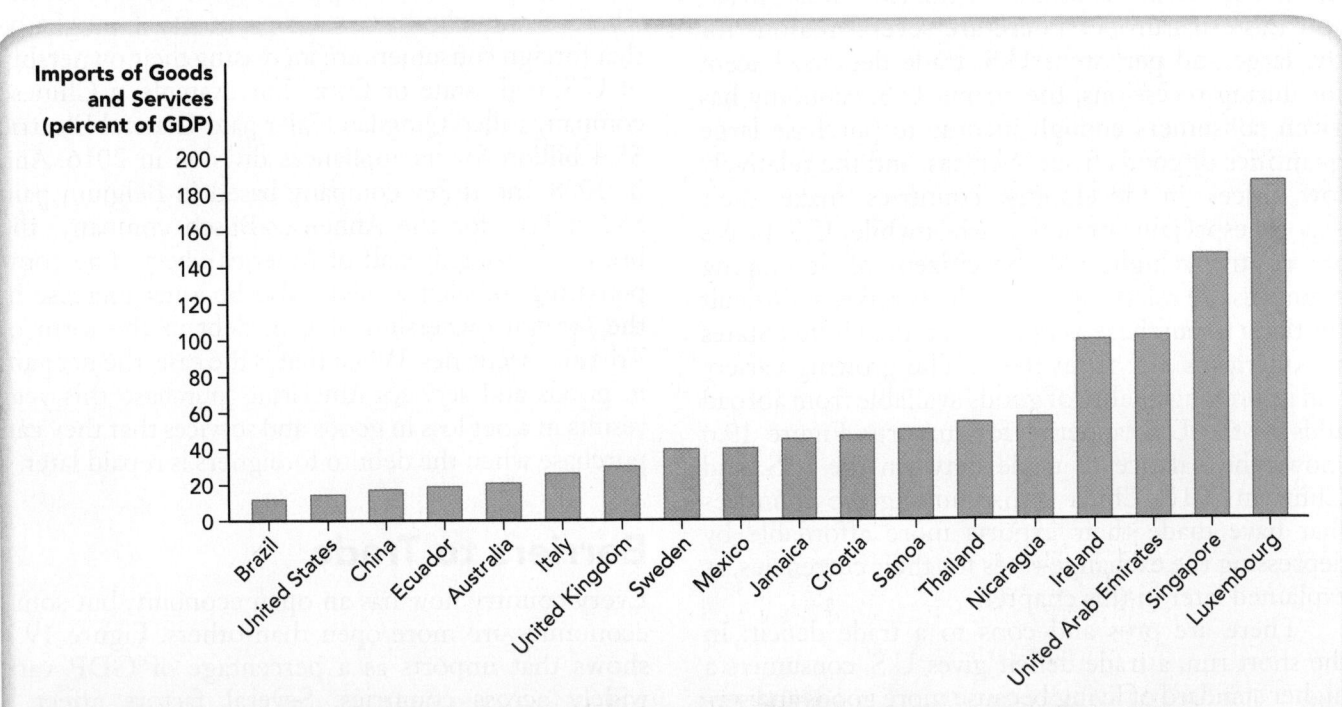

FIGURE 19.7 Imports of Goods and Services as a Percentage of a Country's GDP, 2016
International trade is an important part of every country's economy, but some economies are more open than others. Imports as a percentage of GDP range from 12 percent in Brazil to 191 percent in Luxembourg.

and sand, which are costly to transport. There are also arguments against trade based on

- National security
- National pride
- The protection of workers in declining industries
- The protection of young industries

It can be a matter of national security for a country to make certain products regardless of whether it has a comparative advantage in producing them. No country wants to rely entirely on other countries for things like food or energy, which would render the country helpless if its relationships with key trading partners fell apart.

When a good is important to a country's cultural identity, like tea is to Japan and wool clothing is to Ireland, the country might produce that good for reasons that relate more to national pride than to efficiency.

Some barriers to trade are erected to protect workers. As production shifts toward a country's comparative advantage, workers in declining industries lose their jobs and will remain structurally unemployed until or unless they can obtain the skills required for employment in other industries. For example, in the 1990s, clothing manufacturer Fruit of the Loom employed more than 11,000 workers in Kentucky. Then the company started closing its U.S. plants and moving its operations to countries that have a comparative advantage in textile manufacturing, such as Honduras. In late 2014, the company ended its manufacturing in Kentucky altogether by closing a plant in Russell County and laying off its last 600 workers. As a result, the unemployment rate in Russell County rose from 11.1 percent to a peak of 12.4 percent two months after the closing. Fortunately, the rise in unemployment was only temporary, because Kentucky was also *adding* jobs in *its* areas of comparative advantage. Many workers underwent new training and secured jobs in health care, transportation, construction, and business management, among other industries. One year after the plant closing, the unemployment rate in Russell County was below 8 percent.

Relatively new domestic industries known as *infant industries* may not be competitive at the international level, but a period of protection from lower-priced imports might allow them to develop a comparative advantage. **Protectionism** is the practice of limiting international trade to protect domestic industries and workers. The primary tools of protectionism are *tariffs* and *quotas*.

TARIFFS

A tax on an import is called a **tariff.** The good news about tariffs is that they help domestic industries and provide revenue for the government. Early in American history, tariffs provided most of the revenue for the U.S. government. At their height in 1825, 97.9 percent of all federal government revenue came from tariffs. However, as policy makers began to understand the benefits of free trade, the use of tariffs diminished. Income and payroll taxes were adopted in the early 1900s and became the main sources of revenue for the government. By 1944, tariffs provided only about 1 percent of the federal government's revenues, which is still the case today.

The bad news about tariffs is that they raise prices for domestic consumers. Figure 19.8 shows the U.S. market for bobblehead dolls. The upward-sloping supply curve shows the supply from U.S. firms; the demand curve is for U.S. consumers. If the United States had a closed economy, 5 million dolls would sell for the no-trade equilibrium price of $15 each. Suppose that when trade is unrestricted or "free," an unlimited quantity of dolls can be imported for the equilibrium price in the world market, which is $9. In the absence of a tariff, domestic firms are unable to charge more than the world price. At the $9 world price, domestic firms are willing to supply 3 million dolls. However, domestic consumers demand 7 million dolls for $9. Four million imported dolls make up the difference between the 7 million dolls demanded and the 3 million dolls supplied by domestic firms.

Now suppose that the United States imposes a tariff of $3 per imported bobblehead doll. As Figure 19.9 shows, this raises the amount that must be paid for an imported doll from $9 to $12. Domestic firms can then charge a price of $12 and are willing to supply 4 million dolls for that price. That's an increase of 1 million dolls, compared to the 3 million dolls that firms would

"This is great. They're inflatable trade barriers !"

Cart/cartoonstock.com

protectionism
The practice of limiting international trade to protect domestic industries and workers.

tariff
A tax on an import.

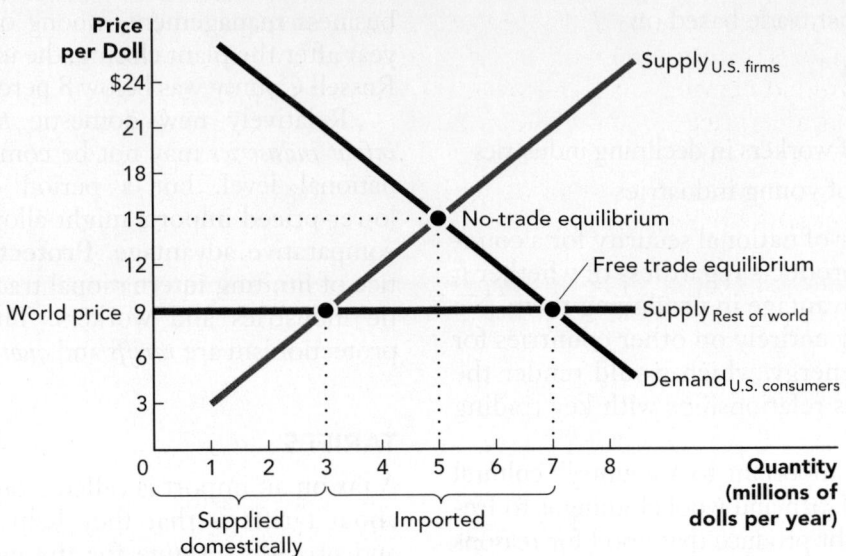

FIGURE 19.8 The U.S. Bobblehead Doll Market with Imports

Without trade, 5 million dolls would be sold at the no-trade equilibrium price of $15. An unlimited quantity of dolls can be imported at the equilibrium world price of $9. With unrestricted "free" trade, domestic firms will be unable to charge more for a doll than the world price of $9. At the world price, domestic firms are only willing to supply 3 million dolls. However, domestic consumers will demand 7 million dolls for $9. The difference between the domestic demand and the domestic supply, 4 million dolls, will be imported.

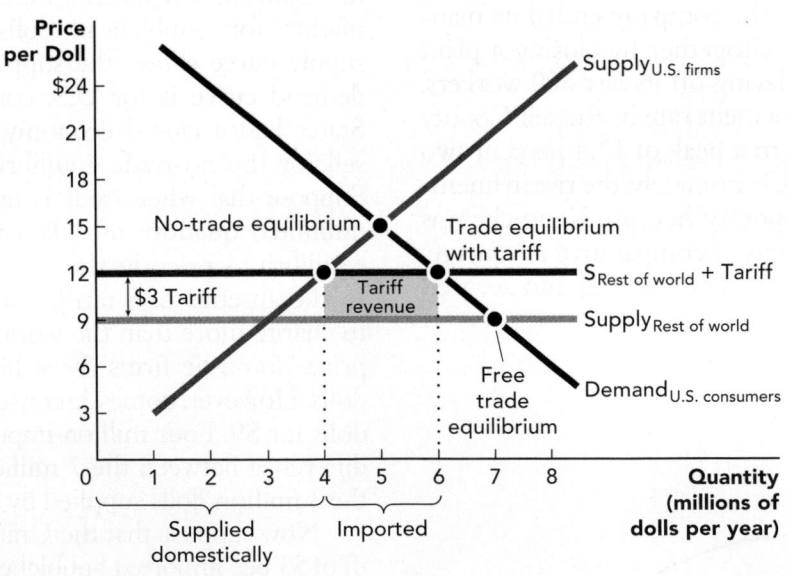

FIGURE 19.9 The U.S. Bobblehead Doll Market with a Tariff

An import tariff raises the cost of dolls supplied by other countries. To buy an imported doll, U.S. consumers pay $9 to the foreign supplier, plus $3 for the tariff, for a total of $12. Domestic firms can then charge a price of $12, for which they are willing to supply 4 million dolls. Domestic consumers demand 6 million dolls for $12. Two million dolls will be imported to make up the difference between the domestic supply and the domestic demand.

International Trade and Finance   **299**

supply at the no-tariff price of $9. With the tariff, domestic consumers demand 6 million dolls for $12, which is a decrease of 1 million dolls compared to the 7 million dolls that consumers would demand at the free-trade price of $9. With the tariff in place, 2 million dolls will be imported to make up the difference between the domestic supply of 4 million and the domestic demand of 6 million. That's a drop of 2 million from the 4 million dolls imported without the tariff. The revenue generated by the tariff will be 2 million × $3 = $6 million.

QUOTAS

A **quota** is a limit on the amount of a good that may be imported within a given period. By restricting the supply of imports, quotas reduce the equilibrium quantity and increase the equilibrium price in the domestic market. Like tariffs, quotas help domestic firms compete with foreign suppliers, but they cause prices to be higher for domestic consumers. Consider sugar, which Americans consume at a rate of about 10.7 million tons per year. To protect domestic sugar-cane and sugar-beet farmers, the U.S. Department of Agriculture (USDA) sets a quota on the amount of sugar that can be imported. In 2018, 1.1 million tons of sugar could be imported before a substantial tariff kicked in.

Suppose the United States imposes an import quota of 2 million bobblehead dolls, as illustrated in Figure 19.10. This prevents the bobblehead market from reaching the free trade equilibrium of 7 million dolls, which would require imports of 4 million dolls rather than 2 million. Instead, consumers face the peach-colored supply curve, which represents the U.S. supply plus the 2 million dolls that can be imported. Imports are not available for less than $9, so the supply$_{U.S. + quota}$ curve doesn't extend below a height of $9. The equilibrium price with the quota is $12. Six million dolls are sold at that price, 4 million of which are supplied domestically. Notice that this quota has the same effect as the $3 tariff on the price, imports, and domestic supply. The difference is that with the quota, no tariff revenue is collected.

RETALIATION AGAINST TRADE BARRIERS

The use of tariffs and quotas is seldom one-sided. When one country feels wronged by a trading partner, retaliation is likely. Early in the Great Depression, the Smoot-Hawley Tariff Act of 1930 increased U.S. tariffs on thousands of imported goods. In response, other countries charged higher tariffs on many goods purchased from the United States. The result was a plunge in U.S. exports. More recently, after the United States proposed tariffs on steel and aluminum in 2018, the European Union quickly threatened to impose retaliatory tariffs

quota
A limit on the amount of a good that may be imported within a given period.

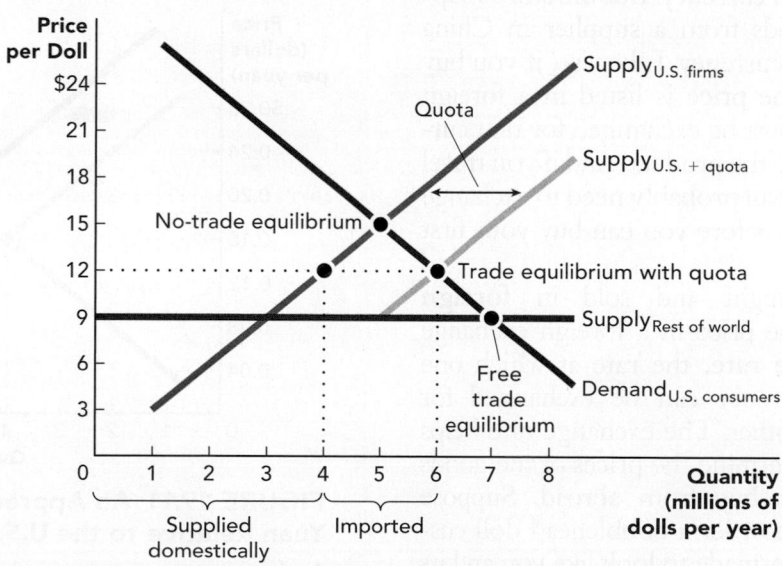

FIGURE 19.10 The U.S. Bobblehead Doll Market with a Quota

If a quota limits bobblehead doll imports to 2 million, U.S. consumers face the peach-colored supply curve that represents the U.S. supply plus the 2 million dolls that can be imported. Imports are not available for less than $9, so the Supply$_{U.S. + quota}$ curve does not extend below $9. The equilibrium price with trade is $12, and the equilibrium quantity is 6 million dolls, 4 million of which are supplied domestically.

on motorcycles, bourbon, and blue jeans made in the United States.

Because trade wars and trade barriers impede the potential benefits of trade, many regional agreements limit the use of tariffs, quotas, and other obstacles to trade. The North American Free Trade Agreement, the Dominican Republic–Central America Free Trade Agreement, and the Asia-Pacific Trade Agreement are a few examples. On a broader scale, since 1947, more than 150 countries have signed the General Agreement on Tariffs and Trade (GATT), the purpose of which is to achieve a "substantial reduction of tariffs and other trade barriers and the elimination of preferences, on a reciprocal and mutually advantageous basis."

In 1994, revisions to the GATT established the World Trade Organization (WTO) to support new agreements on fair trade, help countries work through trade disputes, and monitor national trade policies. For instance, the WTO has worked to resolve a dispute between China and the United States over U.S. tariffs on solar panels, and to prevent more damaging trade wars between these and other countries.

Foreign Exchange Markets

If you go to a store in the United States and buy a bobblehead doll or a pair of jeans made in China, you won't deal directly with foreign currency. But the store's suppliers purchase the goods from a supplier in China with yuan, the Chinese currency. Likewise, if you buy a product online and the price is listed in a foreign currency, your money must be exchanged for that currency before you can buy the product. And if you travel to another country, you will probably need to exchange your currency for theirs before you can buy your first souvenir.

Currencies are bought and sold in **foreign exchange markets.** The price in a foreign exchange market is the **exchange rate,** the rate at which one currency can be exchanged for another. The exchange rate helps determine the prices of the goods you buy from abroad. Suppose you order a bobblehead doll custom-made to look like you and its price is 250 yuan. If the exchange rate is $1 for 10 yuan, you will pay $250 \div 10 = \$25$ for the doll. But if the exchange rate is $1 for 5 yuan, you will pay $250 \div 5 = \$50$ for the doll.

foreign exchange markets
Markets in which currencies are bought and sold.

exchange rate
The rate at which one currency can be exchanged for another.

▲ You can buy Chinese yuan with U.S. dollars in the foreign exchange market.

EQUILIBRIUM IN A FOREIGN EXCHANGE MARKET

A foreign exchange market works just like the markets for goods and services. To buy yuan, the price you would pay is the exchange rate of some amount of U.S. dollars per yuan. In Figure 19.11, the vertical axis measures the price in U.S. dollars per yuan, and the horizontal axis measures the quantity of yuan. The supply curve for yuan is upward sloping because the quantity of yuan that sellers are willing to supply increases as the price paid per yuan increases. The

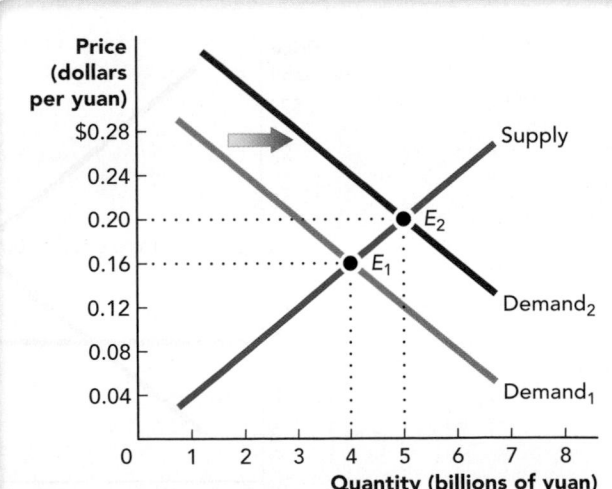

FIGURE 19.11 An Appreciation of the Yuan Relative to the U.S. Dollar

An increase in the demand for yuan in exchange for dollars causes the yuan to appreciate, which means the dollar price of each yuan increases. For example, after the demand increases from Demand₁ to Demand₂, the dollar price of each yuan increases from 16 cents to 20 cents.

demand curve for yuan is downward sloping because as the dollar price per yuan falls, goods from China cost fewer dollars, so consumers holding dollars demand a larger quantity of yuan with which to buy a larger quantity of Chinese goods.

The equilibrium price, or exchange rate, for yuan is found at the intersection of the supply curve and the demand curve, as shown by E_1 in Figure 19.11. An increase in the demand for yuan in exchange for dollars, illustrated by the shift from Demand$_1$ to Demand$_2$, causes the yuan to *appreciate* in value. A **currency appreciation** is an increase in the price of one currency in terms of another currency. A decrease in the supply of yuan in exchange for dollars also causes the yuan to appreciate. When the yuan appreciates relative to the dollar, the dollar price of each yuan increases. For instance, at the new equilibrium E_2 in Figure 19.11, the price of each yuan is 20 cents, up from 16 cents at E_1.

When the demand for yuan decreases, as shown in Figure 19.12, or the supply of yuan increases, the yuan will *depreciate* in value. A **currency depreciation** is a decrease in the price of one currency in terms of another currency. When the yuan depreciates relative to the dollar, the dollar price of each yuan decreases. For example, when the decrease in demand moves the equilibrium from E_1 to E_2 in Figure 19.12, the price of each yuan falls from 16 cents to 12 cents. Next, we'll look at forces that shift supply or demand in the foreign exchange market.

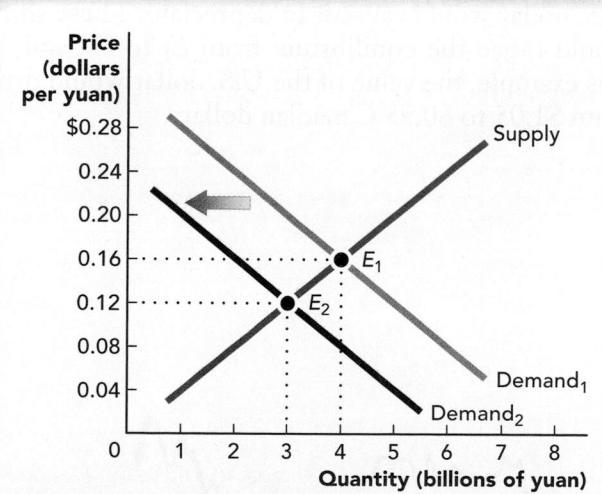

FIGURE 19.12 A Depreciation of the Yuan Relative to the U.S. Dollar

A decrease in the demand for yuan in exchange for dollars causes the yuan to depreciate, which means the dollar price of each yuan decreases. For example, after the demand decreases from Demand$_1$ to Demand$_2$, the dollar price of each yuan decreases from 16 cents to 12 cents.

WHY CURRENCIES APPRECIATE AND DEPRECIATE

Exchange rates are a key determinant of each country's levels of imports and exports. When Brazil's currency, the *real* (pronounced "ray-AHL"), appreciates, it takes fewer real to buy a given quantity of imported goods, so imports into Brazil increase. It also takes more foreign currency to buy Brazil's exports, so exports from Brazil decrease. A depreciation of the country's currency has the opposite effect: The country's imports decrease and its exports increase. In this section we explore the factors that determine exchange rates, which include tastes and preferences, government involvement, relative prices, and relative interest rates.

Tastes and Preferences

Suppose the tastes and preferences of U.S. consumers changed such that they wanted clothing and toys from Norway instead of China. In the foreign exchange market for yuan purchased with U.S. dollars, the demand for yuan would decrease, which would cause a depreciation of the yuan relative to the dollar. There would be a corresponding *appreciation* of the dollar relative to the yuan. For example, suppose the depreciation of the yuan brought the exchange rate for yuan down from $0.20 per yuan to $0.10 per yuan. At the same time, the dollar would appreciate relative to the yuan, because each dollar would buy $1 \div $0.10 = 10$ yuan instead of $1 \div $0.20 = 5$ yuan.

Now consider what would happen in the foreign exchange market for the Norwegian currency, the kroner, purchased with U.S. dollars. The new interest in goods from Norway would increase the demand for kroner with which to buy Norwegian goods. This would cause an appreciation of the kroner relative to the dollar, and a corresponding depreciation of the dollar relative to the kroner.

Government Involvement

It is common for governments to hold reserves of other countries' currencies. In 2018, China's foreign exchange reserves exceeded $3.1 trillion. Some governments manipulate exchange rates by buying or selling their currency in the foreign exchange market. For instance, the Chinese government sometimes buys U.S. dollars with yuan. This causes the U.S. dollar to appreciate relative to the yuan, which makes China's exports less expensive for Americans to buy. China's devaluation of the yuan is controversial because it gives

currency appreciation
An increase in the price of one currency in terms of another currency.

currency depreciation
A decrease in the price of one currency in terms of another currency.

China what can be seen as an unfair advantage in trade, and it increases the U.S. trade deficit with China. Many other countries, including Libya, Algeria, Saudi Arabia, Singapore, and Taiwan, have been accused of intentionally devaluing their currencies.

In some countries, the governments or central banks buy and sell currencies in an effort to maintain a **fixed exchange rate** between their currency and a particular foreign currency. For example, Belize buys and sells the Belize dollar and the U.S. dollar to fix, or "peg," the exchange rate at one U.S. dollar per two Belize dollars. Fixed exchange rates remove the uncertainty of market-determined rates. A fixed exchange rate that devalues the domestic currency has the added benefit of promoting exports, as already discussed. Other countries that peg their currencies to the U.S. dollar include Djibouti, Qatar, and the Bahamas. Denmark and Bulgaria are examples of countries that peg their currencies to the euro, which is the currency of 19 countries in Europe.

fixed exchange rate
An exchange rate that is kept stable by currency purchases and sales by a country's government or central bank.

floating exchange rate
An exchange rate determined by market forces.

A fixed exchange rate also has its drawbacks. By pegging its currency to another currency, a country makes itself more vulnerable to changes in the other country's economy. If the U.S. dollar depreciates relative to the euro, the Belize dollar that is pegged to the U.S. dollar also depreciates relative to the euro. And some central banks have difficulty maintaining the large foreign currency reserves needed to manipulate the foreign exchange market. For these and related reasons, most countries allow the exchange rate for their currency to fluctuate. In the absence of currency manipulations, a country's exchange rate is determined by market forces, and the country is said to have a **floating exchange rate.** Figure 19.13 shows the floating exchange rate between the U.S. dollar and the Canadian dollar over a recent one-year period.

Relative Price Levels
The supply and demand for a country's goods depends partly on how that country's prices compare to the prices in other countries. If the United States experienced a bout of inflation and Canada did not, the prices of U.S. goods and services would increase relative to the prices of Canadian goods and services. U.S. customers would then increase their imports from Canada to take advantage of Canada's relatively low prices. Before they could buy more Canadian goods, U.S. importers would need to supply more U.S. dollars in exchange for Canadian dollars, which would shift the supply curve for U.S. dollars to the right as shown in Figure 19.14.

Meanwhile, consumers in Canada would demand fewer imports from the United States due to the higher U.S. prices. If the demand for U.S. imports is elastic, imports would decrease more than in proportion to the price increase. Canadian consumers would then need fewer U.S. dollars, so the demand curve for U.S. dollars would shift to the left. Both the increase in the supply and the decrease in the demand for the U.S. dollar would cause it to depreciate. These shifts would move the equilibrium from E_1 to E_2, and, in this example, the value of the U.S. dollar would drop from $1.05 to $0.95 Canadian dollars.

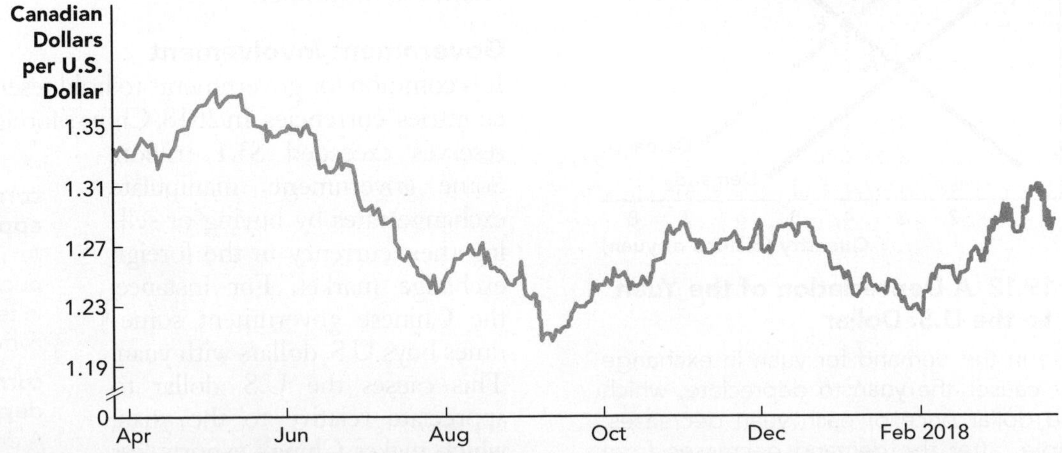

FIGURE 19.13 Canadian Dollars per U.S. Dollar
The exchange rate between the Canadian dollar and the U.S. dollar is influenced by tastes and preferences, government policies, relative price levels, and relative interest rates.

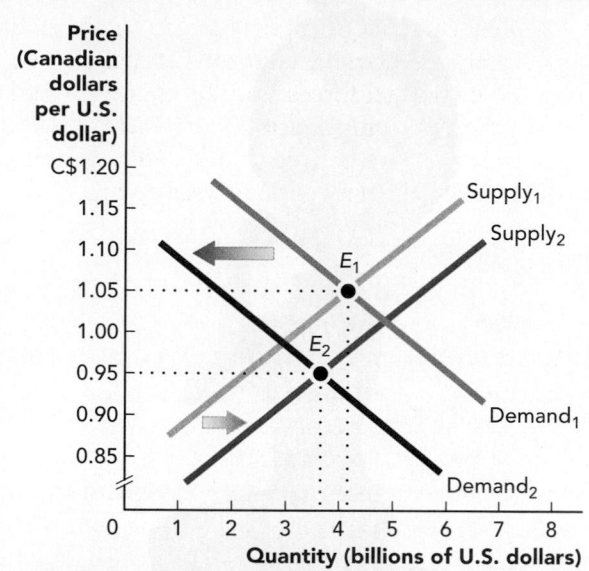

Price (Canadian dollars per U.S. dollar)

C$1.20
1.15
1.10
1.05
1.00
0.95
0.90
0.85

Supply₁
Supply₂
E₁
E₂
Demand₁
Demand₂

0 1 2 3 4 5 6 7 8

Quantity (billions of U.S. dollars)

FIGURE 19.14 An Increase in Relative Prices

If prices in the United States increased relative to prices in Canada, U.S. consumers would buy more Canadian goods. To do so, more U.S. dollars would be supplied in exchange for Canadian dollars, shifting the supply curve from Supply₁ to Supply₂. The higher U.S. prices would also cause Canadian consumers to buy fewer U.S. goods. If their demand for U.S. imports is elastic, the decrease in imports would be large relative to the increase in prices, so Canadian consumers would not need as many U.S. dollars to buy the new quantity of imports. This would shift the demand curve for U.S. dollars from Demand₁ to Demand₂. Both the decrease in the demand for U.S. dollars and the increase in the supply of U.S. dollars would cause the U.S. dollar to depreciate.

Relative Interest Rates

People with savings to deposit in interest-bearing accounts want to put their money where interest rates are high. If the interest rates paid on bank deposits in Japan rise above the interest rates in other countries, foreigners with substantial savings will shift their money into Japanese banks. But first, they must exchange their money for Japan's currency, the yen. So when interest rates rise in Japan, the demand for yen in the foreign exchange market increases.

Like the foreign savers, Japanese savers want to deposit their money where it will earn the most interest. Before the rise in Japanese interest rates, those savers would exchange their yen for the currency of another country with higher interest rates. After the rate increase in Japan, Japanese savers will no longer need to exchange their yen for another currency in order to receive the highest possible interest payments. So an increase in interest rates in Japan causes a decrease in the supply of yen in the foreign exchange market. Both the increase in demand and the decrease in supply of yen cause it to appreciate as a result of an increase in the interest rates paid in Japan.

Recall from Chapter 17 that monetary policy causes interest rates to rise or fall. Now you also know that interest rates affect exchange rates. This allows central banks to influence international trade by changing interest rates that change exchange rates. For example, with expansionary monetary policy, a central bank could decrease domestic interest rates, which would decrease the value of the domestic currency, which would make the country's exports cheaper for foreign consumers to buy.

SUMMARY

The members of your family may specialize in particular tasks when it comes to maintaining your home and supporting your family. The workers in your community specialize in particular jobs. Likewise, the countries of the world specialize in the production of particular goods and services sold in the global economy. Whenever one country can make a good at a lower opportunity cost than another country, that comparative advantage makes it possible for each of those countries to gain from trade. Those gains are the reason every country has an open economy.

Not everything about international trade is desirable, however. When a good is imported, the people who would have made the good domestically must try to find work producing something else, which might require a whole new set of skills. To import goods is to become vulnerable to fragile relationships with trading partners. Trade can also prevent the development of industries that could flourish domestically if given a chance.

A country's balance of payments accounts summarize its international transactions over a particular time period. Money spent overseas comes back, for instance, as purchases, income, investments, loans, or gifts. When expenditures on U.S. imports exceed receipts for U.S. exports, the resulting trade deficit must be offset by some other type of inflow from abroad. For example, a net outflow of dollars for goods and services might lead to a net inflow of dollars for the purchase of U.S. real estate or for loans to fund the government's debt.

Tariffs and quotas are among barriers to trade that many countries erect to protect domestic industries. By taxing or limiting imports, tariffs and quotas increase domestic prices and increase the quantity of goods supplied by domestic firms. However, other countries typically retaliate against trade barriers by increasing their own trade barriers. The result is escalating trade wars and the loss of potential gains from trade. Free-trade agreements and organizations such as the World Trade Organization were formed to discourage trade barriers and prevent damaging trade wars.

The foreign exchange markets resemble the markets for most goods and services, except that, in a foreign exchange market, one country's currency is bought and sold in exchange for another country's currency. Consider the foreign exchange market for U.S. dollars in exchange for Japanese yen. When the supply of dollars decreases or the demand for dollars increases, the dollar appreciates, meaning that it is worth more yen. When the supply of dollars increases or the demand for dollars decreases, the dollar depreciates, meaning that it is worth fewer yen. Factors that influence the supply and demand in foreign exchange markets include government purchases of foreign currencies, the relative price levels between countries, the relative interest rates between the countries, and the tastes and preferences for imported goods, such as baseball bats and bobblehead dolls.

Royal Bobbles

▲ Virtually anything could be made in the U.S. economy, but Americans embrace international trade because, as much as we can do on our own, we can do even more to improve our standard of living with trade.

KEY TERMS

open economy, p. 288
closed economy, p. 288
comparative advantage,
    p. 289
absolute advantage, p. 290
consumption possibilities frontier
    (CPF), p. 292
terms of trade, p. 292

balance of payments accounts,
    p. 294
balance of trade, p. 294
trade surplus, p. 294
trade deficit, p. 294
protectionism, p. 297
tariff, p. 297
quota, p. 299

foreign exchange markets, p. 300
exchange rate, p. 300
currency appreciation, p. 301
currency depreciation, p. 301
fixed exchange rate, p. 302
floating exchange rate, p. 302

PROBLEMS FOR REVIEW

1. True or false: When one country has an absolute advantage over another country, there are definitely opportunities for mutually beneficial trade. Explain your answer.

2. Use the graph to answer each of the following questions:

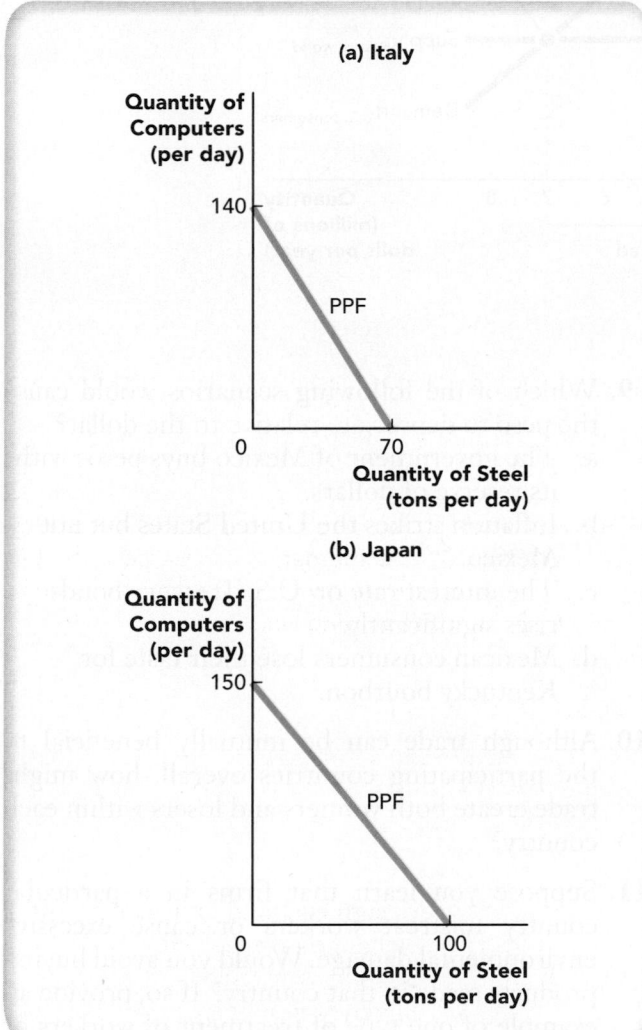

(a) Italy

Quantity of Computers (per day)

140

PPF

0   70

Quantity of Steel (tons per day)

(b) Japan

Quantity of Computers (per day)

150

PPF

0   100

Quantity of Steel (tons per day)

a. What is Italy's opportunity cost of producing one computer?
b. What is Japan's opportunity cost of producing one computer?
c. Which country has a comparative advantage in computer production?

d. Which country has a comparative advantage in steel production?
e. Which country has an absolute advantage in computer production?
f. Which country has an absolute advantage in steel production?
g. If these countries specialize and trade, which country should specialize in computer production?

3. Calzonia and Pizzaland both make calzones and pizza, but Pizzaland chefs are less proficient than Calzonian chefs in the dough-folding process that converts pizza ingredients into calzones. Workers in Calzonia can make at most 10 calzones per hour, and at every level of production the opportunity cost of one calzone is one pizza. Workers in Pizzaland can make at most 12 calzones per hour, and every time they decrease calzone production by 1, they can make 1.5 additional pizzas.

a. Draw graphs of the PPFs for Calzonia and Pizzaland with the quantity of pizzas measured on the vertical axis.
b. If Calzonia trades calzones for pizzas from Pizzaland, what is the range of prices, in terms of pizzas per calzone, that would make both countries better off from trade?
c. Suppose that Pizzaland makes only pizza, Calzonia makes only calzones, and the terms of trade are 1.25 pizzas from Pizzaland for each calzone from Calzonia. On the graph for part a, draw the consumption possibilities frontiers for Calzonia and Pizzaland and label the CPF_C and CPF_P.

4. Answer the following questions on the basis of the information provided in problem 3:

a. Which country has a comparative advantage in pizza production?
b. Which country has a comparative advantage in calzone production?
c. Which country has an absolute advantage in the production of calzones?
d. Which country has an absolute advantage in the production of pizzas?

5. Explain one pro and one con of U.S. trade deficits.

6. Use the graph to answer the following questions:

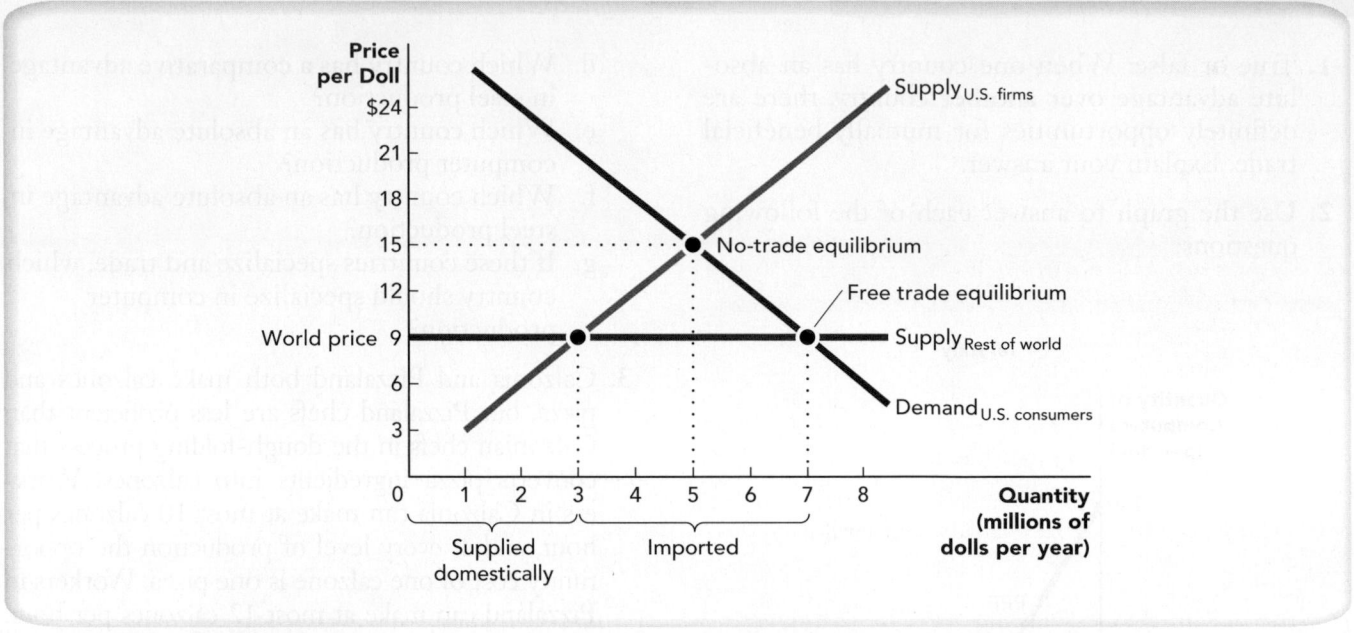

a. What is the smallest tariff that would lead all bobblehead dolls to be supplied by U.S. firms?

b. In the absence of a tariff, what is the smallest quota that would have no effect on international trade?

7. Which of the following equalities must hold for a country?
a. Imports = exports
b. Incoming gifts and donations = outgoing gifts and donations
c. Foreign investments in real estate = domestic investments in real estate
d. Value of receipts from other countries = expenditures on international transactions

8. Draw a graph of the foreign exchange market for Mexican pesos purchased with U.S. dollars. Label the equilibrium exchange rate ER_1 and the equilibrium quantity Q_1. Show how the graph would change if cars made in Mexico became more popular among U.S. consumers. Label the new equilibrium exchange rate ER_2 and the new equilibrium quantity Q_2.

9. Which of the following scenarios would cause the peso to depreciate relative to the dollar?
a. The government of Mexico buys pesos with its reserve of dollars.
b. Inflation strikes the United States but not Mexico.
c. The interest rate on U.S. Treasury bonds rises significantly.
d. Mexican consumers lose their taste for Kentucky bourbon.

10. Although trade can be mutually beneficial to the participating countries overall, how might trade create both winners and losers within each country?

11. Suppose you learn that firms in a particular country mistreat workers or cause excessive environmental damage. Would you avoid buying products made in that country? If so, provide an example of one type of treatment of workers or the environment that you would consider unacceptable. If not, explain why not.

absolute advantage A country's ability to make more of a good than another country using a given quantity of resources.

accounting profit Total revenue minus total explicit cost.

adverse selection When one party takes advantage of information the other party lacks when the second party is deciding what to buy or sell.

aggregate demand curve A curve that shows the quantity of all final goods and services demanded in an economy at various price levels.

asymmetric information When either the buyer or the seller has more information than the other party.

automatic stabilizers Tax and transfer-payment policies that automatically dampen fluctuations in economic activity.

average total cost Total cost divided by the quantity of output.

average variable cost A firm's variable cost divided by the quantity of its output.

balance of payments accounts A summary of a nation's transactions with other countries over a specified time period.

balance of trade The difference in value between a country's exports and imports.

bar chart (bar graph) A chart in which rectangular bars indicate the value of a dependent variable for each value of an independent variable.

barter The exchange of goods and services for other goods and services.

behavioral economics The study of how economic decision making is influenced by the limits of the human mind.

black market An illegal market.

Board of Governors of the Federal Reserve A seven-member board that manages the operations of the Federal Reserve.

boom A time of great expansion in economic activity.

bounded rationality The limits on optimal decision making that result from people's limited cognitive skills, information, or time.

bounded willpower The limits on self-control that prevent people from achieving difficult but worthwhile goals.

budget constraint The set of points on a graph that represents all the combinations of two goods that exhaust a consumer's budget.

budget deficit The excess of government expenditures over government revenues over a given period, usually one year.

budget surplus The excess of government revenues over government expenditures over a given period, usually one year.

business cycle The alternation between expansions and contractions in the economy's level of output.

capital The manufactured goods used to produce other goods or services.

capital depreciation Wear on capital during the production process that depletes the capital's value.

cartel A group of producers that conspires to restrict the quantity of output and increase their profits.

ceteris paribus A Latin phrase that means "other things remaining unchanged."

change in demand A shift in the entire demand curve, indicating a change in the quantity demanded at each price.

change in supply A shift of the supply curve, indicating a change in the quantity supplied at each price.

circular-flow diagram A diagram that shows how goods, services, and money flow throughout an economy.

classical theory Economic theory rooted in the idea that the economy can stabilize itself.

Clayton Antitrust Act Legislation that prohibits anticompetitive actions such as price discrimination, mergers, and exclusive trade agreements between firms when such actions would substantially decrease competition in a market.

closed economy An economy that does not engage in international trade.

coinsurance When the insured pay some percentage of the costs incurred.

collateral An asset a borrower forfeits to a lender if the borrower doesn't repay the loan.

command economy An economy in which economic decision making is centralized and decisions are made by the government or citizen groups rather than market forces.

commercial banks Banks that are primarily in the business of accepting deposits, making loans, and providing similar services to firms and the general public.

commodity money Money that has value apart from its use as money.

communism An economic system under which legislators from a single political party—the Communist party—determine production levels and wage rates.

comparative advantage The ability to make a good at a lower opportunity cost than another country.

compensating wage differential A wage premium that compensates for the exceptional burdens of a job.

complements in consumption Goods for which a decrease in the price of one good causes an increase in the demand for the other good(s).

complements in production Goods or services produced together using the same inputs.

Consumer Price Index (CPI) A measure of variation in the overall price level of goods and services purchased by typical consumers.

consumer surplus The difference between the most a consumer would be willing to pay for a good and the amount the consumer actually pays.

consumption possibilities frontier (CPF) A graph that displays all the combinations of two goods that could be consumed in a country within a given time period.

contractionary monetary policy Monetary policy designed to slow the economy down and fight inflation.

copayment A fixed amount of money that someone with insurance must pay each time the individual incurs a cost covered by the insurance.

copyright A legal right given to the creator of an original work to be the only seller of that work.

corporation A type of firm that exists as a legal entity distinct from its owners.

credit unions Not-for-profit financial cooperatives with the central mission of providing affordable loans for the working class.

cross-price elasticity of demand A measure of how the price of one good affects the quantity demanded of another good.

crowding out The effect of more government spending causing less private investment.

currency Bills and coins used as money.

currency appreciation An increase in the price of one currency in terms of another currency.

currency depreciation A decrease in the price of one currency in terms of another currency.

cyclical unemployment Unemployment caused by contractions in the economy.

deadweight loss The loss of consumer or producer surplus caused by an inefficient quantity of output.

debt The accumulation of past budget deficits, minus past budget surpluses.

deductible The amount that insurance customers must pay before their insurance starts covering costs.

deflation A decrease in the general price level of goods and services.

demand curve A curve that illustrates the relationship between the price of a good and the quantity demanded.

demand schedule A table that indicates the quantity of a good or service that would be demanded in a given period at various prices.

dependent variable A measure whose value is influenced by another variable.

depression An economic downturn loosely defined as a 10 percent or more decrease in output over the period of a year.

derived demand Demand for a factor that is derived from the demand for whatever the factor produces.

developing countries Countries whose citizens experience a relatively low quality of life.

diminishing marginal utility The decrease in the marginal utility received from a good as more of it is consumed.

discount rate The interest rate that Federal Reserve Banks charge financial institutions for short-term loans.

discouraged workers People who are willing and able to work and have looked for a job in the past year, but who have not looked for a job in the past four weeks because they have given up on finding a job.

discretionary spending Government spending authorized by annual appropriations acts.

diseconomies of scale An increase in a firm's long-run average total cost as the level of output increases.

disposable income The income that remains for recipients to spend or save after they have paid their taxes.

dividends A portion of profits a firm distributes to its shareholders.

dominant strategy A strategy that is best for one player in a game regardless of what the other player does.

duopoly An oligopoly dominated by two firms.

economic development A combination of economic growth and a broader set of non-material improvements in the quality of life.

economic growth An increase in the productive capacity of an economy.

economic profit Total revenue minus total cost, with total cost including both total explicit cost and total implicit cost.

economics The study of decision making under conditions of scarcity.

economies of scale A decrease in a firm's long-run average total cost as the level of output increases.

economy A system for coordinating the production and distribution of goods and services.

efficient A condition that is satisfied when no alternative allocation of a resource can make some people better off without making other people worse off.

elastic demand When the price elasticity of demand is greater than 1.

entrepreneurship The willingness and ability to take risks, initiate activities, innovate, and organize the other factors of production to provide goods and services.

equation of exchange An equation that expresses the relationship between the money supply (M), the velocity of money (V), the price level (P), and real GDP (Y): $MV = PY$.

equilibrium point The point on a graph where the supply curve and the demand curve intersect.

equilibrium price The price that brings the market to the equilibrium point.

equilibrium quantity The quantity that is both demanded and supplied at the equilibrium price.

excess reserves Reserves that can be lent out.

exchange rate The price of one country's currency in terms of another country's currency.

excise tax A tax on a particular good or service.

exclusive dealing agreement An agreement that prevents a buyer from making purchases from the competitors of a seller.

expansionary fiscal policy Government policy that shifts the aggregate demand curve to the right.

expansionary monetary policy Monetary policy designed to stimulate the economy.

explicit costs Costs that involve actual payments of money.

exports Goods or services sold to foreign buyers.

externalities Side effects felt by people other than those causing the effects.

factor markets All of the buyers and sellers of factors of production in the economy.

factors of production The resources or inputs used to create goods and services.

federal funds rate The interest rate that banks charge each other for short-term loans.

Federal Open Market Committee (FOMC) The body within the Federal Reserve System that is ultimately responsible for making monetary-policy decisions.

Federal Reserve System The central bank of the United States.

fiat money Money that has value because the government says it does.

final goods and services Goods and services purchased by their ultimate consumer rather than by a firm for use in producing something else.

firm Any enterprise that employs factors of production and sells goods or services.

fiscal policy The use of government spending, taxes, and transfer payments to help stabilize the economy.

fixed cost The cost of fixed inputs such as capital, the quantity of which cannot be varied in the short run.

fixed exchange rate An exchange rate that is kept stable by currency purchases and sales by a country's government or central bank.

fixed input An input whose quantity cannot be varied in the short run.

floating exchange rate An exchange rate determined by market forces.

foreign direct investment (FDI) An investment made to acquire a lasting interest in a firm operating in another country.

foreign exchange markets Markets in which currencies are bought and sold.

foreign trade effect The substitution away from domestic goods and services and toward foreign goods and services that occurs when the domestic price level rises (and the opposite substitution when the domestic price level falls).

fractional reserve banking system A banking system that allows banks and thrifts to lend out all but a fraction of the money they receive as deposits.

free ride To enjoy the benefits of a good without paying for it.

frictional unemployment Unemployment caused by the need for workers and employers to spend time searching for each other.

full employment The level of employment when there is no cyclical unemployment.

full-employment (or potential) output The level of real GDP that can be produced with full employment.

game theory The study of behavior among players whose decisions are interdependent.

Gini coefficient A measure of income inequality that equals 0 if incomes in a country are equal, and equals 1 if the richest person earns all the income.

gold standard A monetary system in which the value of money is measured in terms of gold.

government An organization of individuals with the authority to lead and govern.

government failure When governments implement policies that allocate resources inefficiently.

gross domestic product (GDP) The total value of all final goods and services produced within a country in a given time period, typically a year.

horizontal axis (x-axis) The solid horizontal line along which the x-variable is measured in a coordinate graph.

household A person or group of people living together and sharing income.

human capital Workers' skills, knowledge, and experience.

hyperinflation A period characterized by very high rates of inflation.

implementation lag The delay between the recognition of a problem and the implementation of a solution.

implicit costs Costs that do not involve a direct outlay of money.

import tariff A tax on goods or services purchased from another country.

imports Goods or services purchased from foreign firms.

incentive A reward or punishment that guides a decision.

income effect The change in consumption resulting from the change in the purchasing power of a consumer's income after a price change.

income elasticity of demand A measure of how changes in income affect the demand for a good.

independent variable A measure whose value is not influenced by another variable.

inelastic demand When the price elasticity of demand for a product is less than 1.

inferior good A good for which the demand decreases when income increases.

inflation An increase in the general price level of goods and services.

inflationary gap The gap between the actual output level and the full-employment output level when an economy produces more than its full-employment level of output.

interest rate effect The decrease in investment that occurs when a rise in the price level causes an increase in the interest rate (or the increase in investment that occurs when a fall in the price level causes a decrease in the interest rate).

intermediate goods Goods purchased by firms that either become part of another good or are used up in the production of a good.

Keynesian theory Economic theory centered on the idea that government involvement is sometimes needed to stabilize the economy.

labor The physical and mental contribution of people to the production process.

labor force Everyone who is aged 16 or older, not on active military duty, not institutionalized, and employed or recently looked for a job.

land The earth and everything drawn from it, including water, minerals, plants, and animals.

law of demand When other influences remain unchanged, consumers will demand more of a good or service at lower prices than at higher prices.

law of diminishing returns As more of a variable input such as labor is added to a fixed input such as ovens, the marginal product of the variable input eventually declines.

law of supply When other influences remain unchanged, firms will supply a larger quantity of a good or service at higher prices than at lower prices.

leakage In the context of the spending multiplier, this is something that takes money out of the cycle of spending and respending within the economy, such as saving, taxes, or imports.

limited liability company (LLC) A firm that does not sell stock, and is a distinct legal entity that shields its owners from creditors and litigants.

long run The time period during which the quantities of all inputs can be changed.

long-run aggregate supply curve A curve that shows the relationship between real GDP and the price level in the long run.

long-run equilibrium A situation in which no firm has an incentive to enter or exit the market.

luxury A good with an income elasticity greater than 1.

M1 The portion of the money supply that consists of currency in circulation, checkable deposits, and traveler's checks.

M2 The portion of the money supply that consists of M1 and "near money" (such as deposits in savings accounts and investments in certificates of deposit under $100,000) that is harder to exchange for goods and services than cash or checkable deposits.

macroeconomic equilibrium The state of the economy in which aggregate demand equals aggregate supply.

macroeconomics The study of the economy as a whole.

mandatory spending Government spending required by laws other than annual appropriations acts.

marginal cost The additional cost of supplying one more unit of a good or service.

marginal external benefit The increase in the external benefit created by the purchase of one more unit of a good.

marginal external cost The amount by which one more unit increases the external cost.

marginal private benefit The purchaser's benefit from one more unit of the good.

marginal private cost A firm's cost of providing one more unit.

marginal product The increase in output gained from an additional unit of an input, leaving the quantities of other inputs unchanged.

marginal propensity to consume (MPC) The fraction of new income that is spent.

marginal propensity to save (MPS) The fraction of new income that is saved.

marginal revenue product (MRP) The contribution one more worker would make to a firm's revenue.

marginal social benefit The sum of the marginal private benefit and the marginal external benefit.

marginal social cost The sum of the marginal private cost and the marginal external cost.

marginal utility The utility received from consuming one more unit of a good.

market A collection of buyers and sellers of the same good or service.

market economy (capitalist economy) An economy in which households own the factors of production.

market failure When markets do not allocate resources efficiently.

market power A firm's ability to influence the price consumers pay for its good.

medium of exchange Something that is widely accepted as payment for goods and services.

menu costs The costs to firms of updating price lists to keep up with inflation.

microcredit The extension of small loans to impoverished borrowers.

microeconomics The study of scarcity and choice at the level of individual decision makers.

minimum efficient scale The smallest quantity at which a firm's long-run average total cost is minimized.

mixed economy An economic system that has characteristics of traditional, market, and command economies.

model A simplified representation of a real-life situation.

monetarist theory Economic theory that emphasizes limited growth in the money supply as a means of controlling inflation.

monetary policy Policies the Federal Reserve uses to manage the money supply and interest rates in efforts to stabilize the economy.

money Anything that is generally accepted in exchange for goods and services.

money multiplier A ratio that indicates the largest amount of money that can be created with each $1 of excess reserves.

monopolistic competition Competition that exists in a market under three conditions: (1) Firms can easily enter or exit the market; (2) there are many firms competing in the market; and (3) the firms and their products are not identical.

monopoly A market with only one firm.

moral hazard The problem of people taking more risks when they are insured against the consequences.

movement along the demand curve When a change in the price of a good causes a change in the quantity demanded.

movement along the supply curve A change in the quantity supplied that is caused by a change in the price of the good or service.

natural monopoly A market in which the long-run average total cost for a single firm decreases for every increase in output the market could reasonably desire.

natural rate of unemployment The unemployment rate when there is full employment in the economy.

necessity A good with an income elasticity between 0 and 1.

negative externalities Undesirable effects felt by people who were not involved in the decisions that created those effects.

net interest spending A government's interest payments on its debt, minus interest income the government receives.

nominal value The actual amount paid or received for a good or service.

nominal wages The actual number of dollars workers receive as compensation.

non-excludable good A good others can't be excluded from using.

non-rival good A good the same unit of which can be used by more than one person at the same time.

normal good A good for which the demand increases when income increases.

normative economics The type of economics that deals with judgments about the way things should be.

oligopoly A market dominated by a small number of firms.

open economy An economy that engages in international trade.

open market operations The Fed's purchases and sales of Treasury securities.

opportunity cost The value of the next-best alternative foregone by making a choice.

optimal consumption rule Money should be allocated among goods such that the marginal utility per dollar spent on each good is the same.

origin The point at which the two axes in a coordinate graph meet and the value of each variable is zero.

outside lag The delay between a policy change and its resulting effect on the economy.

partnership A firm that is similar to a sole proprietorship, except that two or more people own and control it.

patent A grant of the right to be the only seller of an invention for a designated period of time.

peak The transition from an expansion to a contraction in the economy.

perfect price discrimination When each customer is charged the highest price he or she is willing to pay.

perfectly competitive market A market in which (1) there are many buyers and sellers; (2) every firm sells the same standardized product; (3) buyers and sellers have full information about the product and its price; and (4) it is easy for firms to enter and exit the market.

perfectly elastic demand When any price increase causes the quantity demanded of a good to fall to 0.

perfectly inelastic demand When consumers demand the same quantity of a good regardless of the price.

pie chart A circular chart made up of pie-shaped slices that show a larger value broken down into smaller pieces.

point A value for both the *x*-variable and the *y*-variable on a coordinate graph.

positive economics The fact-based, descriptive side of economics.

positive externalities Desirable effects felt by people who were not involved in the decisions that created those effects.

precautionary demand The demand for money that can be used to cover unexpected expenses.

price ceiling An artificial upper limit on the price of a good or service.

price discrimination When the same good is sold to different customers at different prices.

price elasticity of demand A measure of consumers' sensitivity to price changes.

price elasticity of supply A measure of how responsive firms are to changes in the price of the good they are selling.

price floor An artificial lower bound on the price of a good or service.

price-taker A firm that takes the market equilibrium price as given.

private goods Goods that are rival and excludable.

producer surplus The amount by which the price exceeds the marginal cost of each unit sold.

product markets All of the producers and consumers of goods and services in the economy.

production function A relationship showing the quantity of each input that a firm uses and the quantity of output that the firm can produce as a result.

production possibilities frontier (PPF) A model that shows all the alternative combinations of two goods that could be produced in an economy within a given time period using every available resource efficiently.

profit Total revenue minus total cost.

progressive tax A tax system under which high-income people pay a higher proportion of their income in taxes than low-income people do.

proportional tax A tax system under which everyone pays the same proportion of their income in taxes.

protectionism The practice of limiting international trade to protect domestic industries and workers.

public good A good that is both non-rival and non-excludable.

purchasing power The value of an amount of money expressed in terms of what one could buy with it.

quality of life A broader measure of citizens' comfort and satisfaction that comes partly from the standard of living, but also from more subjective sources of happiness such as health, recreation, environmental quality, freedom, security, and family life.

quantitative easing A substantial expansion of the money supply achieved with central bank purchases of securities from banks and other financial institutions.

quantity theory of money The theory that an increase in the money supply merely causes a proportional increase in the price level.

quota A limit on the amount of a good that may be imported within a given period.

real GDP per capita Real GDP divided by the number of people in the population.

real value A nominal value adjusted to remove the effects of inflation.

real wages Wages adjusted for inflation to indicate their purchasing power.

real wealth effect The decrease in the quantity of goods and services demanded as a result of a decrease in consumers' real wealth that is caused by inflation (or an increase in the quantity of goods and services demanded as a result of an increase in consumers' real wealth that is caused by deflation).

recession A significant decline in economic activity spread across the economy, lasting more than a few months.

recessionary gap The gap between the actual output level and the full-employment output level when an economy produces less than its full-employment level of output.

recognition lag The delay between the onset of a problem and the realization that it exists.

regressive tax A tax system under which low-income people pay a higher proportion of their income in taxes than high-income people do.

rental rate The cost of a unit of capital.

required reserves Reserves that cannot be lent out.

research and development (R&D) Work directed toward the creation or improvement of products or processes.

reserve requirement The percentage of total deposits that a bank cannot lend out.

reserves The deposits that banks have not loaned out.

sales tax A tax applied to a wide variety of goods and services.

savings and loan associations (S&Ls) Financial institutions whose primary focus is to provide mortgage loans.

savings banks Banks established to help working-class families save money.

Say's law Supply creates its own demand.

scarcity A condition that exists when the supply of something doesn't satisfy everyone's desires for it.

scatter diagram A diagram with many points that correspond to observations of two variables.

seasonal unemployment Unemployment caused by a change in the need for workers due to a change in seasons.

shareholders Investors who buy a corporation's stock.

Sherman Antitrust Act Legislation that restricts anticompetitive behavior by firms, such as the consolidation of several companies under the control of one business enterprise known as a *trust*.

shoe-leather costs The costs individuals incur in their efforts to minimize inflation's erosive effects on the value of their money.

short run The time period during which the quantity of at least one input cannot be changed.

short-run aggregate supply curve A curve that shows the quantity of all final goods and services supplied in an economy in the short run at various price levels.

slope The rate at which a line rises or falls from left to right.

socialism An economic system under which general assemblies and councils of workers and consumers make economic decisions, sometimes with oversight by a central government.

sole proprietorship A business owned and controlled by an individual.

speculative demand The demand for money used to take advantage of investment opportunities or avoid losses due to anticipated changes in the value of alternative investments.

spending multiplier The total amount of spending that results from each $1 of new spending injected into the economy.

stagflation A combination of stagnating real GDP and inflation in an economy.

standard of living A measure of the material wealth available to help people live comfortably.

sticky nominal wages Nominal wages that change only when contracts are renegotiated, not every time the price level changes.

stock A share of ownership in a corporation.

store of value Something that can be used to make purchases in the future.

structural unemployment Unemployment caused by a mismatch between the skills workers have and the skills employers seek.

substitutes in consumption Goods for which an increase in the price of one good causes an increase in the demand for the other good(s).

substitutes in production Goods or services for which the inputs used to provide each of the goods or services could otherwise be used to provide more of the other(s).

substitution effect The change in consumption resulting from a change in the relative prices of two goods.

sunk cost A cost that has already been paid and cannot be recovered.

supply curve A curve that illustrates the relationship between the price of a good or service and the quantity that firms are willing to supply.

supply schedule A table that indicates the quantity of a good or service that would be supplied in a given period at various prices.

supply shock A sudden and unexpected change in aggregate supply.

supply-side fiscal policy Fiscal policy that focuses on increasing aggregate supply to increase an economy's output and decrease the inflation rate.

tacit collusion When firms follow the same strategy without discussing it—as part of an unstated or implied agreement.

tariff A tax on an import.

tax incidence The way the burden of a tax is divided among the affected parties.

terms of trade The rate at which one good is exchanged for another.

thrifts Bank-like institutions that include credit unions, savings banks, and savings and loan associations.

time value of money The principal that it's better to have any given amount of money sooner rather than later.

total cost The fixed cost plus the variable cost.

total revenue The total amount that a firm receives from selling a good.

total utility The combined utility an individual receives from all the units he or she consumes.

trade deficit A deficit that exists when a country's imports exceed its exports.

trade surplus The surplus that exists when a country's exports exceed its imports.

trademark A word, phrase, symbol, or design that distinguishes the products of one firm from those of its competitors.

traditional economy An economy in which economic decisions are made on the basis of precedent.

transaction costs The costs of completing a transaction, such as negotiating a policy or purchasing a good, not including the price of the good itself.

transactions demand The demand for money used to make typical day-to-day purchases.

transfer payments Government payments to individuals or firms for which no good or service is provided in return.

Treasury securities Documents that constitute promises by the U.S. Treasury to repay money that the federal government has borrowed.

trough The transition from a contraction to an expansion in the economy.

tying agreement An agreement that requires a buyer to purchase a second product from the seller.

underemployed workers People who are working fewer hours than they want or are overqualified for their positions.

unemployment rate The percentage of the labor force that is unemployed.

unit of account A standard measure for prices and economic comparisons.

unit-elastic demand When the price elasticity of demand is 1.

utility The satisfaction or happiness that individuals feel.

variable cost The cost of variable inputs such as labor, the quantity of which can be varied in the short run to change the quantity of output.

variable input An input whose quantity can be varied in the short run.

variables Measures that can take on more than one value.

velocity of money The number of times the average unit of currency is spent in one year.

vertical axis (*y*-axis) The solid vertical line along which the *y*-variable is measured in a coordinate graph.

wage The cost of a unit of labor.

Note: **Bold** indicates key terms; page numbers followed by *f* and *t* indicate figures and tables, respectively.